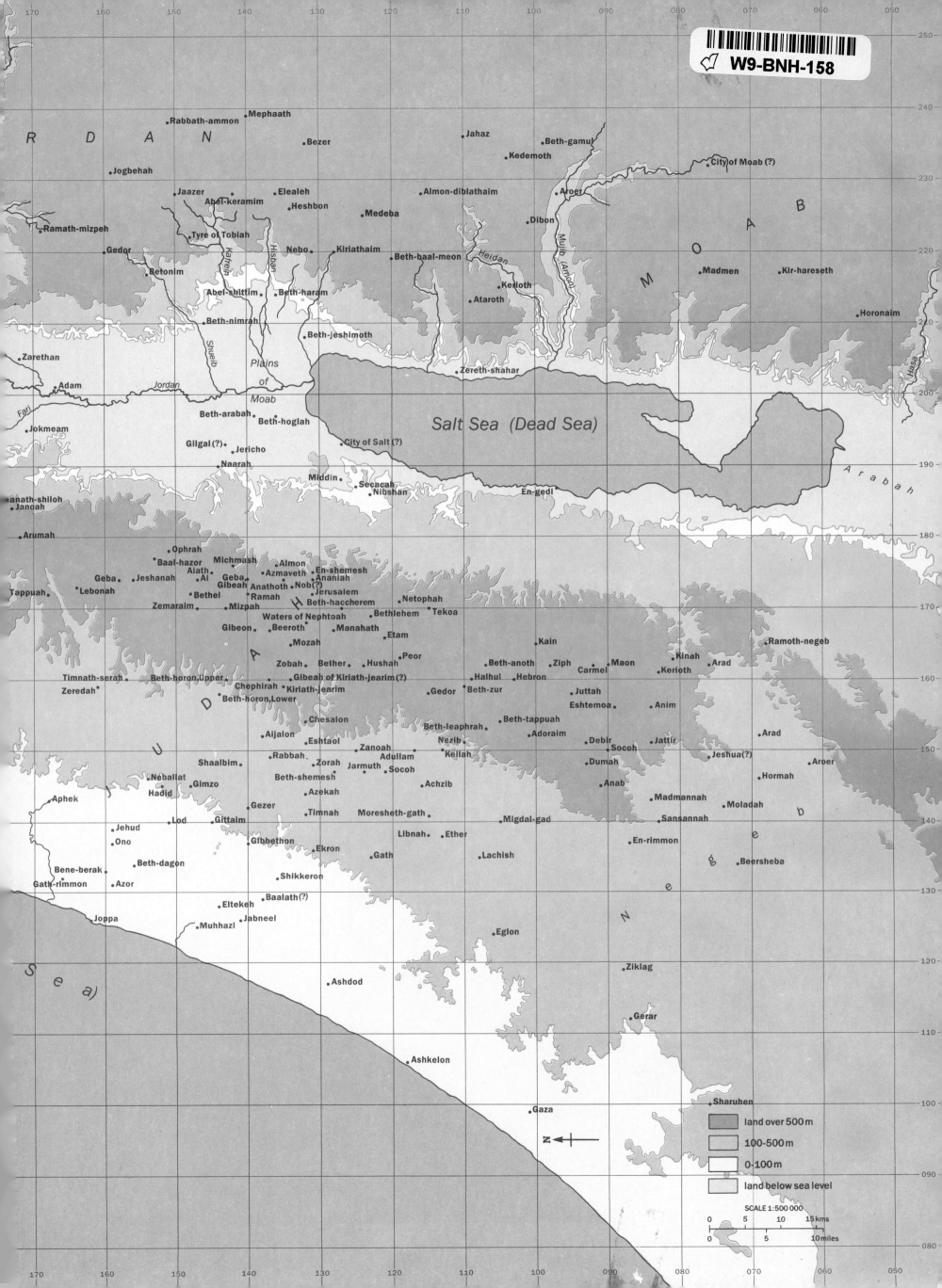

THE HARPER
ATLAS
OF THE
BIBLE

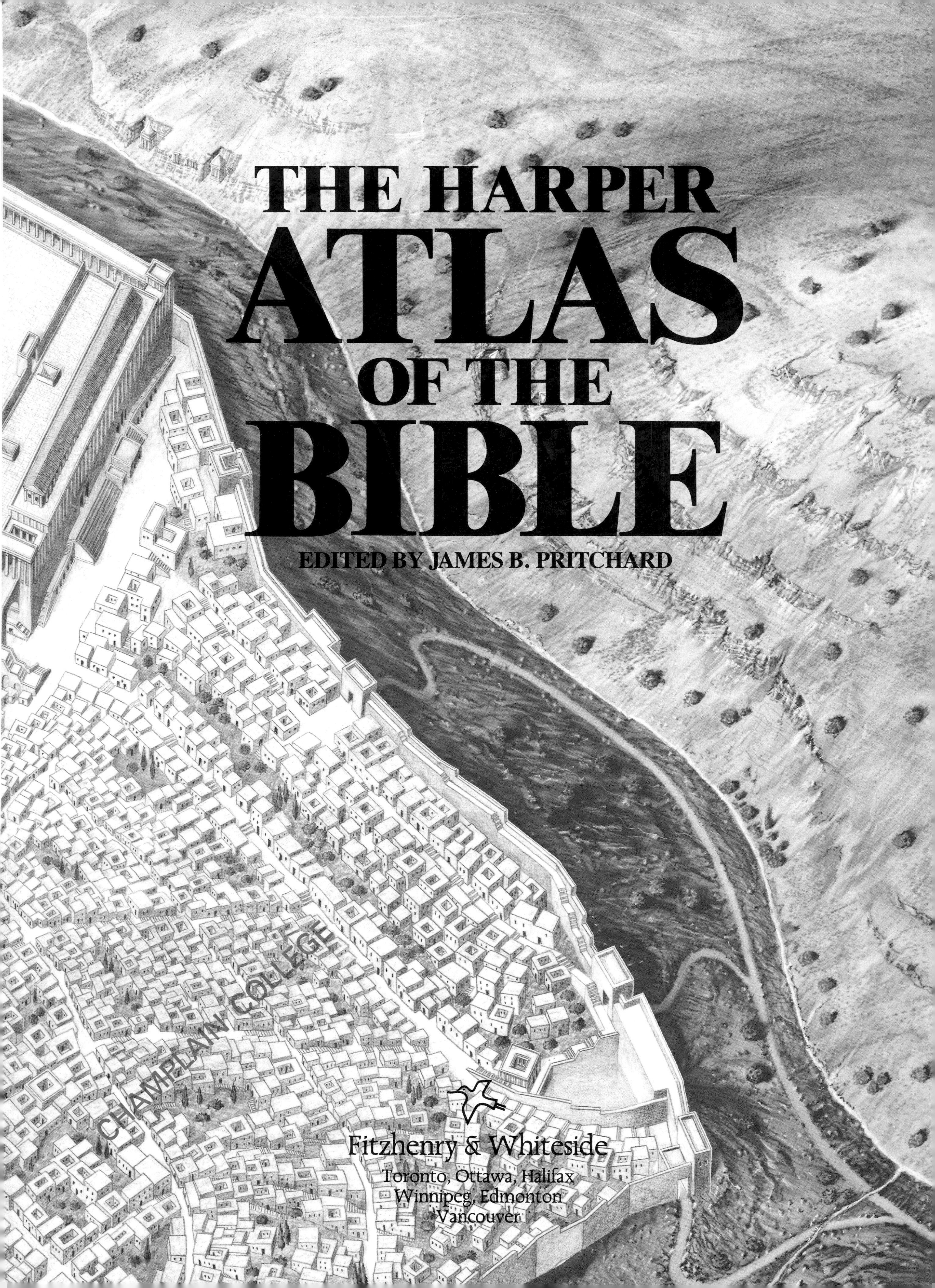

THE HARPER
ATLAS
OF THE
BIBLE

EDITED BY JAMES B. PRITCHARD

Fitzhenry & Whiteside

Toronto, Ottawa, Halifax
Winnipeg, Edmonton
Vancouver

Published in Great Britain as
THE TIMES ATLAS OF THE BIBLE

FIRST EDITION

Maps, illustrations and typesetting
Swanston Graphics, Derby
Irene K. Bates
Andrew Bright
Anne Hall

Alison Ewington
Duncan Mackay
Paul Middleton
Rex Nicholls

Colour processing
Ensign Graphics, Hull

Editorial direction
Robert Allen
Penelope Warren

Design, map design and art direction
Ivan Dodd Designers

Ian Smith

Place-name consultant
P.J.M. Geelan

Index and glossary
P.J.M. Geelan
Barbara James

Printed and bound in Italy by
SAGDOS, Milan

Fitzhenry & Whiteside Limited
195 Allstate Parkway
Markham, Ontario L3R 4T8

ISBN 88902-935-0

THE land lying from 'Dan even to Beersheba', the Holy Land, has been mapped more frequently over the centuries than any comparable area of the earth's surface. This unique focus of attention is not surprising: two world religions emerged in this small and relatively unproductive region and their writings, books collected into the Bible, bear unmistakably the imprint of its geography.

Our aim in this atlas is to show the features of the land and to locate ancient places by making use of the most recent explorations and discoveries. In addition to these objectives, shared by others who draw historical maps, we have sought to impose upon the maps information given in the Bible and other texts about important events. Coloured lines, arrows and other graphic conventions have been employed to trace the course of particular episodes extending from the migration of Abraham to Paul's missionary journeys.

The historical materials found in the Old Testament, the Intertestamental books, and the New Testament are of a kind that can be portrayed graphically. The record is replete with wars, campaigns, destructions, rebellions; routes of conquerors and exiles; the rise and fall of empires, the divisions of kingdoms; and heroic events in which patriarchs, judges, and prophets are involved. It is the joining of such dramatic events with geography that is our major objective.

The time span covered is a long one, as, indeed, is that of the Bible itself. In the first section, 'In the Beginning', we have dealt with the origins of such elements as agriculture, animal husbandry, urbanization and metallurgy, as their origins have become known from archaeological research. Data coming from as far back as Palaeolithic times provide answers to concerns of the Bible about the beginning of civilization. Prehistory is treated cryptically and as a matter of genealogy in the first part of Genesis, where Cain is said to have been the first farmer, Abel the first keeper of sheep, Enoch the first to build a city, and Tubal-cain the forger of metals. At the other end of the time span we have gone beyond New Testament times into the Christian era to the building of Byzantine churches in Palestine.

Important light has been shed upon the geography of the Holy Land in recent times by discoveries in Egypt. The scattered references in the Bible to the settlements before the Hebrews came into Canaan from Egypt have now been augmented by Egyptian records. In a section on the era of Egyptian supremacy in Canaan we have mapped the land from the rich information coming from the Execration Texts, the Amarna letters, and the boastful records of conquests by Tuthmosis III, Amenophis II, Sethos I, and Ramesses II. The earliest recorded names in the land appear in these records of Israel's later enemies to the south.

Israel's hostile neighbours to the east have also provided information on historical geography. For over three centuries Assyria invaded the land, pillaging and destroying its towns. Yet they left records written on stone and clay of their routes, their victories and lists of products taken as tribute. The campaigns of such Assyrian monarchs as Shalmaneser III, Tiglath-pileser III, Sargon, and Sennacherib have enlarged considerably our knowledge of historical geography.

A major concern of the atlas is with everyday life. It is understandable that biblical, as well as other ancient writers took for granted a knowledge of familiar details of their day-to-day life. In the planning of the atlas we have defined geography so as to include the physical environment and the well-established practices of trade and commerce, means of communication, methods of warfare and defence, city planning, and the proper burial of the dead. These and other basic subjects, such as land, climate, plants and animals, popular pagan cults, temples, and the use made of writing, have been included. These thematic items provide a background for the historical events.

A notable departure from previous atlases is in the method used for projecting maps. The general awareness in the space age of the curvature of the earth's surface prompted us to replace a flat projection with a more realistic one. In addition, the older convention of placing north at the top of the map has often been modified for the purpose of design or to suggest a more natural way of looking at the particular subject depicted. However, a sufficient number of maps have been drawn with a north orientation to prevent the reader becoming disoriented. The endpapers have maps showing Old and New Testament sites plotted according to the standard Palestine grid.

In order to make use of the results of the most recent scholarship we have enlisted the help of some 50 scholars from a dozen different countries, many of whom are specialists in a particular discipline. Biblical history of various periods, archaeology both in Palestine and in other parts of the ancient Near East, Assyriology, Egyptology, and Classics are some of the fields of competence represented. We have asked each major contributor to sketch maps with a list of places to be shown, to write a text of explanation, make suggestions for illustrations, and for comments through the various stages of production. From these contributions the editors, designers, and cartographers have dealt with the more practical matters of production.

In any volume of multiple authorship it is desirable to maintain a degree of uniformity. In the matter of chronology we have employed dates found in the most recent edition of the *Cambridge Ancient History*, which is a widely used reference. It is well known that there are conflicts in views among scholars about such matters as the text of the Bible, its literary criticism and its historical interpretation, to mention but a few areas. In the interest of producing a book of standard reference that may be used by readers who hold widely different views, we have attempted to give alternate positions on matters where there is not a generally accepted opinion. The sense of fairness on the part of contributors has been appreciated by those responsible for editing the contributions to the atlas.

The 'Index of Place-Names' is more than the listing of the names appearing on the maps. It is a gazetteer that lists the alternative names by which a place was known, the location of the ancient site on the modern map of the land (Arabic and/or Hebrew names), and the grid reference according to the standard grid system used for Palestine. Uncertainty about the location of ancient sites is indicated by interrogation points. In general we have followed the opinions of the contributors about identifications.

There is a long tradition of producing geographical works on Palestine. A standard bibliography of works on travel and pilgrimages lists more than 300 maps drawn from the 4th through to the 18th century. Since 1800 many more have appeared. In the preparation of the atlas we have indeed stood on the shoulders of giants. One particular debt is that to Yohanan Aharoni, who published in 1964 his *Carta's Atlas of the Bible* (in Hebrew), in which he made use of 171 maps to relate major events to their geographical setting. To Aharoni we are indebted for an innovative concept, one which we have seen fit to continue. Certain of his conclusions have never been superseded by later research and we therefore thank his widow, Miriam Aharoni, for permission to include this material.

If one reflects on our knowledge of the times and events of the Bible he cannot but be aware of how much of the past has been lost. Yet a survey of the past century of research demonstrates that some of what had been forgotten can be recovered – witness the increment to history which has come from Ebla, Ugarit, the caves around the Dead Sea and Masada, to mention but a few, and augurs well for the attempts yet to be made to solve old problems.

James B. Pritchard
Philadelphia 1987

CONTENTS

OLD TESTAMENT

INTER-TESTAMENTAL PERIOD

NEW TESTAMENT

CHRONOLOGY

The dates assigned to the principal characters and events of the Bible can vary considerably. New discovery and the reassessment of older evidence make it difficult to have a consensus about chronology, particularly among the large number of contributors to the Atlas. In order to achieve something of a consistency in matters of terminology and date we have made use of the dates given in the third edition of the *Cambridge Ancient History*, now in the progress of publication. Those who prefer another system of chronological notation can easily make adjustments from those available in the CAH. For the dates of the Babylonian and Assyrian kings not listed in CAH we have followed J. A. Brinkman in A. Leo Oppenheim, *Ancient Mesopotamia*, 1964, pages 341, 347; for the kings of Israel and Judah not yet appearing in the CAH volumes we have depended upon E. R. Thiele, *The Mysterious Numbers of the Hebrew Kings*, 1965, page 205.

The names and dates for the archaeological periods in Palestine are from two sources. For the earlier, prehistoric periods we have used those suggested by O. Bar-Yosef in his contributions to this volume. The dates and designations for the Bronze Age and onward are taken from the chronological table appearing at the end of the *Encyclopedia of Archaeological Excavations in the Holy Land*, IV, edited by M. Avi-Yonah and E. Stern, 1978. However, it must be remembered that other terms and dates have had a wide use. For example, there are two other schemes for designating the periods from the latter part of the Early Bronze through the early Middle Bronze Age (*c* 2350-1750). One divides the span into the 'Intermediate EB-MB Period' and a 'Middle Bronze I Period' (corresponding roughly to the traditional MB II A period). Yet another system makes use of 'EB IV A-C' for the period covered in our table by EB IV and MB I (2350-2000).

DATE BC	PERIOD	CULTURE	SITES	SUBSISTENCE
1 500 000	Lower Palaeolithic	Lower Acheulian Upper Acheulian Acheulo-Yabrudian	'Ubeidiya Gesher Benot-Ya'acov Umm Qatafa cave Ma'ayan Baruch Tabun cave Zuttiyeh	scavengers and gatherers
90 000	Middle Palaeolithic	Mousterian	Sukhul Qafzeh Tabun Kebara	hunters and gatherers
40-38 000	Upper Palaeolithic	'Transitional industry' and 'Ahmarian' 'Levantine Aurignacian'	Boker Tachtit Erq el-Ahmar El-Wad Hayonim Boker	
17 000 12 500 10 300	Epi-Palaeolithic	Kebaran Geometric Kebaran Mushabian	Ein-Gev Kebara Haon Hefsibah	*gathering?* wild cereals and pulses? hunters and gatherers hunting – gazelle, fallow deer, wild boar, wild cattle, ibex, hare,
10 300 8500		Natufian Harifian Khiamian	El-Wad 'Eynan Hayonim Abu Salem Salibiya IX	hunters and gatherers *fishing* – lakes and sea, *hunting* – gazelle, ibex, wild cattle, wild boar, *gathering* – pulses, wild cereals
8300 8000 7500	(Pre-pottery Neolithic A)	'Sultanian' and unnamed desert culture	Jericho Nativ Hagdud Gilgal Nahal Oren	farmers hunters and gatherers *agriculture* – domesticated emmer wheat, barley and pulses, figs, *hunting* – gazelle, fox , wild boar, cattle, goat *herding* – gazelle
7500	Early Neolithic (Pre-pottery Neolithic B)	Tahunian and unnamed desert culture	Jericho 'Ain Ghazal Abu Ghosh Beisamun Amman	*herding* – goats and sheep *hunting* – gazelle *agriculture* – domesticated cereals, pulses, flax, wild barley, oats, pistachio, acorns, peas and vetch
6000 5000 4800 4500	Late Neolithic or Pottery Neolithic	'Yarmukian' Pottery Neolithic B	Sha'ar HaGolan Jericho Munhata Teleilat el-Ghassul Batashi Nahal Essaron Nizzanim Giveat Haparsah Kadesh-barnea	cultivation of crops *herding* of animals some *hunting* and *collecting* in the deserts *agriculture* and *herding*
4500 3500 3400	Chalcolithic	'Ghassulian' Beersheba culture	Teleilat el-Ghassul, later phases En-gedi Bir es-Safadi Tell Abu Matar Ghrubba Wadi Rabah Beersheba Tell Abu Matar Bir es-Safadi En-gedi Nahal Mishmar Azor Hadara Bene Beraq Giv'atayim Tabaqat Fahl (Pella) Golan sites Neve Ur	orchard maintenance (olives) *agriculture, horticulture* and *herding* mixed farming – sheep, pig, goat, cattle, wheat, barley, olives *hunting* and *herding* in the deserts *herding* – use of wool and milk products copper production ivory workshops copper treasure
3150 2850	Early Bronze Age I A-C Early Bronze Age II			

CLIMATE	TECHNOLOGY	SOCIAL ORGANIZATION	ARCHITECTURE
		(little is known) small groups	
		small bands	
		small bands	
wet and cold some warming	microlithic tools some bone tools pounding tools use of bow	small bands	flimsy huts
wet and cool wet some warming	use of bow and simple arrows, elaborate bone industry (basketry?), plastered silos, art objects, use of pestle and mortar, sickles	mobile small bands in desert sedentary camps in the Mediterranean belt	building houses with posts
wet and cool	plano-convex bricks	villages on arable lands, small bands in deserts	Nahal Oren – oval houses and mud plaster Jericho – walled town, round houses, sunken floors mud-brick, round or oval stone-built
wet and cool (desert lakes) becoming wet	basketry, primitive looms, elaborate bows and arrows, heat treatment of flints, white ware in Syria obsidian from Anatolia, arrowheads, sickle blades, borers, chisels, adzes, picks, querns, grinders, microliths, plaster figures, plastered skulls, groups of plaster figures, white ware	sedentary villagers and small bands in desert	lime plaster production 'Ain Ghazal/Amman – rectangular houses, plaster floors Beidha VI-I – semi subterranean round houses, stone built , timber frame burnished and painted plaster floors and walls Jericho-walled town, rectangular houses, plaster floors, temple shrine
warm a spell of dryness becoming wet/warm	Burnished red on cream pottery, arrowheads and sickle blades, common polished axes burnished red-on-cream pottery, arrowheads and sickle blades common	semi-permanent villages	Jericho/Munhata – pit dwellings
a spell of dryness wet, with some summer rains, warm	pottery pottery developed ceramic industry, cornet cups etc., wall paintings, fenestrated stands painted pottery, bow rims, multiple vessels, animal figurines, churns rare. Flint knapping, fan scrapers, few arrowheads ? tournette advent of copper metallurgy relations with Beersheba and Golan	tribal chiefdoms sedentary villagers Neonate burials in jars or on sherds in corner of rooms, under floors bodies in subterranean galleries burial mound, pottery ossuaries for secondary burial	Jericho – rectangular mud-brick houses Pit dwellings Teleilat el-Ghassul – pit dwellings succeeded by large rectangular mud-brick buildings on stone foundations, courtyards, stone and plaster lined storage pits, walled enclosure, twin temples En-gedi – walled enclosure, gatehouse, twin temples rectangular brick-built houses rectangular houses of stone

EVENTS INFLUENCING THE HISTORY OF PALESTINE	DOMINANT FOREIGN POWERS	ARCHAEOLOGICAL ERA	BIBLICAL BOOK
		c 2650-2350 Early Bronze Age III	
c2400 Ebla archives			
		c2350-2200 Early Bronze Age IV	
		c2200-2000 Middle Bronze Age I	
		c2000-1750 Middle Bronze Age IIA	
c1792-1750 Hammurabi's laws			GENESIS
		c1750-1550 Middle Bronze Age IIB	
c 1674 Hyksos take control of Egypt			
	KINGS OF EGYPT **Eighteenth Dynasty**		
c1573 Kamosis campaigns in Canaan	1570-1546 Amosis		
c1565 Amosis expels the Hyksos			
	1546-1526 Amenophis I	**c1550-1400** Late Bronze Age I	
	1525-c1512 Tuthmosis I		
	c1512-1504 Tuthmosis II		
c1482 Tuthmosis III begins to build his empire in Palestine	1503-1482 Hatshepsut		
c1482 Battle of Megiddo	1504-1450* Tuthmosis III		
	1450-1425 Amenophis II		
	1425-1417 Tuthmosis IV		
c1400 Alphabetic writing at Ugarit	1417-1379 Amenophis III		
c1375 Beginning of Amarna correspondence	1379-1362 Akhenaten (Amenophis IV)	**c1400-1300** Late Bronze Age IIA	
	1364-1361* Smenkhkare		
	1361-1352 Tutankhamun		
	1352-1348 Ay		
	1348-1320 Horemheb		
c1318 Sethos I's campaign to the coastland	**Nineteenth Dynasty**		
c1300 Battle of Qadesh	1320-1318 Ramesses I	**c1300-1200** Late Bronze Age IIB	
c1284 Ramesses II's treaty with the Hittites	1318-1304 Sethos I		
	1304-1237 Ramesses II		EXODUS

* Co-regency with predecessor

EVENTS INFLUENCING THE HISTORY OF PALESTINE	DOMINANT FOREIGN POWERS	ARCHAEOLOGICAL ERA	BIBLICAL BOOK
	KINGS OF EGYPT (Cont.)		NUMBERS
	1236-1223 Merneptah		JOSHUA
c1230(?) Merneptah's battle with "Israel"			
	1222-1217 (?) Amenmesses		JUDGES
	1216-1210 (?) Sethos II		
	1209-1200 (?) Merneptah Siptah		
	Tewosret		
	Twentieth Dynasty		
c1200 Invasions of the Sea Peoples	1200-1198 Sethnakhte	**c1200-1150**	
	1198-1166 Ramesses III	Iron Age IA	
	1166-1160 Ramesses IV		
	1160-1156 Ramesses V		
	1156-1148 Ramesses VI	**c1150-1000**	
	1148-1147 Ramesses VII	Iron Age IB	
	1147-1140 Ramesses VIII		
	1140-1121 Ramesses IX		
	1121-1113 Ramesses X		
	1113-1085 Ramesses XI		
			I SAMUEL
			II SAMUEL
c1000 Phoenician trade begins in the Mediterranean		**c1000-900**	I CHRONICLES
David assumes throne in Jerusalem		Iron Age IIA	
c965 Solomon assumes the throne in Israel			I KINGS
			II CHRONICLES

EVENTS INFLUENCING THE HISTORY OF PALESTINE			DOMINANT FOREIGN POWERS	ARCHAEOLOGICAL ERA	BIBLICAL BOOK
	KINGS OF ISRAEL AND JUDAH		**KINGS OF ASSYRIA**		
	Israel	**Judah**			
931 Division of the Hebrew Kingdom	**931-910** Jeroboam I	**931-913** Rehoboam	**934-912** Ashur-dan II		I KINGS
924 Shishak invades Palestine					II CHRONICLES
		913-911 Abijah			
	910-909 Nadab	**911-870** Asa	**911-891** Adad-nirari II		
	909-886 Baasha				
				c900-800 Iron Age IIB	
			890-884 Tukulti-Ninurta II		
	886-885 Elah				
	885 Zimri		**883-859** Ashurnasirpal II		
	885-874 Omri				
	874-853 Ahab				
		870-848 Jehoshaphat			
			858-824 Shalmaneser III		
853 Ahab defeated by Shalmaneser III at Qarqar	**853-852** Ahaziah				
	852-841 Joram	**848-841** Jehoram			
841 Jehu pays tribute to Shalmaneser III	**841-814** Jehu	**841** Ahaziah			II KINGS
		841-835 Athaliah			
		835-796 Jehoash/Joash			
			823-811 Shamshi-Adad V		
	814-798 Jehoahaz				
			810-783 Adad-nirari III		
	798-782 Joash/Jehoash	**796-767** Amaziah		**c800-600 (586)** Iron Age IIC	
	782-753 Jeroboam II		**782-773** Shalmaneser IV		
			772-755 Ashur-dan III		
		767-740 Uzziah/Azariah			AMOS
	753-752 Zechariah		**754-745** Ashur-nirari V		HOSEA
	752 Shallum				
	752-742 Menahem		**744-727** Tiglath-pileser III		ISAIAH
	742-740 Pekahiah				
738 Menahem's tribute to Tiglath-pileser III	**752-732** Pekah	**740-732** Jotham			
734 Ahaz's tribute to Tiglath-pileser III					
732 Tiglath-pileser III places Hoshea on throne	**732-723** Hoshea	**732-716** Ahaz/Jehoahaz I			MICAH
			726-722 Shalmaneser V		
722 Fall of Samaria			**721-705** Sargon II		
712 Sargon II's campaign to Ashdod		**716-687** Hezekiah			
701 Lachish attacked by Sennacherib			**704-681** Sennacherib		
		687-643 Manasseh			
			680-669 Esarhaddon		
670 Manasseh pays tribute to Esarhaddon			**668-627** Ashurbanipal		

EVENTS INFLUENCING THE HISTORY OF PALESTINE		DOMINANT FOREIGN POWERS	ARCHAEOLOGICAL ERA	BIBLICAL BOOK
	JUDAH (Cont.) **643-641** Amon **641-609** Josiah			
		626-624? Ashur-etel-ilani Sin-shumu-lishir		JEREMIAH ZEPHANIAH
612 Fall of Nineveh **609** Josiah slain by Nechoh II of Egypt	**609** Jehoahaz II **609-598** Jehoiakim	**-612** Sin-sharra-ishkun **611-609** Ashur-uballit II **CHALDEAN DYNASTY** **625-605** Nabopolassar **605-562** Nebuchadnezzar II		NAHUM HABAKKUK (DANIEL)
597 Nebuchadnezzar II conquers Jerusalem Jehoiachin deported to Babylon	**598-597** Jehoiachin **597-586** Zedekiah			
587 Fall of Jerusalem and beginning of Exile			**586-332** Babylonian and Persian Periods	OBADIAH
				EZEKIEL
561 Release of Jehoiachin **559** Cyrus becomes king of Persia		**561-560** Evil-Merodach **559-556** Neriglissar **556** Labashi-Markuk **555-539** Nabonidus		
545 Fall of Sardis				
539 Fall of Babylon				
530 Cambyses becomes king of Persia				
c 525 Cambyses takes Egypt **522** Darius I king of Persia **c 520** Rebuilding of temple at Jerusalem				HAGGAI ZECHARIAH
490 First Persian invasion of Greece Battle of Marathon **486** Xerxes I king of Persia				
480 Second Persian invasion of Greece Battles of Thermopylae, Salamis and Plataea (479)				MALACHI
464 Artaxerxes I king of Persia				(ESTHER)
? Ezra reads Law in Jerusalem				
Nehemiah rebuilds walls of Jerusalem				NEHEMIAH
423 Darius II king of Persia				
410-411 Jewish temple at Elephantine destroyed				
404 Artaxerxes II king of Persia Egypt rebels against Persia				
? Ezra reads Law in Jerusalem				EZRA
				RUTH
				JONAH
359 Artaxerxes III king of Persia				JOEL

EVENTS INFLUENCING THE HISTORY OF PALESTINE	DOMINANT FOREIGN POWERS	ERA	BIBLICAL BOOK

EVENTS INFLUENCING THE HISTORY OF PALESTINE

336	Alexander the Great Darius III king of Persia
332	Alexander the Great destroys the Persian Empire
323	Beginning of rule of the Seleucids Death of Alexander
305	Beginning of the Ptolemies

SYRIAN-EGYPTIAN WARS

274-271	Ptolemy II fought Antiochus I.
260-253	Ptolemy II fought Antiochus II.
246-241	Ptolemy III fought Seleucus II.
219-217	Ptolemy IV fought Antiochus III.
202-200	Ptolemy V fought Antiochus III.
	Treaty of Apamea imposed on Antiochus III by Rome
175-4	Seleucus IV attempts to raid Jerusalem Temple treasury. Jason appointed High Priest
170-168	Ptolemy VI fought Antiochus IV.
169-168	Antiochus IV invades Egypt
168	Antiochus IV ejected by the Romans
166-60	Campaigns of Judas Maccabaeus Jonathan becomes High Priest

THE HASMONAEANS

died 160	Judas Maccabaeus
142-134	Simon Thassis
134-104	John Hyrcanus (Yehohanan)
104-3	Aristobulus I (Yehudah)
died 104	Antigonus (Mattityah)
103-76	Alexander Jannaeus (Yehonatan)
76-67	Alexandra Salome
67-63	Aristobulus II (Yehudah)
63-40	Hyrcanus II (Yehohanan)
died 49	Alexander

c 65

DOMINANT FOREIGN POWERS

THE PTOLEMIES

305-283	Ptolemy I Soter
283-246	Ptolemy II Philadelphus
246-221	Ptolemy III Euergetes I
221-204	Ptolemy IV Philopator
204-180	Ptolemy V Epiphanes
180-145	Ptolemy VI Philometor (with Ptolemy VIII, Euergetes II and Cleopatra II 170-164) with Cleopatra II 163-145)
145-116	Ptolemy VIII Euergetes II (restored)
116-107	Cleopatra III and Ptolemy IX Soter II (Lathyrus)
107-101	Cleopatra III and Ptolemy X Alexander I
101-88	Ptolemy X Alexander I and Cleopatra Berenice
88-81	Ptolemy IX Soter II
80	Cleopatra Berenice and Ptolemy XI Alexander II
80-58	Ptolemy XII Neos Dionysus (Auletes)
58-56	Berenice IV (at first with Cleopatra Tryphaena)
56-55	Berenice IV and Archelaus
55-51	Ptolemy XII, Neos Dionysus (restored)
51-30	Cleopatra VII Philopator

THE SELEUCIDS

305-281	Seleucus I Nicator
281-261	Antiochus I Soter
261-246	Antiochus II Theos
246-226/5	Seleucus II Callinicus
226/5-223	Seleucus III Soter
223-187	Antiochus III Megas ('the Great')
187-175	Seleucus IV Philopator
175-164	Antiochus IV Epiphanes
164-162	Antiochus V Eupator
162-150	Demetrius I Soter
150-145	Alexander Balas
145-140	Demetrius II Nicator
145-142/1 (or 139/8)	Antiochus VI Ephiphanes
138-129	Antiochus VII Sidetes
129-126/5	Demetrius II Nicator (restored)
126/5-123	Cleopatra Thea
126/5-96	Antiochus VIII Grypus
126	Seleucus V
114/13-95	Antiochus IX Philopator (Cyzicenus)
95	Seleucus VI
95	Antiochus X Eusebes Philopator
95-88	Demetrius III Philopator Soter
95	Antiochus XI Epiphanes Philadelphus
95-84/3	Philip I
87	Antiochus XII Dionysus
84/3	Philip II

ERA

332-152 Hellenistic I Period

152-37 Hellenistic II Period (Hasmonaean)

BIBLICAL BOOK

ESTHER

DANIEL

EVENTS INFLUENCING THE HISTORY OF PALESTINE	DOMINANT FOREIGN POWERS	ERA	BIBLICAL BOOK

EVENTS INFLUENCING THE HISTORY OF PALESTINE

Death of Pompey the Great

THE HASMONAEANS (Cont.)
40-37 Antigonus (Mattityah)
37-4 BC Herod the Great
died 35 Aristobulus III

Galatia becomes a Roman Province

4 BC-AD 6 Herod Archelaus ethnarch in Judaea
4 BC-AD 33/4 Philip tetrarch in Batanaea etc.
4 BC-AD 39 Herod Antipas tetrarch in Galilee and Peraea

AD

6-41 Judaea becomes a Roman province under a procurator

30 Beginnings of Jesus public ministry
c 32 Crucifixion of Jesus
33-4 Conversion of Paul
36 ? Paul's 1st missionary journey
37 Agrippa I tetrarch in Batanaea etc.
40 So-called Edict of Claudius
40 Agrippa I adds Galilee and Peraea to his rule
41-44 Agrippa I king over all Judaea, Samaria etc.
44-66 Judaea under direct Roman rule
49-51 Paul's 2nd missionary journey
c 50-53 Agrippa II king of Chalcis in Lebanon
51-52 Gallio proconsul of Achaia
c 50 The Jerusalem Conference
Paul writes Galatians and 'previous letter'
52-56 Paul's 3rd missionary journey
53-92/3 Agrippa II king of Batanaea etc. and (later) parts of Galilee and Peraea
66-70 First Jewish Revolt

130-135 Second Jewish Revolt

DOMINANT FOREIGN POWERS

ROMAN EMPERORS
16 Jan 27 BC — 19 Aug AD 14 Augustus
17 Sept 14 — 16 March 37 Tiberius
16 March 37 — 24 Jan 41 Gaius
24 Jan 41 — 13 Oct 54 Claudius
13 Oct 54 — 9 June 68 Nero
10 June 68 — 15 Jan 69 Galba
15 Jan 69 — 14 April 69 Otho
2 Jan 69 — 20 Dec 69 Vitellius
1 July 69 — 24 June 79 Vespasian
24 June 79 — 13 Sept 81 Titus
14 Sept 81 — 16 Sept 96 Domitian
16 Sept 96 — 25 Jan 98 Nerva
25 Jan 98 - 8 Aug 117 Trajan
11 Aug 117 — 10 July 138 Hadrian

ERA
37-AD 324 Roman Period

BIBLICAL BOOK
c 70 Gospel of Mark
c 80 Gospels of Matthew and Luke; Acts of the Apostles
c 90 Johannine writings
c 110 Letters of Ignatius

THE Natufian culture was originally defined by D. Garrod and R. Neuville in the 1930s on the basis of archaeological finds from Mt Carmel and the Judaean Desert caves and rockshelters. The image of the Natufians as the last cave dwellers in southwest Asia was later changed when large open-air sites were discovered within the Mediterranean vegetational belt and the margins of the steppic Irano-Turanian belt.

The Natufian culture is dated to 10,800-8,500 BC on the basis of radiocarbon determinations and commonly subdivided by archaeologists into Early Natufian (10,800-9,300 BC) and Late Natufian (9,300-8,500 BC).

The Natufian sites represent both base camps rich in archaeological remains and transitory stations where stone artefacts are often the only remains found. Natufian base camps contain dwelling structures, rare storage facilities, single and communal burials, art objects, rich bone industry, pounding stone tools and some grinding tools.

The flint assemblages are dominated by microliths (small stone tools) which were produced from short and broad bladelets as well as small flakes. Among the microliths, the lunates (pieces of stone shaped like a crescent moon) are the most common type. In the Early Natufian lunates were often shaped by retouching both sides of the tool (Helwan retouch) while the abrupt, edge blunting retouch characterized the Late Natufian. The use of microburin (boring) technique, with which oblique snapping of bladelets was achieved, is not a chronological but a social marker. It was used by certain Natufian groups for a long time but not by other contemporary groups. This special technique possibly originated in the North African technological world and was introduced to the Levantine region during the preceding millennium when the Mushabians penetrated into Sinai.

Natufian base camps such as 'Eynan ('Ain Mallaha), Hayonim Cave and Terrace, or the recently discovered site at Wadi Hammeh, contain well-built dwellings. The houses at 'Eynan and the rooms in the Hayonim Cave are semisubterranean, circular or oval, 14-29ft in diameter, with stone-built walls up to 2ft 6in-3ft high. In a special semicircular building in 'Eynan, which is about 30ft in diameter, stone-lined postholes indicate that the superstructure was made of unpreserved organic matters (branches, hides, etc). The use of a simple lime-plaster began in this period mainly for coating dwelling walls and the rare storage pits which are well recorded in 'Eynan.

During the Early Natufian era burials were often communal and body decorations were quite common. The communal graves are interpreted as indicating family graves. The position of the corpse is either supine, semiflexed or entirely flexed. In the Late Natufian single burials are more common and body decorations are rare. The uneven distribution of body decorations, where males owned more than females and certain individuals more than others, probably indicate a degree of social hierarchy. The decorations, as exposed during the excavations of the graves, were placed on the head, around the neck, the thighs or the wrists. Ornaments were made of either bone pendants, dentalium shells or both. Sea shells originated mainly from the Mediterranean shores, although a few were obtained by exchange from the Red Sea region.

Art objects are few and include carved gazelles on sickle handles made of bones from El-Wad and from a cave at Kebara. Schematic human stone figurines have been found at El-Wad and 'Eynan. Rare animal figurines carved in limestone have been discovered, such as the gazelle (Um ez-Zuweitina), the tortoise ('Eynan), and a double figurine of a dog and an owl (Nahal Oren). A cluster of incised slabs were found in the Hayonim Cave on which a fish figure can be traced as well as several examples of the 'leader' pattern. The Natufian artistic expressions were an innovation for the region at their time and possibly show increased social activity, perhaps in order to support the social cohesion of the various groups.

It is a typical Natufian characteristic that animal bones, antlers and horns were used for manufacturing sickle shafts, various points, skin burnishers, rare harpoons (see opposite page), rare hooks (see opposite page), pendants, etc. The Natufian culture was the first prehistoric entity in southwest Asia to use this type of raw material intensively.

Hide working and basketry is inferred from the way that bone tools were used. A similar inference can be made for the use of bows and arrows. Stone 'shaft straighteners', as well as edge damage on microliths, testify to the presence of Natufian archery. However, samples of these organic remains need be found in a dry desert cave before this reconstruction can be validated.

Natufian subsistence strategy was based on hunting (gazelle, fallow deer, wild boar), fishing (mainly in freshwater lakes), trapping (birds, mainly migratory ducks), gathering and harvesting plants. Despite the flimsy evidence of charred botanical remains, it seems that wild cereals and pulses, wild fruits (pistachio, almonds, acorns, etc) were intensively collected and formed the main bulk of Natufian diet. This observation is supported by the studies on the Strontium/Calcium ratios in human bones (which when compared to the Strontium/Calcium ratios in herbivore and carnivore bones in the same sites indicate the general composition of the diet).

Pounding stone tools, often made of local limestone, such as mortars, bowls, cup-holes and pestles are found in abundance in Natufian base camps. Some, mostly pestles but occasionally mortars, were made of basalt. Their presence in sites far away from the sources of this raw material indicate that they were exchanged over large distances.

The Early Natufian base camps were the first sedentary communities as evidenced by common animals such as house-mice and the sparrows, in the microfaunal assemblages retrieved in these sites. Their sedentary way of life is also indicated by the presence of numerous burials inside the settlement area often interpreted as demonstrating the ownership of the group over its territory. Each of the Early Natufian base camps had its own identity expressed in the combination of the body decorations. Although the length of annual occupation is unknown it clearly seems that the base camps (villages or hamlets as they are sometimes called) maintained their character over a long period.

With the increase in population, intensification of exploitation was unavoidable and Late Natufian communities expanded their territories and established new sites in the more steppic regions of the Levant. The new localities include sites such as Mureybit and Abu Hureira on the Middle Euphrates, Rosh Zin and Rosh Horesha in the Negeb Highlands, etc.

Climatic fluctuations around 8,500-8,300 BC gave good reasons for accelerating the process of plant domestication in the Mediterranean belt which led to the emergence of farming communities and enforced a special adaptive strategy on marginal Late Natufian groups.

The Harifian in the Negeb and northern Sinai shows a Natufian-derived culture with a highly mobile settlement pattern. In winter Harifians dispersed in small groups in the sandy lowlands of the western Negeb and northern Sinai. Aggregation took place in summer time in the Negeb highlands. Their economic basis was more similar to that of hunter-gatherers than to the evolving communities of the farmers-hunters. Intensive gathering of plant foodstuffs, and possibly exchange with groups who controlled the areas where wild cereals were more abundant, enabled them to last for several centuries. The archaeological remains clearly reflect the elaborate long distance exchange network, oriented toward the Red Sea sources in which numerous marine shells were used.

The disappearance of the Harifian culture occurred at the same time as the establishment of the earliest farming communities along the 'Levantine corridor' which stretched from the Middle Euphrates, through the Damascus basin and into the Lower Jordan Valley.

IN THE BEGINNING

HUNTERS AND GATHERERS: PRODUCERS OF FOOD

Climatic amelioration following the last glacial period made possible a rapid expansion, c 12,500-11,000 BC, of bands of hunter-gatherers into hospitable regions of the Levant. Sometime after c 11,000 BC, however, food resources diminished due to climatic crisis and the expanding populations were forced to reorganize themselves into an entity known as the Natufian culture.

> 'CUSH BECAME THE FATHER OF NIMRUD; HE WAS THE FIRST ON EARTH TO BE A MIGHTY MAN. HE WAS A MIGHTY HUNTER BEFORE THE LORD...' GEN 10.8-9

3

PERIOD	SITE	GAZELLE % (0-100)	FALLOW DEER (0-60)	CAPROVINES (0-80)	CATTLE (0-100)	WILD BOAR (0-80)	RED DEER (0-40)	ROE DEER (0-40)	HARTE-BEEST (0-40)	EQUIDS (0-40)	NUMBER OF FINDS
HARIFIAN	ABU SALEM										(1143)
NATUFIAN	ROSH HORESHA										(977)
	RAKEFET CAVE										(911)
	KEBARA B.										(242)
	HAYONIM TER.										(4523)
	HAYONIM CAVE B.										(357)
	MALLAHA										(880)
	NAHAL OREN V										(1350)
	NAHAL OREN VI										(113)
GEOMETRIC KEBARAN A	HEFSIBAH										(59)
	NAHAL OREN VII										(855)
	EIN-GEV IV										(53)
	EIN-GEV III										(31)

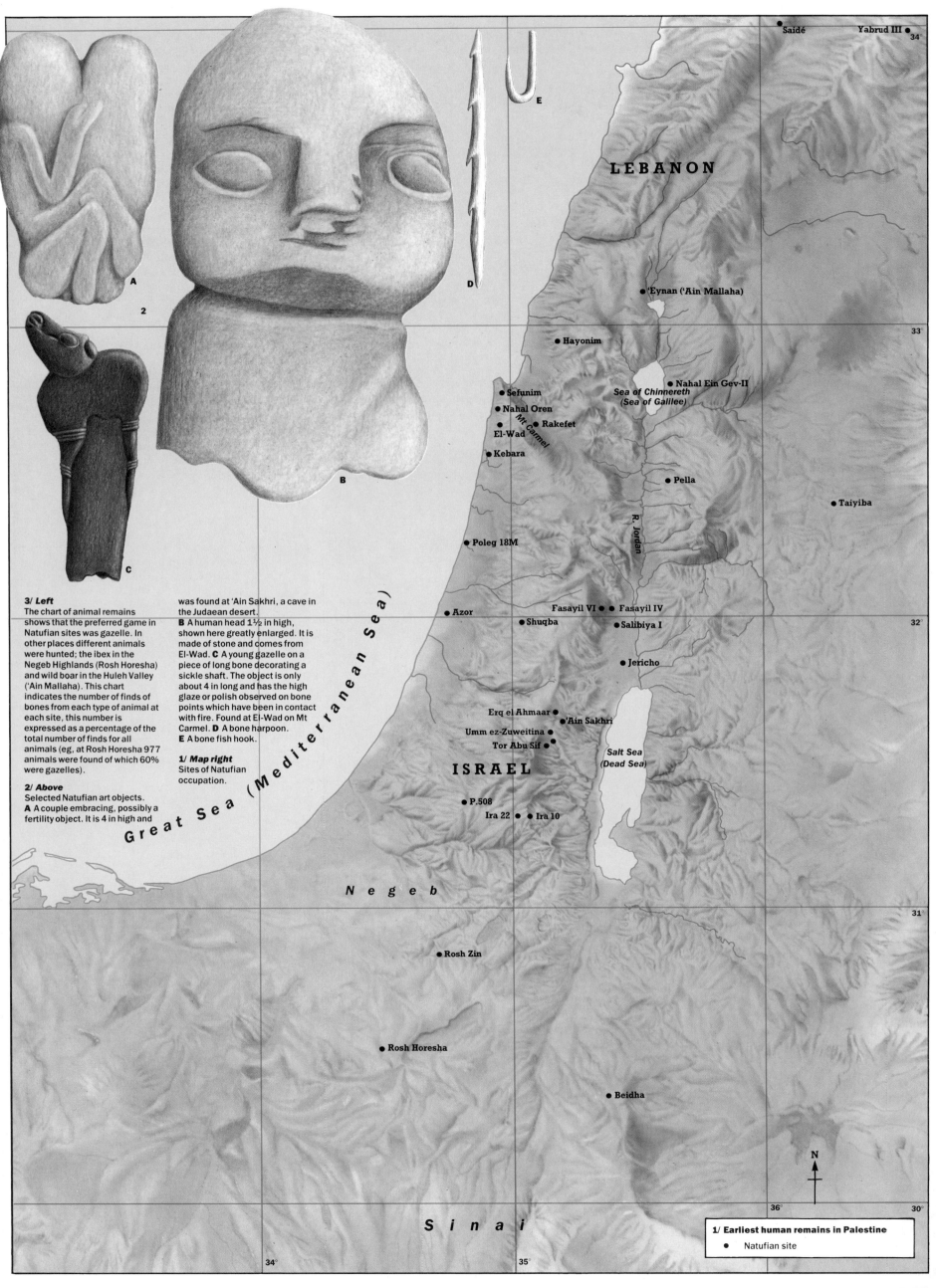

3/ Left
The chart of animal remains shows that the preferred game in Natufian sites was gazelle. In other places different animals were hunted; the ibex in the Negeb Highlands (Rosh Horesha) and wild boar in the Huleh Valley ('Ain Mallaha). This chart indicates the number of finds of bones from each type of animal at each site, this number is expressed as a percentage of the total number of finds for all animals (eg, at Rosh Horesha 977 animals were found of which 60% were gazelles).

2/ Above
Selected Natufian art objects.
A A couple embracing, possibly a fertility object. It is 4 in high and was found at 'Ain Sakhri, a cave in the Judaean desert.
B A human head 1½ in high, shown here greatly enlarged. It is made of stone and comes from El-Wad. **C** A young gazelle on a piece of long bone decorating a sickle shaft. The object is only about 4 in long and has the high glaze or polish observed on bone points which have been in contact with fire. Found at El-Wad on Mt Carmel. **D** A bone harpoon. **E** A bone fish hook.

1/ Map right
Sites of Natufian occupation.

LEBANON

Saidé
Yabrud III
34°

33°

'Eynan ('Ain Mallaha)

Hayonim

Nahal Ein Gev-II

Sea of Chinnereth
(Sea of Galilee)

Sefunim
Nahal Oren
Rakefet
Mt Carmel
El-Wad
Kebara

Pella

R. Jordan

Taiyiba

Poleg 18M

Fasayil VI Fasayil IV
32°

Azor
Shuqba
Salibiya I

Jericho

Erq el Ahmaar
'Ain Sakhri
Umm ez-Zuweitina
Tor Abu Sif

Salt Sea
(Dead Sea)

ISRAEL

P.508
Ira 22 Ira 10

Great Sea (Mediterranean Sea)

N e g e b

31°

Rosh Zin

Rosh Horesha

Beidha

N

S i n a i

34°
35°
36°
30°

| **1/ Earliest human remains in Palestine** |
| ● Natufian site |

25

PERMANENT settlements begin to appear in the ancient Near East as early as the 9th and 8th millennia BC. Jericho and Nahal Oren in Palestine, Mureybit in Syria, Çayönü in Anatolia and Ganj Dareh in Iran are probably the best known.

Evidence of permanent settled life increases greatly during the 7th millennium BC, almost certainly due to the gradual development of agriculture and animal husbandry.

Throughout the Neolithic period, from c 8300-4800 BC, most communities still relied mainly on hunting and gathering to supplement diets based on a gradually increasing production of domesticated cereal and animal food. The all-important process of domestication seems to have been random and probably occurred in a number of different places at the same time, though it is obvious from the well-documented evidence of trade that these early groups did not exist in isolation and interchanges of ideas almost certainly took place.

From the 6th millennium BC regional variations appear in Palestine, representing different tribal migrations which occurred. There is some evidence of increasing aridity in the climate of the Near East; this may have affected settlement in marginally climatic zones. The most intensive and widespread Neolithic settlement in Palestine occurred between 7500 and 6000 BC, known as the Pre-Pottery Neolithic B. Major settlements at Jericho, Munhata, Beidha and 'Ein Ghazal (Amman) show a general uniformity of culture although there were regional differences. The well-constructed, multi-roomed rectangular buildings were

IN THE BEGINNING

VILLAGES OF FARMERS

In the Bible, Genesis gives an account of the early beginnings of human settlements and farming. The earliest settlements in Palestine occurred in the Neolithic or New Stone Age, when man gradually changed from hunting and gathering to the first permanent settlements based on agriculture and animal husbandry.

often finished with a fine burnished lime plaster on walls and floors. The same plaster was used to line storage pits both inside the building and in courtyards, and to produce a group of remarkable male and female figures at 'Ein Ghazal. This evidence of what may be ancestor worship is known from a number of sites, including Jericho and Mureybit (Syria). One building at Jericho has been identified as a cult centre. At Beidha, rectangular buildings begin to appear.

Flaked and ground stone tools, which occur in large quantities, show some continuity from the earlier period; tools with large blades, show a possibly increasing interest in wood technologies. Flint arrowheads point to a continuing reliance on hunting for some food. Obsidian was still imported from Anatolia and there appears to have been an intensification in trading of shells, produce and semi-precious stones.

Most of the Pre-Pottery Neolithic B sites in Palestine were abandoned around 6000 BC, though some sites continued. When occupation begins again in the middle of the 6th millennium there is a different pattern of settlement and greater regional variety. This may be due to the differing origins of the newcomers.

Many later Pottery Neolithic sites in Palestine show an initial occupation by pit dwellers but on most sites large, rectangular houses where built. This perhaps shows a final settlement by previously nomadic groups already well acquainted with permanent architecture. In the flaked stone industries sickle blades are more common; this is probably an indication of a greater reliance on cultivated cereals. The main meat supply now appears to come from domesticated animals. The wide range of traded goods which existed in the earlier periods continued and there was close contact with sites in the Lebanon.

'AND GOD SAID "BEHOLD I HAVE GIVEN YOU EVERY PLANT YIELDING SEED WHICH IS UPON THE FACE OF THE EARTH, AND EVERY TREE WITH SEED IN ITS FRUIT; YOU SHALL HAVE THEM FOR FOOD. AND TO EVERY BEAST OF THE EARTH, AND TO EVERY BIRD OF THE AIR, ...I HAVE GIVEN EVERY GREEN PLANT FOR FOOD."'
GEN 1.29-30

3/ Left
Jericho was the largest known permanent settlement in Palestine. Shown here is part of Jericho's defence system, with a ditch and massive dry stone walls dating from Pre-pottery Neolithic A.

4/ Right
Pre-pottery Neolithic B house with a plaster floor from 'Ein Ghazal.

5/ Far right
Stone tower from Jericho, Pre-pottery Neolithic A.

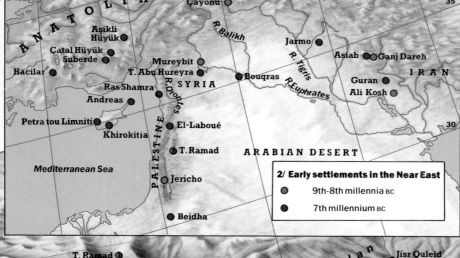

6/ Right
A painted plaster figure, with shell inlay to make eyes, from Jericho.

7/ Below
A skull from Jericho with the features built up in plaster.

2/ Early settlements in the Near East
- 9th-8th millennia BC
- 7th millennium BC

1/ Earliest settlements in Palestine
- 9th-8th millennia BC
- 7th millennium BC
- excavated site of 6th-5th millennia BC
- Chalcolithic period -4th millennium BC

THERE was a great increase in the number of settlements in Palestine and Jordan during the 5th-4th millennium BC, which is known as the Chalcolithic period, (from the Greek word for copper). However, there is a strong thread of continuity from the very first settlements onwards.

Today, many sites of the 5th-4th millennium BC are known and have been excavated. Settlements varied greatly in size but the largest are, naturally, located in the most favourable environments. The many settlements in the Negeb and Sinai were probably connected with the mining and production of copper and turquoise. The classical appearance or assemblage of these sites is known as Ghassulian, after Teleilat el-Ghassul, the site at the north-east corner of the Dead Sea where it was first recognized.

Within the past 30 years discoveries at sites in the region of Beersheba and in the hills immediately to the west of the Dead Sea, show a clear relationship to the later levels at Teleilat el-Ghassul and the name Ghassul-Beersheba is now used to describe the culture. Radiocarbon dating suggests occupation at these sites continued after Teleilat el-Ghassul because pottery shapes which appear only in the latest settlement at Teleilat el-Ghassul are common from the earliest levels of the Beersheba sites and some flaked stone tools and weapons are common to both. Although only a few copper objects are known from the last settlement at Teleilat el-Ghassul, Beersheba developed a highly sophisticated metal industry. A great hoard of copper objects from a cave at Nahal Mishmar remains the most remarkable

IN THE BEGINNING

METALWORKERS

The most notable feature of the Chalcolithic period was the great increase in the population of Palestine. Though local cultures continued, new groups entered the country bringing with them new skills, particularly that of metal working. However, the main basis of the economy continued to be agricultural. There was also a striking flowering of art, associated with religion, seen particularly in wall paintings.

collection of early metal objects in the Near East.

The settlement at Teleilat el-Ghassul was a large, open, site of some 60 acres, with solidly constructed rectangular houses of mud brick, often on stone foundations. In the Beersheba region, part of the initial occupation was troglodyte but there are also well built rectangular houses.

Religious cult centres existed in both areas. At Teleilat el-Ghassul a walled enclosure contained two large spectacular buildings which produced many ceramic vessels and figures, usually associated with religion. An almost identical but much more complete enclosure has been excavated at En-gedi and, there also, the objects suggest a cult centre. Other religious buildings have been identified at Gilat and at Megiddo. Recent excavations in the Golan have identified domestic house shrines, with basalt figures of both

human and animal deities. Evidence suggests that the deities worshipped were agricultural. At Teleilat el-Ghassul clay figurines of animals were placed in storage jars, with remains of cereals and olives.

As with many early societies the flowering of art seems to have been associated with religious practice. Spectacular wall paintings at Teleilat el-Ghassul seem to portray religious subjects. One shows a procession of ceremonially dressed and masked human figures approaching what is, perhaps, a shrine. The leading figure holds a sickle-shaped object in his right hand which curves back over his right shoulder. Similar sickle shaped objects in ivory have been found at Safadi. Human and animal figures attest to the importance of religion. Taken in conjunction with the ivory and metal creations of the Beersheba communities they also vividly illustrate the highly developed artistic abilities of the Chalcolithic people.

Amongst the most interesting creations of the Chalcolithic ceramic artists are ossuaries or burial chests. Large numbers of these have been found on sites in Palestine. At Teleilat el-Ghassul no adult burials were found but some 40 burials of new-born babies, beneath the walls and floors of houses, may point to foundation sacrifice.

Towards the end of the 4th millennium BC new cultural traits appear which herald the birth of the walled urban societies of the Bronze Age.

'ZILLAH BORE TUBAL CAIN; HE WAS THE FORGER OF ALL INSTRUMENTS OF BRONZE AND IRON.'　　　　GEN 4.22

1/ Map below
Permanent settlement occurred in Palestine as early as 9th millennium BC.

2/ Map below left
Permanent settlement increased greatly in the 7th millennium BC.

8/ Right
Examples of Ghassulian culture in the Jordan Valley. **A** pottery cornet cup from Teleilat el-Ghassul. **B** Basalt pestle and mortar from Sanctuary B at Teleilat el-Ghassul. **C** Two pottery bowls from Tabaqat Fahl, c 3500-3300 BC. **D** Polished bone palette, c 3700 BC. **E** Fan scraper probably used for the preparation of hide from Teleilat el-Ghassul. **F** Fenestrated Stand, from Sanctuary B at Teleilat el-Ghassul. **G** Unusual twin cornet vessel from Teleilat el-Ghassul, c 3700 BC. **H** Pottery figure from Teleilat el-Ghassul, found at Sanctuary B, c 3700 BC. **I** Pottery figure of a sheep, c 3700 BC.

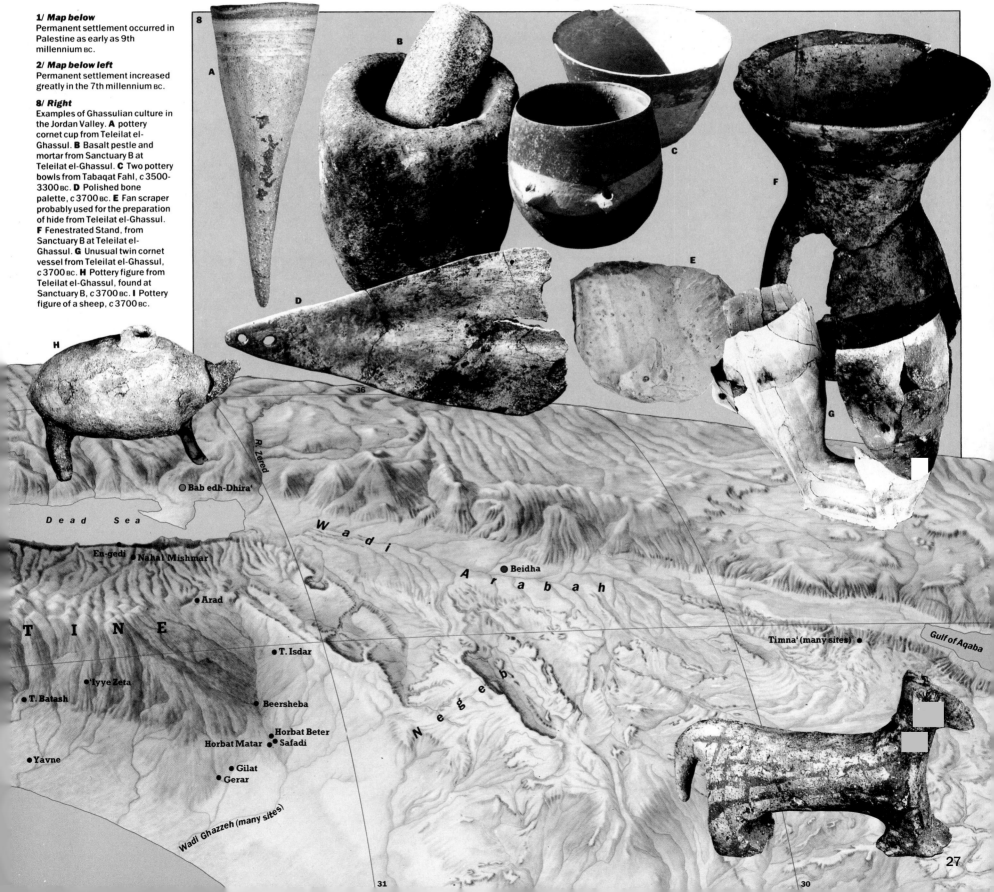

BY about 3000 BC many of the villages which had spread throughout the habitable regions of Palestine in the Chalcolithic period had been abandoned, to be replaced by a smaller number of walled towns, sited generally on major routes and functioning as local market centres and, in all probability, as collection and distribution points in the trading network linking the country with Egypt.

Unlike the contemporary towns of inland Syria, where commercial and cultural contacts with Sumer led to the growth of a rich, literate civilization, such as excavation has revealed at T. Mardikh (ancient Ebla), the Early Bronze Age towns of Palestine were small and unprepossessing, and their inhabitants lacked the art of writing. Their most imposing features were their defences. Walls were built of rough stones or of unbaked mud brick, and varied considerably in strength and design. At Arad (see diagram 3), one of the best preserved sites, the wall was furnished with semicircular bastions at regular intervals, exactly as is depicted on a wall painting in an Egyptian tomb of the 5th Dynasty (see illustration 4), where a Palestinian town is being attacked. At Jericho both square and semi-circular towers were in use, while square mud brick towers also flanked the simple but strong gateway at T. el-Far'ah(N). As time progressed the fortifications often grew more complex by a process of addition and modification, and by the end of the period some towns were surrounded by double or even triple lines of walls, with passages in between and with various outworks to impede enemy attacks.

At the few sites excavated there are signs of incipient town planning. At Arad an area separated by a wall from the rest of the town has been interpreted as a 'royal enclosure' containing a 'palace' and administrative buildings. Nearby is a double temple. At Arad also, and at Ai, large artificial reservoirs to conserve the winter rains were incorporated into the plan. At Megiddo and T. el-Far'ah(N) there is a suggestion of a grid arrangement, with houses grouped in blocks separated by narrow lanes. As for the buildings themselves, there is considerable diversity both in design and in size, although one basic plan does seem to

IN THE BEGINNING

'COME, LET US BUILD OURSELVES A CITY…'

Towards the end of the 4th millennium developments took place in the Levant which led, at the beginning of the Early Bronze Age around 3000 BC, to the appearance of towns. The evolution of urban societies had a profound effect on civilization. Large buildings such as fortifications and temples were erected and this required a complex system of social, economic and political organization.

have been popular for temples and houses alike, namely a rectangular structure with the entrance in the long side and often with benches along the other three.

Any wealth which accrued to the Palestinians from their trading activities seems to have had little beneficial effect on the local crafts and industries, which remained at a low level compared with those of contemporary Egypt and Mesopotamia. A few cylinder and stamp seals, which reflect but do not imitate Mesopotamian originals, are about the only items which can be termed art. In copper metallurgy (and despite the terminology this, and not bronze, was the metal used in the Early Bronze Age) there is nothing to indicate that the high technical achievements of the preceding Chalcolithic period were maintained, though this may be due to lack of evidence since metal objects would have been constantly melted down and re-used. The few tools and weapons known were made in simple, open moulds. Only in the pottery can real technological progress be seen for, compared with earlier pottery, the clay is now more carefully prepared, the wheel comes into common use, and the firing is better controlled, this latter development being demonstrated by a well-preserved kiln found at T. el-Far'ah(N). Two types of Early Bronze Age vessel – a graceful jug and a large ovoid storage jar – are of particular

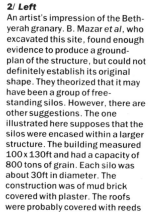

1   Water reservoir and girdle of buildings around it
2   Official buildings
3   Sacred precinct
3a The large twin temples
3b The small twin temples
4   Palace
5   Markets
6   Western gate
7   Dwellings
8   South-western gate

2/ Left
An artist's impression of the Beth-yerah granary. B. Mazar *et al*, who excavated this site, found enough evidence to produce a ground-plan of the structure, but could not definitely establish its original shape. They theorized that it may have been a group of free-standing silos. However, there are other suggestions. The one illustrated here supposes that the silos were encased within a larger structure. The building measured 100 x 130ft and had a capacity of 800 tons of grain. Each silo was about 30ft in diameter. The construction was of mud brick covered with plaster. The roofs were probably covered with reeds and mud.

3/ Above
Excavations at Arad have enabled a partial reconstruction to be made of the city. The black outline diagram shows the total area of the site. The round defensive towers accord well with Egyptian descriptions of such features, as can be seen from illustration 4.

1/ Map below
Urbanization in the Early Bronze Age is shown here. Our information about EBA Canaan comes from Pharaoh Phiops I's (c 2332-2283 BC) descriptions of his campaigns there.

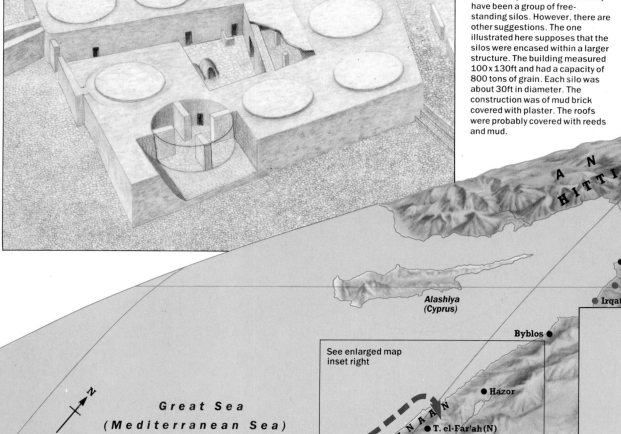

interest, since exported examples have been found in Egypt, providing tangible proof of the oil trade.

The number of times the fortifications of Jericho, T. el-Far'ah(N) and Ai, for example, were repaired and strengthened suggests that this was not a peaceful period. Perhaps inter-town rivalry contributed most to the insecurity, but Egyptian records also testify to military intervention from that country, and some of the destructions apparent in the archaeological record may be attributable to these campaigns. But some of the Early Bronze Age towns seem to have been abandoned peacefully, several (for example Arad and T. el-Far'ah(N)) within a few centuries of their foundation, and before the end of the period, and it is possible that this was because of a gradual decline in the Egyptian trade. There were internal, Egyptian, reasons for this decline, but developments in Syria might also have played a part. Recent discoveries at T. Mardikh (Ebla), south of Aleppo, have demonstrated the spectacular flourishing of civilization there, drawing its inspiration from Sumer. Judging from the clay tablets found there, this city exercised some sort of political hegemony after c 2400 BC as far south as Damascus, and had commercial relations over an even wider area. This must have been detrimental to Egypt's role in the Levant, and probably also explains the increasing number of objects of northern origin found in Palestine during the later part of the Early Bronze Age.

The withdrawal of Egyptian influence from Palestine appears to have had a disastrous effect on urban life there. Although a few Palestinian towns are mentioned in the Ebla texts the archaeological record shows conclusively that the final centuries of the 3rd millennium were a time of far-reaching economic and social readjustment. Town walls and public buildings were destroyed or neglected, not to be rebuilt until the beginning of the Middle Bronze Age II in c 2000 BC. Urban communities disintegrated and disappeared, and the country became once more as it had been in the 4th millennium, a land of agricultural villages and pastoral encampments.

New groups of semi-nomadic peoples (identified by some scholars with the biblical Amorites) may well have appeared and contributed to the decline of urbanism. But the most recent evidence suggests that it was the collapse of the economic system which was the primary cause of the changed conditions. Trade with Egypt had been the stimulus for urbanization in 3000 BC and its demise was to bring about the end of the Early Bronze Age urban interlude.

'"COME, LET US BUILD OURSELVES A CITY, AND A TOWER WITH ITS TOP IN THE HEAVENS, AND LET US MAKE A NAME FOR OURSELVES, LEST WE BE SCATTERED ABROAD UPON THE FACE OF THE WHOLE EARTH."' GEN 11.4

4/ Right
Egyptians attack an Asiatic fortress. From a tomb at Deshasheh.

5/ Below
The gates of T. el-Far'ah(N) built of mud brick on stone foundations.

1/ The campaigns of Pharaoh Phiops I
land route
sea route
Early Bronze Age cities
city engaged in trade with Ebla

MANY movements of peoples between Babylonia and the west are recorded in early documents, though the Genesis account of Abraham's migration gives no details of the precise route, method or time of travel until Canaan is reached. There is a theory that the migration between 'Ur of the Chaldees' in S. Babylonia and Haran to the north was related to the worship of Sin, the moon god who was worshipped in both cities, but this is not now widely accepted. Similarly any identification of the biblical Ur with places of the same name to the west or north of Haran has been disproved. Among detailed surviving itineraries is one of an army or caravan moving by named stages from near Ur and up the R. Tigris via Ashur and Nineveh before striking westwards to Haran ('cross-roads') in the early 18th century BC. Another describes the nine-

ABRAHAM'S MIGRATION

According to the Bible, Abraham was the earliest of the Hebrew patriarchs and was summoned by God to leave his home in Ur and journey to Canaan where he was to become the father of a nation. Although the biblical account gives many details of the journey, it is impossible to trace its route with any certainty. Scholars also disagree strongly about the time at which Abraham lived (estimates from 3000 to 1000BC have been given) and some would question his historicity.

month journey by Zimri-Lim, king of Mari c1760BC, routed up the R. Euphrates and R. Khabur thence to Haran and on to Aleppo (Khalab). Since the return journey was down the R. Orontes and then home by the desert route to Mari, Abraham might have moved south to Canaan initially by that same river valley, though the desert track from Haran down the R. Balikh then via Damascus is the more likely.

Abraham's journey northward is more reminiscent of a family caravan than of a specific trading mission or part of the sort of Amorite tribal migration which was common between Mesopotamia and the northern desert fringes. Such movements of semi-nomads between Babylonia, eastern Palestine and Syria, via Jebel el-Bishri, took place when the travellers moved between towns with which their families had associations. (For the probable route taken by

THE MOSAIC LAW

The Lord said to Moses, 'Come up to me on the mountain, and wait there; and I will give you the tables of stone, with the law and the commandment, which I have written for their instruction...' EX 24.12

'...you shall give life for life, eye for eye, tooth for tooth, hand for hand, foot for foot, burn for burn, wound for wound, stripe for stripe.' EX 21.23-25

'...But if the ox has been accustomed to gore in the past, and its owner has been warned but has not kept it in, and it kills a man or a woman, the ox shall be stoned and its owner also shall be put to death.' EX 21.29

THE LAWS OF HAMMURABI

'I, Hammurabi, am the king of justice, to whom Shamash committed law. My words are choice; my deeds have no equal; it is only to the fool that they are empty...'

'If a seignior has destroyed the eye of a member of the aristocracy, they shall destroy his eye.'

'If he had broken another seignior's bone, they shall break his bone.'

'If a seignior's ox was a gorer and his city council made it known to him that it was a gorer, but he did not pad its horns or tie up his ox, and that ox gored to death a member of the aristocracy, he shall give half a mina of silver.'

3/ Right
The most important single document on life and society in ancient Babylonia is this c 7ft high black diorite stela, inscribed with about 250 laws and with a scene at the top showing the sun-god Shamash committing the laws to Hammurabi, king of Babylon, 1792-1750BC. Once it was set up in Babylon, but some five centuries later was taken as a trophy of war by king Shurruk-Nahhunte of Elam to Susa, where it was discovered in three pieces by Jacques de Morgan during his excavation of the winter of 1901-2 and then taken to the Louvre.

1/ Map below
The ancient Near East was not a trackless waste but, from the Early Bronze Age was covered with an extensive network of trade routes.

2/ Map above
Inset is a reconstruction of the ziggurat (temple tower) of Babylon.

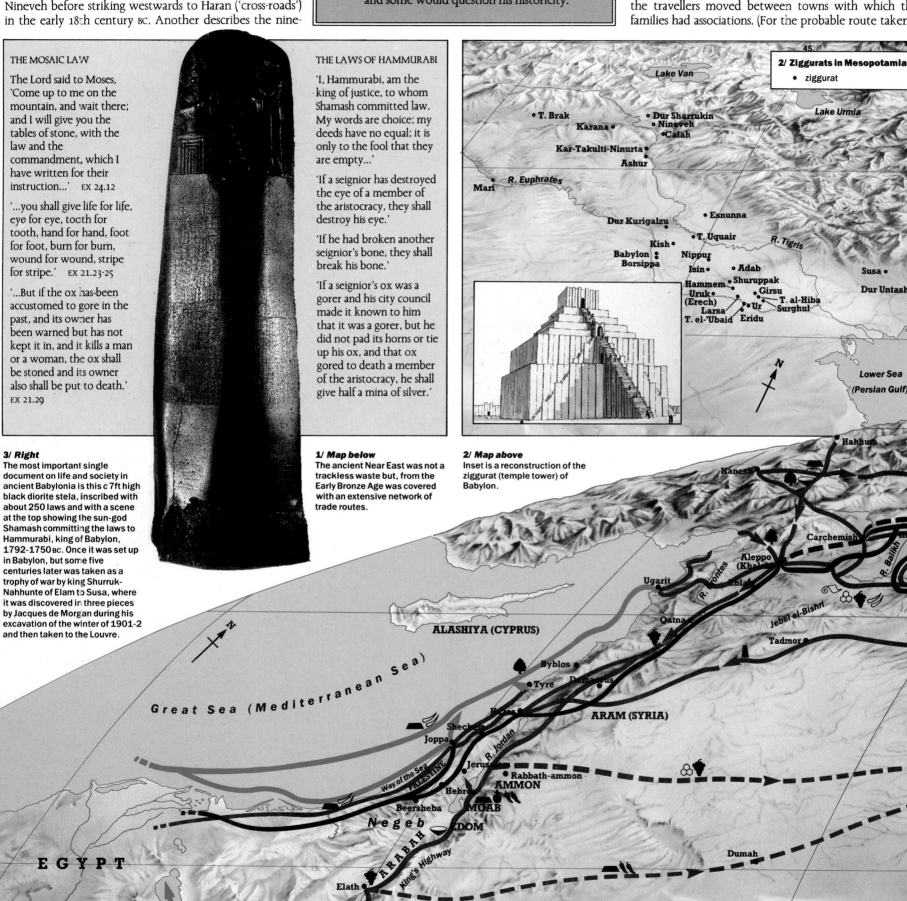

2/ Ziggurats in Mesopotamia
● ziggurat

the patriarchs around the Fertile Crescent see Map 1.)

The route, which extended from the R. Balikh to Haran and south to Aleppo and then via Qatna, Damascus and Hazor along the Palestinian ridge to Shechem and south to Hebron (Mamre) and Beersheba, is well attested. There were settlements between towns at c 17-mile intervals and the track was never more than a day's march from habitation and water.

INTERNATIONAL ROUTES AND TRADE

Already in the 2nd millennium the major cities record their imports of non-local items such as gold, silver, precious stones and wine together with the commodities essential to their industrial and technological processes (eg, copper, tin, oil) as well as luxury items, textiles, precious objects and furnishings. The interchange of luxury commodities trans-mitted via court officials, diplomats and specialists (eg, physicians) formed part of international relations and exchange of ideas. The major route followed in and near Palestine was named the 'Way of the Sea' and was the Philistine road from Egypt. It was supplemented by sea-routes both to the Philistine coastal cities and to the northern ports such as Joppa, Byblos, Tyre and Ugarit. Sea trade from Africa and S. Arabia into the southern ports was supplemented by caravans bringing gold and spices from Sheba through Tema to Dumah for Babylonia or westwards to join the 'King's Highway' through Midian, Edom, and Moab into Palestine or northwards to Rabbath-ammon and on to Damascus. Valuable wood from Lebanon was floated down the coast or dragged to the major streams for transit to the eastern cities as tribute. In the north tin from sources east of Mesopotamia was exchanged for copper, some tin reaching Canaan via Hazor from Mari.

NOW THE LORD SAID TO ABRAM, "GO FROM YOUR COUNTRY AND YOUR KINDRED AND YOUR FATHER'S HOUSE TO THE LAND THAT I WILL SHOW YOU. AND I WILL MAKE OF YOU A GREAT NATION, AND I WILL BLESS YOU, AND MAKE YOUR NAME GREAT, SO THAT YOU WILL BE A BLESSING. I WILL BLESS THOSE WHO BLESS YOU, AND HIM WHO CURSES YOU I WILL CURSE; AND BY YOU ALL THE FAMILIES OF THE EARTH SHALL BLESS THEM-SELVES." SO ABRAM WENT, AS THE LORD HAD TOLD HIM; AND LOT WENT WITH HIM. ABRAM WAS SEVENTY-FIVE YEARS OLD WHEN HE DEPARTED FROM HARAN. AND ABRAM TOOK SARAI HIS WIFE, AND LOT HIS BROTHER'S SON, AND ALL THEIR POSSES-SIONS WHICH THEY HAD GATHERED...' GEN 12.1-5

THE FLOOD FROM THE EPIC OF GILGAMESH

The Assyrian version of the story of the Flood was discovered on a clay tablet found at Nineveh (see right). The tablet, now in the British Museum, is 6in high and forms part of an epic poem which is especially interesting when compared with some of the events in the book of Genesis.

Utnapishtim, the hero of the flood from Shuruppak, tells of the flood

Shuruppak – a city which thou knowest,
And which on Euphrates' banks is situate –
That city was ancient, as were the gods within it,
When their heart led the great gods to produce the flood.

The god Ea orders Utnapishtim to make preparation
'Man of Shuruppak, son of Ubar-Tutu,
Tear down this house, build a ship!
Give up possessions, seek thou life.
Forswear worldly goods and keep the soul alive!
Aboard the ship take thou the seed of all living things.
The ship that thou shalt build,
Her dimensions shall be to measure.
Equal shall be her width and her length.'

Utnapishtim proceeds to build the ship and load it
On the fifth day I laid her framework.
One whole acre was her floor space,
Ten dozen cubits the height of each of her walls,
Ten dozen cubits each edge of the square deck.
I laid out the contours and joined her together.
I provided her with six decks,
Dividing her thus into seven parts.
Her floor plan I divided into nine parts.
I hammered water-plugs into her.
Whatever I had of all the living beings I laded upon her.
All my family and kin I made to go aboard the ship
The beasts of the field, the wild creatures of the field,
All craftsmen I made go aboard.

The rain-storm
Six days and six nights
Blows the flood wind, as the south-storm sweeps the land.
When the seventh day arrived,
The flood-carrying south-storm subsided in the battle,
Which it had fought like an army.

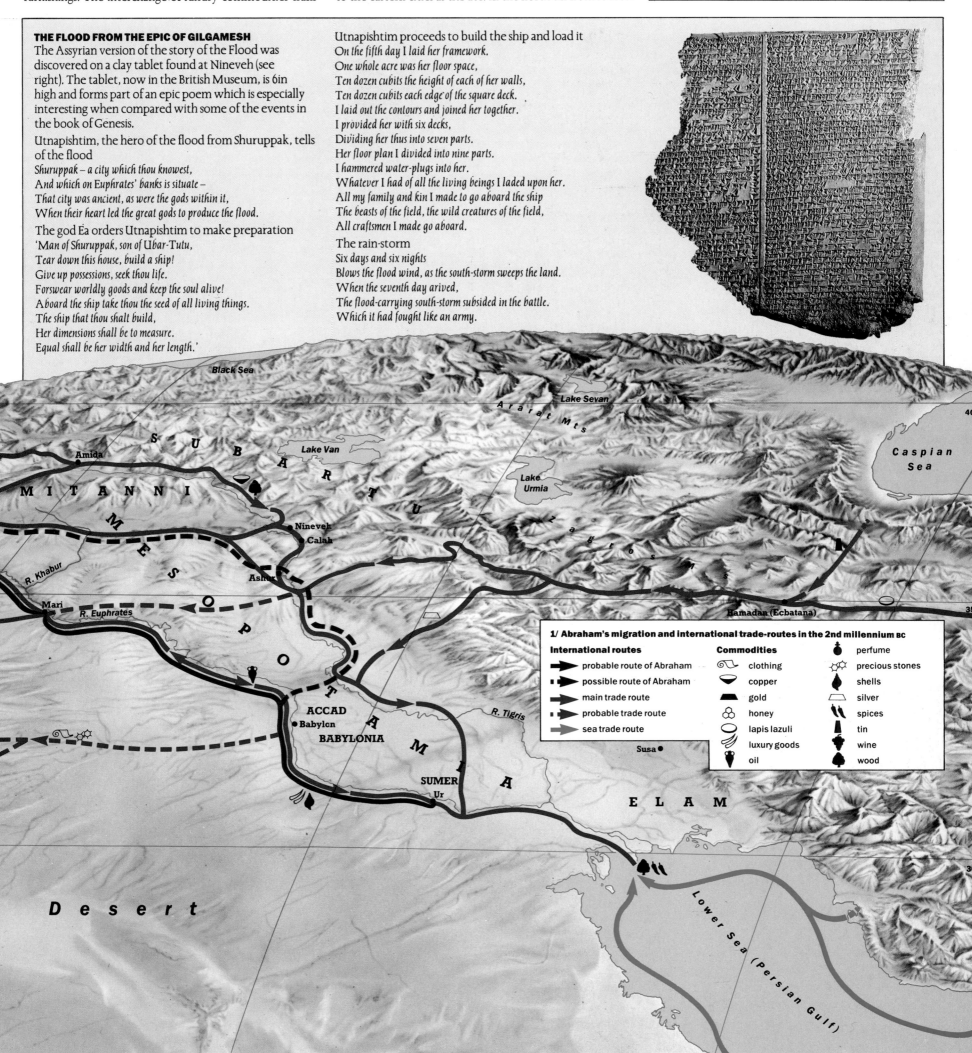

1/ Abraham's migration and international trade-routes in the 2nd millennium BC

International routes
- ➤ probable route of Abraham
- ▪➤ possible route of Abraham
- ➤ main trade route
- ▪➤ probable trade route
- ➤ sea trade route

Commodities
- clothing
- copper
- gold
- honey
- lapis lazuli
- luxury goods
- oil
- perfume
- precious stones
- shells
- silver
- spices
- tin
- wine
- wood

THE society found by the patriarchs among the Canaanites was composed of city-states (eg, Shechem, Gerar) and urban communities (eg, Hebron). They were pastoralists themselves but engaged in agriculture when permitted to do so (GEN 26.12-14). They also strove to gain acceptance in the urban settlements (eg, GEN 19.1-14). Contacts with Egypt were prominent though no Egyptian rule in Canaan was recognized (but Canaan was a descendant of Ham along with Egypt, GEN 10.6). The patriarchs generally confined themselves to the central hill country, along the watershed route from Shechem to Hebron, via Bethel, and on to the biblical Negeb at Beersheba. Their only foray towards the coast was to Gerar (perhaps T. Abu-Hureireh, modern Hebrew T. Haror), where they encountered the Philistine city-state ruled by Abimelech (GEN 20 and 26). No historical or cultural detail in the patriarchal narratives finds any echo in Bronze Age historical documents. It is sometimes proposed that they came in the Middle Bronze Age I (c 2200-2000 BC) but this view does not take account of the fact that, at that time, there were no city-states, no contacts with Egypt and no settlements in the Beersheba area. The areas they usually frequented were those where the Canaanite cities were few and widely separated. It is instructive to compare maps of the patriarchal wanderings with those of the Execration texts (see Map 3 and illustration below) in the MBA and of the campaigns by the 18th Dynasty pharaohs and of the el-Amarna letters. There is a generally negative correlation. On the other hand, the racial groups mentioned in the patriarchal narratives are also radically different from those of the Middle and Late Bronze Ages. The peoples round about are the Philistines,

WANDERINGS OF ABRAHAM AND ISAAC IN CANAAN

According to Israelite tradition, the fathers of the nation came from Ur of the Chaldees, via Haran to Canaan, and after moving to Egypt to escape from famine, they settled at Hebron (GEN 12). Dating the patriarchal wanderings is a debatable subject but it is believed that they took place between the end of the Bronze and the beginning of the Iron Age (c 1300-1150 BC).

the Midianites, and the Ishmaelites (besides the Edomite, Moabite and Ammonite nations who are said to have descended from important figures in the stories themselves). There is good reason to suppose that the patriarchal accounts derive from the milieu of the end of the Bronze and beginning of the Iron Age, and are retold from the standpoint of the late Israelite monarchy.

CANAAN IN THE MIDDLE BRONZE AGE

During the MB I, the absence of urban settlements throughout southern Canaan permitted the influx of semi-nomadic pastoralists who established very poor villages or simple campsites, often along the courses of the stream beds (especially in Transjordan) and occasionally on the ruins of the Early Bronze cities. Their material culture is known mainly from extensive burial grounds discovered throughout the land. They appear to have come in off the steppe

lands bordering on the Arabian desert. The most dense concentration of campsites, and a few fortified settlements are known there. They had no apparent contacts with Egypt, which itself was in a period of weakness.

Urban centres began to spring up again in the MB IIA (2000-1750 BC). The impetus came from the north (Phoenicia-Syria), especially along the coastal plain.

The city-state culture continued to flourish in MB IIB (1750-1668 BC). Strong commercial ties with Egypt are now evident for the southern as well as for the northern coast. More urban centres, fortified by ramparts, come into being. Meanwhile the commercial colony founded at Avaris had grown since its establishment in MB IIA. Imports there became especially plentiful from southern Canaan.

In the final stage, MB IIC (1668-c 1550 BC), the colony at Avaris became a political capital whose rulers gained control over the entire delta and part of Middle Egypt (15th Dynasty). Their scarabs and those of their officials are known in S. Canaan up to the Carmel range. The rulers were called Ḥqꜣw Ḫꜣswt, 'rulers of foreign lands' (the Hyksos of Manetho); they evidently extended their authority into southern Canaan.

WRITTEN SOURCES IN THE MIDDLE BRONZE AGE

Very few written sources exist that shed light on Canaan in the MBA. An Egyptian 'novel' (which might be a true copy of a funerary inscription) about a high-ranking political exile, Sinuhe, describes life in Canaan-Syria. Sinuhe encounters pastoralists in the Sinai whose leader recognizes him from frequent visits to Egypt. He makes his way to Byblos where the strong Egyptian presence forces him to 'turn back' to the land of Qedem (perhaps east of Chinnereth)

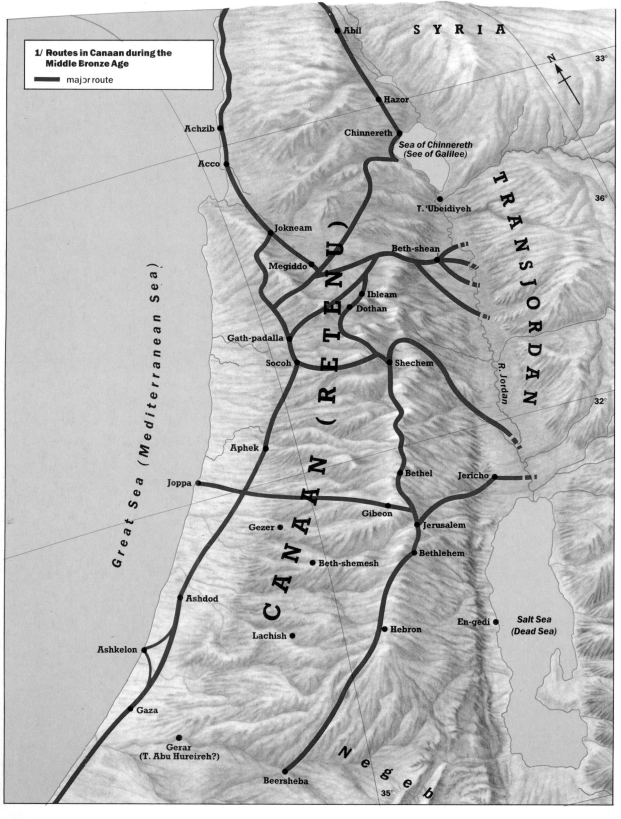

SYRIA

Abil

Hazor

Achzib

Chinnereth
Sea of Chinnereth (See of Galilee)

Acco

T. 'Ubeidiyeh

TRANSJORDAN

Jokneam

Beth-shean

Megiddo

Ibleam
Dothan

Gath-padalla

R. Jordan

Socoh

Shechem

G r e a t   S e a   (M e d i t e r r a n e a n   S e a)

Aphek

Bethel   Jericho

Joppa

Gibeon

Gezer   Jerusalem

Beth-shemesh   Bethlehem

Ashdod

En-gedi   *Salt Sea (Dead Sea)*

Lachish   Hebron

Ashkelon

C A N A A N   (R E T E N U)

Gaza

N e g e b

Gerar
(T. Abu Hureireh?)

Beersheba

1/ Map left
Main routes in Canaan during the Middle Bronze Age.

2/ Map near right
The wanderings of Abraham in Canaan.

3/ Map far right
Towns mentioned in Egyptian Execration texts.

4/ Above
An Execration figure. In this form of magic, a curse was inscribed on the clay and was made effective by smashing the figure. Such texts provide us with the names of foreign rulers considered by the Egyptians as enemies.

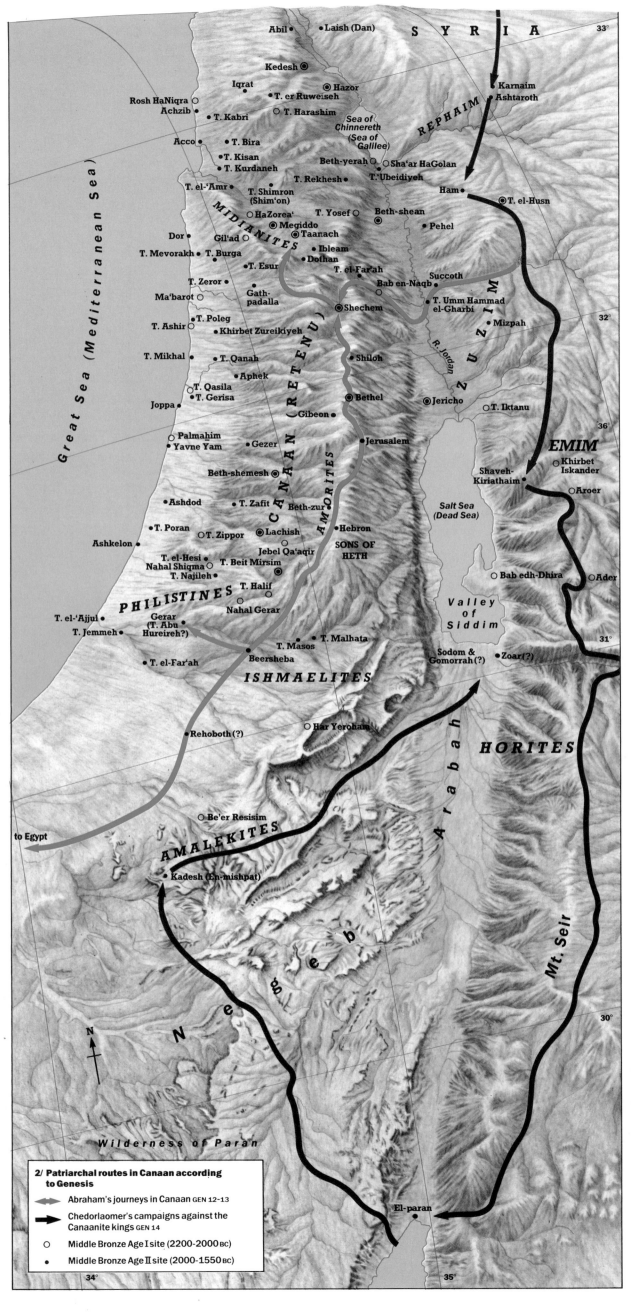

where he is accepted into the family of a local ruler bearing a typical west Semitic name. He is given a feudal fief and serves his new father-in-law as military commander. His adopted home was a sophisticated society with all the branches of agriculture (grain crops, orchards, cattle).

Three collections of magical (Execration) texts, on small saucers or on figurines, list the potential enemies of pharaoh, including the foreign rulers of Retenu (Canaan). The older group, c 1900 BC, contains few recognizable towns but the latest group, c 1800, mentions many places known from the Bible and other later texts. The names of the rulers are all west Semitic, either Amorite or Canaanite, proving affinity with the Amorite populations of the N. Syrian states and the dynasties now ruling the main cities of Mesopotamia (including Hammurabi of Babylon). The pattern of Canaanite city-states, clustered mostly on the plains, continues through the LBA. Only Shechem and Jerusalem are listed in the hill country (the lesser ranking towns of Shiloh, Bethel and Beth-zur are not mentioned). Some development towards centralization may be discerned from the earlier to the later Execration texts but not a trend from nomadism to urbanism as formerly assumed.

'ABRAM WAS SEVENTY-FIVE YEARS OLD WHEN HE DEPARTED FROM HARAN. AND ABRAM TOOK SARAI HIS WIFE... AND THEY SET FORTH TO GO TO THE LAND OF CANAAN. WHEN THEY HAD COME TO THE LAND OF CANAAN, ABRAM PASSED THROUGH THE LAND TO THE PLACE AT SHECHEM, TO THE OAK OF MOREH. AT THAT TIME THE CANAANITES WERE IN THE LAND. THEN THE LORD APPEARED TO ABRAM, AND SAID, "TO YOUR DESCENDANTS I WILL GIVE THIS LAND".' GEN 12.4-7

2/ Patriarchal routes in Canaan according to Genesis

➤ Abraham's journeys in Canaan GEN 12-13

➤ Chedorlaomer's campaigns against the Canaanite kings GEN 14

○ Middle Bronze Age I site (2200-2000 BC)

● Middle Bronze Age II site (2000-1550 BC)

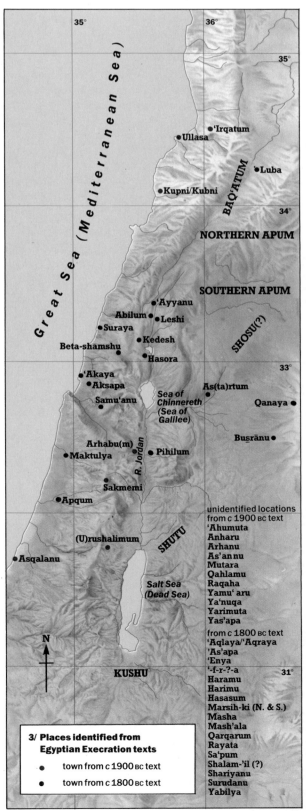

unidentified locations
from c 1900 BC text
'Ahumuta
Anharu
Arhanu
As'an nu
Mutara
Qahlamu
Raqaha
Yamu' aru
Ya'nuqa
Yarimuta
Yas'apa

from c 1800 BC text
'Aqlaya/'Aqraya
'As'apa
'Enya
'-f-r-?-a
Haramu
Harimu
Hasasum
Marsih-ki (N. & S.)
Masha
Mash'ala
Qarqarum
Rayata
Sa'pum
Shalam-'il (?)
Shariyanu
Surudanu
Yabilya

3/ Places identified from Egyptian Execration texts

● town from c 1900 BC text

● town from c 1800 BC text

THE initiative for Jacob's journey had come mainly from his mother Rebekah who wished him to escape from Esau, who planned to kill Jacob because he had stolen the blessing of their father Isaac. Both Rebekah and her husband, Isaac, were direct descendants of Abraham, who had also lived in Haran for many years. To maintain the family link, Jacob's mission was to choose his wife from the relatives of Rebekah's brother Laban, an Aramaean.

Haran was a major city in northwest Mesopotamia, about 850 miles from Jacob's home in Beersheba. It is situated on the R. Balikh, an eastern tributary of the Euphrates, as is reflected in the comment that Jacob's company had to cross 'the river', ie the Euphrates, on their return journey. Haran had two claims to fame, its position on international trade routes, and as a centre for the worship of Sīn, the moon-god. Haran is associated with the term 'Paddan-aram', effectively identical with Aram-Naharaim ('Aram of the two rivers'), the area between the R. Khabur in the east and the great bend of the Euphrates to the west of it.

Jacob's route from Beersheba took him through the hill country passing near Hebron, Jerusalem, Shiloh, and Shechem. The major incident on the journey took place at Bethel, known in those days as Luz. Here Jacob encountered God through a dream (GEN 28.12-17). From Bethel the road passed through Damascus and continued to Haran by one of two routes. The major road went north via Hamath and east via Carchemish, and a southern route went via Tadmor to Mari and Babylon.

· At Haran Jacob moved in with Laban's household and married his two cousins Leah and Rachel (GEN 29.16-30.43). Jacob returned to Palestine probably through Damascus, and then headed south in Transjordan along the King's Highway. This important road passed through towns such as Ramoth-gilead and Rabbah on its way to Edom, where Esau lived, and then on to the Red Sea. Jacob's haste to leave Paddan-aram made this direct road a natural choice, but despite giving Jacob three days' start, Laban caught-up with him somewhere in the highland region of Gilead, covering the distance in a mere seven days. After a rather tense and ill-tempered confrontation, the two men concluded a covenant and commemorated their agreement by heaping up stones as a permanent but inanimate witness at Galeed ('heap of witness'). From there Jacob continued toward the R. Jabbok where he experienced another divine encounter. Jacob called the place Penuel ('the face of God'). The feud with Esau was reconciled. Esau returned southward to the stern heights of Edom, but Jacob crossed the Jordan. After settling temporarily at Shechem and later at Bethel, he was finally reunited with his father at Hebron.

THE CITY OF MARI
Mari, on the west bank of the Euphrates some 200 miles southeast of Haran, was first discovered in 1933. Early in the course of digging there appeared what has become known as the Palace of Zimri-Lim (see plan 4). This building provides a tangible record of what life was like in this region of the Euphrates during the first half of the 2nd millennium BC. The cuneiform tablets – some 25,000 texts have been found – are more explicit. Trade was carried on from Mari with Canaan, Hattushash in Anatolia, and even with the centres of commerce in Alashiya (Cyprus) and Crete. Shipments of tin from Hazor and Laish (Dan) are mentioned. Some texts describe the phenomenon of divine revelation through dreams. Others deal with diplomatic and legal matters, treaties and even the trivial letters of schoolboys. One chides his mother for failing to clothe him properly: 'While

JACOB'S JOURNEY TO HARAN

Important stories about the patriarchs have their setting far beyond the borders of the land of Canaan where they eventually came to dwell. Haran in the land of the Aramaeans, located east of the Upper Euphrates, was a stopping place for Abraham; Isaac took Rebekah for a wife there; and Jacob spent 20 years in Haran tending the flocks of Laban. Archaeology has greatly increased our knowledge of this region, particularly for the first half of the 2nd millennium BC, a period within which many scholars would place the patriarchs. An area hitherto known only for its pastoral economy appears to have had a flourishing trade.

wool was being consumed in our house like bread,' he wrote, 'you were making my clothes cheaper... By cheapening and scrimping my clothes you have become rich.'

EBLA IN NORTH SYRIA
Contemporary with Mari was Ebla, discovered in 1964 at T. Mardikh, 36 miles southwest of Aleppo. The site is best known for the thousands of cuneiform tablets which provide details about international trade and politics over the area extending from Lower Mesopotamia to Palestine for the period from c2400 to 2250BC. T. Mardikh was also occupied in the later Old Syrian period (c2000-1600BC). It is in this later period that architectural features have been found which provide significant connections with Canaan.

> '"...GO TO PADDAN-ARAM TO THE HOUSE OF BETHUEL YOUR MOTHER'S FATHER; AND TAKE AS WIFE FROM THERE ONE OF THE DAUGHTERS OF LABAN YOUR MOTHER'S BROTHER."'
> GEN 28.2

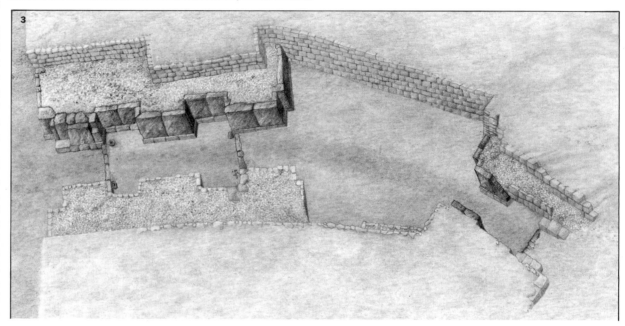

2/ Above
A ground plan of the Great Temple at Ebla (T. Mardikh). It was used during the first half of the 2nd millennium BC, and is an early example of a familiar plan of temple. It is fairly certain that the 10th-century design of temple (see Solomonic temple in Jerusalem page 86) was derived from this tradition, well-established in Syria a thousand years earlier.

3/ Above
The south-west gate of Ebla. The city was surrounded by a rampart about 100ft wide and 65ft high. Entrance was through a gate with double doors. This type of city-gate was probably a predecessor of Israelite city gates (see page 86).

4/ Above right
The city of Mari in the 2nd millennium BC. The palace of Zimri-Lim contained over 260 courts and rooms.

5/ Below right
Part of a fresco from the palace of Zimri-Lim.

6/ Below far right
Zimri-Lim ruled Mari from about 1800BC until his defeat in c1760 by Hammurabi of Babylon.

1/ Map right
GEN 28-29 describes how Jacob left Canaan and went to Haran, where he married his two cousins Leah and Rachel. He eventually returned home and was united with Isaac at Hebron. Both journeys were marked by unique encounters with the Lord at Bethel and Penuel (see text).

1/ Jacob's Journeys to Haran
→ Jacob's probable route
→ other major route

Great Sea
(Mediterranean Sea)

Gerar

Beersheba

Kadesh-barnea

N e g

SHUR

E G Y P T

R. Nile

Red Sea

Sinai

Elath

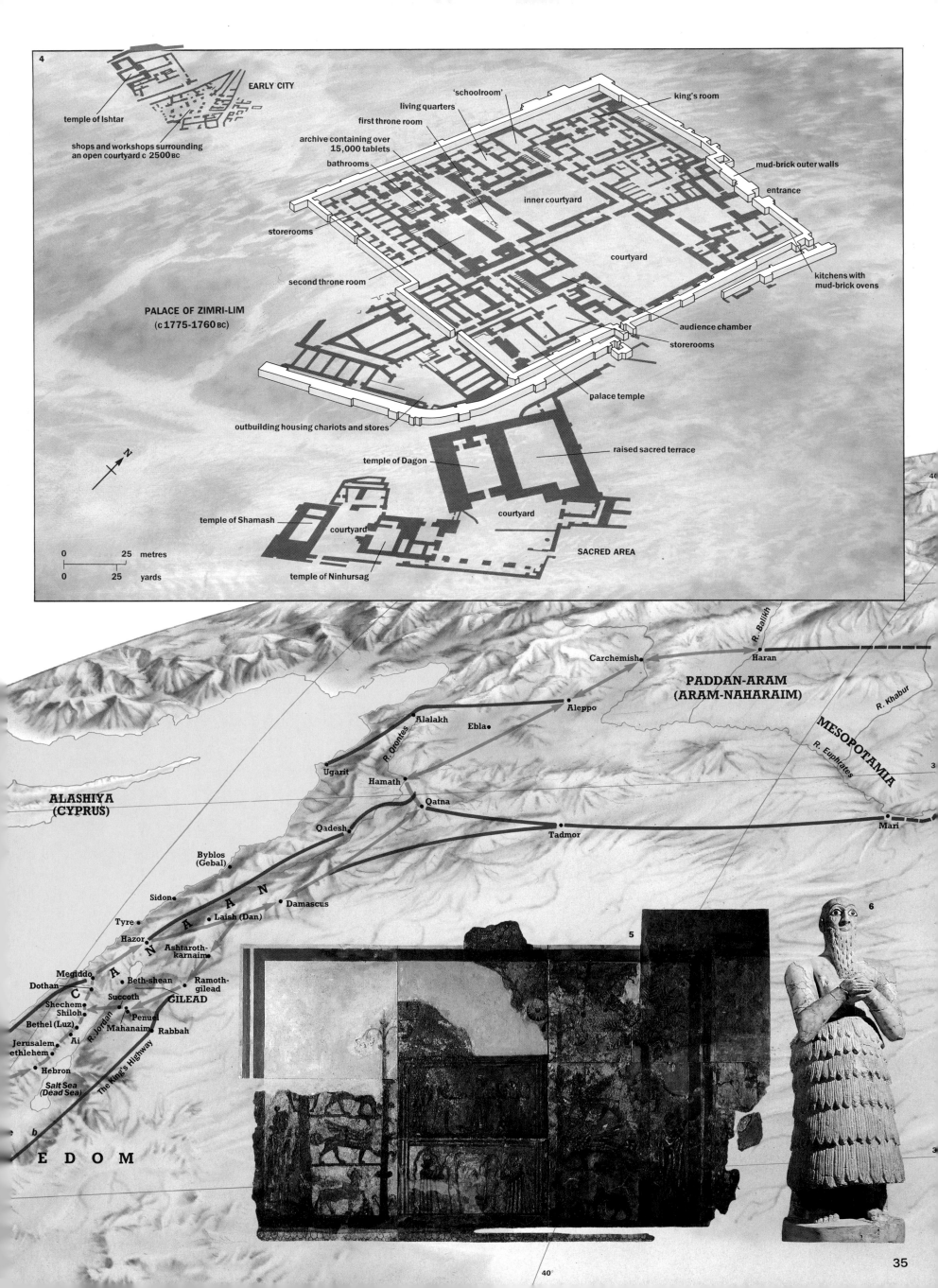

EARLY CITY

temple of Ishtar

shops and workshops surrounding
an open courtyard c 2500 BC

PALACE OF ZIMRI-LIM
(c 1775-1760 BC)

archive containing over
15,000 tablets

bathrooms

'schoolroom'

first throne room

living quarters

king's room

inner courtyard

mud-brick outer walls

entrance

storerooms

courtyard

second throne room

kitchens with
mud-brick ovens

audience chamber

storerooms

palace temple

outbuilding housing chariots and stores

temple of Dagon

raised sacred terrace

temple of Shamash

courtyard

courtyard

temple of Ninhursag

SACRED AREA

N

0	25	metres
0	25	yards

Carchemish

Haran

R. Balikh

**PADDAN-ARAM
(ARAM-NAHARAIM)**

Aleppo

R. Khabur

MESOPOTAMIA

Alalakh

Ebla

R. Orontes

Ugarit

Hamath

R. Euphrates

**ALASHIYA
(CYPRUS)**

Qatna

Qadesh

Tadmor

Mari

Byblos
(Gebal)

Sidon

Damascus

Tyre

Laish (Dan)

Hazor

Ashtaroth-
karnaim

Megiddo

Dothan

Beth-shean

Ramoth-
gilead

Shechem

Succoth

GILEAD

Shiloh

Penuel

Bethel (Luz)

Mahanaim

Rabbah

Jerusalem

Ai

R. Jordan

ethlehem

Hebron

Salt Sea
(Dead Sea)

The King's Highway

E D O M

C A N A A N

C

b

THE story of Joseph as told in GEN 37-50 ties in well with what we know of Egypt during the 13th and Hyksos Dynasties (see below). The Midianite or Ishmaelite traders (the Bible uses both names) who brought him there were but one group among many which visited Egypt in the first half of the 2nd millennium BC. The Canaanite townships of Shechem and Dothan which feature in Joseph's travels in GEN 37 are also attested in external sources for this general period. Excavations at both sites show important and flourishing settlements at the time (Middle Bronze Age). Shechem is also named in Egyptian sources in the 19th/18th centuries BC. It is significant that one large Egyptian household of c 1740 BC contained the names of 79 domestic servants, over half of them being 'Asiatics' with Semitic names such as Jacob, Issachar and Asher. It is piquant to note that the sum of 20 shekels reputedly paid for Joseph (GEN 37.28) was the correct average price for a slave around the 18th century BC, as can be seen from the famous stela of Hammurabi and in contemporary legal tablets from the city of Mari. Whilst many Asiatics spent their life in Egypt in this humble fashion, others are known to have reached very high office, just as Joseph eventually did.

The other feature of the Joseph narrative which accords well with what we know of the time is the account of his brothers coming to look for grain at the time of famine in their own land. Egypt was a fertile country and would normally produce crops in excess. There are records of starving foreigners arriving to ask for assistance. However, sometimes the harvest failed repeatedly and an event such as this may be basis for the tradition of the seven lean years which also appears in the Joseph narrative. Certainly an inscription from the Hellenistic period speaks of seven years of famine.

Many other details of the biblical account reflect Egyptian practices. From a section of an ancient prison register and other monuments we may observe the Egyptian prison system at work in Joseph's general period. Major prisons had a director (cf the role of the captain of the guard in GEN 39) and keepers like the keeper or warder of GEN 39.22. Such prisons 'filed' inmates under seven entries from name and sex through to a final discharge tick, equivalent to 'case closed'. The initial cause of Joseph's imprisonment was the evidence and lies of his owner's wife (GEN 39). In ancient Egyptian literature, such sexually adventurous women occur, during this period (Papyrus Westcar) and later (Papyrus D'Orbiney – see page 39). Butlers or cupbearers were prominent at the courts of the pharaohs, and came to play important roles in administration at the king's direct command. So the appearance of a royal butler and baker in the Joseph narrative is no surprise. Joseph's reported ability to interpret dreams accords with a current belief in the importance of such practices and there exist manuals which give instruction in this art. When he was appointed to high office he was given a collar of gold and the royal seal, which we also know was the regular custom. Finally the manner in which he was embalmed and laid in a coffin was not a Hebrew custom but was typical of the practices of the Egyptians.

THE COMING OF THE HYKSOS

At about the time of Joseph, Egypt had come under the control of a group of foreign rulers whom we call the Hyksos. This name (in Egyptian it was *Hik-khoswet* and later *Hik-shos*) meant 'chiefs of foreign countries'. They were a Semitic people and racially they had more in common with the Hebrews than they did with the native Egyptians.

From the 19th and 18th centuries BC, in the later 12th Dynasty, a growing number of these Semitic foreigners from neighbouring Canaan had found places in Egyptian society, high or low, attached to large households or serving such institutions as temples and their administrations. During the 13th Dynasty the flow grew, and eventually we find that at least one pharaoh had a Semitic name (Khendjer, cf Semitic *hanzir*, 'boar'). During the century from about 1750 to 1650 BC, one or more West-Semitic chief may have succeeded in becoming local ruler of part of the East Delta (the so-called '16th Dynasty'). As the 12th and 13th Dynasty kings had the key centre of Ro-waty (and possibly a summer residence there), adjoining Avaris, such local 'naturalized' foreign chiefs may have become involved with Egyptian royal politics of the day. Certainly, at about 1650 BC, one of these Hyksos rulers finally took the Egyptian throne not only in the East Delta but back in Memphis itself (with Itj-towy, its administrative satellite 'new town'), founding a new regime, the so-called 15th or Hyksos Dynasty.

The new rulers imposed their control over all Egypt, treating as vassals both the line of the 13th Dynasty, restricted to Thebes and the south, and a shadowy 14th Dynasty in the West Delta. The summer capital was extended (or changed)

EMERGENCE OF ISRAEL: PATRIARCHAL TRADITIONS

THE SALE OF JOSEPH AND HIS ENTRY INTO EGYPT

According to Genesis, Jacob's son Joseph was the object of envy on the part of his brothers who sold him to slave-traders travelling to Egypt. However, Joseph eventually rose to high office and, when a famine struck Canaan, his brothers were forced to come to Egypt in search of grain. The Bible recounts how, instead of taking revenge on his relations, Joseph forgave them and provided them with food. Egypt's reputation as a fertile land producing an abundance of crops would certainly have encouraged people starving in poorer countries to migrate there in search of assistance.

to Avaris itself, centre of the worship of the god Seth, nearest equivalent of the weather gods of the Levant such as Baal, Teshub, Adad or Tarkhuns.

The Hyksos kings adopted Egyptian royal style and retained a basically Egyptian bureaucracy, but introduced fellow-foreigners into the administration. The extent of the authority of the Hyksos kings in Canaan is uncertain; the concept of a vast 'Hyksos Empire' lacks sufficient factual foundation. Certainly king Apophis was termed 'Ruler of Retenu' by his opponent Kamosis of Thebes; this could imply rule of part of Palestine. The distribution of Hyksos royal scarab-seals in Canaan, plus a broken stone lintel with remains of royal titles of about this age from near Yibna, would combine to suggest a sphere of direct rule as far north as Joppa, and reaching along the western foothills of Canaan from Gezer to T. Beit Mirsim. Stray finds would extend communications as far as Jericho and Carmel. Much more distant trade or diplomacy might lie behind the objects naming king Khyan found in Crete and at Boğazköy in Asia Minor, but perhaps not a small lion figure found in Baghdad (later loot from Egypt?).

The rulers of Thebes became active opponents of the Hyksos rule during c 1560 – 1540 BC. Seqenenre possibly died in battle with them, while Kamosis restricted them to the East Delta when he swept through Egypt to the very gates of Avaris. But it took ten years for his brother Ahmosis I (founder of the 18th Dynasty and Empire or New Kingdom) to expel the last Hyksos king, Khamudy, from Egypt, and a three-year siege of Sharuhen (T. el-Far'ah (S)) to break their power in southern Canaan. From the Egyptian determination to keep such invaders firmly at bay was born the Egyptian empire in the Levant.

'SO WHEN JOSEPH CAME TO HIS BROTHERS, THEY STRIPPED HIM OF HIS ROBE ... AND CAST HIM INTO A PIT ... THEN THEY SAT DOWN TO EAT, AND LOOKING UP THEY SAW A CARAVAN OF ISHMAELITES, COMING FROM GILEAD, WITH THEIR CAMELS BEARING GUM, BALM, AND MYRRH, ON THEIR WAY TO CARRY IT DOWN TO EGYPT. THEN JUDAH SAID TO HIS BROTHERS, "WHAT PROFIT IS IT IF WE SLAY OUR BROTHER AND CONCEAL HIS BLOOD? COME, LET US SELL HIM TO THE ISHMAELITES, AND LET NOT OUR HAND BE UPON HIM, FOR HE IS OUR BROTHER, OUR OWN FLESH."'
GEN 37.23-27

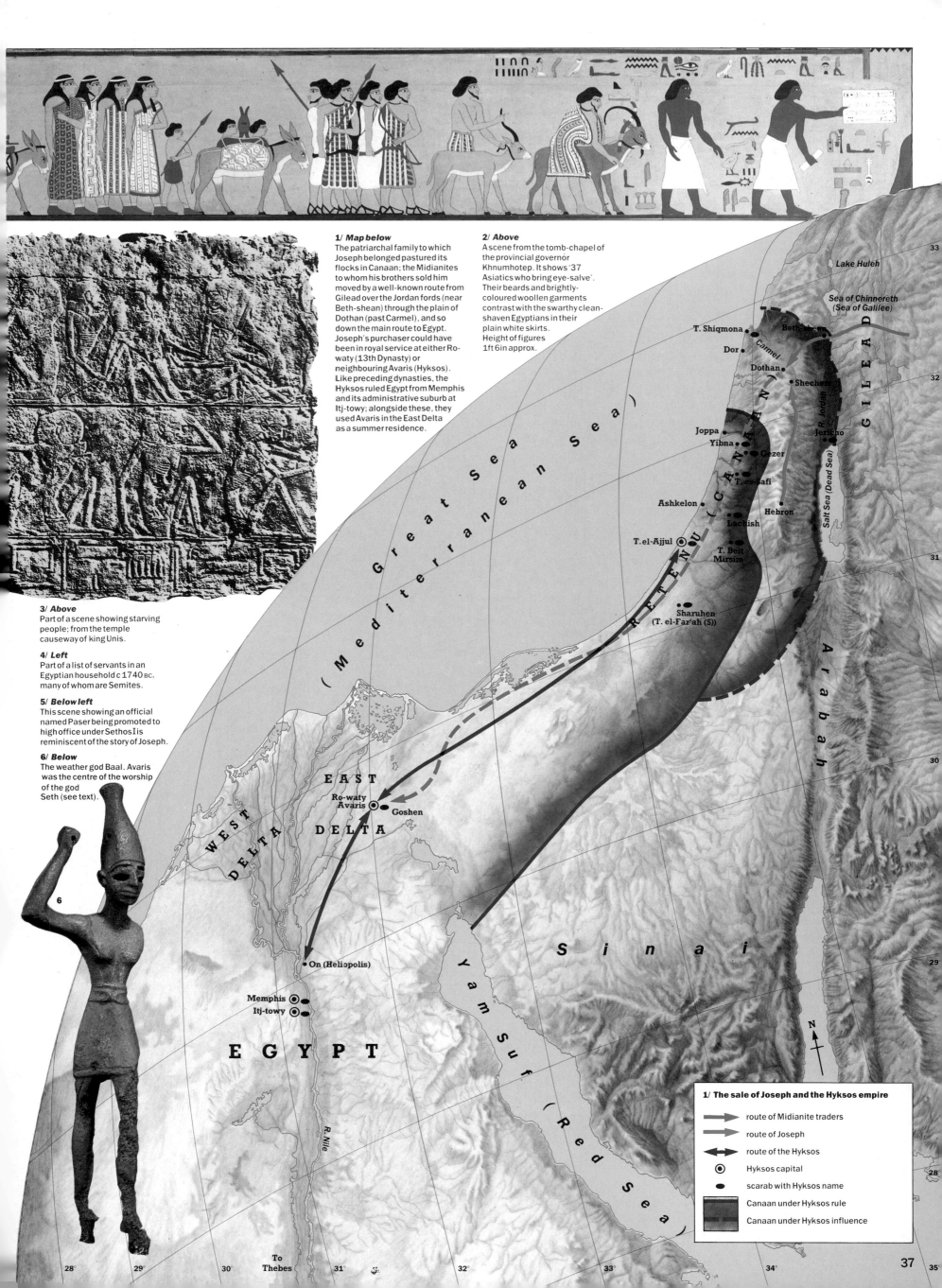

1/ Map below
The patriarchal family to which Joseph belonged pastured its flocks in Canaan; the Midianites to whom his brothers sold him moved by a well-known route from Gilead over the Jordan fords (near Beth-shean) through the plain of Dothan (past Carmel), and so down the main route to Egypt. Joseph's purchaser could have been in royal service at either Ro-waty (13th Dynasty) or neighbouring Avaris (Hyksos). Like preceding dynasties, the Hyksos ruled Egypt from Memphis and its administrative suburb at Itj-towy; alongside these, they used Avaris in the East Delta as a summer residence.

2/ Above
A scene from the tomb-chapel of the provincial governor Khnumhotep. It shows '37 Asiatics who bring eye-salve'. Their beards and brightly-coloured woollen garments contrast with the swarthy clean-shaven Egyptians in their plain white skirts. Height of figures 1ft 6in approx.

3/ Above
Part of a scene showing starving people; from the temple causeway of king Unis.

4/ Left
Part of a list of servants in an Egyptian household c 1740 BC, many of whom are Semites.

5/ Below left
This scene showing an official named Paser being promoted to high office under Sethos I is reminiscent of the story of Joseph.

6/ Below
The weather god Baal. Avaris was the centre of the worship of the god Seth (see text).

Lake Huleh

Sea of Chinnereth
(Sea of Galilee)

T. Shiqmona
Dor
Dothan
Carmel
Beth-shan
Shechem
GILEAD

Joppa
Yibna
Gezer
Jericho
R. Jordan

T. es-Safi

Ashkelon
Lachish
Hebron

T. el-Ajjul
T. Beit Mirsim
Salt Sea (Dead Sea)

Sharuhen
(T. el-Far'ah (S))

Arabah

Great Sea
Mediterranean Sea

RETENU (CANAAN)

EAST
Ro-waty
Avaris
Goshen
WEST DELTA
DELTA

On (Heliopolis)

Memphis
Itj-towy

Sinai

EGYPT

Yam Suf (Red Sea)

R. Nile

N

6

1/ The sale of Joseph and the Hyksos empire

→ route of Midianite traders
→ route of Joseph
↔ route of the Hyksos
⊙ Hyksos capital
• scarab with Hyksos name
▬ Canaan under Hyksos rule
▬ Canaan under Hyksos influence

A MAJORITY of the population of ancient Egypt were peasant farmers working their own small plots of land, or tenant farmers and agricultural labourers on the estates of the Crown, the temples and the nobility. Their daily life was regulated by the annual flooding of the Nile which provided water for irrigation and more importantly the rich silt which made Egypt the most fertile land of the ancient Near East. As the flood waters receded in October the boundaries of the various plots and estates would be marked out, the irrigation channels cleared and repaired, and the planting of crops would begin.

The two principal crops were emmer wheat and barley. The first was used to produce bread and the second to manufacture beer, the two staple items of the ancient Egyptian diet. Flax was another important crop and was used in the production of linen garments. Small garden plots yielded vegetables such as lettuces and lentils, while vineyards were to be found on the great estates. Cattle and poultry were reared to supply meat.

As the crops ripened in the fields, tax assessors would appear to note the quantities and fix the contributions of each owner. These taxes would be paid in kind out of the crop and stored in the state granaries. In normal times there would have been enough food for the entire population with a surplus to spare. A low Nile could lead to a diminished crop yield and successive occurrences might

DAILY LIFE IN ANCIENT EGYPT

Due to the exceptional fertility of the lands watered by the Nile, Egypt developed into one of the most advanced civilizations of the ancient world. Its complex administration, great armies, building techniques and decorative art, all helped to make it an important and influential power in the ancient Near East.

lead to famine conditions.

During the annual inundation when the land could not be worked, the farming population was liable to conscription for work on the various state building projects alongside the specialized core of full-time workers which must have existed. Wealthier sections of the population could buy exemptions from this labour tax by providing substitutes.

Little has survived of the towns and villages of ancient Egypt apart from certain specially built workmen's villages. The houses in these sites were located along narrow streets and entered by one doorway off a lane. They consisted of three or four rooms mostly leading off one another. A

staircase led up to the flat roof where the family would spend much of their time in the hot summer evenings. The houses were made of mud brick which was plentiful. Mud of the right consistency was mixed with water and then straw would be kneaded in to bind the mixture. A mould was used to form the bricks and then these were left to harden in the sun. Two types of brick were produced, the smaller for houses and the larger for official buildings.

Ordinary homes were sparsely furnished apart from wooden boxes housing family possessions which were taken out when needed. Furniture consisted of small stools, chairs and tables varying in quantity and quality with the resources of the owner.

The agricultural villages probably differed little from those of the workmen except that the village plan and the size of the houses would have been more irregular. Naturally the nobility and high officials would have had much larger houses with more spacious rooms, more furniture, and even enclosed gardens.

EGYPTIAN ADMINISTRATION

The everyday life of the ordinary Egyptian was overseen by a hierarchy of officials. The king stood at the top of the social order. Normally he would have inherited his position from his father but, in times of unrest, the ruling dynasty could be overthrown to make way for a new family often with a military background. The royal residence and hence

1/ Map below right
The Nile creates a ribbon of fertile land through Egypt. In the south the New Kingdom capital of Thebes can be seen. In the north are Memphis, Avaris and Pi Ramesse – all major administrative centres.

2/ Top right
A statue of a scribe, with eyes inlaid with quartz, crystal and ebony, from Saqqara, 5th Dynasty. The figure is of painted limestone and about 1ft 6in high.

3/ Right
The palace of Amenophis III at Malqata, near Thebes, built during the 18th Dynasty.

Key
1 Large audience hall
2 Large audience hall
3 Small audience hall
4 Columned antechamber of the great hall of the harem
5 Throne room
6 Bathroom
7 Antechamber to king's bedroom
8 King's bedroom
9 Kitchens
10 South Palace

4/ Below palace plan
A wooden tomb model of a granary. The belief in an afterlife for which one must prepare by taking along provisions has left us with models such as this.

5/ Bottom left
Another tomb model, this time of a man ploughing with a two-handled plough drawn by oxen.

6/ Bottom, second from left
This tomb painting, depicting a harvest comes from the tomb of Nakht at Thebes. It dates from the reign of Tuthmosis IV and is roughly 2ft 6in high.

7/ Bottom, third from left
A workers' village at Deir el-Medina, near Thebes. It was in villages like this that the labour force, on which the Egyptians depended for their great construction projects, lived.

8/ Bottom right
A modern photograph of a labourer making bricks from mud and straw, as described in the Bible.

Great Sea (Mediterranean Sea)

the capital city was not fixed. Thebes rose to prominence at the beginning of the New Kingdom and remained the religious capital and a royal residence, but it was too far south to be an effective site, especially when Egypt became more involved with the affairs of Western Asia. The northern capital of Memphis always retained its prestige, while new northern residences were created such as Avaris under the Hyksos and Pi Ramesse (now Qantir) built near the ruins of Avaris by the Ramessides. The actual task of administration was carried out by two viziers, one for Upper Egypt and one for Lower Egypt.

There were numerous officials under the viziers from overseers of the treasury, the granary, and the cattle, down to minor officers such as town mayors. Each of the important offices had its own staff of scribes, door-keepers and other attendants. The vizier was also initially responsible for the administration of the vast temple properties where a second separate bureaucracy existed. A third existed for the army which was also under the authority of the vizier. Every transaction involving the movement of goods to and from royal storehouses was in theory meticulously recorded although there is evidence of corrupt officials. The army consisted of both conscripts and volunteers and provided a means of promotion for the most humble villager if he showed promise and could attract the right patrons. Valour in battle often led to military decorations and land grants which were tenaciously preserved by the descendants of the original owner. Military men were frequently chosen to fill the top civilian and priestly posts. The rise through the civilian ranks was more difficult as a general knowledge of the scribal arts was a minimum requirement for a bureaucratic post.

Scribal families would obviously pass their skills on from father to son, while local scribes probably took on pupils. The vast amount of written material from the village of the royal workmen at Thebes indicates a high level of literacy among these craftsmen and implies that literacy was probably more widespread than has hitherto been estimated. The literature enjoyed by these workmen consisted of both ethical wisdom literature and popular adventure stories and bawdy tales of the gods. The most popular work was a satire which ridiculed the life of a soldier and praised that of a scribe (see page 50). Ironically it was the successful military man who often gained the greater rewards.

One privileged section of the community consisted of the numerous priests who served in the great temples of the major gods of Egypt. Their function was to propitiate the gods by carrying out the prescribed rituals in the temples.

Each day the shrine of the god or goddess would be opened and the divine image would be clothed in new garments and symbolically fed with appetizing meals. On special holy days the divinity would be placed on a palanquin and carried by priests to the forecourt of the temple where the image could be viewed by the general populace who were barred from entering the temple proper. Occasionally the god would venture forth from the temple to be carried in procession to a neighbouring temple dedicated to himself or to his consort. These days would be great festive occasions. The priests would also carry the image of the divinity whenever he was consulted for an oracular decision. The god would be asked to adjudicate in disputes over offices or land. It is not entirely clear how this was accomplished but probably by the movement of the palanquin to signify consent or refusal. Apart from religious duties, the priests administered the resources of the temples. Favoured gods such as Amon-Re received large endowments from the Crown and owned vast estates.

Entry into the priesthood was normally hereditary although the Crown could confer priesthoods on favoured courtiers and military men as rewards for service. Because of the power and wealth of certain priesthoods, the appointment to the post of high priest was a major political decision. These positions could well be filled with an outsider not drawn from the ranks of the hereditary priests. However, the priesthoods of the great temples did not have a monopoly on religious worship. There were many small chapels at which the individual could pray directly to the gods. In the workmen's community at Deir el-Medina and possibly at other small villages, the ordinary inhabitants themselves acted as priests in their local temples, carrying the divine image in local processions.

THE STORY OF THE VIRTUOUS YOUTH
Egyptian writing is mainly known to us from memorial inscriptions found in temples and tombs. These usually contain boastful, and often exaggerated, claims to military victory on the part of various pharaohs. However, there was also some popular literature and the following folk tale is an example of it. It comes from the Papyrus D'Orbiney, dated about 1225 BC, and tells of the attempted seduction of a moral young man by his elder brother's wife. Having had her advances angrily rejected she then accuses the young man of attempting to rape her. This part of the story bears a marked resemblance to the biblical incident of Joseph and Potiphar's wife (GEN 39.7-18).

The brothers are called Anubis and Bata, after Egyptian gods, and the story has mythological overtones, even though its primary purpose is to entertain.
'Then he sent his younger brother saying: "Go and fetch us seed from the village." And his younger brother found the wife of his elder brother sitting doing her hair ... Then she said to him: "How much is it that is on your shoulder?" And he said to her: "Three sacks of emmer, two sacks of barley, five in all, is what is on my [sic] shoulder." So he spoke to her. Then she talked with him saying "There is great strength in you! Now I see your energies every day!" And she wanted to know him as one knows a man. Then she stood up and took hold of him and said to him: "Come, let's spend an hour sleeping together! This will do you good, because I shall make fine clothes for you!" Then the lad became like a leopard with great rage at the wicked suggestion which she had made to him, and she was very, very much frightened. Then he argued with her, saying, ... "What is this great crime which you have said to me? Don't say it to me again!"'

> '... FOR IT IS CLEAR TO ANY INTELLIGENT OBSERVER, EVEN IF HE HAS NO PREVIOUS INFORMATION ON THE SUBJECT, THAT THE EGYPT TO WHICH WE SAIL NOWADAYS IS, AS IT WERE, THE GIFT OF THE RIVER AND HAS COME ONLY RECENTLY INTO THE POSSESSION OF ITS INHABITANTS.'
> HERODOTUS, THE HISTORIES, BOOK II

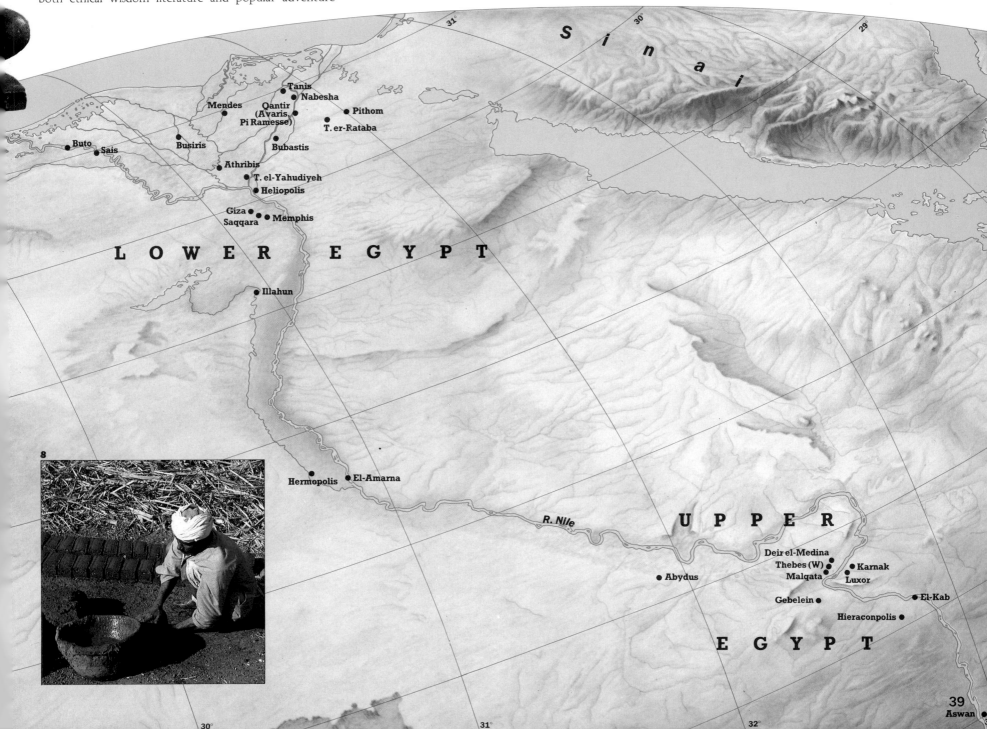

8

LOWER EGYPT

Buto · Sais · Busiris · Mendes · Qantir (Avaris, Pi Ramesse) · Tanis · Nabesha · Pithom · T. er-Rataba · Athribis · Bubastis · T. el-Yahudiyeh · Heliopolis · Giza · Saqqara · Memphis · Illahun

Sinai

Hermopolis · El-Amarna

R. Nile

UPPER EGYPT

Abydus · Deir el-Medina · Thebes (W) · Malqata · Karnak · Luxor · Gebelein · Hieraconpolis · El-Kab

THE Hyksos, meaning 'foreign rulers', were a west-Semitic speaking people with strong cultural ties to the east Mediterranean littoral (the area which later became Phoenicia).

The Hyksos invaded Egypt in c 1674 BC and instigated a regime (the 15th Dynasty) which subjugated Egypt for 108 years. The Hyksos kings ruled over the Nile Delta and Middle Egypt from their capital Avaris, and tolerated a weak native vassal at Thebes in the south. Though the extent of their control over Retenu (Canaan) and Syria whence they had come is not easy to assess, scarabs of Hyksos kings are found in Retenu especially from the coastal plain, and Avaris was in receipt of Syrian 'tribute' brought by sea in large flotillas. Recent excavation at Delta sites occupied or founded by the newcomers has proved that the Hyksos retained their 'Middle Bronze' IIB culture from western Asia, and seldom adopted native Egyptian customs.

THE DECLINE OF THE HYKSOS
The struggle to free Egypt from Hyksos occupation originated in Thebes. The lead was taken by a family of erstwhile vassals to the Hyksos, the 17th Dynasty, who may have been, at least in part, of Nubian descent. The third king of this dynasty, Kamosis, broke the shaky peace that existed in the empire by attacking Hyksos proteges in Middle Egypt with his limited militia and Nubian auxiliaries. However, while he was able to wreak havoc at Nefrusy and Cynopolis, and to disrupt communications between the Hyksos and the king of Cush in the Sudan, Kamosis apparently lacked the required forces and the siege equipment to destroy Avaris. It is recorded that he saw the walls of the Hyksos capital, but retired to Thebes, possibly unable to withstand a concerted Hyksos counter-thrust.

His brother Amosis finished the work. Seizure of Memphis, the old Egyptian capital, early in the reign was followed in about his tenth regnal year by a series of destructive attacks on Avaris itself. Heliopolis and the border-fort of Sile were subsequently taken, and Avaris fell in the eleventh year of Amosis' rule. Thereafter the Egyptian forces pursued the remnant of the Hyksos into the region of Gaza where the Hyksos stronghold of Sharuhen capitulated after a three-year siege.

THE 18th DYNASTY
For 80 years following the Hyksos expulsion, the prospect of a renewed assault on Egypt by these 'foreign rulers' was seriously entertained by the pharaohs of the early 18th

BETWEEN GENESIS AND EXODUS:
400 YEARS OF EGYPTIAN SUPREMACY

EGYPTIAN EXPANSION UNDER TUTHMOSIS III

The death of Joseph, at the end of Genesis, is followed by the life of Moses and the Exodus narrative. These events were separated by a considerable period of time (the Bible suggests a figure of about 400 years). During this era Egypt was the major power in the Near East, and it is from Egyptian records that we learn of the events which occurred in Canaan at this time. The Hyksos rulers, who it is thought occupied Egypt at about the time of Joseph, were expelled by the native Egyptians and a succession of pharaohs then proceeded to make their influence felt as far north as Mitanni. Pharaoh Tuthmosis III was a particularly strong ruler who carried out many military campaigns to confirm Egyptian influence over neighbouring lands.

Dynasty. We know little of Amosis' military activity in Canaan, except for his assault on Sharuhen and a possible attack on the Phoenician coast.

The campaign of Amosis' two successors must be construed as responses, on a more ambitious scale, to the growing power in the Orontes basin (Syria) and the founding of the Hurrian state of Mitanni and Tunip on the Orontes. Tuthmosis I marched even further afield to engage the Mitannian forces themselves within sight of the Euphrates. Under the sickly Tuthmosis II, Egypt seems to have withdrawn from the Syrian sphere; his attack on the Shasu (in the Negeb?) only being a minor punishment of troublesome bedouin.

It must be stressed that none of these campaigns resulted in an Egyptian 'empire' in western Asia. While Egypt's sphere of influence may well have been extended, her military activity amounted to nothing more than an *ad hoc* series of punitive or pre-emptive raids.

PHARAOH TUTHMOSIS III
Tuthmosis III led campaigns into Asia almost every year, during the 20 years of his rule (see chart). The sources for Tuthmosis III's campaigns in western Asia are historically more reliable than those of most other military enterprises in the ancient world. Based on the official day-book of the

king's house, incorporating an official log and booty-lists, the so-called 'annals' were carved on the walls of the Temple of Amun at Thebes, and cover the 20-year period from the 22nd to the 42nd year of the king. Intended partly as a memorial to the god in recognition that he had given Tuthmosis victory, and partly for priestly reference, the annals were never intended to be seen by the mass of the people, and so lack propaganda, which means that they are more realistic than many other accounts.

While Tuthmosis may have undertaken punitive campaigns in the Gaza area when his aunt, Hatshepsut, still ruled, the morrow of her death (late winter c 1482 BC) found a

THE CAMPAIGNS OF PHARAOH TUTHMOSIS III

No.	Year	Enemy	Locale	Diplomatic gifts made to Tuthmosis
1	22-23	Qadesh coalition	Megiddo	
2	24	(Tour of inspection?)	Palestine (?)	Gifts from Assyria
(3)	25	(?)	Retenu	Plant collection
(4)	26(?)	(?)	(?)	
5	29	cities of Phoenician coast	Phoenician coast	
6	30	Qadesh, Sumura, Ardata	S. Syrian & Phoenician coast	
(7)	31	Ullaza	Phoenician coast	
(8)	33	Mitanni	N. Syria	Elephant hunt, gifts from Hittites and Babylon
(9)	34	3 unamed cities	N. Syria (Nukhashshe)	Gifts from Alashiya (Cyprus)
10	35	Mitanni	N. Syria, city of 'Aruna	
(11)	36	(?)	(?)	
12	37	(?)	(?)	
13	(38?)	(?)	N. Syria (Nukhashshe)	Gifts from Alashiya and Alalakh
14	39	Shasu	S. Palestine or Transjordan	
15	40	(?)		
16	41	(?)		
17	42	Ingata, Tunip 3 cities near Qadesh, Mitanni		

4/ Top
A procession of bearded Asiatic prisoners, with 12 of the 115 names of places that Tuthmosis conquered. From the temple of Amun, Karnak.

5/ Above
A victorious Tuthmosis III holding a batch of prisoners by the hair. Also from the temple of Amun.

1/ Map above right
The Asian campaigns of the 17th and 18th dynasties.

2/ Map below right
Pharaoh Tuthmosis III was the most important pharaoh of the 18th dynasty, and during the many campaigns of his rule (see chart above) he managed to extend Egyptian authority in Canaan in order to stem the growing power of Tunip and the Mitannian empire.

3/ Map above far right
At the battle of Megiddo, 1482 BC, Tuthmosis III defeated the Canaanites (see text).

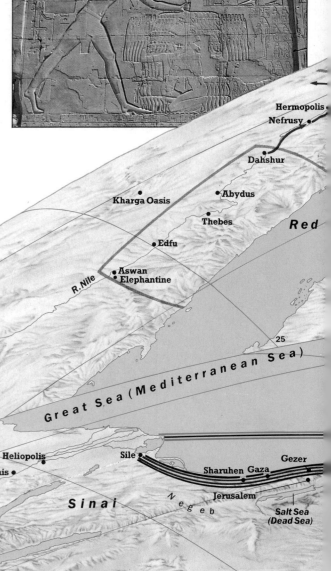

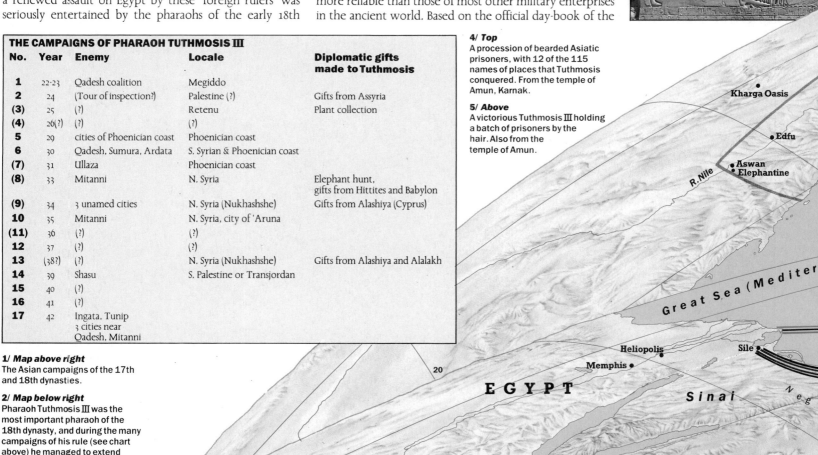

Hermopolis
Nefrusy
Dahshur
Kharga Oasis
Abydus
Thebes
Red
Edfu
Aswan
Elephantine
25
Heliopolis
Sile
Gezer
Memphis
Sharuhen Gaza
EGYPT
Sinai
Negeb
Jerusalem
Salt Sea (Dead Sea)
20
Thebes
Red Sea
R. Nile
Great Sea (Mediterranean Sea)
25

coalition of Syrian cities under the leadership of the king of Qadesh resolved to move against Egypt. The hostile coalition mustered their forces in the plain of Esdraelon beneath the walls of Megiddo, but Tuthmosis III's speed in marching his own troops to this staging area within three weeks pre-empted their plans. The subsequent battle and siege of Megiddo resulted in a sweeping Egyptian victory and the subjugation of most of Canaan.

BATTLE OF MEGIDDO
The battle of Megiddo, fought in mid-May 1482 BC, displays the tactical genius and daring of Tuthmosis III. The Canaanite coalition, under the leadership of the king of

Qadesh, had gathered on the plains of Megiddo which they had turned into a staging area for their projected move against Egypt. Tuthmosis' rapid march pre-empted this but the Canaanite forces still held the best tactical position.

Not knowing, however, by which of the three possible routes the Egyptians intended to negotiate the Carmel range, and not having sufficient troops to cover them all, the Canaanites were obliged to try to outguess Tuthmosis. They opted for a disposition of troops whereby two of the routes, the narrow pass and the road from Taanach, would at least be placed under observation, if not wholly blocked; but the result was an overextension of their line which was militarily unsound.

When Tuthmosis, rejecting his officers' more cautious advice, decided to march his army single file through the narrow pass, thus opting for the most direct route to Megiddo, he took the enemy completely by surprise. At noon the vanguard debouched into the plain, and an hour later Tuthmosis planted his headquarters on the banks of the brook south of Megiddo. In great haste the Canaanites withdrew their forces from the Taanach road and redeployed them between the Egyptians and the city walls, and darkness fell with the two opposing lines of troops facing each other.

The battle began at first light with a forceful charge by Tuthmosis himself in the centre of the line. This was the only manoeuvre required: the Canaanites broke and ran.

Megiddo was subsequently placed under siege, and six months later it capitulated.

TUTHMOSIS' LATER CAMPAIGNS
Subsequent Egyptian activity was directed towards reducing the power of Tunip on the middle Orontes, and checking the spread of the Mitannian empire from beyond the Euphrates (see chart showing campaigns). Tuthmosis' grand strategy was masterful. By the fifth campaign we find him moving up the Phoenician coast to secure the ports so that future communication with Egypt could proceed by sea. The sixth campaign witnessed the invasion of the territory of Qadesh itself, and the eighth (the most important in the view of contemporaries) the defeat of the army of Mitanni beneath the walls of Carchemish.

> HIS MAJESTY ORDERED A CONFERENCE WITH HIS VICTORIOUS ARMY, SPEAKING AS FOLLOWS: "THAT WRETCHED ENEMY OF QADESH HAS COME AND HAS ENTERED INTO MEGIDDO. HE IS THERE AT THIS MOMENT. HE HAS GATHERED TO HIM THE PRINCES OF EVERY FOREIGN COUNTRY WHICH HAS BEEN LOYAL TO EGYPT, AS WELL AS THOSE AS FAR AS NAHARIN AND MITANNI, THEM OF HURRU, THEM OF KODE, THEIR HORSES, THEIR ARMIES, AND THEIR PEOPLE, FOR HE SAYS – SO IT IS REPORTED – I SHALL WAIT HERE IN MEGIDDO TO FIGHT AGAINST HIS MAJESTY."
> INSCRIPTION FROM THE TEMPLE OF KARNAK, ANET 234

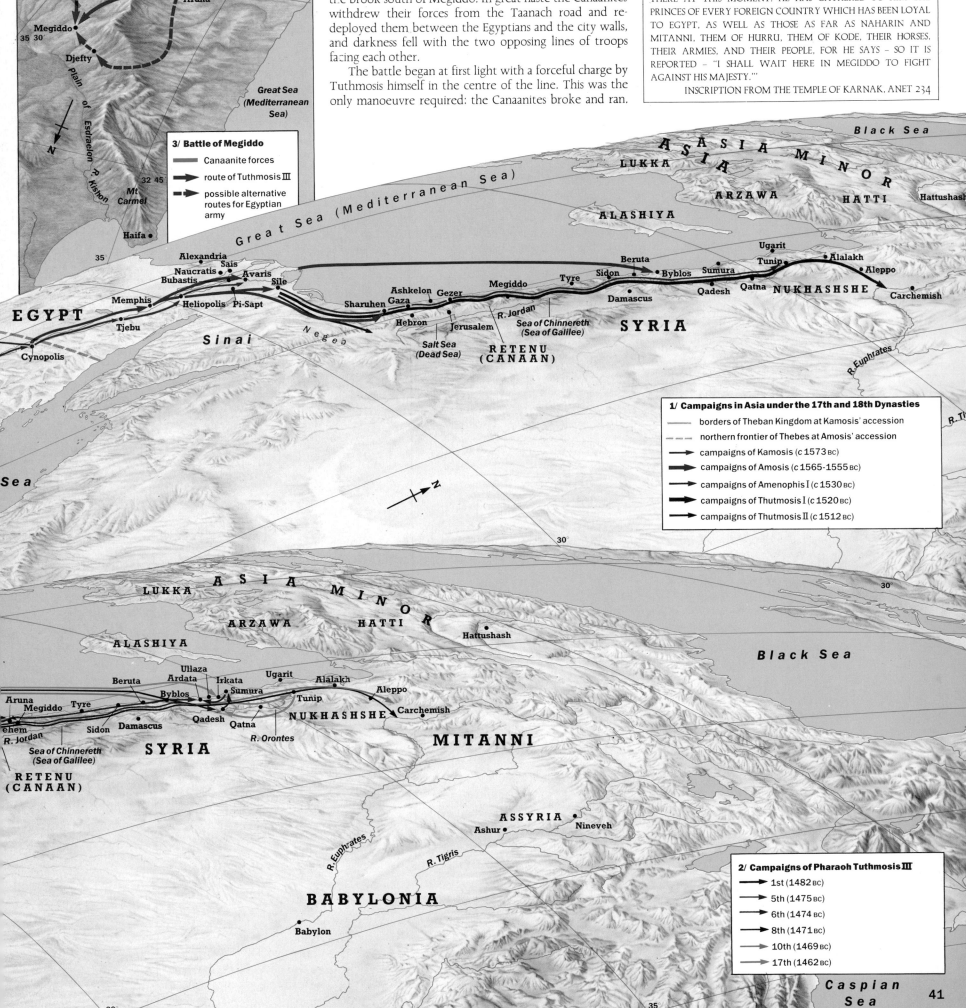

3/ Battle of Megiddo
- Canaanite forces
- → route of Tuthmosis III
- ⇢ possible alternative routes for Egyptian army

1/ Campaigns in Asia under the 17th and 18th Dynasties
- borders of Theban Kingdom at Kamosis' accession
- northern frontier of Thebes at Amosis' accession
- campaigns of Kamosis (c 1573 BC)
- campaigns of Amosis (c 1565-1555 BC)
- campaigns of Amenophis I (c 1530 BC)
- campaigns of Thutmosis I (c 1520 BC)
- campaigns of Thutmosis II (c 1512 BC)

2/ Campaigns of Pharaoh Tuthmosis III
- 1st (1482 BC)
- 5th (1475 BC)
- 6th (1474 BC)
- 8th (1471 BC)
- 10th (1469 BC)
- 17th (1462 BC)

ENMITY between Egypt and Mitanni continued into the reign of Pharaoh Amenophis II, the son of Pharaoh Tuthmosis III. Near the end of his life, the latter pharaoh appointed his son co-regent (1450 BC); the unrest in Egypt's Syrian provinces called for a young and vigorous ruler. In his own third year of reign, just before the death of Tuthmosis III, Amenophis had to lead a military expedition to the land of Takhsi, an area bordering on the territories of Qadesh (to the north of it) and Damascus (to the south of it). It is possible that two cuneiform letters found at Taanach and dated by their script and archaeological context to the mid-15th century BC, may relate to this campaign. A certain Amenophis (without royal titles) rebuked the ruler of Taanach for not reporting to Gaza. In another letter, he orders him to be at Megiddo the next day with his troops, horses and tribute payment. Whether there is any connection or not, the 'first campaign' of Amenophis II was only recorded on a stela erected in a temple at Amada. By the time of his return, Amenophis may have been greeted by the news that his father was dead or dying. Seven recalcitrant rulers were slain on this campaign and their bodies displayed as trophies on the wall of the capital city (one was sent to Nubia as a warning).

When the young king became sole ruler, he had to face up to the challenge of his arch rival, Mitanni. The earliest rebellion of the Takhsi rulers was symptomatic of unrest in Egyptian-held territory. It was time to carry the fray deep into the area under Mitanni control. Two campaigns are recorded; they appear together on a stela at Memphis, with a mostly parallel text on another from Karnak. When the version of Amenophis' feats after becoming sole ruler were recorded, it was decided to renumber them; the campaign of Year 3 was no longer recorded but may be alluded to in the introduction of the Memphis stela. A similar practice of renumbering campaigns was apparently applied to the early Nubian exploits of Tuthmosis III (before his famous campaign against Megiddo, see page 40).

In his new official 'first campaign', Amenophis II departed from Egypt in his seventh regnal year. The first conflict took place at a place called Shamshu-'Adam. The same town appears as No 51 on the topographical list of Tuthmosis III; it is followed by Anuhartu (biblical Anaharath in lower Galilee, JOSH 19.19). Therefore, the distinguished Israeli archaeologist Aharoni identified it with the Adamah in Naphtali (JOSH 19.36) which he located on the Horns of Hattin. Edel, the scholar who edited Amenophis' two stelae, argued from a combination of dates in the Memphis and Karnak texts that Shamshu-'Adam must have been only a day away from Qatna in southern Syria. In any case, the texts take up the story with Amenophis crossing the R. Orontes at a point where mounted troops from Qatna could attempt to harass the Egyptian ranks. The next paragraph finds Amenophis on his way back to Egypt. A short, poorly preserved topographical list of his at the Karnak temple helps to fill in the gap; its northernmost town is Khalab (Aleppo). Whatever the pharaoh did at Khalab, it was not mentioned; perhaps his 'success' was questionable. Nevertheless, he arrived at the city of Niyi (Qal'at el-Mudiq) where he was received with fawning respect. An intelligence report which he received, indicated a local attempt to dislodge an Egyptian garrison at a

BETWEEN GENESIS AND EXODUS:
400 YEARS OF EGYPTIAN SUPREMACY

MILITARY CAMPAIGNS OF PHARAOH AMENOPHIS II IN THE LEVANT

Internal problems within Egypt led to revolts in Canaan. Amenophis undertook two campaigns to demonstrate his power. Details have been found on Egyptian monuments but these accounts have to be read critically as they refer only to victories and never mention defeats.

place, the name of which can be taken as a faulty writing of Ugarit. Amenophis went in person to that city, quelled the rebellion and restored order. Ten days after his arrival at Niyi, he camped at Salqa, a town associated with Ugarit as the source for boxwood and which was known to the kingdom of Alalakh. Although it has been argued that Ugarit was too far from Niyi to have been visited from there, it is possible that Amenophis II did make a sortie to Ugarit during his visit to Salqa. The question remains open; but the Egyptian presence was probably to protect a diplomatic-commercial mission and need not imply that the city was a vassal of Egypt.

After plundering the village of Mansatu, Amenophis was cordially received by Hassilā ('The Rock') and Yanqa, two unidentified towns north of Qadesh. The ruler of the latter also made obeisance to pharaoh who later gave a demonstration of his prowess with the bow. Afterwards, Amenophis went hunting in the forest of Lebo' (= Lebo-Hamath; NUM 34.8, et al). The next station was Khashabu, in the Lebanese Beqa'a Valley. Resistance there was quickly put down and the city submitted. On his way back to Egypt, Amenophis II captured a Mitannian chariot warrior in the 'Valley of Surina', possibly the biblical Plain of Sharon. This man was evidently on a diplomatic mission to stir up trouble behind pharaoh's back.

Two years later, in Year 9, Amenophis II was once again on the road to Retenu (Canaan). This time the action took place deep in Egyptian-controlled territory. The first town visited was Aphek; its ruler greeted the Egyptian king. The next station was Yaham. The army plundered villages west of Socoh (as in I KINGS 4.10). The ruler of another town, the name of which has been defaced, closed his gates but an entrance was forced and the people captured. This was probably Gath-padalla of the Tuthmosis list (No 70) and the Amarna letters. An appearance of the god Amon that night portended the climactic battle on the following day. It took place near Migdol and the unidentified Adoren. Pharaoh won and reputedly guarded the prisoners by himself all night.

The principal Canaanite attempt had failed. Two more of the rebel towns remained to be punished. Amenophis marched unhindered through the pass to the Valley of

Jezreel and proceeded to Anuhartu (Anaharath, JOSH 19.19), probably T. Rekhesh (= T. el-Mukharkhash) in the Tabor Valley (Wadi el-Bira). After punishing that town, pharaoh returned to the military base in the vicinity of Megiddo (written slightly defectively). A contingent was sent to nearby Geba-somen ('The Hill of Eight': Abu Shusheh = T. Shush) where the ruler was summarily arrested and another ruler appointed in his place.

These inscriptions of Amenophis II also give a glimpse into the social strata of the Levant during the 15th century BC. His lists of booty record the rulers, the oligarchs who supported them, including the chariot warriors, and the geographical groups such as Canaanites and people of Nugasse (Syria north of Tunip) as well as bedouin and the 'outcasts' ('apiru).

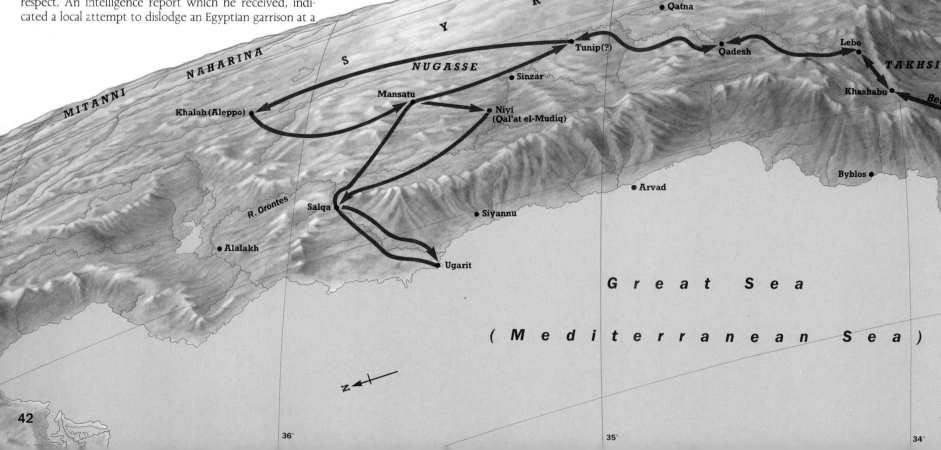

AMENOPHIS II DESCRIBES HIS CONQUESTS

The following is an extract from accounts given on stelae found at Memphis and Karnak. In these the pharaoh gives a boastful version of his campaigns and lists the booty taken:

'His majesty proceeded to Retenu on his first victorious campaign to extend his frontiers, made from the property of them who are not loyal to him, his face terrible like (that of) Bastet, like Seth in his moment of raging. His majesty reached Shamash-Edom. He hacked it up in a short moment, like a lion fierce of face, when he treads the foreign countries. (His) majesty was in his chariot, of which the name was: "Amon, the valiant..." List of the booty of his arm: living Asiatics: 35; cattle: 22.

'His majesty crossed the Orontes on dangerous waters, like Rashap. Then he turned about to watch his rear, and he saw a few Asiatics coming furtively, adorned with weapons of warfare, to attack the king's army. His majesty burst after them like the flight of a divine falcon. The confidence of their hearts was slackened, and one after another fell upon his fellow, up to their commander. Not a single one was with his majesty, except for himself with his valiant arm. His majesty killed them by shooting. He returned thence, his heart glad like Montu the valiant, when he had triumphed. List of what his majesty captured within this day: two princes and six maryanu*, in addition to their chariots, their teams, and all their weapons of warfare.

2 and 3/ Far left and left
The paintings (far left) from the tomb of Amenophis II, show three gods 'giving life' to the dead pharaoh. From top to bottom the gods are: Osiris, Anubis and Isis. The statue (left) depicts Amenophis and comes from the so-called 'Valley of the Kings' on the west bank of the Nile at Thebes.

4/ Below
Amenophis II was noted for his skill with the bow. Here he is shown firing from a chariot travelling at full speed and piercing a copper ingot 2 or 3 in thick.

'His majesty, going south, reached Ni. Its prince and all his people, male as well as female, were at peace with his majesty, (for) their faces had received a bedazzlement. His majesty reached Ikat. He surrounded everyone rebellious to him and killed them, like those who had never existed, put on (their) side, upside down. He returned thence in joy of heart, with this entire country in bondage to him.

'Rest in the tent of his majesty, in the neighborhood of Tjerekh on the east of Sheshrem. The settlements of Mendjet were plundered. His majesty reached Hetjra. Its prince came out in peace to his majesty, (10) bringing his children and all his goods. Submission was made to his majesty by Unqi. His majesty reached Kadesh. Its prince came out in peace to his majesty. They were made to take the oath of fealty, and all their children as (well). Thereupon his majesty shot at two targets of copper in hammered work, in their presence, on the south side of this town. Excursions were made in Rebi in the forest, and there were brought back gazelles, maset, hares, and wild asses without their limit.

'His majesty proceeded by chariot to Khashabu, alone, without having a companion. He returned thence in a short moment, and he brought back 16 living maryanu on the two sides of his chariot, 20 hands at the foreheads of his horses, and 60 cattle being driven before him. Submission was made to his majesty by this town.

'While his majesty was going south in the midst of the Plain of Sharon, he met a messenger of the Prince of Naharin, carrying a letter of clay at his throat. He took him as a living prisoner at the side of his chariot. His majesty went forth in chariot by a track to Egypt, (15) with the marya as a living prisoner in the chariot alone with him.

'His majesty reached Memphis, his heart joyful, the Mighty Bull. List of this booty: maryanu: 550; their wives: 240; Canaanites: 640; princes' children: 232; princes' children, female: 323; favourites of the princes of every foreign country: 270 women, in addition to their paraphernalia for entertaining the heart, of silver and gold, (at) their shoulders; total: 2,214; horses: 820; chariots: 730, in addition to all their weapons of warfare. Now the God's Wife, King's Wife, and King's [Daughter] beheld the victory of his majesty.

'Year 9, 3rd month of the first season, day 25. His majesty proceeded to Retenu on his second victorious campaign, against the town of Apheq. It came out in surrender to the great victory of Pharaoh – life, prosperity, health! His majesty went forth by chariot, adorned with weapons of warfare, against the town of Yehem. Now his majesty captured the settlements of Mepesen, together with the settlements of Khettjen, two towns on the west of Socho. Now the Ruler was raging like a divine falcon, his horses flying like a star of heaven. His majesty entered, and (20) its princes, its children, and its women carried off as living prisoners, and all its retainers similarly, all its goods, without their limit, its cattle, its horses, and all the small cattle (which) were before him.

'Thereupon his majesty rested. The majesty of this august god, Amon, Lord of the Thrones of the Two Lands, came before his majesty in dream, to give valor to his son, Aa-khepru-Re. His father Amon-Re was the magical protection of his person, guarding the Ruler.'

*maryanu=nobles

> 'AND THE LORD WILL MAKE HIMSELF KNOWN TO THE EGYPTIANS; AND THE EGYPTIANS WILL KNOW THE LORD IN THAT DAY AND WORSHIP WITH SACRIFICE AND BURNT OFFERING, AND THEY WILL MAKE VOWS TO THE LORD AND PERFORM THEM.'
> ISA 19.21

1/ Map below
Amenophis was forced to make two incursions into foreign territory to maintain his authority. The first campaign took him far to the north where he re-established his authority at Khalab and Ugarit. The fact that a second campaign was launched two years later implies that his first effort failed. The second campaign was concerned specifically with Retenu and the pharaoh punished any towns which were rebellious.

1/ The two campaigns of Pharaoh Amenophis II

route of first campaign

route of second campaign

DURING the two centuries for which we have documentation for Ugarit's civilization (1400-1200 BC) no city of the ancient Near East has provided such a rich and diverse profile. Indeed, the disasters at the end of the 13th century which brought to an end most of the great Bronze Age civilizations of the Levant, snuffed out the glory of Ugarit at its peak. It would be centuries before the Phoenician cities to the south would once again mirror the sophistication of Ugarit's culture.

Ugarit and its port of Makhadu (modern Ras Shamra and Minet el-Beida respectively), formed the centre of a huge trading and cultural network which covered the Levant and stretched as far as Anatolia and Greece. We know of this remarkable Near Eastern culture from archaeological records discovered at Ras Shamra itself, and also from written records found in Ebla, Mari, Egypt and the Hittite capital of Hattushash (modern Boğazköy). The city was already established in the 5th century BC when it was referred to in the Early Bronze Age records of the city of Ebla as the city of 'Ugarat'.

The kingdom of Ugarit covered some 1,300 square miles of well watered, partly forested and fertile countryside. Its capital covered over 52 acres and was heavily fortified.

Large donkey caravans converged on the city from Syria, Mesopotamia and Anatolia to exchange goods with merchants from Canaan and Egypt as well as the maritime traders who arrived by ship from Alashiya (Cyprus) and Kaptaru (Crete) and the Aegean. The city of Ugarit functioned as a bazaar where its own goods and those from abroad could be imported, exchanged and exported. Furthermore, Ugarit's industries – textiles, ivory, metal,

agricultural products, timber, ceramics, handicrafts – converted raw materials into manufactured goods for further trade. A fleet of ships numbering many hundreds, controlled by the Crown and crewed by experienced seamen, ventured to markets as far away as Egypt and Crete, and perhaps beyond. These Syrian merchants appear to have dominated the maritime trade in the eastern Mediterranean for most of the Late Bronze Age. Two recent excavations of ships from the 14th and 13th centuries BC off the south coast of Turkey (at Kaş and at Cape Gelidonya) illustrate the variety of goods carried by these merchant ships – copper, tin, tools, chemicals, glass ingots, faience and amber beads, ceramics (Canaanite, Cypriot and Mycenaean), ivory (elephant and hippopotamus), jewellery,

luxury goods, semi-precious stones and perishables such as textiles, timber and foodstuffs for which some physical evidence survives. In addition these ships revealed that merchants carried weights reflecting the various standards in use in different areas, personal seals, and equipment for manufacturing metal goods en route.

The medium of exchange was primarily silver, although the basic system was a form of barter of goods of equivalent values. Tin, without which the Bronze Age civilizations could not have functioned, was trans-shipped from Ugarit in ingot form as the recently excavated ships have shown. Furthermore, ships also transported livestock which included sheep, goats, bovines, and, occasionally, much more exotic animals.

Ugarit was a cosmopolitan city where one could find residents from virtually everywhere in the Levant – representing diverse ethnic and linguistic groups. They encountered a rich culture which recorded no less than ten different languages in five different scripts, one of which, alphabetic cuneiform, was probably developed in the local scribal academy. Through international treaties and via a sophisticated legal system, the merchants were assured safety and correct dealings. The political skills of Ugarit's rulers allowed the kingdom to participate in international trade by walking a tightrope between the two major powers of the era, Hatti and Egypt, although bound to the former by vassal treaty for much of the period.

'JUDAH AND THE LAND OF ISRAEL TRADED WITH YOU: THEY EXCHANGED FOR YOUR MERCHANDISE WHEAT, OLIVES AND EARLY FIGS, HONEY, OIL, AND BALM.'
EZEK 27.17

BETWEEN GENESIS AND EXODUS: 400 YEARS OF EGYPTIAN SUPREMACY

UGARIT—A CENTRE OF TRADE AND INFLUENCE

Ugarit is of interest not only because it was a major trading centre, but more particularly because it was here that a hoard of alphabetic cuneiform tablets was found written in a Semitic language related to the Hebrew of the OT. Study of these tablets shows a relationship, both in their subject matter and language, between them and the literature of the Hebrews who were to become the dominant group living in Canaan.

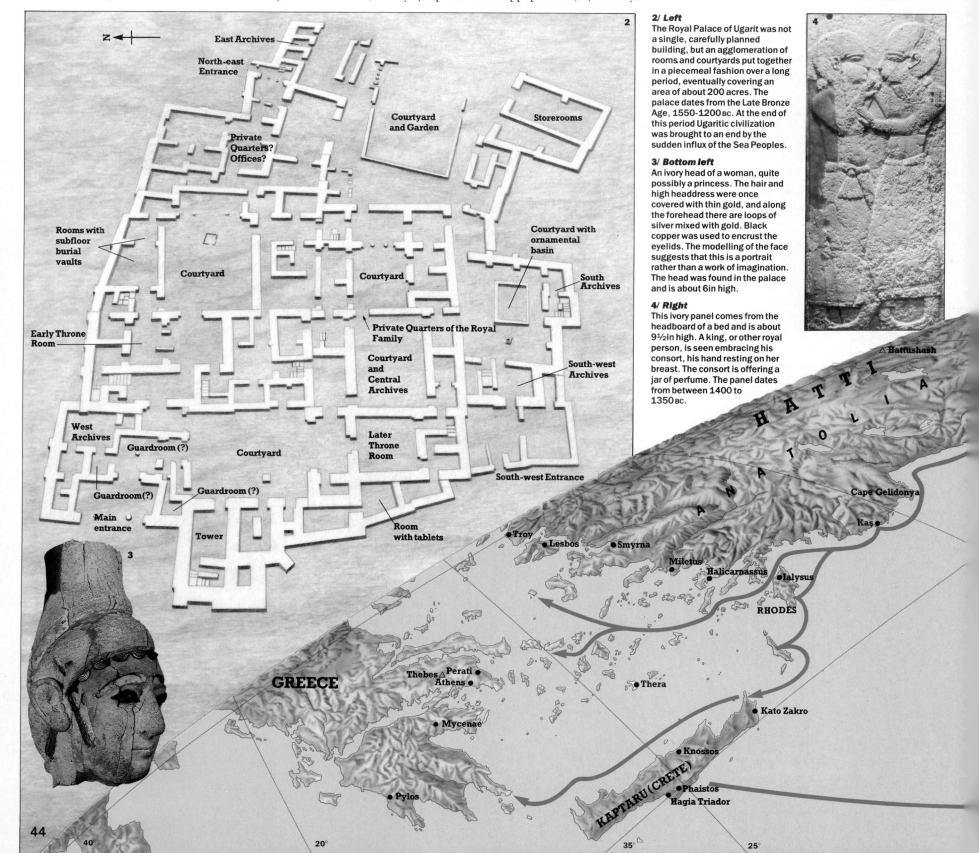

2/ Left
The Royal Palace of Ugarit was not a single, carefully planned building, but an agglomeration of rooms and courtyards put together in a piecemeal fashion over a long period, eventually covering an area of about 200 acres. The palace dates from the Late Bronze Age, 1550-1200 BC. At the end of this period Ugaritic civilization was brought to an end by the sudden influx of the Sea Peoples.

3/ Bottom left
An ivory head of a woman, quite possibly a princess. The hair and high headdress were once covered with thin gold, and along the forehead there are loops of silver mixed with gold. Black copper was used to encrust the eyelids. The modelling of the face suggests that this is a portrait rather than a work of imagination. The head was found in the palace and is about 6in high.

4/ Right
This ivory panel comes from the headboard of a bed and is about 9½in high. A king, or other royal person, is seen embracing his consort, his hand resting on her breast. The consort is offering a jar of perfume. The panel dates from between 1400 to 1350 BC.

Map and palace plan labels:
N, East Archives, North-east Entrance, Private Quarters? Offices?, Courtyard and Garden, Storerooms, Rooms with subfloor burial vaults, Courtyard, Courtyard with ornamental basin, South Archives, Private Quarters of the Royal Family, Courtyard, Courtyard and Central Archives, Early Throne Room, South-west Archives, West Archives, Guardroom (?), Courtyard, Later Throne Room, Guardroom (?), Guardroom (?), Main entrance, Tower, Room with tablets, South-west Entrance

HATTI, ANATOLIA, Hattushash, Cape Gelidonya, Kaş, Troy, Lesbos, Smyrna, Miletus, Halicarnassus, Ialysus, RHODES, GREECE, Thebes, Perati, Athens, Thera, Mycenae, Kato Zakro, Pylos, Knossos, Phaistos, Hagia Triador, KAPTARU (CRETE)

40°   20°   35°   25°

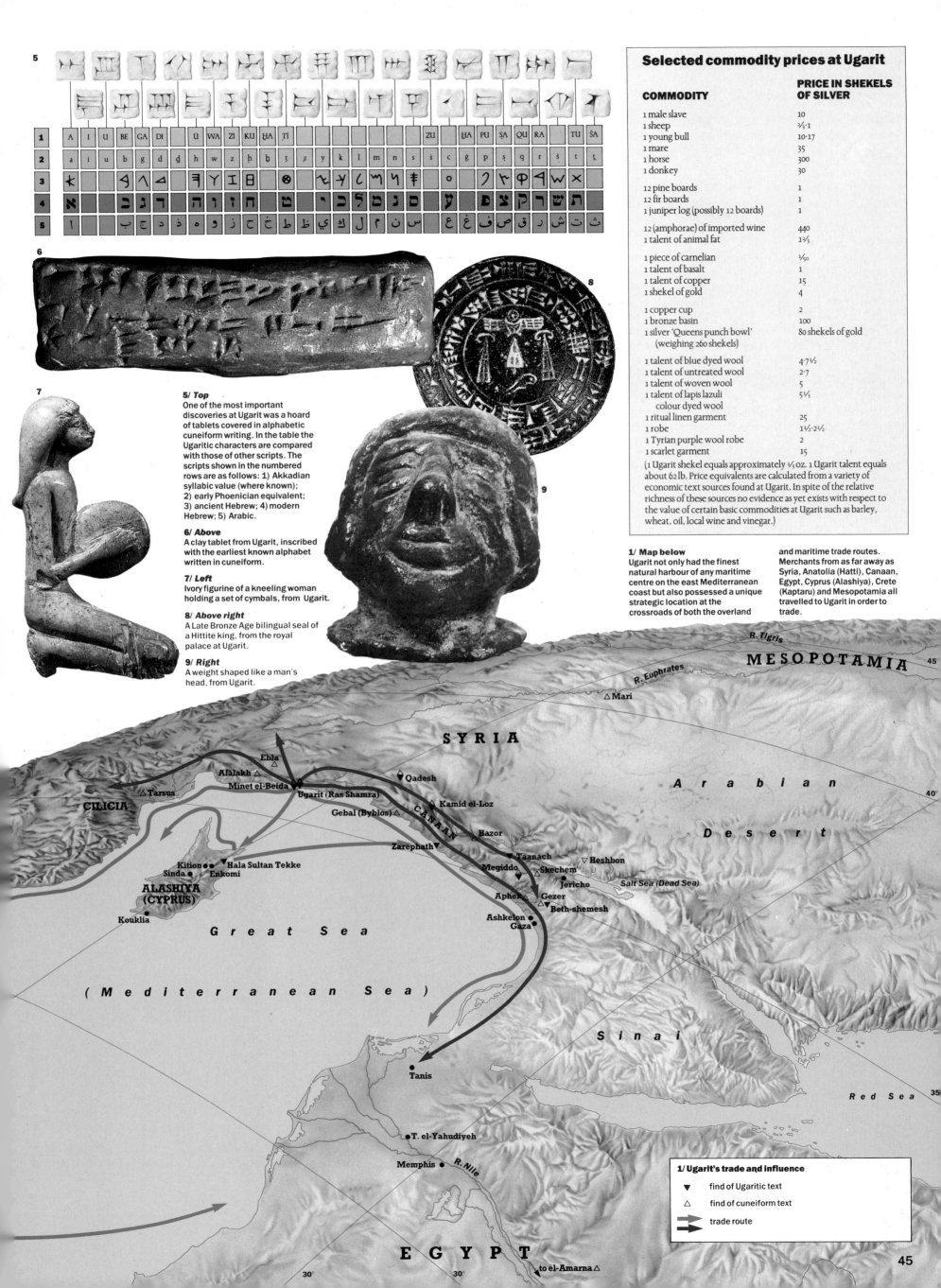

Selected commodity prices at Ugarit

COMMODITY	PRICE IN SHEKELS OF SILVER
1 male slave	10
1 sheep	⅔-1
1 young bull	10-17
1 mare	35
1 horse	300
1 donkey	30
12 pine boards	1
12 fir boards	1
1 juniper log (possibly 12 boards)	1
12 (amphorae) of imported wine	440
1 talent of animal fat	1⅔
1 piece of carnelian	½₀
1 talent of basalt	1
1 talent of copper	15
1 shekel of gold	4
1 copper cup	2
1 bronze basin	100
1 silver 'Queens punch bowl' (weighing 260 shekels)	80 shekels of gold
1 talent of blue dyed wool	4-7½
1 talent of untreated wool	2-7
1 talent of woven wool	5
1 talent of lapis lazuli colour dyed wool	5⅓
1 ritual linen garment	25
1 robe	1½-2½
1 Tyrian purple wool robe	2
1 scarlet garment	15

(1 Ugarit shekel equals approximately ⅓ oz. 1 Ugarit talent equals about 62 lb. Price equivalents are calculated from a variety of economic text sources found at Ugarit. In spite of the relative richness of these sources no evidence as yet exists with respect to the value of certain basic commodities at Ugarit such as barley, wheat, oil, local wine and vinegar.)

5/ Top
One of the most important discoveries at Ugarit was a hoard of tablets covered in alphabetic cuneiform writing. In the table the Ugaritic characters are compared with those of other scripts. The scripts shown in the numbered rows are as follows: 1) Akkadian syllabic value (where known); 2) early Phoenician equivalent; 3) ancient Hebrew; 4) modern Hebrew; 5) Arabic.

6/ Above
A clay tablet from Ugarit, inscribed with the earliest known alphabet written in cuneiform.

7/ Left
Ivory figurine of a kneeling woman holding a set of cymbals, from Ugarit.

8/ Above right
A Late Bronze Age bilingual seal of a Hittite king, from the royal palace at Ugarit.

9/ Right
A weight shaped like a man's head, from Ugarit.

1/ Map below
Ugarit not only had the finest natural harbour of any maritime centre on the east Mediterranean coast but also possessed a unique strategic location at the crossroads of both the overland and maritime trade routes. Merchants from as far away as Syria, Anatolia (Hatti), Canaan, Egypt, Cyprus (Alashiya), Crete (Kaptaru) and Mesopotamia all travelled to Ugarit in order to trade.

1/ Ugarit's trade and influence

▼ find of Ugaritic text
△ find of cuneiform text
➤ trade route

THE archive of about 380 texts and fragments from the ruins of el-Amarna (the official modern name of Akhetaten) in Egypt introduces us to the first great international period in ancient history. The documents are written in the cuneiform script and except for one in Hittite and one in Hurrian, they are all in various dialects of the Akkadian language, the tongue of Mesopotamia. This language was commonly used for international correspondence. The texts from Canaan, however, contain examples of local inflection and syntax.

The period reflected in the Amarna tablets is that of the 14th century BC. The documents are mostly letters written to or by Pharaohs Amenophis III (1417-1379), Amenophis IV (better known as Akhenaten) (1379-62) and Tutankhamun (1361-52). Those addressed to the former were brought to the new capital city of Akhetaten when Amenophis IV moved the foreign office there in about the sixth year of his reign. All of the tablets were discarded when the city was abandoned by Tutankhamun in about 1358.

Internationally, Egypt was at peace and enjoyed a special treaty relationship with Mitanni, the Hurrian kingdom of northern Syria. Diplomatic relations were also enjoyed with Babylonia during the Kassite era. Most of the Amarna letters that came from Mitanni and Babylon date to the reign of Amenophis III, but there are some letters that date from the early part of the reign of his son, the 'heretic' Amenophis IV a time when the kingdom of Mitanni was threatened by the Hittite kingdom rejuvenated by its king, the energetic Suppiluliuma. In the end the Hittites conquered Mitanni and gained control over the city states of northern Syria, actions which threatened Egyptian territories in Canaan. Diplomatic contact with the newly independent Assyria is also documented in the Amarna letters, as well as relations with Alashiya (probably a major city state of Cyprus).

The Amarna letters supply us with a good picture of Canaan at this time. The area of direct Egyptian control conformed more or less to the borders of the land of Canaan (NUM 34.1-12) with the addition of the states of Qatna, Qadesh (on the Orontes) and Amurru (on both sides of the Nahr el-Kebir, the classical Eleutherus). International recognition of Canaan as a legal–political entity is confirmed by a document from Ugarit in which the 'sons [citizens] of Canaan' had to pay an indemnity to the 'sons [citizens] of Ugarit'. The Egyptians maintained several centres for administrative purposes in Canaan; their commissioners were posted at Gaza, Sumur (Simyra) and Kumidi. They also had a supply base governed by a commissioner at Yarimuta (unidentified) and a major quartermaster and ordnance base at Joppa. The troops posted at Beth-shean manned the garrison for the Egyptian authorities; their main task was watching over the caravan route which crossed the Jordan

2/ Near right
Triumphal stela of Pharaoh Sethos I from Beth-shean. The king makes an offering before Re-Har-akhte who holds a sceptre in his right hand and a *ankh* in his left. It is made of basalt, *c* 8ft high.

3/Right
Sethos I being led by the goddess Isis into the presence of Amun-Re and Mut. From a wall of the great hypostele hall at Karnak.

4/ Far right
Pharaoh Sethos I before the goddess Isis, on a pillar of a doorway in the 4th corridor of the tomb of Sethos at Thebes.

5/ Extreme right
The cedars of Lebanon were famous in the Near East for use as building material. Sethos I received cedarwood as tribute.

BETWEEN GENESIS AND EXODUS:
400 YEARS OF EGYPTIAN SUPREMACY

THE AMARNA TABLETS AND SETHOS I's CAMPAIGNS

During the Amarna Age (*c* 1400-1350 BC) Egyptian control over Canaan became less intense because Egypt was at peace with the Mitanni to the north. An archive of clay tablets found at el-Amarna dates from this period and includes letters from Canaanite rulers describing the turbulent local situation in Palestine. The tablets are also important because they name places in Canaan, at a time when the Bible is silent. In *c* 1318 BC, Pharaoh Sethos I, one of the pharaohs of the new 19th dynasty in Egypt, campaigned to reassert Egyptian control over the area.

on the way to Damascus. Other contingents of support or garrison troops were posted at some of the city states, eg, Jerusalem. Those units were recruited from Nubian (Cushite) and other subject peoples. Renegades ('apiru) were recruited in Canaan for service in Nubia.

The commissioners and other officials were actively involved in the affairs of the various city states, frequently carrying out instructions from the pharaoh himself. There is no basis for the assumption that Amenophis IV neglected his empire. On the contrary, he kept himself well informed on matters of state and issued directives for dealing with troublemakers.

Canaanite society can be seen as organized into small city-states with one town at the centre and in some cases with subordinate neighbouring towns around it. All the villages nearby were subject to the overlordship of the local king and his band of noblemen. The latter were usually those capable of furnishing a chariot with its horses and squires. The council of these oligarchs supported the king and advised him on policy. On occasion they even ousted one ruler in favour of another. The land was cultivated by tenant farmers working for the nobles; they also served as infantry. Every city-state was subject to tribute payments and its fighting men were subject to call-up whenever the Egyptian king required them to march with his army.

Two additional groups appear in the Amarna texts, the bedouin (Sutu) and the outlaws/renegades ('apiru). They served as 'legionaires' under Egyptian representatives but often were found acting independently, creating a threat to the city-state populations. The 'apiru were runaways who for various reasons had to flee from their home countries (city-states). They tended to band together in isolated places like the forested hillsides of the Lebanon or the sparsely settled hill country around Shechem, or on the ridges of Upper Galilee. As a social phenomenon, they were documented throughout the 2nd millennium BC and from all parts of the Fertile Crescent. We know that they came from many language groups and had no relation to the pastoral nomads on the desert steppes (the Sutu). There is no proof that the term 'apiru was related to 'ibrim, nor that there was any connection between the 'apiru, the patriarchs, and the Israelite nation. Whenever they appeared in the Amarna letters, it was because they were engaged in violent or subversive activity on behalf of one or other of the city-state rulers. They had a major role in founding the

dynastic state of Amurru on the northern border of Canaan.

The Amarna texts represent correspondence discarded with the abandonment of Akhetaten. The collections of letters dealing with individual incidents that took place in Canaan can be viewed as self-contained case files. They include many details of the troublesome affairs which the Egyptian authorities had to administer. For example, letters contain details of the ruler of Jerusalem's disputes with coastal neighbours. In one set of letters we also read about the ruler of Gubla (Byblos), Rib-Haddi, who warned Amenophis III of 'Abdi-Ashirta, who at the time was subverting the local regimes of northern Phoenicia and forming an independent coalition. As a result Egyptian troops were sent and 'Abdi-Ashirta met his death. But his sons, especially Aziru, revived their rebellious father's policy when Amenophis IV came to the throne, and evidently gained support from senior Egyptian officials. Aziru was allowed to unite the towns in the area into a territorial buffer state over the protests of Rib-Haddi (who was finally ousted from his own town and murdered). Aziru went to Egypt but upon his return, probably near the end of Pharaoh Amenophis' life, he went over to the Hittites.

SETHOS I'S CAMPAIGNS

Egypt's prestige had fallen considerably during the Amarna period. However, the advent of a new royal dynasty in *c* 1320 BC helped restore her position abroad. Under Pharaoh Sethos I in particular, Egyptian control was once more firmly extended into the Jordan valley.

The military campaigns of Sethos I are notoriously difficult to quantify. We are thrown back on to vaguely worded triumphal inscriptions which include the military

5

THE AMARNA TABLETS

The following text is a translation of (6) the Amarna tablet below. Yahtiri, governor of Gaza and Joppa, *c* 1400 BC, writes to Pharaoh for permission to come to Egypt to serve in his army:

'To the king my lord, my pantheon and my Sun-god I speak: thus says Yahtiri, your servant, the dust of your feet. At the feet of the king my lord, my pantheon and my Sun-god, seven and seven times I fell. Moreover, I am a faithful servant of the king my lord. I looked here and I looked there, but there was no light; I look to the king my lord and there is light. And even though one brick might move from beneath its neighbour, I will not move from beneath the feet of the king my lord. And let the king my lord ask Yanhamu, his deputy! When I was young he brought me to Egypt, and I served the king my lord, and I stood in the gate of the king my lord. And let the king my lord ask his deputy whether I guard the gate of Azzati and the gate of Yapu. And I, with the troops of the king my lord will go wherever they go. And now indeed have I set the front of the king's yoke upon my neck, and I will bear it'.

The tablet below right (7) was written in *c* 1375 BC by Tushratta, King of Mitanni, complaining about the detention of his envoys in Egypt:

'To Naphururiya [Amenophis IV] king of Egypt, my brother, my son-in-law, who loves me and whom I love, I speak: thus says Tushratta King of Mitanni, your father-in-law, who loves you, your brother. I am well. May it be well with you! May it be exceedingly well with your estates, with Teye, your mother, the queen of the land of Egypt, Taduhepa, my daughter, your wife, the remainder of your wives, your sons, your houses, your chariots, your soldiers, your country, and whatever is yours.

Pirizzi and Tulupri, my messengers, have I sent to my brother as express messengers, and ordered them to hurry exceedingly. Indeed I sent them off with [only] a small party. Earlier I said to my brother "I shall detain Mane, my brother's messenger, until my brother releases my messengers, and they come back."

And now my brother will by no means release them so that they can return, but has detained them exceedingly! Why? Are my messengers not birds, that fly away and come back? Why does my brother agonize so over the messengers? Why should the one not... in the presence of the other, and that one not hear the greeting of the other? Every day we ought to be exceedingly happy! Let my brother speedily release my messenger so that I may hear my brother's greeting and rejoice!

Indeed I do love my brother, and I will despatch my messenger to my brother for good things; meanwhile let me hear good things for my brother! For my brother is good, and my brother will do what I wish, and not make my heart grieve.

And all the words which I spoke to your father, Teye your mother knows them all. No other person knows them, and you might ask Teye your mother all about them.'

reliefs on the north wall of the hypostyle at Karnak, the lists of place-names, and the two triumphal stelae at Beth-shean.

At the end of May in his first regnal year (about 1318 BC), perhaps as little as three months after he had ascended the throne as sole ruler, Sethos received intelligence that the headman of Hammath, in concert with the town of Pella, was harassing the towns of Beth-shean and Rehob. Perhaps simultaneously word was brought that the bedouin Shasu (*Sutu*), a large settlement of whom was located in southern Transjordan, had irrupted into the Negeb and north Sinai, thus posing a threat to Egypt's land-route to Asia. Neither was a particularly serious threat, but the incidents were probably used by Sethos as an excuse to attack the Hittites under the guise of local punitive action. The army, which was quickly mustered, easily defeated the *Sutu*, took Gaza, and moved up the coast. Probably from Acco Sethos despatched three divisions to quell the disturbance Hammath had fomented, again with noteworthy success.

From here details of the campaign become more doubtful. The Karnak reliefs depict the felling of timber in the Lebanon by Canaanite chiefs, while the place-name lists mention a sequence of places along the Phoenician coast (Tyre, Uzu and Ullaza being the best known), and it is not unreasonable to assume that these mark the main itinerary of the expedition. (A stela of Sethos was, in fact, recovered from Tyre.) Reference to Takhsi, Tunip, Qadesh and Hazor may belong to a subsequent campaign, when Sethos had decided to re-open the old Egypto-Hittite conflict.

Thus the thrust of Sethos' first campaign was directed at the Phoenician coast, and at securing coastal facilities in preparation for the attack on the Hittites. It also brought the Egyptians into direct conflict with the *Sutu*, an ethnic element of rising importance in the area.

1/ Map below
Clay tablets, part of a bureaucratic archive from el-Amarna, name places in Canaan which can thus be proved to have existed in the 14th century BC. The map also shows Sethos I's campaigns in 1318 BC to restore Egyptian authority.

6 and 7/ Below
Two of the Amarna tablets are shown. A translation (by Dr I. Finkel of the British Museum) appears in the text above. These tablets have proved to be a vital source of information not only about Egyptian affairs, but also about those of Egypt's near neighbours, such as Canaan.

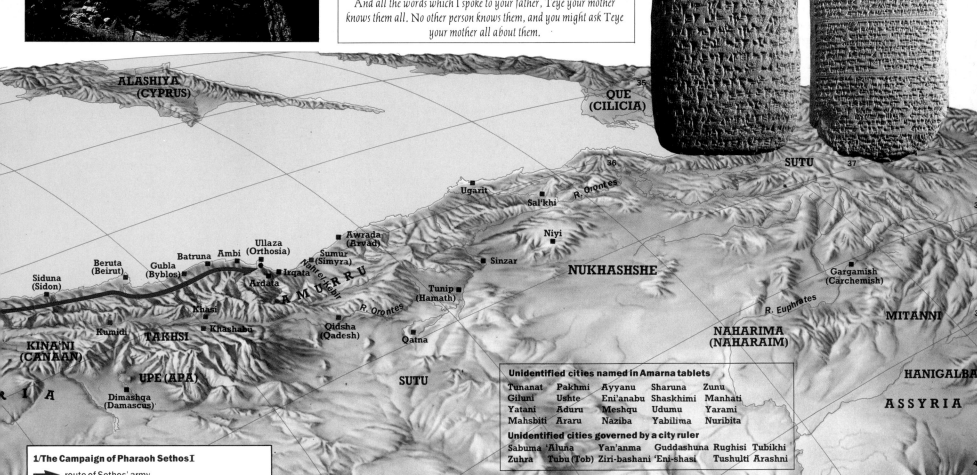

1/The Campaign of Pharaoh Sethos I

→ route of Sethos' army
1 first division of Amun
2 first division of Re
3 first division of Sutekh
→ route of armies from Hammath and Pella
→ route of *Sutu*

1/ Cities named in the Amarna tablets

■ city
■ city governed by Egyptian ruler
■ centre of Egyptian authority

Unidentified cities named in Amarna tablets

Tunanat	Pakhmi	Ayyanu	Sharuna	Zunu
Giluni	Ushte	Eni'anabu	Shaskhimi	Manhati
Yatani	Aduru	Meshqu	Udumu	Yarami
Mahsbiti	Araru	Naziba	Yabilima	Nuribita

Unidentified cities governed by a city ruler

Sabuma	'Aluna	Yan'anma	Guddashuna	Rughisi	Tubikhi
Zuhra	Tubu (Tob)	Ziri-bashani	'Eni-shasi	Tushulti	Arashni

PHARAOH Ramesses II spent a decade at least trying to recapture Egypt's Syrian possessions. In his fourth year (1300 BC), he swept north through Canaan and along the Lebanese coast, past Tyre and Byblos, at each of which he left a royal inscription marking his passage. Probably he went as far as Simyra, to reaffirm Egyptian control over the coastal strip, formerly encroached on by the mountain kingdom of Amurru immediately behind it. This done, Ramesses then struck in a surprise attack at Amurru itself, forcing its ruler to acknowledge Egyptian overlordship. The ruler sent a hasty message to the Hittite king Muwatallis, announcing his involuntary switch of allegiance.

So successful had this 'First Campaign of Victory' been, that the jubilant young pharaoh launched a second next year to re-conquer Qadesh, and so open the way into North Syria. Having mustered at the East-Delta capital Pi-Ramesse, and left Egypt via the border-fort at Sile, the entire force took the customary coast-road to Gaza. There, Ramesses II divided his force into two unequal parts. A trusted elite corps was sent up the coast to guarantee the Egyptian hold on the Phoenician ports and coastline, keep check on Amurru, then strike inland to rendezvous with Ramesses just outside Qadesh itself. The pharaoh meanwhile led the main force by the inland route, from Canaan, past the east side of Galilee and the south end of the Anti-Lebanon range, then into the broad Beqa'a valley to Kumidi (renamed 'Town of Ramesses in Cedar Valley'), and so north to the Qadesh ridge opposite Hermil/Arnam, with a view

RAMESSES II OF EGYPT IN CONTEST WITH THE HITTITE EMPIRE

Prominent in the international politics of the early 13th century BC was the determined attempt by Pharaoh Ramesses II to recover for Egypt the central Syrian territories of Amurru and Qadesh – both lost in the el-Amarna period by Akhenaten, and recaptured only briefly by his own father, Sethos I. Reconquest of these two petty states was vital if Ramesses II was ever to invade North Syria as far as the west bend of the Euphrates, and so emulate the great Levantine power of Pharaohs Tuthmosis I and III of two centuries previously.

north to Qadesh itself on its 'tell' or ruin-mound. The king then encountered two bedouin who professed the wish to bring over their tribes from Hittite to Egyptian allegiance, volunteering the report that Muwatallis, the Hittite king, was skulking far away in Aleppo. This news was too good to be true – the bedouin had been 'planted' by the astute Hittite king to lull the pharaoh into a false sense of security, ripe for a surprise attack. And the trick worked perfectly. Unaware that his foe was in fact stationed just east of Qadesh, Ramesses raced across the south Orontes ford with his personal retainers (followed by the Egyptian 1st Division, of the god Amun), to begin setting-up camp to the north-west of Qadesh itself.

However, as the Division of Re approached across the plain to where the camp was being set up, two Hittite spies were suddenly surprised by Egyptian scouts, seized and interrogated by the pharaoh: so, the awful truth of his predicament emerged. Immediately the vizier and aides were sent off to hasten the arrival of the 3rd and 4th Divisions (of the gods Ptah and Seth), and members of the royal family sent out of the way of impending conflict.

At that moment, the Hittite chariot-force swept west over the Orontes, straight into the unsuspecting and unprepared 2nd Egyptian Division on the march, scattered them, and wheeled north harrying fugitives and attacking the troops of Amun's division still establishing camp. Ramesses himself stayed calm, rallied his immediate aides, and led six desperate charges against the foe, now upon the camp. At this vital juncture there suddenly arrived the elite force under its seasoned commanders who were able quickly to move to the attack. Caught from two sides, the Hittite chariotry wavered and then broke. Ramesses and the elite force then drove the Hittites pell-mell back east to the Orontes, leading to a mad scramble back across the river, doubtless to the consternation of the Hittite king. The crisis over, the Egyptian 3rd and 4th Divisions finally arrived.

Next day, Ramesses launched his own surprise counter-attack upon the Hittite force; but as the stolid Hittite infantry stood their ground, this proved abortive.

So Muwatallis then proposed the renewal of peace, doubtless in terms of the status quo as it had existed before the war: as before, Amurru and Qadesh would remain Hittite, while Egypt retained the coastland up to Simyra. Although these terms did not please him, his army had no more stomach for battle, and Ramesses II then returned south to Egypt, to celebrate his hollow triumph of personal bravery. Behind him, Muwatallis reclaimed Amurru and Qadesh, and even invaded the Egyptian province of Upe (including Damascus). However, he in turn suffered the loss to Assyria of the province of Hanigalbat (within the west bend of Euphrates) while occupied with the pharaoh.

With a refurbished army, in Year 8 (1296 BC), Ramesses marched back into Canaan. First, he had to crush unrest in Galilee and probably in Transjordan (Moab and Seir/Edom), before going on to recover the province of Upe and strengthen his hold in the Phoenician coastlands. Only then could he march through the Eleutherus valley to attack Dapur within Amurru – a conquest marked by erecting his statue in that town. No sooner was Ramesses back home, than Dapur rebelled (ie, returned to the Hittite fold). By Year 10, he was back north again, and personally led another attack on Dapur, even disdaining to wear his body-armour. These northern 'strikes' were no doubt intended to outflank Qadesh and break into North Syria; but so long as the powerful Hittite centres at Aleppo and Carchemish remained untouched, raids on lesser city-states like Dapur were doomed to failure, and even Ramesses gave up these attempts in the light of these stark facts.

There had been no aggressive Hittite response to these Egyptian attacks on North Syria – Muwatallis was followed by his son Mursil III who, after seven years of insecure reign, was ejected from office by his uncle who took power as Hattusil III. The dethroned king eventually fled to Egypt for refuge, whence Hattusil demanded his extradition by Ramesses – a demand which the pharaoh refused. Hattusil threatened war (bringing Ramesses II as far as Bethshean, in Year 18, 1286 BC). But when the new king of Assyria once more seized the Hittite client-province of Hanigalbat (this time, permanently) and threatened Carchemish, even Hattusil realized that he could not take on two great powers. So, in due time he opened negotiations with Egypt, culminating in the notable treaty of peace and alliance with Ramesses II in his Year 21 (1283 BC). After a few hiccups, Egypto-Hittite relations became so close that Hattusil III married off two of his daughters to the pharaoh, in Ramesses II's Year 34 (1270 BC) and up to a decade later.

> 'THE GREAT PRINCE OF HATTI SHALL NOT TRESPASS AGAINST THE LAND OF EGYPT FOREVER... AND USER-MAAT-RE- SETEP-EN-RE, THE GREAT RULER OF EGYPT SHALL NOT TRESPASS AGAINST THE LAND [OF HATTI, TO TAKE] FROM IT FOREVER... IF ANOTHER ENEMY COME AGAINST THE LANDS OF USER-MAAT-RE... AND HE SEND TO THE GREAT PRINCE OF HATTI, SAYING: "COME WITH ME AS REINFORCEMENT AGAINST HIM," THE GREAT PRINCE OF HATTI SHALL [COME TO HIM]...'
> TREATY BETWEEN EGYPTIANS AND HITTITES, 1284 BC

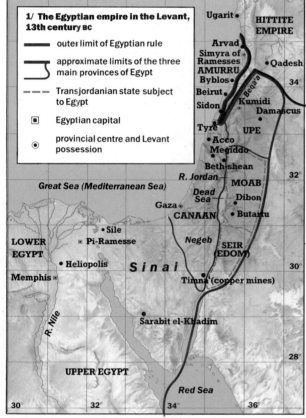

1/ The Egyptian empire in the Levant, 13th century BC

— outer limit of Egyptian rule

⌐ approximate limits of the three main provinces of Egypt

--- Transjordanian state subject to Egypt

■ Egyptian capital

◉ provincial centre and Levant possession

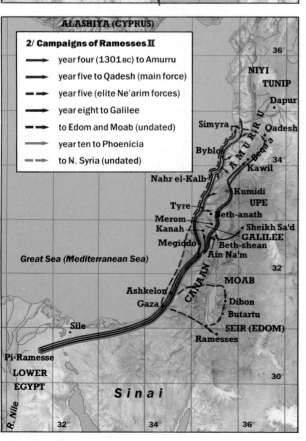

2/ Campaigns of Ramesses II

→ year four (1301 BC) to Amurru

→ year five to Qadesh (main force)

--→ year five (elite Ne'arim forces)

→ year eight to Galilee

--→ to Edom and Moab (undated)

→ year ten to Phoenicia

--→ to N. Syria (undated)

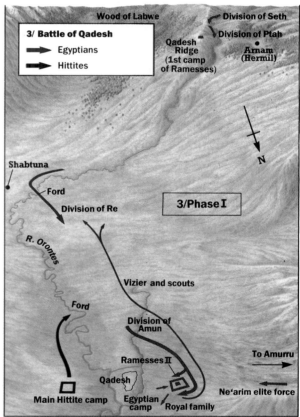

3/ Battle of Qadesh
→ Egyptians
→ Hittites

3/Phase I

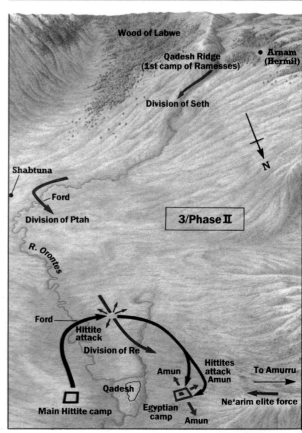

3/Phase II

4/ Left
The battle of Qadesh from the Ramesseum at Thebes. The Hittites are floating in the river. One soldier is attempting to pull his comrade to the shore.

5/ Above
Ramesses II shown holding prisoners by the hair, a common convention in Egyptian art to show the subjection of foreign enemies to the king.

1/ Map far left (top)
Prior to the el-Amarna period (mid-14th century BC), Egypt's empire had been organized into three main provinces, each under a 'Governor of Northern Foreign Countries'. (1) Canaan, which essentially consisted of Western Palestine, from Galilee to the Negeb, between the Jordan/Dead Sea and the Mediterranean. (2) Upe, the oasis of Damascus, and the Beqa'a valley west of it, across the Anti-Lebanon range. (3) Amurru, in two parts: the Lebanon mountain ranges (occupied by the kingdom of Amurru), and the Lebanese/Phoenician coastland below them.

2/ Map far left (bottom)
The campaign of Year 4 (1300 BC) is attested directly by a dated monument found at Byblos, and a rock-inscription still at the headland of Nahr el-Kalb (Dog River). Year 5 saw the Battle of Qadesh. The king advanced to Qadesh by the inland route, sending a support-force along the sea coast to secure his western flank and then to meet him at Qadesh; its arrival saved him in the tactical trap sprung on the pharaoh at Qadesh by the Hittite king Muwatallis.
Year 8 witnessed an onslaught on disloyal townships in Galilee, the recovery of Upe, and an attack on Dapur in Syria proper.

Year 10 is the date of a third inscription of Ramesses II at Nahr el-Kalb, and possibly of his renewed attack on Dapur in Syria. These wars then died down until a threat of war probably brought Ramesses out to face Hattusil III; a stela of Year 18 at Beth-shean may reflect these events.

3/ Battle of Qadesh Phase I near left
Ramesses II and the Division of Amun make camp north-west of Qadesh. Learning of the Hittite presence he sends a vizier and scouts to bring up the Divisions of Seth and Ptah; and members of his family are sent away from danger. The Division of Re march down the Qadesh plain towards Ramesses' camp.

3/ Phase II below near left
The Hittite chariots ford the Orontes, charge into the Egyptian Division of Re, and wheel north to scatter the Division of Amun.

3/ Phase III below
Ramesses II counter-charges the Hittite force as it attacks his camp; the newly-arrived Ne'arim elite force also attacks, from the west, disrupting the Hittites.

3/ Phase IV right
Ramesses and the elite force push the Hittites back into the Orontes, as the Divisions of Seth and Ptah arrive.

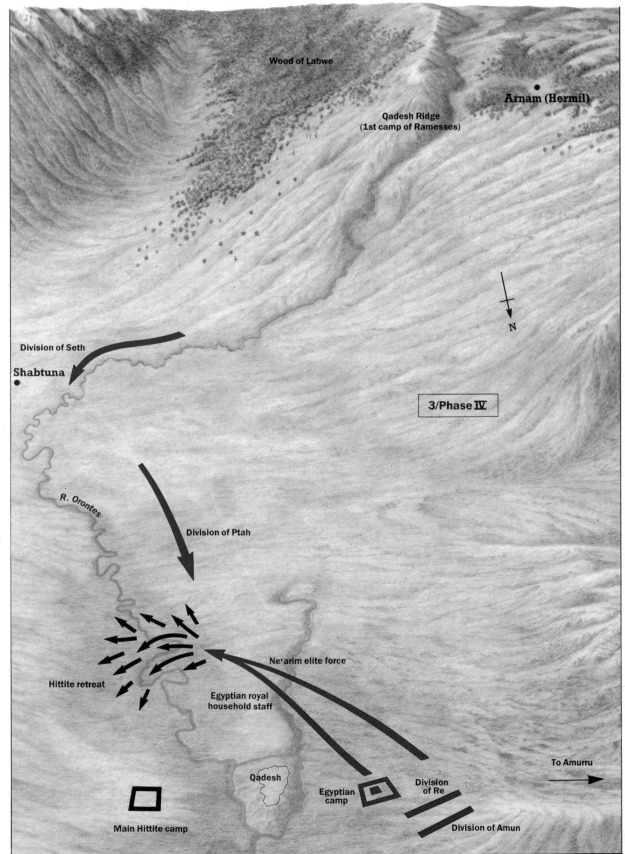

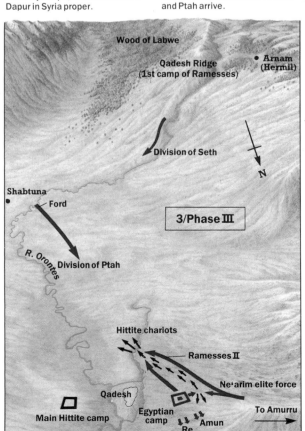

MANY centuries before the age of Ramesses II and Merneptah, Egyptian scribes had used irony and humour to proclaim the advantages and superior career-prospects open to those who trained diligently to become skilled scribes (as opposed to all 'lesser' callings). Under the empire, with wider administrative horizons reaching far into the Levant, the scribal curriculum was duly extended and modernized to match. Within the two centuries from Tuthmosis III to Ramesses II, the Egyptian civil and military administration would have built up a considerable body of knowledge – travel information – on the principal routes through Canaan and Syria to other kingdoms, stopping points, obstacles, lengths of time needed, and the like, for royal envoys abroad, and armies in the field.

Composed under Ramesses II and still popular under Merneptah and his successors, the satirical letter was designed to give instruction in various subjects to budding scribal administrators – constructing building ramps, transporting obelisks, erecting a colossal statue, organizing supplies for a military expedition abroad, and finally a sampling of the geography and routes in Syro–Palestine.

THE SATIRICAL LETTER IN PAPYRUS ANASTASI I
Found in the 19th century by a Greek merchant Anastasi, this document is cast in the form of a letter from one scribe (Hori) to another (Amenemope), in which Hori turns his sarcastic wit to showing up the ignorance and incompetence of his colleague in the matters covered. In the Syrian geography section, Hori depicts his correspondent as an envoy who falls prey to various misadventures. The portion on geography can be viewed in seven segments and is important for its description of Syria and Canaan.

SECTION I
Mention of the most distant places opens the account: the Hittite land. This includes Upe (Egypt's northernmost Syrian province) and Simyra of Ramesses (Egypt's north point in Phoenicia), and Aleppo and Qadesh, major Hittite centres in north and south Syria, reached from the coast by the narrow Eleutherus valley also known as the Magur (later Greek Makra), a vital pass through the Lebanese mountain-ranges.

SECTION II
From Syria and Mount Shawi, the scribe outlines the main coast road south through a series of well-known seaports of antiquity: Byblos, Beirut, Sidon, Sarepta (biblical Zarephath) to the island port of Tyre and its mainland counterpart Uzu, passing the Litani river-mouth nearby. Then, over the narrow coastal pass of Selaim (now Ras en-Nakura) and down to Acre (biblical Acco), before turning inland to Achshaph not far from Megiddo, and looking across the mountain-ridges of User (now Carmel) and Shechem to south and south-east.

SECTION III
From Achsaph and the Megiddo plain, the envoy might ride over to Hazor, south through Hammath by Galilee lake, and then down to Yenoam, back over to Adummim, in a circle.

SECTION IV
The next section has two circuits in the north-east. First, from the north end of the Beqa'a valley (Takhsi and Taminta areas) through Qadesh and Dapur, then back south to Arnam/Hermil. Second, going south from the Beqa'a (and Damascus) through Upe, the scribe looks south to Qiryat 'Anab and Adurun and the south border-forts of Upe.

SECTION V
Back near Megiddo, the scribe takes his reader on another short circle, from the Qina brook to Rehob, up to the strategic fort of Beth-shean and the Jordan river-ford below it, then back west to Megiddo.

3/ Right
Papyrus Anastasi I, the document which provides us with a great fund of information about the training and work of Egyptian scribes, as well as giving an insight into the geography of the Levant during the 2nd millennium BC, comes from the collection of a 19th century Greek merchant named Anastasi. He was employed by the Swedes as their consul general in Egypt and lived in Alexandria. During his service in Egypt he made a collection of antiquities which was eventually split up and sold in several countries including Sweden, the Netherlands and Great Britain. His collection of papyri arrived in London in 1839.
Papyrus, an early form of paper, was made from the pith of a reed.

THE LEVANT AS SEEN BY AN EGYPTIAN SCRIBE
Most accounts left us by the Egyptians are the boastful tales of pharaohs describing their military exploits. However, there are other records which give us an insight into the ancient Near East at that period. Among these is the satirical letter contained in Papyrus Anastasi I. Far from being a pompous account of victories it is an ironical, often humorous and sometimes risqué document which purports to be a letter from one scribe to another. The papyrus is important because it describes Canaan and provides us with information about the lands directly concerned in the Bible story.

SECTION VI
From Megiddo, the scribe pictures his rival as penetrating the narrow, rocky ravine (through the Carmel ridge) on his way south to Joppa where a gentler assailant awaits him: 'The narrow ravine is infested with bedouin hiding in the bushes, men seven or nine feet tall from head to toe, ferocious and merciless, heedless of pleas. You're on your own, no one to help you... Your path is strewn with boulders and pebbles, overgrown... the abyss yawns on one side, and the mountain towers up on the other ... You think the enemy is after you, and you panic! You reach Joppa, finding the meadows in full bloom, you push into one, and find the pretty girl looking after the gardens. She makes up to you, and gives you a sample of her embrace – but you are found out, must confess, and are judged as a chariot-warrior, and sell your best shirt to pay the fine!'

SECTION VII
At Gaza, repairs are effected. The geography ends with a gazetteer of the 12 principal forts and wells along the Sinai coast road from Sile on the Egyptian border to Gaza, Egypt's administrative centre in Canaan (see map 1).
1. Sile, a border-fort, also called 'the Ways of Horus', near el-Qantara.
2. Dwelling of the Lion/Ramesses II, probably at T. el-Habwe.
3. Migdol ('stronghold') of the King, and Well of Hasina, probably at T. el-Her.
4. Fort and Tract of Udjo of Sethos I/Ramesses II and Well of Tract of Unam; possibly at Katiyeh.
5. Outpost and royal fort of Sethos I/Ramesses II, and a well; near Bir el-Abd?
6. 'New Town' of His Majesty, and Well Ibseqeb; location uncertain (south of centre of Lake Sirbonis).
7. The Well of Sethos I, alias Sebi-el; location uncertain – near Bir el-Mazar?
8. The Twin Wells (also: Sweet Well, and Well of Sethos I); location uncertain – perhaps near Umm el-Ushush and Abu Mazruh.
9. 'New Town' of His Majesty, and fort by the Well Haberet – at el-Arish?
10. Well of Sethos I/Nikhasu of the Prince – between el-Arish and Raphia.
11. Rapah – Raphia, modern Rafa.
12. Gaza – the gateway to Egyptian-ruled Canaan.

'THE PRINCES ARE PROSTRATE, SAYING: "MERCY!"
NOT ONE RAISES HIS HEAD AMONG THE NINE BOWS.
DESOLATION IS FOR TEHENU; HATTI IS PACIFIED;
PLUNDERED IS THE CANAAN WITH EVERY EVIL;
CARRIED OFF IS ASHKELON; SEIZED UPON IS GEZER;
YANOAM IS MADE AS THAT WHICH DOES NOT EXIST;
ISRAEL IS LAID WASTE, HIS SEED IS NOT;
HURRU IS BECOME A WIDOW FOR EGYPT!
ALL LANDS TOGETHER, THEY ARE PACIFIED;
EVERYONE WHO WAS RESTLESS, HE HAS BEEN BOUND BY THE KING OF UPPER AND LOWER EGYPT...'   THE ISRAEL STELA

5 and 5a/ Below
The 'Israel' stela made of black basalt is inscribed with a triumphal hymn to the victory of Pharaoh Merneptah over Canaan, 13th century BC. It names places in Canaan, and it specifically mentions the word 'Israel' (see 5a), showing that a people calling themselves by this name had settled in Canaan at this time.

1/ Map below left
The author of the 'Satirical Letter' picks out the main coast-roads from central Phoenician down to Joppa and Gaza, some of the important inland routes linked with the coast, two short runs in Galilee and the Plain of Jezreel, and the famous military road between Egypt and Palestine.

2/ Map right
Pharaoh Merneptah quickly crushed any signs of revolt in Canaan after his father's death. His forces struck successively at Ashkelon, Gezer and Yenoam, engaging also with elements from the people of Israel, then settling in the hill-country of Canaan. Merneptah established two strongpoints, one in Canaan in the hills and one just south of Tyre, to guard his interests in Canaan and Phoenicia, besides renaming and maintaining the former post at

4/ Right
The mummified body of Pharaoh Merneptah was discovered by an expedition led by the French archaeologist Loret in 1898. The body had been placed in the tomb of Pharaoh Amenophis II (see page 43) in the Valley of the Kings.
Merneptah, coming to the throne at 60, ruled for only ten years and left no important buildings as monuments to his reign. His funerary temple at Thebes was built, in part, from stone taken from the temple of Amenophis III.

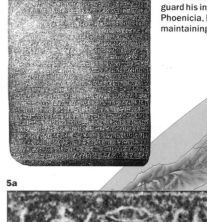

1/ Routes in Papyrus Anastasi I	
————	I
– – –	II
————	III
– ▪ –	IV
————	V
————	VI
– – –	VII
◉	Egyptian administrative centre
▣	Egyptian capital
‿	ford
1 ▆	fort

ALASHIYA (CYPRUS)

Sido
Sarepta
Tyre • Uzu
Selaim • Hazo
Acco •
Adummim
Achshaph
Yenoam
Megiddo •
Bedouin
Ravine • Beth-shean
Reho •
Shechem
R. Jordan
Joppa

Great Sea
(Mediterranean Sea)

Salt Sea
(Dead Sea)

Gaza ◉ 12

Rapah 11
10

el-Arish 9

CANAAN (RETENU)

1 2 3 4 5 6 7 8

LOWER
EGYPT
▣ Pi-Ramesse

▆ 1 Sile

Sinai

33   33° 30'   34°   34° 30'   35°

AT the death of Ramesses II in extreme old age in his sixty-seventh year of sole reign, the throne passed to his thirteenth son Merneptah 1236 BC (scholars suggest dates as varied as 1238/1224/1213 BC for this event), a man already turned 60 at least. Almost half a century of peace had elapsed since the famous Egypt-Hittite treaty (see page 48) without any more known military activity by Egypt in Canaan. The accession of a new king was always a temptation to restless spirits to try to escape the Egyptian yoke, but Merneptah was determined to allow no diminution of his authority compared to his famous father.

To check any dissident activity, the elderly pharaoh dispatched a punitive expedition to Canaan in his first or second year, possibly led by his son, the Crown Prince Sethos (later Sethos II). The blows fell on the towns of Ashkelon, Gezer and Yenoam, in south, south-central and north Canaan respectively, and defeat was inflicted on a 'new' people, Israel, still settling in the hill-country, as the hieroglyphic writing clearly implies. This allusion in a triumphal hymn of Merneptah (the so-called 'Israel Stela') of his fifth year is the first mention of Israel in ancient documents, and sets that people's initial entry into Canaan at an undetermined date prior to the first five years of Merneptah, ie, before 1236 BC or other date adopted for Merneptah's accession. A series of war-scenes in the great temple of the god Amun at Karnak in ancient Thebes can now be attributed to Merneptah (not to Ramesses II as earlier thought); the lower scenes show the fall of Ashkelon and a

BETWEEN GENESIS AND EXODUS:
400 YEARS OF EGYPTIAN SUPREMACY

THE CAMPAIGN OF PHARAOH MERNEPTAH

The fact that Merneptah was forced to undertake a punitive expedition against Israel is the best evidence we possess that a nation of that name actually existed in the 13th century BC and was living in Canaan.

second town (Gezer?); the upper scenes would then have shown the taking of Yenoam preceded by a battle with the Israelites (possibly classed by the Egyptians with the semi-nomadic Shasu, also mentioned). The capture of Gezer is also mentioned on a Nubian monument of Merneptah.

By Year 3 of the king, a postal register shows the frequent arrivals and departures of royal messengers based on the Delta capital and travelling via the border-fort of Sile. Besides the expected links with Gaza, a letter goes to the Prince of Tyre, and three centres of royal rule are mentioned. The 'Wells of Merneptah' (doubtless with a fort) were probably the (Me-) Nephtoah of the Bible (JOSH 15.9 and 18.15), being 'on the (mountain) ridge', and locatable at Lifta, just north-west of Jerusalem. Such a strongpoint would have enabled Merneptah's agents to keep an eye on the growing conflicts between the Canaanite vassals and

their new Israelite neighbours. A second centre of rule was the Castle of Merneptah near Selalim (a slip for Selaim?), probably a new fort to guard the coastal pass at Ras en-Nakura just south of Tyre. A third centre, 'the Town of Merneptah in the district of Pi-Aram', is most likely the Beqa'a centre Kumidi, renamed from its former epithet 'Town of Ramesses II in the Cedar Valley', but with note being taken of new inhabitants of the region – early Aramaeans, first detectable about 150 years earlier under Amenophis III.

This picture of the peaceful links of Egypt with her satellites in Canaan, Upe and the Phoenician coastlands is further reinforced by evidence of Merneptah's rule from Lachish in south Canaan, in Year 4. Here were found fragments of potsherds ('ostraca') in Egyptian script of the time, with dates corresponding to the limits of Merneptah's regnal years (but not those of his successors), bearing accounts of grain-harvest – tribute levied by Merneptah's inspectors of the local ruler of Lachish. Until then, at least, Merneptah's empire still matched that of his father, a position maintained also in Nubia and on the Libyan frontier after epic conflicts in his fifth year. Thus, he was able to leave an outwardly intact realm to his successors.

'IN THAT DAY THE EGYPTIANS WILL BE LIKE WOMEN, AND TREMBLE WITH FEAR BEFORE THE HAND WHICH THE LORD OF HOSTS SHAKES OVER THEM. AND THE LAND OF JUDAH WILL BECOME A TERROR TO THE EGYPTIANS...' ISA 19.16-17

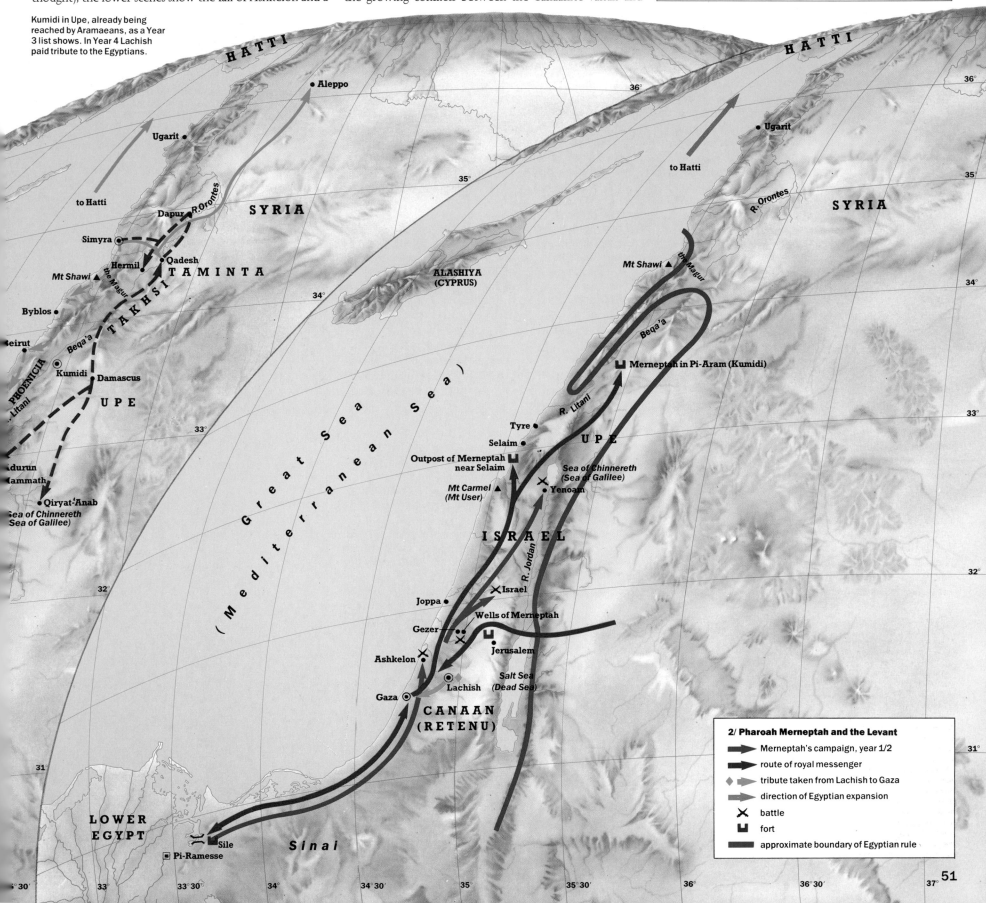

Kumidi in Upe, already being reached by Aramaeans, as a Year 3 list shows. In Year 4 Lachish paid tribute to the Egyptians.

2/ Pharoah Merneptah and the Levant
Merneptah's campaign, year 1/2
route of royal messenger
tribute taken from Lachish to Gaza
direction of Egyptian expansion
✕ battle
⊔ fort
approximate boundary of Egyptian rule

POTTERY of the Mycenaeans, who first visited the Levant with the Minoans, is found at about 100 excavated sites in the Levant and Egypt. Their distinctive wheel-made pots are usually found with large deposits of Cypriot hand-made wares, illustrating international commerce in goods, people and ideas in the Late Bronze Age.

THE EMERGENCE OF THE MYCENAEANS

At the end of the Aegean Early Bronze II or during Early Bronze Age III (c 2300-2000 BC) many settlements in mainland Greece were destroyed, probably by invaders from Anatolia, speaking a language which eventually became Greek. A reduced, impoverished and ethnically mixed population survived. In Crete the first palaces were built about 1930 BC in direct development from earlier Minoan society, enlivened by contacts with the Levant and Egypt. Minoan trading, and occasionally settlement, reached Sicily, western Anatolia, the Levant and Egypt.

During the Middle Bronze Age (c 2100-c 1600 BC) the Greek mainland gradually recovered, in population and cultural institutions. By the end of the period the Mycenaeans were prosperous and powerful, commanding a fertile plain in southern Greece, acquainted with but not riding the horse, and trading with the Cyclades and Crete.

At the end of Middle Minoan II or beginning of III (c 1700 BC), the Cretan palaces were rebuilt after destruction by earthquake. In the second palatial phase, until the end of Late Minoan IB (c 1450 BC) Mycenaean and Minoan cultures converged. The earliest shaft graves in Greece show admiration for Minoan life.

The effect on Minoan Crete of the eruption of Thera in Late Minoan IA is still a debatable question, but it may have accelerated a new relationship with the Mycenaeans. In Late Minoan IB co-operation between them was close, particularly in technology and trade. Joint enterprise can be traced at the Minoan settlement Trianda-Ialysos in Rhodes, in Cyprus, the Levant and Egypt. Pottery finds confirm the reality of representatives of the 'Islands in the Midst of the Sea' depicted in the Theban tomb chapels of Egyptian officials. Scenes in the chapel of Rekhmire, the last vizier of Tuthmosis III and first official of his successor Amenophis II reflect and help to date the Mycenaean takeover at Knossos at the end of Late Minoan IB, and the shift of influence from Crete to the mainland and Mycenae.

MYCENAEAN TRADE WITH CYPRUS, THE LEVANT AND EGYPT

Archaeological research shows that military force helped to achieve and maintain Mycenaean supremacy, stimulated the need for improved defences and weapons, and sustained efforts to obtain copper from Cyprus, and tin and luxuries from further east. Mycenaean (and a minimum of Minoan) goods, were perhaps distributed through the international market of Ugarit (see pages 44-45), where palace archives list commodities of likely Aegean origin, but Cyprus was always the prime target. The vast amount of Mycenaean pottery found in Cyprus is proof of trade which included perishables, domestic and perfumed oil, wine, herbs, wool, leather. Agents organized trading contacts and were sources of information and news. Exported pottery of Mycenaean LIA 2 and early IIIB travelled far beyond Cyprus (Sesebi, above the Second Cataract of the Nile in Nubia, is the most distant find). It travelled as part of shipments of Cypriot hand-made base ring and white slip wares (base ring juglets are thought to have been containers for opium). Study of stone anchors in Cyprus and the Levant has identified the origin of some Levantine ships. Since Mycenaeans needed the oriental trade it is likely that Aegean ships carried the metals home, together with exotic goods, known from excavation at Aegina, Athens, Mycenae, Gournia and Kommos in Crete.

The excavation of a Late Bronze Age shipwreck off Kaş, in south-west Turkey (now called the Ulu Burun wreck) was begun by George Bass in 1984. Its international cargo included copper, tin and glass ingots; Syro-Palestinian amphorae, one packed with Cypriot pottery, others with traces of grapes, olives, unidentified seeds; Mycenaean IIIA 2 and Syrian pottery; artefacts and ornaments in faience, amber, gold and silver; bronze weapons and tools. The ship may have been a Levantine merchantman sailing to Rhodes and the Aegean. It probably foundered in the reign of Akhenaten.

Except at El Amarna, the capital of Egypt under Akhenaten, and at Deir el-Medina, the artisan village at Thebes, no varied or large deposits of Mycenaean pottery have been found in Egypt, perhaps because it was at the end of the trade route, or because few Egyptian cities have been excavated. The Mycenaean stirrup jar, however, was copied in clay, faience and calcite. Two appear in a repre-

sentation at the Ramesseum of Ramesses II's camp before the battle of Qadesh, others are depicted in the tomb of Ramesses III at Thebes.

In the cities of the Levant, menaced by confrontation between Hittites and Egyptians, by internal faction and external attack, Aegean imports were comforting luxuries which gave social status in life and death.

DECLINE AND END OF MYCENAEAN TRADE

At a date, not yet precise, in the 19th Dynasty of Egypt, the trade between Mycenae and the Levant declined. Fine exports were replaced by local imitations and derivatives. In Cyprus wheel-made pottery replaced hand-made wares. Aegean society became unstable, perhaps because of disastrous harvests, earthquake, local warfare or social discontent. People began to leave the Mycenaean centres, and soon were arriving in Cyprus in mixed groups, seeking new homes. Some established precarious footholds at Maa-Palaiokastro, and Pyla-Kokkinokremmos. Others reached the Levant coast. Those who succeeded in settling in Cyprus adapted their culture to a new environment, and maintained tenuous contact with their homelands. The international network pioneered by Minoan seafarers was broken by the Sea Peoples (see pages 54-55).

MYCENAEAN POTTERY

Mycenaean pottery combined Helladic ceramic tradition (the potter's wheel was used at Lerna in early Helladic III) with Cycladic and Minoan inventiveness. About 140 shapes catered for domestic, commercial and ritual needs. Pots were usually thrown, but some special shapes and most figurines were hand-made. In the period of widest export potters worked in a highly organized industry, employing skilled and unskilled labour. All Mycenaean pottery was unglazed and porous, and although burnishing before firing could reduce porosity, containers used for long term storage or transport had to be lined with resin, easily obtainable in the Aegean. Potters used separated slips, or added alkali or salt in firing to produce a surface sheen on fine pots. Shape and decoration owed much to Crete, but standardization reduced invention and spirit. Colour variation in body and decoration show that kilns were vertical, like the Late Bronze kilns excavated at Sarafand in Lebanon or like simple modern kilns in the Mediterranean. A Mycenaean pot is recognized by its buff to pink surface and body, and disciplined form decorated in ferrous colours from orange to black.

The shapes most commonly found abroad are storage jars (for packaging Aegean specialities), but bowls, vessels for drinking and ritual occasions were also exported. The stirrup or false-necked jar, Minoan in origin, was designed for liquids, with a narrow pouring spout, and handle across the top like an inverted stirrup. This popular shape was a hall-mark of Mycenaean activity, and survived after the Mycenaeans were forgotten. Some pottery was custom-made for the export market, particularly the Mycenaean version of the eastern 'pilgrim flask' and the amphoroid krater. The krater, better known in Cypriot and Levant sites than in Greece, seems too big to drink from, too small to use for burial. Its decoration often celebrates a social, religious or official event, in which chariots and horses are prominent. Kraters were treasured in palace, house and tomb in Cyprus and the Levant coast. Their humourous pictures give an endearing insight into Mycenaean life, and are worthy ancestors of the masterpieces of Classical Greece.

BETWEEN GENESIS AND EXODUS:
400 YEARS OF EGYPTIAN SUPREMACY

CANAAN'S TRADE WITH MYCENAE AND CYPRUS

The era before the coming of the Israelites was marked by a cosmopolitan culture in Canaan. Evidence for international trade with Minoan and Mycenaean centres has been found in quantities of a distinctive imported pottery in Late Bronze Age settlements and tombs. From these archaeological discoveries in Syria and Palestine it is possible to chart the routes from ports to inland cities and to date more precisely the layers of debris by the types of Mycenaean pottery found within them.

'SOME WENT DOWN TO THE SEA IN SHIPS, DOING BUSINESS ON THE GREAT WATERS; THEY SAW THE DEEDS OF THE LORD, HIS WONDROUS WORKS ON THE DEEP.' PS 107.23-24

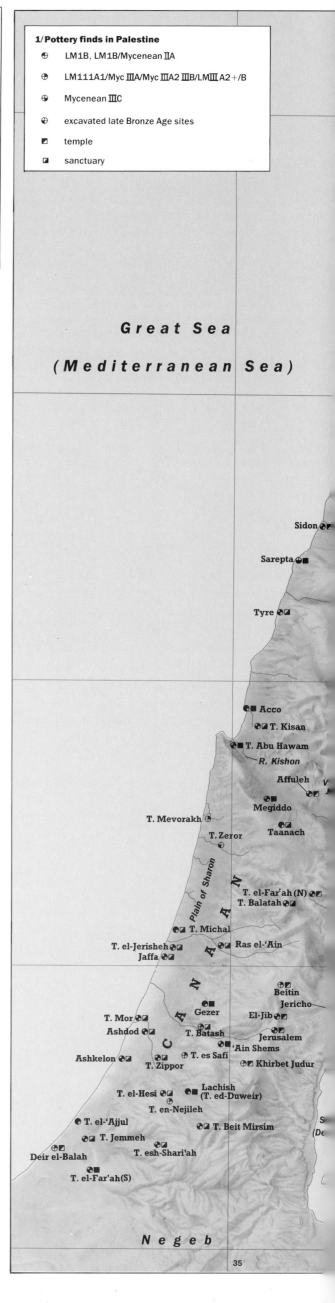

1/ Pottery finds in Palestine

- LM1B, LM1B/Mycenean IIA
- LM111A1/Myc IIIA/Myc IIIA2 IIIB/LMIII A2 +/B
- Mycenean IIIC
- excavated late Bronze Age sites
- temple
- sanctuary

Great Sea
(Mediterranean Sea)

Sidon
Sarepta
Tyre
Acco
T. Kisan
T. Abu Hawam
R. Kishon
Affuleh
Megiddo
T. Mevorakh
T. Zeror
Taanach
T. el-Jerisheh
T. Michal
Ras el-'Ain
Jaffa
Beitin
Jericho
T. Mor
Gezer
El-Jib
Ashdod
T. Batash
Jerusalem
'Ain Shems
Ashkelon
T. es Safi
T. Zippor
Khirbet Judur
Lachish
T. el-Hesi
(T. ed-Duweir)
T. en-Nejileh
T. el-'Ajjul
T. Beit Mirsim
T. Jemmeh
Deir el-Balah
T. esh-Shari'ah
T. el-Far'ah(S)
T. el-Far'ah (N)
T. Balatah

Negeb

35

1/ Map left
This map shows important excavated Late Bronze Age sites where Minoan and Mycenaean pottery has been found, usually together with Cypriote Base Ring and White Slip wares. The quantity varies from a few pots to over a thousand at Ras Shamra (Ugarit), where a group of Aegean traders may have been established. A greater density of sites in the southern Levant is due to search for biblical connections. Contemporary archives and correspondence (eg the Amarna letters) show that the northern Levant had considerable urban populations governed by independent rulers.

2/ Map below
Minoans were pioneers in trade between the Aegean, Egypt and the Levant in the Middle Bronze Age, and perhaps earlier. Mainlanders followed their lead, and generally, but not entirely, replaced them as traders after the destruction of the Palace at Knossos. Minoan shipping may have exploited wind and circulation patterns of surface waters of the eastern Mediterranean and used an anti-clockwise route from Crete to the Nile Delta, returning via the Levant coast and the Dodecanese, while Mycenaean shipping, perhaps because of improved navigation and seamanship, seems to have travelled clockwise through the islands to Cyprus and beyond. Archaeological study and scientific analysis show that the Argolid, in the Peloponnese, was the main source of Mycenaean exported pottery, but other centres, such as Thebes and Athens, also had trading interests.

3/ Below left
Left. Cypriot Base Ring II jug, handmade. Right. Mycenaean IIIA2 flask, wheelmade. Both from Gezer. Late Bronze IIA.

2/ Canaan's trade with Mycenae

- source of exports
- direction of Mycenaean exports
- Minoan trade route

TEXTS from Boğazköy (ancient Hattushash) and Ras Shamra (ancient Ugarit) make it clear that in the 12th century BC invaders came into the eastern Mediterranean by sea, supporting the traditional designation of these invaders as Peoples of the Sea. We even read of three sea battles fought by Suppiluliuma II, the last known Hittite king, against the 'enemy ships from the land of Alashiya' (the Bronze Age name for the island of Cyprus).

As earlier texts from the reign of Suppiluliuma II, as well as those of his immediate predecessors Tudhaliyas III and IV and Arnuwancas III, established Alashiya as a vassal, paying tribute to its Hittite overlord, we have to assume that the enemy ships that fought the Hittites in what were the only recorded sea battles in Hittite history, were those of the Sea Peoples now established in Alashiya and using the island as a base for operations against the surrounding coastal areas. Shortly after this the Hittite empire must have fallen to the invaders. The Hittite capital of Hattushash was burned to the ground in a massive conflagration, and destruction levels are recorded at a series of sites on Cyprus and along the Levantine coast. At Meskene (ancient Emar) this destruction level was associated with a legal text dated to the second year of the reign of the Babylonian king Meli-Sipak (1187 BC). This date is in close agreement with the Egyptian evidence, which puts the great raid by the Peoples of the Sea in the 8th year of the reign of Ramesses III (1190 BC).

A closer look at the dating reveals numerous problems. It is very difficult to find any evidence for Hittite overlords or for resident Sea Peoples on Cyprus. Nor were the massive fortifications of the inland fortress of Hattushash likely to have fallen to a band of sea raiders. It is true that the Egyptian reliefs at Medinet Habu depict whole families on the move, travelling by ox-cart with women and children and household possessions, but these representations seem to depict the contingent which travelled along the coastal strip accompanied by the male warriors who operated from ships that carried only fighting men. The evidence does seem to show the movement of whole tribes of people. This certainly means that any explanation of the forces behind these movements must go beyond Cyprus and the Levant. The traditional dates for the Trojan War (1193-1184 BC) would have the Mycenaean Greeks at Troy at the same time that the Peoples of the Sea were ravaging sites in the eastern Mediterranean. According to

archaeologists, Troy VIIa (the city designated as Homeric Troy) fell at a time when Mycenaean (or Late Helladic) IIIB pottery was being replaced by the new LH IIIC style (see page 52). This IIIB/IIIC transition has come to be dated to c 1190 BC and it is the ceramic context associated not only with the destruction of Troy VIIa but also with the series of destructions in Cyprus (Enkomi and Kition) and all along the Levantine coast. Moreover, it is also the context associated with destructions in Greece itself at Mycenae, Tiryns, Pylos, Gla, Thebes and Orchomenus. At Teichos Dymeion a wall seems to have been built to hold back the invader and a similar construction has been identified at the Isthmus of Corinth.

On the Greek mainland these destructions have been attributed to invaders from the north. In Cyprus and along the Levantine coast these destructions are seen as the work of the Peoples of the Sea. In Palestine, on the other hand, they are seen as archaeological evidence for the conquest of the Promised Land by the children of Israel and as providing

BETWEEN GENESIS AND EXODUS:
400 YEARS OF EGYPTIAN SUPREMACY

CHANGES IN THE WORLD OF CANAAN AND ISRAEL

In the early 12th century BC the Late Bronze Age empires of the eastern Mediterranean came to an end. A new force, possibly of Anatolian origin, the 'Sea Peoples', moved into the area, defeating the Hittites and destroying many sites. After 1200 BC a new culture developed in Syria, the 'Neo-Hittite' or 'Syro-Hittite' culture, which owed much of its origins to the Sea Peoples.

GREECE

Gulf of Kyparissia

Ionian Sea

Gulf of Messenia

37

2/ Settlements in Late Helladic I-IIIB

• settlement

22°

1/ Map below
The coming of the Sea Peoples in c 1200 BC via the routes shown, had important consequences for many place-names along the Mediterranean shore. The Sherden (or Shardana) settled and gave their name to Sardinia, the Sheklesh to Sicily, the Philistines to Palestine, the Ekwash (or Akaiwasa) to Achaea and the Lukka to Lycia.

2 and 3/ Maps above
A wave of destruction and depopulation is believed to have occurred in Greece at c 1190 BC indicated by an abrupt transition from Late Helladic I-IIIB pottery to Late Helladic IIIC (see text).

4 and 5/ Below
Procession of warrior gods and the Hittite king Tudhaliya, in a sanctuary at Yazi Yazilikaya c 1350-1250 BC.

6/ Below right
A small gold image of a Hittite weather god.

ITALY

Mt Olympus • **Athens**
Volos
GREECE Thebes
Gla
Orchomenus
ARCADIA Dendra
CEPHALONIA Teichos **Mycenae**
Dymeion
PELOPONNESE
Malthi • Tiryns
Pylos Sparta • Corinth
ZACYNTHUS **LACONIA**

SARDINIA

SICILY Thapsos •

Ionian Sea **MESSENIA**
CYTHERA

• Nora

Great Sea

the best contemporary evidence for dating the events associated with the Exodus and the conquest.

Archaeology provides no clues to the identity of those responsible for the destruction of the Hittite capital at Boğazköy. What we can say is that, following that destruction, the main centres of power moved from central Anatolia, at Boğazköy, Alaca Hüyük and Maşat, to the south-east, to the areas surrounding Melitene (Malatya), Carchemish and Aleppo. There we find the post-1200 BC development of the so-called Neo-Hittite (or Syro-Hittite) civilization, maintaining certain cultural connections with its Late Bronze Age predecessor but using a different language (Luvian rather than Hittite) and script (hieroglyphic instead of cuneiform). The situation is complicated because the Luvian language and the hieroglyphic writing system are also well attested at the Late Bronze Age sites of central Anatolia.

These Neo-Hittites are almost certainly the Hittites of the Bible, the Hittites that figure in the stories connected with David and the beautiful Bathsheba, whose husband, Uriah the Hittite, David put in the front ranks of the army to increase his chances of getting killed in battle, so that David could have Bathsheba for his own (II SAM 11), or with Solomon the horse-trader, who brought horses from Que (Cilicia) and chariots from Egypt and sold them to 'all the kings of the Hittites and to the kings of Syria.' (I KINGS 10, 28-29). The geographical and political terminology of these stories is in keeping with their Iron Age background, for Que was known to the Bronze Age Hittites as Kizzuwadna and the kings of Aram ruled over an Aramaean state that only developed after 1200 BC.

In the Aegean new elements in the archaeological assemblage can be detected at the end of the 13th century

BC, notably new bronze weapons and a hitherto unknown type of crude, handmade pottery are said to mark the appearance of the northern invaders who put an end to Mycenaean civilization. With the introduction of new weapons went corresponding changes in defensive body armour. Bronze helmets, corselets and greaves became more popular than they had been in Mycenaean times. Greaves were of special importance, offering protection against the new cut-and-thrust sword. For the biblical scholar the most interesting aspect is the remarkable parallel between these new weapons and armour and the new style of fighting they must have entailed. Certain details in the story of David and Goliath, as recorded in I SAM 17 (see page 79) may reflect these developments. The description of the arming of Goliath (I SAM 17,5-7) emphasizes his bronze armour. Goliath seems to fit the description of the 'northern' warriors whose path across the eastern Mediterranean seems to coincide with the destruction of all the major Late Bronze Age sites in the area.

In the search for explanations of events that brought the Late Bronze Age to an end in the eastern Mediterranean, it seems that every trail leads back to Anatolia and Cyprus. How events in the Aegean, Anatolia, Cyprus and the northern Levant relate to the end of the Late Bronze Age in Palestine remains to be worked out in detail.

'A CHARIOT COULD BE IMPORTED FROM EYGPT FOR SIX HUNDRED SHEKELS OF SILVER, AND A HORSE FOR A HUNDRED AND FIFTY; AND SO THROUGH THE KING'S TRADERS THEY WERE EXPORTED TO ALL THE KINGS OF THE HITTITES AND THE KINGS OF SYRIA.'
I KINGS 10.29

3/ Settlements in and after Late Helladic IIIC

• settlement

1/ The Mediterranean world in the 13th-12th centuries BC

➤ land trade route
➤ sea trade route

THE first Book of Kings places the Exodus 480 years before Solomon began to build the Temple, ie, about 1440 BC. This figure conflicts with other data in the Bible and must be regarded as too early; there are several explanations of how it was arrived at. The events in Egypt just before the Exodus can best be placed in the 13th century BC, when the use of foreign labour is well attested and the city of Ramesses (EX 1.11) is often mentioned. Since the Merneptah stela (c 1220 BC) mentions Israel among various names in Canaan, it seems that the Israelites had settled there by then and the Exodus must therefore fall in

FROM EGYPTIAN BONDAGE TO SETTLEMENT IN CANAAN

EXODUS AND THE WANDERINGS

According to the book of Exodus, Moses led the children of Israel from slavery in Egypt to the promised land of Canaan. Though this is one of the major events of the Bible narrative, it is surrounded by controversy.

the earlier part of the century. How much earlier it is impossible to say. There is no reference to it in Egyptian records, but this is hardly surprising, particularly when it is recognized that the numbers of participants must have been far fewer than is indicated in some OT passages which are comparatively late in origin (EX 12.37; compare NUM 1.46 and 26.51). These state that the Israelites who left Egypt numbered some 600,000 male adults, which implies a total company of two million or more. The figures cannot be reduced, as has sometimes been suggested, by a reinterpretation of the Hebrew word for thousands ('elef) as, if this

THE ROUTE

The route of the Israelites through the wilderness is described in a series of itinerary notes scattered through the books of Exodus, Numbers and Joshua (eg. EX 12.37, 13.20 – compare also 13.17-18) and again more compactly in NUM 33.1-49. It is likely that this latter passage supplied many of the details in the main narrative. Certain sections of the journey are described in other books of the OT (DEUT 1.19-3.29; JUDG 11.16-22). Not all of these accounts agree and even where they do, there are sometimes reasons for thinking that harmonization has taken place. The literary process of the composition of the Pentateuch needs to be unravelled before geographical study can proceed very far. The result of this is to show that the earliest accounts contain very little geographical information, only references to key points such as the Red Sea, Mount Sinai/Horeb, Kadesh and the crossing of the River Jordan, and actually laid very little stress on movement from place to place at all. The notion of an Exodus route is due chiefly to NUM 33, 1-49, an itinerary composed on the pattern of similar documents known from other parts of the ancient Near East. It is probable that in NUM 33 the references to Kadesh and Mount Hor originally preceded the mention of Ezion-geber, as is still the case with Kadesh in DEUT 1-2. The idea that the Israelites passed through the wilderness east of Moab and Edom is not present in NUM 33 and is to be traced to editing of the historical books in the period of the Babylonian exile (NUM 21.11-13; DEUT 2.8, 26; JUDG 11.18).

MOUNT SINAI

The location of Mount Sinai (or Mount Horeb as it is known in some texts) is a particular problem and over a dozen sites have been proposed for it. Much of the evidence which has been used in this discussion is insufficiently precise for the purpose (eg. volcanic features in EX 19 may belong to the later elaboration of the Sinai events and need not imply that Mount Sinai was actually a volcano and therefore lay in north-west Arabia) and some of it perhaps relates to a distinct 'mountain of God' (EX 3.1, 4.27, 18.5) rather than to Sinai. The clearest evidence is found in DEUT 1.2: 'It is eleven days' journey from Horeb by the way of Mount Seir to Kadesh-barnea'. This points to the south of the Sinai peninsula, in the region which Christian, Jewish and the oldest Arabic tradition favours, or less likely to a mountain east of the Gulf of Aqaba.

THE 'SEA'

Another important place on the route is the 'sea' where the Israelites were saved from the pursuing Egyptians (EX 14-15). This is sometimes referred to in the Bible as yam suf, which was traditionally equated with the Red Sea (or more exactly the Gulf of Suez). In modern times the Hebrew term has often been thought to mean 'the sea of reeds' and a location for it has consequently been sought in a fresh-water lake in north-eastern Egypt. This later view cannot be sustained in the face of passages like 1 KINGS 9.26, which certainly uses yam suf to refer to the Red Sea (in fact the Gulf of Aqaba), and those texts which place the deliverance at yam suf must be presumed to be referring to the Gulf of Suez (which may have extended further to the north in antiquity). With this conclusion the case for the so-called 'northern route' for the Exodus is considerably weakened. This view, which is upheld by several distinguished students of the problem, relies on the identification of Migdol and Baal-zephon in EX 14.2 with places near the Mediterranean coast and locates the 'sea' at Lake Bardawil, where catastrophes of a comparable kind have occurred. But the names in question prove little, since they are attested elsewhere in eastern Egypt, and EX 13.17 states explicitly that the Israelites did not leave by the coast road, 'the way of the land of the Philistines'.

A southerly direction is therefore to be preferred for the initial stages of the itinerary. The route suggested is a plausible one for traders and mining expeditions, from whose experience it was probably derived. There is evidence of a connection between southern Sinai and Arad already in the Early Bronze Age, and the recent discoveries at Kuntillet 'Ajrud attest the use of 'the way of the Red Sea' in the period of the Israelite kingdoms. Some deviation from the most direct route was required by the traditional belief that the children of Israel were detained in the wilderness by God as a punishment for their disobedience, which followed a loss of confidence after a preliminary exploration of the land (NUM 13-14; DEUT 1-2).

The route of the 'spies' is not described in detail and there appear to be two versions of the story of their mission in the Bible, one implying that they explored the Hebron region only (NUM 13.22-24; DEUT 1.24-25) and the other speaking of a journey through the whole land of Canaan 'from the wilderness of Zin to Rehob of Lebo-hamath' (NUM 13.21 compare 13.1-2).

is done, the computations in NUM 1-2 cease to make sense. They may rather be ascribed to the tendency of later OT writers to inflate population statistics (compare I CHRON 21.5 with II SAM 24.9) coupled perhaps with a reading back into the Exodus period of the total population of Israel at some later time. It may well be that certain of the Israelite tribal groups were in Egypt, but attempts to identify them have produced little agreement.

Whether there was a single historical journey through the wilderness must remain doubtful – those who experienced the deliverance from Egypt may have made their way to Canaan by separate routes in small groups – but geographical study can seek to elucidate the route described in NUM 33 and so discover how later generations of Israelites believed that their forefathers had travelled from Egypt to Canaan. Nevertheless this is no easy task: modern Arabic names provide less help than usual in desert areas and very few of the traditional locations are attested earlier than the 4th century AD. Research has to proceed on the basis of the limited number of places whose identification is relatively certain and choose between various routes linking them which are known from other sources.

'SAY THEREFORE TO THE PEOPLE OF ISRAEL, "I AM THE LORD, AND I WILL BRING YOU OUT FROM UNDER THE BURDENS OF THE EGYPTIANS, AND I WILL DELIVER YOU FROM THEIR BONDAGE. AND I WILL REDEEM YOU WITH AN OUTSTRETCHED ARM AND WITH GREAT ACTS OF JUDGMENT, AND I WILL TAKE YOU FOR MY PEOPLE, AND I WILL BE YOUR GOD; AND YOU SHALL KNOW THAT I AM THE LORD YOUR GOD, WHO HAD BROUGHT YOU OUT FROM UNDER THE BURDENS OF THE EGYPTIANS, AND I WILL BRING YOU INTO THE LAND WHICH I SWORE TO GIVE TO ABRAHAM, TO ISAAC, AND TO JACOB; I WILL GIVE IT TO YOU FOR A POSSESSION. I AM THE LORD."' EX 6.6-8

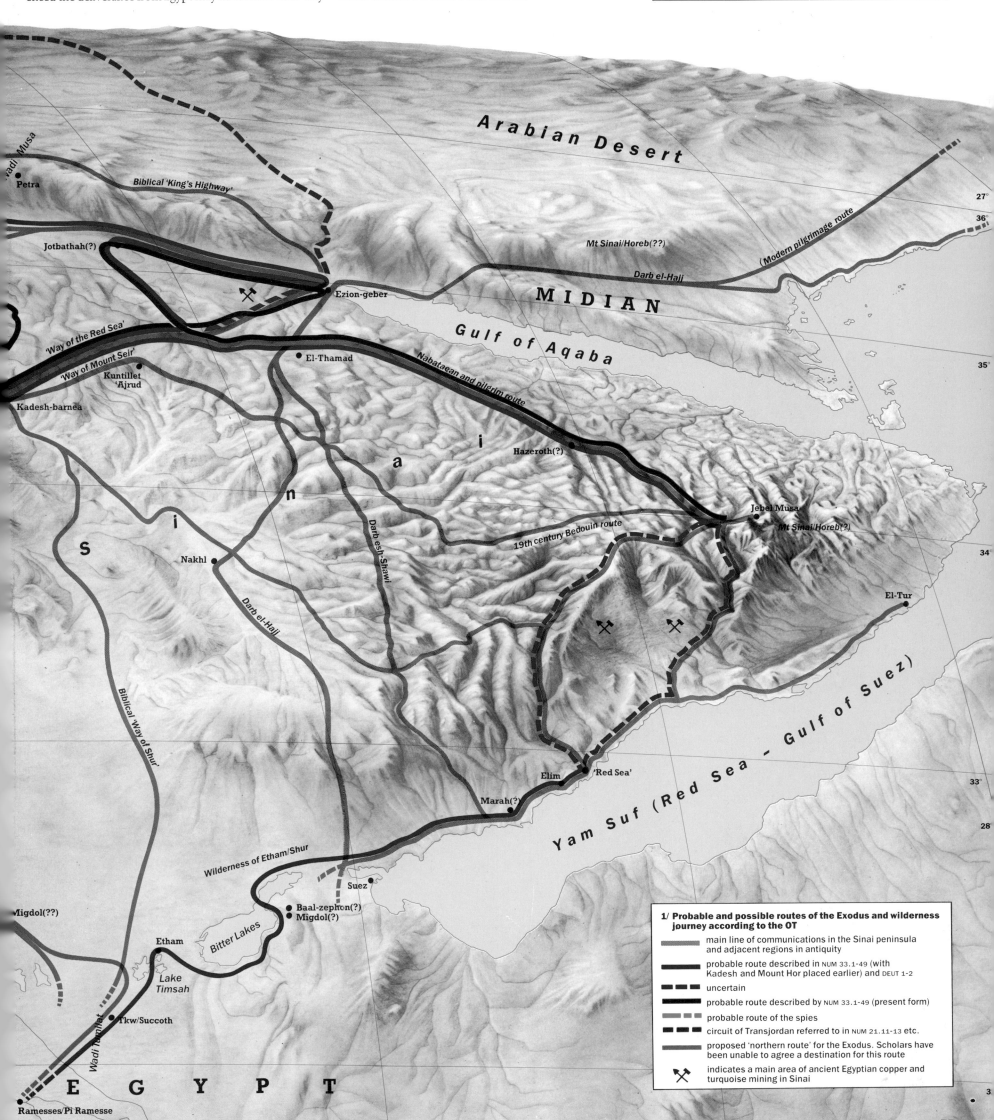

1/ Probable and possible routes of the Exodus and wilderness journey according to the OT

- main line of communications in the Sinai peninsula and adjacent regions in antiquity
- probable route described in NUM 33.1-49 (with Kadesh and Mount Hor placed earlier) and DEUT 1-2
- uncertain
- probable route described by NUM 33.1-49 (present form)
- probable route of the spies
- circuit of Transjordan referred to in NUM 21.11-13 etc.
- proposed 'northern route' for the Exodus. Scholars have been unable to agree a destination for this route
- indicates a main area of ancient Egyptian copper and turquoise mining in Sinai

PALESTINE is characterized by a basic relief of rounded mountains with incised valleys, extending from north to south, and this structure has had an important influence on the layout of the major roads. From west to east, it has a narrow coastal plain followed by a double line of mountains subdivided by a deep longitudinal valley (the rift valley in which the R. Jordan flows).

The climatic variations known in Palestine are largely due to it being a country hemmed in between the sea and the desert. Palestine is located in a subtropical zone, having a short rainy season in the winter and a long dry season in the summer. The amount of precipitation varies greatly in different parts of the country according to location and altitude. The northern mountains of Carmel, Upper Galilee

THE LAND

Palestine represents the south-western tip of the 'Fertile Crescent', and it serves as a natural bridge between the continents of Asia and Africa. Because of the deserts south and east, the sea to the west, and the mountains to the north, all the great continental routes have had to pass through this region. Palestine has always been an important passageway between the two centres of ancient civilization: Egypt and Mesopotamia.

and northern Samaria were once covered with dense woodland because a fair amount of rain fell there. However, only a narrow strip along the Mediterranean coast enjoys a relatively large degree of rainfall. Because the overall amount of precipitation is limited, the rocks are porous and the summer is long, permanent streams are few. The important perennial rivers in the Levant were the Orontes, Litani and Jordan, and these became the focus of the development of urban settlements.

The desert which surrounds Palestine on the east and south frequently served as an area of conflict between settled and nomadic peoples. It was not always the case of nomads raiding the settled areas. Recent surveys in the Negeb have brought to light more than 11,000 new archaeological sites which represent the repeated attempts by settled peoples to occupy this marginal environment. The longest period of continuous settlement in the Negeb was from the Early Iron Age, c 1200 BC, and down to the end of the Ummayad period in AD 750. During the 1st century AD, the Nabataeans were supervising the caravan routes which led across the Negeb from their capital, Petra, to Gaza on the Mediterranean coast. Their main source of wealth was the control of the spice trade between Arabia and the rest of the Levant.

The geological foundations of the land have also had an important influence on human activities. Blocks of stone were quarried from the limestone rocks of Cenomanian, Turonian and Eocene formations. During the Iron Age, ashlars (straight-sided building blocks) were mainly cut out of the soft *nari* limestone and quarries dating from this period have been found at Megiddo, Samaria and Ramat Rahel. During later periods, stone was usually quarried from harder types of limestone such as those known as *meleke* and *mizzi hilu*. Basalt exists in the eastern Galilee and in the Golan; since prehistoric times it has been used as the basic material for making querns (grindstones) and mortars of various sorts. The hard limestones in the hills of Palestine weather into a rich red-brown soil called *terra rossa* which was used for

1/ Map left
The shape of the land has an obvious effect on travel. The map shows the major lines of communication and the position of passes through the high ground. These were important both for trade and for troop movements.

2/ Map below
Palestine not only forms a bridge between Egypt and Arabia to the south and Anatolia and Mesopotamia to the north and east, but is also at the end of sea routes across the Mediterranean and up the Gulf of Suez.

3/ Map right
In Palestine the line which indicates 300mm (12in) of rain separates the fertile northern area from the desert to the south.

4/ Map far right
The geology of a country is directly related to the quality of its soil. In Palestine the most fertile soil is the red-brown *terra rossa* which comes from Cenomanian, Turonian and Eocene rocks.

Biblical routes
1 The road to Bashan
2 The way of the plain
3 The way to the Jordan
4 The way of Beth-horon
5 The way of the Arabah
6 The way of the tent dwellers
7 The way to Moab
8 The way to Edom
9 The way to the land of the Philistines
10 The way of the wilderness of Moab
11 The way of the Atharim
12 The way to Shur
13 The way to the Arabah
14 The way to the Reed Sea
15 The way of the wilderness of Edom
16 The way to Mount Seir

1/ The topography of Palestine
— main road
— minor road
⊢ pass

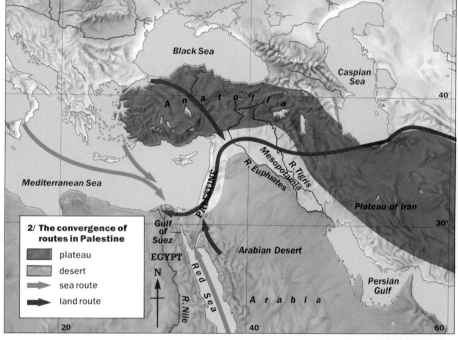

2/ The convergence of routes in Palestine
▮ plateau
▯ desert
→ sea route
→ land route

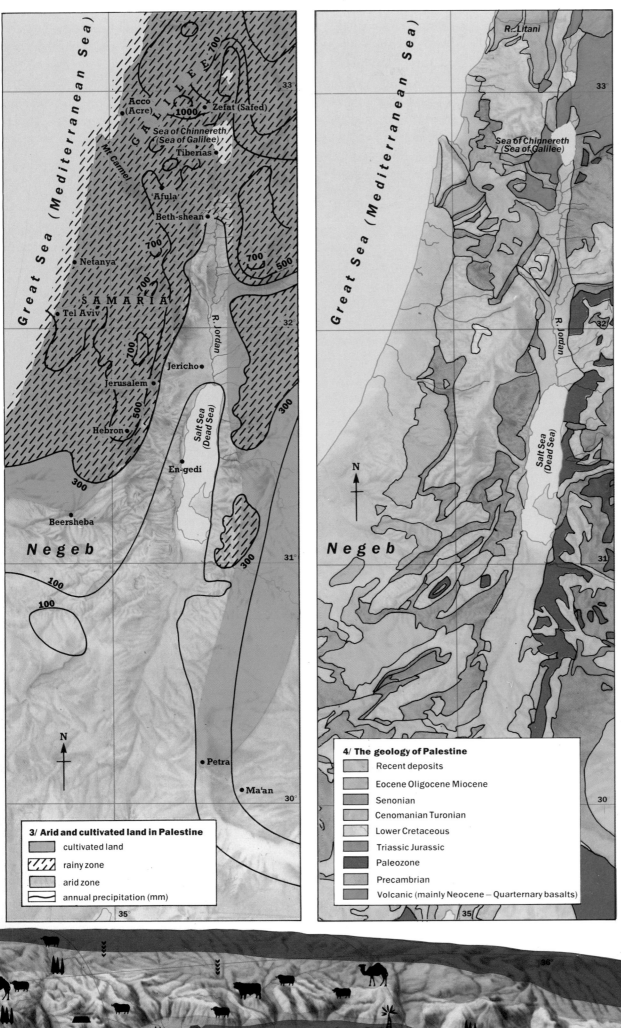

3/ Arid and cultivated land in Palestine

- cultivated land
- rainy zone
- arid zone
- annual precipitation (mm)

4/ The geology of Palestine

- Recent deposits
- Eocene Oligocene Miocene
- Senonian
- Cenomanian Turonian
- Lower Cretaceous
- Triassic Jurassic
- Paleozone
- Precambrian
- Volcanic (mainly Neocene – Quarternary basalts)

farming. The soft limestones tend to erode into a light brown-grey infertile soil known as *rendzina*. Many parts of the coastal plain and the internal valleys, are covered with deep alluvial soil which is usually very fertile. Palestine is not very rich in mineral resources. A thick layer of red Nubian sandstone, containing deposits of copper, is known from parts of the southern Transjordan, the R. Jabbok in central Transjordan, and the Aqaba region. Iron was also mined in the mountains of Transjordan. Salt was obtained from the Mediterranean Sea or from the Dead Sea.

The economy of Palestine has generally been pastoral-agrarian in character. Agriculture has traditionally been based on the well-known Mediterranean triad of grain, wine and olive oil. Barley was usually only grown in areas of poor soils and limited precipitation. The list of the 'seven species' which appears in DEUT 8.8 also includes the fig, pomegranate and the *debas* – 'honey' – of the date. The almond is notably absent from this list even though it does grow in many regions of Palestine and is mentioned elsewhere in the Bible (cf JER 1.11-12; ECCLES 12.5). Grapes and olives were processed in rock-hewn or stone-built installations (cf the wine press in ISA 5.2).

Dry farming was carried out in the highlands but irrigation agriculture was possible in places with permanent springs and perennial rivers. Flood farming was practised in the desert regions of southern Palestine. Terraces were built in serried fashion on the slopes of hills in the highlands. Fields were usually surrounded by stone walls to protect them from grazing sheep and goats. Easy access between the fields and the market places was vital and so in many areas of Palestine a complex network of regional and rural roads was established.

During biblical times, commerce was mainly a monopoly in the hands of kings and rulers, but nomads did play an important role, especially in desert regions. Palestine held an intermediary role in the trade of valuable luxury items. However, it did trade some of its agricultural surpluses such as grain, oil and wine, and various perfumed substances.

There were two main international routes which passed through Palestine: the 'Way of the Sea' (Via Maris) and the King's Highway. The Via Maris was the most important and over it passed messengers, caravans and military expeditions during many different periods. It began in Lower Egypt and extended through the coastal plains of Palestine; among the more important cities located on it are Joppa, Gath, Lod, Ono and Aphek. From the Plain of Sharon the road continued in two directions. One branch passed through the Jezreel Valley, crossed over the Jordan River and led to Transjordan, Damascus and as far as Mesopotamia. The other branch continued northwards to the Plain of Acco and on to Lebanon and Syria. The King's Highway extended along the length of the Transjordan highlands and reached as far as Damascus. It was used as the main route linking north-western Arabia with the northern Levant. The important Transjordanian settlements of Ramoth-gilead, Gerasa, Rabbath-ammon, Dibon, Sela and others were all located along the King's Highway.

> '"AND IF YOU WILL OBEY MY COMMANDMENTS... HE WILL GIVE THE RAIN FOR YOUR LAND IN ITS SEASON, THE EARLY RAIN AND THE LATER RAIN, THAT YOU MAY GATHER IN YOUR GRAIN AND YOUR WINE AND YOUR OIL."' DEUT 11.13-14

5/ Map below
Palestine had sufficient rainfall and adequate soils to produce a variety of crops and livestock.

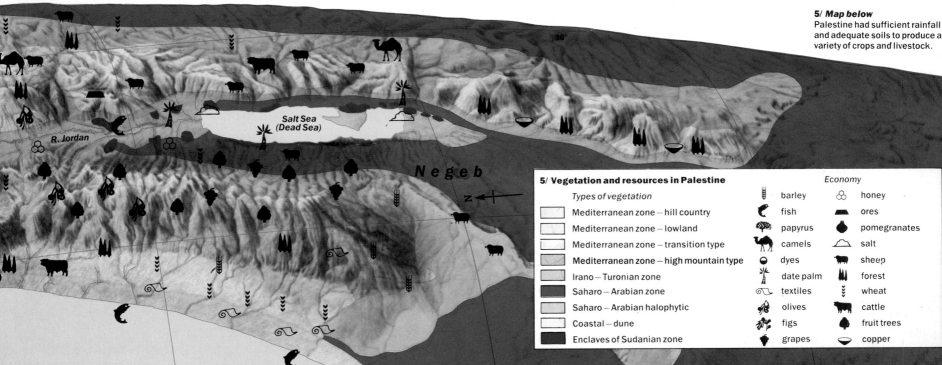

5/ Vegetation and resources in Palestine

Types of vegetation

- Mediterranean zone – hill country
- Mediterranean zone – lowland
- Mediterranean zone – transition type
- Mediterranean zone – high mountain type
- Irano – Turonian zone
- Saharo – Arabian zone
- Saharo – Arabian halophytic
- Coastal – dune
- Enclaves of Sudanian zone

Economy

barley	honey
fish	ores
papyrus	pomegranates
camels	salt
dyes	sheep
date palm	forest
textiles	wheat
olives	cattle
figs	fruit trees
grapes	copper

Since the advent of agriculture in Neolithic times, humanity has had a detrimental effect on the environment in the Levant. Deforestation and the removal of vegetation has resulted in many eroded landscapes. The process of cutting down trees in the hilly regions of Palestine is described in the Bible: 'but the hill country shall be yours, for though it is a forest, you shall clear it' (JOSH 17.18). In certain regions, the regeneration of tree growth and vegetation has been inhibited by the widespread browsing and grazing activities of sheep and goats.

However, a concentration of more than 2,000 plant species, belonging to about 700 genera, are known in the Levant. Because it is situated at the crossroads of three continents, some plant species have migrated from as far away as western Europe, Inner Asia and Central Africa.

FLORA OF THE MEDITERRANEAN ZONE

The Mediterranean Zone is a narrow belt of land, no more than a couple of hundred miles wide. The climate in this zone is characterized by a short and wet winter, with an annual total of between 400-1200mm (15½-47¼in) of rainfall, and a long, dry summer. It originally supported a vegetation of evergreen woodlands and high maquis vegetation which has now largely been destroyed by processes of land clearance. However, remnants still exist in various parts of the Levant. The typical trees are the Aleppo pine (*Pinus halepensis*), the common oak (*Quercus calliprinos*), the Palestine terebinth (*Pistacia palaestina*), the laurel (*Laurus nobilis*), the carob (*Ceratonia siliqua*), and the mastic terebinth (*Pistacia lentiscus*). Associated with them are other types of trees and wild grasses. Degraded or deforested regions are characterized by low garigue and batha bushes and shrubs no taller than the height of a man. Many of them are aromatic and the most widespread type is the thorny burnet (*Poterium spinosum*). The practice of collecting the thorny burnet as firewood or for the burning of lime (cf ISA 33.12) has resulted in a very serious erosion of soils from the slopes of hills.

FLORA OF THE IRANO-TURONIAN ZONE

Loess or thin calcareous soils tend to exist in the Irano-Turanian Zone. The climate is generally characterized by a low rainfall with an annual total ranging between 200-300mm (7¾-11¾in) which serves as the absolute limit for dry-farming (cf GEN 26.12). Only sparse trees and shrubs are to be found in such areas, notably the lotus jujube (*Zizyphus lotus*) and the Atlantic terebinth (*Pistacia atlantica*) which together form a kind of savannah environment interlaced with grassy areas.

FLORA OF THE SAHARO-ARABIAN ZONE

The Saharo-Arabian zone has the poorest flora in the Levant. The area it covers (see map) has an annual total of rainfall which does not exceed 200mm (7¾in) and can be much less. The typical soils, notably hammadas, sands and sebkhas, are not conducive to plant growth. Most plants show some form of adaptation to the extremely dry conditions. Various forms of thorny acacias of African savannah origin grow in the wadi beds and survive on the waters of the occasional flash flood.

FAUNA

A great variety of animals are known from the Levant and among them are about 100 species of mammals, and almost 500 species of birds (about 200 of them resident in Palestine). Their regional distribution roughly corresponds to the three major floral zones in the Levant. However, the borders of these zoogeographic zones tend to be blurred as animals move about, and also because numerous species have been pushed out of their natural habitats by man.

The Bible refers to a large number of different kinds of wild and domesticated animals. Their characteristics were frequently drawn upon in order to enhance various biblical passages. Thus, the speed and agility of the fallow deer was used by Isaiah (35.6) in a passage describing the day of redemption. Many of the wild 'beasts of the forest' (MIC 5.8)

THE FLORA AND FAUNA OF THE LEVANT

The Levant is a meeting place for a great diversity of plant and animal species. It lies at the junction of three major climatic and floral regions. The areas of different vegetation have given rise to numerous species of animals, from large mammals such as the gazelle, to species of lizards, rodents and insects which have adapted themselves to arid regions.

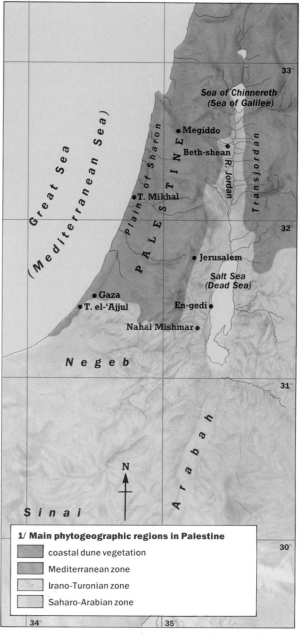

1/ Main phytogeographic regions in Palestine
- coastal dune vegetation
- Mediterranean zone
- Irano-Turonian zone
- Saharo-Arabian zone

no longer exist in the Levant as a result of intensive hunting. Among the extinct animals mentioned in the Bible are the lion, tiger, bear, antelope, wild ox (*Bos primigenius*), Mesopotamian fallow deer (*Dama mesopotamica*), ostrich, crocodile and hippopotamus.

The lion which is described as the 'mightiest among beasts' (PROV 30.30) is frequently mentioned in the Bible (JUDG 14.5; I SAM 17.34; I KINGS 13.24; HOS 13.7-8) but can no longer be found in the Levant. A very clear pictorial representation of the lion appears on an 8th century BC seal which belonged to a servant of Jeroboam II king of Israel (see page 113). Another extinct animal is the 'dishon' which appears in DEUT 14.5 as an edible ruminant and it is probably to be identified with the mountain goat. The creature referred to in Hebrew as 'teo' is probably the Arabian oryx – it was described as a 'unicorn' in the King James version of the Bible (NUM 23.22, 24.8; DEUT 33.17). The ostrich (*Struthio camelus syriacus*), known in Hebrew as 'Ya'en', was frequently mentioned in the Bible as cruel, unclean and stupid (JOB 39.13-18). Ancient rock-carvings of the ostrich have been found in the Sinai Desert. The discovery of five intact ostrich eggs near T. Mikhal, indicate that this large flightless bird inhabited the Plain of Sharon during Chalcolithic times. The crocodile, which originally inhabited the R. Jordan, is clearly mentioned in JOB 41. At the turn of the century, a few crocodiles could still be seen at Nahal Tanninim ('the crocodile river') in the coastal plain of Palestine. The hippopotamus is probably to be identified with the 'Behemoth' mentioned in JOB 40.15-24.

The ibex (*Capra ibex nubiana*) appears in the Bible as the 'ya'el'. Ibex are extremely shy and dislike being observed by man which may explain why God asked Job: 'Do you know when the mountain goats bring forth?' (JOB 39.1). They are described in PS 104.18 as inhabiting the high hills; today they exist in a number of rocky locations in the Sinai, Negeb and at En-gedi near the Dead Sea. David hid from Saul in these 'ibex cliffs' at En-gedi (I SAM 24.1-2). At nearby Nahal Mishmar, objects decorated with ibex horns were found in a copper hoard dating back to Chalcolithic times.

The Sinai leopard (*Panthera pardus jarvisi*) is referred to in a number of biblical passsages (*cf* HOS 13.7-8) and was thought to have become extinct in Palestine until it was observed in 1974 in the cliffs at En-gedi. The leopard was regarded as a sacred animal during ancient times in various parts of the Near East. Wall paintings depicting the cult of the leopard have been found at the Neolithic site of Çatal Hüyük in Anatolia. Stone constructions depicting leopards attacking an antelope have been found in the desert floor next to a structure (temple?) dating from the late 6th millennium BC at Biq'at 'Uvda in southern Palestine. Leopards also appear in ancient wall carvings in Sinai (Wadi Abu-Jada).

Domesticated animals are also mentioned in the Bible and among them are the horse, donkey, goat, sheep and cattle. Insects such as fleas, mosquitoes, and locusts are also sometimes referred to in biblical passages.

'''... THE WOLF SHALL LIE DOWN WITH THE LAMB, AND THE LEOPARD SHALL LIE DOWN WITH THE KID, AND THE CALF AND THE LION AND THE FATLING TOGETHER...'' ISA 11.6

1/ Map left
There are three major climatic and floral zones in Palestine.

2/ Below left
Leopard from mosaic floor, Roman period.

3/ Below left inset
Six leopards attacking a lone oryx or antelope, built out of stones on the desert floor north of Elat. They are probably Neolithic.

4/ Below
Canaanite terracotta fish from T.el-'Ajjul.

5/ Middle
Lion fighting a dog, from a basalt stela found at Beth-shean, 1400 BC.

6/ Bottom
Two camels bearing tribute from Musir to Shalmaneser III. The inscription reads 'Camels whose backs are doubled'. From the black obelisk found at Nimrud in Assyria.

7/ Below
Terracotta gazelle head, 3rd millennium BC found at Byblos.

8/ Centre
A Philistine jar decorated with a bull motif, from Megiddo.

9/ Far right
Ivory comb carved on both sides with similar scenes of an ibex being attacked by a dog. From Megiddo, c 1350 BC.

10/ Below right panel
Animals figure prominently in biblical imagery: (a) 'Foxes have holes, and birds of the air have nests; but the Son of Man has nowhere to lay his head.' (MT 8.20); (b) 'I am the good shepherd. The good shepherd lays down his life for the sheep.' (JN 10.11); (c) 'then shall the lame man leap like a hart' (ISA 35.6); (d) 'Issachar is a strong ass, crouching between the sheepfolds' (GEN 49.14).

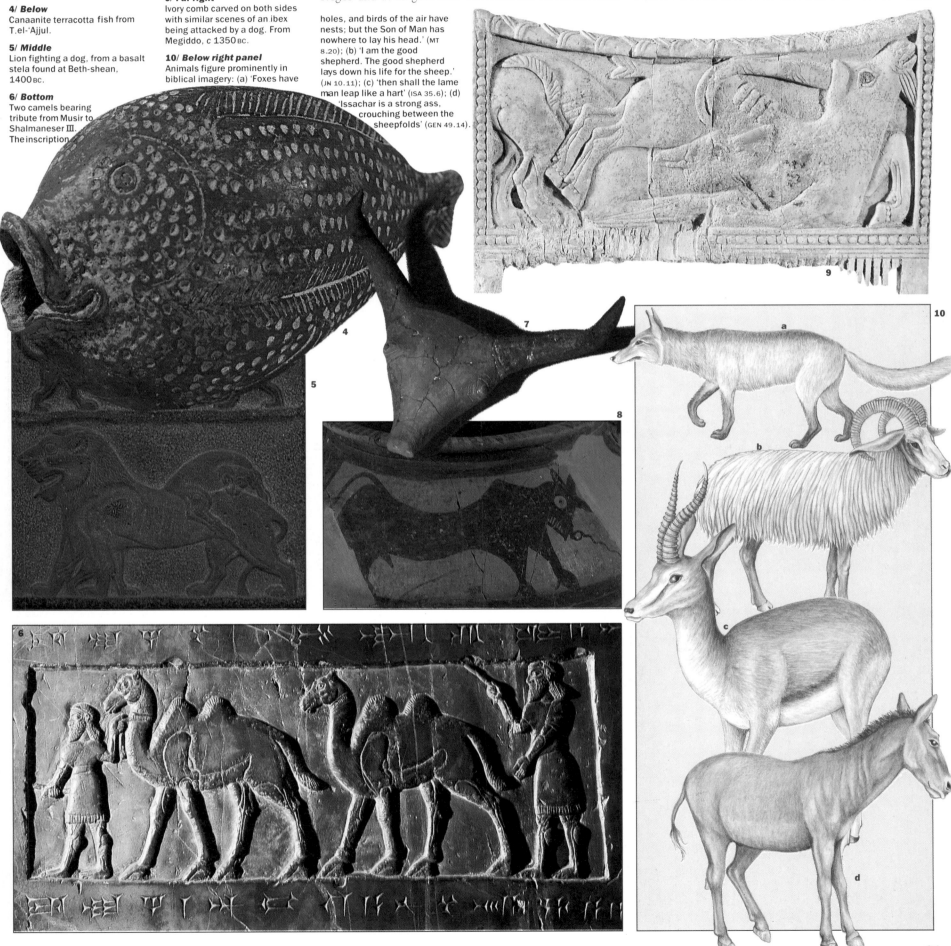

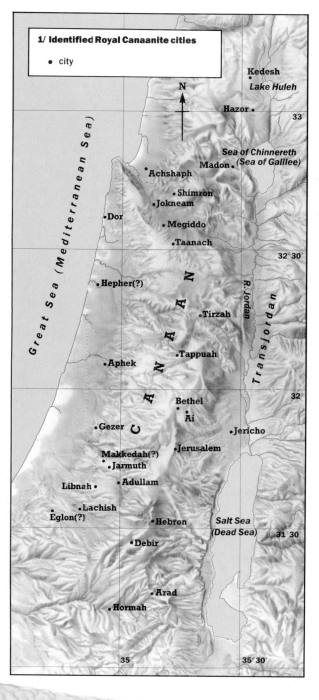

1/ Identified Royal Canaanite cities
• city

Kedesh
Lake Huleh
Hazor
33
Sea of Chinnereth
(Sea of Galilee)
Madon
Achshaph
Shimron
Jokneam
Megiddo
Taanach
32 30
Dor
Great Sea (Mediterranean Sea)
Hepher(?)
Tirzah
R. Jordan
Transjordan
Tappuah
Aphek
32
Bethel
Ai
Gezer
Jericho
C A N A A N
Makkedah(?)
Jerusalem
Jarmuth
Libnah
Adullam
Lachish
Eglon(?)
Hebron
Salt Sea
(Dead Sea)
31 30
Debir
Arad
Hormah
35
35 30

FROM EGYPTIAN BONDAGE TO SETTLEMENT IN CANAAN

CONQUESTS OF JOSHUA IN CANAAN

The Book of Joshua gives an account of the invasion and conquest of Canaan by the Israelites. Biblical and archaeological evidence give a hazy picture of this event. It seems that the 'conquest' was not a sweeping military victory but a gradual process, and indeed the Bible gives lists of cities which were not conquered.

THE way in which Israel established herself in Canaan presents problems. The OT tradition presents us with a very complex picture and a multiplicity of theories have been developed. Chief among these we find the 'single conquest', the 'gradual penetration' and the 'peasant uprising'. Efforts have also been made to produce a synthesis of these theories.

The oldest theory was the belief that there was a conquest of the whole country. In the 13th century BC the Israelites invaded Canaan from Transjordan. The 12 tribes of Israel united in this invasion and quickly conquered the whole country in three campaigns in central, south and north Canaan. All the Canaanites were thought to have been killed during these campaigns. This hypothesis, of which there are many variations, in no way corresponds to what is written in the OT. Indeed, on the basis of a superficial reading of JOSH 1-11 we might well believe that this is the story of a massive conquest of Canaan under the leadership of Joshua. However, the events reported actually took place in the small area inhabited by the tribe of Benjamin. Only in a few short passages do we find any mention of a campaign in the south (JOSH 10.16-42) and in the north (JOSH 11.1-15). JUDG 1 also presents us with a totally different picture. Here we read of operations which were carried out by individual tribes or groups even after Joshua's death. Finally, passages such as JOSH 13.1-7 and JUDG 1.27-36, list many Canaanite cities which were never occupied. These data concur with the fact that long after Solomon many Canaanites still lived unhindered on the land. Apparently the original inhabitants of Canaan were later incorporated into Israel.

A second theory of Israel's settlement in Canaan is that this must have occurred through 'gradual penetration'. Certainly in the OT there are references to groups of people coming to Canaan from elsewhere – and in all

probability from two different directions: one from Kadesh-barnea towards the south and one via Transjordan moving towards the centre and perhaps northwards. No evidence supports the idea of a violent invasion on a large scale. More probably, apart from the two groups which we have just mentioned, other groups entered Canaan, but we are unable to say how the process was actually accomplished. It seems practically certain that, with the exception of some local conflicts, the process was fairly pacific. In the era of the patriarchs we read of the Israelites living mostly in harmony with the local peoples. In the family of Judah there is even mention of marriage with Canaanite women

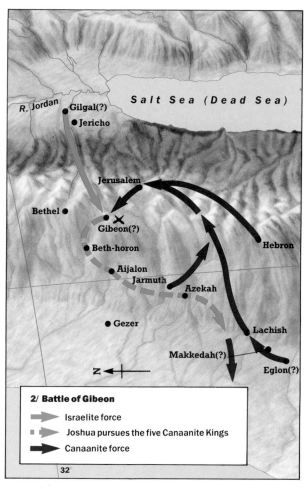

R. Jordan
Salt Sea (Dead Sea)
Gilgal(?)
Jericho
Jerusalem
Bethel
✗
Gibeon(?)
Beth-horon
Hebron
Aijalon
Jarmuth
Azekah
Gezer
Lachish
Makkedah(?)
Eglon(?)

2/ Battle of Gibeon
→ Israelite force
→ Joshua pursues the five Canaanite Kings
→ Canaanite force
32

1/ Map above left
JOSH 12.9-24 lists 31 royal Canaanite cities west of the Jordan. Not all the sites can be identified.

2/ Map above
In JOSH 10.1-13 a league of Canaanite kings attacked Gibeon.

In answer to the Gibeonites' plea for help, Joshua came up from Gilgal and defeated the Canaanites.

3/ Map below
After the battle of Gibeon, Joshua pursued the five Canaanite kings into southern Canaan (JOSH 10.16-39). The decline of the Egyptian 19th dynasty had left this area unprotected and it fell easily to Israelite conquest.

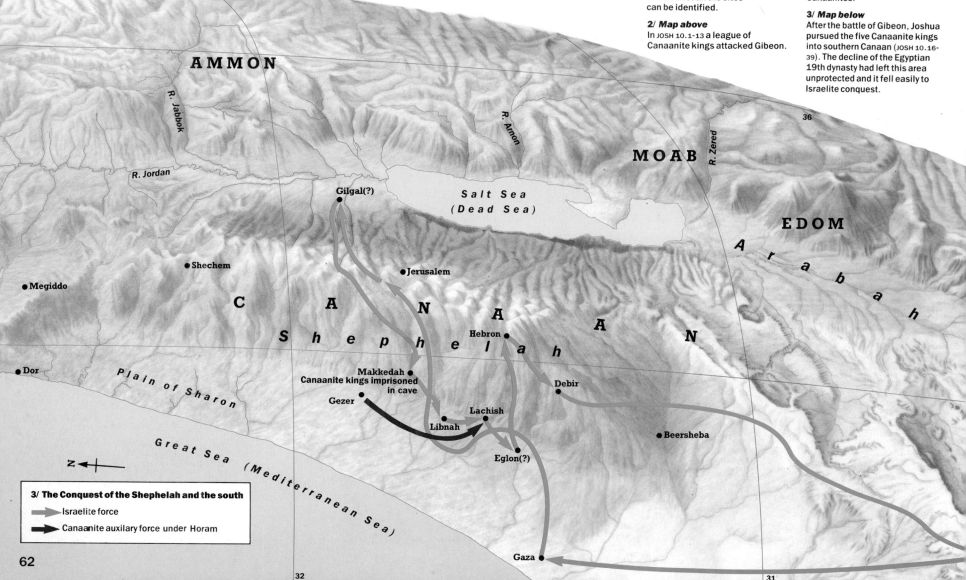

AMMON
R. Jabbok
R. Jordan
R. Arnon
MOAB
R. Zered
36
Gilgal(?)
Salt Sea
(Dead Sea)
EDOM
Shechem
Jerusalem
Megiddo
C A N A A N
Shephelah
Hebron
A r a b a h
Dor
Plain of Sharon
Makkedah
Canaanite kings imprisoned in cave
Debir
Gezer
Lachish
Libnah
Beersheba
Great Sea (Mediterranean Sea)
Eglon(?)

3/ The Conquest of the Shephelah and the south
→ Israelite force
→ Canaanite auxiliary force under Horam

Gaza

32
31

(*cf* GEN 38). References to attacks on Canaanite cities are very limited, while the Canaanite city-states continued to exist for a considerable period of time. Moreover, in JOSH 24 we find references to an agreement between the different tribes, some of whom had always lived in Canaan or had been settled there for so long that those coming later considered them to be indigenous.

A relatively recent explanation of the settlement is the so-called 'peasant uprising'. According to this theory the group which later became known as Israel was created out of different groups. Among these we find the Canaanites who had rebelled against their overlords. These were

joined by the '*apiru* and by the group of Israelites who came to Canaan from Egypt. The emphasis which this latter group placed upon liberation from slavery, and the Exodus from Egypt, made a deep impression on the other two groups. The struggle mentioned in the OT concerns local battles in which only the rulers in a certain area were driven out. Obviously this theory has certain elements in common with the other two. There are references to a conquest, and gradual penetration, but according to this theory it takes place harmoniously, with co-operation from a section of the Canaanite people.

The three settlement models which we have men-

tioned demonstrate that it is impossible to build up a complete picture of what happened. We have to rely on 'snapshots', and our picture of the settlement will be determined to a large degree by which of these snapshots we choose.

'THEN JOSHUA COMMANDED THE OFFICERS OF THE PEOPLE, "PASS THROUGH THE CAMP, AND COMMAND THE PEOPLE, 'PREPARE YOUR PROVISIONS; FOR WITHIN THREE DAYS YOU ARE TO PASS OVER THIS JORDAN, TO GO IN TO TAKE POSSESSION OF THE LAND WHICH THE LORD YOUR GOD GIVES YOU TO POSSESS'"'

JOSH 1.10-11

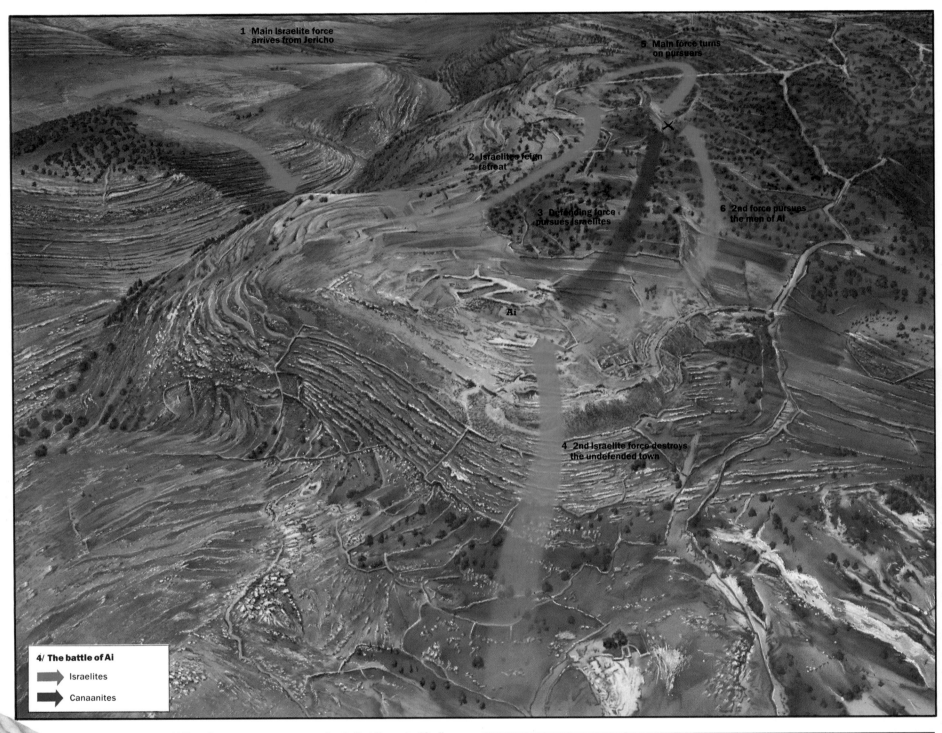

1 Main Israelite force arrives from Jericho

5 Main force turns on pursuers

2 Israelites feign retreat

3 Defending force pursues Israelites

6 2nd force pursues the men of Ai

Ai

4 2nd Israelite force destroys the undefended town

4/ The battle of Ai

➡ Israelites

➡ Canaanites

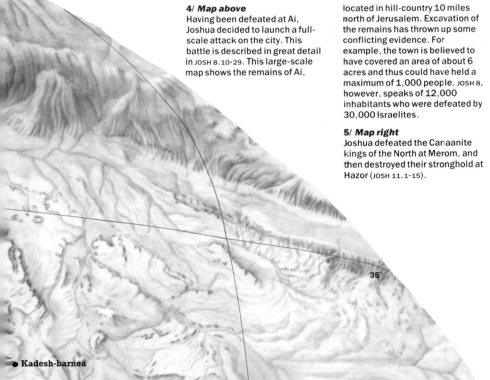

4/ Map above
Having been defeated at Ai, Joshua decided to launch a full-scale attack on the city. This battle is described in great detail in JOSH 8.10-29. This large-scale map shows the remains of Ai,

located in hill-country 10 miles north of Jerusalem. Excavation of the remains has thrown up some conflicting evidence. For example, the town is believed to have covered an area of about 6 acres and thus could have held a maximum of 1,000 people. JOSH 8, however, speaks of 12,000 inhabitants who were defeated by 30,000 Israelites.

5/ Map right
Joshua defeated the Canaanite kings of the North at Merom, and then destroyed their stronghold at Hazor (JOSH 11.1-15).

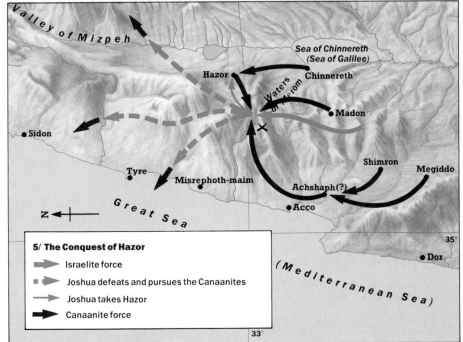

Valley of Mizpeh

Sea of Chinnereth (Sea of Galilee)

Hazor

Chinnereth

Waters of Merom

Madon

Sidon

Tyre

Misrephoth-maim

Shimron

Achshaph(?)

Megiddo

Acco

N

Great Sea

(Mediterranean Sea)

Dor

35°

33°

35°

30°

5/ The Conquest of Hazor

➡ Israelite force

⇢ Joshua defeats and pursues the Canaanites

➡ Joshua takes Hazor

➡ Canaanite force

● Kadesh-barnea

In JOSH 13-17 and JUDG 1 and 3 we find a list of the unconquered Canaanite cities and of the land which was not occupied. The unconquered cities all lay in the area west of the Jordan: in the northern Shephelah, the north of the Plain of Sharon, in the Plain of Jezreel, in the northern coastal plain, in Upper Galilee and one city (Jerusalem) in the central hills. A number of problems arise concerning certain of the unconquered cities mentioned in Joshua and in Judges. Thus it is that we are unable to identify the cities of Kitron and Nahalol in the region inhabited by the tribe of Zebulun, and in all probability the name of the city of Har-heres should be considered as a synonym for Beth-shemesh. Moreover, in JUDG 1.31 Sidon was considered to be one of the unconquered cities whereas everywhere else in the OT this city was placed outside the area accorded to Israel at the time of the settlement. It is also difficult to consider the five city-states of the Philistines – Gaza, Ashkelon, Ashdod, Ekron and Gath which are mentioned in JOSH 13.3 – as Canaanite cities.

In JOSH 13.2-7 and JUDG 3.3 there is reference to the sharing out of the land which had not yet been occupied by the Israelites. These areas were primarily to be found in the south and in the north. In the south this was the land of the Philistines and of the Avvites, while in the north it was those areas which lay approximately to the north of the line Ahlab to Dan and the land of the Geshurites to the east of the Sea of Chinnereth. It was only much later, during the Monarchy, that this land was occupied by Israel.

THE TRIBES AND THEIR BORDERS
In the Book of Joshua we read of how the land of Canaan was divided among the 12 tribes of Israel. This division of territory gives the impression that the 12 tribes occupied their particular piece of territory from the moment they entered the land. Elsewhere in the OT we find lists of the 12 tribes (eg, NUM 26.5-51) which not only give a different order

FROM EGYPTIAN BONDAGE TO SETTLEMENT IN CANAAN

OCCUPATION OF THE LAND

It is likely that the Israelite settlement of Canaan, described in the Books of Judges and Joshua, was not the result of a sudden military conquest but took place over a long period, and there were areas under Canaanite control which remained unconquered for many years. The Bible gives us some information about the 'unconquered cities' and archaeology has provided us with evidence about the sort of houses built by the Israelites in the areas in which they did settle.

of precedence but which also include different names. Indeed, in the Song of Deborah (JUDG 5.14-18), probably the oldest and most authentic text in this respect, mention is made of the names of only ten tribes. We therefore gain a very strong impression that the lists of the 12 tribes which are to be found in Joshua and in Judges – and elsewhere – relate in fact to a later theological reconstruction. The OT data make it clear that certain tribes, those of Reuben and Simeon among others, no longer existed at a very early stage (perhaps even before the entry into the land) and that in an earlier period other tribes and clans, such as Machir and Gilead among others, must also have existed. In actual fact in the OT we are constantly dealing with different groups of tribes. Thus the tribe of Judah is probably a combination of Judah, the tribe of Simeon, and of other clans such as the Calebites. As far as tribal boundaries are concerned changes also took place in the course of time. We know, for example, that the tribe of Dan did not always live in the same area. In JUDG 18 we read that the Danites left the area in which they originally lived in the centre of Canaan and moved north, conquering the Canaanite Laish (Leshem) which then became known as Dan. In JOSH 19.47 we already find an allusion to this event.

EXCAVATED IRON AGE I CITIES
In the period of Iron Age I many Israelite settlements were founded in the hill regions. These were areas which had until then been neither inhabited nor cultivated. An important indication of this fact is to be found in JOSH 17.16-18, where the tribes of Ephraim and Manasseh are instructed

by Joshua to fell forest land in the hill-country in order to create new settlement areas. Most of these Israelite settlements were in the beginning small and were more like unfortified villages. There has been little archaeological research in such small settlements, so we have only sporadic information about the position of such sites. Only in a few cases, where we are dealing with larger settlements, are we able to situate them with more precision. Besides these settlements, archaeological excavation has uncovered a number of new Israelite settlements on sites which were destroyed or deserted in the Middle Bronze Age or earlier.

HOUSE PLANS IN THE PERIOD OF THE SETTLEMENT
During the Early Iron Age the pillared house was common.

2/ Tribes and their borders in JOSH 13-19
DAN name of tribe

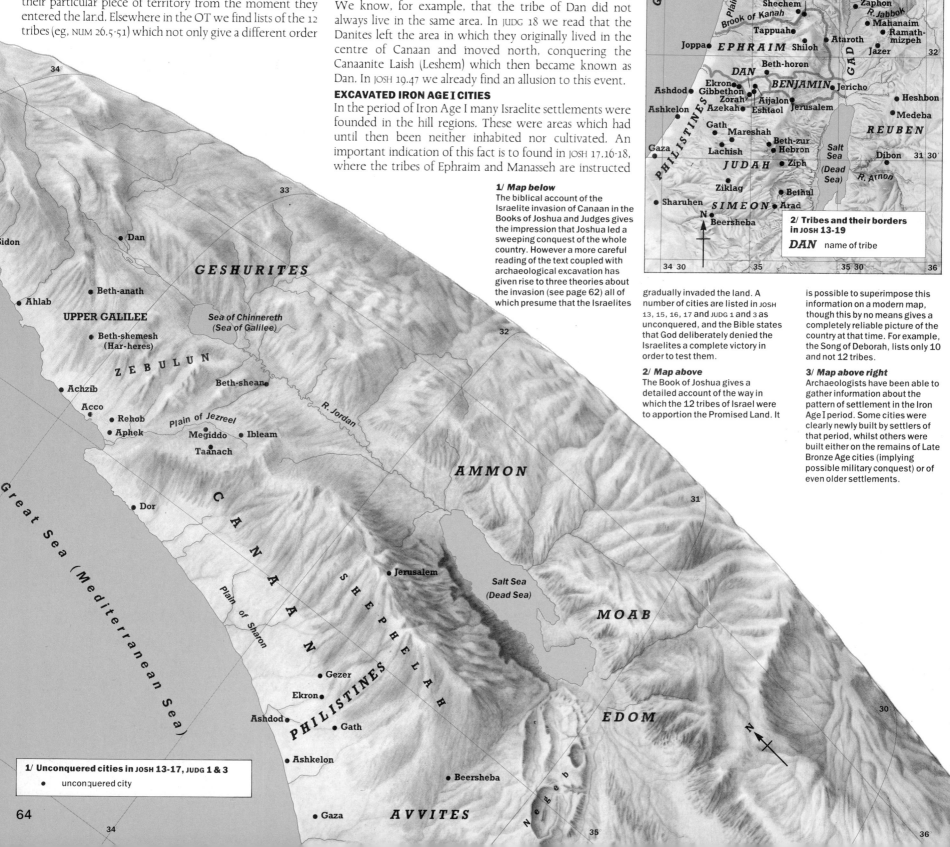

1/ Map below
The biblical account of the Israelite invasion of Canaan in the Books of Joshua and Judges gives the impression that Joshua led a sweeping conquest of the whole country. However a more careful reading of the text coupled with archaeological excavation has given rise to three theories about the invasion (see page 62) all of which presume that the Israelites gradually invaded the land. A number of cities are listed in JOSH 13, 15, 16, 17 and JUDG 1 and 3 as unconquered, and the Bible states that God deliberately denied the Israelites a complete victory in order to test them.

2/ Map above
The Book of Joshua gives a detailed account of the way in which the 12 tribes of Israel were to apportion the Promised Land. It is possible to superimpose this information on a modern map, though this by no means gives a completely reliable picture of the country at that time. For example, the Song of Deborah, lists only 10 and not 12 tribes.

3/ Map above right
Archaeologists have been able to gather information about the pattern of settlement in the Iron Age I period. Some cities were clearly newly built by settlers of that period, whilst others were built either on the remains of Late Bronze Age cities (implying possible military conquest) or of even older settlements.

1/ Unconquered cities in JOSH 13-17, JUDG 1 & 3
• unconquered city

The most popular was the so-called 'four-room' house with one or two rooms subdivided by rows of pillars. Two- and three-room house subtypes are also known. The origins of the pillared house plan are obscure and the four-room house appears in a fully developed form at the very beginning of the Iron Age without any apparent antecedents. The four-room house does not seem to have any forerunner in Canaanite architectural traditions and it seems unlikely to have been derived from the typical Late Bronze Age house with a central courtyard surrounded by rooms on all sides. There is also no evidence that it was of megaron or *bit hilani* inspiration. It has also been suggested that the four-room house plan developed out of a more simple type of pillared house (eg, Building No 90 at T. Eshdar – see drawing below) which, in turn, was derived from a nomadic tent used by the Israelites. It is generally agreed that the homeland of the four-room pillared house, and its variants, was in the central hill country. Those who adhere to this view maintain that the pillared four-room house was a local invention, *c* 1200 BC, which was the result of rapid Israelite adaptation to available resources and to a new rural way of life in the hilly regions. Four-room houses and other pillared structures dating from the Early Iron Age have been found in the central hill country at Ai, Shiloh, Kh. Raddana, and Giloh.

A standard four-room house was built with an entry leading into an internal courtyard separated from rooms on either side by rows of pillars or divider walls. The pillars were built of roughly-shaped stones or sometimes of well-cut monolithic blocks; low curtain walls were frequently built between the pillars. A broadroom was erected at the rear, running across the entire width of the house. The side rooms at the front of the structure were usually paved and appear to have been used as basement-shelters for stabling a small number of sheep and goats, and for the storage of agricultural produce. The storage area was sometimes subdivided by partition walls into small cells. The central courtyard had a plastered floor and was open to the sky; a lot of the food-processing was carried out in this courtyard. The broadroom at the back end of the house was probably mainly used as sleeping quarters. Many of the houses probably had an upper storey rising on three sides of the internal courtyard. The space within the upper rooms would have been necessary for extended families. Access to the external wall of the house was gained by way of a flight of steps parallel to the upper storey of the house. Wooden ladders may also have been used from the internal courtyard. At sites in the hilly regions, the walls of the houses were built of roughly-hewn blocks of stone and the roofs consisted of wooden beams covered with layers of branches and clay smoothed down with the help of a cylindrical roof-roller.

During the course of the 11th century BC, the four-room house plan rapidly spread to other non-Israelite regions of the country; to Philistia (eg, T. Qasile Strata X-IX – see drawing 3 below – and T. Sera' Stratum VIII), to the Jezreel Valley (eg, T. Megiddo Stratum VIB) and to Transjordan (eg, Sahab near Amman and Kh. Medeiyineh). However, this house plan never really became very popular in the non-Israelite regions and earlier structural traditions were maintained. The four-room house plan was also adopted during the 11th century BC at Israelite settlements in the Negeb Desert. Numerous pillared houses have been unearthed at T. Masos in the Beersheba region. They were built out of mud-brick on stone foundations and the pillars were constructed out of stone segments. A new type of pillared structure (Building No 1039) has been identified at T. Masos; it lacks the end broadroom and perhaps it is the Early Iron Age prototype of the well-known pillared storehouses which have been found in settlements of the Later Iron Age Monarchy. At T. Masos a number of 'courtyard houses' of Canaanite tradition appear side by side with the pillared houses of Israelite origin. One of these structures (House No 480 – see drawing 2 below) has a central pillared courtyard with rooms arranged around it on four sides; it bears a general resemblance to Late Bronze Age structures found at Beth-shean VI (House 1500), Gerizim, Amman, T. Halif and to Egyptian type houses of New Empire date. Another 'courtyard house' at T. Masos (Structure No 402) has an indented mud brick exterior wall which was clearly of Egyptian influence.

The four-room house plan remained a dominant characteristic of Israelite dwellings throughout the Iron Age and down to the early 6th century BC. Examples of four-room structures dating from the Iron Age II are known from Hazor Stratum VA, T. el-Far'ah, T. en-Nasbeh Stratum I (all shown below), Jerusalem, T. Beit Mirsim Stratum A, Beth-shemesh and Beersheba Stratum II. They are also known from small rural villages (eg Kh. Jema'in in Samaria) and even from isolated agricultural farms (eg, Kh. er-Ras south-west of Jerusalem).

> 'SO THE MEN WENT AND PASSED UP AND DOWN IN THE LAND AND SET DOWN IN A BOOK A DESCRIPTION OF IT BY TOWNS IN SEVEN DIVISIONS; THEN THEY CAME TO JOSHUA IN THE CAMP AT SHILOH, AND JOSHUA CAST LOTS FOR THEM IN SHILOH BEFORE THE LORD; AND THERE JOSHUA APPORTIONED THE LAND TO THE PEOPLE OF ISRAEL, TO EACH HIS PORTION' JOSH 18.9-10

4/ Below
In the early Iron Age (12th century BC) at the time of the settlement of Canaan by the Israelites, a change in the construction of houses has been observed by archaeologists. Instead of building rooms around a central courtyard, houses consisted of a number of rooms subdivided by pillars and known as the 'four-room' house. Some believe that this simple style of architecture arose because the Israelites had to build houses very quickly in their new home-land. Excavation has revealed (eg at T. Masos in the Negeb) that houses were often built in a chain to protect the settlement from outside attack.
The plans below show the development of housebuilding from the time of the settlement onwards. The houses are as follows:
1) T. Masos, building no.454, Stratum I (Iron Age I)
2) T. Masos, building no.480, Stratum IIa (Iron Age I)
3) T. Qasile, Stratum IXB (Iron Age I)
4) T. Esdar, building no.90, Stratum III (Iron Age I)
5) T. el-Far'ah, building no.327 (Iron Age I)
6) T. el-Far'ah, building no.328 (Iron Age I)
7) Hazor, Stratum VA (Iron Age II)
8) T. Goren, Stratum V (Iron Age II)
9) T. Beit Mirsim, Stratum A (Iron Age II)
10) T. en-Nasbeh (Mizpah), building no.2, Stratum I (Iron Age II).

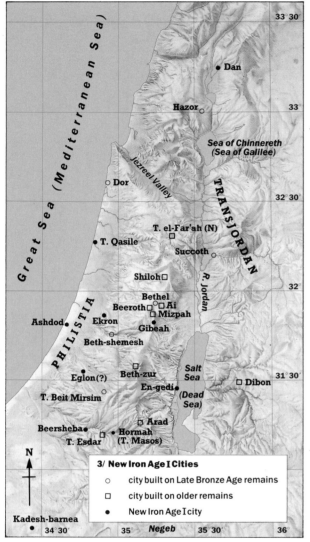

3/ New Iron Age I Cities
- ○ city built on Late Bronze Age remains
- □ city built on older remains
- ● New Iron Age I city

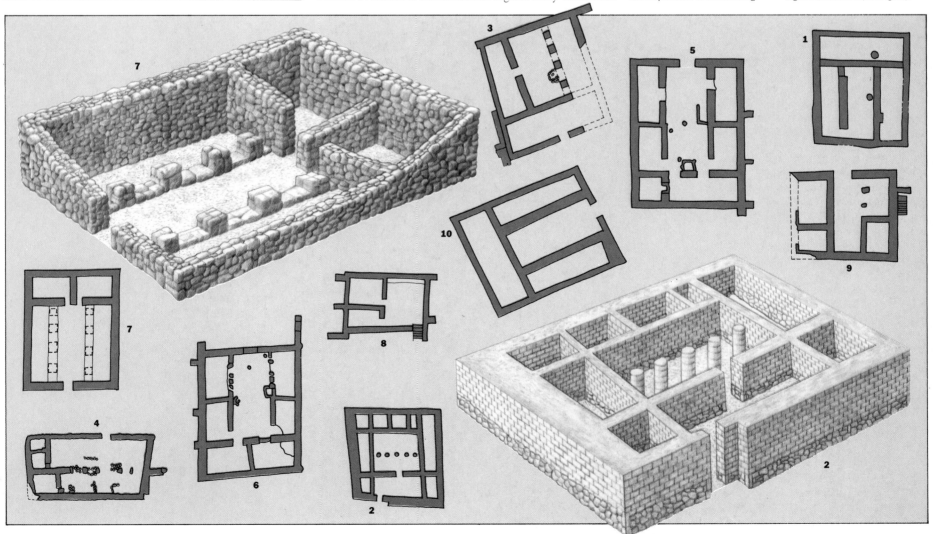

MANY sites in Anatolia, Syria and Palestine were destroyed during the Late Bronze Age. Following this destruction, at some sites, a new kind of pottery, of Aegean type, appears which was used by the settlers of the ruins. The archaeological evidence is borne out by Egyptian documents which record the arrival of groups of peoples called 'Peoples of the Sea', of which one group, the Philistines, settled in and gave their name to Palestine.

In the fifth year of Pharaoh Merneptah (1236-1223 BC) groups of Sea Peoples allied themselves with the Libyans in an attempt to invade Egypt. In addition to the Sherden, the peoples named are the Sheklesh, Lukka, Tursha and Aka-washa (Achaeans). However, the Philistines and the groups closely associated with them are not mentioned until the reign of Pharaoh Ramesses III (1198-1166). The archaeological evidence, particularly at sites such as Beth-shean which remained under Egyptian control through the reign of Ramesses III, shows a number of Philistine burials during this period.

The Tale of Wen-amon (mid-11th century BC) vividly illustrates the chaos existing in the Levant and the lack of Egyptian control over peoples nominally under their domination. The story is told by a priest of the god Amon who is sent to Byblos to purchase lumber for the sacred barge of the god (see Map 1). He is treated with little respect by the rulers of the cities he visits. He is robbed during his stay at Dor, a city belonging to the Tjekker and nominally under Egyptian control. He then has to flee and is pursued

FROM EGYPTIAN BONDAGE TO SETTLEMENT IN CANAAN

THE PHILISTINES

The period encompassing the end of the Late Bronze Age and the beginning of the Iron Age is one of great complexity and instability. It saw the collapse of the great Mycenaean and Hittite empires, the end of the Canaanite city-states and the decline of Egyptian power. There were great movements of people throughout the Mediterranean and the Near East. The reasons for this upheaval are unknown but could well have been due to some natural disaster which caused hitherto settled peoples to become temporarily nomadic. It is during this period that the Israelite tribes and the Philistines arrived and began to settle in Canaan.

by the Tjekker in their fleet of 11 ships as far as Cyprus. This story is of great importance because of its reference to the Tjekker, one of the Sea Peoples closely allied to the Philistines, and to their city of Dor, in the northern coastal plain, just north of the Philistine settlement area.

The 12th century BC reliefs and inscriptions of the mortuary temple of Ramesses III at Medinet Habu are the most important records we have of the arrival of the Sea Peoples. The inscriptions record the destruction of the Hittite empire and the attempts by the Sea Peoples to invade Egypt. The reliefs depict and describe the two great battles with the Sea Peoples, one on land, fought in Phoenicia or Syria, and the other on the sea, probably fought in the Nile Delta.

In the land battle the Sea Peoples are shown fighting in chariots; their families travel with them in ox-drawn carts with solid wheels, similar to a type of cart still used in parts of Anatolia. They are clearly differentiated in their appearance, dress and arms. Three groups are distinguishable by their headdresses: the Philistines, Tjekker and Denyen (Danuna) wear high 'feathered' headdresses; the Sherden, who in this battle are fighting for the Egyptians, wear horned helmets, and the Sheklesh have fillet headbands.

1/ Map left

On his way to buy cedarwood from Byblos, c.1100 BC, Wen-amon spoke of a new group, the 'Sea-Peoples'. Also in the 12th century, the tribe of Dan journeyed through the same area (see text).

In the great naval battle, the Sea Peoples are shown in their fighting ships, with duck-shaped prow and stern, powered only by sail. Here the Sherden are shown fighting with the other Sea Peoples against the Egyptians. Both groups carry round shields and wield long broadswords. They wear panelled kilts with tassels and corselets, reminiscent in design of Mycenaean armour.

The evidence of these exceedingly important reliefs makes it clear that one group of Sea Peoples fought the Egyptians in a great land battle but were not decisively defeated. They were strong enough to attempt to invade Egypt by sea, this time in alliance with another of the Sea Peoples, the Sherden, when they were defeated and eventually settled permanently in Palestine. This group included the Philistines, Tjekker and Denyen or Danuna. The latter group may have some connection with the tribe of Dan who, according to the biblical account (JUDG 18) did not succeed in taking possession of the area allocated to them and had to migrate from the Shephelah to the Canaanite city of Laish in the north (see Map 1).

The arrival of a new Philistine cultural element made itself known in a number of different ways. Many sites, some of them quite large, were destroyed, and upon the ruins are found a new type of pottery, not indigenous to the area, which clearly derived from Aegean, mainly Mycenaean types. More recent excavations of sites with this new, Philistine, culture have also shown that a new type of architecture appears, along with new burial customs and a different type of religious cult.

Many of the large mounds with Philistine material show much evidence of Egyptian influence; this is not surprising as we know that they were first settled in Palestine during a time of Egyptian control and only gradually, as Egyptian power declined and finally ceased, did they expand into the surrounding countryside and found their own cities. Two sites are particularly important. Ashdod, in central Philistia and T. Qasile on its northern borders.

At T. Qasile, the first unmistakable Philistine temples were found. No exact parallels for the temples' architecture have been found in Palestine though some features show Canaanite influence. However, small sanctuaries excavated at Mycenae, Cyprus, and the island of Melos resemble the Qasile temples in a number of ways.

Among the objects found in the Qasile temple complex were cult vessels and a socketed bronze double axe, which has Aegean connections.

The cult vessels excavated at Philistine sites include ring kernoi (libation vessels), animal, bird and human-shaped vessels, rhyta (one-handled cups with a bottom often in the form of a lion's head), cup-bearing kraters and terracotta figurines. The terracotta female figurines are clearly derived from Mycenaean prototypes not previously known in Canaan. A unique example from Ashdod, of the 12th century BC, has the body merging into a chair or couch and almost certainly represents a goddess (see page 69). We do not know what gods the Philistines worshipped when they arrived in Canaan but their deities of later times, Dagon, Ashtoreth and Beelzebub, are of Canaanite origin.

Burial customs are generally a good indicator of cultural affinity and those of the Philistines show the same mixture of Aegean, Egyptian and Canaanite elements that characterise other aspects of their culture.

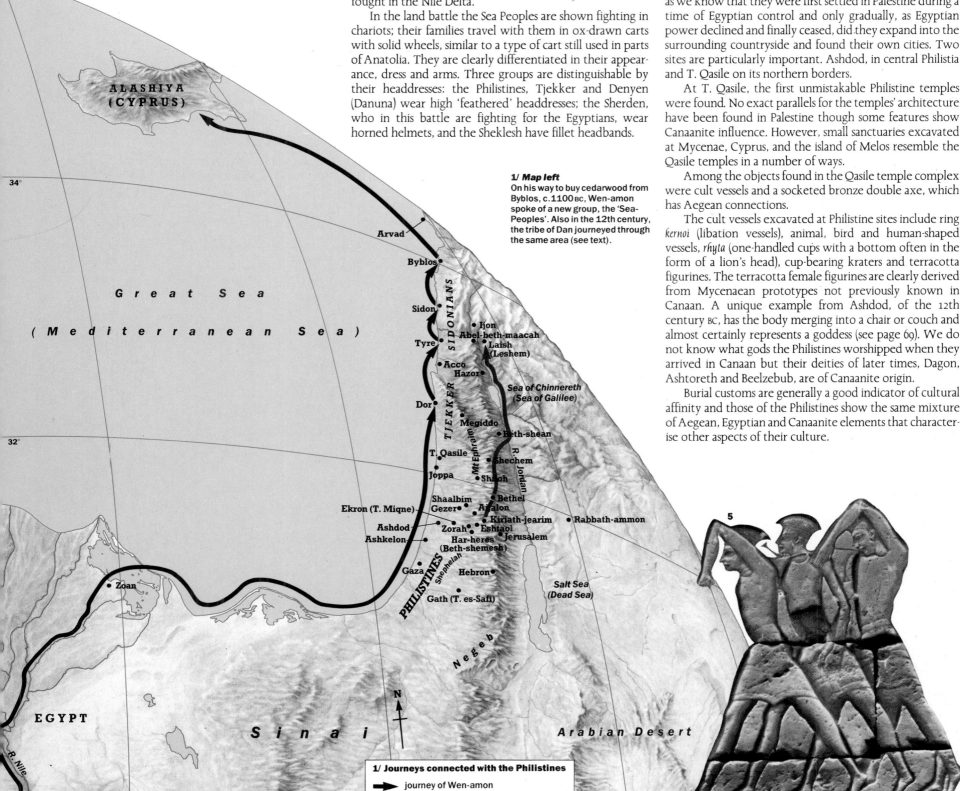

ALASHIYA (CYPRUS)

Great Sea (Mediterranean Sea)

34°

Arvad

Byblos

SIDONIANS

Sidon
Ijon
Abel-beth-maacah
Tyre
Laish (Leshem)
Acco
Hazor
TJEKKER

Dor
Sea of Chinnereth (Sea of Galilee)
Megiddo
Beth-shean

32°

T. Qasile
Mt Ephraim
Shechem
Joppa
Shiloh
R. Jordan
Shaalbim
Bethel
Ekron (T. Miqne)
Gezer
Aijalon
Ashdod
Kiriath-jearim
Rabbath-ammon
Zorah
Eshtaol
Ashkelon
Har-heres (Beth-shemesh)
Jerusalem
PHILISTINES
Gaza
Shephelah
Hebron
Salt Sea (Dead Sea)
Gath (T. es-Safi)

EGYPT

Zoan

Negeb

N

Sinai
Arabian Desert

R. Nile

1/ Journeys connected with the Philistines

→ journey of Wen-amon

→ journey of the tribe of Dan

30°
Noph
Red Sea

32°
34°
36°
38°

Egyptian garrisons in the area in the Late Bronze Age brought to Canaan the practice of burial, often multiple, in anthropoid clay coffins. Such garrisons from the 12th century BC onwards included Philistine soldiers, and some scholars conclude that this burial practice was specifically Philistine. A coffin of this type, with a lid showing a typical Philistine/Sea People headdress has been found at Beth-shean, a site which we know from biblical sources (I SAM 31.8-13; II SAM 21.12) to have been occupied by the Philistines.

Another unusual burial custom is the practice of cremation. An example of this has been found at Azor and belongs to the second half of the 11th century BC, the earliest example of this type of burial in Palestine.

Philistine pottery is a large and varied homogeneous group, locally made, painted in black and red, usually on a

3

2/ Map right
The term 'Philistine' mentioned in the Bible is apparently a general term for the Sea Peoples who settled in Canaan in the 13th and 12th centuries BC. Iron was introduced into the area by the Philistines, and excavation shows that the use of iron increased and became widespread in the 11th and 10th centuries BC.

3/ Above right
Scene from the temple of Ramesses III at Medinet Habu, showing a famous battle with the Philistines, who are easily distinguished by their 'feathered' headdresses (see text).

4/ Right
Libation stand found at Ashdod, 1ft 2in high. Late Philistine, or Iron Age I period.
The stand supporting the libation bowl has moulded figures of musicians and above is a procession of animals, partly incised and partly in relief.

5/ Below left
Bas-relief from the temple of Ramesses III, at Medinet Habu. Height c 3ft, 12th century BC.

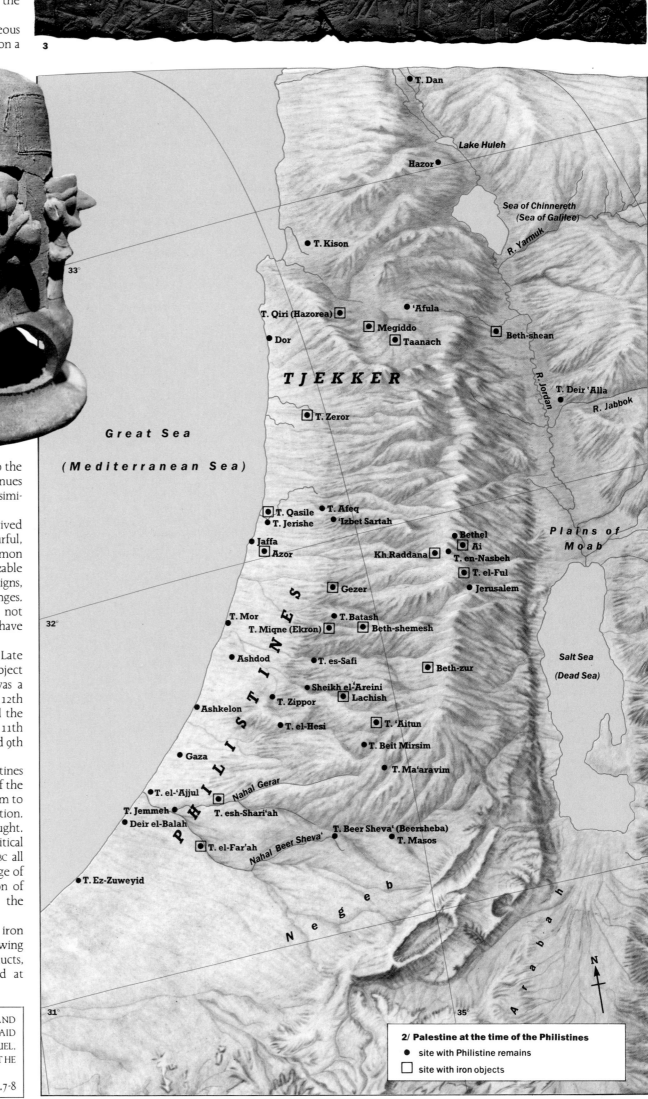

2/ Palestine at the time of the Philistines
- site with Philistine remains
- □ site with iron objects

white-slipped background. It appears in levels dated to the first half of the 12th and the 11th century BC and continues until the 10th century BC when the Philistines were assimilated into the local culture.

The decoration of the pottery is also mainly derived from Mycenaean prototypes and is varied and colourful, with a highly developed artistic sense. Birds are a common motif, but the most striking and readily recognizable feature is the many types of geometric and linear designs, such as spirals, semi-circles, chevrons, zig-zags and lozenges. Animals and humans are rarely portrayed but are not unknown. Cult vessels show similar decoration but have different shapes.

Though iron was to some extent known in the Late Bronze Age, such finds are sporadic and the type of object generally found, such as jewellery, shows that it was a luxury product. Relatively small amounts are found in 12th century BC Canaan but it is clear that bronze was still the major metal. The use of iron increased during the 11th century but it only became widespread in the 10th and 9th centuries.

It has been generally accepted that the Philistines introduced iron into Palestine and that their control of the metal industry was one of the factors that enabled them to achieve military superiority over the rest of the population. The picture is no longer as clear-cut as formerly thought. The upheavals in the area and the economic and political chaos that occurred at the end of the 13th century BC all over the Mediterranean may have resulted in a shortage of copper and tin, the materials used in the production of bronze. This may have provided an incentive for the development of iron technology.

Study of the excavated material shows that most iron tools and weapons of this period come from sites showing Philistine occupation or influence. Very few iron products, and even fewer bronze objects, have been found at Canaanite or Israelite sites.

...THE LORDS OF THE PHILISTINES WENT UP AGAINST ISRAEL. AND WHEN THE PEOPLE OF ISRAEL HEARD OF IT THEY WERE AFRAID OF THE PHILISTINES. AND THE PEOPLE OF ISRAEL SAID TO SAMUEL, "DO NOT CEASE TO CRY TO THE LORD OUR GOD FOR US, THAT HE MAY SAVE US FROM THE HAND OF THE PHILISTINES.'"
I SAM 7.7-8

THE period of the judges is one of the most important eras in Israel's history. It is now that Israel begins to emerge into the light of day, eventually to establish herself as a significant power on the map of the ancient Near East. However, the records of the period are fragmentary, to the extent that it is impossible to arrange the events in chronological order. At best, only a general picture of the nature of Israel and its type of life and experience can be developed.

THE CANAANITE CITY-STATES
The period was one which marked a transition between the stage when Palestine was ruled by a number of independent Canaanite city-states, under the overall control of Egypt, and the stage when it was under the sole rule of an Israelite king. Egyptian control was so seriously weakened, both by attacks from outside and by economic problems at home, that the Canaanite city-state system which it protected broke down, thus allowing the development of a decentralized tribal society; this in turn was succeeded by a monarchic system which in some respects reintroduced

FROM EGYPTIAN BONDAGE TO SETTLEMENT IN CANAAN

THE HEROIC AGE OF THE JUDGES

The roots of Israel lie in the time before the foundation of the monarchy under Saul. Then Israel was a tribal society, living in a land which she believed to have been given her by God and defending it under the leadership of charismatic leaders, or judges, raised up by God to meet particular emergencies as they arose.

characteristics of the old city-state system.

Canaanite society in the city-states was marked by a sharp distinction between ruler and ruled, rich and poor, and by the existence of various guilds of workers such as cloth manufacturers, chariot makers, builders, etc. This form tended to appear once more under the Israelite monarchy, even though modified by the influence of Israel's tribal past. Tribal society is the social form adopted by Israel in the period of the judges, and this sharply distinguished her from the neighbouring Canaanites.

THE TRIBAL ECONOMY
Israel's tribalism was egalitarian and was based on a pastoral-agricultural economy: the Gideon story tells of Midianite raids in Israel's fields, their destruction and looting of crops

and animals (JUDG 6.1-6). The growing of wheat and barley, the tending of sheep, goats and cattle, and the cultivation of vineyards, were fundamental to tribal life, and outside this pastoral-agricultural mix there was probably no significant contribution to the tribal economy. The Book of Judges occasionally mentions cities, but it was only in exceptional cases that these were anything more than unfortified settlements inhabited by those involved in their agricultural occupations.

SOCIAL STRUCTURE
In Israelite tribal society the fundamental social and economic unit was the extended family. This was a largely self-sufficient unit, owning property and having few occupations apart from the tending of livestock and the growing of crops. The wider association to which the family belonged was the clan, which functioned as the social context within which the families intermarried and found material aid and protection. The tribe was a much more fluid and changeable entity. It was both a social and territorial unit, but, being constituted by groups who lived next to each other in a particular area and banded together to resist occasional attacks from outside, rather than on the basis of kinship, it was subject to continual change in its internal clan membership and indeed in its very existence.

A SEGMENTARY SOCIETY
This social structure encouraged independence on the part of clans and families. Trade was probably more or less non-existent, external pressure was occasional and, in any case, involved only isolated groups; thus, there was little need for the creation of more comprehensive social structures. The form of life was determined more from the bottom than from the top, so that it was the clan or family, rather than 'Israel', which was of primary importance to the

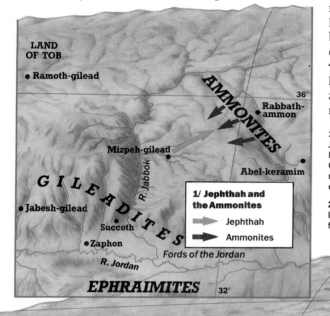

1/ Left
Jephthah, brought back from the land of Tob, is made head of Gilead to lead them in successful resistance to Ammonite expansion (JUDG 11.1-12.7).

2/ Bottom left
In a two-phased operation, Sisera first moved against Barak's forces

gathered at Mt Tabor; the decisive battle took place at Taanach by the waters of Megiddo (JUDG 15.9), probably as a result of the arrival of troops from Ephraim, Benjamin and Machir. Sisera's flight took him to his death at the hands of Jael at the 'Oak of Zaanannim'.

1/ Jephthah and the Ammonites

→ Jephthah
→ Ammonites

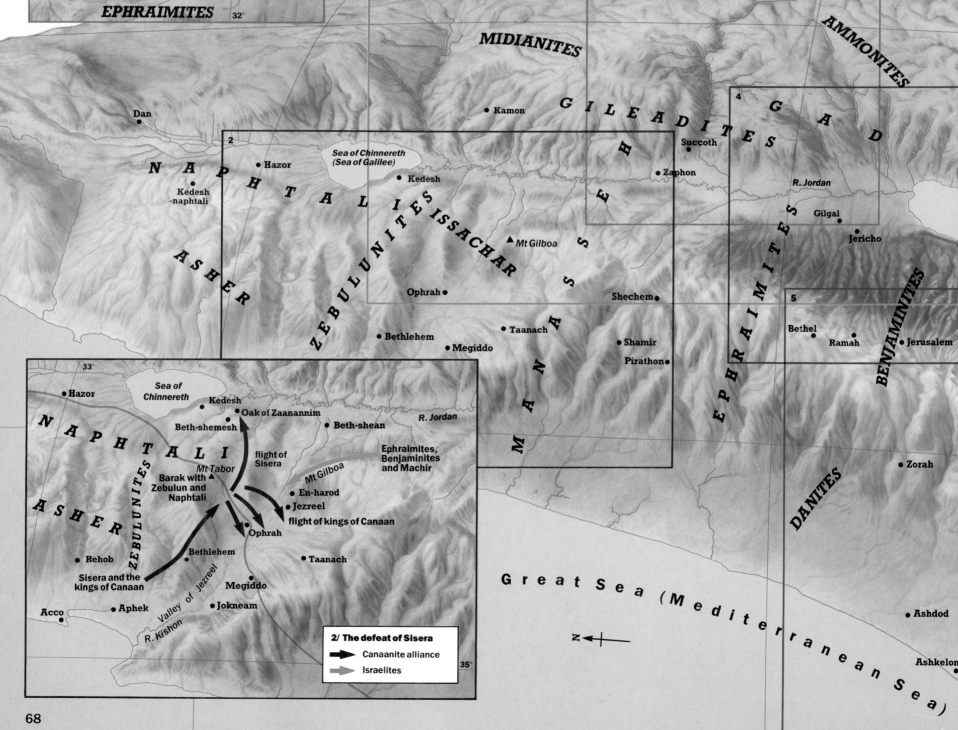

2/ The defeat of Sisera

■ Canaanite alliance
■ Israelites

3/ Below right
Gideon, at the head of a small band drawn from his clan of Abiezer, which belonged to the tribe of Manasseh, mounts a surprise attack on the camp of Midianite crop raiders and expels them from Israelite territory (JUDG 6-8).

4/ Bottom near right
Having killed Eglon the Moabite king after delivering tribute to him, probably at the city of palms (Jericho), Ehud of Benjamin summoned help from Ephraim. By seizing the Fords of the Jordan, the Israelites cut off the Moabite retreat and inflicted a decisive defeat (JUDG 3.12-30).

5/ Bottom far right
In the Samson saga the Israelite hero of the tribe of Dan leads no army, but with his own strength kills Philistines and destroys their fields until finally, betrayed by Delilah, he meets his death in the Philistine temple at Gaza.

7/Left
A Philistine fertility figurine from Ashdod (c 12th century BC). Nicknamed the 'Ashdoda' it is in the form of both a woman and a bed.

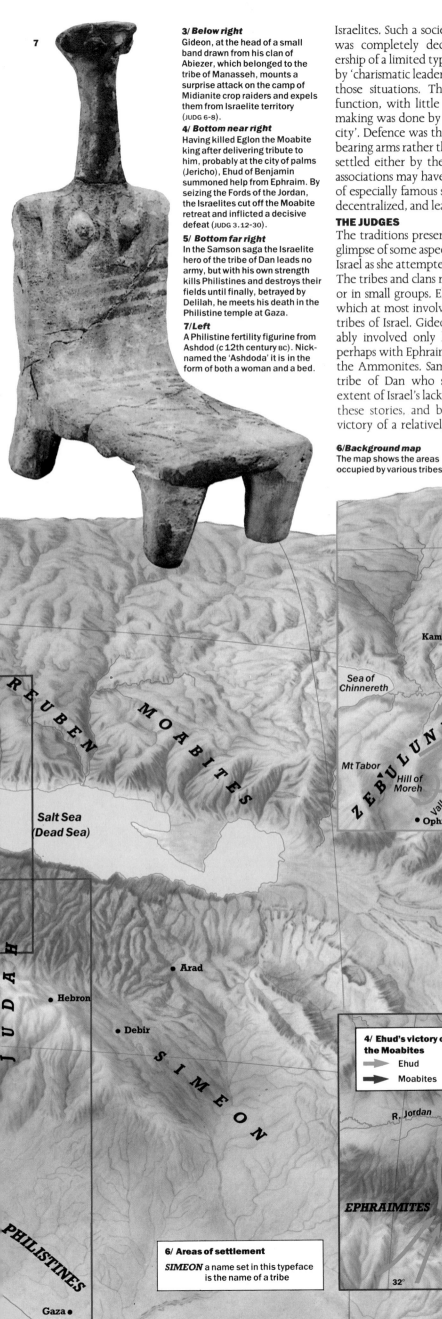

Israelites. Such a society is best described as segmentary, it was completely decentralized. Occasional unified leadership of a limited type was afforded in times of emergency by 'charismatic leaders' who came forward to deal with just those situations. The elders exercised a representative function, with little real power, while effective decision making was done by general assemblies of the 'men of the city'. Defence was the responsibility of all those capable of bearing arms rather than a professional army. Disputes were settled either by the elders or by 'judges'. Limited cultic associations may have existed in Israel for the maintenance of especially famous sanctuaries, but society in general was decentralized, and leagues of any nature were exceptional.

THE JUDGES
The traditions preserved in the Book of Judges afford us a glimpse of some aspects of the experience of pre-monarchic Israel as she attempted to consolidate her hold on the land. The tribes and clans rarely acted together, but rather singly or in small groups. Ehud led a battle against the Moabites which at most involved Benjamin and Ephraim among the tribes of Israel. Gideon's repulsion of the Midianites probably involved only his own clan of Abiezrites together perhaps with Ephraim. Jephthah led Gilead to victory over the Ammonites. Samson was likewise a local hero of the tribe of Dan who skirmished with the Philistines. The extent of Israel's lack of effective unity is well illustrated by these stories, and by JUDG 4, the record of a significant victory of a relatively wide tribal alliance led by Deborah and Barak over the Canaanites, to which, however, so many tribes failed to contribute (JUDG 5.15-17).

Although a chronological ordering to events cannot be established in detail, it is possible to reconstruct something more than a totally static picture. Israelite tribalism emerged primarily in the mountain areas of Palestine, while the Canaanite city-state system continued for some time to dominate the plains (JUDG 1.27-35).

With the significant exception of JUDG 4, the events of the period of the judges are located in those less accessible districts lying largely outside the city-state range of control. The victory over Sisera, recorded in JUDG 4, marks the first appearance of Israelite tribes in the plains, and a significant stage in the development by which Israel under the monarchy came, though not without setbacks, to dominate Palestine.

'THEN THE LORD RAISED UP JUDGES, WHO SAVED THEM OUT OF THE POWER OF THOSE WHO PLUNDERED THEM. AND YET THEY DID NOT LISTEN TO THEIR JUDGES; FOR THEY PLAYED THE HARLOT AFTER OTHER GODS AND BOWED DOWN TO THEM; THEY SOON TURNED ASIDE FROM THE WAY IN WHICH THEIR FATHERS HAD WALKED, WHO HAD OBEYED THE COMMANDMENTS OF THE LORD, AND THEY DID NOT DO SO. WHENEVER THE LORD RAISED UP JUDGES FOR THEM, THE LORD WAS WITH THE JUDGE, AND HE SAVED THEM FROM THE HAND OF THEIR ENEMIES ALL THE DAYS OF THE JUDGE...' JUDG 2.16-18

6/Background map
The map shows the areas occupied by various tribes.

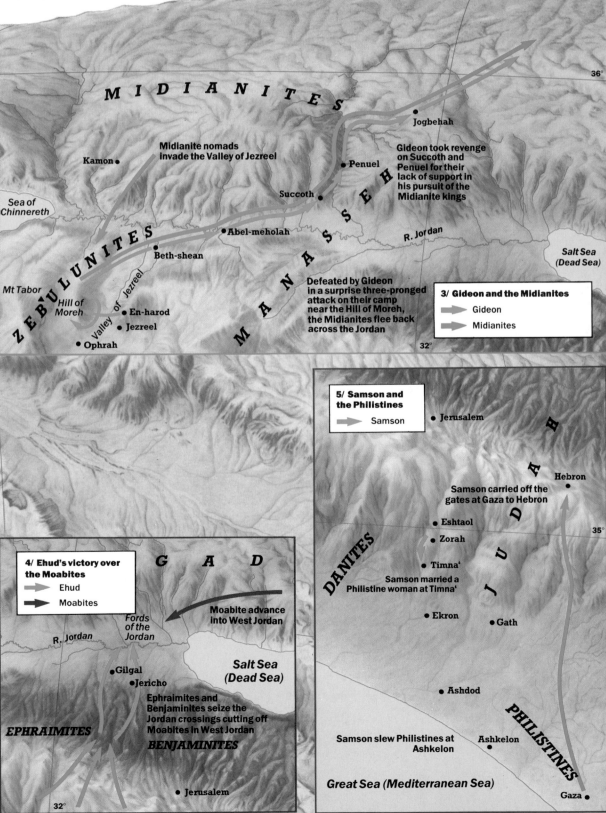

MIDIANITES

Jogbehah

Midianite nomads invade the Valley of Jezreel

Kamon

Gideon took revenge on Succoth and Penuel for their lack of support in his pursuit of the Midianite kings

Penuel

Succoth

Sea of Chinnereth

MANASSEH

Abel-meholah

R. Jordan

ZEBULUNITES

Beth-shean

Salt Sea (Dead Sea)

Mt Tabor

Hill of Moreh

Valley of Jezreel

En-harod

Jezreel

Defeated by Gideon in a surprise three-pronged attack on their camp near the Hill of Moreh, the Midianites flee back across the Jordan

3/ Gideon and the Midianites
→ Gideon
→ Midianites

Ophrah

REUBEN

MOABITES

Salt Sea (Dead Sea)

JUDAH

Hebron

Arad

Debir

SIMEON

5/ Samson and the Philistines
→ Samson

Jerusalem

Hebron

Samson carried off the gates at Gaza to Hebron

Eshtaol

DANITES

Zorah

JUDAH

Timna'

Samson married a Philistine woman at Timna'

Ekron

Gath

Ashdod

4/ Ehud's victory over the Moabites
→ Ehud
→ Moabites

GAD

Moabite advance into West Jordan

Fords of the Jordan

R. Jordan

Salt Sea (Dead Sea)

Gilgal
Jericho

Ephraimites and Benjaminites seize the Jordan crossings cutting off Moabites in West Jordan

EPHRAIMITES

BENJAMINITES

Jerusalem

Samson slew Philistines at Ashkelon

Ashkelon

PHILISTINES

PHILISTINES

6/ Areas of settlement
SIMEON a name set in this typeface is the name of a tribe

Gaza

Great Sea (Mediterranean Sea)

Gaza

69

THE Egyptian pharaohs in the Late Bronze Age ruled in Palestine through local vassal governors resident in the major cities. These cities were located primarily in the lowlands (the coastal plain and the Jezreel Valley), whereas the hill country seems to have been less densely populated and with fewer cities of significant size (such as Shechem and Hebron).

Notable changes in this situation occurred near the end of the 13th century, which, because of the changes, archaeologists designate as the end of the Bronze Age and the beginning of the Iron Age (1200-586 BC). One of the changes marking the transition to the Bronze Age was that in spite of the efforts of Pharaohs Ramesses II (1304-1237 BC) and Merneptah (1236-1223 BC) (see pages 48-51), Egyptian authority in Palestine faded. Indeed Ramesses III (1198-1166) was hard pressed to defend Egypt itself from the Sea Peoples.

Secondly, many of the major cities which had flourished in Palestine during the Bronze Age met with destruction during approximately the 13th century (not necessarily all at the same time or with the same cause). Some of these cities were re-built almost immediately, others not. The Iron Age phases of those which were re-built tended to be smaller in size and with less impressive structures.

The third piece of evidence of a new age was that there was a population increase in the hill country, as indicated by the emergence of numerous villages at previously unoccupied sites.

Finally, generally speaking, Iron Age technology and styles represented less sophisticated continuation of those of the Bronze Age. Yet there were some notable developments, such as terrace farming, plaster-lined cisterns, and more extensive use of iron. These technological developments rendered settlement of the hill country much more practical.

Thus the artefactual remains recovered by archaeologists in Palestine from the beginning of the Iron Age seem to confirm what is suggested by the meagre written records available from the period – namely, that the end of the Late Bronze Age was a turbulent and unsettled time, characterized by the break-down of old authority structures, a heterogeneous population, and demographic shifts.

IRON AGE KINGDOMS

Gradually, by approximately 1000 BC, there emerged a new configuration of political alignments which included a coalition of Philistine cities along the coastal plain, a string of Phoenician cities along the coast further north, and several small kingdoms in the interior (Israel, Judah, Ammon, Moab, and Edom). The Aramean kingdoms of Aram and Syria, especially the kingdom of Damascus, also exerted significant influence in Palestinian affairs. These city-states and modest, local kingdoms existed alongside each other, competed, warred, and made alliances with relatively little outside interference until the latter decades of the 8th century when all of Syro-Palestine succumbed to the Assyrian empire. Thereafter, even though most of the cities and local kingdoms survived for another hundred years or so, they no longer retained any real or lasting independence. Once again, as in the late Bronze Age, Syro-Palestine was

THE INSTITUTION OF THE MONARCHY

THE EMERGENCE OF THE IRON AGE KINGDOMS IN SYRO-PALESTINE

The Bronze Age saw the rise and decline of several empires. The Late Bronze Age (1550-1200 BC) was an age of empire for the Egyptians and Hittites, both of whom sought control of Syro-Palestine. Palestine, because of its proximity, fell within Egyptian influence, especially following the reign of Pharaoh Tuthmosis III (c 1504-1450), when it was essentially an Egyptian province.

dominated by foreign empires – first the Assyrians, then the Babylonians, after that the Persians, and after the Persians the Greeks.

ISRAELITE KINGDOMS

Naturally the Bible gives prime attention to the Israelite kingdom which emerged under Saul, David and Solomon at approximately 1000 BC, and split into two separate kingdoms (Israel and Judah) after Solomon's death. One should not conclude, however, that these two Israelite kingdoms towered above their immediate neighbours in political or economic importance, or that the Israelites stood totally apart in terms of cultural and religious patterns. Even the biblical writers recognized that a close kinship existed between the Israelites, Moabites, Ammonites, Edomites, and Arameans, which they expressed in genealogical terms (GEN 19.30-36; 25.21-28; 36; DEUT 26.5). Likewise, the archaeological record indicates cultural continuity rather than uniqueness with regard to the Israelites and the neighbouring countries.

The Israelite kingdoms were centres in the hill country west of the Jordan, and weak kings (such as Jehu of Israel and Joash of Judah) were hard pressed to defend even that. But stronger kings (such as David, Solomon, Omri (see page 98), Ahab, and Jeroboam II (see page 112) were able to exercise authority over significant portions of the coastal plain, the Jezreel Valley and Galilee, much of the Transjordan, and the Negeb. It was with regard to these areas surrounding the central hill country that Israelite territorial interests conflicted with those of the Philistines, Phoenicians, Arameans, Ammonites, Moabites, and Edomites.

PHILISTINES

The Philistines came to the region as part of the general Sea Peoples migrations mentioned in Egyptian texts from the end of the Late Bronze Age. Actually very little is known about the Sea Peoples (see page 54) except that they apparently were non-Semitic and originated in the Aegean area. This is illustrated by Philistine pottery, for example, which is reminiscent of Aegean prototypes. The Philistines settled along the coastal plain, where they established five

---

EGYPT
Egypt had already passed its zenith before the Israelite and Judaean monarchies appeared on the scene, but it continued to exert considerable cultural influence upon the surrounding peoples, and its pharaohs continued to dabble in Syro-Palestinian politics.

EDOM
The Edomites lived south of the Dead Sea, on both sides of the Arabah. Although much of their territory was very arid, the region around Bosrah, the chief Edomite city, was good farm land. Probably it was Edomite tribes who conflicted with the kings of Jerusalem so frequently, and the fact that Edomites barred Judaean access to the Gulf of Aqabah was one of the chief causes of the conflict.

PHILISTIA
Philistines settled on the southern Syro-Palestinian coast near the beginning of the Iron Age. Often at war with the Israelites, they gave their name to the whole region. 'Palestine' is derived from 'Philistia,' the land of the Philistines.

MOAB
Northern Moab was much disputed territory which probably changed hands between the Moabites, Ammonites, Israelites, and Arameans of Damascus. Moab proper, south of the R. Arnon, was not so easily accessible to outsiders. The opening chapter of the Book of Ruth is set in Moab. King Mesha of Moab paid annual tribute to Ahab, but rebelled against Israel after Ahab died.

PHOENICIA
The Phoenicians belonged to the same race with essentially the same 'Semitic' language as the Canaanites, Israelites, Moabites, etc. They occupied the Syro-Palestinian coast north of approximately Mt Carmel and became experienced seamen. Solomon depended heavily upon them in his shipping venture from the Gulf of Aqabah as well as in connection with his various building activities.

AMMON
The chief city of the Ammonites was Rabbath-ammon, situated at the head of one of the main tributaries of the R. Jabbok. Although a relatively modest kingdom, the Ammonites were often in conflict with the Israelites. No doubt much of the warfare concerned territorial claims in Gilead and Northern Moab.

ARAM
'Aram' was the ancient name for Syria; and one of the several strong Aramaean city-states, Damascus, played the most important role in Israelite affairs. Damascus competed with Israel and Ammon for control of the northern Transjordan (Bashan and Gilead). On at least one occasion, during the reign of Hazael in the 9th century, Damascus dominated much of Syro-Palestine.

ISRAEL AND JUDAH
Except during the reigns of David and Solomon there were two Israelite kingdoms. The northern kingdom known as 'Israel' or 'Ephraim' and the southern kingdom known as 'Judah'. Israel ceased to exist as an autonomous kingdom after its defeat by Assyria in 722 BC. Judah survived the long years of Assyrian domination, but was destroyed by the Babylonians in 587 BC.

HITTITES
Although the old Hittite empire which flourished in Anatolia during the Late Bronze Age had passed from the scene, several cities in northern Syria contemporary with the Israelite monarchies were still known as 'Hittite' cities. Their connection with the old Hittite empire is unclear, and only rarely do they figure in the biblical narratives.

ASSYRIA AND BABYLONIA
Two rival city-states which emerged as empires during the late Iron Age, dominated Mesopotamian affairs. The Assyrian empire (8th-7th centuries BC) incorporated all of Syro-Palestine and much of Egypt. The northern Israelite kingdom was destroyed by the Assyrians and became an Assyrian province. The collapse of the Assyrian empire was followed by a period of Babylonian imperialism. The Babylonians destroyed Jerusalem and carried many Judaeans into exile.

Nile Delta

EGYPT

Great Sea (Mediterranean Sea)

Sea of Chinnereth (Sea of Galilee)

Valley of Jezreel

ISRAEL

Sinai

Ashkelon • • Ashdod
Gaza • **PHILISTIA** • Ekron
Shechem •
R. Jordan

• Jerusalem

Transjordan

Gath • **JUDAH**
• Hebron

AMMON
R. Jabbok
Rabbath-ammon •

Salt Sea (Dead Sea)

Negeb

MOAB

E D O M

Arabah | R. Arnon

1/ Map below
Kingdoms in Syria and Palestine at c 1000 BC.

2/ Left and below
Examples of Philistine pottery. The language of the Philistines, who arrived in Palestine from the end of the Late Bronze Age is unknown, as no Philistine inscriptions have yet been uncovered by archeologists. However, the Philistines did leave behind an important part of their cultural heritage in the style and decoration of their pottery. It is believed to have derived from an Aegean prototype, and is distinguished by its geometric and linear designs. It was often painted in black and red on a white background. The main shapes include bowls, stirrup jars and kraters with two handles.

2

ARAMAEANS

Several Aramaean city-states flourished in the area approximated by present-day Syria. The Aramaeans spoke a Semitic language very closely related to Hebrew and which eventually became an international language throughout the Middle East. Classical geographers referred to the region of the Aramaean cities as 'Syria'; and 'Aram' normally is translated 'Syria' in the ancient Greek versions of the Bible. Damascus was the most prominent Aramaean city in close proximity to the Israelites, and certain of the kings of Damascus figure significantly in the biblical narratives (eg, II SAM 8.5-12; I KINGS 11.23-25; etc).

Ammon was essentially a city-state, with its chief city (Rabbah, or Rabbath-ammon) situated on a southeastern branch of the River Jabbok where it springs at the edge of the desert. Further south and parallel to the Dead Sea on the east was the land of Moab – a strip of cultivable land about 20 miles wide, rolling plateau, sandwiched between the Dead Sea escarpment and the desert. A steep river canyon, the River Arnon of ancient times separated northern Moab from Moab proper and rendered the former more vulnerable to outside encroachment. Northern Moab might be thought of as a continuation of Gilead, the Transjordanian highlands east of the River Jordan. This Gilead–northern Moab region was good agricultural land, so naturally the Ammonite and Moabite kings sought to control as much of it as possible, as did the Israelite kings west of the Jordan and occasionally even the Aramaean kings of Damascus. The Israelites claimed all of this disputed region on grounds that Moses had taken it from an ancient Amorite king.

Settled south-east and south-west of the Dead Sea, on both sides of the Arabah, were the Edomites – mostly villagers and semi-nomadic tribal groups. The region immediately southeast of the Dead Sea represented the best agricultural land available to the Edomites. Here would have been the centre of Edomite population and their chief city, Bosrah (present-day Buseirah). However, the numerous wars between the Israelites (Judaeans) and Edomites probably were primarily to do with conflicting interests in the region southwest of the Dead Sea, particularly attempts on the part of Israelite (and Judaean) kings to gain access to the Gulf of Aqabah and control the city port of Ezion-geber.

main cities: Ashdod, Ashkelon, Ekron, Gath, and Gaza. Other groups of Sea Peoples may have settled along the Palestinian coast as well, but were not distinguished from the Philistines by the biblical writers. Eventually it was the Philistines whose name was given to the whole region – ie, the name 'Palestine' is derived from 'Philistia'.

Still further north along the coast, where good ports encouraged sea trade (ie, northward from approximately Mount Carmel), were the Phoenician cities. The Phoenicians were part of the indigenous Semitic population of Syro-Palestine who developed extensive maritime trade and established colonies on distant Mediterranean shores (eg, Carthage in North Africa). Tyre and Sidon were major Phoenician cities in close proximity to the Israelites and thus are mentioned often in the Bible (eg, II SAM 5.11; I KINGS 5.2; 7.13-46; 9.26-28; 10.11-12, 22; EZEK 27-28; ISA 23; JER 25.22; AMOS 1.9-10; JOEL 3.4).

> 'NOW THESE ARE THE NATIONS WHICH THE LORD LEFT, TO TEST ISRAEL BY THEM... THESE ARE THE NATIONS: THE FIVE LORDS OF THE PHILISTINES, AND ALL THE CANAANITES, AND THE SIDONIANS, AND THE HIVITES WHO DWELT ON MOUNT LEBANON, AND FROM MOUNT BA'ALHERMON AS FAR AS THE ENTRANCE OF HAMATH.'
> JUDG 3.1-4

1/ Kingdoms of the Iron Age

ALASHIYA (CYPRUS)

Anatolia

HITTITES

R. Orontes

PHOENICIA

Tyre Sidon

ARAM

Damascus

ASSYRIAN INFLUENCE

R. Euphrates

BABYLONIA

THE Bible presupposes a first-hand knowledge of the geography and place-names of ancient Palestine. One would expect this, as most of the biblical materials emerged from people who were living on the land. The stories in I-II SAM about old Eli, the prophet Samuel, and the kings Saul and David are especially attentive to geographical detail and refer to numerous local places by names which would have been well known to the ancient Israelites.

Unfortunately, there are some difficulties involved in mapping the biblical stories, to the extent that all such maps are hypothetical in varying degrees. Locations of the major cities of ancient Palestine can be established with a reasonable degree of certainty. Difficulties often arise, however, with less prominent villages and landmarks. Consider, for example, the story of Saul's search for his father's asses in I SAM 9-10 (see Map 2). One reads in verses 4-5 that he passed through the hill country of Ephraim, the land of Shalishah, the land of Shaalim, the land of Benjamin, and eventually reached the land of Zuph. Except for the references to Ephraim and Benjamin, which point to the

THE INSTITUTION OF THE MONARCHY

MAPPING BIBLICAL NARRATIVES

Locating biblical place names on a modern map has been a major concern of scholars for the past century and a half. Although immense progress has been made by archaeologists, geographers and historians, the exact location of many places mentioned in the Bible remains unknown and some site identifications are fiercely contested.

central hill country north of Jerusalem as the general setting of the story, none of the 'lands' mentioned in these three verses can be located with confidence.

Sometimes more than one ancient city or village bore the same name, or a very similar name, which presents

further difficulties. For example, the names 'Geba', 'Gibeah', and 'Gibeon' are all based on an old Semitic word which meant 'hill'. Accordingly, one encounters biblical references to 'Geba of Benjamin', 'Geba of Saul', 'Gibeah of Benjamin', 'Gibeah of Saul', 'Gibeah of Phinehas', 'Gibeon', and a particular hill (or 'Gibeah') near Kiriath-jearim – all in contexts which point to the hill country north of Jerusalem. Scholars agree that these were not all the same place; yet recognize that they were not all different places either, and disagree on exactly how many different places were in fact involved.

Still further problems arise in cases where the ancient manuscripts of the Bible are difficult to translate, or where they present variant readings. II SAM 24 reports that David conducted a census of his kingdom, for example, and verses 5-7 describe the area covered by the census officials. Unfortunately, the syntax of these verses seems garbled in the standard Hebrew manuscripts, and it is unclear whether some of the words should be translated as proper names:

'They crossed the Jordan and camped at Aroer, south [?], the city in the middle of the valley, Gad and to Jazer. And they came to Gilead and to the land of Tahtimhodshi [?] and they came to Dan-yaan [?] and they went around to Sidon and they came to the fortress of Tyre and to all the cities of the Hivites and Canaanites; and they went out to the Negeb of Judah, Beersheba.'

Some of the ancient Greek manuscripts (those of the so-called Lucianic recension) provide a less garbled text for these verses, but also with slightly different implications.

The story of how David killed the giant Goliath in I SAM 17 is not so difficult to follow geographically. Most of the places mentioned are well known (see page 79). Note, however, that the story reflects a common folk theme – innocent young lad accomplishes heroic deed and receives great riches along with the hand of king's daughter in marriage – and includes details which conflict with information provided in other biblical passages. One would assume from I SAM 16.14-23, for example, that David had already left Bethlehem and joined Saul's court before the Goliath incident. II SAM 21.19 credits another Bethlehemite, Elhanan, with killing Goliath. According to II SAM 5, Jerusalem did not

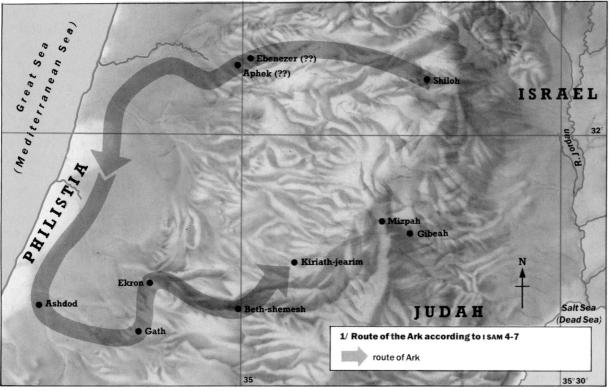

1/ **Route of the Ark according to** I SAM 4-7

→ route of Ark

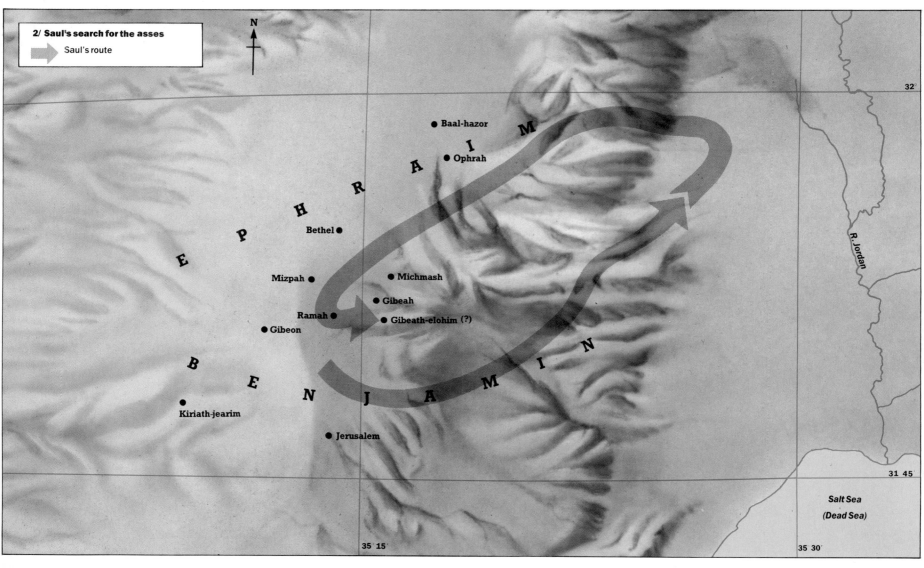

2/ **Saul's search for the asses**

→ Saul's route

1/ Map left
Mapping the route of the wanderings of the Ark highlights the problems of site identification (see text).

2/ Map below
The description of Saul's search for the asses in I SAM 9-10 is a

tantalizing mixture of place names of which some can be located on a modern map, but most of which cannot (see text).

3/ Map right
The route taken by Edward Robinson in his attempt to identify biblical sites (see text).

fall into Israelite hands until after Saul's death. In short, the story poses another mapping difficulty – how to treat stories which are of doubtful historicity. That both scholars and general readers differ on the historicity of biblical events further complicates the matter.

Often the question to be posed is not whether a particular story is legend *or* history, but whether it mixes legend *with* history. The account of the travels of the Ark in I SAM 4.1–7.2 is a case in point (see Map 1). The narrative begins with the Ark at Shiloh in the charge of the old priest

Eli and his two ill-behaved sons. Then the scene shifts to Aphek and Ebenezer, where the Israelite and Philistine armies are camped in preparation for battle. Battle is joined and it appears that the Philistines will be victorious, whereupon the Israelites bring the Ark into the fray in hopes that this will turn the tide. It does not; the Philistines rout the Israelites, Eli's sons are killed, and Eli himself dies upon hearing the news. What is worse, the Philistines capture the Ark and take it to Ashdod, one of their chief cities. But now the Ark begins to bring troubles upon the Philistines – the statue of their god Dagon collapses before it and the people of Ashdod are struck by a plague. The Ark is transferred to Ekron, another Philistine city, with similar results. Finally, in desperation, the Philistines place the Ark on a cart yoked to two milch cows and drive them away. The cows pull the Ark to Beth-shemesh where it is taken into custody by Levites. The Levites take it to the house of Abinadab at Gibeah (or 'the hill') near Kiriath-jearim. There it remains, presumably, until David transferres it to Jerusalem (the story seems to continue in II SAM 6).

This story also presents what many would regard as legendary overtones and seems to conflict with information provided elsewhere. If the Ark was with the Philistines or at Kiriath-jearim from the time of Eli's death until David transferred it to Jerusalem, for example, how does it happen to be on the scene at one of Saul's battles and in the hands of one of Eli's descendants (see I SAM 14.3)? Another intriguing aspect of the story is that it includes motifs and details which other stories in I SAM associate with Samuel and/or Saul. Note that Samuel likewise is reported to have had two ill-behaved sons who misused their priestly office. Samuel and Saul both are involved in major battles with the Philistines – Samuel's occurred at Ebenezer, Saul's near Aphek. Saul's battle also ended with disastrous defeat for Israel including the death of Saul and his sons. Did the careers of Eli, Samuel, and Saul actually include these striking similarities? Or is it possible that these stories present us with a somewhat garbled folk memory which tends to blend together three of Israel's early heroes?

The issue is sharpened when one considers more closely the implications of the different stories regarding the locations of Aphek and Ebenezer. One would assume from the story of the travels of the Ark summarized above that Aphek and Ebenezer were situated near to each other and somewhere on the Philistine frontier. Yet the account of Saul's last battle clearly places its Aphek much further north, near Mount Gilboa (I SAM 29.1; 31.1), while the story of Samuel's battle at Ebenezer places the latter deep in the central hill country near Mizpah (I SAM 7.12). Do these stories preserve authentic memory of two different Ebenezers, two different Apheks, and three major Philistine battles? Or were there only two battles – one at Ebenezer near Mizpah and the other at Aphek near Gilboa – which are remembered out of context and blended together in the story of the Ark?

THE JOURNEY OF EDWARD ROBINSON
It was not until 1838 that modern research in biblical geography can be said to have begun. In that year Edward Robinson, an American scholar who had a thorough training in the Bible, travelled up and down the land recording accurately the modern names of towns and villages; in 1852 he made a similar expedition. Thus with an accurate knowledge of modern Arabic place-names he proceeded to propose biblical names on the basis of a simple proposition: ancient names cling tenaciously to places even though peoples and languages have changed. The echo of ancient Hebrew names, he maintained, could frequently be heard in the sounds by which villagers identified their home.

An example of his method is to be seen in the results obtained on a two-day trip, 4-5 June 1838, through the area north of Jerusalem, ancient Benjamin and southern Ephraim. In the name Anata he could hear Anathoth, the home of Jeremiah; (el) Jib he took as a shortened form of Gibeon, where the sun was said to have stood still; er-Ram was Ramah; Jeba' was probably the site of Geba; Mukhmas was Michmash, the place of Jonathan's victory over the Philistines; Beitin, the site of Bethel.

Since Robinson's day archaeology has produced evidence for identifications. The discovery of ruins dated to periods when a site is said to have been inhabited increases the possibility of equating place names.

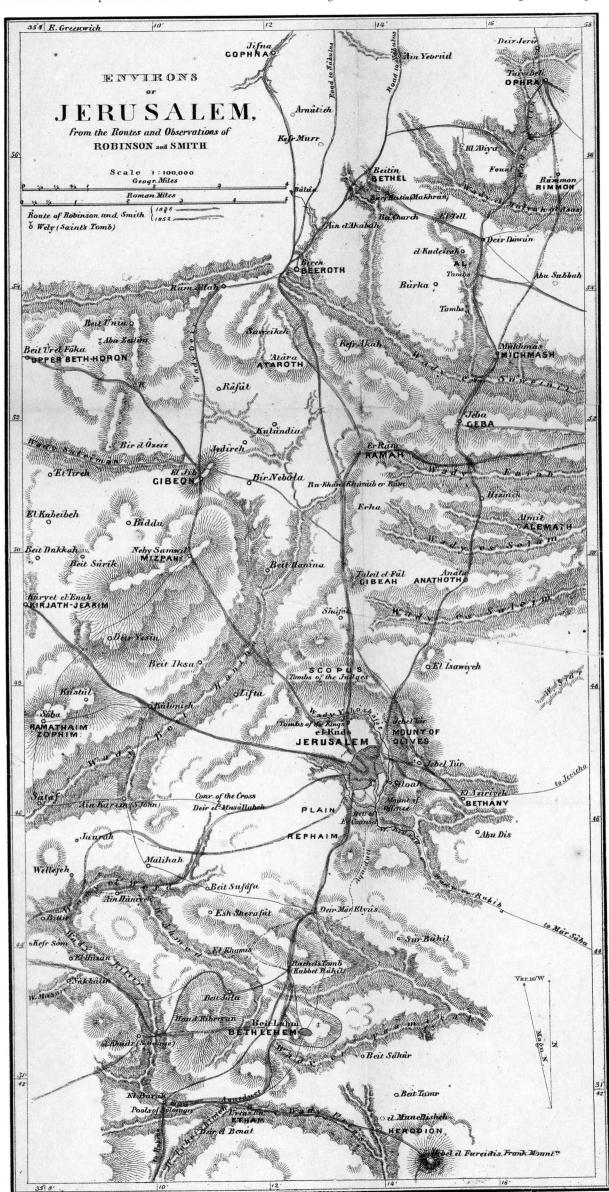

ENVIRONS
or
JERUSALEM,
from the Routes and Observations of
ROBINSON and SMITH.

Scale 1:100,000
Geogr. Miles

'WHEN THE PHILISTINES CAPTURED THE ARK OF GOD, THEY CARRIED IT FROM EBENEZER TO ASHDOD: THEN THE PHILISTINES TOOK THE ARK OF GOD AND BROUGHT IT INTO THE HOUSE OF DAGON AND SET IT UP BESIDE DAGON.'
I SAM 5.1-2

SAUL lived approximately 1000 BC and belonged to the small Israelite tribe of Benjamin which was overshadowed by (if not a sub-branch of) the neighbouring tribe of Ephraim. Both tribes were settled in the hill country north of Jerusalem, along with various other population elements such as Hivites and Archites. Jerusalem was not yet a city of prominence, of course, and the villagers of the hill country were vulnerable to oppression from all sides. Thus Saul emerged on the scene as a local military hero who led the Benjaminite-Ephraimite resistance against surrounding enemies, especially the Philistines. Proclaimed king by his countrymen in response to his early victories, Saul spent the remainder of his career, a reign of unknown duration, defending what thus became the fledgling kingdom of Israel. His public career ended the same way it had begun, in battle. Both Saul and his son Jonathan were killed while fighting the Philistines on the slopes of Mt Gilboa.

Saul accomplished two major victories early in his career, one against the Philistines in his own Benjaminite neighbourhood, at the strategic crossing of a steep valley which separated Gibeah and Michmash (I SAM 13.2–14.46); and one against the Ammonites who were attacking the city of Jabesh in Gilead (I SAM 11). Although the defeat of the

THE INSTITUTION OF THE MONARCHY

THE KINGDOM OF SAUL

By proclaiming Saul as their king, the Israelites entered a new phase of their history. Traditional segmented society gave way to centralized political power. David would solidify and expand the kingdom; Solomon would oversee its transformation into a typical oriental monarchy. Eventually the kingdom would be divided and then conquered by its powerful neighbours. But briefly Israel was a united and independent monarchy of some importance.

Ammonites is reported first in the Bible, it is doubtful that Saul could have collected an army and undertaken a military campaign so far afield as Gilead unless he had already expelled the Philistines from his own home area. More likely, therefore, Saul's first military venture was the surprise seizure of Gibeah which controlled the southern end of the crossing and may have had a small fortification of some sort. When Philistine reinforcements arrived, they camped at Michmash on the opposite (northern) side of the

crossing and began to raid the countryside (see especially I SAM 13.16-18). The turning point in the struggle occurred, according to the biblical narrative, when Jonathan made a surprise raid on the Philistine camp. The Philistines were routed and fled the hill country (see Map 2). It should be noted that the biblical narrative which reports this early episode in Saul's career presents some historical difficulties. There is some evidence to suggest, for example, that Saul, rather than Jonathan, was the hero of the Michmash raid in the original telling of the story. Be that as it may, the Philistines were expelled from the hill country and Saul established his residence at Gibeah.

The biblical account of the Jabesh-gilead victory in I SAM 11 begins, therefore, with Saul residing at Gibeah (see Map 1). The Ammonites attacked Jabesh, a Gileadite city with Israelite tribal connections, and when the Jabeshites appealed for a peace settlement, the Ammonite king offered impossible terms: 'On this condition I will make a treaty with you, that I gouge out all your right eyes, and thus put disgrace upon all Israel' (I SAM 11.2). Thereupon the Jabeshites, having heard no doubt of Saul's recent victory over the Philistines, sent to Gibeah for help. Saul hurriedly mustered an army, marched to Jabesh, and saved the day.

Two other military campaigns, recorded in I SAM 15.1-9 and 31.1-7 respectively, give some impression of the extent of Saul's domain by the end of his career. The first of these passages describes a raid conducted by Saul against the Amalekites, a semi-nomadic people who roamed the Negeb and often raided the villages of the hill country south of Jerusalem (eg, I SAM 30.1-3). Possibly some of the villagers of this region appealed to Saul for protection against the Amalekites in the same way that the Jabeshites had called on him for protection against the Ammonites. Saul defeated the Amalekites and then set up a victory monument at Carmel, a town southeast of Hebron. Possibly this was to signify his claim to political authority over the area. That he exercised some degree of political authority in the southern hill country is suggested also by the fact that Saul was able to move more freely in that region in pursuit of David while the local people are pictured reporting to Saul from time to time on David's whereabouts (I SAM 23.6-14; 24.1; 26.1).

The second military action which gives some indication of the extent of Saul's kingdom by the end of his reign is the one recorded in I SAM 31.1-7, the final battle with the Philistines in which he and Jonathan met their deaths (see Map 3). The Philistines camped at Aphek on the eve of the battle, which itself was fought on the slopes of Mt Gilboa at the southeastern end of the Jezreel Valley. Presumably Saul controlled the central hill country as far north as the Jezreel, therefore, and possibly an attempt on his part to secure control of the valley itself was what occasioned the battle. By the same measure, his kingdom obviously did not include Galilee.

One should not think of Saul's kingdom as having a highly organized administration or precisely defined boundaries in any case. Certainly in peripheral areas the degree of Saul's authority will have varied from time to time, depending on whether his troops were present or

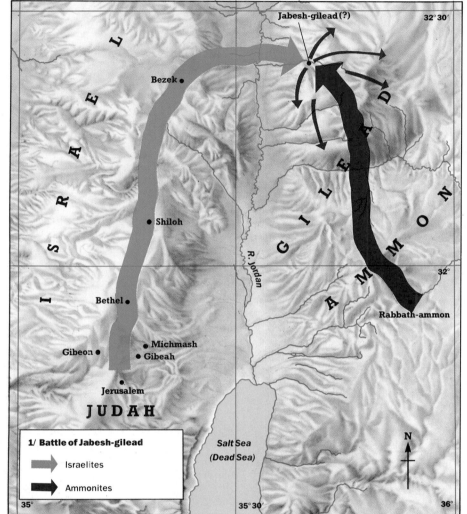

1/ Map left
According to I SAM 11 Saul was sent for by the Jabeshites when they were attacked by Ammonites. He came up from Gibeah and scattered the Ammonite army.

2/ Map right
I SAM 14 describes a battle between Israelites (led by Saul and Jonathan) and the Philistines at Michmash. This reconstruction of the clash tells the story in 10 stages:
1 Saul is at Geba with 600 men.
2 The Philistines had a blocking force at the passage of Michmash.
3 Saul moves to Migron.
4 Jonathan and his armour bearer carry out a raid.
5 In a surprise attack Jonathan kills some Philistines.
6 There is panic in the Philistines camp at Michmash.
7 A frontal assault by Saul's force adds to the Philistines' confusion.
8 The Philistines are defeated.
9 They retreat to the north and west.

3/ Map below
Saul's final battle, in which he and Jonathan were killed, took place on Mt Gilboa. The Bible story comes from I SAM 31:
1 The Philistines are at Aphek.
2 They advance along the Via Maris to Shunem.
3 Saul's army is on Mt Gilboa.
4 Saul encamps at Jezreel.
5 Before the battle he goes to consult the witch of En-dor.
6 In the ensuing battle Saul and his three sons are killed.
7 Their bodies are taken to Beth-shean.
8 The Israelites flee to Gilboa.
9 Saul is finally buried at Jabesh.

1/ Battle of Jabesh-gilead
- Israelites
- Ammonites

whether the local people needed his protection against other threats. But even in the Benjamin-Ephraim-Gilead zone, the core of his territorial domain, some cities may have remained independent. Note also that Jerusalem was never incorporated into his kingdom (see II SAM 5.6-8).

Actually very few details are known about Saul's reign, other than the military actions mentioned above and his dealings with David. Moreover, there are conflicting reports on how it happened that David, from the tribe of Judah and the village of Bethlehem, came to join Saul's court. Whatever the circumstances, David quickly gained a reputation as a daring and successful Philistine fighter, became close friends with Jonathan, and married Michal, Saul's daughter. Eventually, and probably with good reason

as it turned out, Saul began to regard David as a threat even to his own position as king, and also to Jonathan's chances of ascending the throne. Thus Saul sought to kill David, who escaped to the vicinity of Adullam, southwest of Jerusalem. There David was joined by others who opposed Saul for one reason or another. When Saul learned of David's whereabouts in the Adullam vicinity, David and his men transferred to the 'wilderness' area southeast of Hebron, where Saul, with support from the local people, continued to search and pursue. Finally, still on the run from Saul, David joined the Philistines and placed his army in their service. Specifically, he allied himself with Achish, the Philistine ruler of Gath, who in turn, as a mark of favour, assigned to David the city of Ziklag.

Thus it transpired that David and his men were allied with the Philistines at the time of the battle of Mt Gilboa in which Saul and Jonathan were killed, and actually marched with the Philistines to Aphek on the eve of the battle. The Philistines, however, fearing that they might switch sides during the fighting, sent David and his troops back to Ziklag (I SAM 29). The battle was a disaster for Israel, with Saul's kingdom left in shambles.

'AND SAMUEL SAID TO ALL THE PEOPLE, "DO YOU SEE HIM WHOM THE LORD HAS CHOSEN? THERE IS NONE LIKE HIM AMONG ALL THE PEOPLE." AND ALL THE PEOPLE SHOUTED, "LONG LIVE THE KING!"'
I SAM 10.24

Michmash

Philistines blocking force

Jonathan surprises and slays Philistines

Jonathan and armour bearer

Geba

Saul's force attacks Philistines

Migron (??)

Saul's army

Philistine's retreat

2/ Battle of Michmash
Israelites
Philistines

TRANSJORDAN

Mount Gilboa

Beth-shean

Bodies of Saul and his sons taken to Beth-shean

Israelites flee after battle

Shunem

Saul visits En-dor

Jezreel

Philistine forces

Saul's army

Battle of Gilboa

To Aphek

3/ Battle of Gilboa
Israelites
Philistines

In the later Stone Age the usual method of burial in Palestine was 'inhumation'. The body was laid in a shallow hole dug into the ground, often beneath the surface upon which people lived. A few objects were sometimes buried with the body – a jar or two, simple items of adornment, and occasionally a cult object. Such provisions indicate that Stone Age people believed in some kind of existence after death. That belief continued in later periods, when burial practices became more elaborate.

By the Chalcolithic period (5th-4th millennium BC), there was considerable diversity of funerary practice. Burials were often made in containers resembling houses or shrines. About 50 circular cist-graves belonging to an extensive Chalcolithic mortuary complex, have recently been unearthed at the site of Shiqmim in the Negeb desert. Also from this period are clay ossuaries (bone containers) which were placed in cave-tombs.

During the Early Bronze Age (3150-2200 BC) (the era of the first great Canaanite city-states) the people of Palestine not only buried their dead in natural or man-made cave tombs but also practised cremation. This latter practice is attested at Bab edh-Dhira, located on the eastern edge of the Lisan Peninsula, where charnel houses have been found. Bodies may have been brought from considerable distances for reburial at this large funerary site. Cremation was occasionally practised in later periods, but was never the predominant form of rites for the dead.

From about 2100 BC until Judah's final days at the end of the Iron Age (c 600 BC), the dominant kind of tomb was a low chamber cut from the rock, approached by a shaft or passageway and closed with a single stone or pile of rubble. The shape of the chamber was often roughly circular, but

TOMBS AND BURIAL PRACTICES

Almost all ancient peoples conducted the burial of the dead within a religious context. Their practices stemmed from the belief that there was a realm into which the spirit of the deceased person might enter and live in eternal contentment. Objects left with the dead were thought to accompany the spirit into the afterlife.

rectangular and irregular forms were also used; the size of chambers varied from between 3 and 10ft. These tombs served as burial vaults primarily for families. Sometimes family tombs were enlarged and used repeatedly for several centuries. As previously, persons were buried with weapons and foodstuffs, in the expectation of an afterlife.

At the height of the Canaanite culture in the Middle Bronze Age, around the 18th-17th centuries BC, not only food offerings and personal items of apparel were left in tombs but also beds, tables, stools, baskets, gameboards and many other objects of everyday life. The re-use and sometimes enlargement of earlier tombs was a common practice, and tombs frequently consisted of several interconnected chambers. Sometimes burials, usually multiple, were made in cist graves, and infants were often interred in jars under the houses in which their families lived.

Many of the same assumptions and practices continued during the early centuries of the Israelite period, the Iron

Age (c 1200-600 BC). Occasionally new cultural influxes brought variations, such as the preference for anthropoid sarcophagi which some archaeologists attribute to the Philistines. Although the most frequent form of burial was that in which the body was laid on its back in a rock-cut chamber, the position of bodies varied considerably, and sometimes large quantities of bones were piled up in a tomb, having been pushed into a heap when there was need for new interments. Large quantities of funerary objects often accumulated in tombs, particularly those which contained many burials. Jars continued to be used occasionally for the interment of infants, and cremation continued to be practiced by some.

Toward the end of the Iron Age single-grave burials began appearing, and by the Persian period were frequent. Fewer food offerings were deposited with burials and proportionately larger numbers of small, varied objects were interred, such as mirrors, cosmetic implements, jewellery, amulets, and weapons. In some places in Palestine, small vessels imported from Syria, Egypt or Greece, containing small quantities of costly perfumes, were popular.

During the Hellenistic period (332 BC–AD 37) tombs began to undergo change in both form and content. Rock-cut tombs became more uniform in plan and were provided with narrow loculi (burial slots) radiating out from a central chamber, and tomb walls began to be painted. Multiple chambers again became frequent. There was a continuing trend away from burying the dead with objects of everyday life and toward the use of token funerary gifts such as vials of unguents and terracotta lamps. Carved stone sarcophagi began to appear in more elegant tombs.

Hellenistic influences continued into the Early Roman

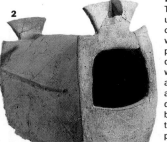

2/ Left and below
This pottery ossuary from Azor was used by people of the Ghassulian culture (c 4000–3300 BC). In it were placed the bones of a dead person after the flesh had decayed. Dolmens (see below) were made of large stone slabs and formed the burial chambers of ancient tombs. The date of the dolmens of Palestine is uncertain, but many authorities now place them in the Middle Bronze I period.

3/ Above
A representative group of Early Bronze Age pottery, including a large bowl with a red slip and burnish on the exterior and a buff interior, several jugs, a *pithos* or large storage jar, and a square stand thought to have been used as an incense burner. These items are from T. Arad.

4/ Right
A section through a Middle Bronze Age tomb at Dhahr Mirzbaneh with some of its contents surrounding it. These rock-cut tombs are particularly common and could vary in size. They were intended primarily for families but could accommodate other groups such as warriors slain in battle.

5/ Left
Tomb P19 was discovered by Kathleen Kenyon at Jericho. It dates from the Middle Bronze II (2000-1500 BC) period and is a very fine example of a multiple simultaneous burial, unusual in this period, in which the bodies have been laid out side by side surrounded by their funeral offerings of furniture, a wooden table and a stool with a string seat, storage jars, which contained grain and wine and/or oil, bowls, which contained pieces of meat, and jugs probably containing beer.
Tombs of this type often consisted of several chambers which were interconnected. It was a common practice not only to enlarge the tomb but also to re-use chambers after removing the bones from earlier burials. Ancient Jericho was not a very large city but has become famous for its rich archaeological finds, among which were many intact Canaanite tombs such as this one.

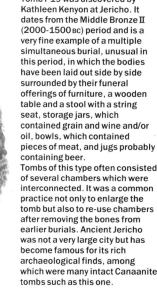

Sea of Chinnereth
(Sea of Galilee)

Beth-shear

P A L

Dor

Great Sea

(Mediterranean Sea

1/ Map right
The map will help to locate the findspots of the tombs and grave goods illustrated. However, it should be remembered that these finds are usually not unique and the same or similar grave types may well occur in other locations. The picture which emerges from such finds is one of changing fashions in funerary practice which nevertheless overlie a continuation of certain beliefs.

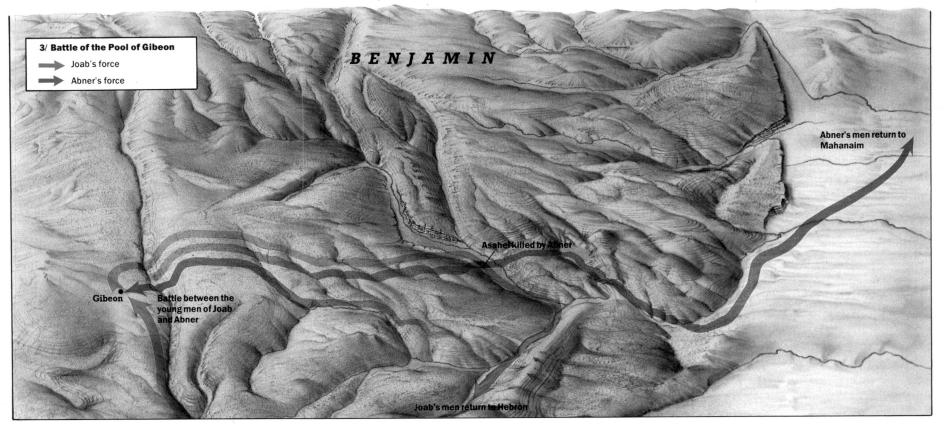

3/ Battle of the Pool of Gibeon
→ Joab's force
→ Abner's force

B E N J A M I N

Abner's men return to Mahanaim

Asahel killed by Abner

Gibeon ● ← Battle between the young men of Joab and Abner

Joab's men return to Hebron

Judaean Hills

Valley of Elah

rout of Philistine force

4/ Battle of the Valley of Elah
→ Israelites
→ Philistines

4/ Map left
After David slew Goliath in the Valley of Elah, the Israelites fell upon the Philistine army and drove them back towards Philistia. This map illustrates the account in I SAM 17.

3/ Map above
II SAM 2.12-32 describes the battle between Joab and Abner at the Pool of Gibeon. The map shows the pursuit of Abner's men by Joab's force and the death of Asahel.

pluralistic constituency than Saul's Israel.

One is not surprised to read in the biblical account, therefore, that at some point after establishing himself in Jerusalem David had to put down two rebellions. One of these was led by Absalom his son, apparently the crown prince the other by Sheba, a Benjaminite.

Appealing to popular grievances, and drawing support from both Israelites and Judaeans, Absalom had himself crowned king in Hebron and then marched on Jerusalem. David evacuated the city followed by a core of loyalists and fled to Mahanaim in Transjordan (the same city from which Ishbosheth had attempted to rule). Thus Absalom actually ruled in Jerusalem for a short time, and had he moved quickly against David's fleeing army, the course of history may have turned out quite differently. Absalom delayed until he had lost the tactical advantage, however, and then, when he did pursue, was himself killed in the resulting battle. II SAM 18.9-15 describes how Joab executed him when the long hair for which he was famous became entangled in the branches of a tree.

The second rebellion was initiated by Sheba, a Benjaminite, and seems to have received less widespread support. It was quickly crushed, in any case, and Sheba himself beheaded, having fled to Abel-beth-maacah. Since Sheba was from the same tribe as Saul, and his call was directed specifically to the Israelites exhorting them to reject David's rule, the possibility must be considered that he hoped to revive the Saulide kingdom and place one of Saul's descendants on its throne.

'We have no portion in David,
    and we have no inheritance in the son of Jesse;
every man to his tents, O Israel!' (II SAM 20.1)

David's execution of Saul's remaining descendants, on the other hand, which is reported in the biblical account immediately following the Sheba incident (II SAM 21.1-14), may have been an added precaution on David's part lest there be any future attempts to revive the Saulide dynasty. Only Mephibosheth, a cripple son of Jonathan, was spared; and he apparently was confined to the royal court in Jerusalem (II SAM 9).

'THEN KING DAVID WENT IN AND SAT BEFORE THE LORD, AND SAID "WHO AM I, O LORD GOD, AND WHAT IS MY HOUSE, THAT THOU HAST BROUGHT ME THUS FAR? AND YET THIS WAS A SMALL THING IN THY EYES, O LORD GOD; THOU HAST SPOKEN ALSO OF THY SERVANT'S HOUSE FOR A GREAT WHILE TO COME, AND HAST SHOWN ME FUTURE GENERATIONS, O LORD GOD! AND WHAT MORE CAN DAVID SAY TO THEE? FOR THOU KNOWEST THY SERVANT, O LORD GOD! BECAUSE OF THY PROMISE, AND ACCORDING TO THY OWN HEART, THOU HAST WROUGHT ALL THIS GREATNESS..."' II SAM 7.18-21

THE most important areas of territorial expansion under David were firstly the Jezreel Valley and Galilee, which was taken largely at the expense of Hadadezer, king of Zobah; secondly the Transjordan, perhaps also taken at the expense of Hadadezer, but encroaching as well on traditional Ammonite and Moabite territory; and finally the Negeb, where David encountered Edomite resistance (see Map 2).

Early in his reign, David formed an alliance with Nahash, king of the Ammonites, which apparently remained in effect until Nahash died. Then hostilities erupted, with the result that David sent troops commanded by Joab to attack Rabbah, the chief Ammonite city. Eventually the city fell and Ammonite prisoners were consigned to forced labour (II SAM 10-12). It was in connection with the Ammonite war that David came into conflict with Hadadezer, the Aramaean king of Zobah.

ARAMAEAN WARS

David's Aramaean wars are mentioned in three biblical passages which unfortunately present a number of interpretational difficulties (II SAM 8.3-12; 10.6-19; and I KINGS 11.23-25).

Essentially the circumstances surrounding this conflict seem to have been as follows: the Ammonites, with their city under siege by David's soldiers, appealed to Hadadezer, who represented a major power in southern Aram at the time. Hadadezer dominated Damascus, for example, and probably considered Galilee and the northern Transjordan as belonging to his realm as well. Hadadezer responded with troops drawn from various Aramaean cities within his sphere of influence, but was defeated by David's army in two resulting battles – one before the gates of Rabbah, and one at Helam somewhere in the Transjordan. Thereupon Hadadezer withdrew and exerted no further influence in the Transjordan. Hadadezer also lost control of Damascus at that time to a marauding band led by Rezon.

David, accordingly, expanded his domain to include territory usually associated with Damascus (presumably some of the area between Damascus and Gilead). Possibly it was in this connection also that David gained possession of Galilee and territory as far north as the vicinity of Sidon.

Naturally Toi of Hamath, a longstanding enemy of Hadadezer, was pleased with the turn of events. Thus Toi sent his son to David with congratulations and gifts. Whether David invaded the heartland of Hadadezer's realm is unclear, depending on one's interpretation of II SAM 8.7-8. 'And David took the shields of gold which were carried by the servants of Hadadezer and brought them to Jerusalem. And from Betah and from Berothai, cities of Hadadezer, King David took very much bronze.' Does this passage mean that he actually took Betah (read Tibhath with I CHRON 18.8) and Berotha? And where were these cities located? In any case, the claim that David 'subjected' Aram is to be regarded as editorial exaggeration.

WARS WITH MOAB

David is reported to have defeated the Moabites as well, and to have executed by arbitrary selection two-thirds of the prisoners captured (II SAM 8.2). It is significant to note in this regard, moreover, that his census officials began at the

DAVID'S CONSOLIDATION OF THE KINGDOM

David was more successful than Saul in extending the frontiers of his domain and he was also more successful in dealing with the Philistines. However, the Philistines probably remained a potential threat during the reigns of both kings. David apparently remained on good terms with the Phoenicians, who continued to dominate the Mediterranean coast as far south as Mt Carmel.

Arnon (see pages 70 and 100). Even if David conducted military campaigns into Moab proper, the geographical isolation of that region would have rendered impractical any sort of permanent rule from Jerusalem.

Likewise, the report that David defeated the Edomites and placed garrisons in their land (read 'Edomites' rather than 'Aramaeans' in II SAM 8.13-14) should not be interpreted to mean that he established Jerusalemite control over all Edomite associated territory. The one battle reported took place 'in the Valley of Salt', probably to be identified with present-day Wadi el-Milh (which means 'Valley of Salt' in Arabic) between the Dead Sea and Beersheba. Presumably, therefore, it was Edomite-related tribal groups along his southern frontier which David defeated and garrisoned.

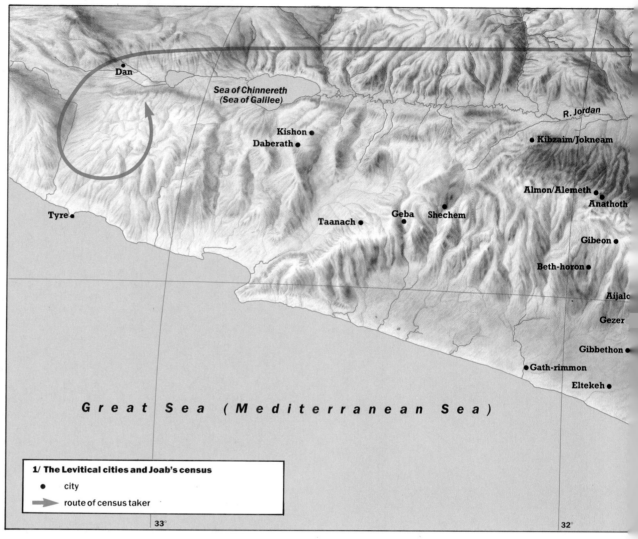

1/ The Levitical cities and Joab's census

●   city

➤   route of census taker

1/ Map above
From the description of David's census of the kingdom which was carried out by Joab and some of the army commanders (see II SAM 24.1-10) and from the lists of

Levitical cities (JOSH 21, I CHRON 6) it is possible to map places which existed at the time of David, although the location of some cities remains uncertain (see text).

2/ The kingdom of David

– – –   border of kingdom

➤   David's campaigns

Perhaps David wished also to secure access to the Gulf of Aqaba, although it was actually Solomon who developed the commercial potential of this port.

'UNCONQUERED' AND LEVITICAL CITIES

Two city lists which are not specifically associated with David in the Bible may nevertheless pertain to his reign. One of these is the list of 'unconquered cities' in JUDG 1.21; 27-36 (see page 64). Apparently these were cities with largely non-Israelite populations which remained independent until incorporated into the Israelite monarchy. Saul may have annexed some of them, but probably it was David who brought most of them under control. The other list is that of the Levitical cities recorded in two versions (JOSH 21.8-42, I CHRON 6.54-81). This Levitical list seems schematic in its present form – four cities listed for each of the 12 tribes – and earlier scholars generally regarded it as fictitious. The more recent tendency is to see it as an essentially authentic list, dating from the time of the monarchy, which was schematized by later editors. It is noteworthy, for example, that the cities listed, rather than representing an even geographical spread, tend to be clustered in areas which remained outside 'Israelite' control until David's conquests. There are indications, on the other hand, that David made heavy use of the Levites in his administration. Possibly, then, the Levitical cities served as administrative centres especially, although not entirely, in the areas which David had incorporated secondarily into the kingdom.

In summary, the area under David's direct control by the end of his reign must have included most of western Palestine (excluding Philistia and some Phoenician presence along the Mediterranean coast north of Mt Carmel) and a large portion of the Transjordan (from the Arnon northward to somewhere in the vicinity of Damascus). This is in keeping with the towns from which David's 'mighty men' were recruited (see II SAM 23.8-39, and the Chronicler's supplement in I CHRON 11.42-47) and with the coverage of Joab's census (see II SAM 24, I CHRON 21.1-26), although it must be kept in mind that there are interpretational problems with both texts. Most of the place-names in the list of David's 'mighty men' cannot be identified. Those which can be identified were situated largely, but not entirely, in the central hill country – eg, Kabzeel, Bethlehem, Tekoa, Anathoth, Gibeah, Gilo, and Carmel. The census is described only in very general fashion, on the other hand. and presents serious translation problems (see comments on pages 72-73).

Biblical atlases often depict David's kingdom as including much more extensive territory than attributed to him above on essentially two grounds. Firstly, certain biblical passages credit Solomon with a much more extensive realm. I KINGS 4.24 reports, for example, that Solomon 'had dominion over all the region west of the Euphrates from Tiphsah to Gaza, over all the kings west of Euphrates'. Secondly, since no wars of conquest are reported for Solomon, it is assumed that therefore he inherited this mini-empire from David, However, this line of reasoning does not take into account the editorial hyperbole characteristic of the biblical account of Solomon's reign. Moreover, embedded in the sweeping claims regarding Solomon's fabulous wisdom, wealth, and far-flung empire, are occasional details which suggest a territorial domain of more modest proportions – certainly no larger than that described above for David.

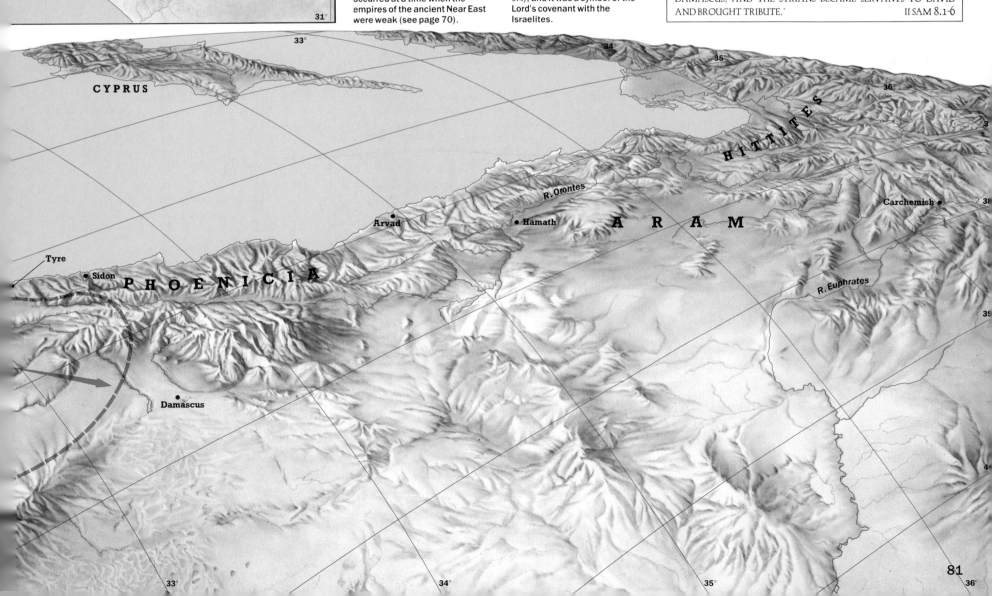

2/ Map below
Estimates of the extent of David's kingdom vary. However, he extended his territory in three areas. To the south David was constantly at war with the Philistines, and he placed garrisons in Edomite territory. David conquered part of Moab, north of the Arnon and defeated the Ammonites.
To the north, although David maintained good relations with Hiram of Tyre, he captured territory from Hadadezer the Aramaean king of Zobah. The expansion of the kingdom occurred at a time when the empires of the ancient Near East were weak (see page 70).

3/ Above
A later but rare depiction of the Ark of the Covenant taken from the 3 rd century AD synagogue at Capernaum. Having regained the Ark from the Philistines (see page 72), David placed it in Jerusalem, which therefore became the capital of his kingdom (see I CHRON 16.1).
EX 37 describes the construction of the Ark. It was constructed from acacia wood with gold inlay, and measured 4 x 2½ x 2½ ft. It contained the tablets with the 10 commandments, a golden urn with manna and Aaron's rod (HEB 9.4), and it was a symbol of the Lord's covenant with the Israelites.

'AFTER THIS DAVID DEFEATED THE PHILISTINES AND SUBDUED THEM AND DAVID TOOK METHEG-AMMAH OUT OF THE HAND OF THE PHILISTINES. AND HE DEFEATED MOAB... AND THE MOABITES BECAME SERVANTS TO DAVID AND BROUGHT TRIBUTE. DAVID ALSO DEFEATED HADADEZER THE SON OF REHOB, KING OF ZOBAH, AS HE WENT TO RESTORE HIS POWER AT THE RIVER EUPHRATES. AND DAVID TOOK FROM HIM A THOUSAND AND SEVEN HUNDRED HORSEMEN AND TWENTY THOUSAND FOOT SOLDIERS: AND DAVID HAMSTRUNG ALL THE CHARIOT HORSES BUT LEFT ENOUGH FOR A HUNDRED CHARIOTS. AND WHEN THE SYRIANS OF DAMASCUS CAME TO HELP HADADEZER KING OF ZOBAH, DAVID SLEW TWENTY-TWO THOUSAND MEN OF THE SYRIANS. THEN DAVID PUT GARRISONS IN ARAM OF DAMASCUS, AND THE SYRIANS BECAME SERVANTS TO DAVID AND BROUGHT TRIBUTE.' II SAM 8.1-6

SOLOMON who came to the throne of Israel in *c*965 BC was in a position to be the middle-man in the important trade in horses and chariots between Asia Minor and Egypt (I KINGS 10.28-29). It appears that Solomon's tradesmen were importing horses from the horse-rearing country of Cappadocia via the kingdom of Que, along the coastal region of Cilicia, and were supplying them to Egypt as well as to some of the Syrian kingdoms located to the west of the R. Euphrates. I KINGS 10.29 would seem to indicate that Solomon was obtaining wooden chariots from Egypt. Biblical sources also credit Solomon with maritime operations on the Red Sea and with expeditions of Phoenician-built ships sailing from Ezion-geber to Ophir (I KINGS 9.26-28; 10.11-12, 22). During Solomonic times, the Gulf of 'Aqaba was probably referred to as Ezion-geber. Ophir is usually identified with the land of 'Punt' along the eastern coast of Africa. Gold appears to have been the major import from Ophir and an ostracon found at T. Qasile had a Hebrew inscription referring to 'Gold [from] Ophir [belonging] to Beth-haran'.

Solomon also appears to have had commercial ties with the Queen of Sheba from Southern Arabia (I KINGS 10.1-3). The commercial negotiations between the two rulers took place against the background of a mutual exchange of 'presents' (I KINGS 10.10, 13) which was a well established diplomatic procedure at that time in the Near East. It is perhaps not

1/ Map far right
Solomon's kingdom had 12 tax districts which provided provisions for the royal household.

2/ Map below
Trade routes at the time of Solomon. (*c* 10th century BC).

coincidental that spices were not mentioned in the lists of imports obtained from Ophir, and this may indicate that Solomon and the Queen of Sheba struck a deal leaving the monopoly over the trade of frankincense and myrrh entirely in the hands of the Arabians. The Israelites also traded at

this time with Phoenicia and the Lebanese mountain communities for timber (I KINGS 5.10-11). According to the biblical text, Hiram from Tyre gave Solomon timber of cedar and fir in exchange for large quantities of wheat and olive oil.

EGYPTIAN TRADE
Due to the political weakness of the pharaonic government after the fall of the Ramesside house, Egypt was less active in foreign commerce than she had been up to that time. The closest commercial ties she enjoyed were with the cities of the Phoenician coast. From Byblos she sought the timber of the Lebanon, and gave in return luxury items, including metalwork, stoneware, statuary, papyrus and the aromatic products of Africa. Egypt's trade with the Sudan was virtually cut off after the loss of her African empire (*c* 1070 BC), but began to pick up again in the late 9th century BC with the rise of the independent kingdom of Cush. Thereafter until the coming of the Persians (525 BC) the Thebaid shows much closer contact with the Sudan in terms of artefacts and pottery than with the rest of Egypt. Trade items included gold,

SOLOMON'S BANQUET
'Solomon's provision for one day was thirty cors of fine flour, and sixty cors of meal, ten fat oxen, and twenty pasture-fed cattle, a hundred sheep, besides harts, gazelles, roebucks and fatted fowl.' (I KINGS 4.22)

ASHURNASIRPAL'S BANQUET
'When Ashurnasirpal, king of Assyria, inaugurated the palace in Calah, a palace of joy and (erected with) great ingenuity, he invited into it Ashur, the great lord and the gods of his entire country, (he prepared a banquet of) 1,000 fattened head of cattle, 1,000 calves, 10,000 stable sheep, 15,000 lambs – for my lady Ishtar (alone) 200 head of cattle and 1,000 *sihhu*-sheep – 1,000 spring lambs, 500 stags, 500 gazelles, 1,000 *ducks*, 500 geese, 500 *kurku*-geese, 1,000 *mesuku*-birds, 1,000 *qaribu*-birds, 10,000 doves, 10,000 *sukanunu*-doves, 10,000 other (assorted) small birds, 10,000 (assorted) fish, 10,000 jerboa, 10,000 (assorted) eggs; 10,000 loaves of bread, 10,000 (jars of) beer, 10,000 skins with wine, 10,000 pointed bottom vessels with *su'u*-seeds in sesame oil, 10,000 small pots with *sarhu*-condiment, 1,000 wooden crates with vegetables, 300 (containers with) oil, 300 (containers with) salted seeds, 300 (containers with) mixed *raqqute*-plants, 100 with *kudimmu*-spice, 100 (containers with)..., 100 (containers with) parched barley, 100 (containers with) green *abahsinnu*-stalks, 100 (containers with) fine mixed beer, 100 pomegranates, 100 bunches of grapes, 100 mixed *zamru*-fruits, 100 pistachio cones, 100 with the fruits of the *susi*-tree, 100 with garlic, 100 with onions, 100 with *kuniphu* (seeds), 100 with the ... of turnips, 100 with *hinhinnu*-spice, 100 with *budu*-spice, 100 with honey, 100 with rendered butter, 100 with roasted ... barley, 100 with roasted *su'u*-seeds, 100 with *karkartu*-plants, 100 with fruits of the *ti'atu*-tree, 100 with *kasu*-plants, 100 with milk, 100 with cheese, 100 jars with "mixture", 100 with pickled *arsuppu*-grain, ten homer of shelled *luddu*-nuts, ten homer of shelled pistachio nuts, ten homer of fruits of the *susu*-tree, ten homer of fruits of the *habbaququ*-tree, ten homer of dates, ten homer of the fruits of the *titip*-tree, ten homer of *cumin*, ten homer of *sahhunu*, ten homer of *uriana*, ten homer of *andahsu*-bulbs, ten homer of *sisanibbe*-plants, ten homer of the fruits of the *simbūru*-tree, ten homer of thyme, ten homer of perfumed oil, ten homer of sweet smelling matters, ten homer of ...., ten homer of the fruits of the *nasubu*-tree, ten homer of *zimzimmu*-onions, ten homer of olives.

When I inaugurated the palace at Calah I treated for ten days with food and drink 47,074 persons, men and women, who were bid to come from across my entire country, (also) 5,000 important persons, delegates from the country Suhu, from Hindana, Hattina, Hatti, Tyre, Sidon, Gurguma, Malida, Hubushka, Gilzana, Kuma (and) Musasir, (also) 10,000 inhabitants of Calah from all ways of life, 1,500 officials of all my palaces, altogether 69,574 invited guests from all the (mentioned) countries including the people of Calah; I (furthermore) provided them with the means to clean and anoint themselves. I did them due honors and sent them back, healthy and happy, to their own countries.'

From the Palace of Ashurnasirpal II at Calah

ivory, incense, wood and skins. Beginning with the reign of Nechoh II (610-594 BC) a canal was driven through part of the Wadi Tumilat and shipyards built on the Red Sea. Direct trade with the Delta could thus proceed to Arabia and points accessible via the Indian Ocean, and excavations at T. el-Maskhuta have demonstrated that the trade involved wine and spices. Some time towards the close of the 7th century BC a crew of Phoenicians in Egyptian employ circumnavigated Africa via the Red Sea.

PHOENICIAN TRADE

Most important in the panorama of Mediterranean trade, certainly from the 9th century BC, and possibly already in the 10th, was the unrivalled maritime commerce of the Phoenician cities. Their traders had complete access to Egyptian ports with the result that, not only did items of Egyptian manufacture pass by way of Tyre and Byblos to the rest of the Near East, but also decorative and artistic motifs of Nilotic origin became familiar around the Mediterranean in Phoenician 'guise'. The most travelled routes for Phoeni-

cian merchantmen were those which led to Cyprus, the Aegean, North Africa and the western Mediterranean. To all the communities alongside the Mediterranean shore the resourceful merchants peddled their timber, cloth, purple dye, metalwork and grain, in return for the products of North Africa, the silver and iron of Spain, the opium of Cyprus, and the slaves and manufactures of the Aegean.

In the wake of the traders came permanent colonists, especially in North Africa and Spain: Carthage was traditionally settled at the end of the 9th century BC and Gades in the 8th, and from these and other settlements further expansion resulted in the ringing of the western Mediterranean coast with Semitic-speaking colonies (see pages 90-91).

> 'KING SOLOMON BUILT A FLEET OF SHIPS AT EZION-GEBER, WHICH IS NEAR ELOTH ON THE SHORE OF THE RED SEA, IN THE LAND OF EDOM.'
> I KINGS 9.26

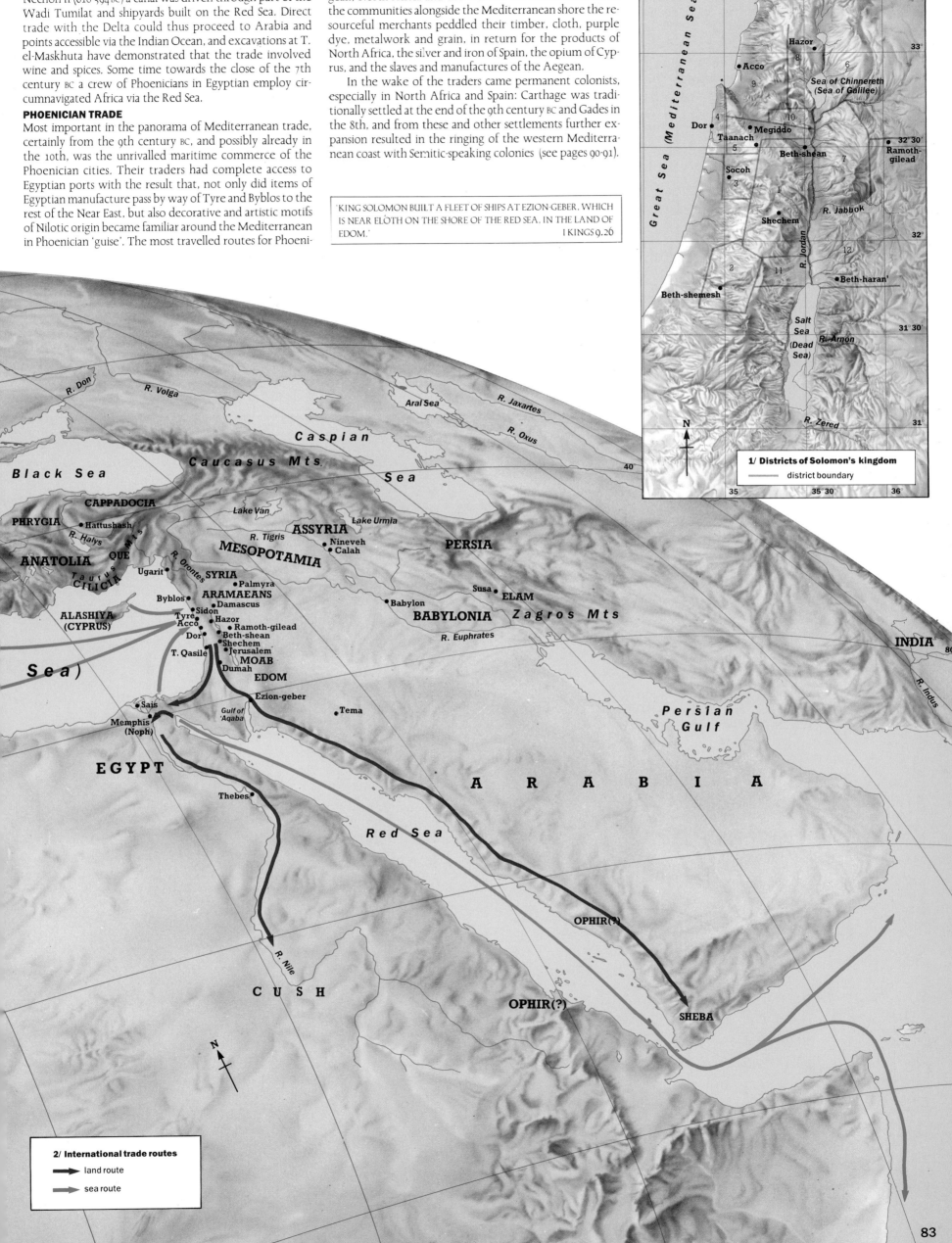

1/ Districts of Solomon's kingdom
— district boundary

2/ International trade routes
→ land route
→ sea route

IN the period of the Judges and the early Monarchy land was owned in common by a village or an extended family. The group property would be divided into smaller units which would be allocated to individual nuclear families by lot on an annual basis. This system prevented the growth of groups of wealthy families with good land and impoverished families with poor land. Gradually, however, this system broke down and land became private property which could be bought and sold, as in the case of Naboth's vineyard (I KINGS 21.1-19).

PLANTING

Grain was sown broadcast on the ploughed and harrowed fields. Olive trees were planted by taking wild or domesticated non-producing root stock and grafting on productive stock (ROM 11.17-24). Grapevines could be grown from seed or rooted from cuttings, and once they had taken root the seedlings were planted out in carefully prepared ground.

From the earliest beginnings of farming, in the Neolithic period (c8300-4800BC), the basic tool used for cultivation was the hoe. It was used to break up the soil before planting and for weeding and thinning the crops. The mattock, a tool for breaking up the soil, was also used in this early period.

The plough may have been known by the Early Bronze Age II, around 2800BC, although the earliest positive evidence occurs only in the early Iron Age, around 1200BC. The biblical plough was an ard, or scratch plough, which penetrated to a depth of a few inches. It had a wooden point, clad with metal – either copper (in the Bronze Age) or iron (in the Iron Age). The ploughman controlled the

THE IMPERIAL AGE OF SOLOMON

TECHNOLOGY OF FOOD PRODUCTION

Everyday life in the ancient Near East revolved around agriculture and the production of food. Learning to make the best use of land was vital. The development of the plough and other tools, and the increasing sophistication of terracing and irrigation techniques, enabled the land to support an ever-increasing population.

point by a handle and draft animals were attached to it by a shaft. In Mesopotamia the plough might also have had an attached seed drill. In Europe the ard was used to plough a field twice, the second time at right angles to the first; this is known as cross-ploughing, a technique which may be referred to in the Bible (ISA 28.24).

TERRACING

Prior to c1200BC most farming in Palestine was carried out on the coastal plain and valley bottoms as there were no tools for farming the steep hillsides economically. By the beginning of the Iron Age the need for arable land had increased, along with the population. Agriculture in the highlands was made possible by the use of stone-built terraces filled with soil. As the forests, which had covered the hills, were gradually cut down, the cultivable land thus created was divided into narrow strips. This was best suited

to the cultivation of vines, figs, pistachios and olives. Vegetables could be grown in the spaces between the trees, thus making maximum use of the land. Cultivation may have been with hoes rather than ploughs because of the small size of the plots and their steepness, and therefore it was more labour-intensive than lowland plough agriculture (see Map 5 page 58).

IRRIGATION

From early in the Neolithic period most farming in Egypt and Mesopotamia was done by the use of irrigation. This involved the diversion and control of the waters of the rivers through the use of a system of canals and sluice-gates. In Egypt, the ancient water-lifting device called a *shaduf* was used and a variety of different water-lifting wheels, some powered by the flow of a river, as at Hama in Syria, and others by donkeys, oxen or, later, camels, were used throughout the Near East.

In Palestine, however, there were no great rivers from which to draw water. Most farming was dry-farming, that is to say, it depended on natural rainfall. There were irrigation schemes but these were usually very small-scale, often confined to a single field, or at most, to a hillside. The water of a spring higher up the slope was conducted into a holding tank and along a small system of stone-built and plaster-lined channels to where it was needed.

Around 3500BC there was a short-lived attempt to operate an agricultural economy at Jawa in the desert east of the Jordan; this used an intricate series of canals, sluice gates and pools. During this period and later, whenever Egypt was weak, agricultural communities were set up in

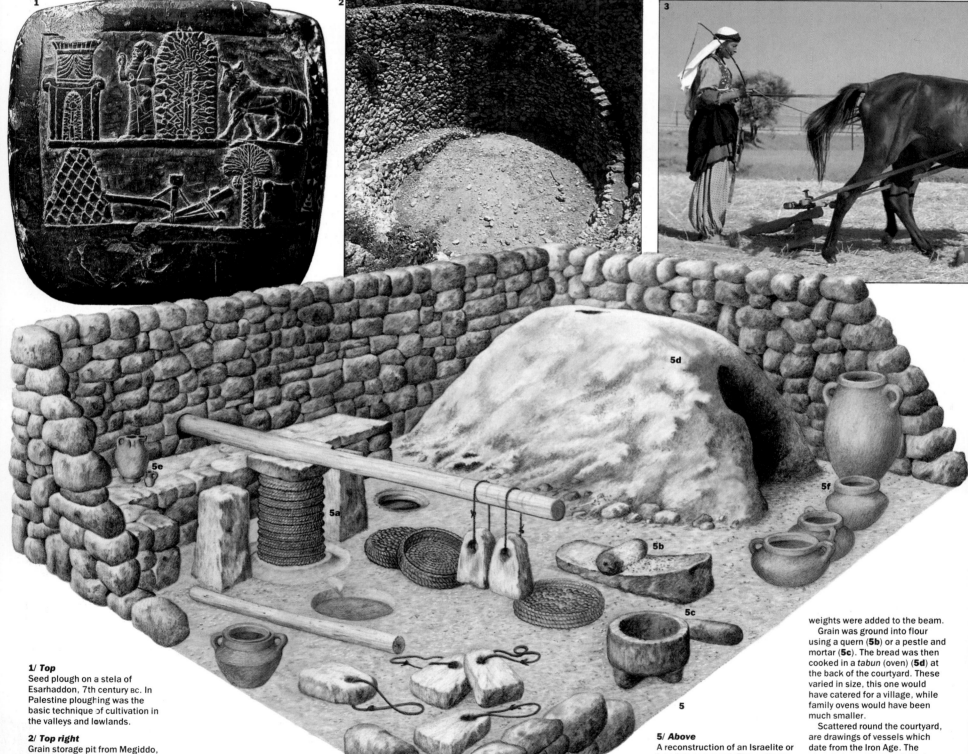

1/ Top
Seed plough on a stela of Esarhaddon, 7th century BC. In Palestine ploughing was the basic technique of cultivation in the valleys and lowlands.

2/ Top right
Grain storage pit from Megiddo, 7th century BC. The remains of a staircase into the pit can be seen.

3/ Top far right
A modern picture illustrating the way that grain has been threshed for many centuries. The threshing sledge was driven over the harvested corn, and the flints on the bottom of the sledge (4/ Far right) released the grain.

5/ Above
A reconstruction of an Israelite or Iron Age courtyard. The walls are typical of Iron Age masonry, with undressed, uneven stones. In the centre (5a) is a press used to crush olives or grapes. They were placed in the wicker baskets and

weights were added to the beam.
Grain was ground into flour using a quern (5b) or a pestle and mortar (5c). The bread was then cooked in a *tabun* (oven) (5d) at the back of the courtyard. These varied in size, this one would have catered for a village, while family ovens would have been much smaller.
Scattered round the courtyard, are drawings of vessels which date from the Iron Age. The storage jar on the bench (5e) was found at Beit Mirsim and was used for storing oil. The juglet next to it acted as a dipper. The cooking pot near the oven (5f) was found at Hazor.

the Negeb and north-western Sinai. These communities had to rely on diverting and storing the limited annual rainfall of the area. Large cisterns stored the water and dams trapped the soil in small, scattered fields which could, retain sufficient moisture to produce crops, thus reducing the risk of drought (see page 160).

HARVESTING
Even before the beginning of the Neolithic period, sickles were used to harvest grain. At first these were made of flint, later of bronze, and then of iron. Harvesting was a highly labour-intensive process which involved the whole community, in addition to any available itinerant labour. Olives were beaten from the trees with long thin sticks. They fell on to cloths spread on the ground beneath the trees. Bunches of grapes were cut from the vines and placed in baskets.

Grain was threshed on threshing floors which were usually of beaten earth, more rarely of stone. The normal method was for an ox to pull a heavy wooden sledge, studded underneath with jagged flints, in circles over the grain, thus cutting up the straw and crushing the husks around the grains. The result of this process was then placed in a broad, flat winnowing basket and tossed in the air to let the breeze carry away the lighter chaff, leaving the heavier grain. The chaff was then collected for use in brickmaking and in the manufacture of pottery.

After harvesting, grain, wine and oil were stored in jars, either storage jars which held about 10 gallons, or *pithoi* of larger capacity. Small numbers of storage jars were to be found in every home. Larger quantities of grain may have been kept in jars in royal storehouses, such as those at Hazor, Megiddo and Beersheba, in large grain silos, such as that from Megiddo, or in underground silos, such as are found at many sites of the Iron Age I period.

FOOD PREPARATION
The art of grinding grain into flour and cooking with it was known to people of the Stone Age. The grinding was done by hand, using a quern: this consisted of a fixed lower stone, called a *metate*, and a movable upper stone or *mano*. It was a very laborious process and had the additional disadvantage of producing grit which got into the bread and gradually wore down the teeth. Bread was baked in small domed clay ovens. These were first heated by building a fire inside, then the coals were raked out and the dough placed inside it to cook.

Grain was also eaten as porridge and as cracked wheat and was fermented to make beer.

Vegetables were widely eaten although the variety was limited. Onions, leeks, beans and lentils were among the most important. These could be eaten raw or boiled.

Meat was a luxury which did not normally form part of the diet because animals could more profitably be used to produce other commodities. It was normally eaten only at sacrificial feasts and as part of the entertainment of an honoured guest. The main meat-providing species were sheep and goats, although some meat was obtained from cattle and birds. The chicken was not introduced into Egypt until the late New Kingdom and may not have reached Palestine until the Intertestamental period. The eating of fish was rare for the Israelites because for part of their history they lacked access to the Mediterranean, so that the Sea of Galilee was their only source. The Roman conquest opened the routes to the coast and consumption of fish was common in NT times. Meat was roasted (on a spit or in an oven), boiled or cooked in oil. Fish might be eaten fresh or, more commonly, pickled or dried.

Because the diet of the common person was so monotonous a variety of seasonings were used. These included salt, onions, leeks, garlic, aniseed, coriander, cummin, dill, thyme, mint, nuts and honey.

Olives and grapes were pressed in stone presses. The oil from the olives was stored in jars, the wine from the grapes either in jars or skins. Olive oil was used in cooking, as a fat for frying, as an ingredient in recipes and as a coating. It was also flavoured with various substances and used as a condiment. Wine was drunk and used in cooking. It was usually mixed with water for drinking and was often flavoured with various substances for variety.

> '... AND GOD SAID TO THEM... "HAVE DOMINION OVER THE FISH OF THE SEA AND OVER THE BIRDS OF THE AIR AND OVER EVERY LIVING THING THAT MOVES UPON THE EARTH." AND GOD SAID, "BEHOLD, I HAVE GIVEN YOU EVERY PLANT YIELDING SEED WHICH IS UPON THE FACE OF THE EARTH, AND EVERY TREE WITH SEED IN ITS FRUIT; YOU SHALL HAVE THEM FOR FOOD. AND TO EVERY BEAST OF THE EARTH, AND TO EVERY BIRD OF THE AIR, AND TO EVERYTHING THAT CREEPS ON THE EARTH, AND EVERYTHING THAT HAS THE BREATH OF LIFE, I HAVE GIVEN EVERY GREEN PLANT FOR FOOD."'
>
> GEN 1.28-31

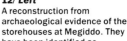

11/ Above
Israelite storehouses at Hazor, built at the time of Ahab.

6/ Top
Peasant women winnowing grain.

7/ Above
Clay model of woman kneading dough. From ez-Zib, 8th century BC.

8/ Below
The shaduf, a water-lifting device.

9/ Below right
An irrigation channel on a macehead from Hieraconpolis, c.3000 BC.

10/ Below far right
A shaduf on an Assyrian relief, from Nineveh, c 700 BC.

12/ Left
A reconstruction from archaeological evidence of the storehouses at Megiddo. They have been identified as 'Solomon's stables' but many experts now consider them to be storehouses and date them to a later period, the reign of Ahab, 9th century BC.

THE eminent Israeli archaeologist Yigael Yadin was the first to observe the similarity of plan between the city gates at Gezer, Hazor and Megiddo, which was not unexpected, since I KINGS 9.15 attributes the rebuilding of these cities to Solomon. The three gates exhibit a common architectural concept and similar dimensions. All three are massive structures with three large gate chambers on either side of the gate passage. The plan of the gatehouses and the fact that only the outer entry was closed by doors indicates that their function was not only military but civic as well.

Archaeology has shown however, that there were several types of city wall at the time of Solomon. At Megiddo the wall leading from the gate is solid but at Gezer the wall is of casemate construction (built with chambers running inside the wall). Moreover the casemates at Gezer seem to belong to a royal citadel confined to the gate area. Also similar city gates attached to solid walls were uncovered at Ashdod (10th century BC) and Lachish (9th-8th centuries). It seems that the rank of the site in the administrative hierarchy (see page 122), the kind of property kept in it, and its regional military role were what determined the type of fortification in each case. Solomon's architects did not feel bound by any schematic dogma.

THE IMPERIAL AGE OF SOLOMON

SOLOMON'S BUILDING PROJECTS

The development of international trade and the centralization of the administrative system of Solomon's kingdom enabled monumental building activities to be conducted on a national level for the first time in the country's history. Excavations of fortified cities and citadels of this time reveal the grand scale of construction, enhanced by the introduction of masonry using ashlar blocks (hewn stones with straight edges).

THE SOLOMONIC CITY OF JERUSALEM

Solomonic activities at Jerusalem converted the embryonic city of David into a royal capital by adding to it the Temple Mount and turning it into a monumental acropolis. The main architectural feature unearthed by archaeologists in the city of David is a stepped stone structure about 50ft high, which evidently served as a retaining wall for the southern end of the raised platform on which Solomon's royal city was built. If this structure is to be identified with the Millo ('the fill'), then the building activities in I KINGS 9.15 proceeded in geographical order from north to south: the house of the Lord, the house of the king, the Millo and the city wall that surrounded the entire city.

The purpose of the Millo was twofold: to make a sharper topographical distinction between the civilian-occupied lower city and the upper royal precinct, and at the same time to expand the area devoted to public buildings (partially at the expense of the area for private houses). As a rough estimate, Solomon enlarged the area of the capital from about 10-12 acres to 20-35 acres. However, this increment was not accompanied by a corresponding increase in population. The additional area was used for monumental building, accommodating a limited number of the royal elite. The overall population most likely did not exceed 1500 during Solomon's reign. It was not the size of the populace but the grandeur of the structures and their luxurious building materials and furnishings that glorified the capital of the United Monarchy.

In the wake of recent advances in our comprehension of the biblical description, backed by the accumulating

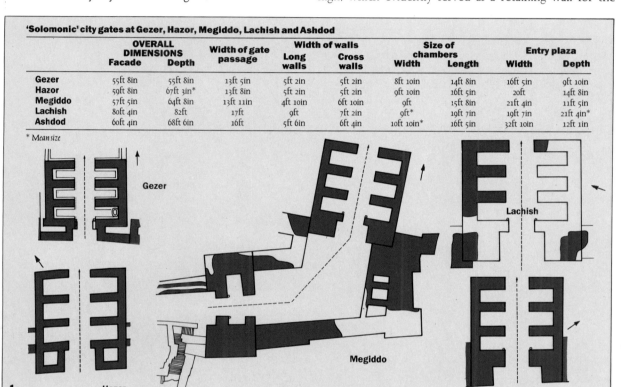

'Solomonic' city gates at Gezer, Hazor, Megiddo, Lachish and Ashdod

| | OVERALL DIMENSIONS | | Width of gate passage | Width of walls | | Size of chambers | | Entry plaza | |
	Facade	Depth		Long walls	Cross walls	Width	Length	Width	Depth
Gezer	55ft 8in	55ft 8in	13ft 5in	5ft 2in	5ft 2in	8ft 10in	14ft 8in	16ft 5in	9ft 10in
Hazor	50ft 8in	67ft 3in*	13ft 8in	5ft 2in	5ft 2in	9ft 10in	16ft 5in	20ft	14ft 8in
Megiddo	57ft 5in	64ft 8in	13ft 11in	4ft 10in	6ft 10in	9ft	15ft 8in	21ft 4in	11ft 5in
Lachish	80ft 4in	82ft	17ft	9ft	7ft 2in	9ft*	19ft 7in	19ft 7in	21ft 4in*
Ashdod	60ft 4in	68ft 6in	16ft	5ft 6in	6ft 4in	10ft 10in*	16ft 5in	32ft 10in	12ft 1in

* Mean size

Gezer

Lachish

Megiddo

1 Hazor

Ashdod

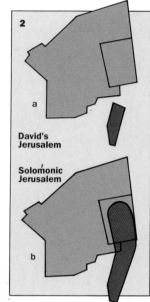

2

a

David's Jerusalem

Solomonic Jerusalem

b

of the passageway into the city. The entrance into Megiddo is provided with the added security feature of an external passageway which forces an attacking army to expose its left flank to defenders upon the wall of the city.

2/ Left
Sketches of the areas of (a) David's Jerusalem (dark tinted area) compared with that of the walled 'Old City' of recent times and (b) Solomon's enlargement of the city northward.

3/ Below
A modern artist's reconstruction of the Jerusalem of Solomon's time based on information supplied by biblical scholars and archaeologists. The terrain is known from various surveys made since 1864 (by Charles Wilson and Charles Warren) as well as from scores of excavations made within the city of Jerusalem over the past century. Details of city wall, gate, houses and public buildings have been extrapolated from what has been learned from excavations of approximately the same period at other cities. Recent evidence has rendered this reconstruction probably more accurate than previous ones.

1/ Left
There are marked similarities in the plans of the city gates of the walled 10th-century BC Gezer, Hazor, Megiddo, Ashdod and that of the gate of Lachish belonging to the 9th-8th centuries. All have three gate chambers on each side

3/ Solomonic Jerusalem

Western Hill

Tyropoeon Valley

City wall

archaeological comparative material, a general consensus is emerging concerning the plan of Solomon's Temple. The Temple and its courtyards covered a considerable area, most probably at the highest (northernmost) end of the city. The plan of the king's palace is less clear. It has been suggested by Professor Ussishkin that all the palace units were incorporated within a single building of the *bit hilani* type. However, such a layout would tend to diminish the scale of the royal court. It is more likely that it consisted of a cluster of palaces, possibly arranged around a common courtyard, similar to the acropolis of Zinjirli (ancient Samal) of the 9th-8th centuries. To Solomon's time is also dated the water system known today as Warren's Shaft. An overall view of Solomon's Jerusalem is presented below.

SOLOMON'S TEMPLE

The description of the Temple appears in I KINGS 6-8; II CHRON 3 and in Ezekiel's vision (EZEK 40-42). For generations, this detailed information has attracted biblical scholars, art historians, architects and archaeologists.

Only recently, and mainly through the exhaustive study of T.A. Busink, a great advance was made in the research. Busink suggests that the tripartite division of the Temple in *ulam* (porch or vestibule), *hekal* (nave or Temple) and *debir*

(inner sanctuary) applies more to the ceremonial signficance of these units than to their structural arrangement. The term used for the main unit, which includes the *hekal* and *debir*, is the 'house' (I KINGS 6.2, 3, 17, etc). The *debir* was most probably a large cabinet made of cedar beams at the rear of the *hekal*, while the *ulam* was evidently an unroofed passage open at the front, protected by two side walls.

The 'house' measured 60 x 20 cubits (about 90 x 30ft), surrounded by lower storerooms (*yasi*) on three sides. Two ceremonial pillars, made of copper, called Jachin and Boaz, stood in front of the Temple, apparently between the walls of the *ulam*. The plan follows the tradition of the longroom Temple type (Megaron) excavated in several Middle and Late Bronze Age sites in northern Syria.

The sacrificial altar, the 'molten sea' (bronze basin) and the ten stands for lavers of bronze (*mekonot*) (described in I KINGS 7. 23-39) stood in the courtyard in front of the Temple. The ten lampstands of pure gold, the golden altar, golden table and golden utensils (I KINGS 7.48-49) were inside the *hekal*. The cherubim of olivewood overlaid with gold (I KINGS 6.23-28) were in the *debir* alongside the Ark of the Covenant with 'the two tables of stone, which Moses put there at Horeb, where the Lord made a covenant with the

people of Israel.' (I KINGS 8.9).

The entire Temple was panelled with precious cedar wood and inlaid with gold: 'And the whole house be overlaid with gold' (I KINGS 6.22).

The city of Jerusalem, its palaces and Temple, represent an architectural achievement that justifies the reaction of the Queen of Sheba on her visit to the royal court of Solomon: 'I did not believe the reports until I came and my own eyes had seen it...' (I KINGS 10.7).

'THEN HE CALLED FOR SOLOMON HIS SON, AND CHARGED HIM TO BUILD A HOUSE FOR THE LORD, THE GOD OF ISRAEL. DAVID SAID TO SOLOMON, "MY SON, I HAD IT IN MY HEART TO BUILD A HOUSE TO THE NAME OF THE LORD MY GOD. BUT THE WORD OF THE LORD CAME TO ME, SAYING, 'YOU HAVE SHED MUCH BLOOD AND HAVE WAGED GREAT WARS; YOU SHALL NOT BUILD A HOUSE TO MY NAME, BECAUSE YOU HAVE SHED SO MUCH BLOOD BEFORE ME UPON THE EARTH. BEHOLD, A SON SHALL BE BORN TO YOU; HE SHALL BE A MAN OF PEACE. I WILL GIVE HIM PEACE FROM ALL HIS ENEMIES ROUND ABOUT; FOR HIS NAME SHALL BE SOLOMON. AND I WILL GIVE PEACE AND QUIET TO ISRAEL IN HIS DAYS. HE SHALL BUILD A HOUSE FOR MY NAME. HE SHALL BE MY SON, AND I WILL BE HIS FATHER. AND I WILL ESTABLISH HIS ROYAL THRONE IN ISRAEL FOR EVER' ".'   I CHRON 22.6-10

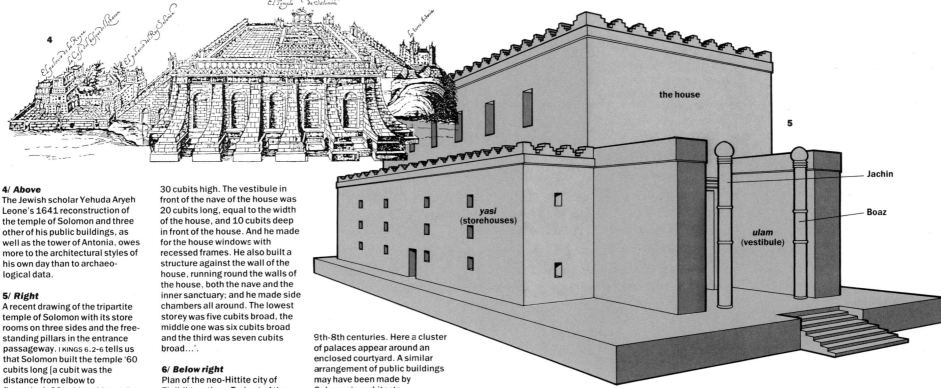

4/ Above
The Jewish scholar Yehuda Aryeh Leone's 1641 reconstruction of the temple of Solomon and three other of his public buildings, as well as the tower of Antonia, owes more to the architectural styles of his own day than to archaeological data.

5/ Right
A recent drawing of the tripartite temple of Solomon with its store rooms on three sides and the free-standing pillars in the entrance passageway. I KINGS 6.2-6 tells us that Solomon built the temple '60 cubits long [a cubit was the distance from elbow to fingertips], 20 cubits wide, and

30 cubits high. The vestibule in front of the nave of the house was 20 cubits long, equal to the width of the house, and 10 cubits deep in front of the house. And he made for the house windows with recessed frames. He also built a structure against the wall of the house, running round the walls of the house, both the nave and the inner sanctuary; and he made side chambers all around. The lowest storey was five cubits broad, the middle one was six cubits broad and the third was seven cubits broad...'.

6/ Below right
Plan of the neo-Hittite city of Zinjirli (southern Turkey) of the

9th-8th centuries. Here a cluster of palaces appear around an enclosed courtyard. A similar arrangement of public buildings may have been made by Solomon's architects.

the house

5

Jachin

Boaz

yasi (storehouses)

ulam (vestibule)

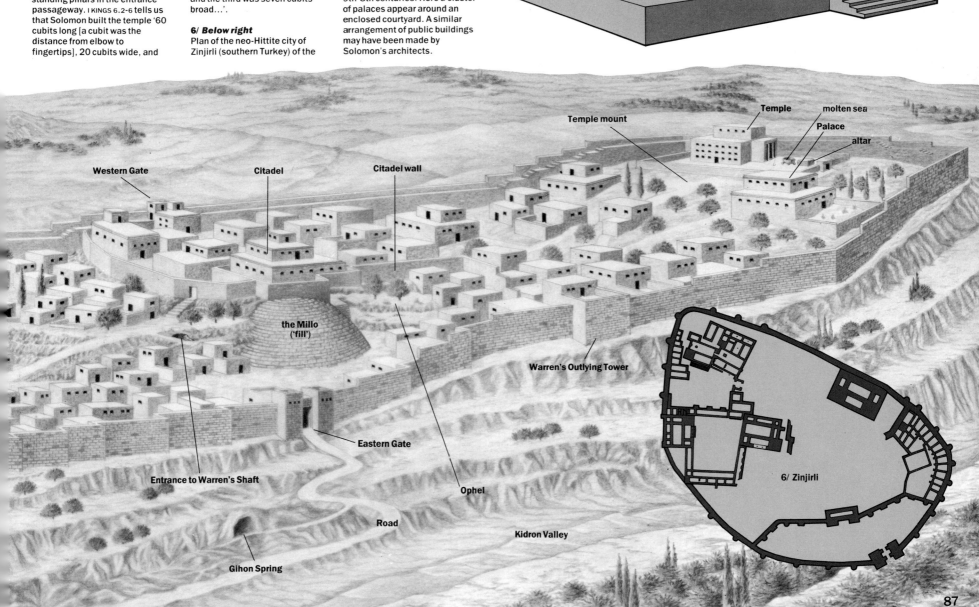

Temple mount

Temple

molten sea

Palace

altar

Western Gate

Citadel

Citadel wall

the Millo ('fill')

Warren's Outlying Tower

Eastern Gate

Entrance to Warren's Shaft

Ophel

Road

Kidron Valley

Gihon Spring

6/ Zinjirli

IN Canaanite religion, a temple was probably considered to be the dwelling place of a god or several gods. The earliest temples hitherto found in Palestine are similar to contemporary houses, usually with the addition of a walled courtyard, where much of the ritual took place. Worshippers assembled in the court to deliver tribute, receive oracles, prepare sacrifices and participate in covenant meals. Over the course of many years the structure of the temple gradually became more sophisticated.

CHALCOLITHIC PERIOD (c 5000-3150 BC)
One of the best preserved early temples, found at En-gedi, dates from this period. It consists of a broad room entered from one of the long sides, together with an annex, a walled courtyard with a stone-lined basin in the centre and a well-built gatehouse as part of the enclosure wall.

Similar buildings were found at Teleilat el-Ghassul, Megiddo, Ai and Arad, though the last building is slightly later in date.

EARLY BRONZE AGE (c 3150-2200 BC)
The distinctive Canaanite broadroom temple first appears in this period. Three examples have been excavated at Megiddo, the earliest dating from around 2500 BC. All had a broad room, open porch and court. Two columns supported the roof and against the rear wall, facing the entrance was an altar with four steps. Just south of the building, behind the rear wall, there was an open-air altar or high place, 25ft wide and 5ft high with steps leading to the top; it was surrounded by a wall. The stones of the altar

THE IMPERIAL AGE OF SOLOMON

TEMPLES IN PALESTINE

Temples are as old as man's first permanent settlements. The first cult places were outside, perhaps by a sacred tree or well. They were eventually enclosed, though much of the ritual was still conducted in the open air of the now walled courtyard. At many sites temples have been re-used or rebuilt. The earliest Palestinian temples were of the broadroom type, but later other varieties developed. The most famous temple of all, that of Solomon in Jerusalem, was a longhouse structure.

were covered with soot from fires.

MIDDLE BRONZE AGE (c 2200-1550 BC)
The Megiddo temples were destroyed at the end of the Early Bronze Age but one was rebuilt to a slightly different plan: the altar was converted into a raised niche – the earliest cult niche so far found in Palestine.

A temple of the broadroom type was also found at Nahariya. The finds from the courtyard there indicate that meals were an important part of the cult. Small pottery bowls, each with seven cups, were used as offertory vessels and finds of clay doves, usually associated with this type of bowl, may indicate that the temple was dedicated to the goddess Astarte.

Another type of temple is also known from the Middle Bronze Age. These are known as 'Migdal' temples because of their thick walls and towerlike entrances which make them look like fortresses. This type of building has been found at Megiddo, Shechem, T. Kittan and at Hazor.

LATE BRONZE AGE (c1550-1200 BC)
Numerous temples of the Late Bronze Age have been found in Palestine and many larger sites have produced more than one.

There are similarities to the temple architecture of Megiddo in the four superimposed Canaanite temples of Hazor. These clearly show the development of temple architecture from the broadroom plan to what became the typical Canaanite and Israelite tripartite building which consisted of an entrance porch and a main room with cult niche or Holy of Holies.

The two earlier temples, the first one dating from the Middle Bronze Age, were built on the broadroom plan, with a cult niche. The temple of Stratum II had two courtyards – an inner and an outer. The former was reached through a propylaeum or gateway. Benches lined the walls in the gate house and on both sides of the entrance were two small raised platforms or tables. (cf the description of the north gate of the inner Court in Jerusalem, EZEK 40.35-7). Among the finds of the inner Court, where the main feature was an 'altar of burnt offering', were fragments of clay liver models used for divination, including one with an

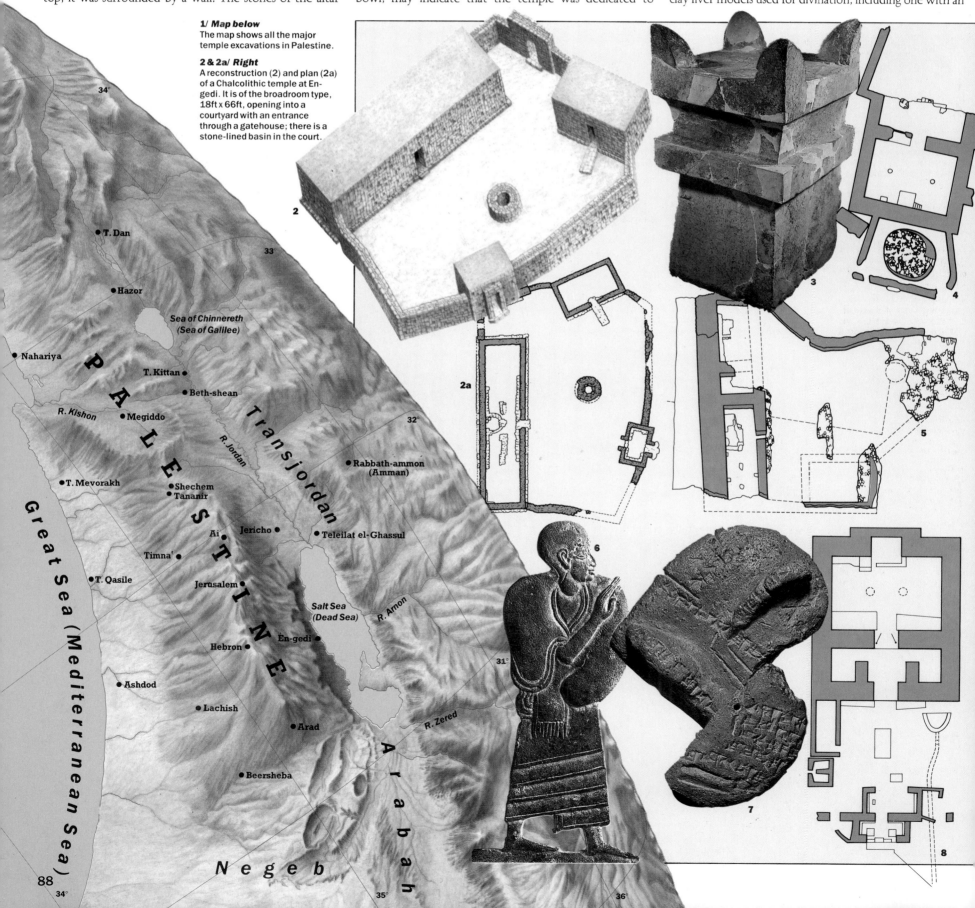

1/ Map below
The map shows all the major temple excavations in Palestine.

2 & 2a/ Right
A reconstruction (2) and plan (2a) of a Chalcolithic temple at En-gedi. It is of the broadroom type, 18ft x 66ft, opening into a courtyard with an entrance through a gatehouse; there is a stone-lined basin in the court.

Akkadian cuneiform inscription. The court had a cobble floor with a drainage channel.

In the main room of the latest temple several cult objects were found, as well as libation tables, incense altars, seals and bronze figurines. Two columns, one on each side of the temple entrance, are reminiscent of the position of the pillars Jachin and Boaz in the Temple of Jerusalem.

Connected with the temples is a basalt statue of a deity which originally stood on a bull; on its breast was a four-pointed star within a circle. The same emblem has also been found on an incense altar and on one of the seven stelae discovered in the vicinity. This emblem and the basalt bull indicate that the temple was dedicated to the Canaanite storm/weather god, Baal.

Another important temple of this period comes also from Hazor, and it is called the 'Stelae Temple'. It is of the broadroom type and also has a raised cult niche. Benches lined the walls and finely worked stones which rested on the floor served as offertory tables. In the cult niche were found ten basalt stelae and the statue of a seated male figure holding a bowl. On his chest was an inverted crescent. One stela bears a relief of two hands stretched upwards towards a crescent and a disc. These symbols probably mean that the temple was dedicated to a moon god.

At Beth-shean the Late Bronze Age temples show strong Egyptian influence and one of them, like the Mekal temples of the Iron Age, seems to have been part of a palace–temple complex. This is not surprising as the city was under direct Egyptian control for most of the Late Bronze Age. The same type of temple architecture also occurs in a structure excavated at Lachish.

A temple complex, occupying the entire mound, has been found at T. Mevorakh. Among the finds was a coiled bronze snake, similar to a copper serpent of the same period from the temple found at Timna'.

The series of superimposed buildings from Lachish known as the Fosse Temples may not actually be temples. The unusual architecture and the tremendous hoards of pottery, only a few showing signs of use, found both inside and outside the buildings, correspond more to a potter's workshop than a temple complex.

Opinion is also divided on other Bronze Age 'temples' such as the square buildings found at Tananir, Amman and at Hazor. These are thought by some to be buildings used for secular purposes.

IRON AGE (c1200-600 BC)

At the end of the Bronze Age many of the cities throughout Palestine were destroyed and the temple areas of cities such as Megiddo, Shechem and Hazor were abandoned. However, at Beth-shean, which was still under Egyptian control, the cult tradition was preserved and it is clear that the religious pattern of the Iron Age had its roots in the previous period.

Only two Iron Age sites have so far produced buildings correctly identified as temples: a series of superimposed Philistine temples found at T. Qasile and an Israelite temple which has been excavated at Arad.

The temple at Arad was in use from c 900-600 BC. It is the earliest Israelite, as opposed to Canaanite, temple to be discovered. It was built in the northwest corner of the citadel, with an eastward orientation. The temple consisted of a main room with raised cult niche and a courtyard. Benches lined the walls of the main room. In the cult niche was found a *massebah* (standing stone). Two incense altars were found on the steps of the niche. The courtyard was divided into two and in the larger outer area was found an altar built of unworked stones, conforming to the regulations laid down in EX 20.25. Two column bases were found, one on each side of the entrance to the main room, recalling the pillars in Solomon's Temple.

Finds of ostraca (notes scratched on fragments of pottery) show unmistakably that this was an Israelite temple: in one letter there is a reference to the 'House of Yhwh'.

The biblical evidence suggests that there were other Israelite shrines or temples in Palestine in addition to the main Temple of Jerusalem but archaeological evidence has so far unearthed only that at Arad.

> 'WHILE THE MAN WAS STANDING BESIDE ME, I HEARD ONE SPEAKING TO ME OUT OF THE TEMPLE; AND HE SAID TO ME "SON OF MAN, THIS IS THE PLACE OF MY THRONE, AND THE PLACE OF THE SOLES OF MY FEET, WHERE I WILL DWELL IN THE MIDST OF THE PEOPLE OF ISRAEL FOR EVER. AND THE HOUSE OF ISRAEL SHALL NO MORE DEFILE MY HOLY NAME..."'
> EZEK 43.6-7

9/ Left
A fortress-temple discovered at Shechem. It dates from the MBA and measures 86ft x 69ft 6in.

10/ Below
This temple was found at Beth-shean and spans the period from LBA to Iron Age I. It measures 49ft long, and from 43 ft to 46ft 6in wide.

11/ Below (photograph)
The cella of the Israelite temple at Arad with two incense altars at the opening and two *massabahs* (standing stones) beyond. The measurements are c 5ft square.

12/ Bottom
An EBA twin temple at Arad. One of the temple rooms measures c16ft x 34ft and has benches around the walls. The other, slightly larger, may have been one or three rooms.

3/ Above centre left
A small limestone altar, 1ft 9in high, from Megiddo. Dating from the 10th century BC, it has projections on top which are probably symbolic horns.

4/ Above left
The plan of an EBA III temple at Megiddo, with courtyard, porch and altar room. The altar room is 29ft 6in x 46ft.

5/ Left
A Chalcolithic/EBA I temple at Megiddo. The width of the best preserved room is 13ft.

6/ Below far left
A bronze plaque showing a Canaanite dignitary. It comes from Hazor and dates from the LBA. Height: 3½in.

7/ Below centre left
Two fragments of a clay liver model used in divining. It comes from Hazor and dates from the 15th century BC. The length of the larger piece is 3in.

8/ Below left
An LBA I temple at Hazor, with an entrance from the courtyard into a porch before the broadroom cella with a screened cultic niche. The building is 59ft x 66ft.

13/ Right
A cylindrical fenestrated incense stand from Beth-shean. Height of restored vessel is 25½ins.

14/ Far right (top)
A photograph of the reconstructed Canaanite shrine at Hazor, dating from the 13th century BC. Within, were a statue of a seated man, 10 stelae, and an offertory table.

15/ Below right
Plan of shrine (fig. 14). It measures 15ft 6in x 11ft.

16/ Below far right
A decorated stela from the Hazor shrine. Two hands stretch upwards as in supplication. Above are a crescent with disc within and two tassel-like circles suspended from the centre of the crescent.

17/ Below
A ritual scene, though from Susa in Mesopotamia not Palestine, showing worship in practice. This bronze mould dates from the 12th century BC and is about 3in high.

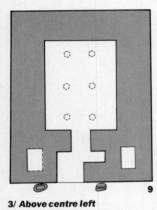
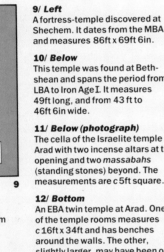

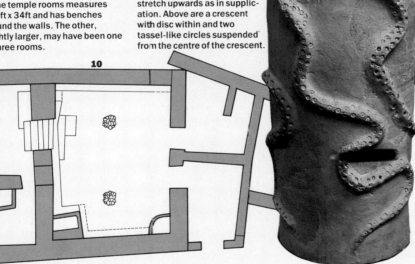

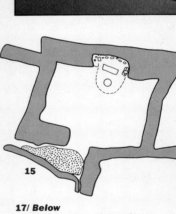

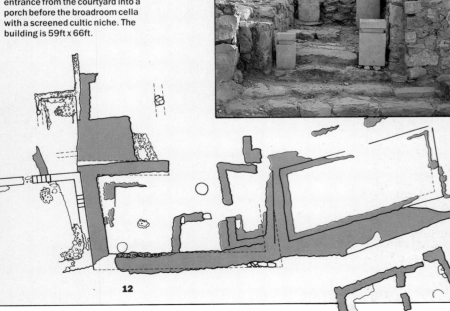

When the Levant recovered from the chaotic events which caused the collapse of the Bronze Age empires in the 12th century BC, both Israel and its Phoenician neighbours developed into important regional entities. They inherited much from their Canaanite past, including closely related languages, but with significant differences. Remaining divided into city-state kingdoms in culture, religion and political organization, the Phoenicians were the inheritors of Canaanite tradition.

Geographical conditions were one reason for the development of the two peoples in different directions. While the Israelite kingdom was mainly agricultural, the fertile but narrow coastal plain encouraged the Phoenicians to look outwards. There were natural resources available: timber (especially cedar), fish and the murex shell from which a highly prized purple dye was extracted. However, like their Canaanite ancestors, the Phoenicians were sailors, traders and craftsmen, producing and selling luxury goods of the highest quality, especially in bronze, ivory, precious metals and textiles.

They traded in the Levant and sailing all over the Mediterranean and beyond, the Phoenicians developed markets and acquired raw materials from places hitherto unknown to the Near East. Their ships (the 'ships of Tarshish' as they are known in the Bible) sailed as far as the Straits of Gibraltar and beyond into the Atlantic. Gold, ivory and slaves, along with other exotic goods, came from Africa; metal ores, especially silver and tin, came from Spain, and copper from Cyprus. Foreign products such as faïence and glass were imported and redistributed abroad and were later imitated and produced locally. Outside the homeland, commerce was handled by Phoenician agents and artisans, such as metal workers, ivory carvers, seal engravers, etc living abroad.

The Phoenician presence in foreign parts, at first temporary, gradually grew into trading stations and, later, colonies, first of Sidon and especially, Tyre, and later, in the west, as part of the Carthaginian empire.

These early trading posts would have had a counting house or storage buildings such as were found at Toscanos (in Spain) and Motya (in Sicily). Some gradually became permanent settlements. These grew into a network of substantial towns and cities along the shipping routes on

THE IMPERIAL AGE OF SOLOMON

ISRAEL'S RELATIONSHIP WITH PHOENICIA

The Phoenicians were direct descendants of the Canaanites. They occupied the narrow coastal plain from around Acco, in the south, to near Tripoli, in the north. Adventurous sailors and traders, they travelled and established colonies all over the Mediterranean and beyond in search of raw materials and markets for their goods. Though the Bible regarded Phoenician religion as a dangerous threat, the Phoenicians were for a long time on friendly terms with Israel, and indeed there were always close ties between the two peoples.

the islands and coasts of the Mediterranean.

Claims by classical writers that Gades (modern Cadiz, on Spain's Atlantic coast) and Utica and Lixus in North Africa were founded about 1100 BC cannot be verified. The earliest Phoenician material so far found in the west has been tentatively dated to the 9th century BC, not without dispute. By the 8th century BC, however, Phoenician settlements were flourishing in many places. Traders were active in Spain, particularly in the south and around the Guadalquivir basin (known as Tartessos to the Greeks and sometimes proposed as the biblical Tarshish) where there were rich metal deposits.

In Cyprus Phoenician influence is discernible from the 11th century BC; by the 9th the Tyrians had established a large settlement at Kition (Larnaca). In the Aegean, finds in Crete indicate the presence of Phoenicians in the early Iron Age. Further west there is some evidence of their activity in Sicily and Sardinia at about the same time.

According to classical tradition the greatest of all Phoenician colonies, Carthage, was founded in 814/3 BC at the height of Tyrian expansion in the Mediterranean, though the earliest material so far found there seems to date from the beginning of the 8th century BC.

Another impetus for the continued expansion and development of colonies abroad was the growing oppression by Assyria which looked greedily at the wealth of these small kingdoms.

The riches which flowed into the Phoenician city-states, of which Sidon and Tyre were the most powerful, rendered them much sought after as partners in political and commercial alliances. Phoenician deities were often worshipped abroad – the ruler of Damascus set up a stela to the Tyrian god Melqart, the same deity worshipped by Jezebel, the Sidonian wife of king Ahab, in Israel.

The alphabet, probably the most important legacy of the Phoenicians, was generally adopted and passed on by the Greeks to the western world.

Collaboration between the Phoenicians and Israel obviously made economic sense: Israel controlled important sections of international trade routes (for example, to the Red Sea and South Arabia) and could supply agricultural products such as corn, wine, oil and balsam (EZEK 27.17). A cuneiform tablet of the 7th century BC refers to Phoenician grain merchants in Assyria using a Judaean grain measure. In return the Phoenicians provided craftsmen of great skill and fine luxury goods for sale, both of which were highly prized in Israel. Alliances established by David and Solomon and renewed by the House of Omri were strengthened by the dynastic marriages of Jezebel and Athaliah into the royal families of Israel and Judah.

The Phoenicians were closely involved with Solomon's building programme (II CHRON 2) and a joint venture to Ophir. Though perhaps not purely Phoenician in style and craftsmanship, Solomonic and later royal buildings in places such as Jerusalem, Megiddo and Samaria show the collaboration between Phoenician and Israelite workmen referred to in the biblical account of Solomon's building programme (I KINGS 5.18; II CHRON 2.13-14).

Inscriptions show that the Phoenicians were widely present in Israel and Judah, not only in Galilee and the coastal plain but also inland, even in places as remote as Kuntillet 'Ajrud, in the Negeb. Phoenician carved ivory has been found in quantity at Samaria and at other sites. Israelite potters copied Phoenician motifs. Engraved metal vessels and *tridacna* shells (large clams) used as cosmetic palettes were fashionable, though finds of such luxuries are rare in Israel, perhaps because they were carried off by the Assyrians. Ivory, probably of Phoenician workmanship, was

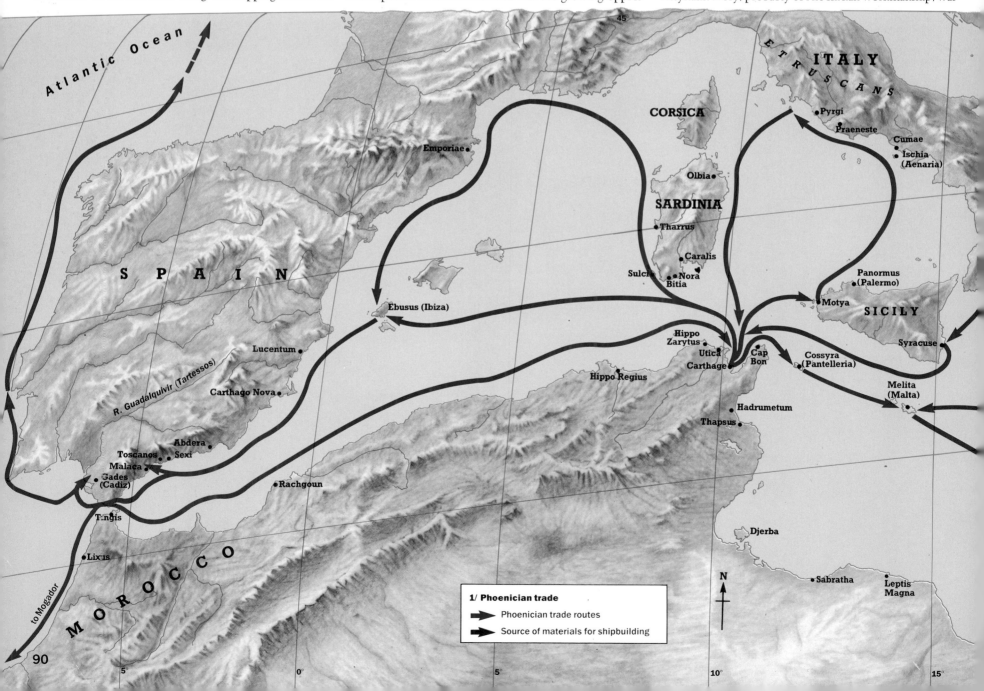

1/ Phoenician trade

→ Phoenician trade routes

➤ Source of materials for shipbuilding

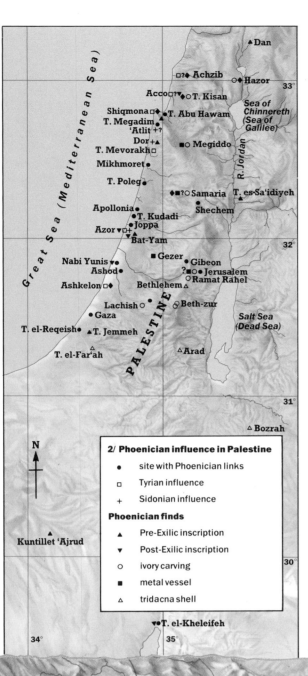

included in the tribute paid by Hezekiah to the Assyrian king Sennacherib, and metal bowls apparently of Judaean origin but Phoenician in style were found among the booty stored by the Assyrians at Nimrud.

EZEK 27 gives a vivid description of Tyrian trade. Yet when Ezekiel was writing the Phoenicians had, for a century and a half, suffered the economic consequences of first Assyrian and then Babylonian pressure, involving tribute, deportations, sieges and destructions.

Under the Persians better days were to dawn. The Phoenicians became favoured members of the Persian Empire. Both Sidon and Tyre regained their original importance and established harbours and territory along the Palestinian coast, on the sea route to Egypt.

Relations between the Phoenicians and the Jewish community after the return to Zion in 538 BC were somewhat different. The Phoenicians now had a massive presence in the coastal plain and their traders settled as far inland as Marisa and Shechem and again at Ezion-geber/Elath, no doubt to secure their routes to the Far East.

In Judah, the poverty of the people meant that there was little demand for the foreign luxuries formerly provided by the Phoenicians, though the discovery at Gibeon of a Phoenician bronze figure shows that these luxuries were not entirely absent.

AND HIRAM [KING OF TYRE] SENT TO SOLOMON, SAYING, "I HAVE HEARD THE MESSAGE WHICH YOU HAVE SENT TO ME; I AM READY TO DO ALL YOU DESIRE IN THE MATTER OF CEDAR AND CYPRESS TIMBER. MY SERVANTS SHALL BRING IT DOWN TO THE SEA FROM LEBANON; AND I WILL MAKE IT INTO RAFTS TO GO BY SEA TO THE PLACE YOU DIRECT, AND I WILL HAVE THEM BROKEN UP THERE, AND YOU SHALL RECEIVE IT; AND YOU SHALL MEET MY WISHES BY PROVIDING FOOD FOR MY HOUSEHOLD." SO HIRAM SUPPLIED SOLOMON WITH ALL THE TIMBER OF CEDAR AND CYPRESS THAT HE DESIRED, WHILE SOLOMON GAVE HIRAM TWENTY THOUSAND CORS OF WHEAT AS FOOD FOR HIS HOUSEHOLD, AND TWENTY THOUSAND CORS OF BEATEN OIL....'
I KINGS 5,8-11

1/ Map below
The map shows the routes by which the Phoenicians were able to trade throughout the whole Mediterranean area and beyond.

2/ Map left
Phoenician influence in Palestine is attested by the finds of artefacts typical of Phoenician workmanship.

3/ Below left
The great temple of Astarte at Kition is the only known example of an early Phoenician temple. Built in the later part of the 9th century BC, on ashlar foundations, it was later rebuilt in the form illustrated.
Inset can be seen examples of Phoenician masonry with its typical use of ashlar blocks and rubble infill.

4/ Below
A Phoenician warship, from a relief in the SW Palace at Nineveh.

5/ Bottom
The dedication of gold plating to a god – from a Phoenician inscription of 391 BC.

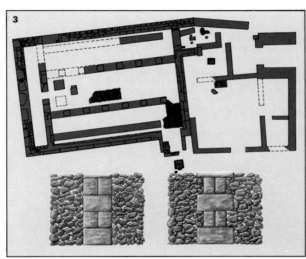

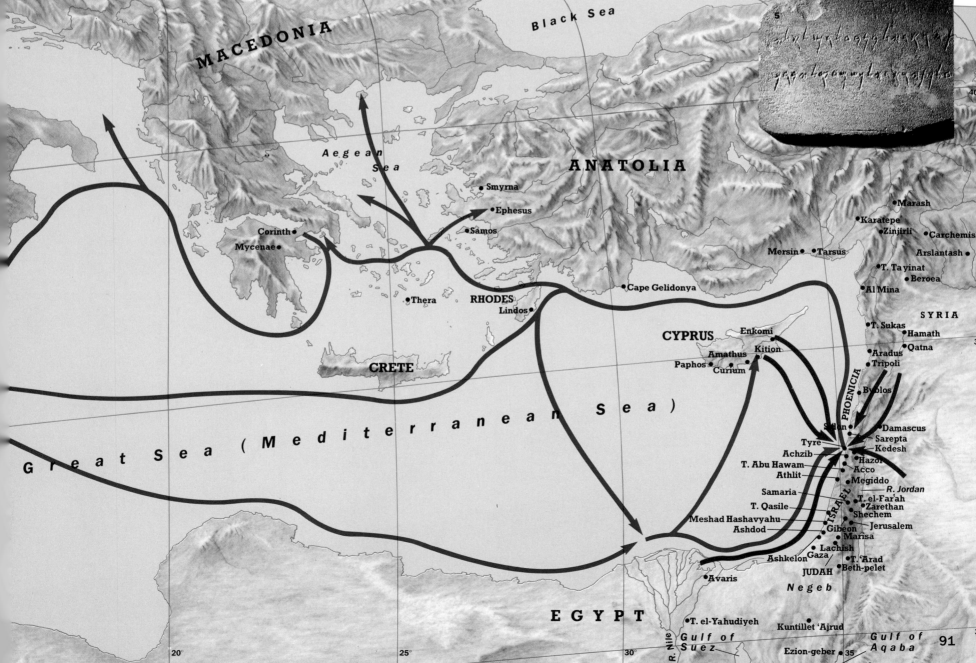

THE ancient Hebrews' world was as widely diversified as our own and, due to their widespread trading contacts they were in touch with countries from Greece and Lydia in the west to Persia in the east, from the Caucasus in the north to Sudan and southern Arabia in the south. Just as we need to know the relations between various countries today, so it was equally important for the ancient Hebrews. However, whereas today we speak of international relations in impersonal political terms, in their society kinship played a much greater role than it does in our own, and so it was normal to think of social relations in terms of the family. By extending the concepts of kinship to the international scene, it was possible to build up a picture in which the relationships between peoples could be expressed as family relationships.

Before the rise of Greek scholarship there was no science of geography in the ancient world. Some maps were religious and cosmological, but most were for practical purposes such as trade, taxation and welfare. There was neither systematic surveying nor cartography according to precise measurements and uniform scale. Not all maps were necessarily drawn on two-dimensional planes; some were linear, consisting of individual roads (later known as *itinerae*) which provided information useful to a traveller, such as distances from one town to another and places of accommodation or dangers to be avoided (for such a map see page 50). Still other maps were descriptions of land ownership which moved in straight lines from one marker or natural feature to another until a boundary was delineated.

GEN 10 is yet another kind of map, it contains information which can be super-imposed on a modern map. The chapter gives, in the briefest fashion, an ethnographic lineage of the peoples of the earth, who are said to have descended from Noah and his three sons, Ham, Shem and Japheth. Within the context of the patriarchal narrative in Genesis such descent was inevitable, in as much as all other males are said to have perished in the Flood. Two broad

A MAP OF THE WORLD FROM GENESIS 10

The Genesis description of the world, which scholars believe was written at the time of the United Monarchy, can be superimposed on a modern map.

streams of tradition can be seen in this larger narrative; an early epic story which existed in its essential form by the time of the Hebrew United Monarchy in the 10th century BC, and priestly traditions that were added to the older narrative as late as the 7th-6th centuries BC, the latter often systematizing and embellishing the earlier material in ways which reflected the knowledge and theological views of the later period. Because they lived at a time when tribal relationships were still a major concern in Hebrew religious thought, the authors of the old patriarchal epic in Genesis tended to see the world from an ethnic perspective. People are categorized not by their geographical locations or their linguistic affinities but by their ethnic origins. Furthermore, each ethnic group is represented eponymously, that is, by a single person who bears the name of the group and is said to be that group's ancestor. The use of eponymous figures led easily to the arrangements of the persons into a single,

2/ Map above right
The world as seen by Strabo in his *Geography*, which dates from the time of Jesus.

3/ Map far right
Hecataeus of Miletus described the world like this in his *Periodos* (c 520 BC).

4/ Photograph far right
An Assyrian clay tablet of about the 7th century BC, on which is incised a cosmological map of the world. Mesopotamia is surrounded by a broad ring representing the cosmic ocean, beyond which lies chaos.

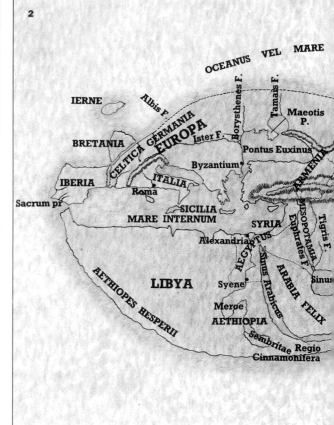

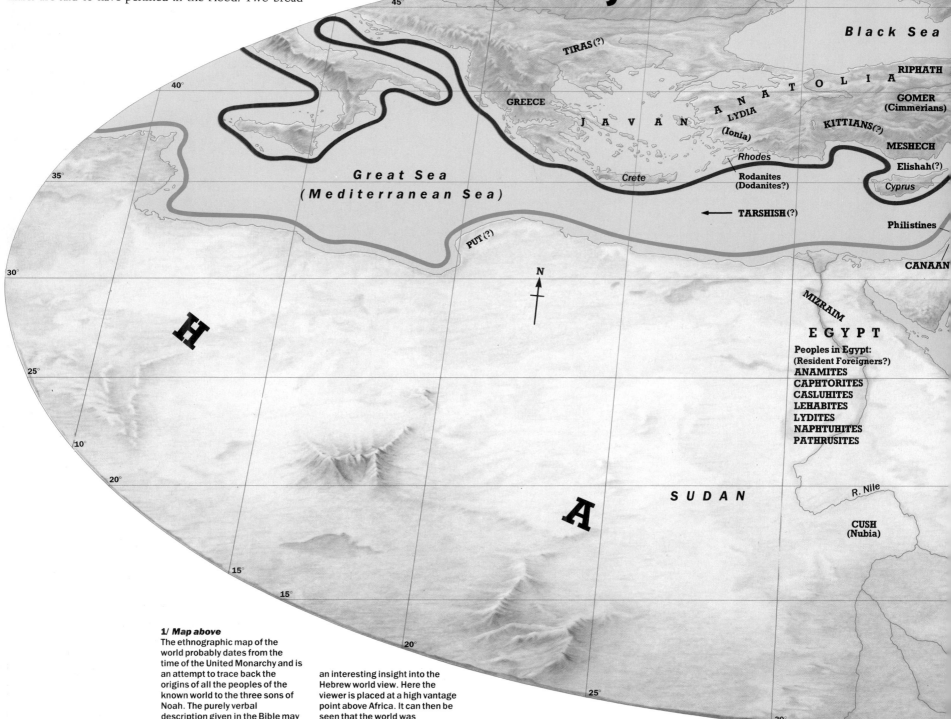

1/ Map above
The ethnographic map of the world probably dates from the time of the United Monarchy and is an attempt to trace back the origins of all the peoples of the known world to the three sons of Noah. The purely verbal description given in the Bible may be plotted on a modern map giving an interesting insight into the Hebrew world view. Here the viewer is placed at a high vantage point above Africa. It can then be seen that the world was considered to be a huge flat disk.

comprehensive lineage. This method was not unique to the Hebrews; it had in fact long been employed, with variations, in epic narratives and priestly records throughout the ancient Near East.

The Hebrew priests of the 7th and 6th centuries BC who edited the earlier epic tradition retained the essentially ethnographic structure of GEN 10, but added to the earliest list some names which reflected their awareness of the larger world – peoples of Asia Minor to the north, Media and Elam to the east, and Cush to the south. Although they seem to have had some interest in geography in its own right, their concerns were heavily theological. They may have wished to have the number of ethnic groups in the world total the cosmic number 70. The centre of the world was, as in the epic narrative, Canaan, the land which the Israelites had taken as their home. The extent of the inhabited earth known to priestly editors was not more than 1,500 miles in any direction from the hub of Canaan/Palestine less than one-twentieth of the earth's actual surface.

'THE SONS OF NOAH WHO WENT FORTH FROM THE ARK WERE SHEM, HAM AND JAPHETH. ... AND FROM THESE THE WHOLE EARTH WAS PEOPLED.'

GEN 9.18-19

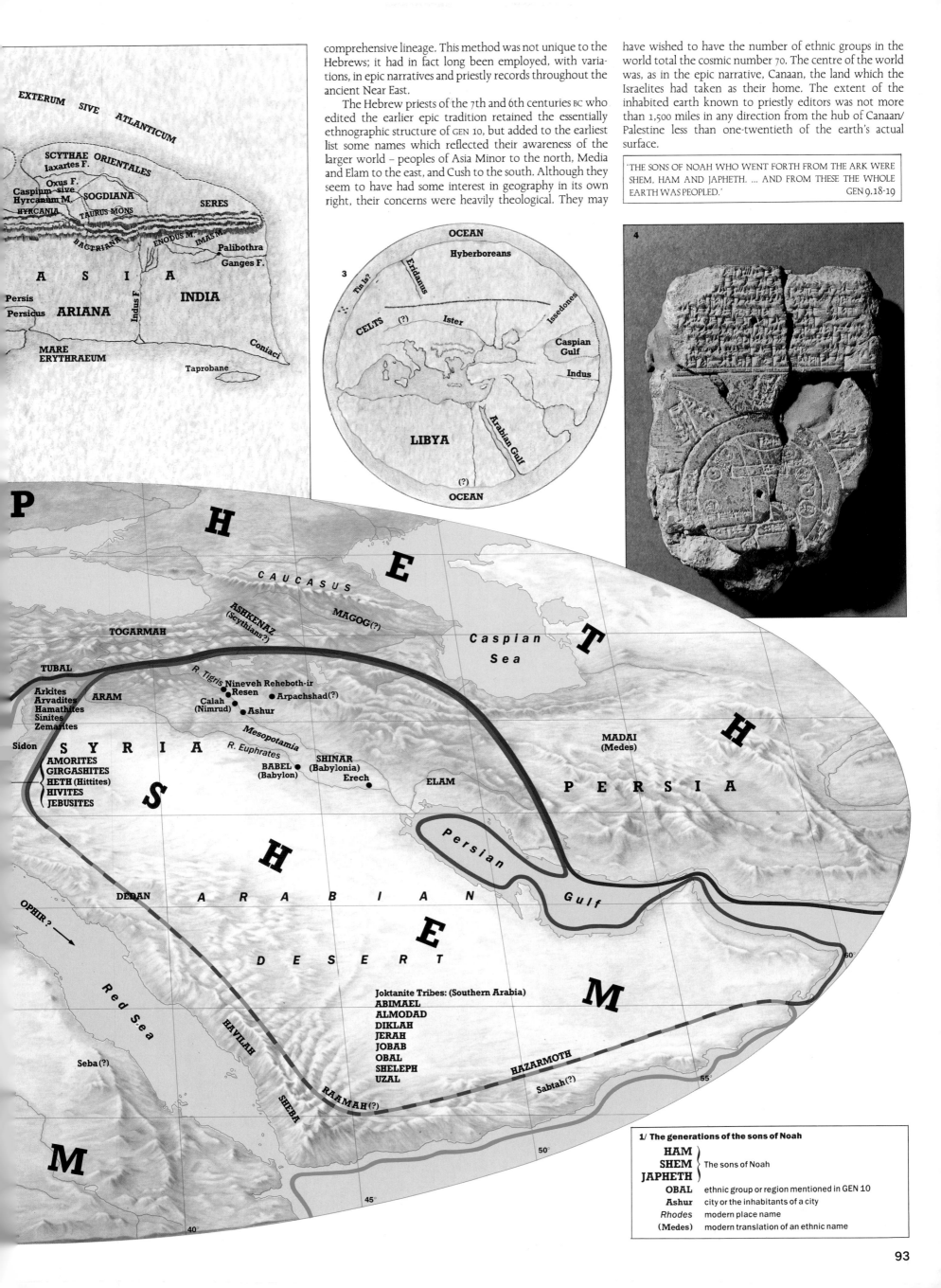

1/ The generations of the sons of Noah

HAM	
SHEM	The sons of Noah
JAPHETH	
OBAL	ethnic group or region mentioned in GEN 10
Ashur	city or the inhabitants of a city
Rhodes	modern place name
(Medes)	modern translation of an ethnic name

Joktanite Tribes: (Southern Arabia)
ABIMAEL
ALMODAD
DIKLAH
JERAH
JOBAB
OBAL
SHELEPH
UZAL

THE survival of examples of ancient writing is, of course, dependent on the durability of the medium to which the writing was committed. Most literate ancient societies have left commemorative inscriptions on stone (sometimes also metal), which by their very nature were intended to survive but which offer only a rather limited type of text (see, eg, pages 43, 106, 123).

Other types of document were written on other media. In Egypt, and places under its influence, writing was normally on papyrus or wood. However, this does not survive well except in arid conditions, such as obtain in Egypt itself. Even so, finds of papyri are seldom massive enough to preserve a full library or archive, though fragmentary hoards are sometimes sufficient to imply the

WRITING AND ITS USES

The discovery and translation of ancient writings, which began in the early 19th century, was a major landmark in our knowledge and understanding of the ancient Near East. The tomb inscriptions of the pharaohs, the Amarna correspondence, the Stela of Hammurabi, the Epic of Gilgamesh and, later, the Dead Sea scrolls are just some of the thousands of texts which have been invaluable in unlocking the secrets of the past.

their own generation and be kept for historical purposes. Libraries, on the other hand, designate collections of documents assembled for purposes other than the purely practical and for which a greater degree of permanence was required. Among these would be classed literary texts, epics, poetry and 'wisdom'. The last group would include texts on religion, mythology, rituals, festivals and incantations; also 'scientific' texts dealing with medicine, mathematics and astrology; and scholastic texts including the vocabularies, syllabaries and lexika required to maintain the writing system itself.

Libraries in this sense are very much less common in antiquity than general archives, though the line is sometimes hard to draw.

LIBRARIES OF THE ANCIENT NEAR EAST

Name	Excavation	No. of texts	Dates	Language	Document type	Comments
Boğazköy (Hattushash)	since 1906	thousands	c 1650-1200 BC	principally Hittite, Akkadian	royal library and archives	Hittite imperial capital, temples and citadel.
Kültepe (Kanesh)	since 1925, 1948	thousands	c 2000-1800 BC	Old Assyrian	merchant colony archives	Assyrian merchant colony in Anatolian city-state.
T. Atchana (Alalakh)	1936-1949	hundreds	c 1700-1400 BC	Akkadian	letters, administrative texts	Small palace of vassal kingdom of Aleppo.
Ras Shamra (Ugarit)	since 1929	thousands	1400-1200 BC	Akkadian, Ugaritic	libraries and archives	Phoenician kingdom, vassal of Hittite Empire.
T. Mardikh (Ebla)	since 1964	thousands	2500-2300 BC	Sumerian, 'Eblaite'	palace archives	Very early Syrian palace, archive remarkably intact.
El-Amarna (Akhetaten)	since 1887	hundreds	c 1417-1362 BC	Akkadian	royal correspondence	Egyptian chancery for relations with Levant.
Meskene (Emar)	1972-1976	thousands	c 1400-1200 BC	Akkadian, Hurrian	palace archives	Hurrian/Semitic vassal kingdom of Hittite Empire.
T. Hariri (Mari)	since 1933	thousands	c 1830-1760 BC	Akkadian	palace archives	Amorite kingdom between Syria and Mesopotamia.
Nimrud (Kalkhu)	since c 1850	more than 1000	c 860-612 BC	Assyrian	palace and temple library and archives	One time capital of Assyria.
Quyunjiq (Nineveh)	since c 1850	thousands	c 700-612 BC	Assyrian	palace library and archives	Last, greatest capital of Assyria.
Qal'at Sharqat (Ashur)	since 1903-1914	thousands	c 1400-612 BC	Assyrian	libraries and archives	Original centre of Assyria.
Yorghan Tepe (Nuzi)	1925-1931	thousands	c 1550-1450 BC	Akkadian	private contracts and letters	Small Hurrian vassal kingdom.
Sultan Tepe (Huzirina)	1950s	hundreds	7th century BC	Assyrian	provincial library	Assyrian provincial city.
Susa	c 1897-1939	thousands	2800-? BC	Akkadian, Elamite	various	Great Elamite capital city.
Babylonian cities	since c 1850	many thousands	3000-300 BC	Sumerian, Akkadian	very various	Centre of Sumero-Akkadian civilizations.

existence of such (see pages 37, 39 and 50).

The clay tablet, which originated in Mesopotamia, is a medium uniquely suitable for survival and thus has transmitted to us the great library and archive collections of the ancient Near East, which often contain many thousands of documents. The languages are principally Sumerian and Akkadian, but thanks to the borrowing of the script and medium, also Hittite and some other languages.

There are some important centres which must have had huge archives that have simply never been discovered, eg, Carchemish and Aleppo.

A distinction should be made between libraries and archives. The latter are essentially practical collections of the documents of law, diplomacy and economics. The documents in general relate strictly to their own times, although some may retain relevance beyond

2/ Above right
Ancient scripts used in Syro-Palestine

1/ Egyptian Hieroglyphic: Papyri circulated in the Levant c 1600-1200 BC, though none has survived. Hieroglyphic writing is preserved on statues from Byblos and Ugarit, and on ivories from Megiddo. Illustrated: part of an ivory pen case with an inscription of Ramesses III.

2/ Akkadian Cuneiform: The Canaanite princes used Cuneiform tablets with the Akkadian language for their correspondence, as is shown by the Amarna letters from Egypt, and the letters found in the Levant itself. Illustrated: a letter from the Pharaoh to the king of Damascus, c 1400 BC (found at Kamid el-Loz).

3/ Ugaritic 'Cuneiform Alphabet': A native Ugaritic script, cuneiform in appearance, is alphabetic in character. The signs are found on school tablets written in the order of the later Phoenician-Hebrew Alphabet. Illustrated: Ugaritic ABC.

4/ Hittite Hieroglyphic from Ugarit: The Hittite administration of Syria employed Cuneiform

1/ Map below
The transmission of languages and their scripts in the Mediterranean, the Near East and as far east as the Indus Valley is shown. A continuous arrow indicates a definite transmission and a dashed arrow represents a probability.

1/ The spread of writing

- Mesopotamian cuneiform
- Egyptian hieroglyphic
- Alphabetic script
- definite transmission
- possible transmission

MESOPOTAMIAN CUNEIFORM

1 The earliest writing consists of pictographic signs on clay tablets from Uruk, from the 'Protoliterate' period (c 3200-2800 BC). These should probably be read as Sumerian, implying that the Sumerians invented the script, but definite proof is lacking.

2 In the Early Dynastic period (c 2800-2400 BC) archaic inscriptions certainly in Sumerian are found on many sites, including Ur and Lagash. The script has developed from pictographic to 'Cuneiform': ie, the signs are made up of wedge (Latin cuneus)-shaped strokes.

3 A late Early Dynastic palace archive has been discovered at Ebla (c 2500-2300 BC) containing some 15,000 tablets, written in Sumerian Cuneiform but also 'Eblaite', a Semitic language. Thus the script was early adapted to write a non-Sumerian language.

4 The Semitic Dynasty of Akkad (c 2400-2250 BC), borrowed Cuneiform for its inscriptions. Akkadian, known in two dialects, Babylonian and Assyrian, replaced Sumerian as the spoken language of Mesopotamia. Sumerian was retained as a learned language. Cuneiform always remained primarily a script for clay tablets but was also carved on stone objects.

5 At Susa a large group of tablets contemporary with the later Protoliterate was found, inscribed in an undeciphered pictographic script different from that of Mesopotamia, but apparently modelled on it. These 'Proto-Elamite' tablets are still being found at several sites across Iran.

6 After 2000 BC Cuneiform Akkadian on clay tablets was widely used as an international means of communication. Other peoples borrowed the script and the tablet for writing their own languages: the Elamites (c 2250-350 BC); the Hurrians (c 2200-1300 BC); the Hittites (c 1650-1200 BC); and latest, the Urartians (c 850-600 BC).

7 The Indus valley cities have produced many short undeciphered inscriptions on seals, etc, c 2500-1800 BC. Links with Mesopotamia by sea or overland across Iran may have transmitted the idea of writing and led to the local invention of the script.

8 In the Persian Empire (c 550-330 BC), a 'Cuneiform' script was used to write the language Old Persian on monumental stone inscriptions. This script is Cuneiform only in appearance; actually it was modelled on the Aramaic alphabet with influence from the Akkadian syllabary.

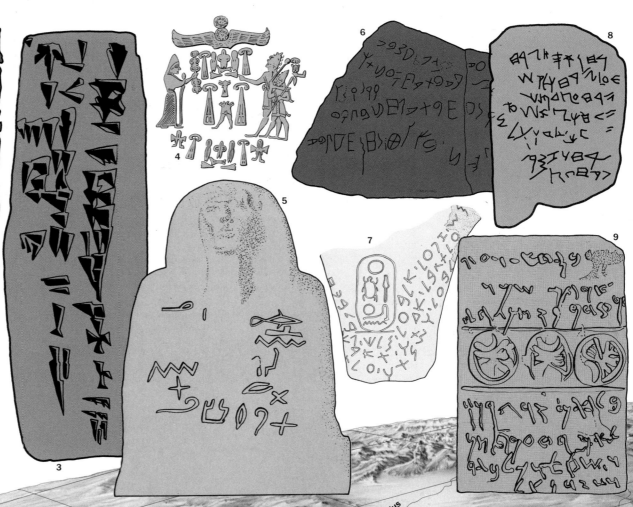

Akkadian, but their own Hieroglyphic script is found on seals validating official documents. This impression of the seal of Tudhaliya IV shows the king's name and titles written in Hieroglyphic.

5/ Sinaitic: At the Egyptian turquoise mines in Sinai linear pictographic inscriptions were found, dating to c 1500 BC. This script links with both Egyptian Hieroglyphic and the Proto-Canaanite Alphabet. This statue inscription, the signs hypothetically identified with alphabetic letters, reads 'to the Lady'.

6/ Proto-Canaanite Alphabet: Among Proto-Canaanite graffiti this sherd, dating to c 1150 BC, shows a complete ABC in the traditional order implying that Proto-Canaanite was already organized for learning as a regular script.

7/ Phoenician Alphabet: The earliest known inscriptions in the true Alphabet are a group on stone by kings of Byblos dating c 1050-850 BC. This statue of the Egyptian Osorkon (914-874 BC) bears an inscription on its breast dedicating it to the Lady of Byblos.

8/ Hebrew Alphabet: OT references imply an early writing among the Hebrews, but examples have not survived. The earliest example, dating probably to c 900 BC, is this small tablet from Gezer on which has been scratched a calendar.

9/ Aramaic Alphabet: The Aramaeans left a corpus of stone inscriptions dated c 850-700 BC, influenced by the contemporary Hittite Hieroglyphic monuments. Illustrated: Aramaic tablet, agreement dated to 635 BC.

EGYPTIAN HIEROGLYPHIC

9 The earliest writing in Egypt is on stone monuments c 3100 BC, where the signs already show the characteristic monumental ('Hieroglyphic') forms. Since the period shows Mesopotamian cultural influences, it is thought that the knowledge of Mesopotamian writing inspired the invention of an original system.

10 The use of Hieroglyphic expanded in the Early Dynastic period (c 3100-2900 BC), surviving largely as tomb inscriptions on stone, wood and ivory, also sealings. It was certainly also written on papyrus, but none survives until c 2600-2500 BC.

11 The script, besides its monumental Hieroglyphic form, developed cursive hand-written forms for papyrus, Hieratic and later Demotic. Unlike Cuneiform, Hieroglyphic was never borrowed directly for writing any other language than its original, Egyptian.

12 In Crete, under Egyptian influence c 2000 BC a native 'Hieroglyphic' script begins to appear on seals and clay dockets. This developed into two linear scripts, A and B. Linear B (c 1400-1200 BC) has been deciphered and shown to write Mycenaean Greek.

13 Cyprus has two indigenous scripts, the undeciphered Cypro-Minoan on clay (c 1500-1200 BC), and the Cypriot syllabary (c 750-300 BC), descended from the earlier script and used for writing monumental inscriptions in Greek and an unknown language.

14 The Hittites employed a Hieroglyphic script for seals and monumental inscriptions, c 1500-700 BC, but the language written was Luvian not Hittite. Probably the Luvians constructed their own script with a knowledge of the Aegean and perhaps also the Egyptian scripts.

15 Many Egyptian Hieroglyphic inscriptions dating c 2700-1000 BC were discovered at the Egyptian mines in Sinai. Beside these there is a small group of linear pictographic inscriptions, 'Proto-Sinaitic', connected both with Hieroglyphic and with the Proto-Canaanite alphabet.

THE ALPHABET

16 North and South Arabian scripts appear at an uncertain date, probably c 500 BC, and the latter gave rise to Ethiopic. These scripts may have split off the developing alphabetic tradition as early as the Proto-Canaanite stage, ie, before 1000 BC.

17 Scattered graffiti in a linear pictographic script on various objects dating to c 1500-1100 BC come from Canaan. Termed Proto-Canaanite, the signs are found arranged in alphabetic order c 1150 BC. A system of writing on perishable material may be inferred.

18 In Ugarit a 'cuneiform alphabet' was used c 1400-1200 BC to write the local language, and this is also found at other sites in Canaan. The signs were arranged in alphabetic order, and the script is thus closely linked to the Proto-Canaanite linear alphabet.

19 From Byblos an undeciphered 'Pseudo-Hieroglyphic' script on stone and metal, dated uncertainly c 2000-1000 BC, occurs. More significant, the earliest readable inscriptions in the true Alphabet are found here in a group of Phoenician inscriptions on sculpture.

20 The Hebrews adopted the Alphabet c 1150-1050 BC, and would have written mostly on papyrus, of which almost none survives. Preserved contemporary documents from the Hebrew kingdoms c 620-595 BC are sparse: ostraca, seals, and very few stone inscriptions.

21 The Aramaeans adopted the Phoenician-Hebrew Alphabet after 900 BC, and established their script and language into Mesopotamia. Aramaic became the administrative language of the Persian Empire, c 500-330 BC, thereby disseminating their Alphabet widely from Anatolia to India.

22 Phoenician colonization c 1000-700 BC took them to the west, to Carthage, Malta, Sardinia and Spain, and their language and script went with them. As usual, survivals are mostly stone inscriptions, not very representative of their general literacy.

23 By c 800 BC, the Greeks had adopted the Phoenician Alphabet and remodelled it for their language. At first many different local forms of the Alphabet are attested, but by 400 BC the Ionic Alphabet had been adopted as the common script.

24 In Anatolia several peoples adopted a variant of the Alphabet, probably from the Greeks, and left stone inscriptions, etc: Phrygian (from c 750 BC), Lydian, Carian (from c 600), Lycian (from c 500). These Anatolian writings continued until Alexander's conquest, when they were superseded by Greek.

25 Greek colonization of the west, Sicily, S. Italy and S. France in the period c 800-500 BC effectively Hellenized the coastal areas, and established the Greek language and script. Each colony used its own metropolis' variant of the Alphabet.

26 The Etruscans began writing after 700 BC. Earliest attested inscriptions are from c 650 BC. Their Alphabet was probably the Euboean variant borrowed from Cumae. They maintained their script and their still largely undeciphered language until the 1st century AD.

27 Early Rome was under strong Etruscan influence, and borrowed much, including the Alphabet. Most of the letters of the alphabet passed directly from the Greek through the Etruscan (A B E H I K M N O Q T) though some in variant forms (D L P R S V). Three acquired new values (C, F and X), and three were later additions (G, Y, Z).

SOLOMON'S reign is often considered a 'golden age', but even during his lifetime, much of the territory taken by David had been lost. Damascus had revolted and established a new Aramaean monarchy (see page 104). Tyre controlled part of Galilee, and an Egyptian campaign in Philistia resulted in the loss of Ekron and its north-west territory. Nevertheless, the kingdom left by Solomon in 928 BC to his son Rehoboam, was considerable, and had his successor shown wisdom, the 'United Monarchy' might well have lasted. However, Rehoboam's failure to recognize the deep-seated division between north and south resulted in the dissolution of a major power into two minor kingdoms.

Rehoboam's accession to the throne in Jerusalem and Judah was automatic: the dynastic principle was favoured in the south and his acceptance as Solomon's heir was unquestioned. In the north, however, charismatic leadership was customary and the choice of Rehoboam was not a foregone conclusion. Also, the rift between north and south had widened since Saul's death. His son, Eshbaal, had been murdered by David's supporters, thereby ensuring a Judaean kingship, and further northern resentment had been engendered by David placing the re-captured Ark of the Covenant in Jerusalem (see page 78). The northern tribes had been bound into the united kingdom by treaty rather than by any inherent concept of unity. Thus it was necessary for Rehoboam, after his accession in Jerusalem, to travel to Shechem to renew this covenant. At the meeting was Jeroboam ben-Nebat, who, for dissident activities, had been banished by Solomon and had taken refuge with Pharaoh Shoshenq I of Egypt (known in the Bible as Shishak). At the assembly, the northerners appeared willing to accept Rehoboam's kingship, but only given certain conditions, chiefly a reduction in taxation and forced labour which had been imposed by Solomon. Rehoboam requested three days to consult his advisers, then he refused. The reaction was swift: Rehoboam's chief of forced labour was murdered and Jeroboam was proclaimed king.

DIVISION OF THE KINGDOM AND THE CAMPAIGN OF PHARAOH SHISHAK I

King Rehoboam, the son of Solomon, failed to contain the internal tension inherent in the kingdom of Israel, between Judah and the northern tribes. After his accession in 928 BC, there followed a period of almost continuous war between Judah and the north, which weakened the monarchy sufficiently to make it fall prey to Egyptian domination. In 924 BC Pharaoh Shishak taking advantage of the divided kingdom, led a campaign into Israel and captured many cities.

Rehoboam returned to Jerusalem and launched a campaign against the north.

After the assembly at Shechem, there probably followed continuous war between Israel and Judah. Most disputed was the territory of Benjamin, and the border was not fixed for several generations. Initially, it appears to have run south of Bethel, and on the west and east north of Aijalon and south of Jericho respectively (see Map 1).

Such a period of conflict allowed areas conquered under the United Monarchy to break away. The situation in Transjordan is unclear but, since according to the Mesha stela Omri re-conquered Moab, it must be assumed that it had gained independence. That Israel maintained control over at least part of Ammon is clear from Jeroboam's claim to have 'built' Penuel, a site identified as Telul-edh-Dhahab on the Wadi Zerqa. This may have been one of Jeroboam's capitals of the new state. He also enlarged Shechem (T. Balata) and Tirzah (T. el-Far'ah) for use as royal residences.

Shishak, founder of the 22nd (Libyan) Dynasty, became Pharaoh during Solomon's reign. Relations between the two kingdoms were probably peaceful, although Shishak did offer refuge to Jeroboam. With the division of the kingdom it is likely that relations between Egypt and Israel

3/ Major excavated sites in Israel
- site with Iron Age II remains
- state boundary

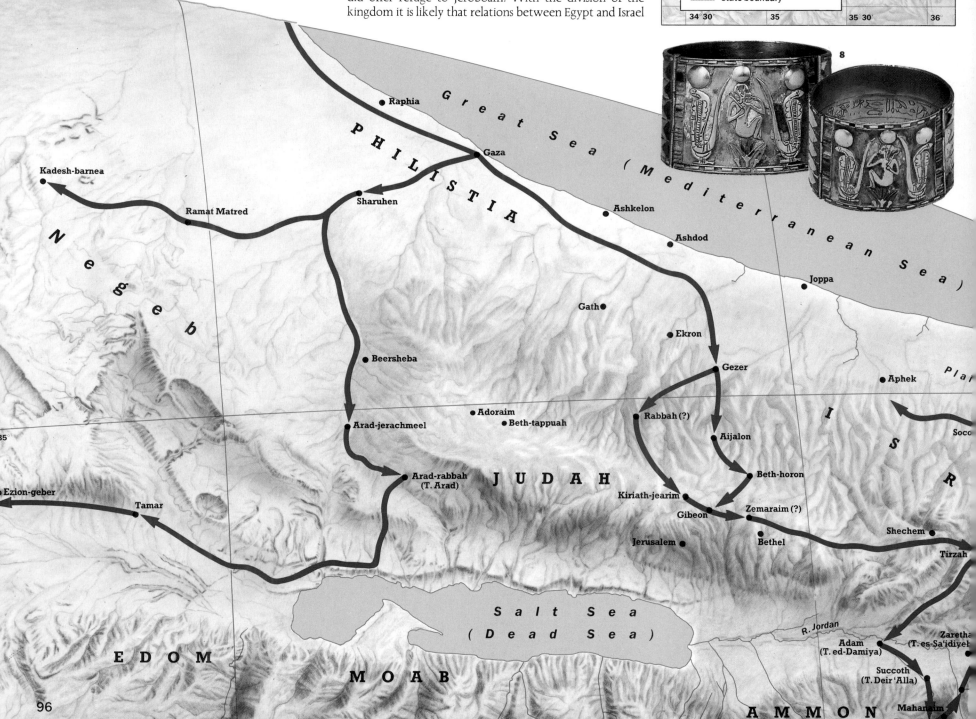

remained initially cordial, and possibly for this reason Rehoboam, fearing that the 'special relationship' between Shishak and Jeroboam might develop into an alliance, fortified cities in the Judaean hills extending south and west from Jerusalem in preparation for an Egyptian invasion (see page 118).

When the invasion came in 924 BC, however, it was not limited to Judah. The OT only describes Shishak as capturing the fortified cities of Judah and receiving the temple and palace treasures from Jerusalem but the Karnak list includes many conquered cities in Israel. That this list represents an actual campaign and not a boast is clear from evidence found at sites mentioned in the inscription.

The campaign route is disputed, due to the incompleteness of the Karnak list and difficulties in identifying many places. The main force probably followed a route through Gaza in Philistia, to Gezer and the Judaean hills. Having received the tribute of Rehoboam, probably at Gibeon, Shishak's army advanced into Israel, possibly taking Shechem – and then Tirzah. The Egyptians then seem to have turned eastwards, crossing the Jordan opposite Adam,

(T. ed-Damiya). The objective of this foray into Transjordan was to capture Jeroboam's residence at Penuel and the cities of Succoth (T. Deir 'Alla) and Zaphon (possibly T. el-Qos). Afterwards, Shishak re-crossed the river at some point north of Zarethan (T. es-Sa'idiyeh) and went to Beth-shean and the Plain of Esdraelon. The Egyptians probably set up a base at Megiddo: a fragment of a commemorative stela of Shishak was found there. When Shishak's army left Megiddo it returned home via the Plain of Sharon and the Via Maris: the exact itinerary cannot be reconstructed as the Karnak inscription breaks off here.

In addition to the major campaign route the Karnak list shows that an army detachment was sent from Gaza to attack settlements in the Negeb. Sharuhen (T. el-Far'ah, (south)?) and Arad (T. Arad) are mentioned and destruction levels at Beersheba and Ezion-geber (T. el-Kheleifeh) may reasonably be attributed to the activities of Shishak.

> 'IN THE FIFTH YEAR OF KING REHOBOAM, SHISHAK KING OF EGYPT CAME UP AGAINST JERUSALEM: HE TOOK AWAY THE TREASURES OF THE HOUSE OF THE LORD.' I KINGS 14.25-26

1/ Map below right
The seeds of division inherent in Solomon's kingdom were brought to fruition during the reign of his son Rehoboam. Israel, under Jeroboam, broke away and continuous war is said to have ensued, which allowed areas such as Moab to gain their independence.

2/ Map below left
On the Great Temple of Amon at Karnak is a topographical list confirming the biblical account that Pharaoh Shishak, taking advantage of the divided kingdom, invaded Israel and 'came up against Jerusalem'. The map shows Shishak's route and the places from the inscription which have been located. There probably was no intention to establish permanent control over Israel – it may best be explained as an Egyptian show of strength.

3/ Map above left
An important innovation during the monarchy was the increasing use of iron. Excavated sites with Iron II remains are a useful source of information for the material culture of this period.

4/ Left
The stela set up by Mesha, king of Moab, to record his victory over Ahab, king of Israel in c860BC. Although Moab broke away from the United Monarchy at this time, it was later reconquered by Omri (see page 100).

5, 6 and 7/ Left
A fragment of an Egyptian victory stela found at Megiddo with the name Pharaoh Shishak. A drawing (6) helps to show the detail more clearly. The reconstruction of the complete stela (7) shows where the surviving fragment would have been.

8/ Far left
A pair of golden bracelets made for Shishak's son, Prince Nimlot. They show the child Horus sitting on a lotus blossom flanked by a pair of uraei or royal cobras.

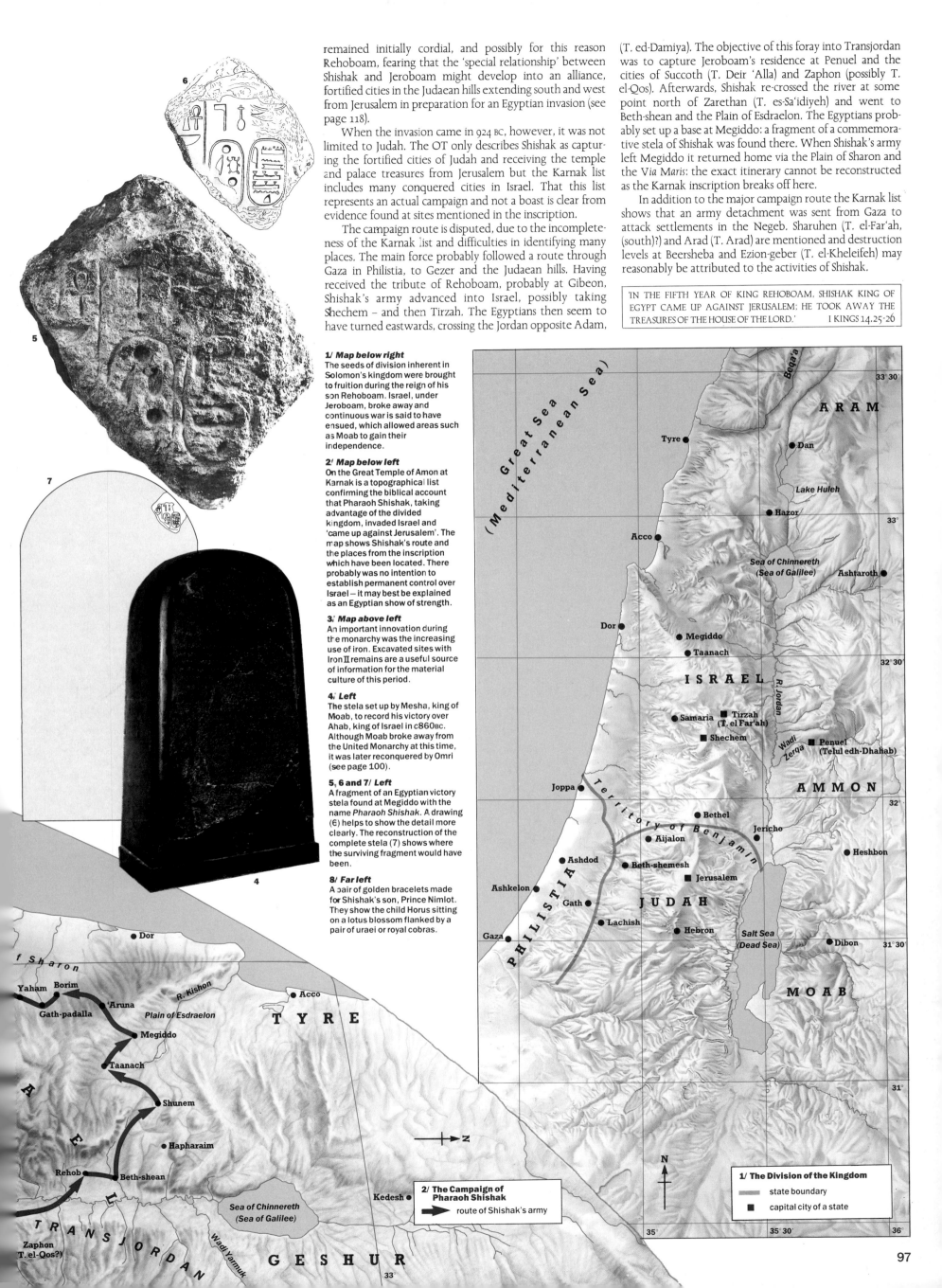

2/ The Campaign of Pharaoh Shishak
→ route of Shishak's army

1/ The Division of the Kingdom
state boundary
■ capital city of a state

OMRI first appears in the Bible as commander-in-chief of the Israelite army, at Gibbethon during a campaign against the Philistines in 885 BC (I KINGS 16.15-18). During the campaign another army commander, Zimri, murdered Elah the king of Israel (886-5 BC), at Tirzah, the capital city, and made himself king. Omri's army proclaimed him king in the field and he then marched against his rival at Tirzah. After a siege of seven days Zimri burnt the royal palace and perished in the flames. The kingdom was in such turmoil during this period that even this event did not give Omri sole control; another group was supporting an alternative ruler, Tibni, whose claim to the throne was probably as legitimate as that of Omri. This rivalry continued until the death of Tibni in 880 BC.

At the beginning of his reign Omri retained Tirzah as his royal residence and capital city. It had already been used, on occasion, by Jeroboam I the first king of Israel (931-910 BC) (I KINGS 14.17), and has been the permanent capital of king Baasha (909-886 BC). Tirzah, the large mound of T. el-Far'ah, is located near two springs, at the head of a fertile valley, modern Wadi el-Far'ah. A number of dressed stones have been found forming parts of several well-built but apparently unfinished buildings, which very likely represent the building activity of Omri.

Another building project achieved during the dynasty of Omri was the construction of Samaria. Some seven miles to the south-west of Tirzah and accessible from there along a south-west valley branching from the upper Wadi el-Far'ah lay the important and ancient city of Shechem. It commanded the most convenient pass across the central range and led to a widening valley, which descended north-westwards to the Plain of Sharon. A little over five miles to the north-west of Shechem, where the valley begins to widen, and where another route runs northwards towards Dothan and Megiddo, was a largely unoccupied hill site. This site, according to the Bible was the property of a private citizen named Shemer, and was purchased by Omri for two talents of silver (I KINGS 16.23-24) as the site for his new capital city. He made this change in 880 BC after Tibni had been successfully eliminated. Omri may have been considering this move for some time but it would not have been practical to build on a virtually virgin site until he had full control of the entire kingdom. According to the OT Omri named his new capital Samaria (today called Sebastiyeh) after its former owner Shemer (I KINGS 16.24).

By acquiring a new site Omri, like David before him, established a capital city with no earlier associations or loyalties to previous kings. The move to Samaria, with its westward orientation may also have reflected a growing association with Solomon's old ally, Phoenicia, ruled at this time by Ethbaal I of Tyre. Indeed there is abundant evidence for close links between Israel and the Phoenicians during the time of Omri's son and successor Ahab (874-853

THE DYNASTY OF OMRI

Omri's reign over Israel (885-874 BC), was so significant in retrospect that the neighbouring Assyrians came to refer to Israel as *bit Humri*, 'house of Omri'. Omri was a usurper whose family background is obscure. Unlike other rulers we do not even know his father's name; he may even have been of foreign or Canaanite extraction. Nevertheless he stabilized the Israelite kingdom and established a dynasty which lasted for over 40 years, through four reigns; and which was distinguished by important building projects. This period was also characterized by prominent activities of the prophets Elijah and Elisha.

BC). Ahab married the daughter of Ethbaal (or Ittobaal), Jezebel, who brought her religion with her to the Israelite kingdom. Phoenician influence is seen in the architectural remains of the period found at Samaria.

Excavations on the citadel of Samaria have shown two early building phases which are ascribed to Omri and Ahab respectively. Omri only lived for six years after moving to Samaria, so his building projects had to be completed by his son, Ahab. The work attributed to Omri includes the construction of a large terrace about 820 by 525 ft in size, enclosed by a massive wall c 5 ft thick which also served in parts as a retaining wall. The wall was made of large well-dressed masonry blocks with somewhat smaller blocks in the upper courses. In the second phase, which is attributed to Ahab, an outer defensive casemate (chambered) wall was built, extending to a total width of 32 ft on the north side and 16 ft on the east. These were connected with an extension of the outer area, the western end of the terrace being carried out a further 98 ft. Though the details of the terrace have not been preserved, it seems, from what survives, that there were substantial rectangular buildings on it which were aligned with the retaining walls. Comparison of this fine masonry with Phoenician work at Tyre and elsewhere suggests that Omri and Ahab enlisted the aid of Ethbaal to supply Phoenician craftsmen for this work. This theory is supported by the discovery of a decorative pilaster capital similar to other examples of the 9th century BC from Megiddo and Hazor which reflect Phoenician inspiration.

Substantial architectural works built during the time of Ahab have also been found at Hazor and Megiddo. Relatively few artefacts can be directly connected with Omri or the members of his dynasty but one possibility is a fine scaraboid seal carved in Phoenician style and inscribed *yzbl*. This may be the Phoenician spelling of the name of Ahab's wife, Yzebel, which appears in the OT as Jezebel.

DECLINE OF THE DYNASTY OF OMRI

An increasing threat to the Israelite kingdom and its neighbours during the 9th century BC was the growing power of Assyria. A coalition of states which included Damascus, Hammath, Arvad and Ammon, as well as Israel, under Ahab, assembled in north Syria, in 853 BC, to attempt to halt the advance of the Assyrian king, Shalmaneser (858-824 BC), and his armies. A major battle was fought at Qarqar (see page 108) in which, though Shalmaneser was not defeated, the Assyrian advance was stopped. In the same year as the battle of Qarqar Ahab was killed during a battle against the Aramaeans at Ramoth-gilead and was succeeded by his son Ahaziah (853-852 BC). Ahaziah had close links with Jehoshaphat, king of Judah: they were both involved in an unsuccessful attempt to revive sea trade down the Red Sea from Ezion-geber. Ahaziah died after a fall in Samaria. He was succeeded by another son of Ahab, Joram (or Jehoram) (852-841 BC). Both the short reign of Ahaziah and that of Joram saw increasingly close links developing with the kingdom of Judah, expressed by dynastic marriages and joint ventures. The idea of monarchy based on a dynastic succession however, was never as deep-rooted in Israel as it was in Judah. Strong rulers were required to hold Israel together. Omri and Ahab succeeded in this but the reign of their two successors, Ahaziah and Joram, saw the decline of the kingdom.

Control of the kingdom was also hampered by the religious fervour of the prophets Elijah and Elisha. The prophet was a lone figure seized upon by God, granted experiences or visions of the divine (Elijah in the cave, Isaiah in the Temple), and compelled inwardly, often at the risk of physical injury or death, to speak the truth as he perceived it to the mightiest in the land. Elijah and Elisha constantly inveighed against the rulers of Israel for allowing the worship of foreign deities. The climax to the unrest came with the revolt of Jehu who seized control of the kingdom and murdered both Joram and Ahaziah, the Judaean king.

5/ Below
Omri built Samaria as his capital city and it remained the capital until 721 BC when it was destroyed by the Assyrians.

A: The Roman city wall of Samaria, strengthened by towers, surrounded an area of c 137 acres.

B: The acropolis or royal quarter of the Israelite kings (enlarged from A).
1 Remains of earliest city wall, the 'inner wall' 5 ft thick, of 'Phoenician' workmanship, enclosing an area of 291 by 583 ft. Believed to be built by Omri. **2** A building in which the carved Phoenician ivories were found (AMOS 6.4). **3** A casemate wall 32 ft thick on one side and 16 ft on the other which enclosed a larger area surrounding buildings attributed to Ahab.

C: Detail of the west end of the Israelite city of Samaria.
1 A storehouse, 59 by 82 ft, in which the inscribed potsherds or ostraca were found (see page 111). **2** The Palace of the Israelite Kings. An impressive building, consisting of a central courtyard surrounded by rooms. 78 by 88 ft. **3** A square block that was possibly the foundation for a tower that fortified the acropolis. **4** A tower now generally dated to the Hellenistic period.

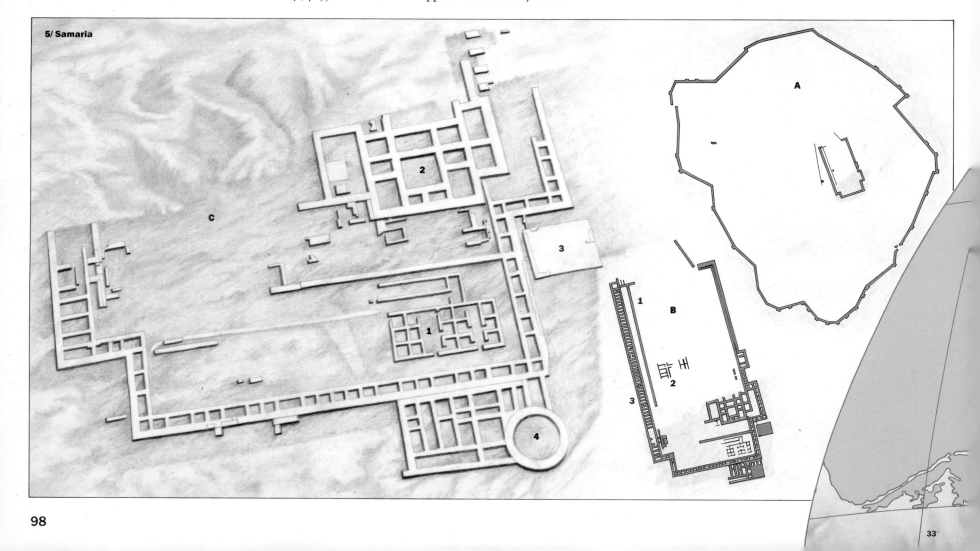

5/ Samaria

33

He then completely wiped out the family of Ahab, including Jezebel and much of the royal family of Judah, who would have been possible avengers for the murders of their kinsmen. In this bloodthirsty fashion the dynasty of Omri came to an end.

'IN THE THIRTY-FIRST YEAR OF ASA KING OF JUDAH, OMRI BEGAN TO REIGN OVER ISRAEL, AND REIGNED FOR TWELVE YEARS; SIX YEARS HE REIGNED IN TIRZAH. HE BOUGHT THE FIELD OF SAMARIA FROM SHEMER FOR TWO TALENTS OF SILVER; AND HE FORTIFIED THE HILL, AND CALLED THE NAME OF THE CITY WHICH HE BUILT, SAMARIA, AFTER THE NAME OF SHEMER, THE OWNER OF THE HILL.'
I KINGS 16.23-24

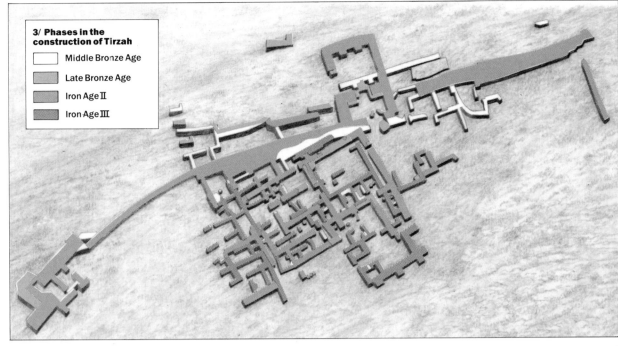

3/ Phases in the construction of Tirzah
- ☐ Middle Bronze Age
- ▨ Late Bronze Age
- ▨ Iron Age II
- ▨ Iron Age III

4

TYRE	ISRAEL	JUDAH
Ethbaal (Ittoba'al I)	Omri (885-) 880-874	Asa 911-870
Baal-azor II	Jezebel = Ahab 874-853	Jehosaphat 870-848
	Ahaziah 853-852 Joram 852-841	Athaliah = Jehoram 841-835 848-841

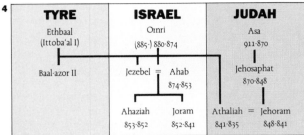

2/ Left
Carved ivory from Nimrud. A woman at the window was a common Phoenician motif.

1/ Map below
Omri secured the throne of Israel in 885 BC, by marching up from Gibbethon to defeat his rival at Tirzah which he made his capital. He later moved to Samaria. During the reign of the House of Omri the first of the major OT prophets, Elijah and Elisha, began their mission.

3/ Above
Excavation at T. el-Far'ah has uncovered Omri's capital Tirzah. It was the capital of Omri's predecessors and it is believed that Omri attacked the city but subsequently rebuilt part of the walls. Remains of the city wall extend for c 344 ft.

4/ Above far left
Genealogical table of the House of Omri.

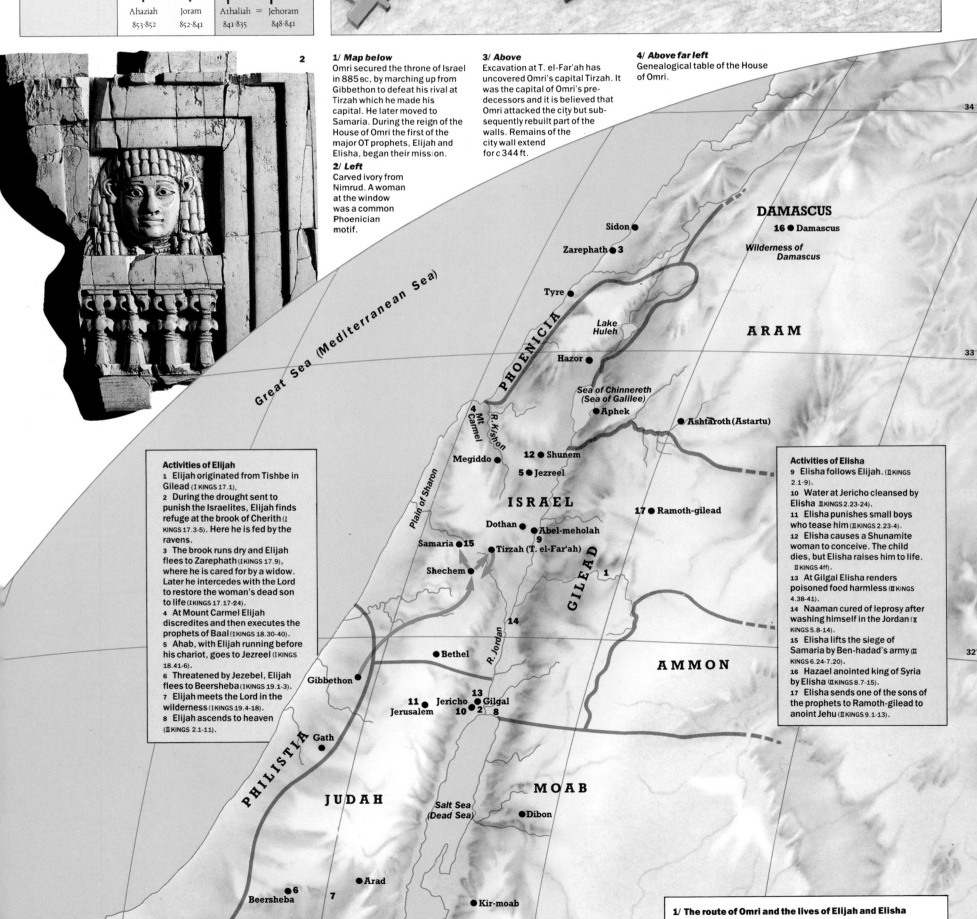

Activities of Elijah
1 Elijah originated from Tishbe in Gilead (I KINGS 17.1).
2 During the drought sent to punish the Israelites, Elijah finds refuge at the brook of Cherith (I KINGS 17.3-5). Here he is fed by the ravens.
3 The brook runs dry and Elijah flees to Zarephath (I KINGS 17.9), where he is cared for by a widow. Later he intercedes with the Lord to restore the woman's dead son to life (I KINGS 17.17-24).
4 At Mount Carmel Elijah discredits and then executes the prophets of Baal (I KINGS 18.30-40).
5 Ahab, with Elijah running before his chariot, goes to Jezreel (I KINGS 18.41-6).
6 Threatened by Jezebel, Elijah flees to Beersheba (I KINGS 19.1-3).
7 Elijah meets the Lord in the wilderness (I KINGS 19.4-18).
8 Elijah ascends to heaven (II KINGS 2.1-11).

Activities of Elisha
9 Elisha follows Elijah. (II KINGS 2.1-9).
10 Water at Jericho cleansed by Elisha II KINGS 2.23-24).
11 Elisha punishes small boys who tease him (II KINGS 2.23-24).
12 Elisha causes a Shunamite woman to conceive. The child dies, but Elisha raises him to life. (II KINGS 4ff).
13 At Gilgal Elisha renders poisoned food harmless (II KINGS 4.38-41).
14 Naaman cured of leprosy after washing himself in the Jordan (II KINGS 5.8-14).
15 Elisha lifts the siege of Samaria by Ben-hadad's army (II KINGS 6.24-7.20).
16 Hazael anointed king of Syria by Elisha (II KINGS 8.7-15).
17 Elisha sends one of the sons of the prophets to Ramoth-gilead to anoint Jehu (II KINGS 9.1-13).

1/ The route of Omri and the lives of Elijah and Elisha
→ route of Omri
17 ● events in the lives of the prophets

MOAB, as a geographical designation, refers to the strip of agricultural land sandwiched between the Dead Sea and the Arabian Desert. The Mujib canyon (the R. Arnon of OT times) separates northern Moab from Moab proper. The region of northern Moab was constantly disputed territory between the Israelites, Ammonites, and Moabites.

The Book of Joshua claims for Israel all of the territory as far south as the Arnon, for example, while other biblical texts (see especially ISA 15 and JER 48) regard everything as far north as Heshbon and Elealeh as belonging to Moab. David, Solomon, Omri, and Ahab dominated northern Moab, but probably were unable to exercise any kind of permanent control over Moab proper because of its geographical isolation. David's census takers began at the Arnon and worked northwards, for example, and king Mesha claims to have recovered specifically northern Moab from Israel (see below). Even the Turkish sultans of more recent times have found it impossible to police the area between the Wadi Mujib and the Wadi Hesa.

Moab was good farm and grazing land in ancient times, as it is today. In time of famine, people from Judah might go to Moab in search of food (which is the setting of the Book of Ruth). Mesha paid annual tribute to Omri and Ahab in kind – lambs and wool.

As well as the Moabite Stone detailing king Mesha's achievements, there are two biblical passages shedding further light on Israelite–Moabite relations during Mesha's reign: II KINGS 1.1, where we read that 'after the death of Ahab, Moab rebelled against Israel', and II KINGS 3.4-27, which describes an unsuccessful attempt on the part of Jehoram to restore Israelite control over Moab. Drawing on both the Moab inscription and the biblical texts, the following description of the relationship between Israel and Moab seems reasonable.

David dominated northern Moab and may have exercised less direct control over Moab proper. Solomon was presumably able to exercise some degree of control over Moab as well, although Moabite–Israelite relations during Solomon's reign are less clear. (Note that Solomon had a

1/ Map right
Principal sites in Moab.

2/ Right
Fragment of a stela discovered near Mt Shihan in Moab, probably dating from the era of the Israelite and Moabite kingdoms.

3/ Below right
Our prime source about ancient Moab comes from the 'Moabite Stone' or 'Mesha Inscription'. Discovered near Dibon in 1868 it is a memorial stela erected by Mesha, king of Moab. It was occasioned by the completion of a sanctuary dedicated to the Moabite god Chemosh, and the inscription reviews the major accomplishments of Mesha's reign. Mesha was proud of having restored Moabite control over northern Moab.

Moabite wife and made arrangements for the worship of Chemosh in Jerusalem.) At some point, possibly during the years of conflict between Israel and Judah which followed Solomon's death, even northern Moab reverted to Moabite hands. Later Omri restored Israelite control over northern Moab and extracted tribute from the Moabite king on a regular basis; Omri's son (Ahab) continued the same policy.

THE REIGN OF MESHA
However, Mesha ascended the throne of Moab approximately mid-way in Ahab's reign and his inscription depicts this event as the beginning of a new era. 'Omri occupied the land of Medeba and [Israel] dwelt there in his time and half the time of his son, forty years; but Chemosh dwelt there in my time.' Actually Mesha probably did not challenge Israelite authority until Ahab died (see II KINGS 1.1; 3.5), and his challenge at that point consisted of refusing to deliver the annual tribute, seizing control of northern Moab, and making preparations for defence against Israel's retaliatory attack which he assumed would occur as soon as a new king was established in Samaria.

The expected Israelite retaliatory attack did not come for several years; in fact not until Ahaziah died and was succeeded by Jehoram. By that time Mesha had secured his position in northern Moab. Jehoram, supported by the king of Judah and possibly of Edom, chose to march around the southern end of the Dead Sea and penetrate the heartland of Moab proper. This narrative reflects a complex literary history and can hardly be taken at face value. Also

ISRAEL AND MOAB

The Israelites and Moabites were close neighbours who shared a common culture and whose respective histories were intertwined. Periods of peaceful relations (as depicted in the Book of Ruth) were interrupted occasionally by periods of hostilities (as depicted in II KINGS 3 and the Mesha Inscription). The Mesha Inscription, which is the most extensive ancient inscription discovered thus far in Palestine, tells how Mesha recovered northern Moab from Israelite control.

1/ Principal archaeological sites in Moab

■ site

the narrative provides very little specific geographical information.

The most likely order of events is as follows: Jehoram marched out from Samaria (Sebastiyeh). After collecting the king of Judah, he marched 'by the way of the wilderness of Edom'. That is, he marched around the southern end of the Dead Sea, which would have led through the traditionally Edomite territory both southwest and south of the sea. Thus they would have approached Moab from the southwest where the terrain is extremely rugged. Although Jehoram devastated the Moabite countryside, he failed to reduce Kir-hareseth where Mesha took refuge. Kir-hareseth is usually identified with modern-day Kerak.

Years later, after Israel had fallen under Syrian domination, Mesha erected the inscription which recounted his successful rebellion against Israel and other deeds.

KING MESHA'S ACCOMPLISHMENTS
Mesha identifies himself as a Dibonite, and the Mesha stela was discovered among the ruins of present-day Dhiban or somewhere in the immediate vicinity. The exact spot of its discovery is no longer known. We learn from the inscription that the stela was erected in connection with the dedication of a sanctuary to Chemosh at a place called Qarhoh. Presumably Dibon served as Moab's capital during Mesha's reign and Qarhoh was some sort of suburb of Dibon, perhaps a royal quarter. Surrounded by rolling agricultural land, Medeba was the key city of northern Moab, as it is today. Note that Omri is said to have occupied specifically 'the land of Medeba'. Lines 9-21 of the inscription recount Mesha's key moves in his recovery of the land of Medeba from Israel, but should not be read as a chronological sequence of events – eg, as the itinerary of a military campaign. Specifically, he attacked, massacred, and looted two Israelite settlements in northern Moab (Ataroth and Nebo); fortified two other sites on the northwestern slopes of the plateau (Baal-meon and Qaryaten); and placed his own loyalists in Jahaz. Apparently Jahaz had been built (or fortified) by the Israelites to serve as a military and administrative base during their occupation of northern Moab. Contrary to Professor Albright's translation of the inscription from the Moabite Stone (see below), there is nothing to suggest that Mesha took Jahaz by force. Possibly the Israelite soldiers and/or administrative officials withdrew rather than attempting to defend the place.

Lines 18-30 of the inscription describe Mesha's accomplishments as a builder. Attention is turned to the sanctuary at Qarhoh, for example, which would have been one of Mesha's recent accomplishments and which occasioned the inscription.

'WE HAVE HEARD OF THE PRIDE OF MOAB, HOW PROUD HE WAS; OF HIS ARROGANCE, HIS PRIDE, AND HIS INSOLENCE – HIS BOASTS ARE FALSE. THEREFORE LET MOAB WAIL, LET EVERY ONE WAIL FOR MOAB. MOURN, UTTERLY STRICKEN, FOR THE RAISIN-CAKES OF KIR-HARESETH.'
ISA 16.6-7

3

The Moabite Stone
This important inscription was discovered intact in 1868; it was subsequently broken, presumably by local bedouin tribesmen, and in 1873 it was taken to the Louvre. (See photograph on page 97.)

The date of the Mesha stela is roughly fixed by the reference to Mesha, king of Moab in II KINGS 3.4 as about the mid-9th century BC.

The following is a translation of the stela:
I (am) Mesha, son of Chemosh-[...], king of Moab, the Dibonite — my father (had) reigned over Moab thirty years, and I reigned after my father, — (who) made this high place for Chemosh in Qarhoh [...] because he saved me from all the kings and caused me to triumph over all my adversaries. As for Omri (5) king of Israel, he humbled Moab many years (lit., days), for Chemosh was angry at his land. And his son followed him and he also said, "I will humble Moab". In my time he spoke (thus), but I have triumphed over him and over his house, while Israel hath perished for ever! (Now) Omri had occupied the land of Medeba, and (Israel) had dwelt there in his time and half the time of his son (Ahab), forty years; but Chemosh dwelt there in my time.

And I built Baal-meon, making a reservoir in it, and I built (10) Qaryaten. Now the men of Gad had always dwelt in the land of Ataroth, and the king of Israel had built Ataroth for them; but I fought against the town and took it and slew all the people of the town as satiation (intoxication) for Chemosh and Moab. And I brought back from there Arel (or Oriel), its chieftain, dragging him before Chemosh in Kerioth, and I settled there men of Sharon and men of Maharith. And Chemosh said to me, "Go, take Nebo from Israel!" (15) So I went by night and fought against it from the break of dawn until noon, taking it and slaying all, seven thousand men, boys, women, girls and maid-servants, for I had devoted them to destruction for (the god) Ashtar-Chemosh. And I took from there the [...] of the Lord, dragging them before Chemosh. And the king of Israel had built Jahaz, and he dwelt there while he was fighting against me, but Chemosh drove him out before me. And (20) I took from Moab two hundred men, all first class (warriors), and set them against Jahaz and took it in order to attach it to (the

district of) Dibon.

It was I (who) built Qarhoh, the wall of the forests and the wall of the citadel; I also built its gates and I built its towers and I built the king's house, and I made both of its reservoirs for water inside the town. And there was no cistern inside the town at Qarhoh, so I said to all the people, "Let each of you make (25) a cistern for himself in his house!" And I cut beams for Qarhoh with Israelite captives. I built Aroer, and I made the highway in the Arnon (valley) I built Beth-bamoth, for it had been destroyed; I built Bezer – for it lay in ruins – with fifty men of Dibon, for all Dibon is (my) loyal dependency.

And I reigned (in peace) over the hundred towns which I had added to the land. And I built (30) [...] Medeba and Beth-diblathen and Beth-baal-meon, and I set there the [...] of the land. And as for Hauronen, there dwelt in it [...And] Chemosh said to me, "Go down, fight against Hauronen." And I went down [and I fought against the town and I took it], and Chemosh dwelt there in my time....

THE epigraphic material recently uncovered at the religious centre of Kuntillet 'Ajrud to the south of Kadesh-barnea in Sinai, provides a complex picture concerning the multiplicity of religious practices existing during the 9th and 8th centuries BC. The Hebrew and Phoenician inscriptions which were found at the site bear the names of El, Yhwh*, Baal and Asherah. Although the monotheistic Hebrew faith precluded the addition of any female deity as consort to Yhwh, pictures and an inscription were found at 'Ajrud which may represent 'Yhwh and his consort'. It has been suggested that the site was a religious way-station established by Athaliah, the daughter of Jezebel, on the pilgrim's route to Mt Horeb (ie, Mt Sinai). Athaliah's hatred of the priests of the House of David is well known from the Bible.

STELAE
The custom of erecting an upright commemorative stone stela for religious purposes can be traced back to very early times (eg, a basalt stone was placed in a niche in a Pre-Pottery Neolithic temple at Jericho). During Canaanite times, the stelae were regarded as a representation or symbol of the male divinity (eg, the stela of Baal: II KINGS 10.26-27). A group of basalt stelae, one carved with uplifted hands and a crescent moon, were found within the recess of a small Canaanite sanctuary belonging to the Late Bronze Age at Hazor Stratum IA (see page 89). The custom of erecting stelae was adopted by the Israelites as a sign of a covenant (eg, 'And Jacob took a stone and set it up as a pillar', GEN 31.45; cf, also the 12 stelae in EX 24.4), as a memorial

THE DIVIDED KINGDOM – ISRAEL

PAGAN CULTS AND THE PRACTICE OF RELIGION

At the time of the Divided Monarchy, when Israel was linked to Phoenicia by commerce and royal marriages, pagan cults were being practised by parts of the local population. At this time, Hebrew monotheism was struggling to resist these Phoenician cults as well as other Canaanite practices which had survived from the Late Bronze Age.

to the dead (eg, the stela on Rachel's grave, GEN 35.20), or as a cultic object (eg, Jacob took a stone and 'set it up for a pillar, and poured oil on the top of it and called the place Bethel' (house of God) GEN 28.18-19). The Israelite practice of setting up stelae for cultic purposes was later inveighed against mainly because they were regarded as stone representations of the divinity. For this reason they were condemned, together with sculpted idols, in LEV 26.1. A stone stela was found within the inner sanctum of an Israelite temple dating from the 9th century BC at T. Arad. Two small altars used for burnt offerings were found in front of the stela. The temple was apparently destroyed when Josiah centralized the Hebrew cult in Jerusalem (II KINGS 23), in accordance with the covenant he had made with God.

An abbreviation for the name of God. See page 192.

ALTARS AND SACRIFICE
The Hebrew word for altar *mizbeah* comes from the word 'to slaughter'. The *mizbeah* was an installation upon which animals were sacrificed and offerings were burnt. The early altars were either built out of mud-brick or of unquarried stone (EX 20.24-26; DEUT 27.5). Altars have been found at the Canaanite sanctuaries at Megiddo, and Lachish. Altars dating from the Iron Age are known from various sites in Palestine, notably at Beersheba where an altar was found which had 'horns' on the top of four corners and a protective snake engraved in its side. The horns symbolized the sacred power inherent in the altar. They were smeared with sacrificial blood (EX 29.12), and grasped by those seeking asylum (I KINGS 1.50; 2.28).

HOLY TREES
Holy trees, symbols of the life force, were also associated with Canaanite cults. Places of worship with sacred trees are frequently mentioned in the Bible (JOSH 24.26) and their use was later condemned by the prophets. Cylinder seals dating from the Late Bronze Age often show a worshipper standing in front of a tree. Other seals dating from the 10th-8th centuries BC, which depict a tree flanked by worshippers, have been found at T. Halif, Lachish, Beth-shemesh, Gibeon, Samaria, and Megiddo. A 'tree of life' with lily flowers being eaten by two ibex was found drawn on a large pithos at the religious centre of Kuntillet 'Ajrud. Gold pendants of the Late Bronze Age from T. el-'Ajjul (near Gaza) and from Ugarit (Ras Shamra) show stylized trees growing out of the navel or the pudenda of a formalized goddess. Sexual intercourse under these holy trees was thought to transmit the potency and vitality of the goddess (HOS 4.13-14). These

(Continued on page 102)

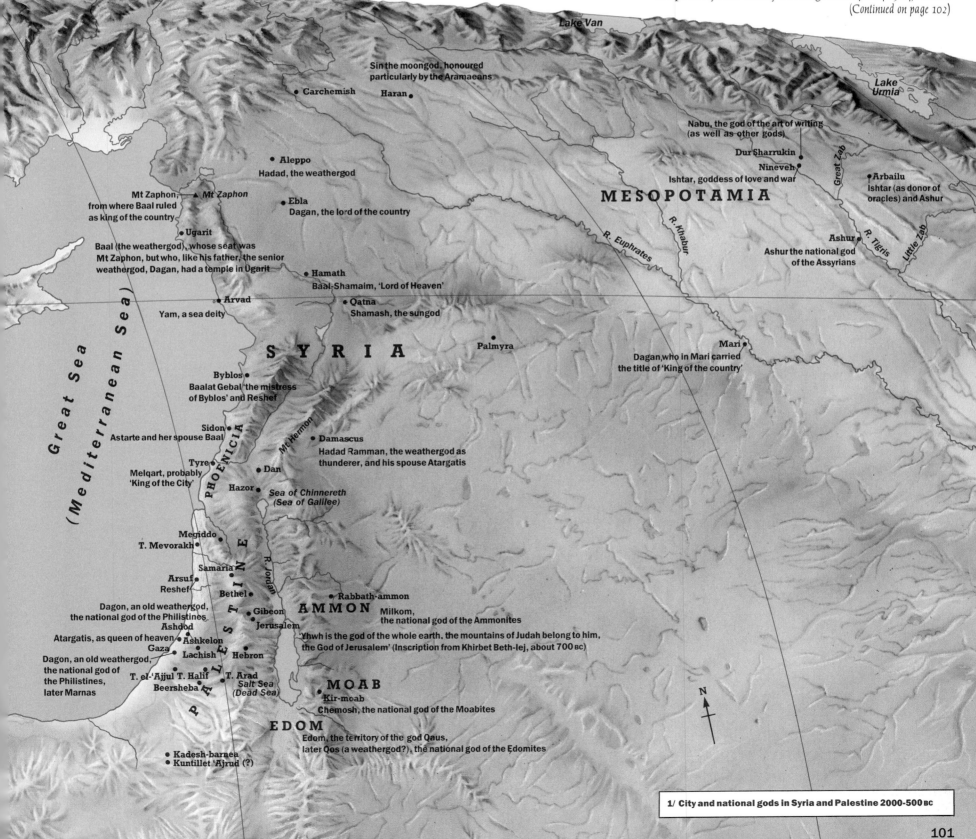

1/ City and national gods in Syria and Palestine 2000-500 BC

(*Continued from page 101*)

female deities could well have been the Asherah or Astarte who are often mentioned in the OT as the consort of the weather god Baal (JUDG 3.7).

THE CULT OF BAAL

Baal ('master') is one of the major gods of the Canaanite cult and in the poems of Ugarit (see page 44) he is associated with a holy mountain called Zaphon. Numerous Canaanite bronzes such as the one from Megiddo, show him as a young man, his right hand raised in a gesture of victory. The discoveries at Ugarit show that the bull was a major symbol of Baal. An Israelite open-air shrine from the time of the judges, in the 12th century BC, has recently been discovered on a hilltop in north-eastern Samaria. A very large (7in long) bronze bull was found associated with this shrine: was this a sacred attribute of Baal or of Yhwh? Bronze bulls of Baal are known from the Late Bronze Age at Ugarit and Hazor. A drawing of a figure with the face of a cow with an inscription 'Yhwh of Shomron' is known from Kuntillet 'Ajrud. Jeroboam is known to have violated the Law by setting up images of golden calves which were offered sacrifices in the temples of Dan and Bethel (1 KINGS 12.28-30).

The altars of Baal in different parts of the country, were frequently replaced by those of Yhwh (JUDG 6.25-32). Baal, as the owner and defender of the fertile lands, fought the sea god Yam. A scarab from T. el-Far'ah(S), 20 miles west of Beersheba, depicts a winged Baal, identified with the Egyptian god Seth, stabbing the horned serpent which personified the sea. However, it is not only the sea which threatens the fertile soil but also the summer drought which was called down upon it by the god Mot. A scarab from T. Kisan, near Haifa, shows the bull of Baal defeating the lion of Mot. Other scarabs of Early Iron Age date, depict the winged Baal standing triumphantly above the lion of Mot.

Nergal (the god of the Underworld) and his spouse Ereshkigal

Utu-Shamash (the sungod) and his spouse Shenirda-Ija

Marduk combative god of creation, national god of Babylonia and his spouse Zarpanitum

Nabu, god of the art of writing and the wisdom; together with Marduk the national god of Babylonia

Zababa, a wargod who had equal status with Ningirsu-Ninurta, and his spouse Inanna-Ishtar (as warrior)

Enlil ('Lord Breath of Wind'), the main god of the Sumerians, Lord of Destiny and his spouse Ninlil

Ninhursag, the great, old mother goddess

Ningirsu-Ninurta, lord of farmland and war, and his spouse Baba, often identified with the goddess of healing Gula

An-Anu, the god of heaven, and his daughter, Inanna-Ishtar, the goddess of love and war, who was later honoured as his spouse

Utu-Shamash, the sungod, and his spouse Shenirda-Ija

Nanna-Sin, the moongod and his spouse Ningal (Canaanite Nikkal)

Enki-Ea, god of the fresh water ocean and of wisdom, and his spouse Damgalnunna-Damkina

BABYLONIA

Caspian Sea

R. Diyala

R. Euphrates

Sippur

Kuta

R. Tigris

Babylon

Kish

Borsippa

Nippur

Adab

Lagash

Erech

Larsa

Ur

Eridu

ELAM

PERSIA

Persian Gulf

1/ City and national gods in Babylonia 2000-500 BC

The god Reshef, standing on an antelope, is frequently shown beside him.

THE CULT OF FERTILITY

The female deity Asherah is referred to in the Bible as the consort of Baal (JUDG 3.7; II KINGS 23.4). These Asherahs and Astartes are often described as fertility goddesses. However, the female partner of the weather god appears to bare her breasts in an erotic pose rather than in a maternal gesture. Ancient Syrian seals which depict her surrounded by stars as the queen of the heavens, baring her breasts to the weather god striding across the hills, seem to confirm this.

An Egyptian stela of the 13th century BC which shows the Canaanite Qudshu ('holiness') between the ithyphallic Min on the left and the warlike Resheph on the right, represents sexuality rather than maternal fruitfulness. It is also quite clear that prostitution was connected with the cult of Asherah (cf II KINGS 23.7). In the same way, the goddess figurines found in Palestine from the 10th-6th centuries BC (described in the Bible as 'teraphim'), are to be regarded not only as 'nourishing goddesses' (dea nutrix) but also as symbols of eroticism (see PROV 5.19). The pillar-shaped body with the clumsily formed arms and breasts contrast with the carefully moulded head with large eyes and curly hairstyle.

Large quantities of these goddess figurines have turned up in Iron Age levels at Jerusalem and other Judaean sites. The fact that intact figurines are very rarely found suggests that they may have been purposely broken.

Maternal traits were usually expressed in animal rather than in human form. The cow suckling her calf, which is a familiar scene in Phoenican and north Syrian ivories, can be regarded as the counter-part of the god in the form of a bull. A drawing of a cow and suckling calf has recently been found on a pithos fragment at Kuntillet 'Ajrud. Suckling gazelles, deer and goats frequently appear on seals from

Palestine dating from the Late Bronze Age and Iron Age. They are sometimes accompanied by a scorpion which, like the dove, had been a creature sacred to the Syrian goddess of love since the 3rd millennium BC, because of its conspicuous mating dance. The lover's vow 'by the gazelles or the hinds of the field' (SONG 2.7; 3.5) refers to the fact that these were animals sacred to the goddess.

The small bronze snakes which have been found in the Late Bronze Age temples of Hazor, Megiddo, T. Mevorakh, Gezer, and in the Early Iron Age shrine at Timna', may have been votive offerings to the goddess. A snake is sometimes depicted in one of the goddess's hands. However, some of these snakes may have been used for protection like the carved snake on the altar at Beersheba. A copper image of a snake set on a pole, was made by Moses to control the 'fiery serpents' which were attacking the Israelites (NUM 21.6-9). This same image, or one very like it, was being worshipped as Nehushtan by the Israelites and so had to be destroyed by Hezekiah (II KINGS 18.4).

The Egyptian divinity Bes was also worshipped in Palestine and was regarded as a protector of pregnant women. He was frequently depicted as a dwarf-like figure, with arms akimbo, and with a characteristic feathered headdress. A drawing of Bes was found on a fragment of a pithos at the religious centre at Kuntillet 'Ajrud. His face was also depicted on pottery vessels dating from the Persian period.

Cherubim are frequently mentioned in the Bible as winged heavenly beings symbolic of protection. The word cherub originally comes from the Akkadian karibu 'a genie'. They appeared in the inner sanctum of Solomon's Temple in Jerusalem (I KINGS 7.29) and even on the throne of God (EX 25.18; I SAM 4.4). A cherub or sphinx, was a winged figure with a lion's body and a female head; they are well known from the Syro-Phoenician iconography dating from the Iron Age. Ivory panels carved with winged cherubim are known from Samaria. A carving of a sphinx, dating from Persian times, apparently protected the entrance to the subterranean quarry-cave in Jerusalem which is known locally as 'Solomon's Quarries', though it is very unlikely that it has any direct connection with Solomon himself.

1/ Map below
The map illustrates the distribution of religious cults throughout Palestine, Phoenicia, Syria and Mesopotamia.

2/ Panel above left
a) A seal cylinder of the Late Bronze Age showing a worshipper standing in front of a tree. **b)** Scarab of the Early Iron Age (1200-1000 BC) show Sumerian carving of the winged Baal standing triumphantly on the lion of Mot. The god Reshef, standing on an antelope, is shown beside him. **c, d, e, f** and **g)** These Iron Age seal amulets from Palestine (both the amulets and their impressions are shown) show suckling deer and goats. They are accompanied by a scorpion which, like the dove, was sacred to the Syrian goddess of love because of its conspicuous

mating behaviour. **h)** A seal amulet from 10th-8th century BC Palestine showing two people standing either side of a sacred tree in an attitude of worship. **i)** The Egyptian god Bes flanked by seraphs, which use their wings to protect themselves from the god of Israel's terrible holiness.

3/ Far left
This cow suckling her calf, from a Phoenician ivory carving, can be seen as the female counterpart of the god Baal in his manifestation as a bull. The idea of a goddess providing nourishment was often conveyed by animal, rather than human, imagery.

4/ Left
A gold pendant of the Late Bronze Age from T. el-'Ajjul shows a tree growing out of the stylized navel of a goddess.

5/ Above left
An Egyptian stela of the 13th century BC shows the Canaanite Qudshu between the ithyphallic Min and the warlike Reshef.

6/ Below left
This bronze bull was discovered at Samaria and is associated with the worship of Baal.

7/ Below
The weather god Baal, seen in a bronze from Megiddo, is shown with his right hand raised in a gesture of victory.

8/ Below right
The trunk-like body and exaggerated breasts of the 'nourishing goddess' contrast with the carefully moulded face. These figures date from the Iron Age. They are never discovered intact, suggesting that they were broken intentionally.

ALL THOSE WHO MAKE IDOLS ARE NOTHING, AND THE THINGS THEY DELIGHT IN DO NOT PROFIT; THEIR WITNESSES NEITHER SEE NOR KNOW, THAT THEY MAY BE PUT TO SHAME. WHO FASHIONS A GOD OR CASTS AN IMAGE, THAT IS PROFITABLE FOR NOTHING? BEHOLD, ALL HIS FELLOWS SHALL BE PUT TO SHAME, AND THE CRAFTSMEN ARE BUT MEN; LET THEM ALL ASSEMBLE, LET THEM STAND FORTH, THEY SHALL BE TERRIFIED, THEY SHALL BE PUT TO SHAME TOGETHER. THE IRONSMITH FASHIONS IT AND WORKS IT OVER THE COALS; HE SHAPES IT WITH HAMMERS, AND FORGES IT WITH HIS STRONG ARM; HE BECOMES HUNGRY AND HIS STRENGTH FAILS, HE DRINKS NO WATER AND IS FAINT.'
ISA 44.9-12

HEZION'S grandson Ben-Hadad I (c 900-c 860 BC) conducted a campaign into Israelite territory in the time of Baasha (909-886 BC) in response to an appeal from Asa of Judah (911-870 BC) with whom he had a treaty of mutual assistance, and who was suffering military encroachments from Israel. Ben-Hadad I also had a treaty with Baasha of Israel, but a payment of treasure from Asa encouraged him to break this and take Asa's side. In this campaign he entered Israel from the north and advanced successfully via Dan and Hazor to the Sea of Galilee. Further details of this campaign are not recorded, but evidence of Aramaean influence in Ammon, the most northerly of the three Transjordanian kingdoms, suggests that this Israelite territory, plus Bashan and Gilead to the north of it, fell to Aram.

There was further conflict between Israel and Aram in the time of Ahab (874-853 BC), when Ben-Hadad II of Damascus (c 860-c 843 BC), known in Assyrian inscriptions as Adad-Idri, invaded Israel from a base in Succoth in Transjordan, and besieged Samaria. He was repulsed, but after some reorganization, he attacked again, only to be defeated once more in the area of the Sea of Galilee, and taken prisoner at Aphek (he was then obliged to grant Israel special trading

rights in Damascus). Substantial fortifications and newly cut shafts to springs of natural water at Megiddo and Hazor are probably to be dated to this time, and to be seen as responses to the Aramaean threat.

The westward expansion of Assyria, a rising power at this time, was temporarily delayed in 853 BC when a number

of Levantine states, including Aram and Israel, unusually allied, combined and confronted Shalmaneser III in a famous battle at Qarqar (see pages 108-9). This co-operation between Israel and Aram did not last, however, and soon after the battle Ahab, with the aid of Jehoshaphat of Judah, sought to regain former Israelite territory in Transjordan and was killed in battle at Ramoth-gilead, a site which many scholars believe to be modern T. Ramit.

Following the death of Ahab there is no record of conflict between Israel and Aram for several decades, but towards the end of the reign of Jehu (841-814 BC) and during the reign of Jehoahaz (814-780 BC), Hazael, the king of Aram (c 843-c 780 BC), who had killed Ben-Hadad II and usurped the throne, extended Aramaean control in Transjordan as far south as Aroer in northern Moab, and thus became a significant threat. Hazael is perhaps known from an Assyrian representation of the Phoenician god Melqart, found at Breij near Aleppo. The inscription on this stone is damaged, but one restoration would identify its dedicator as 'Bar-Hadad son of Izri-Shamsh who was father of the king of Aram', the 'king of Aram' possibly being Hazael, who might therefore have been another son of Izri-Shamsh. The details

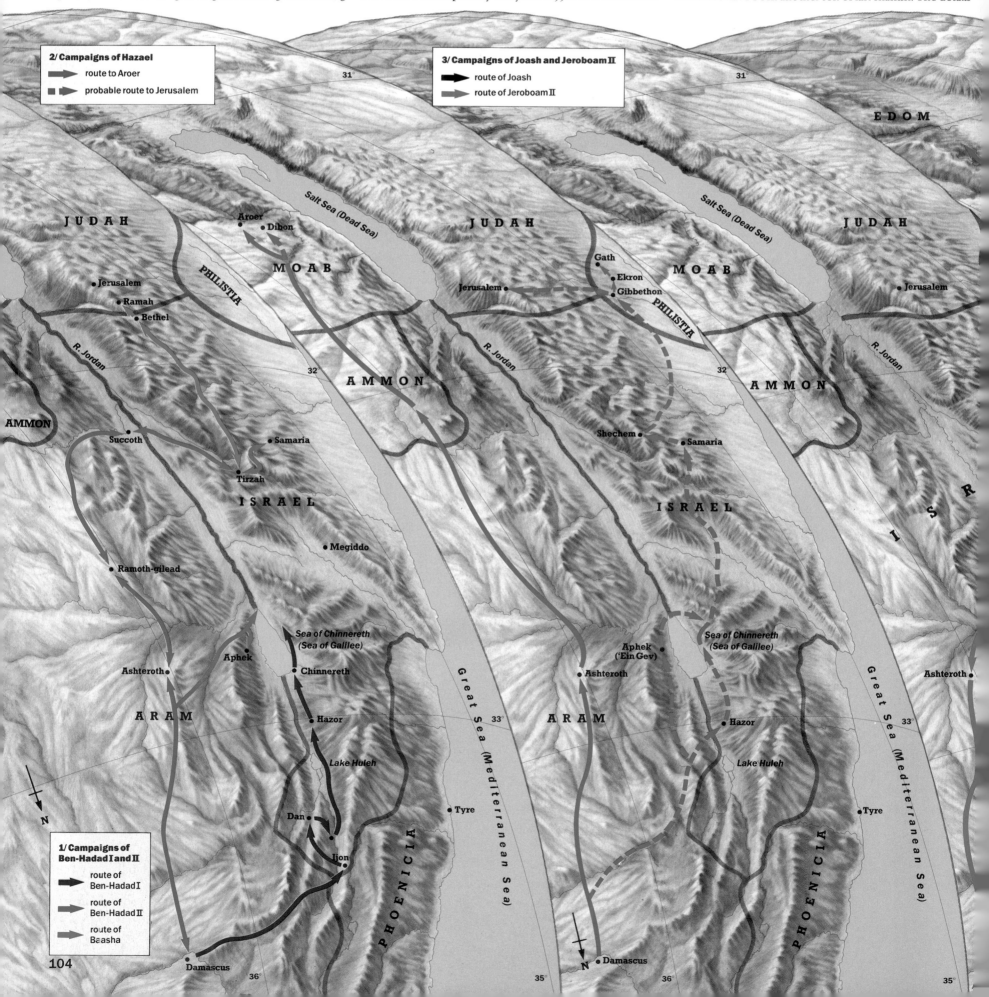

2/ Campaigns of Hazael
→ route to Aroer
▪▪▶ probable route to Jerusalem

3/ Campaigns of Joash and Jeroboam II
→ route of Joash
→ route of Jeroboam II

1/ Campaigns of Ben-Hadad I and II
→ route of Ben-Hadad I
→ route of Ben-Hadad II
→ route of Baasha

of Hazael's operations against Israel are not known, but destruction levels at Hazor, 'Ein Gev, Shechem, and even possibly at Samaria itself, may be traces of his action. It is possible that these were the result of separate incursions, but they may have formed steps in the route of a major campaign conducted by Hazael as far as Gath in Philistia, on which occasion Jehoash of Judah made a payment of treasure to him to keep away from Jerusalem. This action does not seem to have had a permanent effect because it appears that Jerusalem was raided by the Arameans, following which Jehoash was assassinated. The OT states that Hazael took all the Israelite territory east of the Jordan as far as Aroer (II KINGS 10.32-3), and probably including Dibon.

The motive for Aramaean penetration in Transjordan, and also possibly in Philistia, may have been the desire to control the profitable incense trade which came up western Arabia, and the hostility towards Israel may have simply been part of a 'hands off' policy.

In the time of Joash (798-782 BC) and Jeroboam II (782-753 BC) of Israel there was a resurgence of Israelite success against Aram, by now under Hazael's son Ben-Hadad III. Joash is said to have recovered the cities which Hazael had taken from Jehoahaz, and to have achieved a decisive victory at Aphek. This success was continued by Jeroboam II who was able to recover all the Israelite territory in Transjordan which had been lost to Aram, and to occupy Damascus and the whole of the area dependant on it.

The last king of Damascus, Rezin (c 750-732 BC), joined with the former rival Israel, now under Pekah (740-732 BC), and the two together sought to bring Jotham of Judah into an alliance against Tiglath-pileser III, king of Assyria since 745 BC, who was presenting a formidable threat from the north-east.

Jotham, perhaps feeling less threatened by Assyria by reason of its greater distance, refused, so Rezin and Pekah invaded Judah and captured Jerusalem, Rezin at the same time organizing a campaign of conquest through Ammon and Moab as far south as Edom (II KINGS 16.6). To protect himself, Jotham appealed to Assyria for help and in 732 BC Tiglath-pileser took Damascus, killing Rezin, making Aram a part of the Assyrian empire and conducted a major campaign in Israel, as a result of which Pekah was assassinated and succeeded on the throne by Hoshea who was to be the last king of Israel.

SHALMANESER III CONQUERS HAZAEL

Some of what we know about Aram and its rulers comes from Assyrian texts. The following passage is taken from a fragment in which Shalmaneser III describes his campaign in Aram:

In the eighteenth year of my rule I crossed the Euphrates for the sixteenth time. Hazael of Damascus put his trust upon his numerous army and called up his troops in great number, making the mountain Senir, a mountain facing the Lebanon, to his fortress. I fought with him and inflicted a defeat upon him, killing with the sword 16,000 of his experienced soldiers. I took away from him 1,121 chariots, 470 riding horses as well as his camp. He disappeared to save his life (but) I followed him and besieged him in Damascus, his royal residence. There I cut down his gardens outside of the city, and departed. I marched as far as the mountains of Hauran, destroying, tearing down and burning innumerable towns, carrying booty away from them which was beyond counting.

'NOW HAZAEL KING OF SYRIA OPPRESSED ISRAEL ALL THE DAYS OF JEHOAHAZ. BUT THE LORD WAS GRACIOUS TO THEM AND HAD COMPASSION ON THEM... BECAUSE OF HIS COVENANT WITH ABRAHAM, ISAAC, AND JACOB...' II KINGS 13.22-23

1/ Map far left
The first map shows the campaign of Ben-Hadad I going to the assistance of Asa, king of Judah. It also shows the probable route taken by Ben-Hadad II invading Israel, an expedition which failed.

2/ Map second from left
Hazael killed Ben-Hadad II and became king of Aram. He managed to extend Aramaean influence far to the south (down to Aroer in Moab). It is possible, but not proven, that he also launched a campaign into Israel.

3/ Map third from left
Under Joash and Jeroboam II Israel regained strength and was able to push up from Samaria and recover lost territory, eventually occupying Damascus.

4/ Map below
Under Rezin, Damascus joined forces with Pekah of Israel and invaded Judah capturing Jerusalem. Eventually Rezin so provoked the Assyrians under Tiglath-pileser III that they invaded Damascus and killed him. Aram was thus made a part of the Assyrian empire.

5/ Right
The table shows in parallel the reigns of the kings of Aram, Israel and Judah.

6/ Bottom right
The inscription to this stela mentions an unnamed king of Aram, possibly Hazael. The figure represented on the upper part of the stela is the god Melqart who can be seen grasping a battle axe with a rounded blade in his left hand.

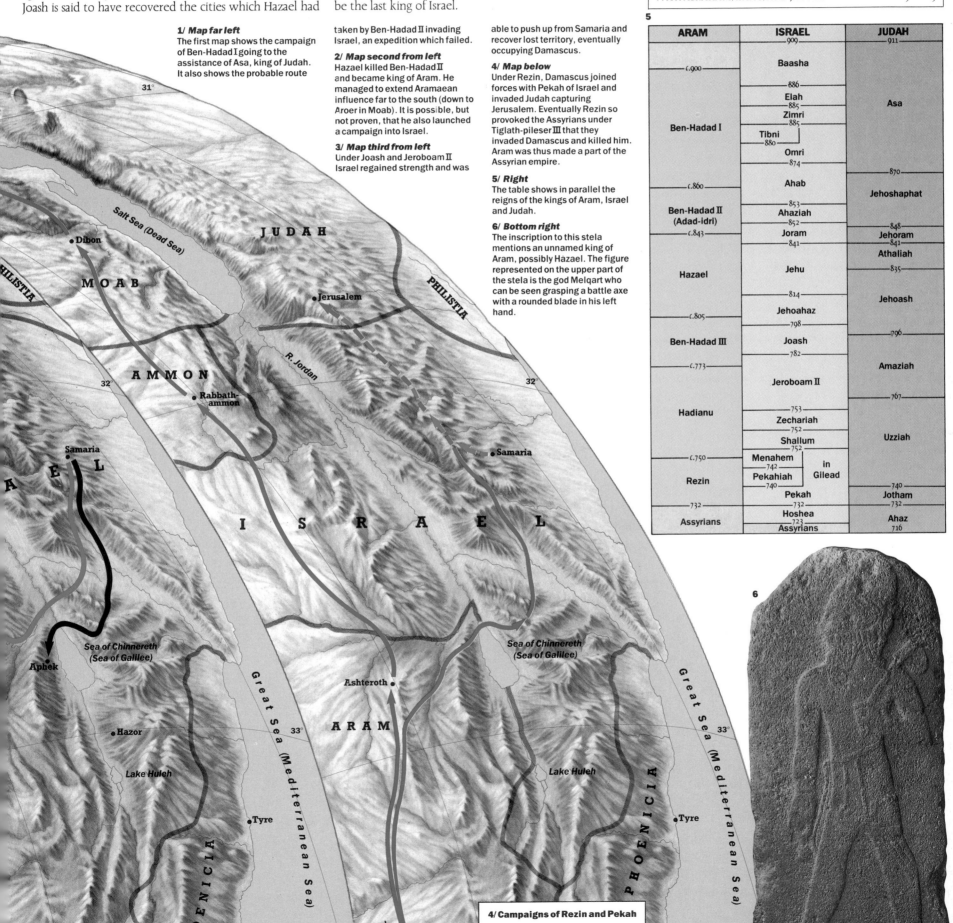

ARAM	ISRAEL	JUDAH
	900	911
c.900	Baasha	
	886	Asa
Ben-Hadad I	Elah	
	885	
	Zimri 885	
	Tibni / Omri 880	
	874	
		870
c.860	Ahab	Jehoshaphat
	853	
Ben-Hadad II (Adad-idri)	Ahaziah 852	848
c.843	Joram	Jehoram
	841	841
		Athaliah
		835
Hazael	Jehu	Jehoash
	814	
c.805	Jehoahaz	
	798	796
Ben-Hadad III	Joash	
	782	Amaziah
c.773		
	Jeroboam II	767
Hadianu		Uzziah
	753	
	Zechariah 752	
	Shallum 752	
c.750	Menahem 742 / Pekahiah 740 in Gilead	740
Rezin	Pekah	Jotham 732
732	732	
Assyrians	Hoshea 723	Ahaz 716
	Assyrians	

4/ Campaigns of Rezin and Pekah
→ route of Rezin
⇢ route of Pekah

It is not surprising that in the surviving literature of the great empires which surrounded ancient Israel there should be little mention of the principal characters and events of the Bible. Israel was small in comparison to such powers as Assyria and Egypt, and at most periods of its history played a minor role in the military and commercial affairs of the larger world. Patriarchs, judges, the three kings of the United Monarchy – Saul, David and Solomon – and the Hebrew prophets are known only from the pages of the Bible. Yet there are a few notable exceptions to this neglect of Israel's heroes. Over a span of two and a half centuries Assyrian kings took pains to enhance and preserve their fame by displaying in their capitals boastful accounts of their triumphs over the monarchs of the kingdoms of Israel and Judah. With the discovery of the ancient palaces of the Assyrian kings at Khorsabad, Nineveh, and Nimrud in the 19th century, details about ancient Israel came to light from sources outside the Bible.

The boxes on Map 1 below contain accounts of events which have survived in the mounds of Assyria, Babylonia, on a stela found in Transjordan, and on a temple wall at Karnak. Carved in stone or written on clay these documents have come down to us unchanged, a testimony contemporaneous with the campaigns, battles, and conquests to which they bear witness. Whenever the Bible speaks of these events the appropriate quotation appears in the box alongside the extra-biblical text.

It is of interest to see the points of agreement or disagreement between the accounts. Some outside sources, like the two inscriptions of Shalmaneser III, mentioning Ahab and Jehu, list events which are not referred to in the Book of Kings. Other Assyrian sources supplement the biblical accounts of events with specific details. Sargon II had engraved on the wall of his palace at Khorsabad that he carried away 27,290 inhabitants of Samaria, and Sennacherib was specific in his boast of having taken 200,150 prisoners from 46 cities belonging to Hezekiah of Judah. Sheshonq I's (Shishak of the Bible) long list of cities conquered in Palestine not only confirms the account of the invasion found in the Bible but provides us with a valuable source for the geography of the 10th century BC. Mesha's stela, erected for all to read of the king's achievements, proclaims to his Moabite subjects that 'Israel has perished forever!' (see pages 96 and 108.) But even the wishful thinking of exaggerated boasts of Israel's enemies serves to link events and kings otherwise known only in the religious writings of ancient Israel with the history of the larger world.

FIXED POINTS IN THE CHRONOLOGY OF THE KINGDOMS OF ISRAEL AND JUDAH

The discovery of ancient documents from the world of the Bible has not only given biblical history a new dimension, but these texts have made it possible to assign precise dates of the Julian calendar to some of the principal events of Israelite and Judaean history.

THE DIVIDED KINGDOM – ISRAEL

LINKS BETWEEN THE BIBLE AND WORLD HISTORY

For modern readers of the Bible the events of the OT often appear to take place in a vacuum. However, the impression that biblical history exists in isolation from the rest of the world can easily be dispelled by looking at Palestine through the eyes of neighbouring (and often hostile) countries, notably Assyria. It can then be seen that many events thought of as 'biblical' were also recorded elsewhere.

The Book of Kings has a double system for recording regnal years. One is the listing of the total number of years for each king's reign. The other is a record of the synchronism between the accession of a king of one kingdom and the regnal year of the king of the other. Although the data are precise – there are some discrepancies, such as the differing totals of the two systems – it was impossible before the discovery of certain Assyrian texts to peg with any precision the dates for Israelite and Judaean kings.

The Assyrian method of keeping track of regnal years was different. There a king was accustomed to designate each year of his reign – the first year was named understandably after the king himself – by an important public official, who was the *limmu*, or eponym, for the year. Scribes kept lists of regnal years, for each of which there were the name of the *limmu*, his title or office, and a record of an important event or events of the year (the panel at the top of the facing page contains an excerpt from a *limmu* list found at the capital city of Ashur). Such lists of regnal years have now become available for the kings who ruled from the beginning of the 9th century BC to almost the end of the 6th.

In one of these sequential lists there appears a notation of a significant event which occurred in the year called after a certain Bur-Sagale, a governor of the province of Guzana during the reign of king Ashur-Dan. It is the statement that 'in the month of Simānu an eclipse of the sun took place.' Since solar eclipses take place with regularity it is possible to compute those which were visible from certain Assyrian cities. A recently published computer print-out gives tables for the occultation of eclipses of the sun at Nineveh from 3000 BC to 0 (see the diagram on the facing page). These astronomical calculations reveal that in the year 763 BC (June 15, 9.33am to 12.19pm) there was an eclipse at Nineveh

which had a magnitude of 99 per cent. Within a span of more than a century this was by far the largest and most complete eclipse of the sun visible at Nineveh (69 years before there was an eclipse of 94 per cent magnitude and 178 years later one of 98 per cent). If we fix 763 BC as the Julian year of the *limmu* Bur-Sagale, we have from the list of sequential *limmus* the absolute regnal years for the Assyrian kings mentioned in the Bible.

These dates have been used, along with the two systems of chronology provided by the Bible, for determining the reigns of the kings of Israel and Judah. A considerable number of problems necessarily remain – there are currently five or six major systems of chronological calculations – but the margin of divergence for the dates of a particular king is only a few years and certain pivotal events of biblical history are firmly fixed.

'[THIS IS] THE PALACE OF ASHURNASIRPAL, THE HIGH PRIEST OF ASHUR, CHOSEN BY ENLIL AND NINURTA, THE FAVOURITE OF ANU AND OF DAGAN [WHO IS] DESTRUCTION [PERSONIFIED] AMONG ALL THE GREAT GODS — THE LEGITIMATE KING, THE KING OF THE WORLD, THE KING OF ASSYRIA, SON OF TUKULTI-NINURTA, GREAT KING, LEGITIMATE KING, KING OF THE WORLD, KING OF ASSYRIA [WHO WAS] THE SON OF ADAD-NIRARI, LIKEWISE GREAT KING, LEGITIMATE KING, KING OF THE WORLD AND KING OF ASSYRIA — THE HEROIC WARRIOR WHO ALWAYS ACTS UPON TRUST-INSPIRING SIGNS GIVEN BY HIS LORD ASHUR AND [THEREFORE] HAS NO RIVAL AMONG THE RULERS OF THE FOUR QUARTERS [OF THE WORLD]; THE SHEPHERD OF ALL MORTALS, NOT AFRAID OF BATTLE ...'
FROM THE PALACE OF ASHURNASIRPAL IN CALAH.

1/ Map below
On this map nine biblical accounts of battles and the payment of tribute over three centuries of Israel's history are compared with reports of the same incidents recorded by Israel's enemies. The quotations from the Bible are all shown as coming from Jerusalem (in diagrammatic simplification). The other texts, written on stone or clay, have been discovered over a wide segment of the Fertile Crescent from Karnak in Egypt to Nimrud in modern Iraq. The precise details assigned to events are made possible by astronomical calculations (see illustrations 2 and 3) and the double system of recording regnal years for the kings of Israel and

---

738 BC
...and Menahem gave Pul [Tiglath-pileser] a thousand talents of silver...
II KINGS 15.19.

734 BC
So Ahaz sent messengers to Tiglath-pileser king of Assyria, saying, 'I am your servant...' Ahaz also took the silver and gold that was found in the house of the Lord...and sent a present to the king of Assyria. II KINGS 16.7-8.

732 BC
In the days of Pekah king of Israel Tiglath-pileser king of Assyria came...Then Hoshea...made a conspiracy against Pekah the son of Remaliah, and struck him down...and reigned in his stead... II KINGS 15.29-30.

722 BC
In the ninth year of Hoshea the king of Assyria captured Samaria, and he carried the Israelites away to Assyria... II KINGS 17.6.

712 BC
In the year that the commander in chief, who was sent by Sargon the king of Assyria, came to Ashdod and fought against it and took it... ISAIAH 20.1.

701 BC
And Hezekiah king of Judah sent to the king of Assyria at Lachish, saying, 'I have done wrong; withdraw from me; whatever you impose on me I will bear.' And the king of Assyria required of Hezekiah...three hundred talents of silver and thirty talents of gold. II KINGS 18.14.

597 BC
And Nebuchadnezzar king of Babylon came to the city, while his servants were besieging it; and Jehoiachin the king of Judah gave himself up to the king of Babylon...The king of Babylon took him...and carried off all the treasures of the house of the Lord...And the king of Babylon made Mattaniah...king in his stead...
II KINGS 24.11-17.

Great Sea (Mediterranean Sea)

PALESTINE

Jerusalem

Dibon

MOAB

EDOM

EGYPT

Sinai

Arabian Desert

R. Nile

Red Sea

Karnak

DIBON
As for Omri, king of Israel, he humbled Moab many years.... And his son followed him.... but I have triumphed over him...while Israel hath perished forever!
MESHA, king of Moab, on stela found at Dibon.

c830 BC
Now Mesha king of Moab was a sheep breeder; and he had to deliver annually to the king of Israel a hundred thousand lambs... But when Ahab died, the king of Moab rebelled against the king of Israel. II KINGS 3.4-5.

KARNAK
[Victories of Sheshonq I over the] Asiatics of distant foreign countries [with list of cities in Palestine and Syria].
AMON TEMPLE, Karnak.

c924 BC
In the fifth year of king Rehoboam, Shishak king of Egypt came up against Jerusalem...
I KINGS 14.25.

Judah. Of particular interest are texts which refer to the Israelites but which are *not* found in the Bible, and two of these have been included in the panels on the far right of the map.

2/ Right
The Assyrian system of chronology depended on *limmus*, or eponyms, for each year (see text).

3/ Below right
The diagram shows the stages, or periods of occultation, during which the sun (white disk) is eclipsed by the moon. The colour bands extending across the map of the Near East mark the zones of centrality (paths of maximum view) for the eclipses of 832, 763, and 585 BC. Within the box at the lower right appears an excerpt from a computer print-out which gives the year, month, day and hour for the various phases of occultation in the eclipses as seen from Nineveh. It is from such astronomical calculations that the Julian year for the Assyrian king Ashur Dan came to be fixed and a synchronism established with the Bible's system of chronology. Because of their dramatic nature (especially when the sun is blacked out during total occultation), eclipses have been observed and recorded throughout history by peoples as diverse as the Chinese and the Assyrians. They were frequently thought to be signs of ill omen and created panic when they occurred.

Excerpt from Assyrian *limmu* list for the years extending from the 9th to the 6th centuries

765 NINURTA-MUKIN-NISHE (governor) of Kirruri — Against Hatarika. A plague.

764 SIDKI-ILU (governor) of Tushhan — in the land.

763 BUR (ISHDI)-SAGALE (governor) of Guzana — Revolt in the city of Ashur. In the month of Simânu an eclipse of the sun took place.

762 TAB-BEL (governor) of Amedi — Revolt in the city Ashur.

761 NABU-MUKIN-AHI (governor) of Nineveh — Revolt in the city of Arrapha.

760 LAKIPU (governor) of Kalizi — Revolt in the city of Arrapha.

(The name of the official by whom the year was known appears in column 1; his title, in column 2; important events of the year, in column 3)

Assyrian and Babylonian kings whose reigns overlapped those of kings of Israel and Judah

SHALMANESER III (858-824)	Ahab, forces defeated in 853 Jehu, paid tribute in 841
TIGLATH-PILESER III (744-727)	Menahem, paid tribute in 738 Jehoahaz, paid tribute in 734
SHALMANESER V (726-722)	Hoshea, capital captured in 722
MERODACH-BALADAN (721-711)	Hezekiah, became an ally in 703 (?)
SARGON II (721-705)	Hoshea, Sargon claims to have taken his capital
SENNACHERIB (704-681)	Hezekiah, paid tribute in 701
ESARHADDON (680-669)	Manasseh, paid tribute in 670
NEBUCHADNEZZAR (604-562)	Jehoiachin, deported in 597
EVIL-MERODACH (561-560)	Jehoiachin, released from prison in 561

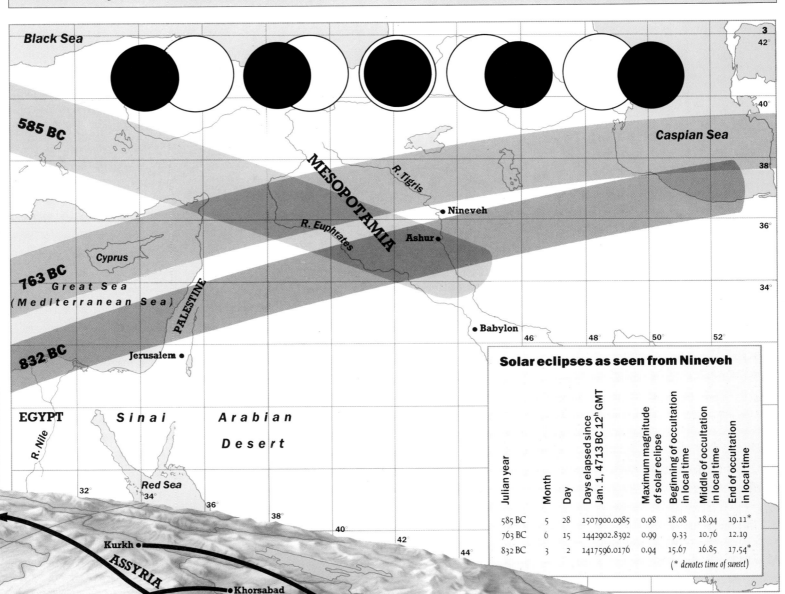

NIMRUD
I received tribute from...Rezon of Damascus, Menahem of Samaria, Hiram of Tyre...and Zabibe, the queen of Arabia.... TIGLATH-PILESER III, on inscription at Nimrud.

[I received] the tribute of...Jehoahaz of Judah.... TIGLATH-PILESER III, on a building inscription on clay from Nimrud.

They overthrew their king Pekah and I placed Hoshea as king over them. TIGLATH-PILESER III, on inscription at Nimrud.

KHORSABAD
I besieged and conquered Samaria, led away as booty 27,290 inhabitants of it. SARGON II, on inscription at Khorsabad.

Azuri, king of Ashdod, had schemed not to deliver tribute [any more].... On account of the misdeeds which he committed I abolished his rule.... I besieged and conquered the cities of Ashdod, Gath [and] Asdudimmu. SARGON II, on inscription at Khorsabad.

NINEVEH
As to Hezekiah, the Jew, he did not submit to my yoke, I laid siege to 46 of his strong cities.... I drove out [of them] 200,150 people.... Himself I made a prisoner in Jerusalem...like a bird in a cage.... Hezekiah himself...did send me, later...30 talents of gold, 800 talents of silver.... SENNACHERIB on a text from Nineveh.

BABYLON
The king of Akkad...laid siege to the city of Judah...and the king took the city.... He appointed in it a [new] king of his liking, took heavy booty from it and brought it into Babylon. NEBUCHADNEZZAR II on a tablet from Babylon.

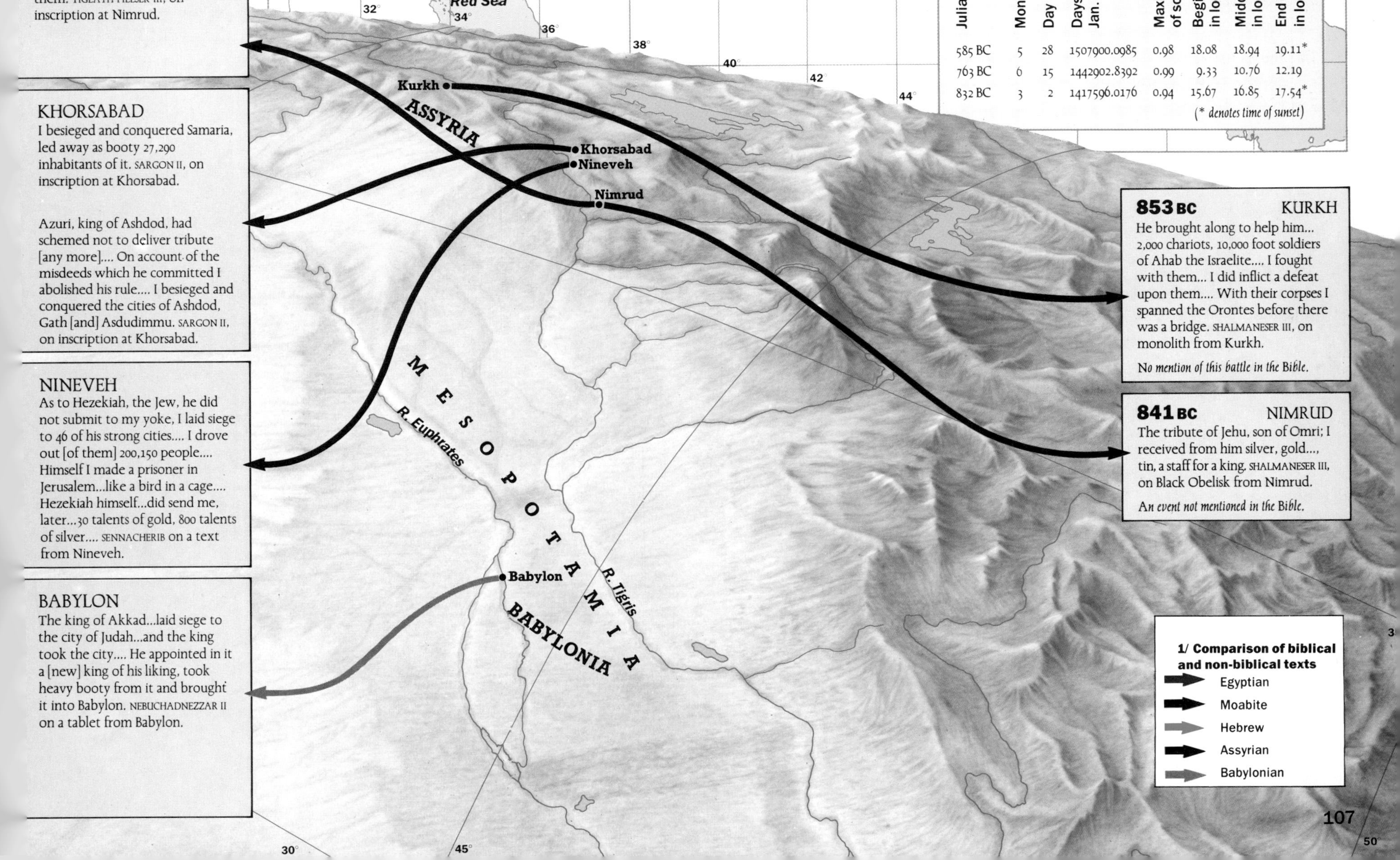

Solar eclipses as seen from Nineveh

Julian year	Month	Day	Days elapsed since Jan. 1, 4713 BC 12h GMT	Maximum magnitude of solar eclipse	Beginning of occultation in local time	Middle of occultation in local time	End of occultation in local time
585 BC	5	28	1507900.0985	0.98	18.08	18.94	19.11*
763 BC	6	15	1442902.8392	0.99	9.33	10.76	12.19
832 BC	3	2	1417596.0176	0.94	15.67	16.85	17.54*

(* denotes time of sunset)

853 BC   KURKH
He brought along to help him... 2,000 chariots, 10,000 foot soldiers of Ahab the Israelite.... I fought with them... I did inflict a defeat upon them.... With their corpses I spanned the Orontes before there was a bridge. SHALMANESER III, on monolith from Kurkh.

No mention of this battle in the Bible.

841 BC   NIMRUD
The tribute of Jehu, son of Omri; I received from him silver, gold..., tin, a staff for a king. SHALMANESER III, on Black Obelisk from Nimrud.

An event not mentioned in the Bible.

1/ Comparison of biblical and non-biblical texts
- Egyptian
- Moabite
- Hebrew
- Assyrian
- Babylonian

Map labels: Black Sea, Caspian Sea, 585 BC, MESOPOTAMIA, R. Tigris, Nineveh, R. Euphrates, Ashur, 763 BC, Cyprus, Great Sea (Mediterranean Sea), PALESTINE, 832 BC, Babylon, Jerusalem, EGYPT, Sinai, Arabian Desert, R. Nile, Red Sea, Kurkh, ASSYRIA, Khorsabad, Nineveh, Nimrud, MESOPOTAMIA, R. Euphrates, R. Tigris, BABYLONIA, Babylon

THE Assyrian economy was based on the kingdom's fertile cornlands, but its position on one of the ancient Near East's major routes of communication (the R. Tigris) early gave it involvement in international trade. From the late 2nd millennium onwards the Assyrian kings sent trading expeditions into neighbouring countries to seek commodities not readily available at home.

A second reason for foreign expeditions was that a long history of raids on the Assyrian plains by the mountaineers to the east and north, and a period of foreign occupation after the middle of the 2nd millennium BC, had impressed upon the Assyrians the need for secure boundaries. The consequent policy of expansion was interpreted in religious terms, so that by the 9th century Ashurnasirpal II (883-859BC), the founder of the 1st-millennium Assyrian empire, explicitly described the aim of his foreign policy in terms of his religious duty to conquer the foes of the national god Ashur and to impose tribute and tax upon subject peoples.

In pursuance of this aim, Ashurnasirpal had a clear strategic plan. He began by securing control of the quadrant of mountain territories to the east and north of Assyria, and followed this with action along the R. Khabur and middle Euphrates from the Babylonian border to Carchemish. In the Khabur and Euphrates regions he subjugated the Aramaeans, a people of nomadic origin who controlled the caravan routes from Syria, and this opened the way for Assyrian advance to the Mediterranean, reached c875 for the first time in two centuries. Coastal cities as far south as Tyre paid tribute.

Ashurnasirpal's son and successor Shalmaneser III (858-824BC) made further penetration in the west. In his early years he concentrated upon the Aramaean state of Bit-Adini (Beth-eden of AMOS 1.5, made into an Assyrian province in 857) and the coalition of states from Carchemish north-westwards. In 853 he moved south-westwards from Aleppo against the mid-Syrian state of Hamath, provoking a strong reaction from a Syro-Palestinian coalition, headed by Hamath, Damascus and Israel. A major battle at Qarqar on the R. Orontes checked the Assyrian advance. Shalmaneser made further attacks between 849 and 845, but despite substantial conquests in Hamathite territory, he failed to smash the coalition. Eventually it collapsed from internal problems, marked by the usurpation of Hazael in Damascus and Jehu in Israel (I KINGS 19.15-18; II KINGS 8.15; 9.14 etc.). This enabled Shalmaneser in 841 to reach Damascus, from where he marched south to the Hauran and then through Israelite territory to Mt Carmel (if this is the correct identification of an Assyrian place-name); Jehu is shown on an obelisk paying tribute. Shalmaneser's subsequent activities in the west were directed against Asia Minor, where he reached Tarsus in Cilicia.

After a setback in Syria under Shamshi-Adad V (823-811), Adad-nirari III (810-783) reasserted Assyrian control between 805 and 796. The key action was the conquest of Damascus, which brought recognition of Assyrian suzerainty, marked by payment of tribute, by other states including Sidon, Tyre, cities in Philistia and Israel under Joash.

In the north the kingdom of Urartu, centred near Lake Van, was developing into a major power. This reacted upon Assyria. By the early 8th century BC the westward expansion of Urartu had weakened Assyrian control in Syria, and may have led Assyria to welcome a strong Israel as a counterpoise to its main southern opponent, Damascus: it is not unlikely that the capture of Damascus by Jeroboam II of Israel (II KINGS 14.28) had the connivance or even the active support of Assyria, which itself attacked that city in 773. It is certain that alliances were used by Assyria to alter the balance of power, as shown by an attempt by Ashur-nirari V (754-745) to control north Syria by treaty with Arpad, although in this instance it proved ineffective against the Urartian advance.

The deteriorating situation in Assyria ended in rebellion, bringing to the throne Tiglath-pileser III (744-727, called 'Pul' in II KINGS 15.19, etc), a vigorous and innovative ruler. Whereas earlier kings had treated conquered regions west of the Euphrates as tribute-paying vassals, Tiglath-pileser introduced the new strategy of establishing directly-ruled provinces in areas which proved troublesome. Vigorous military action pushed back Urartian influence in the west and north-west and established a chain of Assyrian provinces as far as Damascus, with Israel partly under provincial administration and partly tributary (see page 114). Babylonia, unsettled by Chaldaean tribesmen, was taken under direct rule.

The main lines of Tiglath-pileser's policy continued until the end of the empire, with ever-increasing territory, despite local setbacks. Shalmaneser V (726-722) and Sargon II

THE DIVIDED KINGDOM – ISRAEL

ISRAEL'S PAYMENTS OF TRIBUTE TO ASSYRIA

The kingdom of Assyria was located on the Middle Tigris and dated back to the 3rd millennium BC. The military conquests for which the Assyrians have become famous, were prompted to a large extent by the kingdom's lack of secure boundaries and its resultant vulnerability to attack.

(721-705) extended Assyrian control in Syria and Palestine (see page 114) and Sargon defeated Urartu in its own territory and made advances beyond the Zagros. Sennacherib, although best known for his attack on Judah (see page 122), also devoted considerable effort to settling Babylonia, to defence against Elam, and to protecting Assyrian interests to the east and north. For developments under the last two major Assyrian kings, see page 126.

BATTLE OF QARQAR
The Battle of Qarqar in 853, not mentioned in the Bible despite the involvement of a considerable Israelite force, is described in the inscriptions of Shalmaneser III.

In 853, Shalmaneser, whose campaigns had hitherto been confined to north Syria, moved south-westwards via Pethor (NUM 22.5, DEUT 23.4) and Aleppo into territory of Hamath. After taking several fortresses, he was met at Qarqar, east of the R. Orontes, by a powerful coalition headed by Irhuleni of Hamath, Hadad-ezer of Damascus and Ahab of Israel, with supporting forces from several Phoenician city-states and from Egypt (probably the garrison in Gubla [Byblos]), as well as an Arab contingent mounted on camels. According to Shalmaneser the largest chariotry force was that of Israel, amounting to 2,000 chariots; Israel and Hamath each provided 10,000 infantry, against 20,000 from Damascus. Damascus and Hamath, but not Israel, also provided cavalry. The strength of Assyria has been calculated as only half that of the coalition in terms of chariotry, though it had more than twice the cavalry. Shalmaneser claimed to have inflicted an enormous slaughter. This could be true, in view of the operational difficulties likely to have faced the coalition's rapidly assembled force of over 60,000 men under up to 11 commanders, unused to operating as a co-ordinated army. The coalition's resistance was, however, sufficient to check any further major southward advance by Assyria for over a decade.

ASHURNASIRPAL II'S EXPEDITION
It was Ashurnasirpal II (883-859) who re-opened direct Assyrian contact with the Mediterranean after a break of two centuries. Aramaean migrations, from the late 2nd millennium BC onwards, had left the Middle Euphrates and Khabur predominantly Aramaean ethnically, with many trade routes in their control. After Ashurnasirpal had, in his early campaigns, re-asserted Assyrian control in the Khabur and Middle Euphrates areas, he was able in c875 to move from Carchemish, near his most westerly base of Til Barsip,

into north Syria, by a route skirting the powerful state of Hamath. He progressively strengthened his campaign forces by enlisting units from local rulers on his route and by taking hostages in order to protect himself from treachery. After defeating the state of Patina in the Amqi, he went down the R. Orontes, largely unopposed, along the borders of Hamath territory as far as the Lebanon range and then to the Mediterranean. There he met no resistance, and Phoenician states as far south as Tyre sent tribute. It seems likely that the Phoenician states welcomed Assyria as a counterpoise against the Aramaeans, who just before this date had been seeking to gain economic advantage in Palestine (I KINGS 20.34) and who were probably acting in the same way against the Phoenicians. In the long term, however, this campaign of Ashurnasirpal was the first step in the process which by the 8th century BC brought the whole of Syria, Palestine and Phoenicia into the Assyrian empire.

ADAD-NIRARI III'S VICTORY OVER DAMASCUS
The position of supremacy achieved in Syria by Shalmaneser III was eroded by strong Aramaean resistance under his successor. Assyrian control was re-asserted by Adad-nirari III (810-783). Beginning with attacks in 805 and 804 to subdue north Syria, he reached the Mediterranean in 803, and may have made a further march down the Mediterranean coast in 802 to ensure the submission of the Phoenician cities. After a gap during which he was concerned with the east, Adad-nirari mounted another Syrian campaign in 796. He moved south into Lebanon, setting up a camp in Mansuate (in the Beqa'a valley), controlling the road to Damascus. With Damascus cut off from potential allies, Adad-nirari was able to enter the city and receive the submission of its king, Ben-Hadad III.

The geographical, economic and political relationships between Damascus and Israel in the 9th and 8th centuries BC were such that an Assyrian attack on one would inevitably affect the other, and this was clearly apparent here, in that Adad-nirari records Joash of Israel as paying tribute. An alternative interpretation of the data sees an even closer link in assuming an attack by Adad-nirari on Damascus in 803, in direct response to an appeal by Joash under siege by Damascus. On this theory (not represented on the map) Adad-nirari entered Damascus and then passed through Israelite territory to the Mediterranean, receiving the tribute of Joash and Tyre and frightening off the army besieging Samaria; II KINGS 7.6-7 is then assumed to refer to this. But this theory requires a dating for Joash earlier than that usually accepted and is difficult to reconcile with the total Assyrian evidence.

'PROPERTY OF ADAD-NIRARI, GREAT KING, LEGITIMATE KING, KING OF THE WORLD, KING OF ASSYRIA – A KING WHOM ASHUR, THE KING OF THE IGIGI HAD CHOSEN (ALREADY) WHEN HE WAS A YOUNGSTER... AS FAR AS THE GREAT SEA OF THE RISING SUN (AND) FROM THE BANKS OF THE EUPHRATES, THE COUNTRY OF THE HITTITES, AMURRU-COUNTRY IN ITS FULL EXTENT, TYRE, SIDON, ISRAEL EDOM, PALESTINE AS FAR AS THE SHORE OF THE GREAT SEA OF THE SETTING SUN I MADE THEM SUBMIT ALL TO MY FEET, IMPOSING UPON THEM TRIBUTE.'

FROM INSCRIPTION AT CALAH

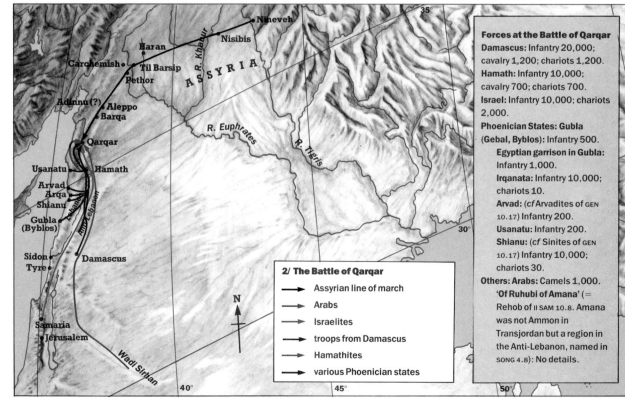

2/ The Battle of Qarqar
→ Assyrian line of march
→ Arabs
→ Israelites
→ troops from Damascus
→ Hamathites
→ various Phoenician states

Forces at the Battle of Qarqar
Damascus: Infantry 20,000; cavalry 1,200; chariots 1,200.
Hamath: Infantry 10,000; cavalry 700; chariots 700.
Israel: Infantry 10,000; chariots 2,000.
Phoenician States: Gubla (Gebal, Byblos): Infantry 500.
Egyptian garrison in Gubla: Infantry 1,000.
Irqanata: Infantry 10,000; chariots 10.
Arvad: (cf Arvadites of GEN 10.17) Infantry 200.
Usanatu: Infantry 200.
Shianu: (cf Sinites of GEN 10.17) Infantry 10,000; chariots 30.
Others: Arabs: Camels 1,000.
'Of Ruhubi of Amana' (= Rehob of II SAM 10.8. Amana was not Ammon in Transjordan but a region in the Anti-Lebanon, named in SONG 4.8): No details.

3/ Right

Ashurnasirpal II wanted to renew the expansionist policies of Assyria and he set out to gain tribute from the coastal cities of Phoenicia. Our only evidence about Ashurnasirpal II's expedition to Phoenicia, is his own account, which is brief and undetailed. The route is virtually certain, until he crossed the R. Orontes, and then it seems that he may have gone south down the east side of the river to the Mediterranean.

4/ Map far right

Adad-nirari was able to take advantage of the Assyrian supremacy achieved by Shalmaneser III over Syria (see Map 2) and he received tribute from Damascus. A stone slab found at Calah boasts of his achievements (see left quotation).

1/ Map below right

Lacking natural boundaries and therefore physical defences from raiders, the Assyrians constantly needed to extend their kingdom in order to secure surrounding territories.
The maximum extent of the Assyrian kingdom was brought about by Ashurbanipal, and the boundaries shown combine maximum military penetration with the maximum area credibly claimed as paying tribute.
The broken line indicates transitory control. Boundary lines have to be denoted by broad sweeps, which cannot claim accuracy at every point. Where there is a sudden change in the direction of a boundary, there is positive evidence either from inscriptional data combined with identified sites or from the demands of geography.

2/ Map below left

At the battle of Qarqar Shalmaneser III defeated a coalition of forces from Phoenicia, Egypt and Israel, and thus gained control over this area (see text).

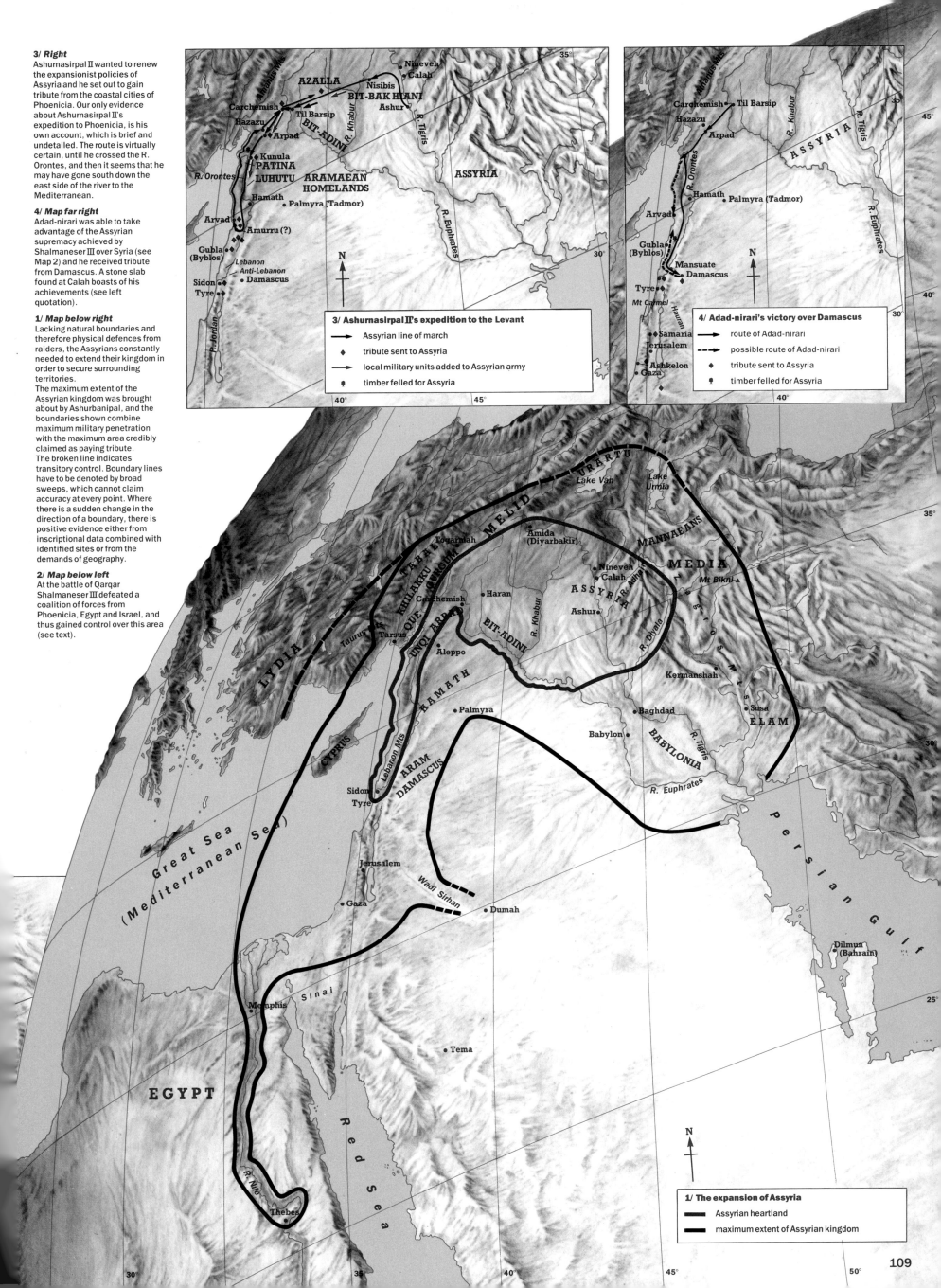

3/ Ashurnasirpal II's expedition to the Levant

→ Assyrian line of march
◆ tribute sent to Assyria
→ local military units added to Assyrian army
♠ timber felled for Assyria

4/ Adad-nirari's victory over Damascus

— route of Adad-nirari
--- possible route of Adad-nirari
◆ tribute sent to Assyria
♠ timber felled for Assyria

1/ The expansion of Assyria

— Assyrian heartland
— maximum extent of Assyrian kingdom

109

IN THE ancient Near East wine was not necessarily the product of grapes (though in Palestine this was most frequently the case). Other fruits such as dates and pomegranates were used and, to increase the variety of flavours available, spices were added. Wine played a prominent role in everyday life in the ancient world from at least 3000 BC, and is frequently mentioned in ancient texts. It was not only drunk for pleasure but was also considered useful as a medicine (I TIM 5.23) and could be applied externally as well as being swallowed (LK 10.34). Old wine was preferred to new, and the final brew had to be strained before it could be drunk.

The harvesting of grapes was a joyous occasion which took place in August and September. The grapes were sun-dried and then pressed by treading. Treading vats consisted of two pits, usually square, cut into rock. The treading pit was higher and larger, usually double the size of the reception pit which was deep and narrow. The treading of the grapes took place with a great deal of dancing and singing (some of the psalms may be grape-treading songs).

The use of mechanical presses is also recorded. A simple one in which the grapes have obviously been wrapped in cloth which is then being stretched (apparently with considerable vigour) is shown in illustration 1. Other devices for pressing have been discovered (one is illustrated on page 84).

Once the juice had been collected in a vat the first stage of fermentation would begin within hours. In a hot climate the process would start readily and progress rapidly – not necessarily the case in colder areas. After the first fermenta-

CRAFTS AND INDUSTRIES

From Neolithic times human intelligence has to a large extent been devoted to the constant discovery and invention of new techniques and processes which could improve the quality of life. Among the most important were the invention of pottery and the discovery of the techniques of working metal.

tion the wine was transferred to skins or jars (thus removing much of the sediment) where fermentation would continue (JER 13.12; 48.11).

POTTERY

In the Neolithic and Chalcolithic Ages pottery making was probably a household activity carried out by women. From the beginning of the Middle Bronze Age, however, or even the Early Bronze Age, pottery was made for the commercial market by professional male potters.

Pottery was mainly used for domestic purposes – for the storage, preparation, and cooking of food. It was also used in commerce, particularly for the storage and transportation of oil and wine (the 'Canaanite commercial jar' became the forerunner of the Classical amphora), and in industry, particularly in metallurgy, where it was the only material suitable for crucibles.

The pottery of biblical times was normally made from a

clay which contained a good deal of iron; this was fired in a well-controlled closed kiln in an oxidizing atmosphere which gave a reddish colour to the finished ware. The clay was first dug, and then weathered in the potter's yard. It then had to be trodden into water until all the air was removed – a skilled process (ISA 41.25), and 'grog' or 'temper', made of finely chopped straw, finely crushed stone (such as flint) or crushed pottery, was added, if necessary, to reduce the plasticity of the clay and to keep it from cracking up as it dried. When the clay was ready it was formed into the desired shape. This might be done by hand, or on a wheel, or by press moulding. If made by hand it was usually built up from coils of clay. Plain ware was decorated by using a slip, by painting, burnishing, incising, or by the addition of raised decoration (appliqué). Although the technique of glazing was known in Egypt from an early date it was never adopted in Palestine. Similarly, though the potter's wheel (JER 18.3) was used in Mesopotamia from at least 3500 BC and was known in Palestine, completely wheel-made pottery only began to be made around 2000 BC.

The earliest pottery was probably baked in the open as in the Neolithic societies of the Americas and sub-Saharan Africa, but by the Early Bronze Age the closed kiln had been adopted. This method of firing was both much more fuel-efficient and better suited to mass production. The results were also more controllable.

METALWORK

Gold was probably the earliest metal to be worked, quickly followed by copper. At first these were worked cold, but

1/ Left
This Egyptian tomb carving shows one method of pressing grapes. It appears that the fruit has been wrapped in a twisted cloth which is then stretched between two wooden poles. The resulting juice flows into a vat below.

2/ Above right
A ceremonial axe head found at Beth-shean. The blade is made of bronze and, at one end, appears to resemble a hand. Some experts believe that this is not native work but is an import. Certainly such blades have been found in other sites throughout the Near East.

3/ Right
A bronze juglet probably from c 8th century BC and thought to be of Phoenician origin.

4/ Right
A stone mould for producing axe heads. This example was discovered at Gezer.

5/ Far right
An assortment of utensils for the storage and application of cosmetics.

11/ Below
Stone relief from Susa, early 1st millennium BC showing a noblewoman spinning. She is seated cross-legged on a stool and her servant stands behind her with a fan.

12/ Below right
A modern Turkish peasant woman can be seen using exactly the same method of spinning as that employed two thousand years ago. This simple method,

6/ Above left
A lamp from Dor showing Persian influence.

7/ Left
This cult vessel represents a seated nude woman with a churn on her head. From Gilat (Chalcolithic period).

8/ Above
A rhyton in the form of a head. It

comes from a tomb in Jericho and dates from c 17th century BC.

9/ Above right
Israelite Iron Age pottery including jugs, a bowl and two flasks.

10/ Right
A modern Egyptian potter using methods which have not changed for millennia.

by c4000 BC the techniques of smelting and casting had been developed. From a very early date the copper ore malachite was used as an ornamental stone because of its beautiful variegated blue-green colour. It is likely that the discovery that the ore could be smelted to produce metallic copper was in some way connected with its use in the ceramic industry, where the requisite temperatures for smelting could have been achieved. This is supported by the fact that from very early in the Pre-Dynastic period in Egypt copper ores were used to make faience-glazed blue beads which were – and still are – held to be good-luck talismans and protection against the evil-eye.

The major source of copper for Egypt was in southern Sinai. The source for Canaan and later for both Egypt and the Israelites was in the southern part of the Wadi Arabah and the north-eastern Sinai peninsula. There is evidence of mining in the Wadi Arabah as early as c4000 BC and it has continued intermittently to modern times.

The processing of copper ore begins with it being broken into small pieces and then placed in a furnace on a bed of charcoal. These furnaces were usually circular with a basin-shaped interior designed to catch the molten metal, thus producing a pudding-shaped copper ingot. Bellows, made of a ceramic bowl with a hollow spout on the side over the top of which a piece of leather was tied, which was pulled up and pushed down, were used to give sufficient forced draft to achieve smelting temperature. An ingot from the first smelting would be spongy and full of impurities and needed to be hammered out and re-smelted

before it could be used for making tools and ornaments.

The temperature necessary for the casting of iron could not be achieved in antiquity so objects of iron were forged by blacksmiths.

At least in the later periods craftsmen were organized in hereditary guilds, who lived and worked together. The metalworking guilds probably made seasonal expeditions to the mining areas, and worked up the ingots into finished products in the neighbourhood of their home cities during the rest of the year.

CLOTH

Organic materials such as cloth do not survive well in a climate with such seasonal variations of temperature and moisture as that of Palestine, so that we have few textiles preserved from antiquity. Recently, however, a cave in the south of the country at Nahal Hemar was excavated which was found to contain a number of pieces of Pre-Pottery Neolithic B cloth, dating from around 7000 BC.

The main fibres used were linen, wool and, in later periods, cotton. The basic dyes were blue, purple, indigo and scarlet (ESTH 1.6; EX 28.31; PS 45.14).

Because of the different lengths and characteristics of the fibres used, the spinning of each one was a specialized skill. Egyptian linen was particularly soft and pliable. It was light and comfortable to wear (GEN 41.42) but durable enough even for such purposes as the sails of ships (EZEK 27.7). In Egypt the woody portion of the flax, from which linen is made, was removed by retting it in running water until the connective tissues decomposed. Linen fabric was exported

in quantity from inland western Syria, from centres such as T. Mardikh/Ebla and from Tyre (II CHRON 2.13-14).

Flax was grown in Palestine from the Early Bronze Age and Galilee, in particular was noted for producing flax of high quality. It was often retted by laying it on house roofs where decomposition was effected by the dew (JOSH 2.6).

Three types of loom were used in the ancient Near East. The Egyptian vertical loom was, according to Herodotus, only used in Egypt. On this the warp beam was at the top and the cloth beam at the bottom, the weft being beaten downward. The Greek vertical loom had the cloth beam at the top, the warps were weighted at the bottom and the weft beaten upwards. Nomadic peoples used a portable horizontal loom which could be held in place either by pegs at each end or by pegs at one end and a belt around the weaver's waist at the other end. In the nomadic societies weaving was done in the household by the women. In the sedentary societies it was, to some extent, done by the women in the home, especially in Egypt, but there were also professional weavers, most of whom were men.

'YOU WILL SAY TO ME THEN, "WHY DOES HE STILL FIND FAULT? FOR WHO CAN RESIST HIS WILL?" BUT WHO ARE YOU, A MAN, TO ANSWER BACK TO GOD? WILL WHAT IS MOLDED SAY TO ITS MOLDER, "WHY HAVE YOU MADE ME THUS?" HAS THE POTTER NO RIGHT OVER THE CLAY, TO MAKE OUT OF THE SAME LUMP ONE VESSEL FOR BEAUTY AND ANOTHER FOR MENIAL USE?'
ROM. 9.19-21

requiring only the most basic equipment, is still widely used in many areas of the world.

13/ Right
A remnant of woollen cloth found at Masada and dating from the 1st century AD.

14/ Below centre right
This highly coloured and intricately patterned Coptic cloth contrasts strongly with the plainer Israelite textiles. The designs used seem rather out of place in the Near East and are reminiscent of central American cultures.

15/ Below far right
The horizontal loom, much favoured by nomadic people of the ancient Near East, is still in use. This example comes from Turkey but is no different from those which would have been in use thousands of years ago. An even more easily portable version, in which one end of the work was secured to the weaver's waist, was also used. It is this which Delilah is described as using in JUDG 16.13-14.

AFTER Adad-nirari III of Assyria had weakened the kingdom of Damascus (806 BC), Israel under Joash and his son, Jeroboam II gained three victories over Aram (II KINGS 13.25), perhaps at Lo-debar and Karnaim (AMOS 6.13) and finally at Aphek (II KINGS 13.17). Jeroboam II was able to subject Damascus and extend Israel's control as far north as Lebo-hamath; in Transjordan his authority extended as far as the Dead Sea (II KINGS 14.28). The herald of this new resurgence on the part of Israel was Jonah from Gath-hepher in Zebulun.

Judah also saw a time of revival in political, military and economic power. The former clash between Israel and Judah (II KINGS 14.8-14) was smoothed over ten years later with the death of Joash (782 BC) and the return of Amaziah to Jerusalem (II KINGS 14.16-17). The power in Judah was, however, in the hands of the co-regent, Azariah/Uzziah, who launched a campaign against the Philistines (II CHRON 26.6) and established strong points in the territory of Ashdod and elsewhere on the coastal plain. His control of the trade routes from Arabia and Sinai was secured by the restoration of Elath, after his father died (II KINGS 14.22); thus he received tribute from the Arabs and also the Meunites (who were in Sinai now; II CHRON 26.7). His son and co-regent, Jotham, overpowered the Ammonites and reduced them to tribute as well (II CHRON 26.8; 27.5). In this way during the first half of the 8th century BC, Israel and Judah controlled practically the same territory as the former United Monarchy (cf I KINGS 4.24).

The inland trade route across Transjordan was first controlled under Jeroboam II, who reorganized the Israelite tribes in this area by means of a census; but after his death, the initiative passed to Judah under Jotham (I CHRON 5.17).

Such a period of prosperity and dominance brought with it a false sense of security and an increase of social injustice on the part of the newly enriched upper classes (AMOS 2.4-8). Possible evidence for royal officials and servants

PEACE AND PROSPERITY UNDER JEROBOAM II

In the 8th century BC Israel and Judah under Jeroboam and Uzziah reached a peak of political importance and a prosperity which rivalled that of the kingdom of Solomon. The wealth of the upper classes led prophets like Amos to speak out against greed and injustice. New light has been shed on the era by the discovery at Samaria, the capital city of Israel, of receipts for oil and wine sent from local estates to the royal storehouses. This collection of ancient Hebrew names from an extra-biblical source provides confirmation of tribal lists and genealogies of the Bible.

living in the capital at Samaria while receiving shipments from local estates may be seen in the Samaria ostraca, a group of over 60 inscribed pottery fragments found during the excavations there. These are scribal notations of commodities received at the royal storehouse, either 'aged wine' or 'purified oil'. As the jars were delivered, the shipment was duly recorded on a sherd and later entered in a ledger. The officials receiving the oil or wine could thus be credited and have the use of their supplies. The same formula on the potsherd may have already been inscribed on the jar itself. The recipients were probably 'eating at the king's table' (cf II SAM 9.10, 13) and being sent just enough from their own estates for use while on duty there. Though the estates may have been part of their own patrimony, they also could have been royal grants of land taken from other citizens (cf I SAM 8.14).

The inscriptions fall into two groups, the one coming from Years 9 or 10 and the other from Year 15 (and perhaps one from Year 17) of the reigning king(s). The former group

records the place from which the commodity was sent and the name of the recipient. The latter group usually adds the name of the clan district as well as the town and also gives the name of the sender; the commodity is generally omitted. Text No 1 of the earlier group has a list of senders with their commodities, all to one recipient. The Hebrew formulation, 'From (the town) ... to (the person)', is so closely paralleled by administrative expressions in the Bible (especially Leviticus) that there can be no doubt as to its meaning.

The names of the recipients often end in the theophoric -yaw that seems to be typical of the northern kingdom (as against -yahu or -yah of Judah). They can receive from more than one place but each steward only sends to the same man. A few notations do not have a recipient; they must represent shipments to the king from royal vineyards.

Fair identifications have been proposed for all but two or three of the town names, based on similar names in the Arabic toponymy of the central Samaria hills. All of the settlements seem to fall in the old tribal district of Manasseh (JOSH 17.7-10). Since Manasseh's town list is missing in the Bible, the Samaria ostraca provide a welcome source of local settlement patterns. The later texts, which also have the name of a clan district, give surprising testimony to the geographical reality behind the geneaological tables in I CHRON and elsewhere. The clans mentioned on the Samaria ostraca are all either male descendants of Manasseh (Abiezer, Helek, [A]sriel, Shechem, Shemida) or the female descendants of Zelophehad (Noah, Hoglah; cf NUM 26.28-34; 27.1-4; 36.10-12; JOSH 17.1-6; I CHRON 7.9-19). The texts show that the biblical accounts of Zelophehad's daughters had an historical basis in fact, and probably represent the legitimisation of certain later arriving clans in the territory. Be that as it may, by matching the clans with the towns associated with them in the inscriptions, one may locate the clan districts themselves. It is noted that the clans named after

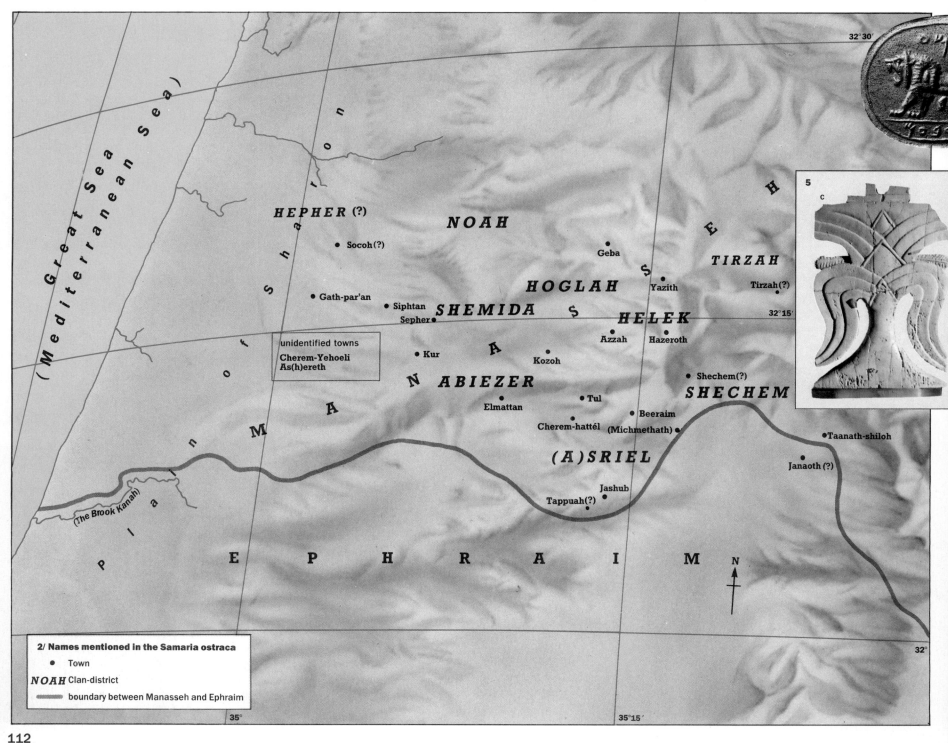

2/ Names mentioned in the Samaria ostraca

● Town

NOAH Clan-district

━━━ boundary between Manasseh and Ephraim

male descendants extend from Mount Ebal south while the daughters of Zelophehad extend from Samaria northwards. The former are seen to have settled in the central hill country while the latter were located in the northern hilly region (formerly occupied by the clans of Issachar?). Another descendant of Manasseh, Hepher, is the eponym of 'the land of Hepher' associated with Socoh on the edge of the Sharon plain (I KINGS 4.10). Comparison of the genealogies of Judah and Caleb (I CHRON chapters 2, 4) reveals that direct descent, such as the line of Hepher, Zelophehad and the daughters, does not mean geographical identity. There is no justification for placing Hepher in the hill country region with or alongside Zelophehad's daughters. Hepher is most likely the rich northeastern part of the Sharon plain.

The southernmost town on the Samaria ostraca, Jashub, if properly placed at modern Yasuf, confirms that the adjacent hills, the 'land of Tappuah' (JOSH 17.8) really belonged to a clan of Manasseh. The border between Manasseh and Ephraim (JOSH 17.7-10; also 16.6-9) thus corresponds to the social reality of the ostraca.

Palaeographically, the ostraca exhibit a script that should be dated to the first part of the 8th century BC. The two groups, from Years 9 and 10 and from Year 15, respectively, show some palaeographical differences which had led scholars to suggest that they came from different reigns, of Joash and Jeroboam II. The use of hieratic numerals on Hebrew texts seemed odd when first discovered in these inscriptions but now it is known to have been standard practice by scribes in Judah as well (eg, in the Arad letters).

> 'IN THE FIFTEENTH YEAR OF AMAZIAH THE SON OF JOASH, KING OF JUDAH, JEROBOAM THE SON OF JOASH, KING OF ISRAEL, BEGAN TO REIGN IN SAMARIA, AND HE REIGNED FOR FORTY ONE YEARS... HE RESTORED THE BORDER OF ISRAEL FROM THE ENTRANCE OF HAMATH AS FAR AS THE SEA OF THE ARABAH...'
> II KINGS 14.23-25

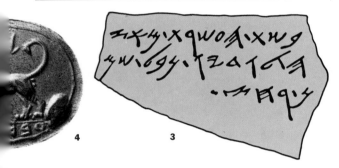

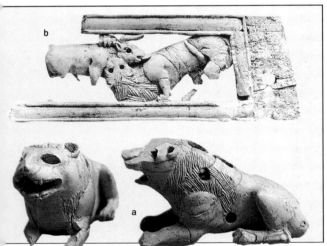

4/ Top left
This seal, inscribed 'Belonging to Shema', servant of Jeroboam', was discovered at Megiddo and can be dated to the 8th century BC.

3/ Top right
The ostraca (pottery sherds on which inscriptions were written) were used as invoices for consignments of wine and oil. Taxes in kind were paid to the royal treasury from various towns in Samaria. The translation of the inscription on the example illustrated is as follows: 'In the tenth year. From Azz/o. (Belonging) to Gaddiau. A *nbl* of fine/oil'.

2/ Map left
The Samaria ostraca can be used to attest the existence of a number of towns at this period. The map shows not only these towns but also clan districts which are mentioned in the ostraca inscriptions.

5a, 5b, 5c/ Above
This group of ivory carvings all date from the late 9th century and are of Phoenician workmanship, thus demonstrating the influence which Phoenicia exercised at the period. They were found in Samaria and appear to have been used as decorations for furniture (holes in the figures were used for fixing them in place). **5a** shows two crouching lions with mouths open, c 2in high. **5b** depicts a lion grappling with a bull. This pierced relief is c 2in high and 5in long. **5c** appears to be a stylized tree or plant, intended decoration for a border. The fact that the Israelites were able to afford these embellishments is an indication of their prosperity.

1/ Map right
The map shows the borders of Israel, Judah and Philistia during the 8th century BC. Also indicated are the cities from which the prophets of this period originated.

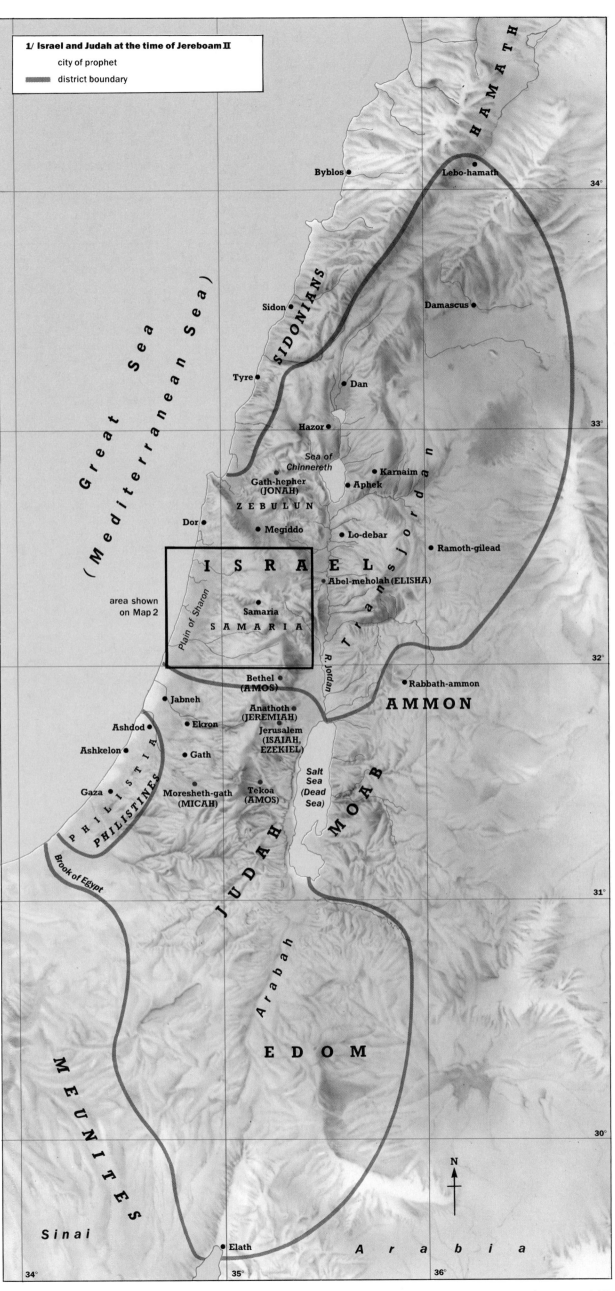

1/ Israel and Judah at the time of Jeroboam II
● city of prophet
▦ district boundary

UNTIL the second half of the 8th century BC, Assyria had treated the R. Euphrates as its western boundary, with dependent states beyond allowed to remain under vassal native kings. With the reign of Tiglath-pileser III (744-727, Pul of the Bible) this changed, and Assyria began to introduce direct provincial rule right to the Mediterranean. A factor in this change of policy was that, during the second quarter of the 8th century BC, Urartu (Ararat), Assyria's northern rival, had expanded westwards to weld into an anti-Assyrian block the north-Syrian states from Melid to Arpad, creating a threat to Assyrian trade routes. After a campaign to settle the mountain areas east of Assyria, Tiglath-pileser attacked the Urartian coalition in the west in 743. The Urartian army was defeated, and Arpad, the main centre of resistance, taken by siege in 740, when it became the capital of an Assyrian province. Its fall is alluded to in II KINGS 19.13 (= ISA 37.13). Tiglath-pileser then moved against Unqi (Patina) at the northern end of the

ASSYRIAN SOVEREIGNTY OVER ISRAEL

The Bible tells in II KINGS 16 how the kings of Syria and Israel attacked Ahaz of Judah, who called upon Tiglath-pileser for assistance. Tiglath-pileser III introduced a new line of Assyrian kings, and a new strategy, so that by 721 Israel was entirely under Assyrian rule, and Judah only survived by dutiful vassaldom.

Orontes; its capital, Kullania (Calneh) was taken in 738 and gave its name to a newly created province. A further Assyrian advance southwards culminated in the creation of the province of Simirra and Khatarikka (Hadrach) in the same year, and the payment of tribute by rulers including Rezin of Damascus, Menahem of Samaria, and the kings of Tyre, Gubla and Hamath.

Meanwhile Tiglath-pileser was combating Urartian influences elsewhere, in 739 in Ullubu (the Dohuk-Zakho region of north Iraq), in 737 in the Median area in north-east Iran and in 735 he moved against Urartu itself.

In 734 Tiglath-pileser returned to the west to extend firm Assyrian control into Philistia. He took Gaza and reached the Brook of Egypt (Wadi el-Arish), subduing the nomadic tribes there and appointing an Arab tribal chief as Warden in north Sinai. He also entered into a relationship with other Arab rulers in northern Arabia and eastern Transjordan. Recent changes of ruler in both Israel and Judah had brought new political alignments, and Pekah of Israel joined with Rezin of Damascus in an anti-Assyrian coalition, which included Tyre, Ashkelon and some of the Arab tribes of north Arabia and Transjordan; the common interest was control of the trade routes from south Arabia. The coalition failed to involve Ahaz of Judah, who, accepting Assyrian suzerainty, invoked assistance against attack (II KINGS 16.6-7; II CHRON 28.16-17). In campaigns in 733 and 732, Tiglath-pileser received a renewal of submission by the Arab tribes and Ashkelon and Tyre; he also defeated the leaders of the coalition. The coastal, northern and Transjordanian sectors of Israel were made into the Assyrian provinces of Du'uru (Dor), Magiddu (Megiddo) and Gal'aza (Gilead), Pekah was deposed, and the rump of Israel was placed under Hoshea as Tiglath-pileser's nominee and vassal.

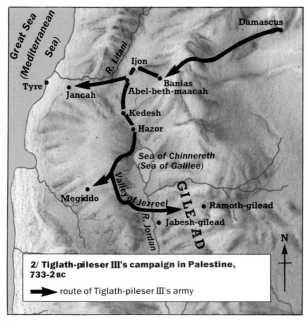

2/ Tiglath-pileser III's campaign in Palestine, 733-2 BC

→ route of Tiglath-pileser III's army

1/ Map Below
Between 744 and 727 BC Tiglath-pileser III carried out a series of campaigns to expand Assyrian influence. His first campaign was against the Urartian coalition in 743 BC. This was followed by a push southwards. Eventually, his influence extended down to the Brook of Egypt. In spite of rebellion by vassal states, he was able to turn his attention to the putting down of a revolt in Babylonia.

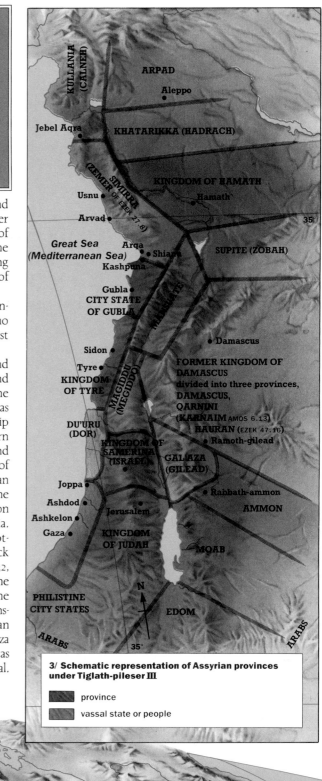

3/ Schematic representation of Assyrian provinces under Tiglath-pileser III

▨ province
▨ vassal state or people

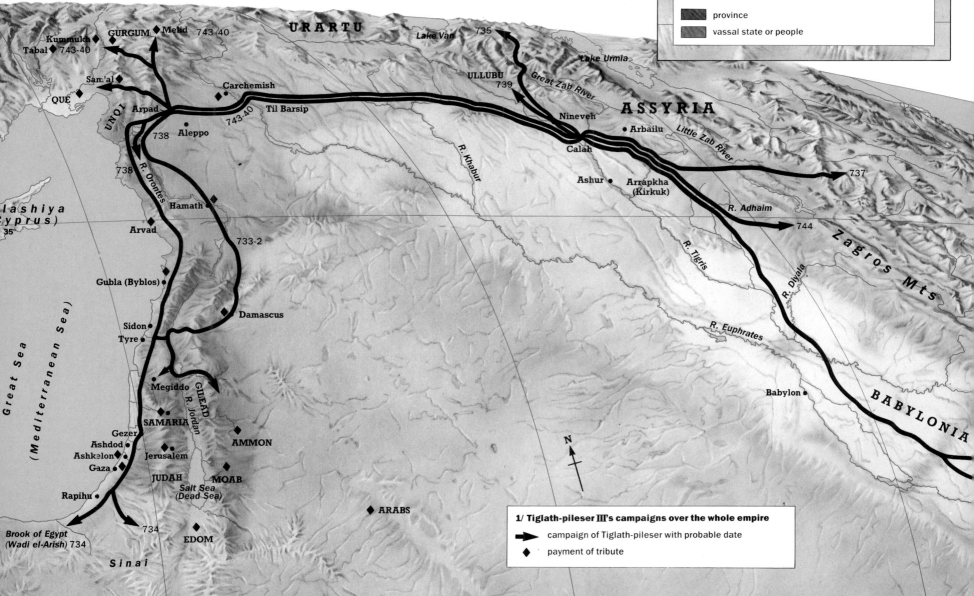

1/ Tiglath-pileser III's campaigns over the whole empire
→ campaign of Tiglath-pileser with probable date
◆ payment of tribute

The kingdom of Damascus was taken under direct Assyrian rule, divided into the three provinces of Damascus, Qarnini (Karnaim) and Khaurina (so written, perhaps for Hauran). In accordance with usual Assyrian policy, parts of the population of both kingdoms were deported and the area repopulated with conquered peoples from elsewhere. Ammon, Moab and Edom remained loosely under Assyrian control as tribute payers, with the further incentive of Assyrian protection against nomadic tribes to their east and south.

The main concern of the rest of Tiglath-pileser's reign was Babylonia, where a revolt broke out under a Chaldaean chieftain. When this had been quelled, Tiglath-pileser took the kingship of Babylon in person from 729.

His briefly reigning successor, Shalmaneser V (726-722), clashed with vested interests in his capital Ashur. The resulting instability weakened Assyria's hold on the west, enabling Egypt to extend influence in Palestine. Hoshea, Assyria's appointee as king of Israel, transferred allegiance

to Egypt. Assyria replied by sending an army against Samaria, which after a two years' siege was taken in late 722. The biblical implication that the conquest took place under Shalmaneser, accords with the Assyriological data since, although Shalmaneser's successor Sargon (721-705) does claim this success in his later records, he says nothing of it in his earliest inscription dealing with events in the west in 720. Israel was made into a province called Samerina, possibly incorporating the earlier Dor, although by the reign of Esarhaddon this was treated as part of Philistia. Part of the population was subsequently deported, and replaced by peoples from elsewhere.

Sargon's accession was linked to the opposition to Shalmaneser, but he quickly restored stability. He faced problems in three areas: Babylonia, where Chaldaean tribes supported by Elam were attempting to oust Assyrian control; the far north, from south of Lake Urmia to Asia Minor, where Urartu was working to establish a chain of vassal states and allies; and Syria and Palestine, where a renascent Egypt was seeking to increase its influence. The most immediate problem was in Babylonia; although a military clash with Elam checked the threat from that quarter, for the time being Sargon was powerless against the Chaldaean leader Marduk-apil-iddina (Merodach-baladan of the Bible), who usurped the throne of Babylon and held it for a decade. In the west a widespread revolt broke out, headed by Hamath, with Arpad, Damascus, Samaria and parts of Phoenicia and Philistia implicated, and Egypt giving support (II KINGS 17.4). Sargon quelled this revolt in 720; it was conflation of his minor action against Samaria at this time with the major siege two years earlier, which allowed him in his later records to claim credit for the original capture of the city.

Subsequent years saw both military and diplomatic successes against Urartian influence in the north, culminating in a treaty with Urartu's former ally Mita (Greek Midas) of Mushki (biblical Meshech) in Asia Minor – powerful from control of the trade routes between Europe and Asia – and a decisive invasion of Urartu itself in 714.

6

> 'IN THE DAYS OF PEKAH KING OF ISRAEL TIGLATH-PILESER KING OF ASSYRIA CAME AND CAPTURED IJON, ABEL-BETH-MAACAH, JANOAH, KEDESH, HAZOR, GILEAD, AND GALILEE, ALL THE LAND OF NAPHTALI; AND HE CARRIED THE PEOPLE CAPTIVE TO ASSYRIA.'
> II KINGS 15.29

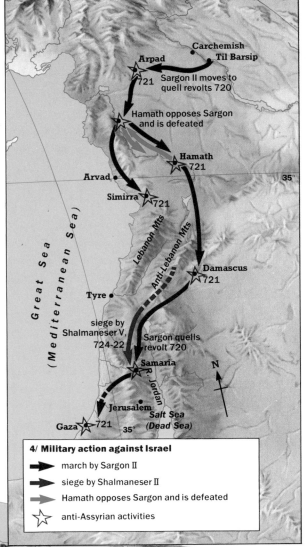

4/ Military action against Israel

→ march by Sargon II

→ siege by Shalmaneser II

→ Hamath opposes Sargon and is defeated

☆ anti-Assyrian activities

2/ Map above far left
A detail of Map 1 showing the campaigns in Palestine in which Tiglath-pileser III defeated the coalition of Israel, Damascus, Tyre, Ashkelon and some Arab tribes.

3/ Map top left
The Assyrians were not mere destroyers. They evolved a sophisticated system of administration by which subject nations could be kept under control.

4/ Map near left
Further attacks on Israel were carried out under Sargon II and Shalmaneser V. Shalmaneser besieged Samaria for two years before it fell.

5/ Map below
The Assyrians appreciated the benefits of deporting defeated populations and replacing them with captives from elsewhere. The resultant social dislocation made it hard for captive peoples to organize resistance.

6/ Top
Sargon II (ruled 721-705 BC), successor of Shalmaneser V (726-722 BC). This relief comes from his palace at Khorsabad built between 717 and 707 BC. The original carving (on limestone) is about 3ft high. The facial details are keenly observed and it seems likely that this is a portrait rather than an idealized representation.

7/ Above
A fresco (about 1ft 4in high) from the summer palace of Tiglath-pileser III. The two figures are high officials of the court. This fresco was painted rather than carved in low relief, the art form for which the Assyrians are noted.

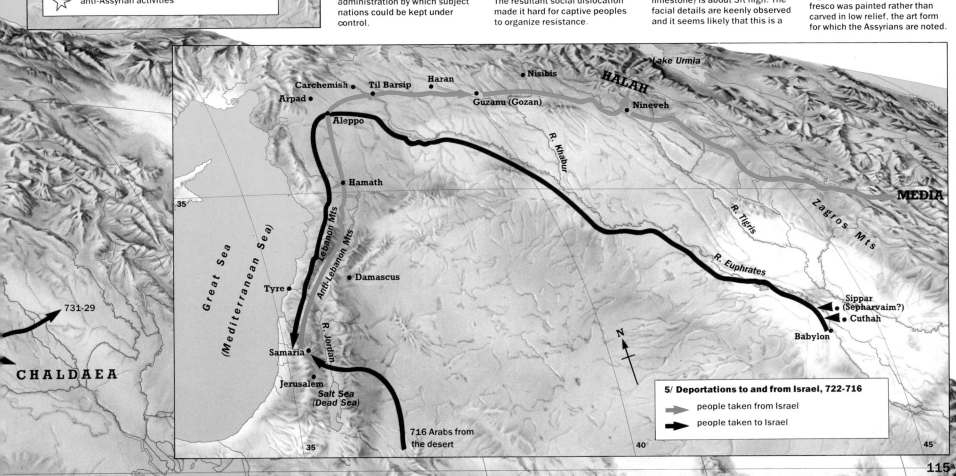

5/ Deportations to and from Israel, 722-716

→ people taken from Israel

→ people taken to Israel

THE end of the 2nd millennium BC was a time of great upheaval in the lands of the Bible (see pages 52-55). The great empires of Egypt and the Hittites had collapsed and throughout the Near East and the Mediterranean there were large movements of peoples wandering and eventually settling in the towns and cities of Canaan and elsewhere. Nomadic and semi-nomadic tribes, including the groups which eventually became the Israelites, Mediterranean peoples such as the Philistines and their brethren, known as the Sea Peoples, driven from their homelands possibly by some natural disaster, were all pushing their way into Canaan. Sometimes they settled among the Canaanites peacefully, but sometimes they conquered the area by warfare. The Sea Peoples settled in the coastal area, the Israelites in the hill country, the Aramaeans in the north, and the Ammonites, Moabites and Edomites in the east.

Except for the Egyptian monuments and inscriptions, there is an almost complete absence of illustrated monuments to shed light on the conduct of warfare during the beginning of this period (the end of the 2nd and the beginning of the 1st millennium BC). Because of this the reliefs of Ramesses III at Medinet Habu in Egypt (see page 66) are of particular importance as they bring vividly to life the desperate hand-to-hand conflict.

The illustrations of Ramesses' campaigns against the Libyans in the west and the Sea Peoples in the east provide us with basic source material to show the methods of battle, weapons and fortifications of the Egyptians and their

WARFARE IN THE 1ST MILLENNIUM BC

War, whether caused by inter-tribal squabbles or by the invasion of alien peoples such as the Philistines, was a constant threat to the peoples of the ancient Near East. Reliefs from Medinet Habu in Egypt, and on the palace walls of the Assyrian kings, give a vivid account of the manner in which warfare was conducted at this time. Archaeological excavation in Israel has shed light on the way in which the Israelites used casemate walls to encircle their towns and shafts to create underground water-systems so that they could endure long periods of siege.

enemies. We see from the reliefs that the Philistines, with their distinctive feather-topped headdress and their brethren, the Sherden, are distinguished by their use of a long straight sword and round shield while the Egyptians use the composite bow and javelin. The few weapons discovered in archaeological excavations complete our knowledge of warfare during this important but still little known period.

It is only from the following period, during the United Monarchy in the 1st millennium BC, that more information on warfare becomes available and the various biblical passages are filled out by evidence from archaeological

excavations. In addition, Assyrian and Aramaean reliefs add to our visual knowledge on these subjects. These reliefs, found in the palaces of Ashurnasirpal II (883-859), Shalmaneser III (858-824), Tiglath-pileser III (745-727), Sargon II (721-705), Sennacherib (704-681) and Ashurbanipal (668-627) at Nineveh, Nimrud and Balawat depict exploits of the Assyrian kings, particularly in war, in great and accurate detail. From them we can see the evolution of various arts of war such as the use of the battering ram, the development of new types of chariot, the methods of fortifying and besieging cities and the weapons used by both the Assyrians and their enemies.

CHARIOTS

The chariot was not used by the Israelites during the early period of their settlement in Canaan. It is only with the establishment of a United Kingdom under David, and mainly after Solomon, that references begin to appear in the Bible. The type of vehicle used in David's and Solomon's time can be reconstructed from reliefs discovered in Syria, at Zinjirli and T. Halaf, dating from the 10th century BC. They were drawn by two horses and had a crew of two, a driver who also used a spear, and an archer. Later, the Assyrians, particularly Tiglath-pileser III, developed the chariot into a heavier vehicle with larger wheels and eight spokes, instead of the earlier six spokes. It supported a crew of three, sometimes four, and eventually four horses were used instead of the earlier two.

WEAPONS

The basic weapons used in the last millennium BC were the sling and the bow. Squadrons of slingers and bowmen were

1

used, the archers in front, protected by shields. Spears, daggers and javelins were personal weapons used in hand-to-hand combat. Protective clothing was worn (I KINGS 22.34), often of leather, but parts of bronze and even iron coats of armour have also been found in excavations. The shield was used for protection; in the Assyrian army sometimes a shield-bearer protected the bowman.

The most terrifying weapon, however, was the battering-ram. These siege weapons were used by building ramps against the slopes of the besieged city; the battering-rams were placed in position to knock down the walls at their weakest point, usually the city gate. The defenders used burning torches, stones, arrows and anything else they could find to keep the enemy from breaching the walls. A series of reliefs from the palace of Sennacherib at Nineveh shows the Assyrian army attacking the Judaean city of Lachish in 701 BC (see page 122). A battering-ram is at the city gate; a soldier from inside it pours water over it to prevent it being set alight by the burning torches being thrown by the Lachishites who also use their bows and throw stones. The double walls of the city are clearly visible. The story told on these reliefs is confirmed by excavations at the site of Lachish where an Assyrian siege ramp has been found close to the city gate. What appears to be a counter-ramp has been discovered inside the city.

FORTIFICATIONS

The main features of early Israelite fortifications are casemate walls and gateways with three pairs of chambers, and twin towers. This type of wall (which consists of two parallel walls connected at intervals by partitions with connected gate) has been found at Megiddo, Hazor, Gezer and many other sites, some of them clearly built to the same plan. Their destruction c920 BC is followed by a new combination of fortifications. Massive solid walls of salients and recesses replaced the casemate walls. The new city gates were smaller (two, then only one pair of chambers, with no towers) but they were more massively built. These major changes are consequences of the development of the art of warfare, and the introduction of new types of weapons, one of which was the battering-ram mentioned above. There is evidence from the reliefs of the Assyrian kings that this new type of weapon makes its appearance from at least as early as the beginning of the 9th century BC.

WATER SUPPLY

One of the methods used by the various armies to subdue enemy cities was to lay siege to them. In order to withstand long periods of sieges (the siege on Samaria lasted 3 years!) a water supply had to be ensured, accessible from within the city walls. To this end the Israelite kings executed formidable engineering projects and a number of fine examples of underground water systems have been found in Palestine; at Jerusalem, Megiddo, Hazor, Gibeon and various other places. Local problems required different plans, but a common solution was to protect or camouflage a spring or water source lying outside the city. Within the city a deep vertical shaft with steps was dug through the rock to around water level and then a tunnel was dug through the rock under the city to the water supply, which enabled the water to flow into the city. The creation of such a water system was a tremendous feat of engineering. King Hezekiah recorded the making of the Jerusalem water supply system in the well-known Siloam inscription and it is clear that it was considered a great achievement both by him and by the writer of Chronicles (II CHRON 32.30).

> ... WHEN THE TUNNEL WAS DRIVEN THROUGH. AND THIS WAS THE WAY IN WHICH IT WAS CUT THROUGH:- WHILE ... WERE STILL ... AXES, EACH MAN TOWARD HIS FELLOW AND WHILE THERE WERE STILL THREE CUBITS TO BE CUT THROUGH, THERE WAS HEARD THE VOICE OF A MAN CALLING TO HIS FELLOW, FOR THERE WAS AN OVERLAP IN THE ROCK ON THE RIGHT AND ON THE LEFT, AND WHEN THE TUNNEL WAS DRIVEN THROUGH, THE QUARRYMEN HEWED THE ROCK EACH MAN TOWARDS HIS FELLOW, AXE AGAINST AXE; AND THE WATER FLOWED FROM THE SPRING TOWARD THE RESERVOIR FOR 1,200 CUBITS, AND THE HEIGHT OF THE ROCK ABOVE THE HEADS OF THE QUARRYMEN WAS 100 CUBITS.'
>
> THE SILOAM INSCRIPTION

2

1/ Left
This scene showing the battle of the River Ulai in 653 BC, gives a vivid idea of hand-to-hand fighting. Depicted is the defeat of Teumnon, king of Elam, by the Assyrian king Ashurbanipal at Til-Tuba on the River Ulai. The relief is from the south-west palace at Nineveh.

2/ Above
A graphic example of Assyrian archery. A detail from relief on the north-west palace at Nineveh, c640 BC.

3/ Below
The chariot was one of the most feared and effective weapons of ancient warfare. These are taken from the bronze bands on the gates of the temple of Mamu

(858-824 BC), built by Shalmaneser III at his palace at Imgur-Enlil, now called Balawat. The chariots were part of an expedition to the Tigris.

4/ Bottom
One of Sennacherib's Assyrian soldier's counting the heads of executed prisoners. A detail of the relief in the south-west palace at Nineveh (704-681 BC).

5/ Right
Plan of Hezekiah's tunnel in Jerusalem, showing how a water supply enabled towns to withstand a siege. Hezekiah's tunnel was a triumph of engineering skill. A squeeze of the Siloam inscription (6) found on one of its walls is reproduced here with a translation (see above).

3

4

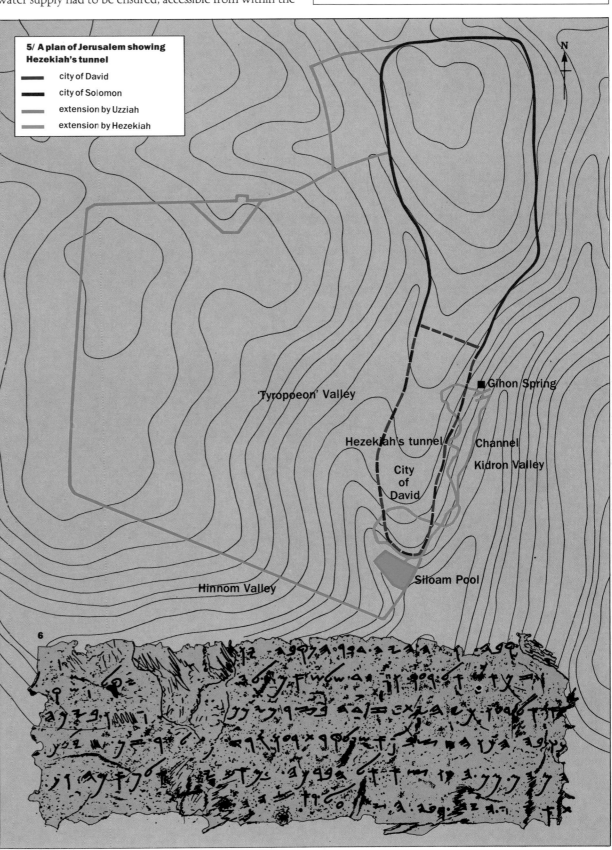

5/ A plan of Jerusalem showing Hezekiah's tunnel

— city of David
— city of Solomon
— extension by Uzziah
— extension by Hezekiah

N

'Tyroppeon' Valley

■ Gihon Spring

Hezekiah's tunnel Channel

Kidron Valley

City of David

Hinnom Valley

Siloam Pool

6

THE division of the kingdom of David and Solomon into the two states of Israel and Judah brought with it the collapse of the empire. With the accession of Rehoboam and his failure to achieve rule over Israel also, Judah emerged as a small and embattled state, reduced in both territory and prosperity. There was continuous war between Israel and Judah through the reigns of Rehoboam and Abijah. The latter's successor, Asa, was faced with pressure from the north in which the Israelite king, Baasha, took and fortified Ramah, a hill with a good view southwards, and from which it was possible to control the route from the coastal plain in the south, and also the main road north from Jerusalem which lay only some five miles away. By enlisting the help of Syria, Asa was able to draw off this threat and fortify Mizpah and Geba against his northern neighbour. Here, running through the midst of the territory of Benjamin, the northern border of Judah remained.

If the Chronicler's information (II CHRON 11.6-10) on Rehoboam's system of fortresses may be taken as a historical record, they are a vivid reflection of Judah's threatened state. Whether built before, or in order to oppose a repetition of, the ravages of Shishak's campaign (see page 96), they signal a concern to protect the heartland of the country where they are concentrated; the coastal plain and even Beersheba lie outside the territory they control.

With the conclusion of hostilities between Judah and Israel under Asa's successor Jehoshaphat, the beginning of a revival on the part of both states may be discerned. The Judaean king entered an alliance with the Omride dynasty, in which he furnished troops for Israelite battles with Syria and Moab; the alliance was sealed by the marriage of his son Jehoram to the Omride princess Athaliah. Other information for the reigns of Jehoshaphat, Jehoram and Ahaziah is, however, scarce: Edom was at first subject to Judah but later broke free. Jehoshaphat attempted, though unsuccessfully, to revive trade on the Red Sea.

The Chronicler (II CHRON 17.2,12) affirms that Jehoshaphat 'placed forces in all the fortified cities of Judah and set garrisons in the land of Judah' and 'built in Judah fortresses and store cities'. This alone is an inadequate basis for crediting him with instituting a comprehensive administrative organization of the kingdom. Yet, there is some probability that such a reform is to be dated to his reign. From the city list in JOSH 15.21-62; 18.21-28 it is possible to derive a series of 12 districts, defined by their cities, which as a whole embrace the known territory of the kingdom of Judah. Some of the cities mentioned, such as Beth-haccherem, Jattir, Juttah and Eshtemoa, are known from archaeology to have been founded only in the Iron II period, and the time of Jehoshaphat is probably the earliest for the origin of the system represented by the list as a whole. Some propose a later date, however, for the reign of

THE DIVIDED KINGDOM – JUDAH

THE RESURGENCE OF JUDAH'S POWER c 750 BC

The major sources for this period are Kings and Chronicles plus a considerable amount of archaeological information. Because of its late origin and uncertainties about its sources, Chronicles presents problems for the historian. It frequently offers different and additional information to that contained in Kings, but its historical reliability is often disputed. This problem is significant in the present context in relation to the fortresses of Rehoboam and the achievements of Uzziah.

Uzziah or that of Josiah. If it is assumed that the list may reflect a continuing and developing situation, rather than a single act of administrative reform, it is probable that the organizational measures of a number of Judaean kings, in-

cluding Jehoshaphat, Uzziah and Josiah, are reflected here.

Following the death of Ahaziah, in the course of the revolt of Jehu in Israel, and the six-year reign of Athaliah, the only non-Davidide to rule in Jerusalem, the Davidic line was represented once more by Joash. About his reign there is little information: he was forced to pay heavily to persuade the Aramaean king, Hazael, to withdraw from Jerusalem, and in the end he was assassinated. It was under his successor Amaziah that Judaean revival began again. He defeated the Edomites but was himself defeated by Israel in a battle the background of which is obscure. Eventually he too was assassinated and was succeeded by his son Uzziah.

The Book of Kings records only that Uzziah built Elath and restored it to Judah, but that must presuppose considerable general expansion southwards on the part of Judah. The Chronicler's much fuller picture (II CHRON 26) is, therefore, given some support: here Uzziah achieved a number of military victories over Arabs, 'Meunites', Ammonites and Philistines. He is said also to have strengthened the fortifications of Jerusalem and built 'towers in the wilderness', and, indeed, major forts, the foundation of

1/ Map right
In II CHRON 11.5-12 there appears a list of fortresses built by Rehoboam at strategic points throughout Judah. One line of forts was built along the border with Philistia, whilst the three forts at Hebron, Beth-zur and Bethlehem were intended to protect a main route which ran along the ridge of the Judaean hills. One puzzle in the biblical account is the mention of a fort at Gath. This could not be the Philistine city as it was still in Philistine hands at this period. It has been suggested that Moresheth-gath was intended, and this would make sense from a strategic point of view.

2/ Map below left
This division of Judah into districts is based on a town list which appears in JOSH 15.21-62. The division is based on the geographical areas of Judah: the Negeb, the Shephelah, the hill country and the wilderness. In the original Hebrew text there are 10 groups of towns, but it is now widely accepted that there were actually 12. Opinions are divided as to the composition of these groups, this map follows the system suggested by Prof. Y. Aharoni.

3/ Map below right
The map shows the way in which Uzziah sought to expand the kingdom in the west and to gain control of the far south.

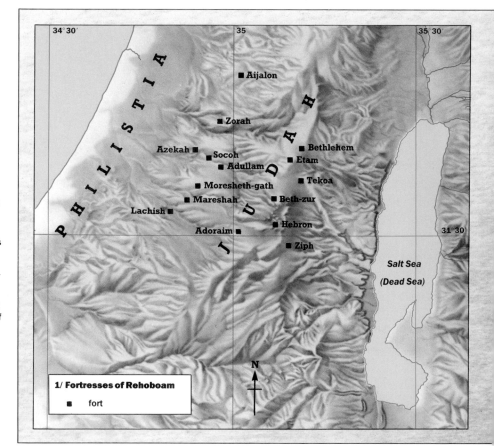

1/ Fortresses of Rehoboam
■ fort

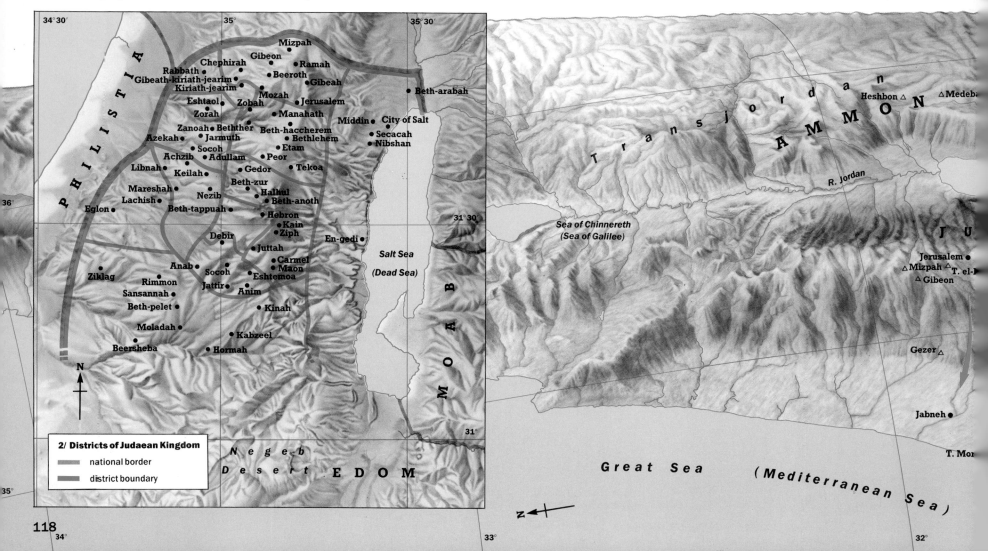

2/ Districts of Judaean Kingdom
national border
district boundary

which may be dated to the 9th or 8th centuries, have been discovered at Arad Rabbah, Ramat Negeb, Tamar, Kadesh-barnea, Jotbathah, Ezion-geber, and other sites in the Negeb. While the detail must remain uncertain, it is clear that Uzziah's reign saw an expansion of Judaean territory and a resurgence of power such as it had not known since the division of the kingdom.

THE ROLE OF PROPHETS IN THE OT

It is at about this time that some of the major prophets of the OT were active and it is therefore appropriate to consider here what part they played in the history and religious life of the nation.

The word 'prophet' is derived from the Greek *prophetes* meaning 'spokesman', and this is itself the term used by the Septuagint for the Hebrew *nabi*. The Hebrew word is probably closely related to the Akkadian *nabu*, 'to call' and may indicate the fact that the biblical prophet felt himself to be 'called' or summoned by God to deliver his message, or perform acts that would indicate the divine will.

Although the earlier prophets, such as Samuel, were also designated as 'seer', and were consulted professionally for advice about impending events, foretelling the future was not the main preoccupation of the prophetic figure as it developed. The main feature was the pronouncement of the divine word.

The fact of being in the control of God is a characteristic common to all the biblical prophets, whether of the early type, such as Samuel, Elijah or Elisha, or of the later 'writing' prophets like Amos or Jeremiah. The earlier records, particularly of the reign of Saul, speak of bands of prophets, who entered into trance-like states. Indeed, Saul at one point joined them, and became 'another man'. This experience of being possessed by the holy spirit is vividly described by Jeremiah and Isaiah, who resisted the 'call' protesting their unworthiness.

The prophet had both a political and an ethical role, the moral dimensions becoming more apparent in the writing prophets. The confrontation between prophet and king is seen at the very beginning of royal power with Samuel and Saul, and continues with Nathan and David, Elijah and Ahab, and with the great political and moral fulminations which have come down to us in the prophetical writings contemporary with the rise and fall of the Assyrian, Babylonian and Persian Empires.

The prophets felt impelled to interpret major political upheavals in divine, moral terms, perceiving God as the power who used nations to further his own purposes.

Within the prophet's own milieu, too, his insistence on moral rectitude, especially on the part of the rich and powerful, was part of his view of the world as a place where physical victory and peace depended on individual and social righteousness. Only repentance and moral regeneration would lead to national redemption. This idea was often expressed in the most beautiful poetic imagery. Some prophets, particularly Amos and Jeremiah, saw urban civilization with all its temptations as especially repellent, and Jeremiah harked back to the wilderness days when the Israelites led a simple life of obedience to their God.

> 'WHEN THE RULE OF REHOBOAM WAS ESTABLISHED AND WAS STRONG, HE FORSOOK THE LAW OF THE LORD, AND ALL ISRAEL WITH HIM.'
>
> II CHRON 12.1

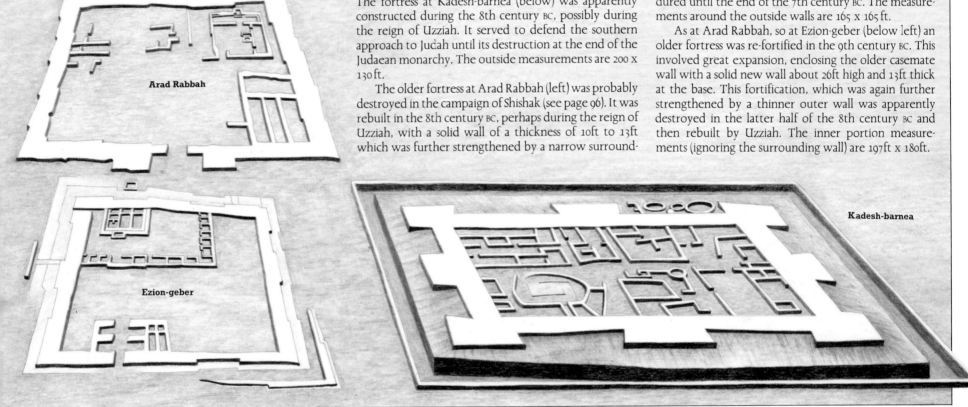

FORTS IN THE NEGEB

The fortress at Kadesh-barnea (below) was apparently constructed during the 8th century BC, possibly during the reign of Uzziah. It served to defend the southern approach to Judah until its destruction at the end of the Judaean monarchy. The outside measurements are 200 x 130 ft.

The older fortress at Arad Rabbah (left) was probably destroyed in the campaign of Shishak (see page 96). It was rebuilt in the 8th century BC, perhaps during the reign of Uzziah, with a solid wall of a thickness of 10ft to 13ft which was further strengthened by a narrow surrounding retaining wall (not shown). This fortification endured until the end of the 7th century BC. The measurements around the outside walls are 165 x 165 ft.

As at Arad Rabbah, so at Ezion-geber (below left) an older fortress was re-fortified in the 9th century BC. This involved great expansion, enclosing the older casemate wall with a solid new wall about 26ft high and 13ft thick at the base. This fortification, which was again further strengthened by a thinner outer wall was apparently destroyed in the latter half of the 8th century BC and then rebuilt by Uzziah. The inner portion measurements (ignoring the surrounding wall) are 197ft x 180ft.

Arad Rabbah

Ezion-geber

Kadesh-barnea

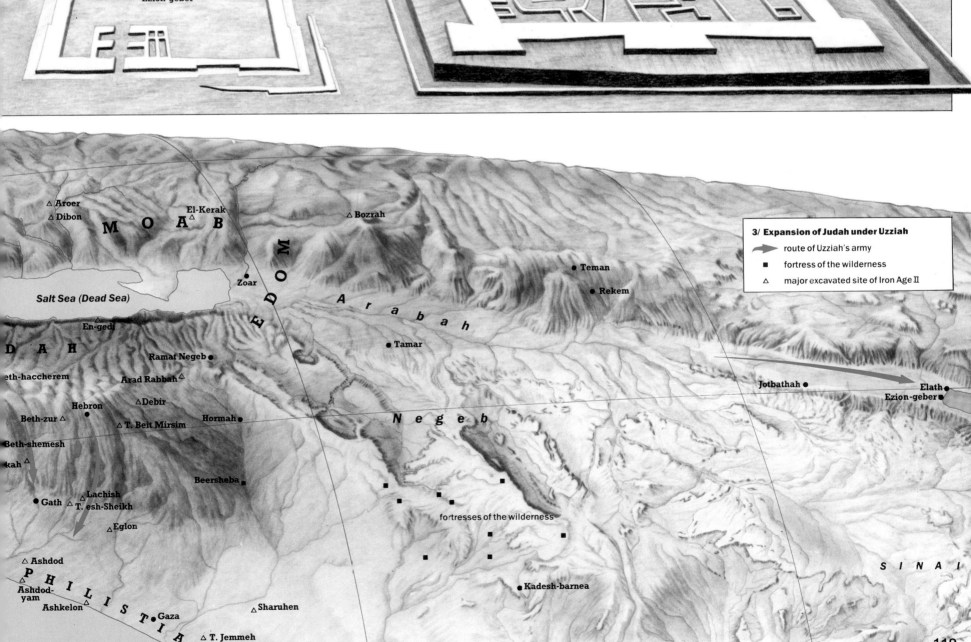

3/ **Expansion of Judah under Uzziah**
→ route of Uzziah's army
■ fortress of the wilderness
△ major excavated site of Iron Age II

FOUR ranks of cities and towns have been identified in this hierarchical scheme. In addition to these ranks were the villages and settlements which accomodated the rural population.

ROYAL CAPITALS

The 9th century capital of Israel at Samaria and the 10th century (reconstructed) capital of the United Monarchy at Jerusalem are the two examples of this category. The acropolis at Samaria is remarkable for its size, superb ashlar masonry and well organized internal arrangements. The summit of the hill was adapted (through quarrying, levelling and infilling operations) to incorporate a large rectangle surrounded by casemate storerooms, which enclosed the royal palace and administrative buildings, in one of which the famous Samaria ostraca were found. The palace faced what could have been an open ceremonial square, while the residences of the court elite lay to its east. Commoners lived in the 'lower city' on the slopes below.

MAJOR ADMINISTRATIVE CENTRES

The importance of the public sector is strongly reflected in the layout of such centres. The complexes that were intended for the use of the administrative officials still maintain their enclosed orthogonal shape even though incorporated into a circular urban plan.

At Megiddo the increasing entrenchment of the

CITY PLANNING — THE HIERARCHICAL ORDER

The large number of Iron Age sites excavated in Israel and the extensive archaeological exposure of many of them provide a sound data base for the study of city planning during the Israelite period. Until recently research has concentrated on finding the 'typical' Israelite city plan. However, a more valid approach is to try to identify the position of each town in the hierarchical sequence of cities according to its role in the central administrative system. The towns can be graded according to general layout, type of fortifications, network of streets, shape of structures, type of building materials and the relative amount of space allocated for public buildings such as palaces and storehouses.

bureaucracy is evident when comparing the unwalled city of the early 10th century BC with the solidly fortified city of the late 10th century. In the latter, the allocation of space for public structures (such as the palace called No 338 by the excavators), the vast shaft for the water system and the

royal storehouses (popularly known as 'Solomon's stables'), cover about 82% of the mound.

An even larger proportion of the area (84%) is estimated for Lachish of the 8th century BC. Here the greater part of the city is occupied by a huge rectangular unit, which encompasses the palace, storehouses and an immense open courtyard. In marked contrast, the civilian population is crowded into small irregular shaped dwellings in a narrow strip between the acropolis and the city wall.

The large open courtyards associated with the residences of the governors in such centres were probably used to accommodate military units whenever they were stationed inside the city. Due to the limited space allocated for private houses, the population was probably much less than is usually estimated for such cities: about 500 persons in 10th century Megiddo and 750 in 8th century Lachish.

SECONDARY ADMINISTRATIVE CENTRES

For smaller, economically less important districts another type of city plan was followed. The best example is Beersheba, where the entire city was apparently a royal administrative centre. Accordingly, the public units, such as the storehouses, water system and the governor's residence, were not confined to a separate quarter but were incorporated organically into the city plan.

Unlike in the previous categories, here the private

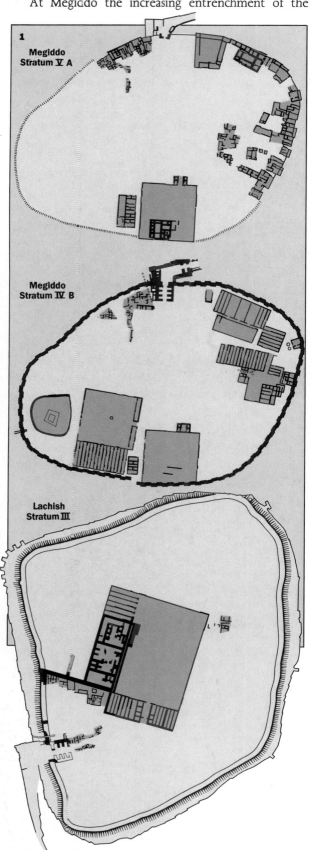

1
Megiddo
Stratum V A

Megiddo
Stratum IV B

Lachish
Stratum III

Note
In all the accompanying diagrams black lines represent actual excavated remains and red lines represent a hypothetical reconstruction by the archaeologist.

2

Beersheba   Stratum II

1/ Above left
The three excavations illustrated, Megiddo Stratum VA (top), Megiddo Stratum IVB (middle), and Lachish Stratum III, show the amount of space devoted to public buildings (see text).
These major administrative centres were primarily for the use of the bureaucracy and, by the late 10th century public structures covered 82% of the mound at Megiddo and 84% at Lachish.

2/ Above
An artist's impression, based on the evidence of excavation, of Beersheba Stratum II.

3/ Right
A plan of Beersheba showing the excavated portions on which the above reconstruction is based.

3

dwellings (most likely living quarters for the junior officers and minor officials) are nicely arranged along the street grid which covers the entire city.

The strict level of planning and the inclusion of public units in the town plan clearly demonstrates the difference between the status of Beersheba and that of other population centres such as T. Beit Mirsim. Due to its well organized and compact layout, Beersheba probably had a population of about 400, though it covers an area of less than 3 acres, as compared to 15 acres at Megiddo or Lachish.

FORTIFIED PROVINCIAL TOWNS

Unlike the administrative centres, these towns lack public buildings, and the main feature that distinguishes them from simple villages is the existence of a fortification wall. However, inside this wall the houses are scattered randomly in an unplanned agglutinative pattern.

The complete lack of planning is well demonstrated by the absence of any clearly defined street network. A good example is T. Beit Mirsim of the 10th-8th centuries BC, where the width of the streets differs considerably even in two neighbouring blocks. Consequently, almost 40% of the area of such towns is not built up. It seems that the main source of livelihood in these provincial towns besides agriculture and herding (perhaps some of the empty space inside the town was used for penning the flocks) was light

industry, as reflected by olive presses, dyeing installations, pottery kilns and the like. Although a defensive wall encircled the town, its function was more likely connected with the overall framework of regional or national defence rather than with the protection of the occupants.

The impact on town planning of the city's role in the hierarchical scheme is well reflected by the main two Iron Age phases at T. en-Nasbeh. Under the United Monarchy (late 11th and 10th centuries BC) this was a small provincial town. After the division of the monarchy at the end of the 10th century, it became a border city and was apparently upgraded in military and administrative status. Since the previous town was not destroyed, the new city wall was built around the old nucleus, but some distance away from it. The intervening space was exploited for public functions such as storage (in numerous silos), the water system (in cisterns hewn partially under the city wall) and accommodations for officers in four-room houses.

Foreign influence on city planning is clearly evident in the plan of Megiddo of the 8th-7th centuries BC, which differs from anything known previously and should probably be considered an example of Assyrian town planning applied to a western provincial capital. It is characterized by a regular grid pattern, somewhat more regular for the north-south streets than the east-west ones. Each block was

65ft-75ft deep and the streets were 8ft-10ft wide (42 and 46 Assyrian cubits). One-third of the city (at the north near the gate) was devoted to a series of palaces. Since there was no clear separation between the official and private sectors, it may be concluded that the entire city was occupied by functionaries of the Assyrian administration.

The classification of cities according to type in Iron Age Israel shows that the majority of the population lived from agriculture, dwelling in villages, hamlets and farmsteads close to their fields and pastures where they worked – and not in cities. Cities were constructed by the royal administration solely for the bureaucracy. They were inhabited by the political, military, economic and religious elite and their servants and subordinates.

'REHOBOAM DWELT IN JERUSALEM, AND HE BUILT CITIES FOR DEFENSE IN JUDAH. HE BUILT BETHLEHEM, ETAM, TEKOA, BETH-ZUR, SOCO, ADULLAM, GATH, MARESHAH, ZIPH, ADORAIM, LACHISH, AZEKAH, ZORAH, AIJALON, AND HEBRON, FORTIFIED CITIES WHICH ARE IN JUDAH AND IN BENJAMIN. HE MADE THE FORTRESSES STRONG, AND PUT COMMANDERS IN THEM, AND STORES OF FOOD, OIL, AND WINE. AND HE PUT SHIELDS AND SPEARS IN ALL THE CITIES, AND MADE THEM VERY STRONG. SO HE HELD JUDAH AND BENJAMIN.' II CHRON 11.5-12

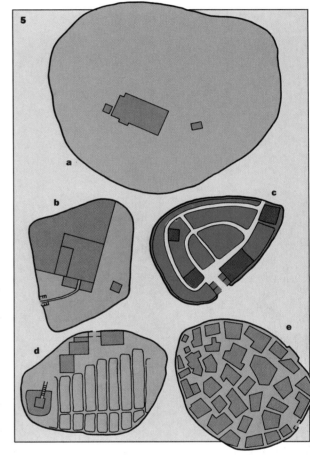

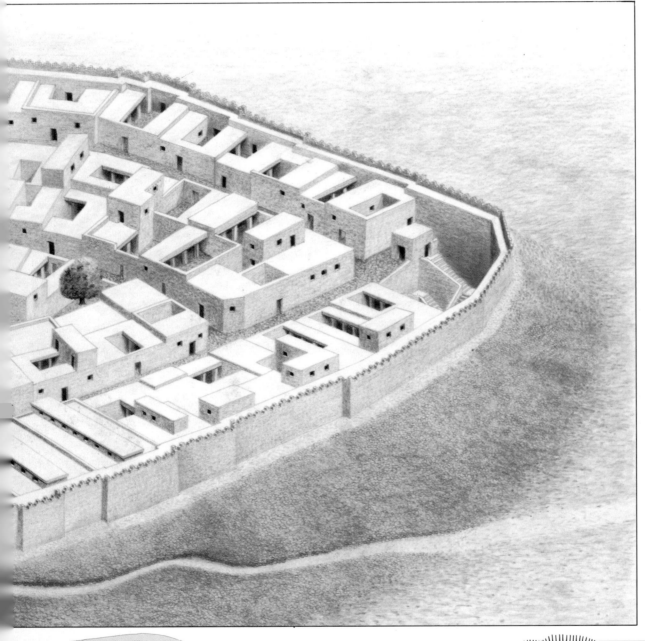

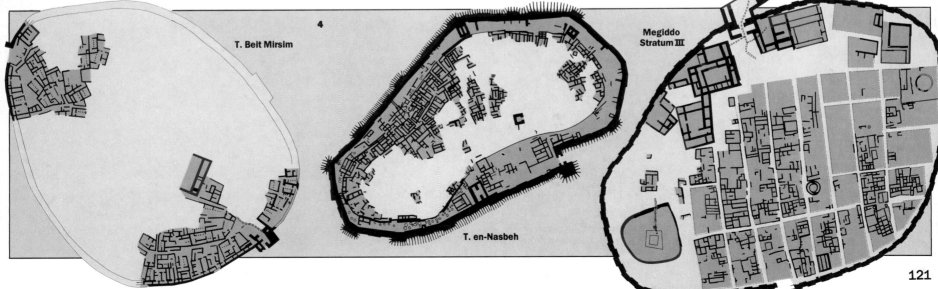

4/ Below
The plans are of, left to right, T. Beit Mirsim, T. en-Nasbeh, and Megiddo Stratum III. The first two are fortified provincial towns, whereas Megiddo was an Assyrian administrative capital characterized by a regular grid pattern.
The fortified towns had a fortified outer wall but the houses were scattered. At T. Beit Mirsim, for example, the width of streets varies considerably in two neighbouring blocks. Such towns, though fortified, were not military camps and the people were engaged in agriculture and light industry.

5/ Above
The towns illustrated show all the types represented in the hierarchical order; they are:
a) Samaria (royal capital),
b) Lachish (major administrative centre), c) Beersheba (secondary administrative centre),
d) Megiddo (Assyrian provincial capital), and e) T. Beit Mirsim (fortified provincial town).

THE western revolt of 721 BC also affected some of the Philistine states backed by Egypt. In 720 BC, Sargon reconquered Gaza and repulsed an Egyptian army which had come to its aid. In 716 BC he extended his formal boundary to the Brook of Egypt (Wadi el-Arish), where he established a military colony. Another aspect of his policy was to encourage trade with Egypt. Subsequent disturbances in Philistia brought action in 712 against Ashdod (ISA 20.1), which had attempted to involve other Philistine states (plus Judah, Moab and Edom) in an anti-Assyrian coalition. Ashdod was made into a province, although anomalously a vassal king was subsequently permitted alongside the Assyrian governor.

Sargon died in 705, probably in battle at Tabal (biblical Tubal) in Asia Minor; ISA 14.15-20 may refer to this. This brought widespread revolt, in which both Hezekiah of Judah and his ally Merodach-baladan of Babylonia (II KINGS 20.12 etc) were involved.

Sennacherib (704-681) acted first in Babylonia. He defeated Merodach-baladan's Chaldaean and Aramaean allies, ravaged the tribal areas, and appointed a Babylonian nobleman as king. After a further campaign to the northern borders of Merodach-baladan's ally Elam, he turned (701) to the west. Here the ringleader of the insurrection, in alliance with some Philistine cities, was Hezekiah of Judah, who had already prepared for a siege by improving Jerusalem's water supply (II KINGS 20.20; II CHRON 32.30). Egypt, under a new

THE DIVIDED KINGDOM – JUDAH

ASSYRIAN ATTACKS ON PHILISTIA AND JUDAH

Tiglath-pileser's successors tightened the Assyrian grip on Palestine. Sargon dealt with the Philistine cities, and when Hezekiah attempted to reverse his father Ahaz's acceptance of vassaldom, Sennacherib invaded Judah. Sennacherib's inscriptions and the Bible give complementary accounts of the siege of Jerusalem from the two sides, and agree closely.

dynasty, now supported the Philistine cities against Assyria.

The Assyrians came down the Phoenician coast, making a show of force against a group of hostile cities headed by Sidon. This brought tribute, signifying loyalty, from rulers of the whole coastline from Byblos to Ashdod, as well as from Judah's neighbours to east and south – Ammon, Moab and Edom – who were likely to welcome a curb upon Judaean expansion. Two Philistine cities stood out – Ekron, whose pro-Assyrian king had been removed to imprisonment in Jerusalem in a rebellion backed by Hezekiah; and Ashkelon, now under a new dynasty, which had seized Joppa and other cities north of Ashdod. Sennacherib took

the latter cities by siege and received the surrender of Ashkelon itself, whose king he replaced with a scion of the former pro-Assyrian dynasty. As he moved to attack Ekron, an Egyptian army approached. A battle at Eltekeh went in Assyria's favour, and Sennacherib advanced to take Timna'. The rebels in Ekron submitted, their pro-Assyrian king eventually being reinstated after release from prison.

With Judah now isolated, Sennacherib undertook its systematic subjugation, beginning with the fortress of Azekah, Philistine Gath (which Hezekiah had annexed), Lachish and Libnah; he speaks of taking 46 walled cities. MIC 1.10-15 may refer to further aspects of this, and archaeological evidence shows destruction of other Judaean sites at this time. From Lachish a column was sent to Jerusalem. A suggestion that ISA 10.28-32 describes a second Assyrian army approaching from the north accords neither with the accounts in II KINGS 18-19 and the Assyrian annals, nor with Assyrian military tactics. Hezekiah made submission, paid heavy tribute, released the king of Ekron, and lost some western territories to the pro-Assyrian kings of Ashdod, Ekron and Gaza.

Sennacherib's major problems during the next 12 years were with Babylonia and Elam; increasingly severe action culminated in his sack of Babylon in 689. In 681 he was murdered by two of his sons (II KINGS 19.37), one of whom has been identified in a cuneiform source as Arad-mulishshi, whose name is represented in the Bible as Adrammelech.

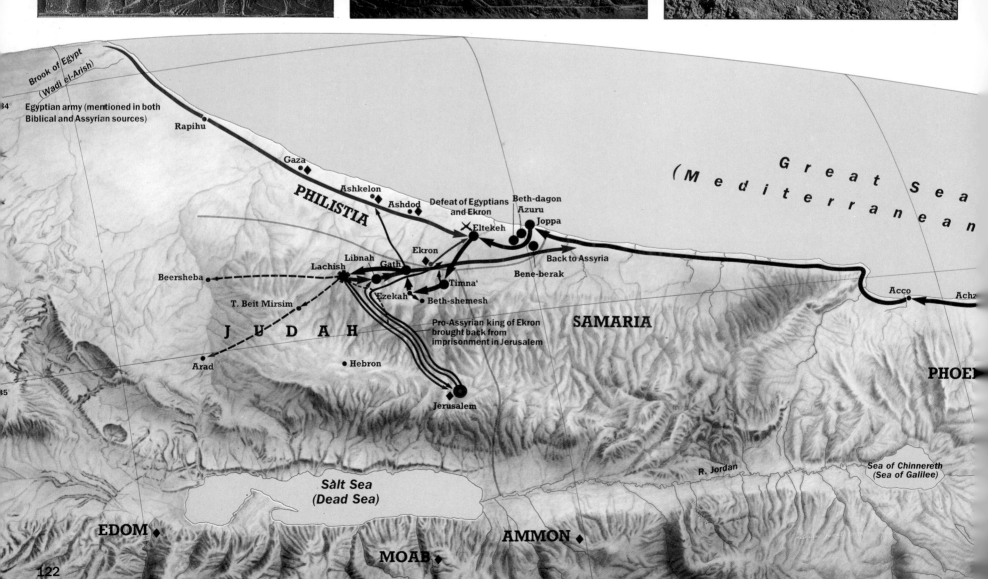

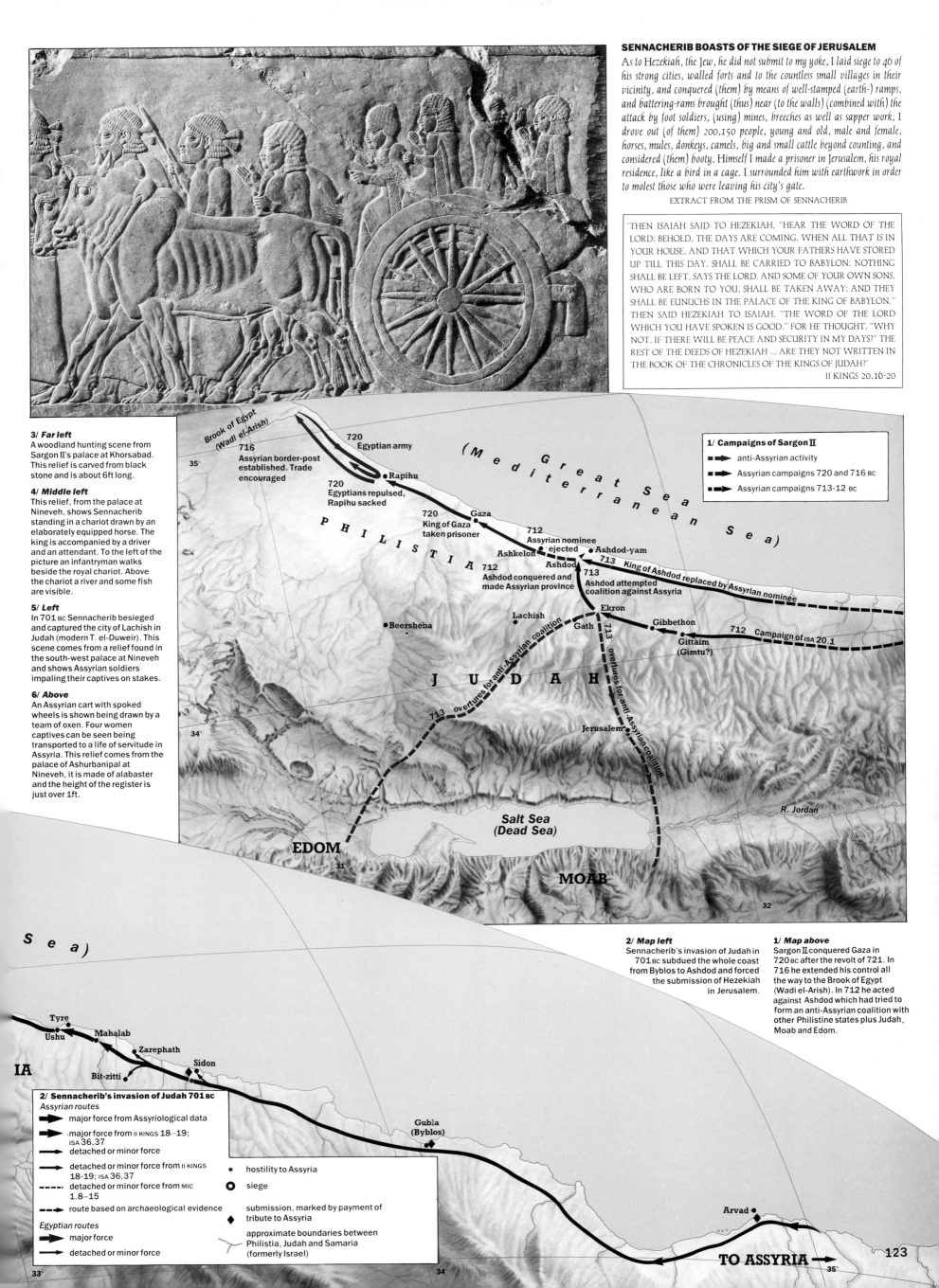

SENNACHERIB BOASTS OF THE SIEGE OF JERUSALEM

As to Hezekiah, the Jew, he did not submit to my yoke, I laid siege to 46 of his strong cities, walled forts and to the countless small villages in their vicinity, and conquered (them) by means of well-stamped (earth-) ramps, and battering-rams brought (thus) near (to the walls) (combined with) the attack by foot soldiers, (using) mines, breeches as well as sapper work, I drove out (of them) 200,150 people, young and old, male and female, horses, mules, donkeys, camels, big and small cattle beyond counting, and considered (them) booty. Himself I made a prisoner in Jerusalem, his royal residence, like a bird in a cage. I surrounded him with earthwork in order to molest those who were leaving his city's gate.

EXTRACT FROM THE PRISM OF SENNACHERIB

'THEN ISAIAH SAID TO HEZEKIAH, "HEAR THE WORD OF THE LORD: BEHOLD, THE DAYS ARE COMING, WHEN ALL THAT IS IN YOUR HOUSE, AND THAT WHICH YOUR FATHERS HAVE STORED UP TILL THIS DAY, SHALL BE CARRIED TO BABYLON; NOTHING SHALL BE LEFT, SAYS THE LORD. AND SOME OF YOUR OWN SONS, WHO ARE BORN TO YOU, SHALL BE TAKEN AWAY; AND THEY SHALL BE EUNUCHS IN THE PALACE OF THE KING OF BABYLON." THEN SAID HEZEKIAH TO ISAIAH, "THE WORD OF THE LORD WHICH YOU HAVE SPOKEN IS GOOD." FOR HE THOUGHT, "WHY NOT, IF THERE WILL BE PEACE AND SECURITY IN MY DAYS?" THE REST OF THE DEEDS OF HEZEKIAH ... ARE THEY NOT WRITTEN IN THE BOOK OF THE CHRONICLES OF THE KINGS OF JUDAH?'

II KINGS 20.16-20

3/ Far left
A woodland hunting scene from Sargon II's palace at Khorsabad. This relief is carved from black stone and is about 6ft long.

4/ Middle left
This relief, from the palace at Nineveh, shows Sennacherib standing in a chariot drawn by an elaborately equipped horse. The king is accompanied by a driver and an attendant. To the left of the picture an infantryman walks beside the royal chariot. Above the chariot a river and some fish are visible.

5/ Left
In 701 BC Sennacherib besieged and captured the city of Lachish in Judah (modern T. el-Duweir). This scene comes from a relief found in the south-west palace at Nineveh and shows Assyrian soldiers impaling their captives on stakes.

6/ Above
An Assyrian cart with spoked wheels is shown being drawn by a team of oxen. Four women captives can be seen being transported to a life of servitude in Assyria. This relief comes from the palace of Ashurbanipal at Nineveh, it is made of alabaster and the height of the register is just over 1ft.

1/ Campaigns of Sargon II
➡ anti-Assyrian activity
➡ Assyrian campaigns 720 and 716 BC
➡ Assyrian campaigns 713-12 BC

Map labels:
Brook of Egypt (Wadi el-Arish)
720 Egyptian army
716 Assyrian border-post established. Trade encouraged
Rapihu
720 Egyptians repulsed, Rapihu sacked
720 King of Gaza taken prisoner
Gaza
712 Assyrian nominee ejected
Ashkelon
Ashdod • Ashdod-yam
713 King of Ashdod replaced by Assyrian nominee
712 Ashdod conquered and made Assyrian province
713 Ashdod attempted coalition against Assyria
Lachish
Beersheba
Ekron
Gibbethon
Gath
Gittaim (Gimtu?)
712 Campaign of ISA 20.1
713 overtures for anti-Assyrian coalition
Jerusalem
Salt Sea (Dead Sea)
R. Jordan
EDOM
MOAB
PHILISTIA
JUDAH
(Great Sea (Mediterranean Sea)

2/ Map left
Sennacherib's invasion of Judah in 701 BC subdued the whole coast from Byblos to Ashdod and forced the submission of Hezekiah in Jerusalem.

1/ Map above
Sargon II conquered Gaza in 720 BC after the revolt of 721. In 716 he extended his control all the way to the Brook of Egypt (Wadi el-Arish). In 712 he acted against Ashdod which had tried to form an anti-Assyrian coalition with other Philistine states plus Judah, Moab and Edom.

Map labels (lower):
Sea)
Tyre
Ushu
Mahalab
Zarephath
Bit-zitti
Sidon
IA
Gubla (Byblos)
Arvad
TO ASSYRIA ➡

2/ Sennacherib's invasion of Judah 701 BC
Assyrian routes
➡ major force from Assyriological data
➡ major force from II KINGS 18—19; ISA 36,37
➡ detached or minor force
➡ detached or minor force from II KINGS 18-19; ISA 36,37
--➡ detached or minor force from MIC 1.8—15
--➡ route based on archaeological evidence
• hostility to Assyria
○ siege
◆ submission, marked by payment of tribute to Assyria
≈ approximate boundaries between Philistia, Judah and Samaria (formerly Israel)

Egyptian routes
➡ major force
➡ detached or minor force

THE kingdom of Judah underwent its severest crisis at the end of the 8th century BC. King Hezekiah had come to the throne in 716 BC and tried to unite 'all of Israel and Judah' in the worship at the Jerusalem Temple (II CHRON 30.1-51). He was thus attracting the remaining Israelites dwelling in the newly formed Assyrian provinces such as Samaria, Megiddo and perhaps Gilead. He seems to have tried to remain inconspicuous during the reign of Sargon II of Assyria (compare his neutrality during Sargon's troubles with Ashdod, ISA 20) but when Sargon died, he followed the lead of many subject nations and raised the flag of revolt. The western league of which he was a leader included the Phoenicians, the Moabites, Ammonites and Edomites and especially some of the Philistine states. Ekron handed their quisling ruler over to Hezekiah and joined the rebels. Gaza remained loyal to Assyria and Hezekiah occupied some of its territory (II KINGS 18.8; I CHRON 4.42-43).

When the Assyrian army under Sennacherib appeared in Phoenicia, some of Hezekiah's allies rushed to surrender and pay their tribute. Judah and Ekron were left alone to bear the brunt of the Assyrian onslaught. Of the 46 Judaean cities captured the foremost was Lachish (see page 122). Though the capital at Jerusalem was not taken (II KINGS 18.13-19.36; II CHRON 32.1-23), the kingdom was devastated and its Shephelah and Negeb districts largely transferred to Philistine control. Thus, Hezekiah found himself without direct access to the major trade routes, especially that from Elath to Gaza. Henceforth, throughout the reign of Manasseh, the Negeb routes and the franchise for running the caravans were in the hands of the North Arabians, who reciprocated by assisting the Assyrians under Esarhaddon in his invasion of Egypt (671 BC).

A familiar trademark of Hezekiah's reign is the presence of wine jars bearing a royal seal impression and one of four place names: Ziph, Socoh, Hebron and the unidentified *mmšt*. Several theories have been propounded to explain the choice of the four places. The distribution of the jars, or more appropriately, their broken handles, reflects the logistic preparations of the war with Sennacherib; so it can not help us to discern the administrative reason for the choice of these four centres. It should only be noted that *mmšt* stamps are more prevalent in the north, while Socoh is found more often in the south. The same type of jar handles often bear private seal impressions and Ramat Rahel and Lachish have provided evidence that these were also jars with the royal seal (the wine jars of this type had four handles). The men whose seals were impressed on the jars were evidently officials who had to inspect and certify the contents. The simplest, most straightforward explanation for the geographical names is that they represent four centres where the royal wineries were located. This is commensurate with similar practices elsewhere, especially in the Aegean world, where the origin of wine was indicated by seal impressions on the jar handles.

The location of the king's vineyards is clearly stated with regard to Uzziah and there is no reason to think that the situation had changed during the later 8th century. The royal husbandmen (vine-dressers) were located 'in the mountains and in the Carmel' (II CHRON 26.10). Since Judah never controlled Mt Carmel in the 8th century, the Carmel region here must be the area around Carmel south-east of Hebron (JOSH 15.55; I SAM 15.12; *et al*), while 'the hills' are the Hebron-Bethlehem district of Judah. Accordingly, when the four place names of the *lmlk* (royal) wine jars are marked on the map of Judah's districts as depicted in JOSH 15, it becomes obvious that there is one winery in each of the three southern districts: Socoh in the southern, Ziph in the south-eastern and Hebron in the west-central. The enigmatic *mmšt* can be placed in the Bethlehem district (preserved only in the Septuagint as verse 59a) where the names have been so seriously corrupted in the Greek manuscripts that many are completely unintelligible. On the other hand, *mmšt* just might be a phonetic spelling for **memša(1)t*, 'government' (cf II KINGS 20.13; ISA 39.2 from the reign of Hezekiah), in which case it might refer to the royal stores in the capital. The evidences for identifying Ramat Rahel with Beth-haccherem are sufficiently strong to refute the recent proposal to locate *mmšt* at Ramat Rahel.

Manasseh was appointed co-regent by his father in 696 BC (II KINGS 21.1). Hezekiah had been ill in 701 and was granted 15 years by the Lord (II KINGS 20.1-7), but he evidently had to wait until Manasseh reached 12 years of age. By the year of Hezekiah's death (686 BC), Manasseh had probably formulated his policy for Judah's survival in the current political constellation. The trade routes were all in the hands of his neighbours; Sennacherib had reduced Judah to the hill country and the wilderness. Manasseh elected to enter into diplomatic relations with the countries round about which

JUDAH UNDER HEZEKIAH AND MANASSEH

King Hezekiah and his son Manasseh (who assumed the throne at the age of 12 and ruled for 55 years) both lived under the shadow of the Assyrian empire. Not only was Judah politically vulnerable but the Jewish religion was also under attack from the influence of Assyrian cults and Manasseh was guilty of encouraging this trend by erecting altars to foreign gods in the courts of the Temple in Jerusalem. These altars were later destroyed by Josiah.

were enjoying the benefits of Assyrian control of southern Levantine commerce. He invited embassies from Tyre and other adjacent countries (perhaps even from the Arabs), and shrines to their respective deities were restored in Jerusalem for their use (II KINGS 21.3; 23.13). Manasseh was playing up to Tyre as did Ahab in the 9th century (II KINGS 21.3). Thus, he sought to overcome the isolation in which Judah found herself after the crushing defeat at the hands of Sennacherib.

For half a century, Judah was kept in this subservient position and Manasseh not only assisted in the corvée work of delivering timber to Assyria for Esarhaddon's palace, he also had to send troops to accompany the Assyrian army under Ashurbanipal in its campaign against Egypt (667/6 and 604/3 BC). However, a change in Judah's fortune came about as a result of the great civil war in Mesopotamia. The Arabs, and apparently also Tyre and some other western states, sided with Ashurbanipal's rebellious brother in Babylon. The Arabs were severely routed and Ashurbanipal sent for the leaders of all the western states to give account of themselves; among them was Manasseh (II CHRON 33.11-17). He renounced all his treaties with Tyre and the other neighbours (indicated by turning away from their gods) and was reinstated. Permission was granted to rebuild the fortresses of Judah; this would indicate that Judah was once again being trusted with supervision of the trade routes.

Judah's relations with her neighbours are often reflected in the oracles of the prophets. For example, the oracles against Moab (ISA 15-16 and JER 48-49) mention several towns in the table land north of the R. Arnon. Most of these same towns also appear in the Mesha inscription of the mid-9th century. It is clear that neither Judah nor Israel had managed to wrench that table-land from Moab in the 8th or 7th centuries.

Judah's expansion under Uzziah (II CHRON 26.6-8) had been neutralized by the losses under Ahaz (II CHRON 28.18) and Hezekiah (at the hands of Sennacherib). Now Manasseh's new lease on life opened the way for a renascence of Judaean power as the decline of the Assyrian empire allowed a degree of freedom to neighbouring states.

HEZEKIAH'S BUILDING ACTIVITIES IN JERUSALEM
Hezekiah is known to have conducted a great many

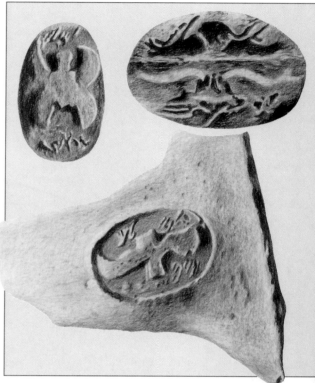

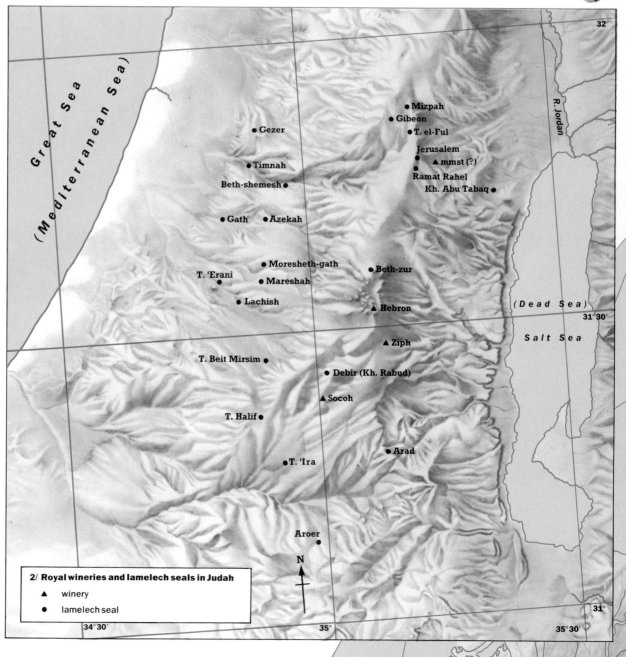

2/ **Royal wineries and lamelech seals in Judah**
▲ winery
● lamelech seal

building activities within the city of Jerusalem during the late 8th century BC. On the eve of the Assyrian siege, Hezekiah 'made a pool, and a tunnel, and brought water into the city' (II KINGS 20.20; cf ISA 22.11; II CHRON 32.2-4, 30). Hezekiah's subterranean tunnel still exists; it was built to divert the waters from the Gihon Spring to the Siloam Pool located within the city walls. A Hebrew inscription which was found during the late 19th century at the lower end of the tunnel, provides details concerning the manner in which the tunnel was hewn (see page 117).

Hezekiah also concentrated on the fortifications of the city. According to II CHRON 32.5, Hezekiah 'built up all the wall that was broken, and raised it up to the towers, and another wall without, and repaired the Millo in the City of David'. The construction of 'another wall without' is probably a reference to a new wall which was built around two residential and commercial quarters of the city: the *mishneh* quarter (II KINGS 22.14) on the Western Hill and the *makhtesh* quarter (ZEPH 1.10-11) in the Central Valley. A series of houses which belonged to the area of the *mishneh* have recently been unearthed in the excavations of the Jewish Quarter. Segments of the fortifications have also been unearthed and part of a tower which may have belonged to a gateway (perhaps the 'Middle Gate' mentioned in JER 39.3). The excavated fortification wall is about 23ft wide and was built above the remnants of houses which originally belonged to the extra-mural suburbs of the city (cf ISA 22.9-11: 'you broke down the houses to fortify the wall').

It has been estimated that the population of Jerusalem at that time numbered about 20,000 individuals. The sudden growth of the city population may have been the result of an influx of refugees who came to Judah following the fall of the Northern Kingdom in 721 BC.

A large subterranean quarry is known to the north of Jerusalem and it was originally referred to by Eshtori Ha-Parchi in AD 1322 as the 'Cave of Hezkia' a clear reference to Hezekiah. The cave is about 700ft long and 345ft wide, and over 196,000 cu yards of *meleke* limestone were extracted from the cave. Pottery found within the cave suggests that it was being used as an ashlar quarry during the 8th century BC.

> 'MANASSEH WAS TWELVE YEARS OLD WHEN HE BEGAN TO REIGN, AND HE REIGNED FIFTY-FIVE YEARS IN JERUSALEM. HE DID WHAT WAS EVIL IN THE SIGHT OF THE LORD, ACCORDING TO THE ABOMINABLE PRACTICES OF THE NATIONS WHOM THE LORD DROVE OUT BEFORE THE PEOPLE OF ISRAEL.'
>
> II CHRON 33.1-2

1/ Map below
By the time of Hezekiah and Manasseh the kingdom of Judah had been reduced greatly in size. It was bounded by Assyrian-controlled Samaria to the north, Philistia to the west and the Transjordanian kingdoms of Edom, Moab and Ammon in the east.

3/ Left
These seals (known as *lamelech* meaning 'to the king') date from the 8th century and were stamped into the wet clay of wine jar handles before firing. They were of two types, one looked like a disc with wings and the other was a scarab or beetle. When the jar had been delivered with its contents in good condition the seal was cancelled by incising concentric circles next to it. All these seals date from 8th century Judah and the greatest numbers have been found at Lachish and Jerusalem.

2/ Map left
We know of royal wineries from seal impressions found on wine jars. Four locations are known at Ziph, Socoh, Hebron and an unidentified site called *mmst*, which scholars believe to have been in the Bethlehem area.

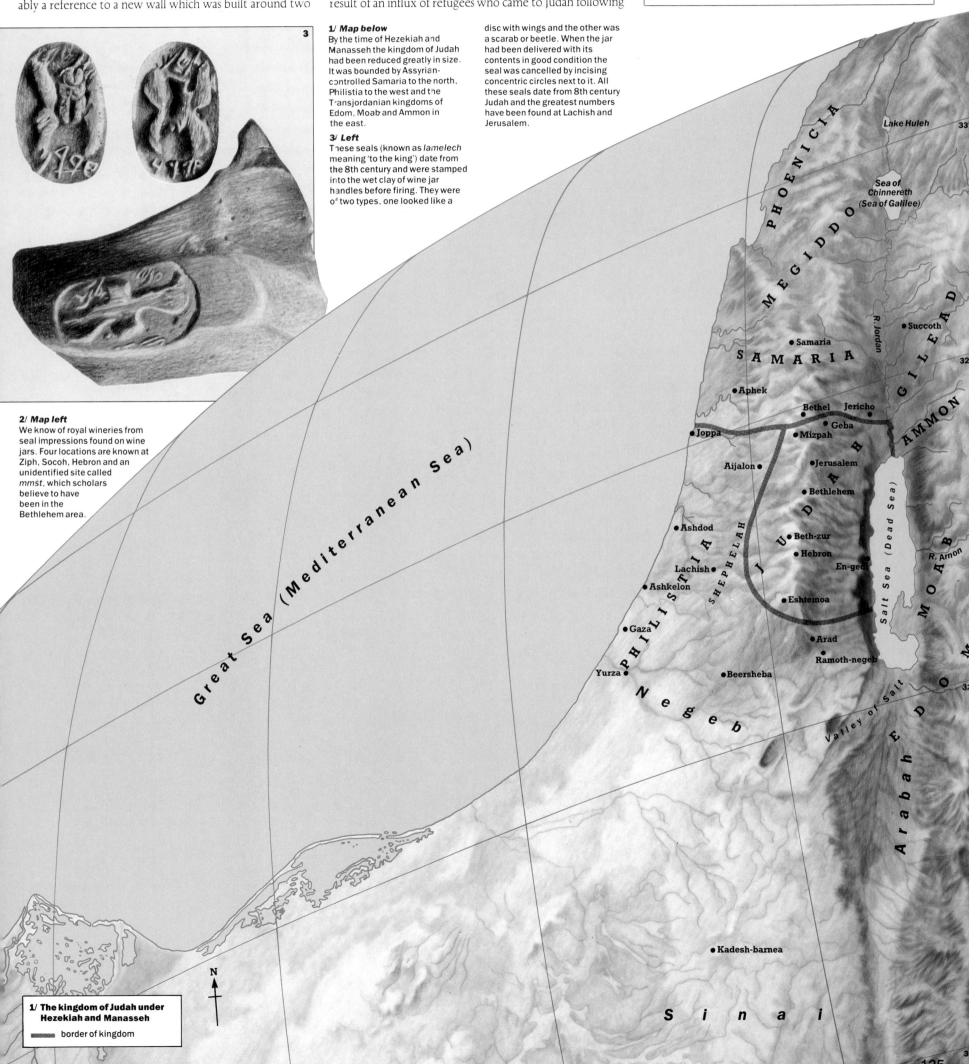

1/ The kingdom of Judah under Hezekiah and Manasseh

▬▬▬ border of kingdom

N

ESARHADDON (680-669), Sennacherib's son and successor, made major innovations in Assyrian imperial strategy. In Babylonia, he reversed his father's harsh policy, by rebuilding devastated Babylon with the help of vassals from the west, among them Manasseh who was a prisoner in Babylon, an incident reflected in II CHRON 33.11. (Other scholars believe that the reference in II CHRON relates to a rebellion of Manasseh in Ashurbanipal's reign). Esarhaddon recognized Babylonian aspirations for nominal independence, by appointing two of his sons (Ashurbanipal and Shamash-shum-ukin) as heirs to rule separately over Assyria and Babylonia. He sought stability by making treaties with his more powerful vassals, notably the Medes, the maritime kingdom of Tyre which controlled the western Mediterranean (though Tyre subsequently rebelled), the Scythian tribes in the north (one of whose kings sought a marriage alliance), and the desert Arabs.

Esarhaddon's attitude to Egypt represented a radical change of policy. Since the reign of Tiglath-pileser III, the Brook of Egypt (Wadi el-'Arish) had been the south-western limit of Assyrian interests. But Egypt had frequently given support to anti-Assyrian movements in Palestine and Phoenicia, and in 669 BC Esarhaddon sought to curb this by invasion through Sinai; an undertaking only made possible through friendship with the Arabs. His plan was to hold the Nile Delta area through native kings supervised by Assyrian officials.

There were no other major territorial changes during Esarhaddon's reign, although pressure from Cimmerians

(biblical Gomer) was eroding Assyrian authority along the northern border, a situation reversed under Ashurbanipal. At Esarhaddon's death, the dual succession left the senior heir, Ashurbanipal (668-627 BC) of Assyria, free to continue his father's policy in Egypt. He undertook two major campaigns there, the first in 667 to quell a rebellion in support of the former king Tirhakah, who had returned from his southern capital of Thebes to re-take Memphis.

The second campaign, in 664, followed another insurrection, associated with an attack on Assyrian garrisons by Tirhakah's Ethiopian successor Tanuatamun. This time Ashurbanipal conquered Egypt as far south as Thebes, and confirmed one of the vassal kings, Nechoh of Sais, as paramount ruler.

Ashurbanipal's control of Egypt strengthened Assyria elsewhere in the west, and this may have led Manasseh of Judah to a pro-Assyrian stance interpreted as apostasy (II KINGS 21). However, control of Egypt depended upon the loyalty of the vassal king, and when Nechoh's successor Psammetichus proclaimed independence, Assyrian withdrawal became inevitable.

In the north, circumstances adverse for Assyria in the long term produced a temporary advance in the area of Assyrian influence, when pressure from Cimmerian tribes ('Gomer and all his hordes' of EZEK 38.6) drove the states of Tabal (biblical Tubal), Lydia under Gyges (the name Gog of EZEK 38.2), north Cilicia (Khilakku), and eventually Urartu (biblical Ararat), to accept vassal status for protection.

Problems were developing elsewhere. Instability in

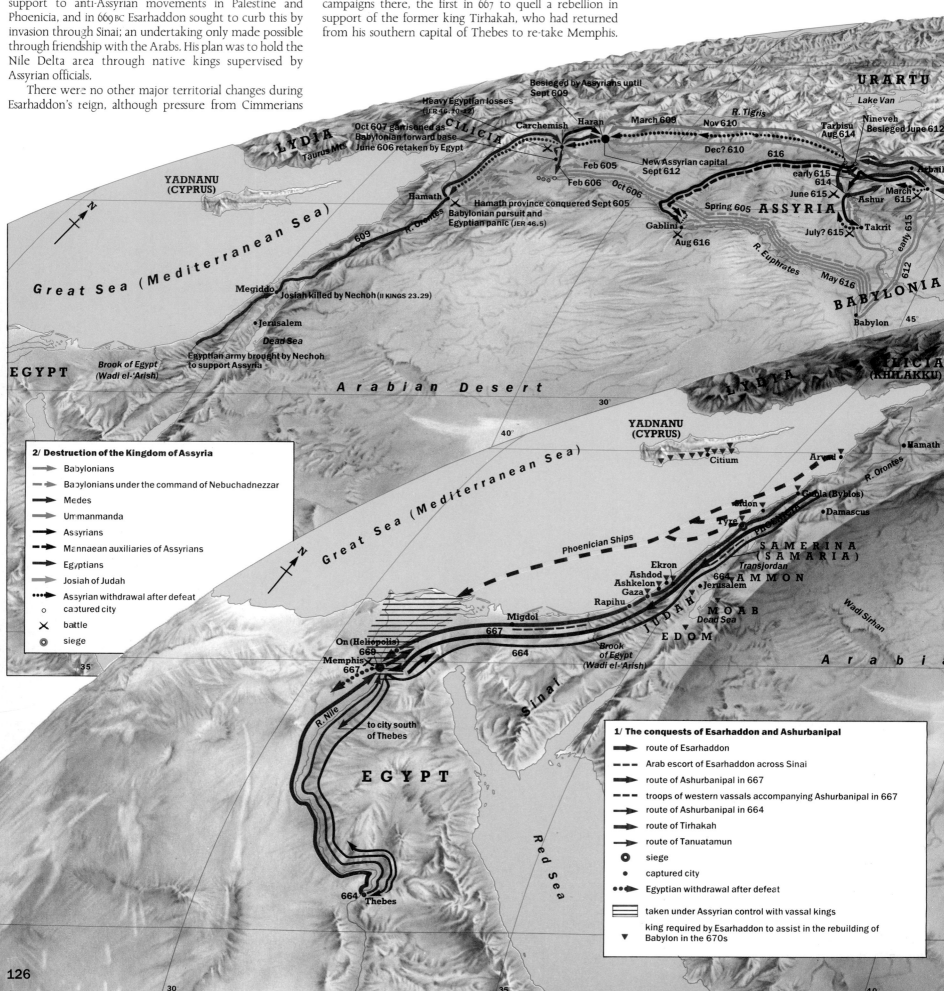

2/ Destruction of the Kingdom of Assyria
- Babylonians
- Babylonians under the command of Nebuchadnezzar
- Medes
- Ummanmanda
- Assyrians
- Mannaean auxiliaries of Assyrians
- Egyptians
- Josiah of Judah
- Assyrian withdrawal after defeat
- o captured city
- × battle
- ◎ siege

1/ The conquests of Esarhaddon and Ashurbanipal
- route of Esarhaddon
- Arab escort of Esarhaddon across Sinai
- route of Ashurbanipal in 667
- troops of western vassals accompanying Ashurbanipal in 667
- route of Ashurbanipal in 664
- route of Tirhakah
- route of Tanuatamun
- ◯ siege
- • captured city
- •••► Egyptian withdrawal after defeat
- taken under Assyrian control with vassal kings
- ▼ king required by Esarhaddon to assist in the rebuilding of Babylon in the 670s

Elam threatened Babylonia and required repeated Assyrian intervention from 667 onwards, producing tensions which led to civil war (652-648) between Ashurbanipal and his brother Shamash-shum-ukin of Babylonia, ending in the latter's defeat and death. Ashurbanipal then, in a series of campaigns, devastated Elam, deporting part of the population to Palestine (EZRA 4.9-10). Arab tribes, which had earlier attacked Assyrian vassals in Transjordan, and subsequently had aided Shamash-shum-ukin, again raided western territories whilst Assyria was involved with Elam, leading to punitive campaigns in the Syrian desert, c644 BC.

Sporadic revolts on the Phoenician coast, though contained, were indications of anti-Assyrian movements in the west, to which some scholars relate II CHRON 33.11.

The death of Ashurbanipal in 627 unleashed many tensions inherent within the empire. But the most significant development, which directly led to the fall of the empire, was the seizing of the kingship of Babylon by a Chaldaean chieftain, Nabopolassar, in 626.

DOWNFALL OF ASSYRIA
Four particular factors contributed to the downfall of the Assyrian empire: 1) a struggle for succession between two sons of Esarhaddon; 2) a Chaldaean chieftain, Nabopolassar, who challenged Assyrian overlordship by assuming the kingship of Babylonia in 626; 3) the Medes who under Cyaxares attacked Assyria, and 4) tribal hordes from the north, known as Ummanmanda, mainly Cimmerians (biblical Gomer, probably the threat from the north foreseen by Jeremiah in JER 6.1) who overran Assyrian territory.

After several years of fighting to break the Assyrian hold on Babylonia, Nabopolassar moved against Assyria itself by 616 BC. In 615 the Medes invaded, and in 614 took the old capital Ashur. A formal alliance between Nabopolassar and Cyaxares followed this success. In 612 Nineveh itself fell to a combined siege by Babylonians, Medes and Ummanmanda, surprisingly quickly, probably because its defences were weakened by flooding (NAHUM 1.8). The Assyrian army withdrew first to Haran, and then, after further attacks by Ummanmanda and Babylonians, to Carchemish. Here they called on Egypt for assistance. The Egyptians, who had had small forces in the area as early as 616, sent a large army northwards under Nechoh. Josiah of Judah, an ally of the Babylonians, attempted to intercept the Egyptians at Megiddo and was killed (II KINGS 23.29). The Egyptians joined the Assyrian remnant at Carchemish. In 605 BC the Crown Prince Nebuchadnezzer, placed in charge of the Babylonian army, attacked the Egyptian army at Carchemish, with massive slaughter (JER 46.2-12). The Egyptian army fled, and according to Babylonian sources the survivors were destroyed in the Hamath district.

THE RISE OF BABYLON
The pact between Nabopolassar and Cyaxares in 614 BC prepared the way for the orderly dismemberment of the Assyrian empire. The principal heir was Babylonia, with the Medes taking control of the most northerly areas in Asia Minor and the regions east of the Zagros. Parts of Syria and Palestine were still under Egyptian influence, and Nebuchadnezzar had to devote several campaigns between 604 and 586 to establishing his authority there. He also took action in Hume (Cilicia) and neighbouring areas in the north-west, a region in which Neriglissar (559-556), the successor after Nebuchadnezzar's briefly reigning son Evilmerodach (II KINGS 25.27), had to undertake a further campaign to consolidate the Babylonian hold.

Nabonidus (Nabunaid) (555-539 BC) introduced a new imperial strategy. Reacting to the firm Median control of the trade routes to east and north of Mesopotamia, he took over control of the trade routes in western Arabia, by seizing the principal oasis settlements, and changing his capital to Yatribu (Medina). Meanwhile the Persian Cyrus had defeated his Median overlord and become ruler of the Median territories, with a vigorous policy of expansion. The long absence of Nabonidus from Babylon, combined with economic problems and unpopular attempts at religious reform, produced internal opposition, as a result of which Babylon surrendered without resistance to Cyrus in 539 BC. The surrender of the whole of the Babylonian empire followed.

1/ Map below
Esarhaddon and Ashurbanipal staved off threats to Assyria from all sides. Esarhaddon rebuilt Babylon and Ashurbanipal in 648 conquered Elam. In the west they tried to curb the power of Egypt, and in 664 BC Ashurbanipal won a major victory and controlled Egypt as far south as Thebes.

2/ Map left
The Assyrian empire could not hold out against a concerted attack. Nabopolassar, king of Babylon, joined forces with the Medes and routed the Assyrians as far west as Carchemish. The Egyptians came to help the Assyrians but at Carchemish a decisive battle in 605 BC destroyed the combined forces.

3/ Below inset
The Babylonians, under Nabopolassar, increased their boundaries as far west as the Great Sea, and down into Egypt.

'FLEE FOR SAFETY, O PEOPLE OF BENJAMIN, FROM THE MIDST OF JERUSALEM! BLOW THE TRUMPET IN TEKOA, AND RAISE A SIGNAL ON BETH-HACCHEREM; FOR EVIL LOOMS OUT OF THE NORTH, AND GREAT DESTRUCTION.' JER 6.1

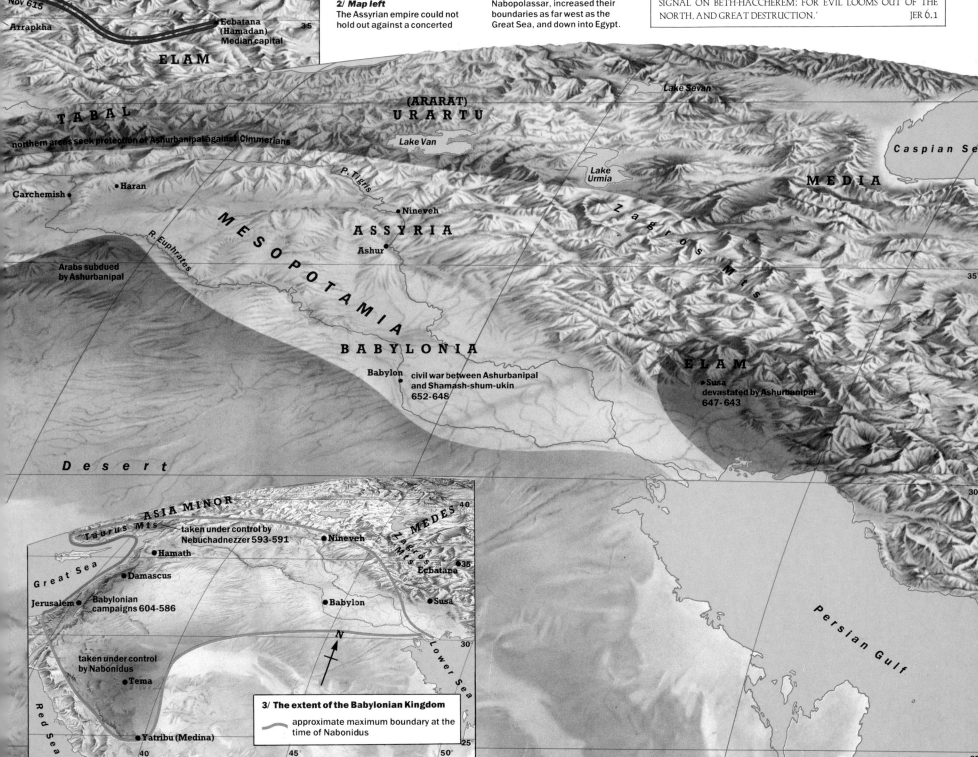

3/ The extent of the Babylonian Kingdom
approximate maximum boundary at the time of Nabonidus

WHEN Amon was assassinated in 641 BC 'the people of the land', the assembly of the common people rather than just the wealthy landowners, made his eight-year-old son Josiah king of Judah (II KINGS 22.1, II CHRON 33,25-34.). Assyria was at the time so weakened by internal problems that Judah was able to break away from her dominance to gain complete independence at the death of Ashurbanipal (c 627 BC). This move was first marked by the purification and repair of the Jerusalem Temple and the extension of Judah's control over former Israelite territory which had become the Assyrian provinces of Samaria (Samerina) and Megiddo (Magiddu).

THE KINGDOM OF JOSIAH

Josiah aimed to restore the area once held by the House of David and thus to reunite the former divided kingdom. From the places listed in his religious reforms it seems that he quickly regained the land of Ephraim to claim to rule from Beersheba to Geba (either modern Jebà or Et-Tell in Ephraim, south-west of Shiloh). He controlled Bethel on the former Israel-Samaria border (II KINGS 17.28) and in the south he took Simeon territory back from Philistia. Archaeological evidence shows that he fortified Arad and En-gedi,.where he stationed Greek mercenaries in readiness against possible Egyptian reprisals. In the north he held sway as far as Naphtali including the Valley of Jezreel and Galilee. Megiddo had been reinforced with storage facilities for a large garrison, probably Egyptian. Since Josiah took a wife from Rumah (Khirbet er-Rumah) he had access to, and even control of, the northern reaches.

This extension of political authority was accompanied by the most radical religious reforms in Judah's history. According to the Deuteronomist historian (II KINGS 22-23; cf II CHRON 34-35) reforms in Jerusalem and Judah were already in hand by Josiah's 18th year when 'The Book of the Law of Moses' was found in the Temple. On the basis of the action which followed, this is generally agreed to be a scroll of Deuteronomy or part of it.

Symbols of Assyrian cults which marked that foreign domination and national humiliation since the reigns of Manasseh and Ahaz were quickly removed. National worship concentrated in Jerusalem where the Temple was no longer the mere Royal chapel it had become. Priests from the abandoned rural shrines throughout Judah were brought in but not allowed to serve as Temple officiants. The laws of Deuteronomy (DEUT 13) which made idolatry a capital offence were enforced as former Israelite territory was regained. False priests were slain and their altars desecrated. In suppressing all pagan ritual and practices male and female prostitutes were removed. All articles made for the gods Baal and Asherah (the Canaanite mother goddess represented by a fertility pole and by statues elaborately bedecked in fine garments) were destroyed.

JUDAH UNDER BABYLON

THE REIGN OF JOSIAH

Josiah, king of Judah (641-609 BC) aimed to recover and extend the glory of David's kingdom by taking over the Assyrian-dominated provinces of Samaria and Megiddo. At the same time he began radical religious reforms by rooting out pagan practices. This attempt to become an independent kingdom eventually led to a clash with Egypt in which Josiah died.

Special attention was paid to blotting out the old Canaanite worship of Molech (Moloch) which had been reintroduced by Ahaz. These rites involved passing children through fire as a dedication to the god; some were even burned to death, though human sacrifice was condemned in Israel (LEV 18.21; 20.2-5) and was considered a particular sin of Samaria and Ammon. Later Carthaginian-Phoenician (Punic) inscriptions c.400-150 BC, in areas where the practice lingered on, seem to indicate that Molech was then a general term for sacrifice or votive offering. Josiah also stamped out solar and astral cults and divination, although pagan shrines at Arad and Lachish indicate some local resistance.

All these actions were accompanied by new administrative arrangements. The tithe was again paid to the Jerusalem sanctuary. Publicly the act of territorial reunification was marked by a great national assembly attended by the king, all officials, priests, prophets and people to hear the public reading of The Book of the Covenant and to respond to its requirements by rededication to the Lord. The enactment of the Passover, possibly for the first time since Joshua's day, was taken to be a political and social as well as religious act signifying the end of dependence on other nations and deities. It also marked the national resolve to resist external pressures and was a time of great optimism reinforced by ideas of dynastic revival.

THE PROPHET JEREMIAH

During the 13th year of Josiah's reign (628 BC) Jeremiah began his important prophetic activity at this time of religious reform. He gave counsel to monarchs up to and beyond the Babylonian capture of Jerusalem in 587 BC and we know more about the life of Jeremiah than of any other biblical prophet. His name means 'May the Lord exalt'. He came of a priestly family from Anathoth in the territory of Benjamin, and he prophesied during the reigns of Josiah, Jehoiakim and Zedekiah (JER 1). He had serious confrontations with the two latter, was imprisoned by Zedekiah,

and rescued from death only through the good offices of an Ethiopian commander (37-38). Despite his protestations he was taken to Egypt by the refugees from Jerusalem (42-43), and it is possible that he died in exile there.

Jeremiah viewed political events in a context that went beyond the narrow confines of the Judaean state. The rise and fall of empires were controlled by a divine hand and the impending invasion by the Babylonians, 'the foe from the north', which he consistently predicted (25 and 28), and which dominated the politics of the time was seen as a punishment for the moral and ritual corruption of the Jewish people. The unwelcome message he brought to his rulers was to accommodate the Babylonians, and that those in exile should 'build houses, and live in them, plant gardens and eat their produce......and seek the welfare of the city' where they had been carried away captive (29.5-7). This appeal was based on his conviction that God would restore the fortunes of his people and once their sins had been expiated the exiles would return and the monarchy be restored in Judah (30-33).

Symbolism recurs throughout Jeremiah's prophecy. He appears with bars round his neck to signify the imminent yoke of Babylonian conquest (27). He unearths a girdle that was buried, and which is now 'good for nothing', to symbolise the damage the people had done to the tight bonds that fastened them to their God. Symbolic imagery occurs in the form of the almond-tree and the boiling pot

4/ Above
From the reign of Josiah, this fragment of a letter in Hebrew was found at Meshad Hashavyahu. It confirms that an Israelite influence was present in the area.

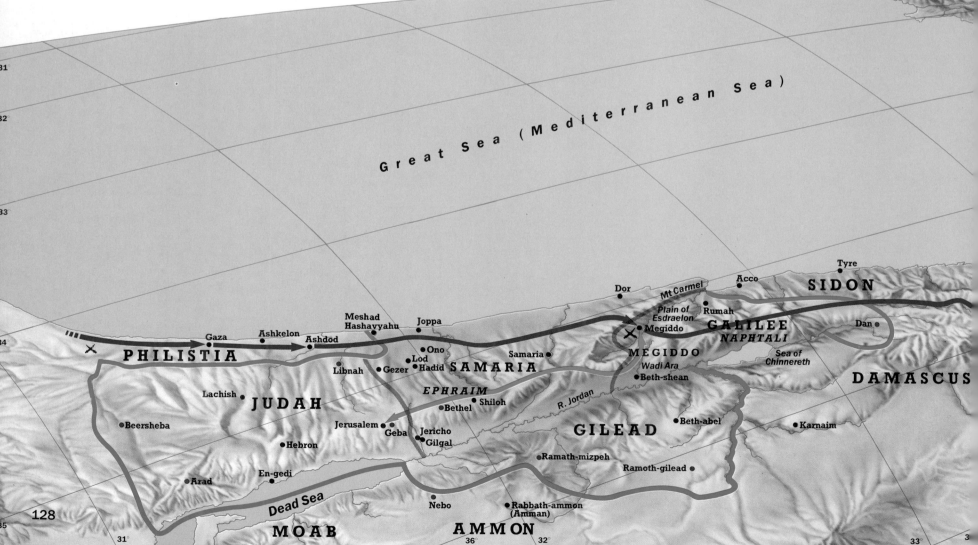

,1), and the book of prophecy that Jeremiah gave to Seraiah, commanding him to tie it to a stone and throw it into the R. Euphrates, for 'thus shall Babylon sink' (51.64).

The principal objects of Jeremiah's denunciations, apart from the political incompetence of Judah's rulers, were moral corruption and the adoption of idolatrous practices including the custom of passing the children through fire (7). The incident with the Rechabites (35) and the prophet's constant appeal to the experience of the Jewish people in the desert after the Exodus (7) may point to an ascetic tendency in his approach to religious practice.

A unique insight into the transmission of prophecy in the OT is provided by Jeremiah's relationship with Baruch, son of Neriah. He was a brother of Seraiah and a loyal friend of the prophet. A vivid account is given of how in the fourth year of Jehoiakim's reign (605 BC) Jeremiah dictated his prophecies to Baruch. Jeremiah commanded him to read them to the people in the Temple, because the prophet was not able to go himself (36.5). The court was informed and ordered Baruch to repeat the prophecies. The content was so inflammatory that the courtiers advised Baruch and Jeremiah to hide, while they took the scroll to Jehoiakim. It was read again, but the king seized it before the reader had finished, cut it in pieces and threw it into a brazier (36.23). Jeremiah on hearing the news dictated the prophecies again to Baruch, and added more besides. It is very likely that large portions of the Book of Jeremiah,

recounting details of the prophet's life in the third person, were added during the re-writing by Baruch.

CAMPAIGNS OF PHAROAH NECHOH

Josiah's new regime was soon to be put to the test. The Saitic kings of Egypt being stronger than the pharaohs who preceeded them, felt confident enough to challenge the rising Babylonian power at the R. Euphrates itself. Psammetichus I had sent the Egyptian army in 610 BC to help the Assyrians and their last ruler Ashur-uballit against the Babylonians and Medes who captured Haran. In the following year the new Egyptian ruler Nechoh II (Nikkû of the Babylonian Chronicle) tried to regain Haran but had once more to abandon the attempt on the approach of the Babylonians. To reach Haran on the R. Balikh the Egyptians must have marched up by stages through Palestine via their garrison posts at Megiddo, Riblah and Carchemish.

Little is known of the last decade of Josiah's reign until in 609 BC Nechoh sent word to Josiah, that he was not going to fight him but required passage to a garrison-post ('the house of my warfare', II CHRON 35.21) – presumably Megiddo or Carchemish. This warning, given as he passed through Philistia into which Josiah dared not enter, alerted Judah to the threat that the Egyptians were supporting Assyria's (its former overlord's) cause.

Josiah moved swiftly to the Wadi 'Ara opposite Megiddo, where the pass across M. Carmel enters the Plain of Esdraelon. He clashed with the Egyptians in open warfare in which they had superiority in chariots and archers. Josiah was badly wounded and died in Jerusalem to which he had been taken.

His 31-year reign was the last distinguished episode in Judaean history and was characterized as doing 'the right in the eyes of the Lord'. Nechoh himself was to fight one final battle against the Babylonians between Gaza and Pelusium in 601 BC. Both sides suffered heavy casualties and the Egyptians never again entered Palestine in force.

1/ Map below
Josiah won back part of Israel's former land from Assyria and this map shows the new extent of his kingdom. In 609 BC Pharaoh Nechoh marched through Palestine to support the Assyrians against Babylon and defeated Josiah at Megiddo. The abolished temples illustrate Josiah's drive against foreign gods.

2/ Above left
From the citadel at Amman 7th century BC, this carved head of a woman 1 ft high, resembles the Egyptian goddess Hathor.

3/ Left
An area of the Tanit precinct (or Tophet) at Salambo, Carthage. Urns held the charred remains of children that had been sacrificed to Molech. Worship of such gods was denounced by Jeremiah and Josiah tried to eliminate them. The rise of Babylon was forecast as divine punishment 'For the sons of Judah have done evil in my sight, says the Lord; And they have built the high place of Topheth... to burn their sons and daughters.' JER 7.30.

> AND THE KING COMMANDED HILKIAH, THE HIGH PRIEST, AND THE PRIESTS OF THE SECOND ORDER, AND THE KEEPERS OF THE THRESHOLD, TO BRING OUT OF THE TEMPLE OF THE LORD ALL THE VESSELS MADE FOR BAAL, FOR ASHERAH, AND FOR ALL THE HOST OF HEAVEN; HE BURNED THEM OUTSIDE JERUSALEM IN THE FIELDS OF THE KIDRON, AND CARRIED THEIR ASHES TO BETHEL, AND HE DEPOSED THE IDOLATROUS PRIESTS WHOM THE KINGS OF JUDAH HAD ORDAINED TO BURN INCENSE IN THE HIGH PLACES AT THE CITIES OF JUDAH AND ROUND ABOUT JERUSALEM; THOSE WHO BURNED INCENSE TO BAAL, TO THE SUN AND THE MOON, AND THE CONSTELLATIONS, AND ALL THE HOSTS OF THE HEAVENS. AND HE BROUGHT OUT THE ASHERAH FROM THE HOUSE OF THE LORD, OUTSIDE JERUSALEM, TO THE BROOK KIDRON, AND BURNED IT AT THE BROOK KIDRON, AND BEAT IT TO DUST AND CAST THE DUST OF IT UPON THE GRAVES OF THE COMMON PEOPLE ... AND HE DEFILED TOPHETH, WHICH IS IN THE VALLEY OF THE SONS OF HINNOM SO THAT NO ONE MIGHT BURN HIS SON OR HIS DAUGHTER AS AN OFFERING TO MOLECH.' II KINGS 23,4-10

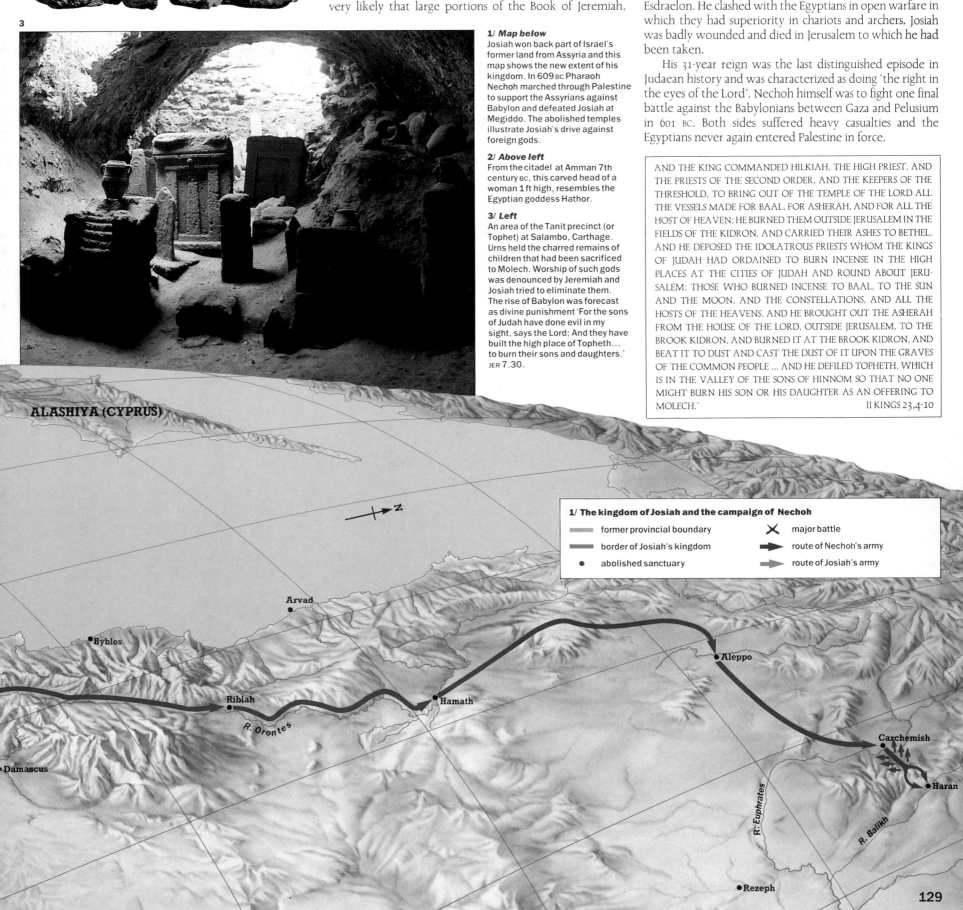

ALASHIYA (CYPRUS)

1/ The kingdom of Josiah and the campaign of Nechoh
- former provincial boundary
- border of Josiah's kingdom
- abolished sanctuary
- X major battle
- route of Nechoh's army
- route of Josiah's army

Arvad
Byblos
Aleppo
Riblah
R. Orontes
Hamath
Carchemish
Damascus
Haran
R. Euphrates
R. Balikh
Rezeph
Tadmor

AFTER Nabopolassar, king of Babylon and founder of the Chaldaean dynasty, had taken over former Assyrian territories in the Upper Euphrates with the help of the Medes and Cimmerians, his son Nebuchadnezzar, as crown prince, led his own army against the north-eastern hill tribes. The Egyptians then set a garrison at Carchemish which forced the Babylonians on the Euphrates at Quramati to retreat. Nebuchadnezzar soon led a force, which included Greek mercenaries, in a reprisal raid. Moving up the east bank of the Euphrates he crossed to the west below Carchemish, surprised the enemy and captured the city in August 605 BC. The Egyptians who fled were cut off and the whole force destroyed so that, according to the Babylonian Chronicle, a reliable source, 'not a single Egyptian escaped home'. The whole region of Hamath was taken over, including Riblah, a former Egyptian stronghold dominating the road south and the routes to the Mediterranean coast. From here the Babylonians claimed sway over Palestine as far south as the Egyptian border at Nahal Musur (Wadi el-'Arish).

Nebuchadnezzar was in the west when, according to Berosus, he 'learned quickly that his father Nabopolassar had died. He set the affairs of Egypt and other countries in order and committed the captives he had taken from the Jews, Phoenicians, Syrians and the peoples belonging to Egypt to one of his friends to conduct the heavily armoured sections of the army with his baggage to Babylon.' The date of Nabopolassar's death is recorded as 16 August, so his son must have ridden with horsemen c 580 miles as directly as possible to Babylon to claim the throne as Nabū-kudurri-usur (Nebuchadrezzar) II on 7 September. Soon thereafter he went back to Syria ('Hatti-land') where he was to campaign almost annually for at least the next ten years.

In 604 BC 'all the rulers of Hatti came before him and he received their heavy tribute'. Jehoiakim of Judah was among those submitting (II KINGS 24.1). Ashkelon refused to submit and was captured with its king and Nebuchadnezzar proceeded to reinforce Arad, Meshad Hashavyahu and other centres against expected Egyptian counter-attacks.

Next year Nebuchadnezzar had to take heavy siege equipment and strong forces across hilly terrain against an unknown city. A papyrus letter found at Saqqara written in hieratic bears an appeal from a ruler, Adon, to his overlord in Egypt for help and states that the Babylonians had reached Aphek. The final objective has not been identified and Gaza, Lachish, Ashdod, Ekron or even the more northerly Tyre or Sidon have been suggested. Nebuchadnezzar took the opportunity of these marches to collect timber from Lebanon for his building work at Babylon.

BATTLE WITH EGYPT
At the end of 601 the Babylonian Chronicle uniquely refers to a major battle with the Egyptians in which both sides suffered heavy losses including chariots and cavalry. It took a year for the Babylonians to re-equip and train a new army. The clash could have taken place in the Gaza plain for it effectively ended Egyptian control in Asia by land. Jehoiakim of Judah changed allegiance to Egypt and the Babylonians now sought an opportunity for revenge.

CAPTURE OF JERUSALEM
During 599-8 the Babylonians encouraged the Qedar Arabs, Moab and Ammon to invade Judah. Then 'on the second day of the month Addar in his seventh year [16 March 597] he captured the city of Judah [Jerusalem] which he had besieged. He seized its king and appointed there a king of his own choice. Taking heavy spoil he sent it to Babylon'. Thus the Babylonian Chronicle records the beginning of the Jewish exile. Documents from Babylon attest the presence of Jehoiachin (son of Jehoiakim) there during the next 30 years.

Disturbances in the next year took Nebuchadnezzar as far north as Carchemish and down the Tigris against a raiding force from Elam (JER 49.34-39). Further unspecified operations in Syria were probably aimed against coastal cities such as Byblos – visited by Pharaoh Psammetichus II about 591 – or Tyre, besieged by the Babylonians for 13 years between 596 and 563. His control extended as far as W. Cilicia (Khume and Piriddu), the base from which Nebuchadnezzar or his representative negotiated for the Medes against Lydia after the battle of the R. Halys,

NEBUCHADNEZZAR AND THE DESTRUCTION OF JERUSALEM

The capture of Jerusalem by the Babylonian king Nebuchadnezzar II in 597 BC, followed ten years later by the destruction of the Temple and the Exile in Babylon, formed a cataclysmic end to Jewish history as recorded in the Old Testament.

Tishri new year reckoning) and the city fell a month later.

The Babylonians ruled Judah through a local governor, Gedaliah, seated at Mizpah (T. en-Nasbeh) and responsible to a district governor at Samaria for territory which included Lachish. Vinedressers were left to tend royal estates in Benjaminite lands north of Jerusalem and send supplies to Babylon, as they had previously to the Judaean court. Sealings on vessels naming 'Eliakim, Jehoiachin's assistant' may indicate the continuing collection or payment of taxes. When Gedaliah was killed by assassins sent from Ammon and Judaeans fled to Egypt, a further Babylonian raid put an end to Ammon's independence and carried off yet more Jews to exile.

At the capture of Jerusalem the Babylonians took a

dated 28 May 585 BC by the solar eclipse recorded then.

THE DESTRUCTION OF JERUSALEM
When Zedekiah planned an anti-Babylonian coalition with Edom, Moab, Ammon, Tyre and Sidon, contrary to the advice of Jeremiah (JER 27.1-11), Nebuchadnezzar was provoked to lay siege to Jerusalem again. After two years, despite an abortive attempt by the Egyptian king, Apries, to intervene, the Babylonians closed in steadily. Hill forts and watch-posts in the surrounding hills were taken and walls breached. The Temple fell in August 587 BC (according to the Nisan calendar, or 586 by the

1/ Map below
Under Nebuchadnezzar the Babylonians dominated the ancient Near East. Using the traditional invasion routes they invaded Judah, destroyed Jerusalem and subjugated the Jews.

major group of army and skilled Judaeans (10,000) off into exile followed, at the fall of the city, by further bands totalling 3,023, 832 and 745 prisoners (JER 52.28-30).

THE REIGN OF NABONIDUS

After the death of Nebuchadnezzar in 562 BC there were three kings of Babylon in seven years, only one of whom died a natural death. Eventually Nabonidus (555-539 BC), the son of a priestess, assumed the throne. In the face of the increasing power of the new Medo-Persian confederation, he seems to have worked to keep the main western trade routes open. He first followed up the action of his predecessor Neriglissar, an official who had taken part in the sack of Jerusalem, and who had campaigned in Cilicia. From Hamath, Nabonidus operated against the forces from Lydia which threatened the trade route into western Anatolia. Afterwards he turned against the Ammananu and then the Arabs and Udummu (which was probably Edom). He claimed the control of Gaza, plus parts of Egypt and Syria. From these areas he called up workforces to engage in the restoration of his family-endowed shrine to the moon god Sin at Haran.

In 552 Nabonidus moved from Edom to adjacent NW Arabia to win military control of an area around the oasis of Tema, which measured about 266 by 106 miles. He stayed there, in virtual voluntary exile, for ten years because of opposition from the Babylonians. This unpopularity had two causes: he had become increasingly eccentric, possibly due to some health problem, and he was suspected of harbouring unorthodox religious views.

Nabonidus finally returned to Babylon (in 542 BC) where his son and co-regent Bel-sharra-usur (the biblical Belshazzar) had been left in charge.

By now the Babylonians had come under considerable pressure from the Medes and Persians, and elaborate defences against any attack on the capital had to be prepared. The flood defences and the 'Median Wall' across the narrow land bridge between the Euphrates and Tigris south of Sippar and Opis became the scene of a pitched battle in which the Babylonians were defeated. According to the Babylonian Chronicle and to Herodotus, the Persian army under the Guti governor Ugbaru took Babylon by surprise. However, he also enjoyed some local collaboration. The sudden fall of the city may have been in part due to a diversion of the river which subverted the defences. Belshazzar was killed and Nabonidus was captured. Cyrus himself entered Babylon on 30 October 539 BC, and brought Babylonian domination of the Near East to an end.

'BY THE WATERS OF BABYLON, THERE WE SAT DOWN AND WEPT, WHEN WE REMEMBERED ZION ... HOW SHALL WE SING THE LORD'S SONG IN A FOREIGN LAND?' PS 137.1,4

2 and 2a/ Below and left
The plan of Babylon (below) is based upon archaeological evidence. The illustration (left) is an attempt to show what part of the city may actually have looked like. The picture represents the portion of the city shaded in grey on the plan.

1. Summer palace
2. Akitu (New Year) house
3. Hanging gardens
4. North citadel (and museum)
5. Reservoir
6. Sin gate
7. Ishtar gate
8. South citadel (royal palace)
9. Vaulted building
10. Emah temple
11. Ishtar temple
12. Nabu-sha-hare temple
13. Greek theatre
14. Marduk gate
15. Zubaba gate
16. Enlil gate
17. Urash gate
18. Ninurta temple
19. Gula temple
20. Esagila (Marduk temple)
21. Etemananki ziggurat
22. Processional way
23. Bridge
24. Lugalgirra gate
25. Necropolis
26. Adad gate
27. Shamash gate
28. Shamash temple
29. Adad temple

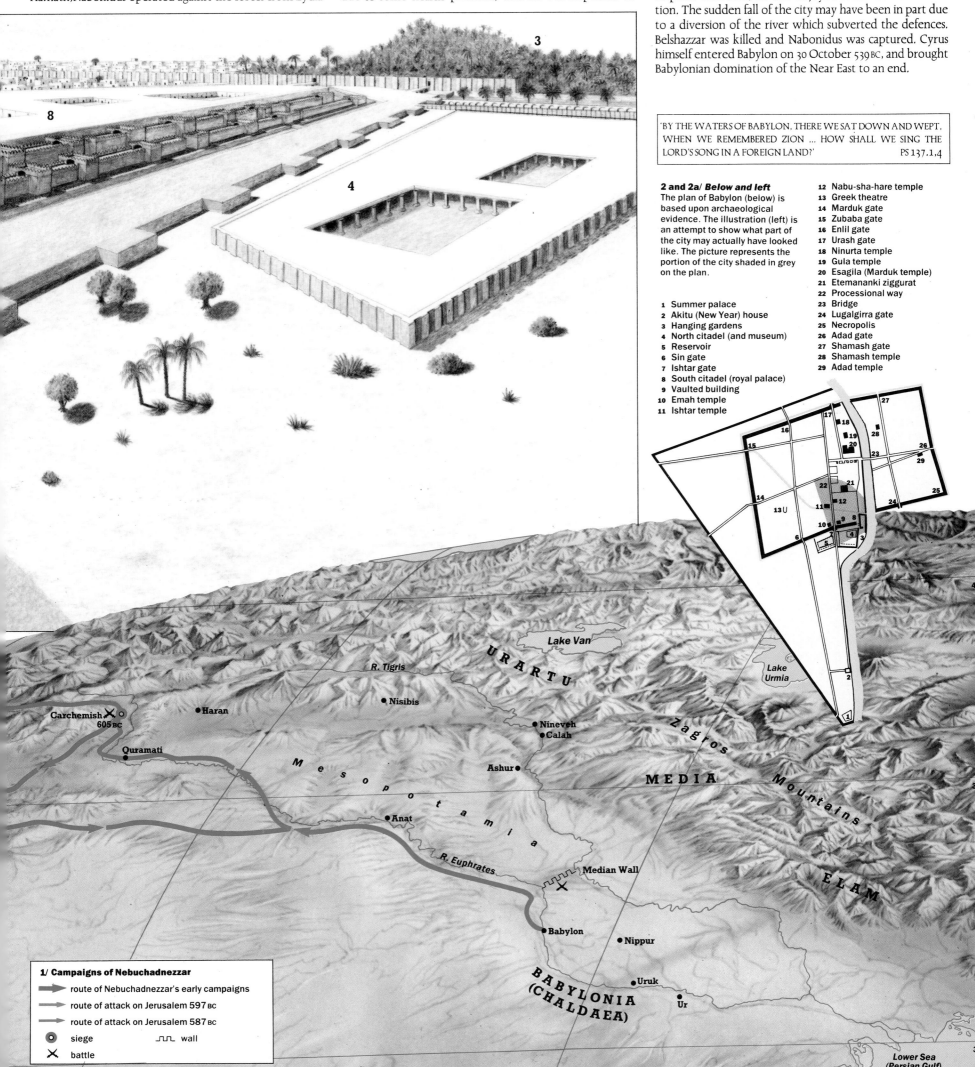

1/ Campaigns of Nebuchadnezzar
→ route of Nebuchadnezzar's early campaigns
→ route of attack on Jerusalem 597 BC
→ route of attack on Jerusalem 587 BC
⊙ siege ⌐⌐ wall
✕ battle

IT IS extremely difficult to give precise dates for much of the material in the Bible, especially the earlier portions. However, we may assume, on linguistic grounds and by comparing it with other Near Eastern literature, that the poetic portions of the Pentateuch and Judges may reflect the oldest strata, to be dated perhaps before 900 BC. Deuteronomy may be identified with the book discovered in the Temple in the reign of Josiah in 621 BC (see II KINGS 22-23).

In the event, it is certain that the Pentateuch (or the Five Books of Moses) had reached its present form, and had already been regarded as Holy Writ, by the time of Ezra (about 400 BC). The prophetical books can be dated more accurately because they often place themselves within an identifiable historical context. Thus Amos and Hosea belong to the 8th century BC, while Joel and probably Jonah belong to the 4th. Jeremiah consistently issues warnings about the imminent Babylonian attack on Jerusalem (end of the 7th century), and Ezekiel reflects circumstances during the Babylonian exile (early 6th century).

The third section of the OT, known as the Hagiographa, was the last to be officially canonized. Rabbis were still discussing the details in the academy at Yavneh (Jamnia) in about AD 100. Attempts to place some of these books in earlier antiquity and thus give them added authority led to the Psalms being ascribed to David, and Proverbs, Ecclesiastes and the Song of Songs to Solomon. There is also a rabbinic view that Job was written by Moses. However there too we are confronted with material from different periods. Some parts of Psalms and Proverbs, for example, may go back to the 8th century, others may be as late as the 2nd century BC. Daniel seems to reflect the Maccabaean struggle of 168-165 BC. The OT contains only a selection of ancient Hebrew literature. There are references in the Bible itself to works which are now lost, e.g the Book of Jashar (II SAM 1.18) and the Book of the Wars of the Lord (NUM 21.14), as well as sources referred to in the historical books.

Conversely, there are books which have survived but which were not included in the Jewish canon. These were later incorporated in the Apocrypha (literally 'hidden items') eg, The Book of Maccabees, and Ben Sira (or Ecclesiasticus). The language of the OT is Hebrew, but parts of Daniel and Ezra are in Aramaic.

THE DEVELOPMENT OF THE BIBLE

The Bible is a library, composed of 63 books, 36 in the OT, and 27 in the NT. In addition, there are 15 books in the Apocrypha which were not accepted into the Hebrew Bible. These books contain a whole literature: poetry, history, law, census records, prophecies, rituals, letters, and more. The Greek name Bible, meaning 'books', reflects this diversity.

The oldest manuscripts of the Bible now extant are those found in the cave at Qumran by the Dead Sea. Scholars are not agreed on their dating, but they predate AD 100. Not all the biblical books are represented there by any means, but those which are, especially Isaiah and Psalms, tend to corroborate the traditional accuracy of textual transmission. Some of the Dead Sea manuscripts still preserve the ancient form of the Hebrew alphabet, in the writing of the tetragrammaton (Yhwh, the four-lettered name of God) – a type of script which has come down to us in a modified form in Samaritan.

For the benefit of Jews who lived in Alexandria in the 3rd century BC, and whose Hebrew knowledge was scanty, the Pentateuch was translated into Greek, in a version known as the Septuagint (from the Greek *Septuaginta* – a reference to the 70 translators who worked on it) and which later embraced the other books of the OT. It is this version, which is frequently quoted in the NT, whose language is entirely Greek.

We have far fewer problems dating the various parts of the New Testament than we have with the Old. We can say with some certainty that practically the whole NT had reached its present form by the year AD 120.

Both the Old and New Testaments were originally written down in separate books, usually in scroll form. It was only with the invention of the codex, that is to say, a manuscript in the form of a modern book, with writing on both sides of the page, that it became possible for larger collections of books to be assembled. The codex form was quickly adopted by the Christians and it was they who were the first to gather the complete Bible (Old and New Testaments in Greek) within the covers of the same book. This exercise was given added impetus by the adoption of Christianity as the official religion of the Roman Empire in the early 4th century. The great vellum manuscripts, the Codex Sinaiticus and the Codex Vaticanus, date from this period, while the equally magnificent Codex Alexandrinus was written in the following century. Earlier manuscripts of the NT, however, survive written on papyrus. A tiny fragment of John in the Manchester University John Ry-

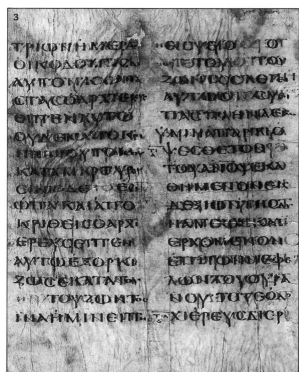

Pentateuch (Hebrew: Torah)
- Genesis
- Exodus
- Leviticus
- Numbers
- Deuteronomy

Early Prophets (Hebrew: Nebiim Rishonim)
- Joshua
- Judges
- I & II Samuel
- I & II Kings

Later Prophets (Hebrew: Nebiim Aharonim)
- Isaiah
- Jeremiah
- Ezekiel
- Hosea
- Joel
- Amos
- Obadiah
- Jonah
- Micah
- Nahum
- Habakkuk
- Zephaniah
- Haggai
- Zechariah
- Malachi

Hagiographa (Hebrew: Ketubim)
- Psalms
- Proverbs
- Job
- Song of Songs
- Ruth
- Lamentations
- Ecclesiastes
- Esther
- Daniel
- Ezra
- Nehemiah
- I & II Chronicles

OLD TESTAMENT

Gospels
- Matthew
- Mark
- Luke
- John

Apostolic Writings
- Acts
- Romans
- I Corinthians
- II Corinthians
- Galatians
- Ephesians
- Philippians
- Colossians
- I Thessalonians
- II Thessalonians
- I Timothy
- II Timothy
- Titus
- Philemon
- Hebrews
- James
- I Peter
- II Peter
- I John
- II John
- III John
- Jude
- Revelation

NEW TESTAMENT

THE BIBLE

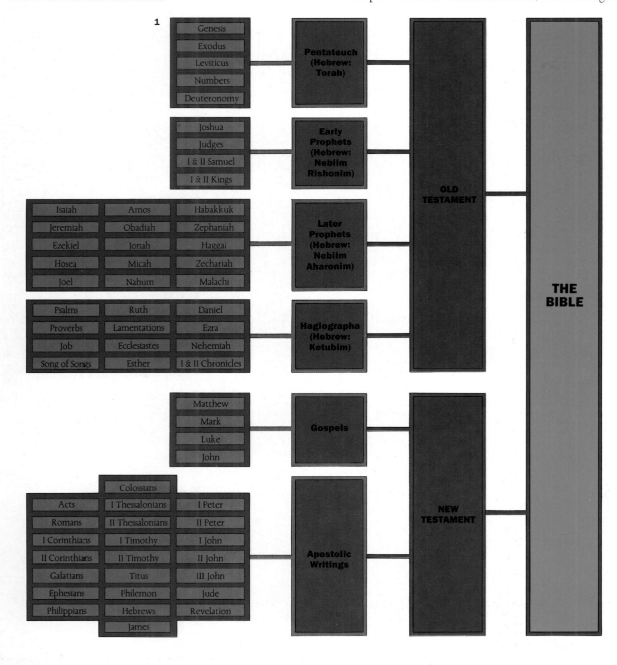

lands Library is attributed to the early 2nd century, and is probably the earliest extant, while important 3rd century papyrus codices form part of the Chester Beatty collection in Dublin.

ORDER OF BOOKS IN THE OT

The number of books in the OT, as well as the order in which they appear, differs in modern editions. The Hebrew Bible and the Jewish translations made directly from it are arranged according to the chronological sequence in which each of its three sections was accepted as canonical: the Pentateuch or Torah, the Prophets or Nebiim, and the Hagiographa or Ketubim. The books of the Torah are Genesis, Exodus, Leviticus, Numbers, and Deuteronomy

and appear in the order familiar to modern English readers. The Nebiim, however, consist of eight volumes divided into two groups of four each, the 'Former Prophets' (Joshua, Judges, Samuel, and Kings) and the 'Latter Prophets' (Isaiah, Jeremiah, Ezekiel, and the Twelve [Minor Prophets]).

The third division, the latest books to be considered authoritative by Jews, consist of 11 miscellaneous works arranged principally by literary types: poetical books (Psalms, Proverbs, Job), the Five Scrolls, or Megillot (Canticles, Ruth, Lamentations, Ecclesiastes, Esther), prophecy (Daniel), and history (Ezra-Nehemiah, and Chronicles). Thus, 24 books came to be regarded by Jews at about the end of the 1st century AD as canonical and have continued to be so regarded. When these books were translated into Greek for Greek-speaking Jews the traditional Hebrew order was modified. The new arrangement seemed to provide a better chronological order (Chronicles was placed along with Samuel and Kings, for example). In time apocryphal books were inserted at what were thought to be appropriate places. Thus it was that the traditional order of the Jewish scriptures was changed. By the middle of the 4th century AD, when the Codex Vaticanus or Codex B was written, the Septuagint consisted of the following books (books of the Apocrypha are in italics): Genesis; Exodus; Leviticus; Numbers; Deuteronomy; Joshua; Judges; Ruth; I-II Kings (=I-II Samuel); III-IV Kings (=I-II Kings); I-II Chronicles; I *Esdras*; II Esdras (= Ezra-Nehemiah); Psalms; Proverbs; Ecclesiastes; Canticles (Song of Songs); Job; *Wisdom of Solomon*; *Ecclesiasticus of Ben Sira*; Esther; *Judith*; *Tobit*; Book of the Twelve (Minor Prophets); Isaiah; Jeremiah; *Baruch*; Lamentations; *Epistle of Jeremy*; Ezekiel; Daniel; *The Song of the Three Children*; *The History of Susanna*; *Bel and the Dragon*.

These canonical books of the Jewish canon rearranged and augmented by the books of the Apocrypha were generally considered to be the Old Testament by early Christians. This tradition of contents and order has been preserved in the Vulgate, the Latin translation of the Roman Catholic Church. Protestant editions of the English Bible began to omit the books of the Apocrypha early in the 17th century and since 1827 most English Bibles have

been printed without the books of the Apocrypha. The order of the canonical books, however, has remained essentially the same as that found in the Septuagint.

The divisions of the books of the Old Testament into chapters and verses for the use in liturgies or for marking a unit for oral translation into another language were made at various times. The standard division into verses seems to have been made by Aaron ben Moses ben Asher in the 10th century. The number of verses in the Pentateuch according to Ben Asher's system is 5,845.

A search for the original text of the books of the Bible has long been a major preoccupation of scholars. Ancient manuscripts in the original languages have been compared and checked with translations made from copies now lost. Of the four polyglot editions of the Bible published between 1514 and 1659 (Complutensian, Antwerp, Paris, and London) the monumental work of Brian Walton, published in London, 1657-1659, is the most extensive. In six folio volumes he gave for the Old Testament a complete Hebrew text with a Latin interlinear translation, the Samaritan Pentateuch, Greek, Latin, Syriac, Arabic, Ethiopic, and Persian versions; for the New Testament one can find in this compendium of textual evidence Greek, Latin, Syriac, Ethiopic, and Persian versions. In addition to these traditional sources for the text there are the most ancient examples of biblical texts found in the caves along the shores of the Dead Sea (see page 161).

'THEN THE KING SENT, AND ALL THE ELDERS OF JUDAH AND JERUSALEM WERE GATHERED TO HIM. AND THE KING WENT UP TO THE HOUSE OF THE LORD, AND WITH HIM ALL THE MEN OF JUDAH AND ALL THE INHABITANTS OF JERUSALEM AND THE PRIESTS AND THE PROPHETS, ALL THE PEOPLE, BOTH SMALL AND GREAT; AND HE READ IN THEIR HEARING ALL THE WORDS OF THE BOOK OF THE COVENANT WHICH HAD BEEN FOUND IN THE HOUSE OF THE LORD. AND THE KING STOOD BY THE PILLAR AND MADE A COVENANT BEFORE THE LORD TO WALK AFTER THE LORD AND TO KEEP HIS COMMANDMENTS AND HIS TESTIMONIES AND HIS STATUTES, WITH ALL HIS HEART AND ALL HIS SOUL, TO PERFORM THE WORDS OF THIS COVENANT THAT WERE WRITTEN IN THIS BOOK....'
II KINGS 23.1-3

1/ Far left
The Bible is a collection of books. The OT is shown here in the traditional Jewish order, which differs from that adopted by the Christian Church (see text).

2/ Above left
A portion of the Book of Leviticus from a Hebrew manuscript of the 10th century AD which was found in Syria.

3/ Left
A page from a codex of the gospels probably written in the 6th century. Letters of gold and silver were written on vellum dyed purple.
The taste for such luxury in editions of the gospels was censured by Chrysostom and Jerome. The passage shown on this page of the Purple Gospels is from Matthew.

4/ Below left
A page from the Codex Sinaiticus, a 4th century Greek codex discovered by Konstantin von Tischendorf at the monastery of St Catherine at Mount Sinai in 1855. It remained in St Petersburg until 1933, when the British Museum purchased it. The page is from the gospel of Luke. The codex, which

contains both Old and New Testaments, consists of 346 sheets of vellum, each page 15 by 13½in. Tischendorf made three visits to St Catherine. His tact and patience in rescuing this valuable piece of textual evidence is an entertaining interlude in accounts of textual criticism.

5/ Above
A page from the Prologue to the first printed Bible of the Vulgate edition, appearing in 1456 and attributed to J. Gutenberg. It is part of a letter from St Jerome to Paulus.

6/ Below
A modern scribe writing a Hebrew manuscript.

7/ Below left
Three Hebrew scrolls with their covers removed, and partly unrolled.

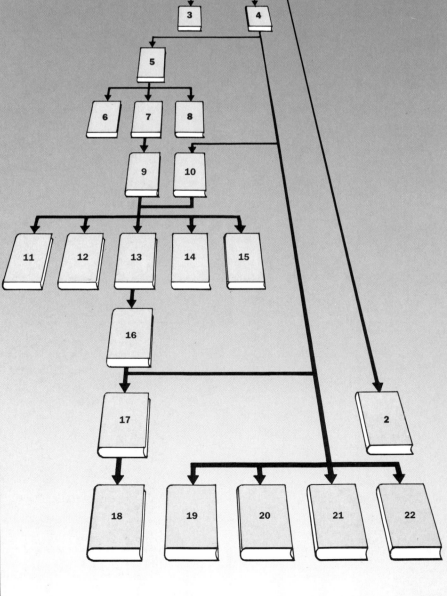

8/ Right   Editions of the Bible
1 The Hebrew canon
2 1916 translation by Jewish Publication Society of America
3 Septuagint
4 New Testament
5 Vulgate translation c 400 by Jerome into Latin
6 Bede's gospel
7 Wycliffe bible, 1384
8 Lindisfarne gospels
9 NT printed in English, 1526 by W. Tyndale
10 Erasmus' translation of NT
11 Coverdale's printed bible, 1535
12 Geneva Bible, 1560
13 Great Bible, 1539
14 Bishop's Bible, 1568
15 Donai Rheims
16 Authorized version, 1611
17 English Revised version, 1881-5
18 Revised Standard version, 1952
19 Jerusalem Bible, 1966
20 New English Bible 1970
21 Good News Bible, 1976
22 New International version, 1979

WHEN in 546 BC the Persian king Cyrus the Great captured the Lydian capital, Sardis, from Croesus and the Persian troops looted the city, Croesus asked Cyrus, 'What are those men doing?' 'Plundering your city', replied Cyrus. 'Not my city, but yours', said Croesus. This event brought Persian rule to the Mediterranean seaboard, and it was not popular. In 498 BC Sardis was burnt again when the Ionians rebelled. The Athenians, anxious to keep the Persians out of the Aegean, supported the rebellion. This led to Persian invasions of Greece, and to the defeat of Darius' army at Marathon (490 BC) and Xerxes' fleet at Salamis (480 BC), and for the next two centuries Greeks and Persians eyed each other warily across the Aegean. In 449 BC the Peace of Kallias barred the Athenians from Cyprus and Egypt, and the Persians from Athenian cities of the Aegean and Ionian coast. Not surprisingly, Persia helped Athens' enemy Sparta in the Peloponnesian War (431-401 BC). In 401 BC some 13,000 Greek mercenaries marched from Sardis to help Cyrus depose his brother, Artaxerxes II of Persia; they were defeated at Cunaxa and escaped north through Armenia to the Black Sea at Trapezus led by Xenophon, who described their long march in his book *Anabasis*. The rebellion, however, demonstrated amply the potential of Greek mercenaries, and the Persians themselves were soon using an Athenian admiral to help evict a Spartan army from Lydia (394 BC) and an Athenian general in an attack on Egypt (374 BC).

The Greek cities of Asia Minor were always unwilling Persian subjects, and the Persian satraps of these regions were frequently tempted to seek independence. In the 350s, the satraps of Asia Minor, Phoenicia and Egypt, relying on mercenary troops, all rebelled, but failed for lack of unity. Philip II of Macedon now prepared to take advan-

THE PERSIAN PERIOD

PERSIA INVADES THE MEDITERRANEAN — THE JEWS BEGIN TO LOOK WEST

In the biblical tradition, the Persian period was remembered for three major events: the restoration of the Temple (520-516 BC), the rebuilding of the walls of Jerusalem by Nehemiah (444 BC) and the promulgation of the Law by the priest Ezra. These were seen as key factors in the restoration of the Jewish community after the disaster of the Exile. In particular, there was a new awareness of the need to preserve the Jewish people and its way of life against external influences.

tage of the weakened empire, and when his son Alexander crossed the Hellespont in 333 BC with 40,000 infantry and 7,000 cavalry, the Persian opposition was composed mainly of Greek mercenaries.

PERSIA'S INTEREST IN EGYPT
The Persians coveted the wealth of Egypt and the ships, trade and timber of the Phoenicians. The satrapy of Abar Nahara, 'Across the River', in which Judah lay, included the province of Phoenicia, and was the gateway of Egypt. When Cambyses invaded Egypt (525 BC), the Phoenicians supplied a supporting fleet, and the Arabs water for the desert route south of Gaza. Cambyses' successor Darius I actively colonized Egypt, opening a canal between the Nile and the Red Sea, encouraging building works at El-Khargeh, the Wadi Hammamat, El-Kab, Busiris, Memphis, Sais and

Edfu, codifying Egyptian law and improving the training of Egyptian priests. However, on his death in 486 BC Egypt rebelled from Persian exploitation, but Xerxes swiftly restored order, removing to Susa the statue of Darius which had been set up at Heliopolis. A full-scale revolt took place in the 460s and 450s, but it collapsed when a supporting Athenian fleet was trapped and destroyed. For the next 40 years Egypt was ruled by the satrap Arsames (some of his correspondence survives), and her southern border was garrisoned by Jewish soldiers on the island of Elephantine (Yeb, near Aswan), who claimed to have been settled there since before Cambyses' time. Their archives, the Elephantine papyri, show that their garrison and temple suffered at local hands during renewed rebellion c 410-400 BC. Egypt remained independent until Artaxerxes recaptured it in 343 BC. But this Persian effort was too late. The Greeks had long coveted Egypt, and in 331 BC under Alexander they acquired her.

THE ISLAND OF ELEPHANTINE
Elephantine was the Greek translation of an ancient Egyptian name meaning 'Elephant place'. It was called *Yeb* in the Aramaic papyri whose appearance in the antiquities market in Aswan at the beginning of this century led to excavations on the island and the discovery of more papyri. These papyri of the 5th century BC evidence the existence of a Jewish community serving as a garrison for the Persian rulers of Egypt. These Jews were already settled in Elephantine by the time of Cambyses conquest of Egypt in 525 BC (their date of arrival is not known; they may have been refugees from the fall of Jerusalem in 587 BC or even from persecution in the 7th century BC).

ANANIAH'S HOUSE
The plan above right illustrates how the Jewish Temple of Yhwh, the God of Heaven, in the fortress of Elephantine, was surrounded by streets and Jewish houses. Their layout, and the history of their ownership in the 5th century BC, can be reconstructed from two sets of family archives from Elephantine: firstly the archive of a Jewish temple official Ananiah, his wife Tamut, his daughter Jehoishma and son-in-law Anani; and secondly, the archive of Mahseiah's daughter Mibtahiah, who married three times and acquired a considerable amount of property.

Ananiah purchased his house in 437 BC. In 434 BC he made over the end nearest the temple, 7 cubits wide by 11 cubits long, to his wife Tamut, perhaps after the birth of their two children – Pilti and Jehoishma. When Jehoishma married in 420 BC, her father drew up a legal document giving her half the stairway and the right of using it. In two later documents, dated 404 and 402 BC, Ananiah confirmed and improved upon this gift, and in a third document 16 months later ceded to Jehoishma the whole staircase and courtyard area at the north-eastern end of the property. By this document Jehoishma's expectations of inheriting this part of the property after her father's death became a reality before it. Nine months later this was followed by the sale of the rest of the property to Jehoishma's husband, Ananiah's son-in-law, for 13 shekels. The property was thus made over to the next generation, apparently on the understanding that the parents would continue to live there and be cared for.

> 'THUS SAYS CYRUS KING OF PERSIA: "THE LORD THE GOD OF HEAVEN, HAS GIVEN ME ALL THE KINGDOMS OF THE EARTH, AND HE HAS CHARGED ME TO BUILD HIM A HOUSE AT JERUSALEM, WHICH IS IN JUDAH."'
> EZRA 1.2

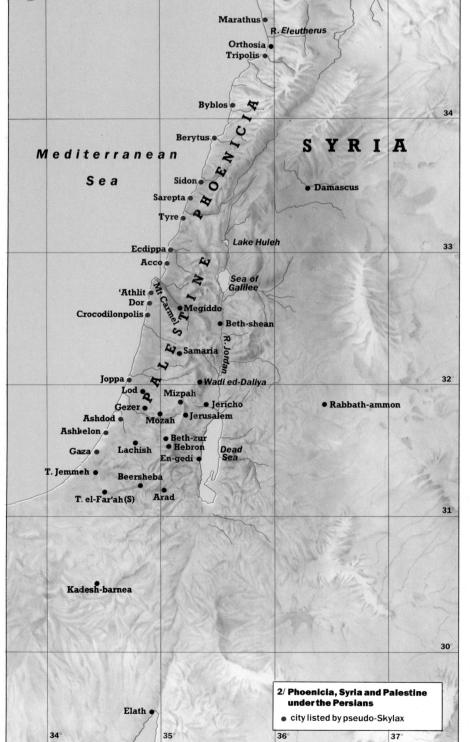

2/ Map left
Evidence for the history of the Persian empire comes mainly from the Bible and from Greek writers, since no Persian historical writings are known apart from Darius I's inscriptions. Important Greek sources include: Herodotus of Halicarnassus (c 490-420 BC); travelled widely, wrote an *Historia* ('enquiry') of the Persian Wars in nine books. Xenophon of Athens (428/7-354 BC); aristocrat, soldier and writer; served on Cyrus' expedition and led the retreat, described in his *Anabasis*. Other important works include his *Hellenica*, a history of Greece, and his *Cyropaedia* and *Memorabilia*.
Skylax of Caryanda (6th-5th century BC); explored Indus and Arabian coast for Darius I; quotations survive in later authors. Wrongly attributed to him is a late 4th century BC description of the Mediterranean Sea giving useful details of the Palestinian coast (for details of towns listed in this description see map left).
Diodorus Siculus of Agyrium (mid-1st century BC); wrote a world history in 40 books, useful for quotations of earlier sources.
Plutarch of Chaeronea (c AD 50-120); lecturer, teacher, writer, best known for his *Lives* of famous Greeks and Romans. Arrian of Bithynia (2nd century AD); wrote a history of Alexander the Great, the *Anabasis*, based on the memoirs of Alexander's general Ptolemy (Ptolemy I of Egypt).

2/ Phoenicia, Syria and Palestine under the Persians
● city listed by pseudo-Skylax

Aradus
Marathus
R. Eleutherus
Orthosia
Tripolis
Byblos
PHOENICIA
SYRIA
Berytus
Mediterranean Sea
Sidon
Damascus
Sarepta
Tyre
Lake Huleh
Ecdippa
Acco
Sea of Galilee
'Athlit
Dor
Mt Carmel
Megiddo
Crocodilonpolis
Beth-shean
R. Jordan
Samaria
PALESTINE
Joppa
Wadi ed-Daliya
Lod
Mizpah
Gezer
Jericho
Rabbath-ammon
Ashdod
Mozah
Jerusalem
Ashkelon
Beth-zur
Gaza
Lachish
Hebron
En-gedi
Dead Sea
T. Jemmeh
Beersheba
T. el-Far'ah(S)
Arad
Kadesh-barnea
Elath

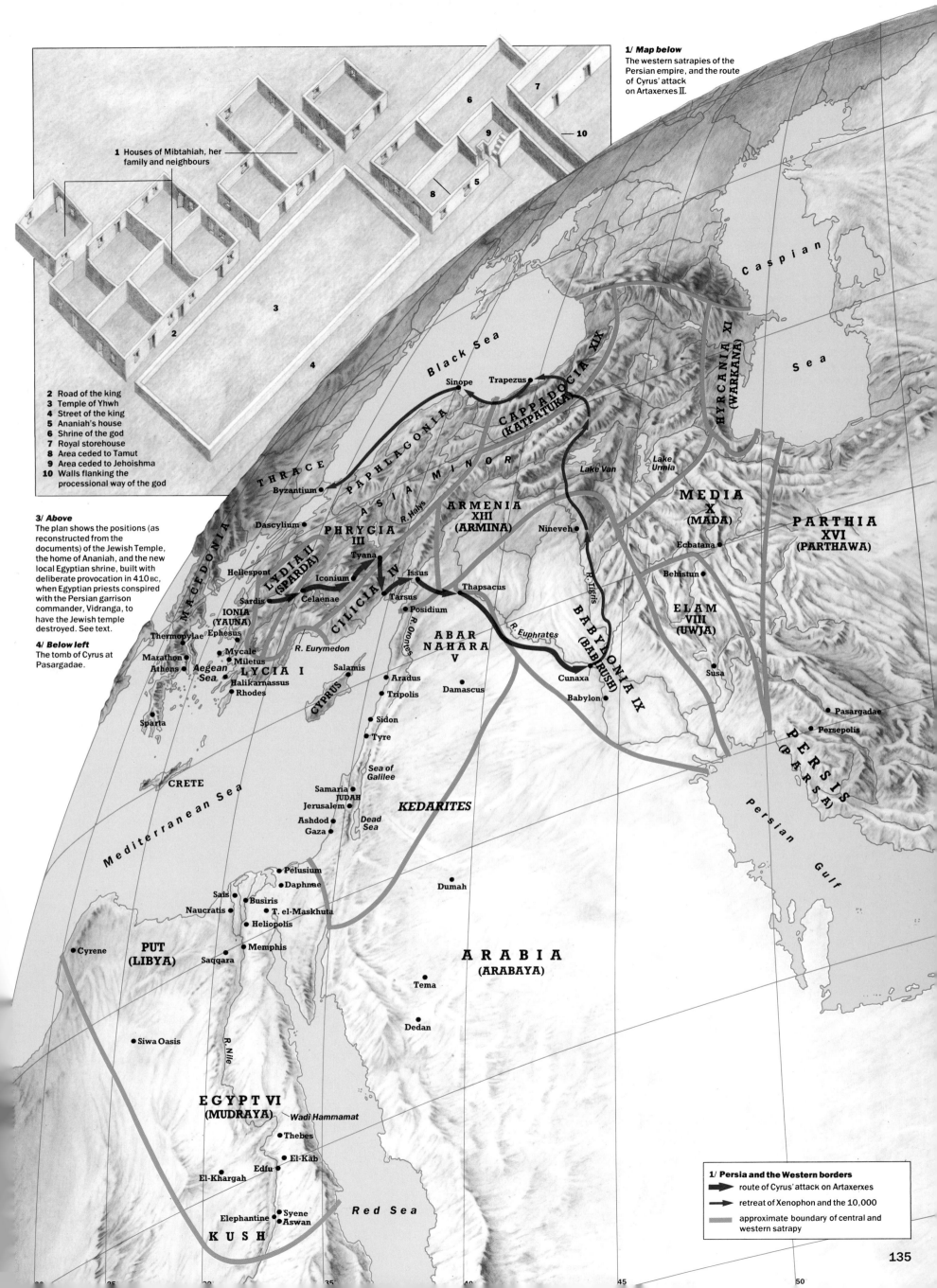

1 Houses of Mibtahiah, her family and neighbours

2 Road of the king
3 Temple of Yhwh
4 Street of the king
5 Ananiah's house
6 Shrine of the god
7 Royal storehouse
8 Area ceded to Tamut
9 Area ceded to Jehoishma
10 Walls flanking the processional way of the god

3/ Above
The plan shows the positions (as reconstructed from the documents) of the Jewish Temple, the home of Ananiah, and the new local Egyptian shrine, built with deliberate provocation in 410 BC, when Egyptian priests conspired with the Persian garrison commander, Vidranga, to have the Jewish temple destroyed. See text.

4/ Below left
The tomb of Cyrus at Pasargadae.

1/ Map below
The western satrapies of the Persian empire, and the route of Cyrus' attack on Artaxerxes II.

THRACE

Byzantium

Dascylium

MACEDONIA

Hellespont

Sardis
IONIA
(YAUNA)
Ephesus
Thermopylae
Mycale
Marathon
Miletus
Athens
Aegean
Sea
Halikarnassus
LYCIA I
Rhodes
Sparta

CRETE

Mediterranean Sea

PAPHLAGONIA
Sinope

ASIA MINOR

PHRYGIA
III
Tyana
Iconium
Celaenae
CILICIA IV
R. Eurymedon

Black Sea

Trapezus

CAPPADOCIA XIX
(KATPATUKA)

R. Halys

ARMENIA
XIII
(ARMINA)

Lake Van

Issus
Tarsus
Posidium
Thapsacus
R. Orontes
ABAR
NAHARA
V
Aradus
Tripolis
Damascus
Salamis
CYPRUS
Sidon
Tyre

Sea of
Galilee
Samaria
JUDAH
Jerusalem
Ashdod
Gaza
Dead
Sea

KEDARITES

R. Euphrates
Cunaxa
Babylon

BABYLONIA
(BABIRUSH)
IX

Nineveh

R. Tigris

Caspian

Sea

HYRCANIA XI
(WARKANA)

Lake
Urmia

MEDIA
X
(MADA)

Ecbatana

Behistun

ELAM
VIII
(UWJA)

Susa

PARTHIA
XVI
(PARTHAWA)

Pasargadae
Persepolis

PERSIS
(PARSA)

Persian Gulf

Pelusium
Daphnae
Sais
Busiris
Naucratis
T. el-Maskhuta
Heliopolis
Memphis
Saqqara

Dumah

ARABIA
(ARABAYA)

Tema

Dedan

PUT
(LIBYA)
Cyrene

Siwa Oasis

R. Nile

EGYPT VI
(MUDRAYA)
Wadi Hammamat

Thebes

El-Kab
Edfu
El-Khargah

Elephantine
Syene
Aswan

Red Sea

KUSH

1/ Persia and the Western borders

→ route of Cyrus' attack on Artaxerxes

→ retreat of Xenophon and the 10,000

— approximate boundary of central and western satrapy

135

PALESTINE in the Persian period (559-332 BC) was included within the satrapy called 'Beyond the River' (EZRA 4.10, 8.36; NEH 2.7,9). In Hebrew the expression was 'eber nahara and in Aramaic 'abar nahara, a term derived from Assyrian administrative usage (ebir-nari), known from the time of Esarhaddon. (See Map 1 on page 135.)

The internal administrative division of the satrapy is not described in written sources though Herodotus mentions four regions on the coast which were occupied by three different nations. In the north was situated Phoenicia whose southern boundary is not mentioned. From Phoenicia 'to the boundaries of the city of Caditis (Gaza), the country belonged to the Syrian. From Caditis to Ienysus (el-'Arish?), the sea ports on the coast belong to the king of Arabia and the land from Ienysus to the Sirbonis lake is Syrian territory' (Herodotus III, 5).

The picture derived from the Greek sources, except for the coastal area, is not accurate, and in order to study the administrative division of the country during the Persian period we must turn to the contemporary biblical sources and from what is known of the Assyrian administrative division. It is the general consensus that the Persians did not alter the internal administrative division of Palestine which was created at the time of Assyrian and Babylonian rule. From the time of Tiglath-pileser III (733 BC) onwards, this Assyrian division in the north of the country was composed of the provinces of Megiddo, Dor and Samaria, and in Transjordan, Hauran, Karnaim (the Bashan) and Gilead. In the Babylonian period, when the southern part of Palestine was also subjugated and the remnants of the independent states were eradicated, new provinces were annexed: Judah, Ashdod and Idumaea (the southern Judaean hills) in the west and Ammon and Moab in Transjordan. Farther south the Kedarite Arabs ruled Gaza, the Negeb and apparently also Edom. Since conclusive contemporary evidence is lacking the establishment of these provinces by the Babylonians is a matter of conjecture, though the existence of the northern provinces in Transjordan in the Babylonian period may perhaps also be indicated by the reference to Hauran and Gilead in EZEK 47.18. Some of the above-mentioned provinces may have been created only at the beginning of the Persian period. In the time of Ezra and

IN THE DAYS OF THE PERSIAN EMPIRE

Persia has retained a special place in Jewish history as the nation which eventually allowed the Jews to return from exile to the land of Israel. The story of the near destruction of the Jews by the evil counsellor, Haman, and their salvation by Esther and Mordecai have entered the Bible as a popular and colourful epic. In spite of the dominance of Persia it is questionable to what extent Persian influence affected the culture of Palestine.

Nehemiah mention is made of the provinces of Samaria in the north, Ashdod in the west and Ammon in the east; the southern region was occupied by Geshem the Arab. The existence of a province of Moab may possibly be indicated by the biblical reference to the 'children of the Pahat-Moab' (EZRA 2.6; NEH 7.11). No reference to Edom is found

1/ Below
The great palace of Persepolis overlooks an extensive fertile plain in the Persian homeland of south-western Iran, and was a principal residence of the Achaemenid kings. Work began in the late 6th century BC with the construction of a terrace some 1,640ft x 984ft in area and 39ft high. The buildings erected on this terrace over the following 50 or 60 years included high-columned audience halls and reception rooms, storerooms for tribute and other valuables, and quarters for a military garrison. Of these structures, only the stone columns and doorways survive. Much of the stonework is decorated with fine low-relief sculptures depicting the Great King enthroned, Persian courtiers and soldiers, and, on the stairways leading to the apadana, a procession of delegations from different parts of the empire bearing gifts or tribute.

and it is possible that in this period it was annexed to Arabian territory. Further contemporary evidence of the existence of the provinces of Samaria and Judah can be found in the Elephantine papyri (see page 134) and in the documents from Wadi ed-Daly'eh.

The subdivision of the medinah ('province') is described in chapter three of Nehemiah which mentions the rulers of the pelekh ('district', 'part', NEH 3.14, 15). The pelekh is further subdivided into half districts (NEH 3.9). According to this roster, Judah was organized into at least five districts.

The archaeological excavations have been also of great value in throwing light on the history of Palestine in this obscure period. A review of the results of the excavations at the various sites allows us to state with a great degree of certainty that already at the start of the period the country was divided into two regions: the mountain region of Judah and Transjordan (and also Samaria to a lesser extent) and the Galilee and coastal plain. At times the border bisecting these cultural areas was as sharp as a partition between two separate countries. Without an understanding of this subdivision of Palestine, it is impossible to grasp the internal development of the culture of the period.

A study of these two areas indicates that the culture of

1/ The royal palace at Persepolis

1 Principal stairway to terrace, gently graded to allow ascent on horseback.
2 Gate tower leading via processional way to Hall of 100 Columns (10) and to courtyard in front of principal audience hall (4).
3 Eastern stairway to apadana, sides decorated with tribute reliefs.
4 Apadana principal audience hall of Darius I with open colonnades on 3 sides and a timber ceiling supported by 36 slender columns nearly 65½ft tall.
5 Tripylon small central palace or vestibule.
6 Tachara or 'winter palace' of Darius I, notable for the use of Egyptian architectural features.
7 Hadish or palace of Xerxes, with reception hall and fine carvings.
8 Palace of Artaxerxes I.
9 Unfinished gate-tower leading to courtyard facing Hall of 100 Columns.
10 Hall of 100 Columns or 'throne hall'; larger in floor area but only half the height of the apadana.
11 Hall of 32 Columns small reception hall.
12 Royal stables and chariot-house.
13 Offices and storerooms of the Royal Treasury.
14 Additional treasury warehouses and storerooms.
15 Garrison quarters.
16 Remains of mud-brick fortification wall with projecting towers.
17 Remains of mud-brick fortification wall separating palace buildings from probable citadel area on higher ground to east.

1/ Royal palace – phases of construction
— 515-480 BC
— 479-450 BC
— 449-330 BC

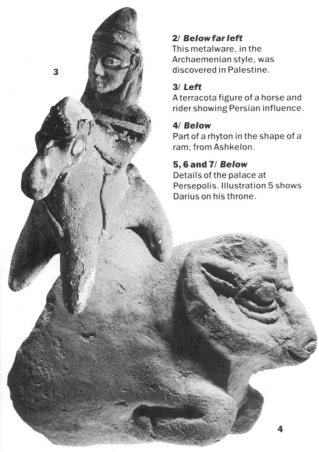

2/ Below far left
This metalware, in the Archaemenian style, was discovered in Palestine.

3/ Left
A terracota figure of a horse and rider showing Persian influence.

4/ Below
Part of a rhyton in the shape of a ram; from Ashkelon.

5, 6 and 7/ Below
Details of the palace at Persepolis. Illustration 5 shows Darius on his throne.

the mountains was basically eastern, being composed of a local culture which continued the Israelite tradition, and of eastern cultural influences such as Assyrian, Babylonian and Egyptian. The culture of the coast, in contrast, contained the essentially western East-Greek, Cypriot and Attic elements. It is thus evident that the material culture of Greece appeared in Palestine much earlier than the Macedonian conquest. At the same time there is no doubt that this was a purely external 'conquest', ie, the products of the Greek culture were adapted to local traditions and customs and no longer possessed the same significance as in their country of origin. The chief carriers of this new Palestinian culture were apparently the Phoenicians, and only to a lesser extent Greek soldiers and colonists.

It thus seems that we are confronted with the astonishing fact that the material culture of Palestine exhibits no influences of the ruling Persians and only some slight influence can be seen in the several pottery types, a few pieces of jewellery and metalware, which were also apparently produced by the Phoenicians.

> "'BEHOLD, I HAVE GIVEN ESTHER THE HOUSE OF HAMAN, AND THEY HAVE HANGED HIM ON THE GALLOWS, BECAUSE HE WOULD LAY HANDS ON THE JEWS.'"
> ESTHER 8.7

THE BOOK OF ESTHER
The Book of Esther is unlike any other book of the Bible in character. It is almost like a tale from the Arabian Nights. The scene is set in Susa; the capital of Persia. King Ahasuerus (probably to be identified with Artaxerxes I who reigned 486-465 BC) has dismissed Vashti his queen, and invites the most beautiful maidens from throughout the land, from whom to choose a new consort. His choice falls on Esther, who unbeknown to him is Jewish. The king's vizier Haman gains the royal assent to destroy the Jews in Persia. The date is fixed by drawing lots (purim). Esther, on the advice of her cousin Mordecai, adopts the dangerous procedure of trying to change the king's mind. She eventually succeeds. The edict is rescinded and Haman is hanged. Mordecai commands the Jews to celebrate their deliverance on the very day (the 14th of the Hebrew month Adar) that they were due to be annihilated. This celebration called Purim is still practised today. The Book of Esther is read from a special scroll and Haman's name provokes loud jeering and rattle-shaking.

THE Greeks were always fascinated by Persia and its wealth, though they affected to despise it. Many Greeks before Alexander went east, eg Skylax, who explored the Indus and the Arabian coast for Darius. In the 4th century BC, many Greeks became Persian mercenaries, and throughout the Persian territory of coastal Asia Minor cities were built or rebuilt in the Hellenistic grid-pattern invented by Hippodamus of Miletus. Hellenization was introduced to Caria by the independent-minded Persian satrap Mausolus; his tomb, the Mausoleum, was one of the seven wonders of the ancient world.

However, Alexander's campaigns (334-323 BC) dramatically quickened the pace of Hellenization. Alexander himself laboured to unite Greeks and non-Greeks, encouraging intermarriage, founding Hellenistic cities, and settling Greek colonists. After his death, his generals continued his policy in their new kingdoms. Cassander held Greece and Macedonia, Lysimachus Thrace, Antigonus and his son Demetrius Poliorcetes ('the Besieger') Asia Minor, Seleucus Babylon and Syria, and Ptolemy Egypt. Further east arose the Indo-Greek kingdom of Bactria; its kings had Greek names, but they soon broke away from western loyalties, and shortly before 100 BC this kingdom developed overland links with China.

The east, however, was hardly flooded with Macedonian settlers (only 15,000 Macedonians campaigned with Alexander, and many returned, homesick for Greece). The Seleucid kings in particular founded new colonies to secure their communications with the east; sometimes merely renaming old towns with Greek names or granting Greek city status to such places for a fee. The Ptolemies similarly renamed cities (eg, Acco became Ptolemais, and Rabbath-ammon became Philadelphia). Both dynasties had large empires to control, and a strong, bureaucratic administration, conducted in Greek and conversant with the local Egyptian or Aramaic, served their need. The spread of Greek language and culture went hand-in-hand with the purposes of government.

HELLENISM IN JUDAH

Inevitably, Greek influence was felt in Judah also. In the late 7th century BC Greek mercenaries served the Egyptians on the Philistine coast; in the 5th century traders from Tyre (doubtless able to speak Greek) appeared at Nehemiah's Jerusalem. By the 4th century, Judah used coins bearing the Attic owl, and Attic red-figure ware was known at Ptolemais and Sebaste. Large quantities of Persian and Hellenistic period storage jars have been dredged up from the sea round Dora and Caesarea, Azotus and Ascalon, indicating regular trade through these ports; a Greek helmet of the same period was found off Azotus. There is evidence of imports from Boeotia in Greece, Cyprus, and Alexandria; jars from 3rd-2nd century BC Rhodes have been found at many sites.

Judah's interest in sea trade is evidenced by a graffito in Jason's Tomb (2nd century BC) in Jerusalem, showing a Greek monoreme chasing a cargo ship. One recalls that Simon the Maccabee decorated his family tomb at Modin, in sight of the sea, with ships (I MACC 13.29). The Maccabees were well aware of the Hellenistic Mediterranean world; Judas Maccabeus himself sent an embassy to Rome (I MACC 8.17), and Jonathan entertained diplomatic relationships with Sparta (I MACC 12.2), to which a few years earlier the ejected high priest Jason had tried to flee for exile (II MACC 5.9). Hellenistic life-style is illustrated by the town of Marisa, populated by colonists from the Phoenician town of Sidon, whose tombs contain Greek inscriptions and wall paintings of animals captioned with Greek names (eg, *rhinoceros*, *elephant*). Hellenistic administration is evidenced by a Greek inscription from Scythopolis (Beth-shean) dating from 195 BC, recording orders issued by Antiochus III and his son to Ptolemaios, the military governor of Coele-Syria and Phoenicia.

Greek writers naturally shared in the Hellenistic discovery of the east. Megasthenes of Ionia wrote on India (*c* 300 BC), and his contemporary Hecataeus of Abdera on Egypt; both included material about the Jews. Two of Aristotle's students, Theophrastus and Clearchus of Soli, also mentioned them. The general tendency was to present them as a race of philosophers. The Jews themselves began to write in Greek. This perhaps happened first in Alexandria, but in Jerusalem itself Eupolemus (mid-2nd century BC; *cf* I MACC 8.17) wrote a Jewish history in Greek, and in the 1st century FC the books ESTHER and I MACCABEES were translated into Greek, and the Hasmonaean king Alexander Jannaeus struck coins bearing both Greek and Hebrew inscriptions, while the Nabataean king Aretas III called himself 'Philhellene' on his coins.

THE GREEKS TURN EAST, JUDAH IN THE HELLENISTIC WORLD

Apart from the brief historical surveys in I MACC 1 and DAN 11, the Bible says very little about this period, as by now the Jewish scriptures were almost complete. They existed in three groups – 'the Law and the prophets and the other books of our fathers' (ECCLESIASTICUS, Prologue). However, the Hellenistic age is important because it saw the translation of the Jewish scriptures into Greek at Alexandria, probably at first for the local Jewish community and later to the benefit of Jews and then Christians throughout the Mediterranean. New writings appeared, some written in Hebrew and translated into Greek (eg, ECCLESIASTICUS, I MACC), and some written in Greek. This was no 'dark age' for the Jews, but a period in which they responded vigorously to the new Hellenistic environment.

'SO HE ADVANCED TO THE ENDS OF THE EARTH, PLUNDERING NATION AFTER NATION... HE ASSEMBLED VERY POWERFUL FORCES AND SUBDUED PROVINCES, NATIONS AND PRINCES, AND THEY BECAME HIS TRIBUTARIES.'
I MACC 1.3-5

1/ Map right
Alexander's campaigns (334-323 BC) took Hellenization to the limits of the known world and beyond, as cities were founded from Alexandria in Egypt to 'Furthest Alexandria' (*Alexandria Eschate*) in Sogdiana. Alexander crossed the Hellespont in 334 BC with about 35,000 men, against the Persians. Having defeated them at the River Granicus in 334, he advanced through Asia Minor into Syria and Egypt, and then moved eastwards into Armenia where he had a second decisive victory against the Persians at Gaugamela in 331. He then advanced through Media and Persia and north to the Caspian Gates and the Hindu Kush. Alexander wanted to find the mythical river, which was thought to encircle the world. However, in India he had to turn back as his troops refused to advance any further into the unknown. Part of the force returned by sea under the leadership of Nearchus, while the rest returned by land through Gedrosia to Babylon, where Alexander died in 323 BC.

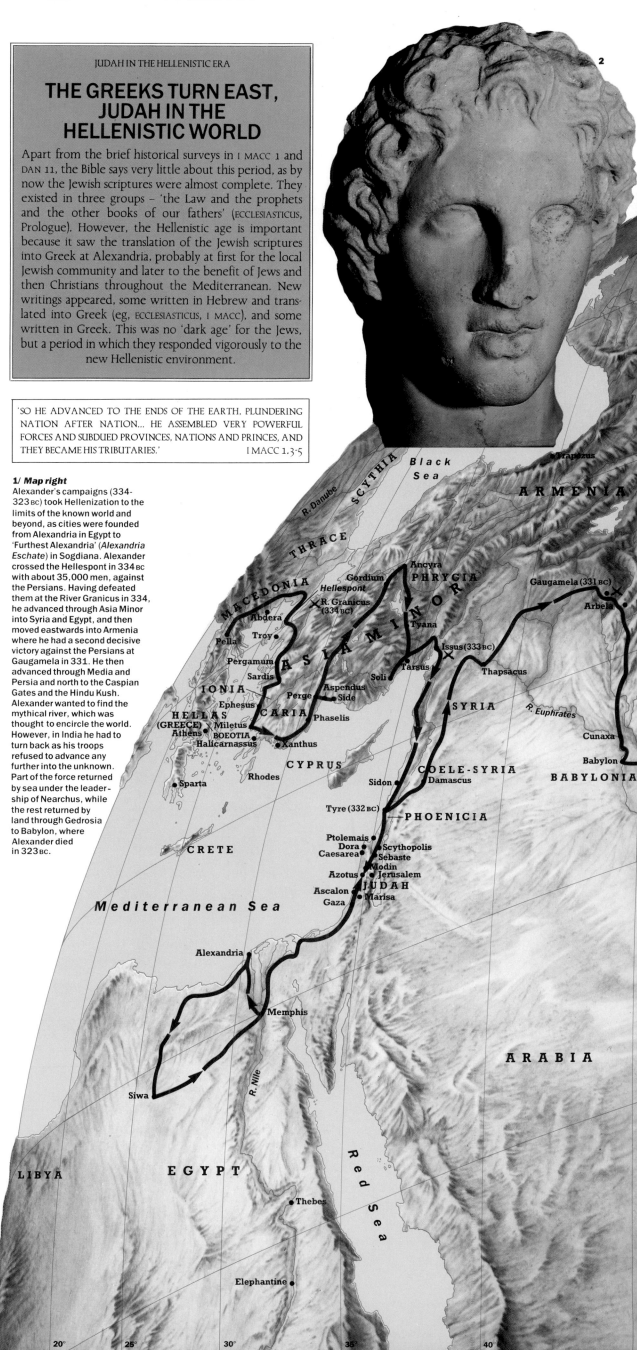

2/ Left
A later depiction of Alexander the Great. In the 2nd century A.D., Flavius Arrianus wrote his *History of Alexander* based on the writings of Alexander's contemporaries; Ptolemy, Aristobulus and Nearchus — Alexander's admiral and boyhood friend.

From this we know that he had grey eyes, a fair complexion and a heavy mane of hair. Unusually for the period, he was clean-shaven.

Aral Sea

R. Jaxartes

R. Oxus

Alexandria Eschate (329 BC)

Maracanda

S O G D I A N A

Ai Khanum

Caspian Sea

Alexandria Margiana

Alexandria Oxiana (328 BC)

Bactra

B A C T R I A

GANDHARA

P A R T H I A

Ortospana (Kabul)

R. Indus

Taxila

HYRCANIA

Alexandria Areion

Alexandria among the Paropamisadae

Bucephala (328 B

M E D I A

Rhagae

Caspian Gates

A R A C H O S I A

R. Hydaspes

Ecbatana

Alexandria Arachosion (330 BC)

Alexandria Prophthasia

D R A N G I A N A

R. Hyphasis

Susa

SUSIANA

R. Tigris

P E R S I A

G E D R O S I A

I N D I A

Charax

Pasargadae

Persepolis (331 BC)

Alexandria in Carmania

P E R S I S

Alexandria Rhambacia

Persian Gulf

Pattala

I n d i a n   O c e a n

1/ Alexander's Campaigns
➤ route of Alexander
➤ route of Nearchus
✕ major battles

50°   55°   60°   65°   70°

HELLENISTIC culture brought with it not only new ideas and customs, but also new buildings to house those institutions which the Greeks regarded as indispensable to civilized life.

THE AGORA
The agora was the centre of public life. From the Hellenistic period the square or rectangular agora was planned, for it had now to be a symbol of civic pride as well as catering to the growing complexity of life and government. The stoa, offering shelter from sun and rain, became an essential component. The long colonnades served for public and private discourse, while the inner part housed shops, banks, and offices. Temples and monuments were often integrated, and a basilica would have appeared where Roman influence was strong. This rectangular roofed hall often functioned as a commercial exchange centre. Essential to the government of the city was the *bouleuterion* which housed the city council.

STADIUM
The unique status of 'sacred' games, of which the supreme examples were the four great panhellenic festivals at Olympia, the Isthmus of Corinth, Delphi, and Nemea, was jealously conserved until the 2nd century AD. By contrast 'cash' contests (*thematitai*) could be organized by any city

JUDAH IN THE HELLENISTIC ERA

INSTITUTIONS OF THE HELLENISTIC CITY

Greek culture, with its great intellectual sophistication and its emphasis on athletic prowess, was a great danger to the Jewish way of life. The Greek emphasis on philosophical speculation attracted many Jews, but was an anathema to the orthodox. Similarly Jewish young men who were attracted to the athletic ideals of the Greeks outraged the modesty of the Jewish community by competing in athletic events naked, in accordance with Greek custom. This Hellenistic culture, epitomized by such institutions as gymnasia, theatres, baths and temples, was spread throughout the Near East and was to have the most profound influence on the course of human history.

with the financial resources to provide prize money to attract worthy contestants. Preserved start and finish lines indicate that the stadium could vary from 195 yards in length (Delphi) to 210 yards (Olympia). The participants ran

in marked tracks. There is evidence of different types of starting-gates, but by the 1st century AD a simple trumpet blast appears to have sufficed. Prior to the introduction of stone seating in the imperial period wooden benches were brought out for each festival. If an appropriate hollow was not available a terrace was cut in a hillside.

GYMNASIUM
Greek education involved training both body and mind. It was centred in the gymnasium which became the focus of communal life and the hallmark of Hellenism. Any barbarian grouping which aspired to the status of a Greek city had to found a gymnasium (II MACC 4.9). The ideal form is described by Vitruvius in *De Architectura*.

'Square or oblong cloisters are to be made with a walk round them of two stadia (this walk the Greeks call *diaulos*). Three of the sides are to be single colonnades; the fourth which has a south aspect is to be double, so that when rain is accompanied by gales the drops may not reach the inside. On the other three sides, spacious *exhedrae* are to be planned with seats where philosophers, teachers of rhetoric and other studious persons can sit and discuss. In the double colonnade, however, these provisions are to be made. In the centre there is to be the *ephebeum* (a large apsidal recess with seats for young men aged between 18 and 20) a third

1/ Bottom left
A general view of Olympia looking across the gymnasium to the palaestra.

2/ Bottom, second from left
The palaestra at Olympia seen from the north east, showing one of the baths in the changing rooms.

3/ Bottom, second from right
The stadium at Delphi, built in the 5th century BC.

4/ Bottom, far right
The theatre at Miletus, Turkey, which dates from the Hellenistic period.

5/ Far right
The temple of Apollo at Corinth, dating from the 6th century BC. Inset are three diagrams showing various temple layouts from the simple to the complex. Also a coin from the reign of Maximus (AD 235-238) can be seen. Depicted on it is the temple of Diana at Ephesus.

6/ Background illustration
The agora of Athens (150 BC).
1 Ilissos River
2 Stadium
3 Acropolis
4 Klepsydra springhouse
5 Eleusinion
6 Houses
7 Pantheon (?)
8 Tower of the winds
9 Agoranomion (?)
10 Roman market
11 Library of Hadrian
12 Roman basilica
13 Monopteros
14 Stoa of Attalos
15 Library of Pantainos
16 Southeast stoa

17 Southeast temple
18 Nymphaion
19 Southeast fountain house
20 Middle stoa
21 East building
22 South stoa II
23 Heliaia (?)
24 Southwest fountain house
25 Civic offices
26 Southwest temple
27 Eponymous heroes
28 Altar of Zeus Agoraios (?)
29 Odeion
30 Panathenaic way

31 Temple of Ares
32 Altar of the 12 gods
33 Poikile stoa
34 Altar
35 Roman stoas
36 Royal stoa
37 Stoa of Zeus Eleutherios

38 Temple of Zeus Phratrios and Athena Phratria
39 Temple of Apollo Patroos
40 Metroon
41 Bouleuterion
42 Propylon to bouleuterion
43 Tholos

44 Strategeion (?)
45 Hephaisteion
46 Arsenal (?)
47 Cross-road sanctuary

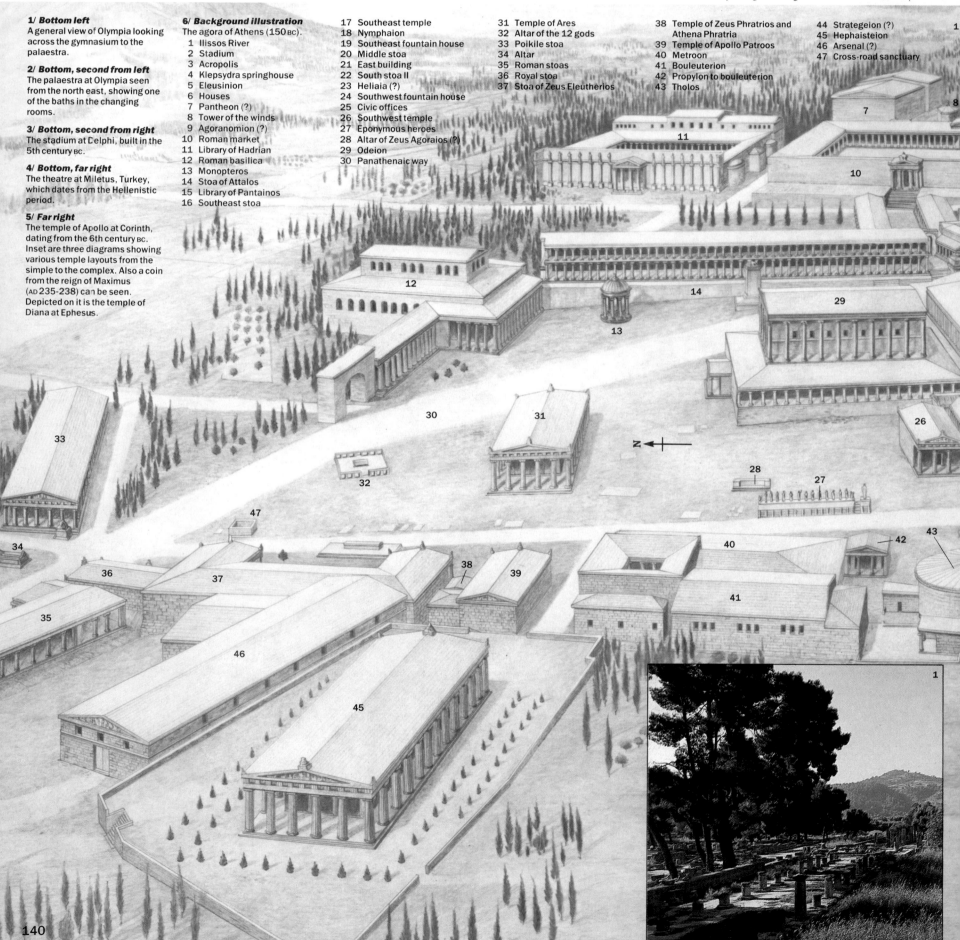

longer than it is wide; on the right the *coryceum* (for exercise with the quintain); next to this the *conisterium* (for athletes to powder themselves); adjoining the *conisterium* at the angle of the colonnade the cold bath which the Greeks call *loutron*; at the left of the *ephebeum*, the *elaeothesium* (for athletes to oil themselves); next to this is the cold room from which the furnace-room is entered at the angle of the colonnade. Adjoining this on the inside in line with the cold room, a vaulted sweating-room is to be placed, twice as long as it is broad, having in the angle of the colonnade the *laconicum* (domed sweating room) constructed as before described. In the palaestra, the cloisters ought to be thus completed and arranged.

'Outside the palaestra three colonnades are to be arranged; the first as you go out of the peristyle; right and left of this, two colonnades with running tracks. Of these three, the one which has a north aspect is to be built double and very wide; the others are to be single. On the sides which adjoin the walls and those which adjoin the columns, they are to have borders 10ft wide to serve as paths. The middle part is to be excavated with steps down from the paths to the level track 1½ft below, and the track is to be not less than 12ft wide. Thus persons who walk about on the paths in their clothes will not be disturbed by the athletes who use oil. Such a colonnade is called *xystos* by the Greeks, whose athletes take exercise in the winter on covered tracks. Next to the covered track and the double colonnade are to be planned open-air walks (which the Greeks call *paradromides* and our people *xysta*). When it is fine weather in winter, the athletes come into the open and exercise there.'

BATHS

Public baths were maintained at the expense of the city, and were accessible even to the very poor. The nominal entrance fee came nowhere near covering the heavy operating cost.

Having stripped in the *apodyterium* bathers went first to the *caldarium*. The cleansing perspiration produced by the dry heat could be supplemented by hot water from the large tub (*labrum*); it was scraped off with the strigil. The bathers were dried and then retraced their steps to the *tepidarium* to cool off gradually, and concluded with a plunge in the cold pool of the *frigidarium*.

THEATRE

Freestanding theatres were rare. They were normally constructed to take advantage of a hillside, often the slope of the acropolis. The staging of dramatic productions was never the most important function, the theatre principally served the needs of the literary and musical side of the festival games. Prizes were offered for new plays, the composition and recitation of epic verse and panegyrics. There were laurels for the best actors, singers and musicians. The theatre also served for meetings (ACTS 19.29-40).

TEMPLE

Religions flourished, and those accorded official recognition had their temples. The essential element was an altar on sacred ground. Where a stoa formed the perimeter of the *temenos* (also *hieron* and *peribolos*) it provided lodging for the priests and space for stalls where visitors might buy votive offerings. The temple was not a centre of congregational worship. Its purpose was to house the image of the god and votive offerings of particular importance. The basic plan has been traced to the 10th century BC and was firmly established by the 6th century BC. Subsequently there were no significant modifications.

'SO THEY BUILT A GYMNASIUM IN JERUSALEM, ACCORDING TO GENTILE CUSTOM, AND REMOVED THE MARKS OF CIRCUMCISION, AND ABANDONED THE HOLY COVENANT.' I MACC 1.14-15

PTOLEMY I Soter was a Macedonian general of Alexander the Great. On the death of Alexander his empire was torn apart by his generals. Ptolemy seized Egypt as his portion of the spoil. The Ptolemies were Greeks, and they focused their kingdom on the Hellenistic world. At the height of their power, they held most of the Levant, the south and south-western coasts of Anatolia, Cyprus, and some coastal areas of Thrace (see Map 1).

PTOLEMAIC INTEREST IN THE LEVANT

Egypt had always coveted Palestine, but in OT times its influence was often weak. Solomon married an Egyptian princess (I KINGS 3.1); after his death Pharaoh Shishak I briefly invaded Judah (see pages 96-7) (I KINGS 14.25). Under Assyrian pressure Israel (724-2 BC) and Judah (701 BC) appealed for help to Egypt, but Egypt was 'a broken reed' (ISA 36.6). When Assyria fell, Pharaoh Nechoh took Judah (609 BC), but soon lost it to Nebuchadnezzar, king of Babylon (605 BC).

After Alexander's death (323 BC), Ptolemy took over Egypt as satrap annexing Cyrenaica and then Syria and Phoenicia to improve his access to the Mediterranean and his defence against his rivals Antigonus and Seleucus. He moved the capital from Memphis to Alexandria, shifting Egypt's focus to the Mediterranean, occupied Coele-Syria and Judah (301 BC) and established control over Cyprus and the Aegean. In 288/7 he took Tyre and Sidon. He thus both secured a defensive ring of territory and also created close contacts with the Hellenistic world. Inevitably this led to collision with the Seleucid empire described in DAN 11.5-44. For the main events of the ensuing wars see below.

After their defeat by Antiochus III at Panion in 200 BC the Ptolemies had little influence on Judah. In 150 BC the Seleucid pretender Alexander Balas, seeking help against his rival Demetrius, allied with Ptolemy VI, marrying his daughter Cleopatra; but the next year Ptolemy attacked Alexander, won the Levant, and had himself crowned in Antioch as king. Both Ptolemy and Alexander died as a result of the subsequent battle, and the Seleucid Demetrius regained the kingdom.

SYRIAN-EGYPTIAN WARS

274-271 BC Ptolemy II fought Antiochus I. Ptolemy celebrated victory with a procession at the festival of Ptolemaieia in Alexandria, 271/270 BC.

260-253 BC Ptolemy II fought Antiochus II. Antiochus gained new territory in Ionia, Pamphylia and Cilicia, and under the settlement terms repudiated his wife Laodicea for Ptolemy's daughter Berenice (DAN 11.6).

JUDAH IN THE HELLENISTIC ERA

EGYPTIAN RULE IN JUDAH — THE REIGN OF THE PTOLEMIES

In the Intertestamental era Egypt once more played a crucial role in the history of the Jewish people. First, it was here that the Jewish scriptures were first translated into Greek – a translation which became known as the 'Septuagint' after its 70 (Greek *septuaginta*) translators. But secondly, Alexandria became the home of a very lively Jewish community, anxious to be included in the citizenship of the capital of Hellenistic Egypt. Contact between Alexandria and Jerusalem was easy, but the Ptolemies' administration and taxation of Judah were probably resented, and the change to Seleucid government in 200 BC welcomed, at least in its early years.

'THEN THE KING OF THE SOUTH SHALL BE STRONG, BUT ONE OF HIS PRINCES SHALL BE STRONGER THAN HE AND HIS DOMINION SHALL BE A GREAT DOMINION. AFTER SOME YEARS THEY SHALL MAKE AN ALLIANCE, AND THE DAUGHTER OF THE KING OF THE SOUTH SHALL COME TO THE KING OF THE NORTH TO MAKE PEACE; BUT SHE SHALL NOT RETAIN THE STRENGTH OF HER ARM, AND HE AND HIS OFFSPRING SHALL NOT ENDURE...' DAN 11.5-6

1/ Map below
The area under Ptolemaic control in the 3rd century BC.

2/ Map right
This large-scale map shows the landscape of the area around Panion (later to be called Caesarea Philippi).
After failing to take Gaza and hold Palestine in 201 BC, Antiochus III withdrew to Syria, and marched south again in 200 BC. Ptolemy V's troops under Scopas marched north to block his route at the head of the Jordan valley, to find Antiochus controlling the higher ground on the southern slopes of Mt Hermon.
In this large-scale map of the battle (based on the work of B.Bar Kochva), the battleground is divided by the Wadi Banias and the Wadi Sa'ar. The Seleucid army

had the advantage of higher ground (especially for its right flank cavalry north of the Banias, and its left flank cavalry south of it), and its Indian elephants were larger and heavier than Ptolemy's African elephants.
North of the wadi, the Seleucid right wing cavalry put the opposing cavalry to flight and swung round to attack the Ptolemaic centre in the rear. Caught between the cavalry and the elephants, Ptolemy's centre phalanx disintegrated. South of the wadi, Ptolemy's centre was successful against the Seleucid phalanx, but could make no headway against the Seleucid elephants blocking their advance. The final result was that Scopas withdrew with 10,000 men (mainly from the southern battlefield) to Sidon, where he was besieged and surrendered.

246-241 BC Ptolemy III fought Seleucus II. Ptolemy attacked in order to support Berenice's son's claim to the Seleucid throne. He failed, but regained territory along the Anatolian seaboard, and captured Seleucia in Pieria (see DAN 11.7-9).

219-217 BC Ptolemy IV fought Antiochus III. Antiochus had initial success, recapturing Seleucia, Ptolemais, Tyre and Gaza, but was defeated decisively at Raphia, 217 BC. Ptolemy regained most of his territory but left Seleucia in Seleucid hands (see DAN 11.10-12).

202-200 BC Ptolemy V fought Antiochus III. Antiochus captured Coele-Syria at Panion, and took Sidon and Gaza, and annexed Judah (see DAN 11.13-16).

170-168 BC Ptolemy VI fought Antiochus IV. Antiochus invaded Egypt in 169 and 168 BC, but in 168 BC was ejected by the Romans ('Kittim', DAN 11.30; see DAN 11.25-30; I MACC 1.16-20; II MACC 5.1).

JEWS IN EGYPT

Under the Ptolemies, the Jewish population in Egypt began to increase. Jews had settled in Egypt after the fall of Jerusalem in 587 BC (cf JER 43.5-7, 44.1), and the Elephantine Papyri reveal a Jewish colony near Aswan acting as a Persian frontier garrison. In 312 BC Ptolemy added Jewish captives from Jerusalem; some, according to the Letter of Aristeus, were later repatriated in exchange for a copy of the Torah which was taken from Jerusalem to Alexandria and translated into Greek for Ptolemy II's library (or, more likely, for the benefit of the growing Jewish population in Alexandria). In the mid-2nd century BC Onias IV, fled to Egypt and built a temple at Leontopolis, either for the local Jewish

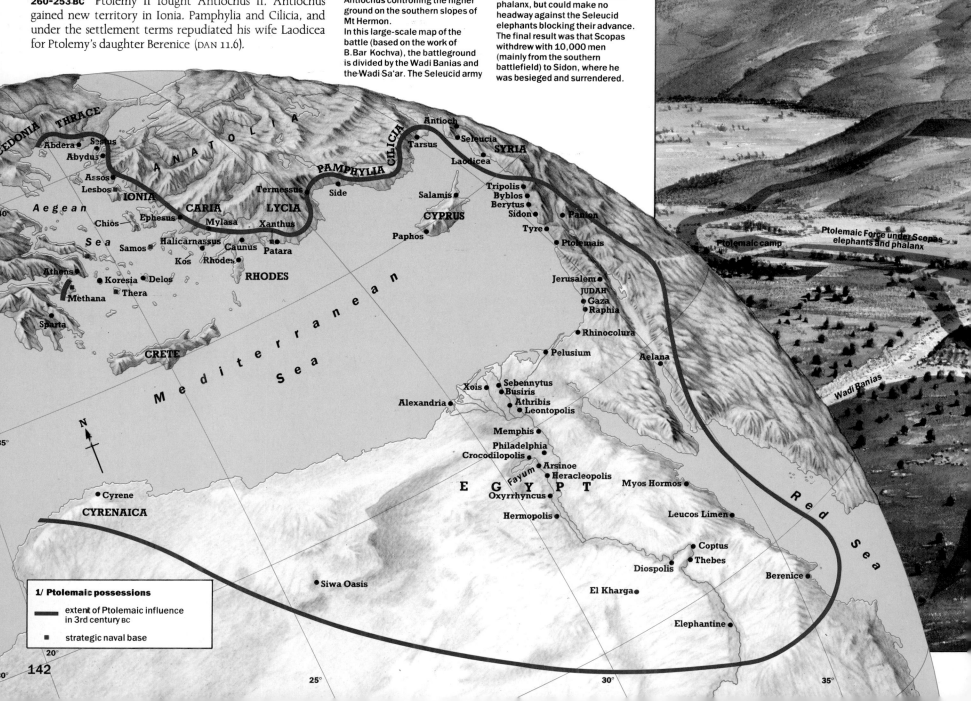

2/ Battle of Panion, 200 BC
→ Seleucid force
→ Ptolemaic force

Ptolemaic Force under Scopas elephants and phalanx

Ptolemaic camp

Wadi Banias

MACEDONIA
THRACE
Abdera
Sestus
Abydus
Assos
Lesbos
IONIA
Chios
Ephesus
Samos
Halicarnassus
Kos
Athens
Koresia
Delos
Methana
Thera
Sparta
ANATOLIA
CARIA
Mylasa
Caunus
Rhodes
Patara
RHODES
LYCIA
Xanthus
Termessus
PAMPHYLIA
Side
CILICIA
Tarsus
Antioch
Seleucia
SYRIA
Laodicea
Salamis
CYPRUS
Paphos
Tripolis
Byblos
Berytus
Sidon
Tyre
Panion
Ptolemais
Jerusalem
JUDAH
Gaza
Raphia
Rhinocolura
Pelusium
Aelana
Xois
Sebennytus
Busiris
Athribis
Leontopolis
Alexandria
Memphis
Philadelphia
Crocodilopolis
Arsinoe
Heracleopolis
Fayum
Oxyrrhyncus
Hermopolis
Myos Hormos
Leucos Limen
Coptus
Thebes
Diospolis
Berenice
El Kharga
Siwa Oasis
Elephantine
Cyrene
CYRENAICA
EGYPT
Aegean Sea
Mediterranean Sea
Red Sea

1/ Ptolemaic possessions
— extent of Ptolemaic influence in 3rd century BC
■ strategic naval base

military garrison, or as a religious centre for all the Jews of the Nile Delta. Ptolemy III was well disposed towards the Jews, and in his reign many appear settled as farmers, artisans, soldiers, policemen, tax collectors, and administrators. Jewish synagogues are known at Alexandria, Crocodilopolis in the Fayum, Athribis, and elsewhere.

EGYPTIAN-JEWISH LITERATURE
Jewish writers flourished in Ptolemaic Alexandria. Demetrius (late 3rd century) wrote a chronology of Jewish history. In the 2nd century, Aristobulus was a teacher and philosopher (cf II MACC 1.10), Artapanus a religious propagandist who wrote a work called *Concerning the Jews*, Ezekiel dramatized the Exodus story in Greek verse, and ·Pseudo-Hecataeus wrote *On the Jews* and *On Abraham*. In 132BC or soon after Ecclesiasticus was translated into Greek.

RELATIONSHIP OF JEWS AND GREEKS IN EGYPT
Some Jews favoured Hellenistic culture while others rejected it. But all Jewish writers were anxious to persuade fellow Jews and gentiles alike that the Jewish traditions compared well with those of the gentiles. Jews might even boast of their contribution to the world of learning and of their loyalty to their host society, in order to demonstrate that persecution was unjustified. However, in III MACC we read that Ptolemy IV tried unsuccessfully to massacre Jews packed into a hippodrome by loosing on them intoxicated elephants. For all its improbabilities, this story reflects the fears of the Jews in alien surroundings.

THE ZENON PAPYRI
In 1915 papyri were found at the Hellenistic town of

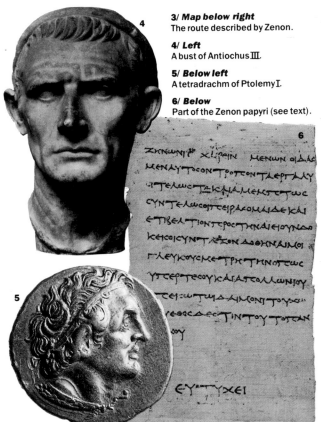

3/ Map below right
The route described by Zenon.

4/ Left
A bust of Antiochus III.

5/ Below left
A tetradrachm of Ptolemy I.

6/ Below
Part of the Zenon papyri (see text).

Philadelphia. These are the correspondence of Zenon son of Agreophon, a native of Caunus who became the right-hand man of Ptolemy II's senior official Apollonius. Several documents concern the journey Zenon made through Judah, Transjordan and Galilee in 259BC (see Map 3). One list gives the itinerary, another the travellers' names, and others details of rations supplied en route. Gifts to Ptolemy II are listed in a letter from Toubias, who commanded a small garrison of military settlers on his estate at Birta of Ammonitis (modern Arak el-Emir). His soldiers included an Athenian, a Macedonian, and a Cnidian: one of them sold Zenon a Sidonian slavegirl.

THE PTOLEMIES	
Ptolemy I Soter	305-283 BC
Ptolemy II Philadelphus	283-246 BC
Ptolemy III Euergetes I	246-221 BC
Ptolemy IV Philopator	221-204 BC
Ptolemy V Epiphanes	204-180 BC
Ptolemy VI Philometor	180-145 BC
with Ptolemy VIII Euergetes II and Cleopatra	170-164 BC
with Cleopatra II	163-145 BC
Ptolemy VIII Euergetes II (restored)	145-116 BC
Cleopatra III and Ptolemy IX Soter II (Lathyrus)	116-107 BC
Cleopatra III and Ptolemy X Alexander I	107-101 BC
Ptolemy X Alexander I and Cleopatra Berenice	101-88 BC
Ptolemy IX Soter II (restored)	88-81 BC
Cleopatra Berenice and Ptolemy XI Alexander II	80 BC
Ptolemy XII Neos Dionysus (Auletes)	80-58 BC
Berenice IV (at first with Cleopatra Tryphaena)	58-56 BC
Berenice IV and Archelaus	56-55 BC
Ptolemy XII Neos Dionysus (restored)	55-51 BC
Cleopatra VII Philopator	51-30 BC

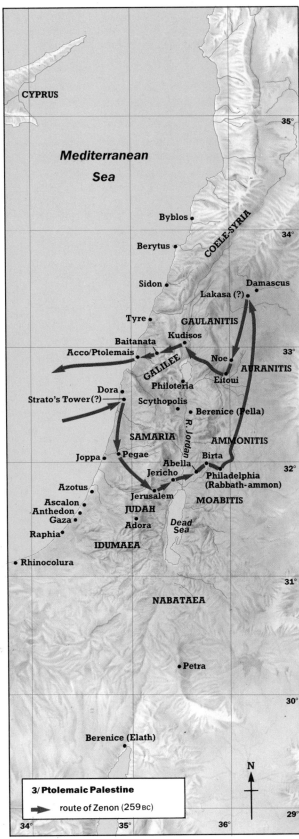

3/ Ptolemaic Palestine
→ route of Zenon (259BC)

THE empire's first capital was at the newly founded Seleucia on the Tigris; but Seleucus' political interests were in the west, where his main rival, Antigonus the One-eyed, was planning to reunite and rule Alexander's former empire. In order to maintain and expand their newly acquired independent kingdoms, Seleucus of Babylon and his son Antiochus, together with Lysimachus of Thrace, and Cassander of Macedon allied against Antigonus and his son Demetrius Poliorcetes, who were trying to hold together the centre of Alexander's empire from their base in western Anatolia.

THE BATTLE OF IPSUS 301 BC

Antigonus commanded 70,000 infantry, 10,000 cavalry, and 75 elephants. Seleucus commanded 64,000 infantry, 10,500 cavalry, 400 elephants, and 120 chariots.

Seleucus advanced from Dorylaeum to the north along the valley towards modern Afyon, the key to the major routes through western and southern Anatolia. Antigonus blocked him just north of Afyon, at modern Sipsin.

The course of the battle was as follows (see Map 2): Demetrius' cavalry routed Antiochus' cavalry and pursued it north up the valley; Seleucus' main force of elephants moved to block Demetrius' return to the battle; Seleucus' mounted archers moved to the empty space on the flank of Antigonus' phalanx (infantry) and harassed them, while Seleucus delayed his central attack in the hope that Antigonus' troops would be demoralized and yield. This succeeded; Seleucus attacked, and Antigonus himself was killed. Demetrius fled west to Ephesus with 5,000 infantry and 4000 cavalry.

Seleucus at this point moved his capital west, first to the port of Seleucia Pieria and then to Antioch on the Orontes. Both were new foundations; Antioch was to become one of the major cities of the Hellenistic and Roman worlds, the 'queen of the east'.

THE EASTERN EMPIRE

The eastern empire was the Seleucid burden. In 308-3 BC Seleucus I campaigned in the Indus valley against Chandragupta, eventually yielding to him Arachosia and Gedrosia in exchange for 300 elephants. Bactria, however, well settled with Macedonian colonists and new Hellenistic cities and linked to the west by a good road, remained Seleucid until 250 BC, when it became an autonomous Hellenistic state under Diodotus.

In 247 BC the less Hellenized Parthia seized independence under Arsaces and Tiridates. In 212-205 BC Antiochus III reduced the Parthian king to vassaldom (so earning for him-

self the title 'the Great'), but recognized Euthydemus as king of Bactria and granted independence to the ruler of the Indus valley in return for money and elephants.

However, after Antiochus' humiliation by the Romans in the Treaty of Apamea (188 BC) when Antiochus was forced to cede his lands in Anatolia and Greece to Roman allies, Rhodes and Pergamum, the Seleucids could no longer hold the east. Antiochus IV (166-5 BC: 1 MACC 3.30 etc., 6.1-16), Demetrius II (141 BC; 1 MACC 14.1-2), and Antiochus VII (129 BC) all tried and failed to regain Parthia, whose king, Mithridates II (124-87 BC), welcomed ambassadors from China.

THE WESTERN EMPIRE

The Seleucids were equally unsuccessful in the west. They never controlled the regions of Armenia, Cappadocia, Pontus and Bithynia. They faced opposition from Pergamum (supported by Rome) in the north-west, the sea power of Rhodes in the south-west, the Galatians in Phrygia, the Romans in Greece, and the Ptolemies along the coast of Asia Minor, Cyprus, Phoenicia and Palestine.

This meant that the Seleucids were in the end effectively limited to Cilicia and Syria, the regions either side of the two main cities, Seleucia and Antioch. Much Seleucid energy was taken up by the struggle with the Ptolemies for the Levant. The acquisition of Coele-Syria, Palestine and Transjordan after the battle of Panion (200 BC) (see page 194) was a major gain for the Seleucids, and this area played an important role in Seleucid politics until the death of Antiochus VII in 129 BC. Antiochus IV's over-anxiety to secure Judaea as a buffer towards Egypt was probably a major factor in his reaction to the Maccabaean rebellion.

SELEUCID ADMINISTRATION

The basis of Seleucid rule was conquest. The rulers were of Macedonian origin, the subjects included varied native peoples from Asia Minor in the west to Bactria in the east, from Hellenistic city-dwellers to nomadic tribes. The Seleucid empire (like the Persian empire) was divided into

JUDAH IN THE HELLENISTIC ERA

THE SELEUCID EMPIRE

The Seleucid empire was the real heir to Alexander's conquests in the east. However, the eyes of its founder, Seleucus, were on the west – Seleucus was, after all, Macedonian by birth – and the centre of gravity of his empire moved westwards to Antioch, Seleucus' new foundation on the edge of the Mediterranean world. The eastern empire receded from view, and only recently has the extent of Greek influence in places like Bactria begun to emerge. The Bible is interested in the Seleucids mainly because their 2nd century rulers became seen as fierce persecutors of Judaism. DAN 11 is an important witness to Seleucid campaigns against the Ptolemies in 3rd-century Palestine, but the main evidence for the Seleucids comes from Greek writers like Polybius and Diodorus Siculus.

THE SELEUCIDS

Seleucus I Nicator	305–281
Antiochus I Soter	281–261
Antiochus II Theos	261–246
Seleucus II Callinicus	246–226/5
Seleucus III Soter	226/5–223
Antiochus III Megas ('the Great')	223–187
Seleucus IV Philopator	187–175
Antiochus IV Epiphanes	175–164
Antiochus V Eupator	164–162
Demetrius I Soter	162–150
Alexander Balas	150–145
Demetrius II Nicator	145–140
Antiochus VI Epiphanes	145–142/1 or 139/8
Antiochus VII Sidetes	138–129
Demetrius II Nicator (restored)	129–126/5
Cleopatra Thea	126/5–123
Antiochus VIII Grypus	126/5–96
Seleucus V	126
Antiochus IX Philopator (Cyzicenus)	114/13–95
Seleucus VI	95
Antiochus X Eusebes Philopator	95
Demetrius III Philopator Soter	95–88 (at Damascus)
Antiochus XI Epiphanes Philadelphus	} twins 95 (in Cilicia)
Philip I	95–84/3 (in Cilicia)
Antiochus XII Dionysus	87 (at Damascus)
Philip II	84/3

2/ Map below left

At the battle of Ipsus in 301 BC, Seleucus I defeated Antigonus, his main rival to the west. Using his elephants to block their path, Seleucus harassed the enemy with his cavalry, and when they were sufficiently demoralized he attacked and routed them. Antigonus was killed and his son Demetrius, fled west to Ephesus with 5000 infantry and 4000 cavalry (see text).

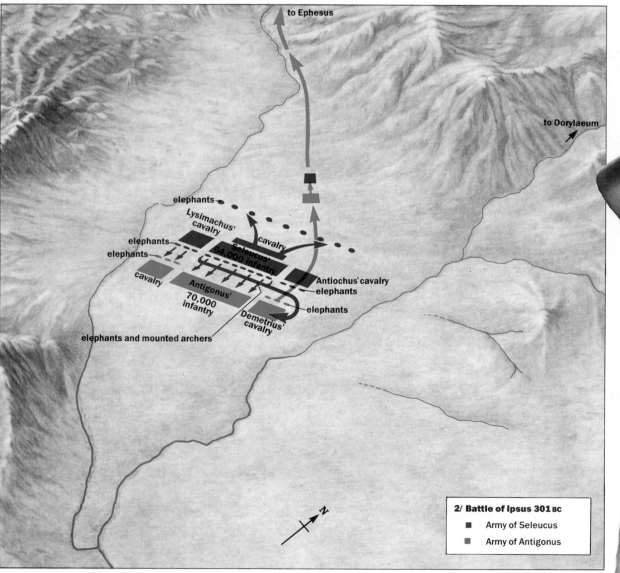

elephants
Lysimachus' cavalry
cavalry
elephants
elephants
Seleucus' 64,000 infantry
cavalry
Antiochus' cavalry
elephants
Antigonus' 70,000 infantry
elephants
Demetrius' cavalry
elephants and mounted archers
to Ephesus
to Dorylaeum

N

2/ Battle of Ipsus 301 BC

- ■ Army of Seleucus
- ■ Army of Antigonus

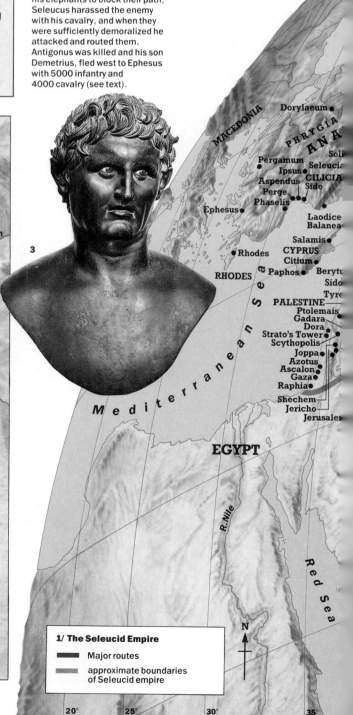

MACEDONIA
Dorylaeum
PHRYGIA
ANA
Pergamum
Soli
Ipsus
Seleucia
Aspendus
CILICIA
Perge
Side
Phaselis
Laodice
Ephesus
Balanea
Salamis
CYPRUS
Rhodes
Citium
RHODES
Paphos
Berytu
Sido
Tyre
PALESTINE
Ptolemais
Gadara
Dora
Strato's Tower
Scythopolis
Joppa
Azotus
Ascalon
Gaza
Raphia
Shechem
Jericho
Jerusalem

Mediterranean Sea

EGYPT

R. Nile

Red Sea

N

1/ The Seleucid Empire

- ▬ Major routes
- ▬ approximate boundaries of Seleucid empire

20°   25°   30°   35°

satrapies. These were subdivided into eparchies.

A major feature was colonization and urbanization of conquered territories. Macedonian soldiers were settled in colonies (*katoikiai* or *klerouchiai*) which began as collective institutions holding property in common but tended to develop into cities with private property-holders. The colonists would take local wives, and their presence would help maintain local peace.

Particularly important was the establishment of new towns, usually with names drawn from the Macedonian homeland (eg, Larissa, Beroea) or from members of the Seleucid dynasty (Antiochia, Laodicea etc). In such cities the king could have more direct control than he could in the older, independent cities, with which he would conclude an 'alliance' and to whom he would carefully proclaim the virtues of *demokratia* and *eleutheria*.

There were also temple cities which had a certain independence and the privilege of *asulia* (ie, asylum *cf* the case of Jerusalem, I MACC 10.43). The aim was to make cities loyal to the crown, and in this way hold the empire together by peaceful rather than military means. Cities

founded by a Seleucid ruler might establish a cult of the ruler, also to help maintain loyalty.

THE ARMY

The army was naturally important to the Seleucid administration: it was needed for conquest and as a symbol of authority. The core of it, the heavy infantry of the phalanxes, was originally composed of Macedonian troops drawn mainly from colonies settled in Syria and Mesopotamia (the army headquarters was at Syrian Apamea). In addition to this local contingents were employed for use as light infantry and cavalry.

The navy operated in the Mediterranean from Seleucia and Ephesus, and in the Persian Gulf. It was drastically reduced by the Romans in 188 BC by the Treaty of Apamea.

1/ Below
The Seleucid empire in the 4th century BC expanded from Babylon to the Indus in the east.

3/ Below left
Seleucus I based his empire on conquest. He was one of the first commanders to realise the importance of elephants in battle, and they were an important factor in the victory at Ipsus in 301 BC (see map).

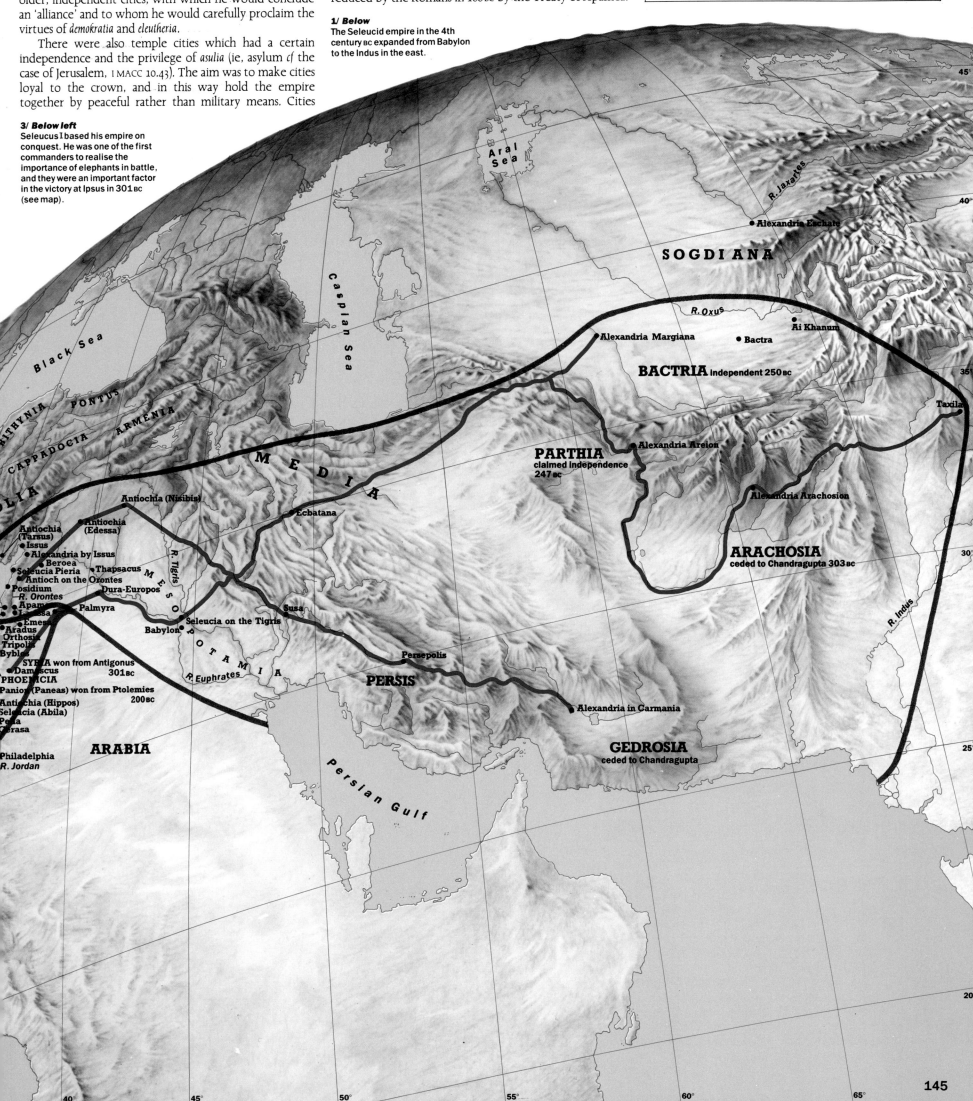

145

WHEN in 200 BC the Seleucids took Judaea (Judah) from the Ptolemies, some Jews may have preferred to remain under Egyptian rule; others used the opportunity to proclaim Judaea's independence, 'In those times many people shall rise against the king of the south; and the men of violence among your own people shall lift themselves up in order to fulfil the vision; but they shall fail.' (DAN 11.14).

These attempts did fail, but Antiochus III responded by granting the Jews tax concessions and the right to live according to their traditional law. Other Jews were in fact anxious to bring Judaea into the cultural context of Hellenism via the Seleucid empire. I MACC 1.11 portrays these Jews as 'lawless men' who 'misled many' by their policy of inviting the Jews 'to make a covenant with the gentiles round about us'. Their political ambitions, coupled with Antiochus IV's ambition to rule Egypt, and the Seleucid need of money to pay off Roman war indemnities, all combined to impel Judaea from peace to civil war and direct rule by the Seleucids within a decade of Antiochus IV's accession in 175 BC.

JEWISH DISCONTENT
The trouble began when Seleucus IV attempted to raise money by robbing the Jerusalem Temple (II MACC 3). 'There was no little distress throughout the whole city. The priests prostrated themselves before the altar in their priestly garments and called toward heaven' (II MACC 3.14).

The high-priest Onias, who had opposed the attempt, was deposed by his brother Jason, who offered Antiochus IV increased tribute in exchange for high-priestly office for himself and Greek city status, with appropriate institutions such as the gymnasium, for Jerusalem. Three years later, Jason himself was similarly ousted by the financial official Menelaus, who was a priest but not of the high-priestly family. Menelaus, however, lost public support by selling the Temple plate to pay his debts to the king, and when Jason tried to regain his position by force, Antiochus saw this as rebellion against Seleucid authority, attacked Jerusalem and pillaged the Temple (167 BC). (His recent eviction from Egypt by the Romans probably increased his frustration and vindictiveness.)

The commissioners left to govern Jerusalem and Samaria added further brutalities. These events reveal that the cause of the Maccabaean revolt was not so much the increasing Hellenization of Judaea (which continued through the 2nd century BC) as the increasingly heavy-handed Seleucid treatment of Jewish opposition to the cynical misuse of the high-priesthood, both by Jews and Seleucids, for political purposes.

THE START OF THE REBELLION
The next development, in the course of events leading up to the Jewish rebellion, was Antiochus' decree, which, according to I MACC, proscribed Jewish sacrifices, sabbath observance, circumcision, and the Jewish Law, and enforced gentile forms of cult in the Temple and elsewhere. II MACC says that Antiochus forced the Jews to abandon their Law, had the Temple rededicated to Olympian Zeus, and initiated the Greek cult of Dionysus.

What mattered most to the Jews was how the decree affected the Law and the Temple. First, the decree of Antiochus cancelled the concession allowing the Jews to govern themselves by their own Law; secondly, it made the Temple like any other Hellenistic city temple, open to all worshippers and so to gentiles, with their unclean offerings such as swine, as well as to Jews. The Jews saw this as religious persecution, 'And behold, our holy place, our beauty, and our glory have been laid waste; the Gentiles have profaned it. Why should we live any longer?' (I MACC 2.12-13); Antiochus probably saw it as the political control of an unruly subject nation. I MACC presents the Maccabees as religious partisans; the rebellion began with the killing of a Jew (Eleazar) as he committed apostasy publicly. However, religion and politics were inseparable, and the rebellion was aimed equally at political change.

THE FIRST CAMPAIGNS
The Maccabees came from the village of Modin in the hills north-west of Jerusalem. Their superior knowledge of the locality made for initial successes. The governor of Samaria was killed by the Maccabees leading a small force against them; a larger force was ambushed as it climbed from the coastal plain through the pass of Beth-horon.

In 165 BC Judas defeated a larger Seleucid army at nearby Emmaus. By December 164 BC (just as Antiochus died) Judas felt strong enough to purge the Temple of its gentile cult and rededicate it, fortify the Temple hill against the Syrian garrison overlooking it, and occupy and fortify Beth-zur to the south. In 163 BC the Maccabees campaigned in Idumaea,

JUDAH IN THE HELLENISTIC ERA

SELEUCID RULE AND JEWISH REACTION – THE MACCABAEAN FIGHT FOR RELIGION AND COUNTRY

The Maccabees were the family of the Jewish freedom fighter Judas ben Mattathias (died 166 BC) who led the opposition to Seleucid rule in Judaea. Under the unstable Seleucid king Antiochus IV, Jerusalem was sacked and laws were enacted persecuting the Jewish religion. However, the Seleucid empire was going into decline and the guerilla war of the Maccabees, combined with intricate political manoeuvring, eventually obtained, (though only briefly) an independent Jewish state.

Philistia, Galilee and Transjordan, rescuing Jewish residents from local harassment and demonstrating Maccabaean strength. When Judas actually besieged the Seleucid garrison in Jerusalem, Lysias, the vice-regent of the young Antiochus V, invaded Judaea, captured Beth-zur, defeated Judas at Beth-zechariah (see Map 2), and besieged his troops in turn in the Temple. A threatened coup in Syria forced Lysias to abandon the siege; he repealed the decree of 167 BC, executed Menelaus (whom he rightly blamed for much of the trouble), but dismantled the Maccabaean defences at the Temple and left 'the Syrian garrison in control of Jerusalem.

A NEW PHASE
In 161 BC Seleucus IV's son Demetrius took over the Seleucid empire. The Hellenizing party of Judaea, led by Alcimus, complained to Demetrius of the Maccabees' continuing resistance. Demetrius made Alcimus high-priest, and sent his general Bacchides in support, to crush the Maccabees. Alcimus purged some former Maccabaean supporters, moderates naively trusting him to restore stability. Judas soon renewed his resistance, however, and Demetrius sent Nicanor, whose initial conciliatory negotiations with Judas dismayed Alcimus and his party. Renewed fighting led to Nicanor's death at Adasa (161/160 BC), the return of Bacchides, and the defeat and death of Judas at the Battle of Elasa (160 BC) (see Map 3).

The Hellenizing party, backed by Syria, now controlled Judaea; but Alcimus died in 159 BC, and after one last abortive campaign Bacchides made peace with Judas and withdrew. This was the turning point; the Syrians still garrisoned Judaea at Jerusalem and other points (I MACC 9.50-53), but the only credible Jewish leader left was Jonathan, who seems to have ruled informally from Michmash (I MACC 9.73).

TOWARDS INDEPENDENCE
Jonathan now bargained with successive contenders for the Seleucid throne to win political concessions. In 152 BC he supported the pretender Alexander Balas in return for the high-priesthood (to which he had no right by descent), thus earning the title 'the Wicked Priest' from the pious community which settled at Qumran about this time.

Jonathan continued to support Balas in spite of rival approaches from Demetrius I, whom Balas defeated in 151 BC. When Jonathan defeated Demetrius II in 147 BC, Balas rewarded him with new honours and new territory, the district of Accaron. However, when Balas died after battle with Ptolemy VI (145 BC), Jonathan promptly allied with Demetrius II, acquiring thereby three Samaritan districts and their revenues. Under pressure from Balas' son Antiochus and his guardian Trypho, Demetrius solicited Jonathan's support, falsely promising to withdraw the Seleucid garrison from Jerusalem. When Trypho and Antiochus ousted Demetrius, they confirmed Jonathan in his position and possessions, and appointed his brother, Simon, Seleucid governor of the coastal region from the Ladder of Tyre to the borders of Egypt.

CONSOLIDATION OF MACCABEE GAINS
Jonathan and Simon now rapidly consolidated their position. Simon replaced the Seleucid garrison at Beth-zur by a Jewish one, garrisoned Joppa, and fortified Adida between Joppa and Jerusalem. Jonathan took Gaza, and campaigned (ostensibly on Trypho's behalf) to defeat Demetrius near the Sea of Galilee and near Hamath in Syria. He blockaded the Seleucid garrison in Jerusalem, and began repairing Jerusalem's walls and rebuilding fortresses in Judaea (probably those established by Bacchides in 160/159 BC and abandoned in 152 BC; I MACC 9.50; 10.12).

When Trypho, alarmed by Jonathan's growing inde-

2/ Battle of Beth-zechariah 163 BC
→ army of Judas
→ army of Lysias

JUDAEA (JUDAH)

route of Maccabee army

flanking cavalry
elephants and infantry

flanking cavalry

light-armed troops

route of Seleucid army

to Beth-zur

Beth-horon

to Jerusalem

defeated Jews flee

Elasa

Berea

JUDAEA (JUDAH)

3/ Battle of Elasa 160 BC
→ army of Judas
→ army of Bacchides

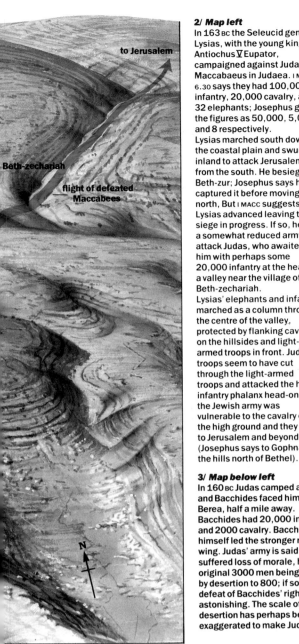

2/ Map left

In 163 BC the Seleucid general Lysias, with the young king, Antiochus V Eupator, campaigned against Judas Maccabaeus in Judaea. I MACC 6.30 says they had 100,000 infantry, 20,000 cavalry, and 32 elephants; Josephus gives the figures as 50,000, 5,000 and 8 respectively.

Lysias marched south down the coastal plain and swung inland to attack Jerusalem from the south. He besieged Beth-zur; Josephus says he captured it before moving north, But I MACC suggests that Lysias advanced leaving the siege in progress. If so, he had a somewhat reduced army to attack Judas, who awaited him with perhaps some 20,000 infantry at the head of a valley near the village of Beth-zechariah.

Lysias' elephants and infantry marched as a column through the centre of the valley, protected by flanking cavalry on the hillsides and light-armed troops in front. Judas' troops seem to have cut through the light-armed troops and attacked the heavy infantry phalanx head-on. But the Jewish army was vulnerable to the cavalry on the high ground and they fled to Jerusalem and beyond (Josephus says to Gophna, in the hills north of Bethel).

3/ Map below left

In 160 BC Judas camped at Elasa, and Bacchides faced him at Berea, half a mile away. Bacchides had 20,000 infantry and 2000 cavalry. Bacchides himself led the stronger right wing. Judas' army is said to have suffered loss of morale, his original 3000 men being reduced by desertion to 800; if so, his defeat of Bacchides' right wing is astonishing. The scale of desertion has perhaps been exaggerated to make Judas'

bravery the more admirable. I MACC describes only the central feature of the battle. It says nothing of the part played by Bacchides' slingers, archers and cavalry – it is possible that Judas' army included light-armed troops and even some cavalry. The crucial attack on Bacchides' right wing which gave way towards the mountain slopes to the east or north-east. Judas' men followed, and the Syrian left wing swung round in their rear. Judas was among those killed.

pendence, captured him at Ptolemais, Simon took over the leadership, and continued to develop Judaea's military and political strength. He completed Jerusalem's walls, made Joppa a military base, rebuilt Judaea's fortresses, took and fortified Gazara, and finally expelled the Seleucid garrison from Jerusalem (141 BC). Simon renewed the diplomatic relationships established earlier with Rome (I MACC 8.17-32; 12.1-4) and Sparta (I MACC 12.5-23), and negotiated the formal abolition of tribute with Demetrius II. All this meant the practical independence of Judaea from the Seleucids (though Antiochus VII soon challenged this), and so I MACC 13.41 notes that in 142 BC, 'the yoke of the gentiles was removed from Israel, and the people began to write in their documents and contracts, "In the first year of Simon the great high priest and commander and leader of the Jews"'.

1/ Map below

After the Maccabees' early campaigns against the Seleucids (see maps 2 and 3), their strategy changed under the leadership of Jonathan. Political manoeuvre worked where military action had been unsuccessful and Jonathan and his brother Simon were able to consolidate the Jewish position, culminating in 141 BC with the expulsion of the Seleucid garrison (see text).

'THEN JUDAS HIS SON, WHO WAS CALLED MACCABEUS, TOOK COMMAND IN HIS PLACE. ALL HIS BROTHERS AND ALL WHO HAD JOINED HIS FATHER HELPED HIM; THEY GLADLY FOUGHT FOR ISRAEL. HE EXTENDED THE GLORY OF HIS PEOPLE. LIKE A GIANT HE PUT ON HIS BREASTPLATE; HE GIRDED ON HIS ARMOUR OF WAR AND WAGED BATTLES, PROTECTING THE HOST BY HIS SWORD. HE WAS LIKE A LION IN HIS DEEDS, LIKE A LION'S CUB ROARING FOR PREY. HE SEARCHED OUT AND PURSUED THE LAWLESS; HE BURNED THOSE WHO TROUBLED HIS PEOPLE. LAWLESS MEN SHRANK BACK FOR FEAR OF HIM; ALL THE EVILDOERS WERE CONFOUNDED; AND DELIVERANCE PROSPERED BY HIS HAND. HE EMBITTERED MANY KINGS, BUT HE MADE JACOB GLAD BY HIS DEEDS, AND HIS MEMORY IS BLESSED FOR EVER. HE WENT THROUGH THE CITIES OF JUDAH; HE DESTROYED THE UNGODLY OUT OF THE LAND; THUS HE TURNED AWAY WRATH FROM ISRAEL.'
I MACC 3.1-8

THE MACCABEES

Judas ben Mattathias	died 166 BC
Judas the Maccabee	160 BC
Jonathan (high priest)	143 BC
Simon (high priest)	134 BC
John Hyrcanus I (high priest)	104 BC
Aristobulus I (high priest)	103 BC
Alexander Jannaeus (high priest)	76 BC
Alexandra Salome	67 BC
Aristobulus II	49 BC
Hyrcanus II (high priest)	30 BC
Antigonus	37 BC

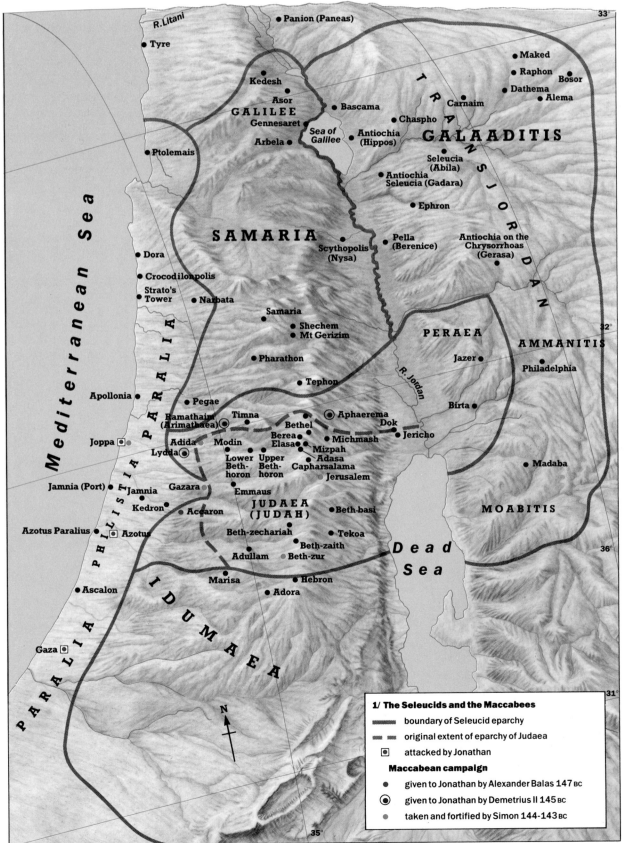

1/ The Seleucids and the Maccabees

- boundary of Seleucid eparchy
- original extent of eparchy of Judaea
- ⊡ attacked by Jonathan
- **Maccabean campaign**
  - ● given to Jonathan by Alexander Balas 147 BC
  - ◉ given to Jonathan by Demetrius II 145 BC
  - ● taken and fortified by Simon 144-143 BC

UNDER Simon, in the 170th year of the Seleucid era (142BC), 'the yoke of the Gentiles was removed from Israel' (I MACC 13.41), and the first year of a new era began. From now until the arrival of the Romans, the Jews were free to develop their own independent state. The main features of the period are the final emancipation from Seleucid rule, the expansion of Judah's territory, the development of the Maccabaean military leadership into a monarchy, and the opposition to this development.

FREEDOM FROM THE SELEUCIDS

Demetrius II (145-140 BC) exempted Judah from tribute, thus granting virtual independence (I MACC 11.30-37). Antiochus VII (138-129 BC) confirmed this, granting Simon the right to mint coinage (I MACC 15.1-9); but on securing his position in Syria, Antiochus changed his mind, demanded the return of territory he claimed as Seleucid, and attacked Simon, though without success. After Simon's death (134BC), Antiochus successfully besieged Simon's son, John Hyrcanus, in Jerusalem, withdrawing only when Hyrcanus paid tribute and gave hostages. However, Antiochus died fighting the Parthians (129 BC), and thereafter the Seleucids were no threat to Judah (though in 108BC the Samaritans enlisted Antiochus Cyzicenus' help against Hyrcanus, and in 88BC the Pharisees called in Demetrius III against Jannaeus).

JUDAH AND HER NEIGHBOURS

The Seleucid collapse gave stronger subjects (in particular the Jews) opportunity to expand. Judah had been a Seleucid eparchy, surrounded by other eparchies: Samaria to the north, Idumaea to the south, Paralia (the coastal strip) to the west, and Galaaditis to the east across the Jordan. Jonathan (152-142 BC) had gained Accaron from Paralia, and Lydda, Arimathaea and Apherema from Samaria (I MACC 10.30; 10.89, 11.28, 34); Simon continued this expansion westwards, annexing Gazara and then the port of Joppa (I MACC 10.76, 13.11, 14.5). Judah's expansion over the next 50 years is easily traced: (a) along the coast, Hyrcanus took Apollonia, Jamnia and Azotus; Jannaeus built on this by annexing Strato's Tower (the later Caesarea) and Dora to the north (though he failed to take Ptolemais, defended by Ptolemy IX Lathyrus), and Anthedon, Gaza, Raphia and Rhinocolura to the south; (b) inland, to the north, Judah's historic rival Samaria had asserted its religious independence by building in the Hellenistic age its own temple on Mount Gerizim near Shechem. Hyrcanus took Samaria in two stages, first defeating the people and destroying the temple, and later (108BC) capturing the cities of Samaria and Scythopolis and the Carmel range. This opened the way for Aristobulus to take Galilee and attack the Ituraeans to the north, annexing part of their territory and forcibly circumcizing the people; (c) to the south, Hyrcanus invaded Idumaea, forcibly Judaizing the people. (One unexpected result was that a century later an Idumaean, Herod, ruled in Jerusalem.) This invasion threatened the Nabataeans (see page 160), whose trading ambitions reached from Petra to the Mediterranean via Gaza in the northwest, and to Syria via the Transjordanian route to the north. Jannaeus finally cut Nabataean access to the sea by destroying Gaza; the route to Syria was cut when Hyrcanus seized the important town of Medeba and Jannaeus extended Judah's control of this region to the southern end of the Dead Sea. Jannaeus also captured a

JUDAH IN THE HELLENISTIC ERA

JEWISH INDEPENDENCE — THE HASMONAEAN MONARCHY

This period represents a high point of Jewish nationalism. For the first time since 587BC, Judah was ruled by Jewish kings, and the nation's boundaries expanded dramatically. This is the period when the Pharisees and Sadducees make their appearance. We begin to see the social situation reflected in the gospels.

1/ Map right
The Hasmonaeans (see chart below) expanded Judah's territory considerably. Hyrcanus captured surrounding cities in Samaria Idumaea and Ammonitis. Aristobulus was able to strike north into Galilee and Jannaeus consolidated the kingdom by extending Judaean control down to the south end of the Dead Sea and by building fortresses at strategic locations on the southern and eastern borders.

2/ Below left
The Masonic Hall is one of the most beautifully preserved stone constructions of the late Hellenistic period in Jerusalem.

The interior measures 60 x 84ft and it is part of a system of underground chambers west of Wilson's Arch in Jerusalem. Archaeologists have identified it with the 'chamber of hewn stone' in the Sanhedrin and the 'council-house' described by Josephus. The Masonic Hall takes its name from the Masons, who for many years used it as a meeting-place because they believed that it had been used for arcane religious rites in the days of Solomon.

3/ Right
The first coins of the independent kingdom of Judah were struck by Hyrcanus, or, according to some scholars, by Jannaeus.

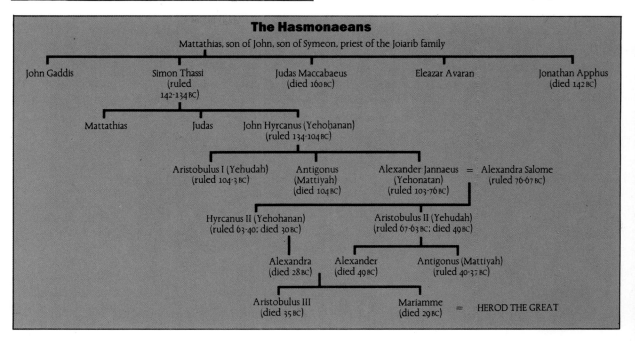

The Hasmonaeans

Mattathias, son of John, son of Symeon, priest of the Joiarib family

John Gaddis — Simon Thassi (ruled 142-134 BC) — Judas Maccabaeus (died 160 BC) — Eleazar Avaran — Jonathan Apphus (died 142 BC)

Mattathias — Judas — John Hyrcanus (Yehohanan) (ruled 134-104 BC)

Aristobulus I (Yehudah) (ruled 104-3 BC) — Antigonus (Mattiyah) (died 104 BC) — Alexander Jannaeus (Yehonatan) (ruled 103-76 BC) = Alexandra Salome (ruled 76-67 BC)

Hyrcanus II (Yehohanan) (ruled 63-40; died 30 BC) — Aristobulus II (Yehudah) (ruled 67-63 BC; died 49 BC)

Alexandra (died 28 BC) — Alexander (died 49 BC) — Antigonus (Mattiyah) (ruled 40-37 BC)

Aristobulus III (died 35 BC) — Mariamme (died 29 BC) = HEROD THE GREAT

number of towns in Galaaditis, Gaulanitis, and Syria; nevertheless, the Nabataean Obodas I defeated Jannaeus in Gaulanitis c 93BC, and his successor Aretas III took possession of Coele-Syria and Damascus in 85BC, and raided Judah, defeating Jannaeus at Adida. The Nabataeans remained a threat to Judah; in 63BC they aided Hyrcanus against Aristobulus, until forced home by the Romans in 62BC. The location of Jannaeus' forts at Alexandrium, Hyrcania, Masada and Machaerus (see map) reveals Jannaeus' concern for his southern and eastern borders.

THE RISE AND FALL OF THE HASMONAEAN MONARCHY

In 142BC Simon had been appointed high priest, military commander and civil ruler, hereditary offices inherited by his son Hyrcanus in 134BC. Hyrcanus' coins (the first Hasmonaean coins minted) are inscribed 'Yehohanan the high priest and the congregation of the Jews'; the inscription suggests that Hyrcanus was firstly presenting himself as a typical Hellenistic ruler, secondly emphasizing his high-priesthood, and thirdly governing with a council and not as an independent autocrat. The coins of Aristobulus and Jannaeus followed the same formula, though some of Jannaeus' bore a bi-lingual inscription, 'Jonathan the king'

(Hebrew), and 'King Alexander' (Greek). By the terms of Jannaeus' will, his wife Alexandra Salome succeeded. Debarred as a woman from priesthood, she appointed her older son Hyrcanus high-priest. When she died, he succeeded, but almost immediately resigned his royal and high-priestly inheritance to his brother Aristobulus (67BC). His coins read, 'Yehudah, high priest, and the congregation of the Jews'. When Pompey removed Aristobulus (63BC), he left Hyrcanus as high-priest, without royal powers. It seems that only Jannaeus put 'king' on his coins.

KINGS AND HIGH-PRIESTS

The Hasmonaeans ruled with difficulty. Simon was assassinated. Hyrcanus I was opposed by the Pharisees; he was told that he should retain royal powers but give up the high-priesthood, from which (they alleged) his mother's status as a slave disqualified him. In fact the Maccabees and Hasmonaeans had no hereditary high-priestly rights, and Jonathan's assumption of high-priesthood in 152BC probably caused the Qumran sect to call him 'the Wicked Priest'. Later when Jannaeus presided as high-priest at the feast of Tabernacles, he was pelted with lemons. Jannaeus' response was a massacre which led to civil war. The Pharisees called in Seleucid Demetrius III against Jannaeus, who later avenged himself by crucifying 800 opponents and killing their families. The Jews nicknamed him 'the Thracian' for his barbarity, and on his deathbed he advised his wife Alexandra to make her peace with the Pharisees. She did so; Josephus comments that though she had the royal title, the Pharisees had the power. However, her ambitious younger son, Aristobulus, led the opposition, and on her death easily forced his brother Hyrcanus to resign the throne and the high-priesthood. However, at this point the even more ambitious Idumaean Antipater, son of Jannaeus' governor of Idumaea, tried to re-establish Hyrcanus as his puppet with the help of Nabataean Aretas III, and they besieged Aristobulus in the temple. Meanwhile, the Romans under Pompey had taken over Syria, and both parties appealed to him. At first Pompey supported Aristobulus, but later he supported Hyrcanus, successfully besieged Aristobulus in the temple, paraded him in his triumph at Rome, and left Hyrcanus as high-priest (but not king). The Hasmonaean attempt to combine kingship and high-priesthood in one person contributed to the failure of Judah's brief period of independence in the midst of centuries of foreign rule.

'WHEN THEIR FATHER DIED, THE ELDEST OF THEM, ARISTOBULUS ... WAS THE FIRST TO WEAR A CROWN, 471 YEARS AND THREE MONTHS AFTER THE RETURN OF THE NATION TO THEIR OWN LAND, SET FREE FROM SLAVERY IN BABYLON.' JOSEPHUS, WAR 1.72

2

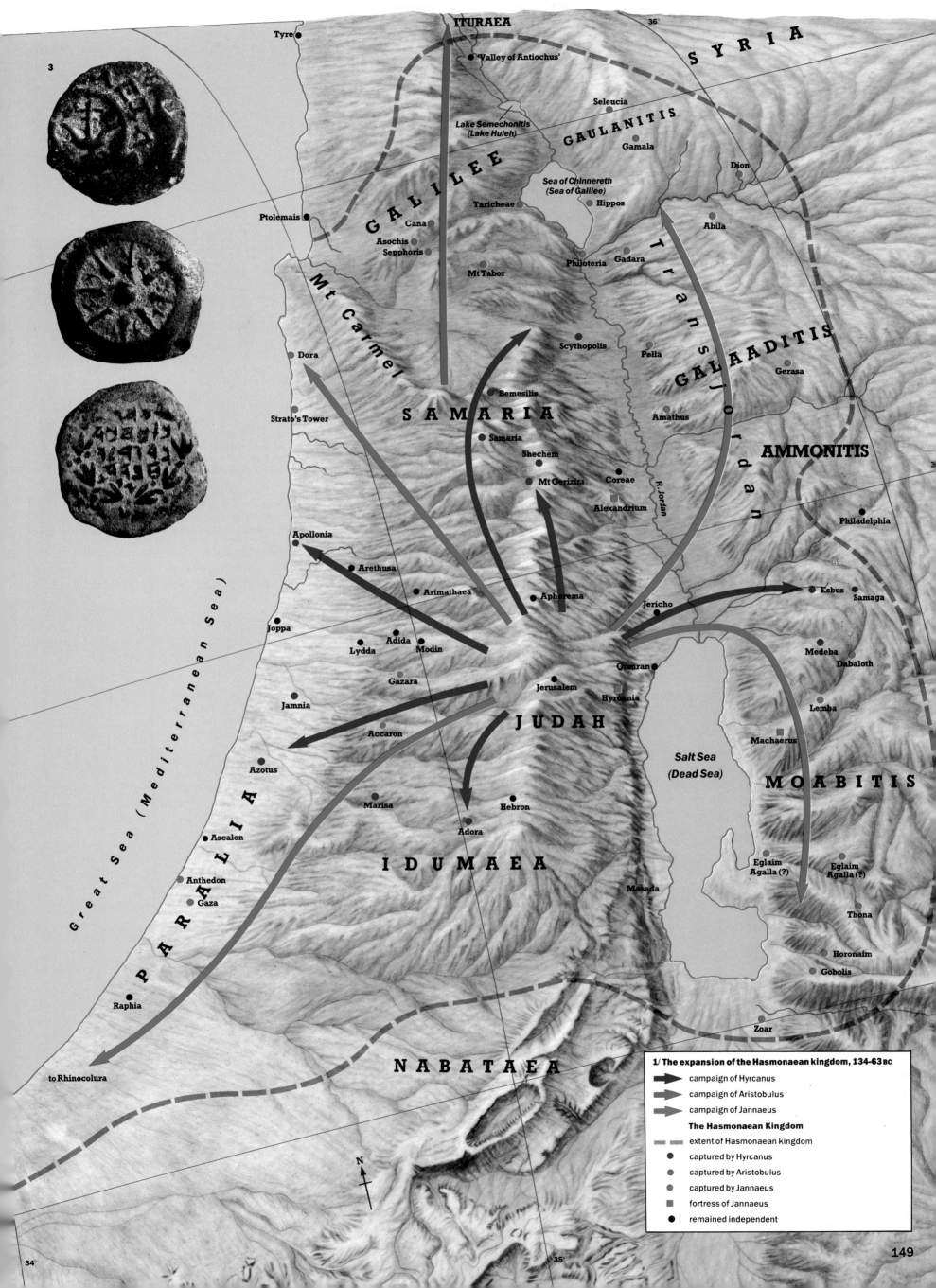

TYRE

ITURAEA

SYRIA

'Valley of Antiochus'

Seleucia

Lake Semechonitis
(Lake Huleh)

GAULANITIS

Gamala

Dion

GALILEE

Sea of Chinnereth
(Sea of Galilee)

Taricheae

Hippos

Abila

Cana

Philoteria Gadara

Asochis
Sepphoris

Mt Tabor

Ptolemais

T
r
a
n
s
j
o
r
d
a
n

G A L A A D I T I S

Scythopolis

Pella

Gerasa

Dora

S A M A R I A

Bemesilis

Amathus

AMMONITIS

Mt Carmel

Strato's Tower

Samaria

Shechem

Philadelphia

Apollonia

Mt Gerizim

Coreae

R. Jordan

Arethusa

Alexandrium

Arimathaea

Esbus

Samaga

Joppa

Apherema

Jericho

Lydda Adida

Qumran

Medeba

Modin

Dabaloth

Gazara

Jerusalem

J U D A H

Hyrcania

Lemba

Jamnia

Accaron

Machaerus

Salt Sea
(Dead Sea)

M O A B I T I S

Marisa

Hebron

Azotus

Adora

Ascalon

I D U M A E A

Masada

Anthedon

Eglaim
Agalla (?)

Eglaim
Agalla (?)

Gaza

Thona

G
r
e
a
t

S
e
a

(
M
e
d
i
t
e
r
r
a
n
e
a
n

S
e
a
)

P
A
R
A
L
I
A

Horonaim

Gobolis

Raphia

to Rhinocolura

Zoar

N A B A T A E A

N

149

1/ The expansion of the Hasmonaean kingdom, 134–63 BC

→ campaign of Hyrcanus

→ campaign of Aristobulus

→ campaign of Jannaeus

The Hasmonaean Kingdom

– – – extent of Hasmonaean kingdom

● captured by Hyrcanus

● captured by Aristobulus

● captured by Jannaeus

■ fortress of Jannaeus

● remained independent

In the 2nd century BC there was a sharp decline in the power of the Greek kings of the eastern Mediterranean world, as Roman merchants, diplomacy and conquest penetrated it. The policy of Rome, whose diplomacy reached far, was consistently to weaken any strong power in the east and at this time she was at war on every front.

To the east, the Macedonian king and the Greek cities were perceived as a threat to Italy itself by the Roman senate. From an allied kingdom Macedonia became first a protectorate (167 BC), and then a province (148 BC), from which Achaea (Greece) was also controlled. It was the respect felt for Rome by a Greek prince that gave her a first foothold in Asia Minor. When Antiochus III the Seleucid emperor was defeated, the Romans had left the Attalid dynasty of Pergamum in control of the western parts of Asia Minor, but in 133 BC the last Attalid died without heirs, and bequeathed Pergamene territories to Rome. They were reconstituted as the Roman province of Asia. At that time other kingdoms in Asia Minor such as Bithynia, Pontus and Cappadocia were still ruled by Iranian princes, heirs to the old Persian satraps who had held authority from the Achaemenids. Rome was drawn into conflict with the ambitious king of Pontus, Mithridates VI Eupator. Sulla forced Mithridates to withdraw from Galatia, Bithynia and Asia, but still recognized him as king of Pontus and 'ally (socius) of Rome'. Afterwards Bithynia came to Rome by bequest.

Meanwhile, however, Mithridates had married the daughter of Tigranes of Armenia, whose conquests were extending into Mesopotamia, Media, Asia Minor and North Syria. While Tigranes pressed on into Syria, Mithridates invaded the new Roman province of Bithynia (74 BC); but the Roman consul Lucullus with five legions stopped both men. He drove Mithridates not only from Bithynia, but from Pontus into Armenia. And when Tigranes, who had reached Damascus in Syria (72 BC), returned to Armenia (69 BC), Lucullus defeated both Mithridates and Tigranes.

'Extraordinary' powers were granted by the senate of Rome to Pompey by special laws of 67 BC and 66 BC. This was because Roman corn supplies had been threatened by pirates who controlled Cilicia. Pompey cleared Cilicia of this threat. Then with command granted to him over the entire Roman east and with powers to undertake whatever

ROME IN THE EAST

With the defeat of the Seleucid Antiochus III in 190 BC, Rome gradually became the ascendant power in the Near East. Between 67 and 63 BC the Roman general Pompey campaigned in Asia Minor and under his 'Eastern Settlement' the Jewish Hasmonaean state was reduced to the provinces of Judaea and Idumaea. Aristobulus was deposed by Pompey, and Hyrcanus was appointed in his place as high priest and ethnarch.

campaigns and settlements he thought necessary, he continued the successes of Lucullus. Mithradates was driven from Asia Minor; Tigranes submitted to Rome; Syria was secured (64 BC); and Palestine was reorganized (64-63 BC).

In his famous 'Eastern Settlement' Pompey formed a line of provinces around the coastline of Asia Minor and North Syria: 'Bithynia et Pontus', 'Asia', 'Cilicia' and 'Syria'. Beyond this the peculiar status of clientela which Rome formed with subordinate allies was employed. Local rulers became 'client-kings', acting as buffer-states against aggression from the Parthian East, and named 'friends' (amici) or 'allies' (socii) of Rome. In northern Mesopotamia Pompey deliberately thwarted Parthian claims, assigning Mesopotamian territory to Tigranes, who kept Armenia. In south Syria too, Pompey left certain princedoms intact – Jewish Judaea and Arab Chalcis (Ituraea) and Nabataea. But it was his general boast when he returned to Rome that he had founded or reconstituted a large number of 'Greek' (Hellenized) city-states at the expense of various lesser kings in Asia Minor and Syria.

The larger Jewish state of Alexander Jannaeus suffered severely, being reduced to Judaea (with Idumaea), Galilee and Peraea (east of the Jordan). The Samaritans retained a small state around Shechem and the temple on Mt Gerizim (Samaria). As for the Hasmonaean princes who had been in control of Judaea, Pompey deposed Aristobulus II (67-63 BC)

2/ Pompey's settlement of the Hasmonaean Jewish State 64-40 BC

- Hasmonaean state before Pompey's settlement
- ■ large towns within the borders of non-Jewish states
- Jewish state after Pompey's settlement
- ○ other independent cities
- Jewish territories ceded to Ituraea and Ptolemais
- ▲ Gabinius' synedria
- Samaritan state
- ⋈ fortress of Jannaeus
- cities of the Decapolis
- ∿ other political boundary

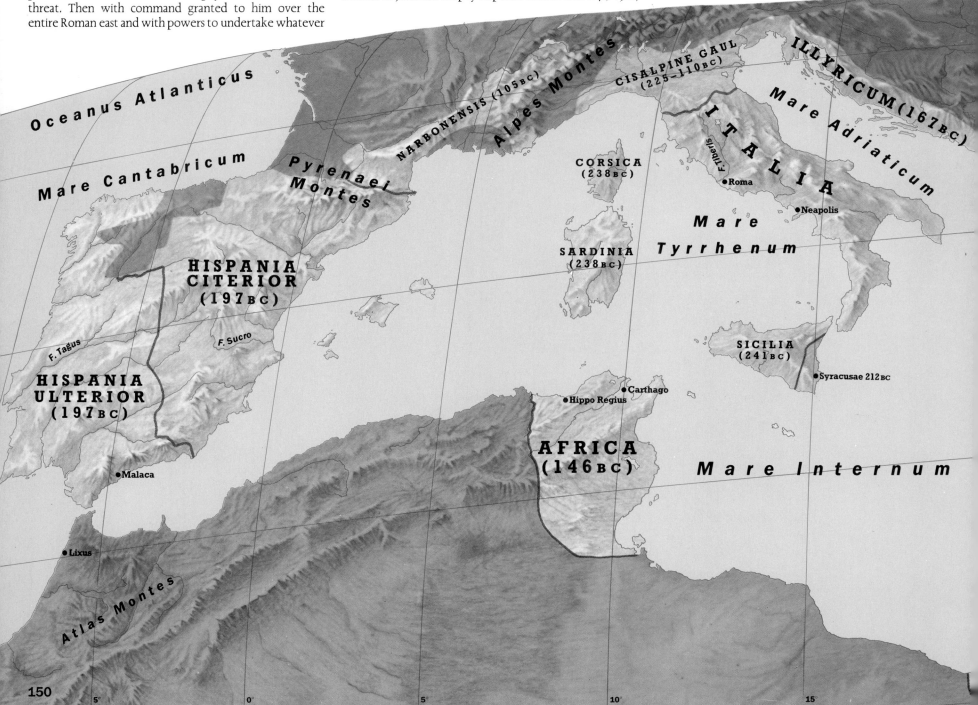

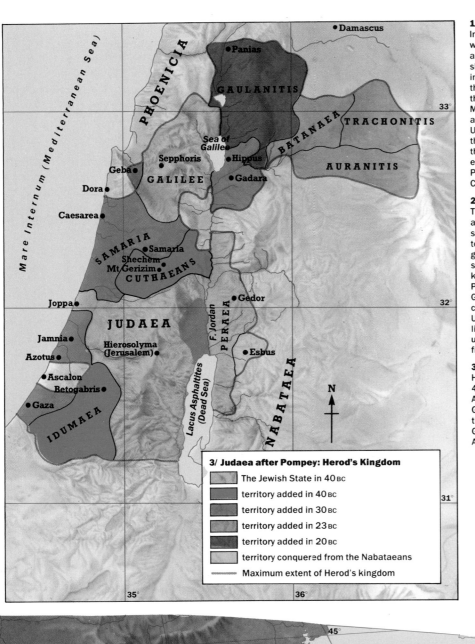

1/ Map below

In the 2nd century BC Rome was at war on every front. To the west as a result of the wars with Carthage, she gained the provinces of Spain in 197 BC and Africa in 146 BC. In the east Roman legions defeated the Seleucids in 190 BC, and Macedonia and Asia were annexed in 148 BC and 129 BC. Under Sulla, Lucullus and Pompey, the Romans gradually defeated the princedoms of Asia Minor and extended their control to Bithynia, Pontus, Cilicia, Syria, Crete and Cyprus.

2/ Map far left

The decline of Seleucid rule had allowed the Hasmonaean Jewish state under Jannaeus (103-76 BC) to expand. In 64 BC the Roman general Pompey and his successor Gabinius reduced the kingdom to Judaea, Galilee and Peraea, and allowed the 20 or so Greek cities which Jannaeus had captured to become independent. Under Gabinius (57-55 BC) a short-lived attempt was made to divide up the Jewish state yet further into five *synedria* (districts).

3/ Map left

Herod became king of Judaea in 40 BC, and soon found favour with Augustus. He was given back Gaza and the coastal cities and the provinces of Batanaea, Gaulanitis, Trachonitis and Auranitis.

3/ Judaea after Pompey: Herod's Kingdom

- The Jewish State in 40 BC
- territory added in 40 BC
- territory added in 30 BC
- territory added in 23 BC
- territory added in 20 BC
- territory conquered from the Nabataeans
- Maximum extent of Herod's kingdom

in favour of his elder brother Hyrcanus II (63-40 BC). He received the title 'High Priest and Ethnarch'.

At this time Rome was troubled by the inadequacies of the old republican system of government, by political faction and by a contest of power between Pompey and Julius Caesar. A series of crises emerged, until finally in 27 BC the period of civil unrest ended. Octavian received the title 'Augustus', extraordinary constitutional powers and control of the most important provinces and armies. Rome, which had become an empire, now had an emperor.

During the time of unrest the 'friends' of Rome had to be politically agile. The Hasmonaean ruler Hyrcanus, had as his able adviser an ambitious Idumaean, Antipater. They switched their allegiance from Pompey to Julius Caesar at the right time to survive. When Antipater died, Mark Antony, friend of Caesar, nominated his sons Herod and Phasael as tetrarchs of the Jewish state. There followed clashes in Syria and at Jerusalem between Parthian and Roman troops supporting different Jewish 'pretenders'. In 40 BC the Roman senate declared Herod 'King of Judaea'; in 37 BC 11 Roman legions under Sosius, lieutenant of Mark Antony, drove the Parthians out of Jerusalem and Herod became king *de facto*. In 31 BC Herod was confirmed by Octavian as client-king, his enmity with Cleopatra serving him well. He held in 31 BC the areas he had governed since 37 BC: Judaea (with Idumaea), Samaria, Galilee, Peraea. In 30 BC he was also granted rule over the Greek cities of Samaria, Hippus, Gadara and all the coastal cities (except the free state of Ascalon). From this time on the areas of Jewish settlement were governed either by the house of Herod or by Roman officials direct.

'POMPEY NEXT DEPRIVED THE JEWS OF THE TOWNS THEY HAD OCCUPIED IN COELE SYRIA, PUTTING THEM UNDER A ROMAN GOVERNOR SPECIALLY APPOINTED; THIS MEANT THAT THE NATION WAS CONFINED WITHIN ITS OWN BOUNDARIES. HE REBUILT GADARA, WHICH THE JEWS HAD RAZED TO THE GROUND, AS A FAVOUR TO A GADARENE AMONG HIS OWN FREEDMEN. HE ALSO FREED FROM THEIR RULE ALL SUCH INLAND TOWNS AS THEY HAD NOT ALREADY DESTROYED – HIPPUS, SCYTHOPOLIS, PELLA, SAMARIA, JAMNIA, AZOTUS AND ARETHUSA.
JOSEPHUS, WAR, BOOK I

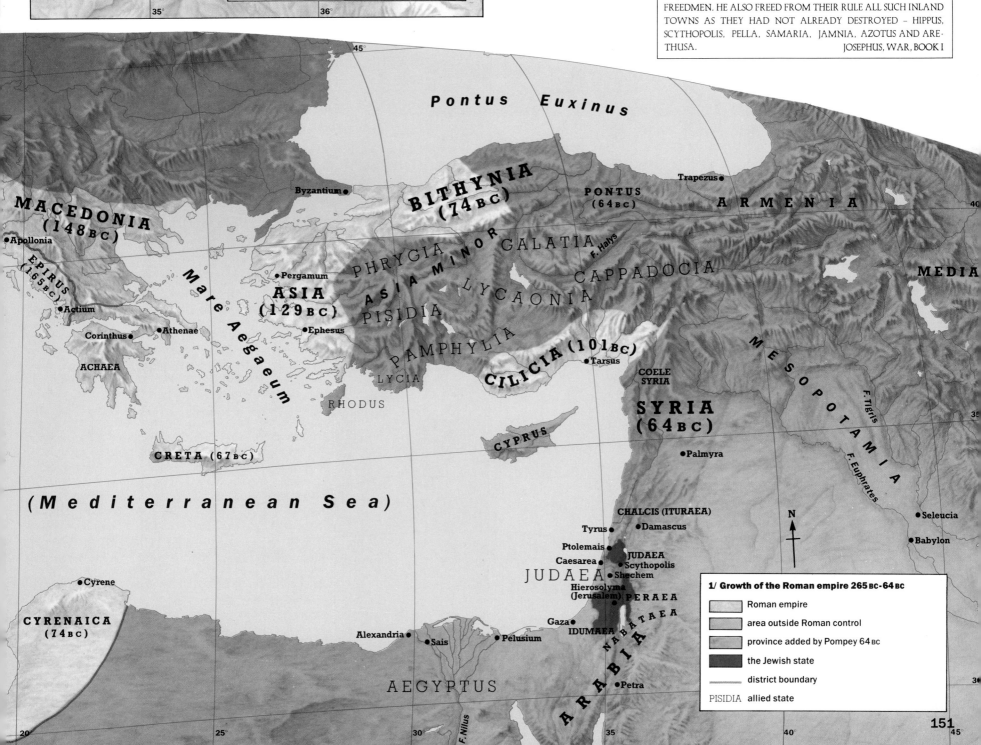

1/ Growth of the Roman empire 265 BC-64 BC

- Roman empire
- area outside Roman control
- province added by Pompey 64 BC
- the Jewish state
- district boundary
- PISIDIA allied state

Q UITE when the institution of the synagogue first began is uncertain. Both the Babylonian Exile after 587 BC and the period following the reaffirmation of the covenant by the Jews led by Ezra in 5th-century BC Judah provide suitable contexts for the inauguration of a regular method for reminding Jews of their Law, but it is only in the 3rd century BC that the earliest papyri from Egypt refer to the existence of a synagogue. By the 1st century AD, however, many sources assume that synagogues have become widespread both in Palestine and in the diaspora. The gospels refer to synagogues in the villages of Galilee, and Acts refers to the many synagogues of Jerusalem. An inscription found in Jerusalem which was set up before AD 70 by a certain Theodotus boasts of the synagogue and hospice which he had erected. Both Acts and the letters of Paul give testimony to the synagogues which were found in every diaspora community and Josephus implies that

THE DEVELOPMENT OF THE SYNAGOGUE

The Greek term *synagōguē* simply means 'assembly', but the word has long been accorded by Jews a more specific meaning. The synagogue, as the focal point of Jewish communities and the main institution through which the study and dissemination of the divine Law was carried on, was one of the most distinctive and important religious achievements of the Jews of late antiquity.

of some diaspora synagogues such as that at Antioch in his day. However, such considerations conflicted in the bigger cities with the more mundane but central task of teaching the Law: the great synagogue of Alexandria is said to have been so huge that those at the back could not hear the blessings and had to wait for a lackey to wave a handkerchief to know when to respond with 'Amen'. Usually, therefore, the larger Jewish communities preferred to set up a number of synagogues for each city.

It should be noted that contemporary references to the magnificence of some synagogue buildings are confined in the 1st century BC to the diaspora. The significance of this imbalance may be partly confirmed by archaeological discoveries. In Palestine, up to now, only three buildings have been claimed by their excavators as synagogues erected before AD 70. Two of these, at Masada and at Herodium, were discovered within royal palaces, and in both cases the Jewish rebels who held the fortresses for a few years after AD 66 converted existing public buildings by the addition of stone benches around the walls. At Gamala on the Golan an impressive edifice found near the town wall has been tentatively dated to the 1st century BC. These buildings were certainly intended for some public use, but whether that included the reading of the Torah, the main function of the synagogue, is less certain. This meagre harvest of archaeological evidence from Palestine for the years before AD 70, in contrast to the considerable remains from the later Roman period and despite extensive excavation, suggests that synagogues in the holy land were not regularly built in a monumental style while the Temple stood in Jerusalem. In the diaspora only slightly more archaeological evidence survives for this early period: the inscriptions dedicated to 'the most high God' which were found within a monumental building of the 1st century BC at Delos show that this was almost certainly a synagogue, and there are also traces of a synagogue at Ostia in the 1st century AD, although little can be said about its design. The scanty archaeological evidence for the diaspora buildings is, however, less significant than in Palestine, as the search for

3/ Right
This artist's reconstruction is based on the archaeological remains of the mid-4th century AD synagogue at Horbat Shema'.

some of these institutions had been in existence for many years. By contrast, the majority of the inscriptions and archaeological remains from ancient synagogues date from the 3rd century AD and after.

The function of the synagogues was to provide for the reading and interpretation for the whole Jewish community of the divine Law as enshrined in the Torah, ie, the Pentateuch. The spread of the synagogue assumes universal acceptance by Jews of this sacred text. Kept in a special case within an ark, the scroll of the Torah was the visual and religious focus of synagogue liturgy. Such veneration for a holy scripture marked out Judaism from other religions in antiquity: most literature produced by Jews in this period consisted of commentary on, or paraphrase of, the Torah, and all Jewish ethics and theology were expressed in its terms. Hence the significance of the weekly readings which ensured that the Torah was available to all those who wished to come and listen.

In many places synagogues were more than just places of teaching. The congregation once assembled could take on a political role, and in cities where Jews were in a minority the synagogue provided a physical focus for the community. Communal funds were deposited there, and the officials of the synagogue fulfilled the tasks of lay leaders. Courts sat in the synagogues and it was there that punishment was sometimes executed (cf ACTS 22.19; 26.11). Hostels for visitors were also sometimes attached to the place of assembly. This social function of synagogues was naturally less prominent among the predominantly Jewish communities of Palestine, where synagogue officers probably lacked any secular authority, but in the cosmopolitan Jewish metropolis of Jerusalem Jews reinforced their regional identities by imitating the diaspora and setting up small synagogues for their own nationalities (cf ACTS 6.9).

This role of the synagogue as the public expression of Jewish identity in sometimes hostile places encouraged the building of large edifices as a testimony to, and reinforcement of, the social significance of the Jews who commissioned them. Thus Josephus writes about the magnificence

1/ Map left
The great majority of synagogue remains throughout the diaspora date from the late Roman and Byzantine periods. In the diaspora fine structures have been uncovered at Ostia, Sardis and Dura-Europos. In their final phases the synagogue at Dura belonged to the mid-3rd century AD and those at Ostia and Sardis were erected in the 4th century or later.

2/ Map below left
The map shows the distribution of synagogue remains in Roman Palestine. There is only scant evidence for synagogues prior to AD 70, Masada, Herodium and Gamala are the only examples. However, in later periods synagogues were built throughout the area.

1/ Synagogue sites in the Diaspora
✳ remains of synagogue
⊛ possible remains of synagogue

2/ Synagogue sites in Roman Palestine
✳ synagogue remains

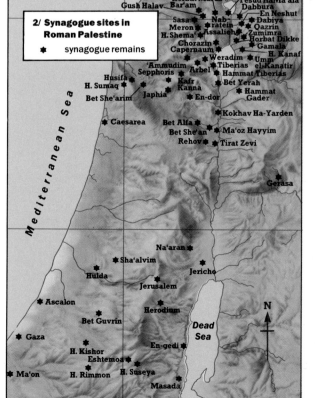

early synagogues outside the holy land has preoccupied archaeologists far less.

It is probable that the greater magnificence of diaspora synagogues before AD 70 reflects their greater religious significance outside Palestine in that period. Since synagogues existed originally only to *teach* the Law, and since Torah was also interpreted informally on a different, perhaps more sophisticated, level by expert scholars (scribes), religious developments in the *observance* of the Law in such matters as the keeping of the Sabbath and the accordance of importance to purity rules took place in 1st century Palestine without the involvement of the synagogues. In Palestine it was possible to be a pious Jew without recourse to a synagogue – John the Baptist was one such Jew. So, for instance, prayer, which provided direct access to the divine, was probably considered an exclusively private form of worship, for MT 6.5 castigates praying in synagogues as ostentatious; in the diaspora, by contrast, synagogues are sometimes described even in this period as 'prayer houses'. Above all, Jews recognized that the most effective worship was through sacrifices in Jerusalem.

'AND HE ENTERED THE SYNAGOGUE AND FOR THREE MONTHS SPOKE BOLDLY, ARGUING AND PLEADING ABOUT THE KINGDOM OF GOD: BUT WHEN SOME WERE STUBBORN AND DISBELIEVED, SPEAKING EVIL OF THE WAY BEFORE THE CONGREGATION, HE WITHDREW FROM THEM, TAKING THE DISCIPLES WITH HIM...'
ACTS 19.8-9

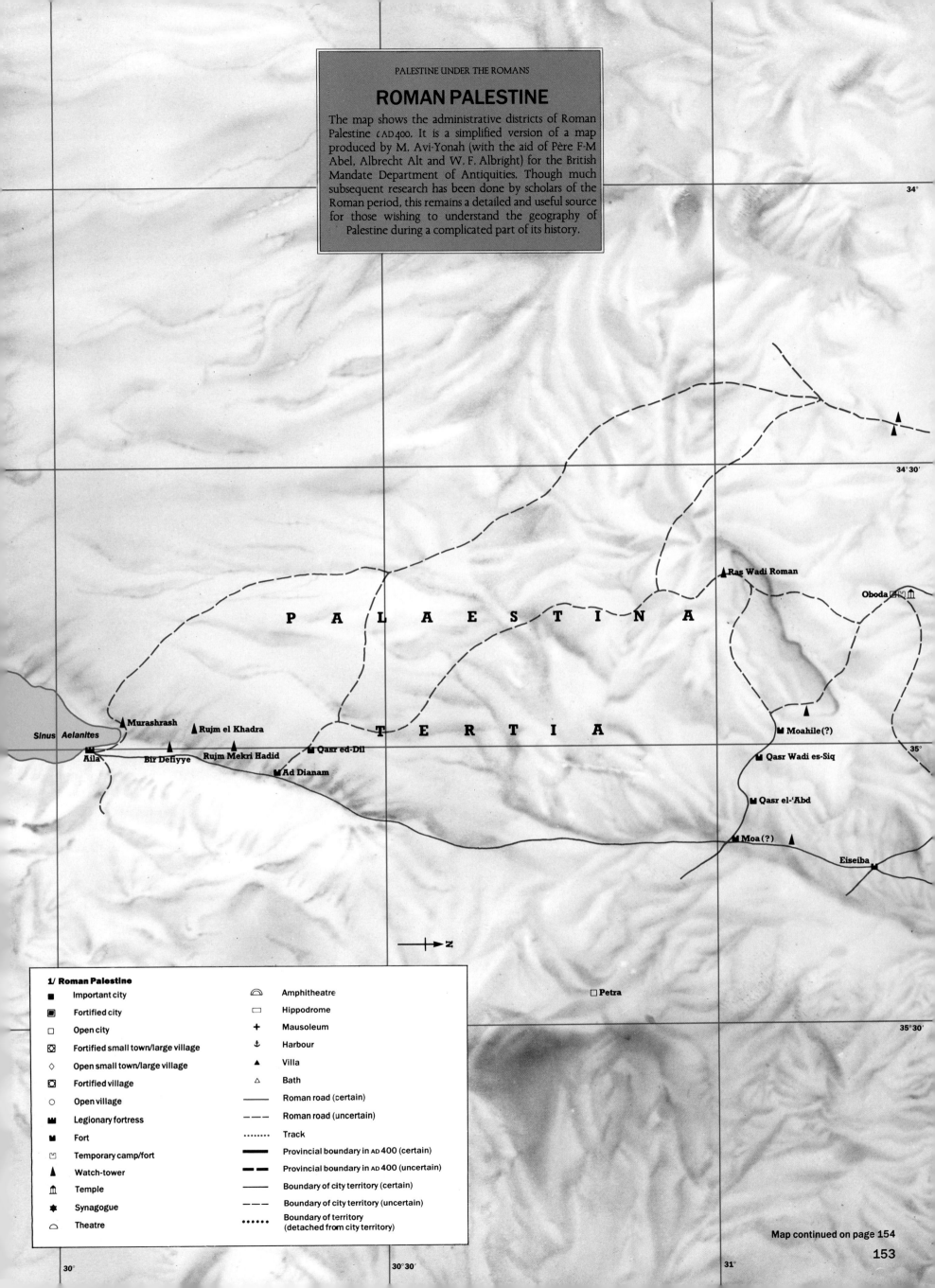

PALESTINE UNDER THE ROMANS
ROMAN PALESTINE

The map shows the administrative districts of Roman Palestine *c* AD 400. It is a simplified version of a map produced by M. Avi-Yonah (with the aid of Père F-M Abel, Albrecht Alt and W. F. Albright) for the British Mandate Department of Antiquities. Though much subsequent research has been done by scholars of the Roman period, this remains a detailed and useful source for those wishing to understand the geography of Palestine during a complicated part of its history.

P A L A E S T I N A

T E R T I A

Ras Wadi Roman

Oboda

Moahile (?)

Qasr Wadi es-Siq

Qasr el-'Abd

Moa (?)

Eiseiba

Sinus Aelanites

Murashrash

Rujm el Khadra

Aila

Bir Defiyye

Rujm Mekri Hadid

Qasr ed-Dil

Ad Dianam

□ Petra

1/ Roman Palestine

■	Important city	⌒	Amphitheatre
▣	Fortified city	⊓	Hippodrome
□	Open city	+	Mausoleum
⊠	Fortified small town/large village	⚓	Harbour
◇	Open small town/large village	▲	Villa
⊡	Fortified village	△	Bath
○	Open village	——	Roman road (certain)
⊞	Legionary fortress	- - -	Roman road (uncertain)
⬓	Fort	⋯⋯	Track
⌒	Temporary camp/fort	▬▬	Provincial boundary in AD 400 (certain)
▲	Watch-tower	▬ ▬	Provincial boundary in AD 400 (uncertain)
🏛	Temple	——	Boundary of city territory (certain)
✹	Synagogue	— —	Boundary of city territory (uncertain)
⌒	Theatre	••••••	Boundary of territory (detached from city territory)

Map continued on page 154

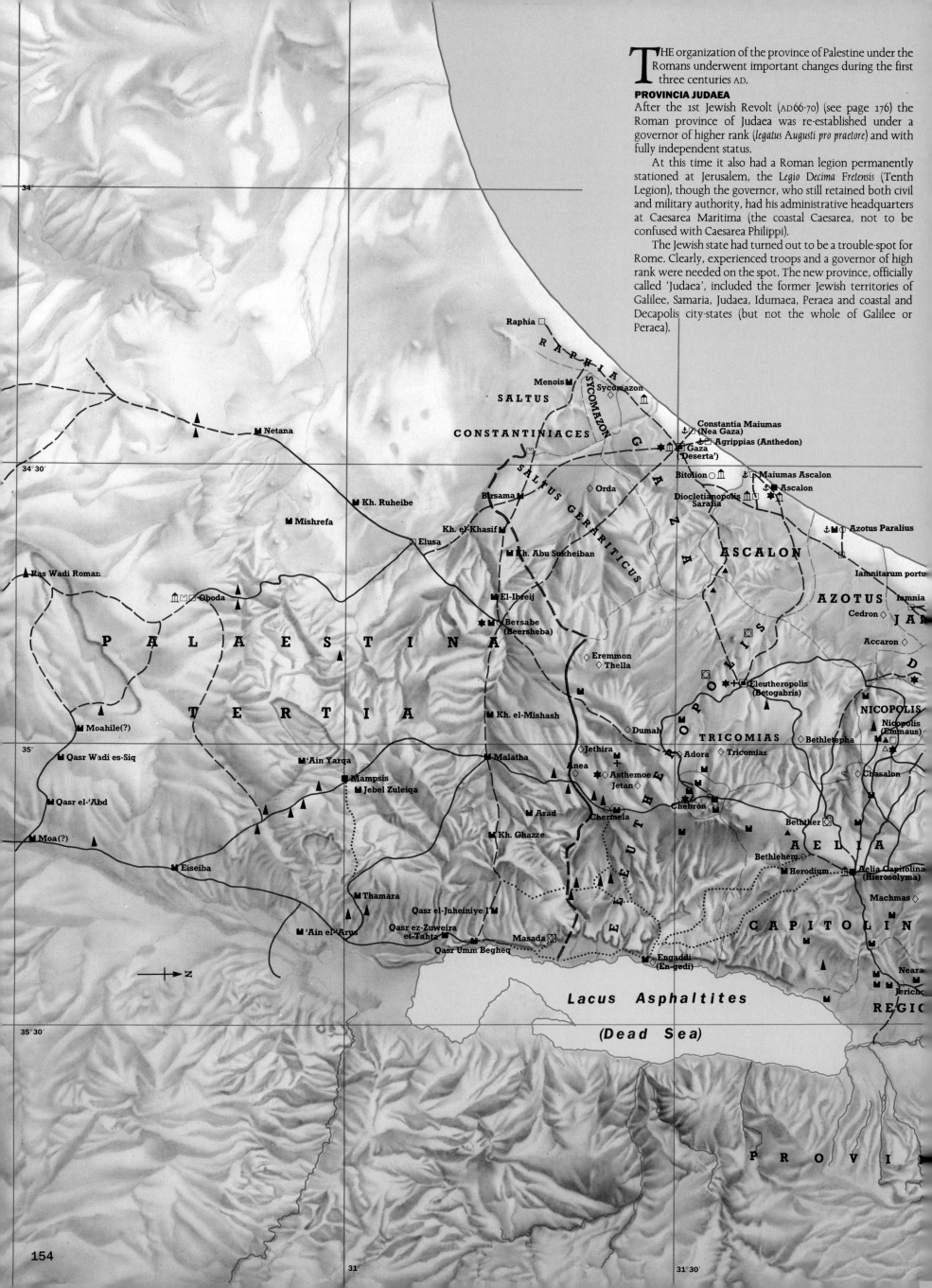

THE organization of the province of Palestine under the Romans underwent important changes during the first three centuries AD.

PROVINCIA JUDAEA

After the 1st Jewish Revolt (AD66-70) (see page 176) the Roman province of Judaea was re-established under a governor of higher rank (*legatus Augusti pro praetore*) and with fully independent status.

At this time it also had a Roman legion permanently stationed at Jerusalem, the *Legio Decima Fretensis* (Tenth Legion), though the governor, who still retained both civil and military authority, had his administrative headquarters at Caesarea Maritima (the coastal Caesarea, not to be confused with Caesarea Philippi).

The Jewish state had turned out to be a trouble-spot for Rome. Clearly, experienced troops and a governor of high rank were needed on the spot. The new province, officially called 'Judaea', included the former Jewish territories of Galilee, Samaria, Judaea, Idumaea, Peraea and coastal and Decapolis city-states (but not the whole of Galilee or Peraea).

34°

34° 30'

35°

35° 30'

Raphia

Menois
Sycomazon
SALTUS
SYCOMAZON
CONSTANTINIACES
Constantia Maiumas (Nea Gaza)
Gaza ('Deserta')
Agrippias (Anthedon)

Netana

SALTUS GERARITICUS
Bitolion
Maiumas Ascalon
Ascalon

Kh. Ruheibe
Orda
Diocletianopolis Sarafia

Birsama
ASCALON

Mishrefa

Elusa
Kh. el-Khasif
Azotus Paralius

Ras Wadi Roman
Kh. Abu Sukheiban
Iamnitarum portu
AZOTUS
Iamnia
Cedron

Oboda
El-Ibreij
Accaron

P A L A E S T I N A
Bersabe (Beersheba)
Eremmon
Thella
Eleutheropolis (Betogabris)
NICOPOLIS
Nicopolis (Emmaus)

T E R T I A
Kh. el-Mishash
Dumah
TRICOMIAS
Bethletepha

Moahile(?)
Jethira
Adora
Tricomias
Chasalon

Qasr Wadi es-Siq
Malatha
Anea
Asthemoe

'Ain Yarqa
Jetan
Chebron

Qasr el-'Abd
Mampsis
Jebel Zuleiqa
Chermela
Bethzer

Moa(?)
Arad
Bethlehem
AELIA

Eiseiba
Kh. Ghazze
Herodium
Aelia Capitolina (Hierosolyma)

Machmas

Thamara
Qasr el-Juheiniye I
CAPITOLIN

'Ain el-Arus
Qasr ez-Zuweira et-Tahta
Masada

Qasr Umm Begheq
Engaddi (En-gedi)
Neara

Jericho

Lacus Asphaltites

REGIO

(Dead Sea)

P R O V I

P R O V I N

N→Z

The city-territories of Caesarea, Sebaste (Samaria) and Scythopolis (Beth-shean) had acted as barriers between areas of Jewish sympathies during the Revolt; even the Jewish 'cities' of Tiberias and Sepphoris in Galilee had been reluctant or unwilling to join the struggle. It seems that awareness of this political fact stimulated Rome to a new strategy of 'urbanization', by which under Vespasian (later Hadrian and Severus) temple-states became city-territories. The villages and estates were administered by a growing class of provincial aristocrats served by local businessmen, Hellenized pro-Roman sympathizers who collected Rome's taxes for her, whose well-being in fact depended on Rome. The enormous new self-governing territories removed a great burden of administration. Moreover the principle of 'divide-and-rule' cut across the loyalties created by 'tribal' or 'ethnic' (national) cultures and religions.

Vespasian (AD 69-79) restored Gabaa, Apollonia, Antipatris (former Pegae-Arethusa), Flavia Joppe (former Joppa), Jamnia and Azotus (former Ashdod) as autonomous city-territories, internally self-governing and not subject to a Jewish authority any longer (though in fact Joppa now had a large Jewish community, which it still retained in the 3rd century AD).

In Galilee, Sepphoris and Tiberias became autonomous, and their territories were soon enlarged to cover all Lower Galilee. The part of the former Samaritan temple-state which had not been absorbed into the city-territory of Samaria-Sebaste was reconstituted now as another city-territory, Flavia Neapolis (modern Nablus). However, Upper Galilee and the Golan remained under the direct administration of the Roman legate based at Caesarea. Jerusalem itself, taken by the Roman troops in AD 70, became a permanent camp and military area, until Hadrian decided to establish a Roman colony there. Parts of Peraea and the Jordan Valley were of special economic significance

to Rome, and were administered direct as imperial estates (including Jericho).

PROVINCIA SYRIA PALAESTINA
In the Second Jewish War (AD 132-5) Bar Kochba for a time destroyed Roman power over a substantial area involving at least Judaea and parts of Samaria. However, the Revolt was overcome (see page 180).

The Roman Emperor Hadrian (AD 117-138) re-founded Jerusalem as a Roman colony, Aelia Capitolina, dedicated to Jupiter. Once more a Jewish Revolt produced a change in provincial status. Now two legions and a governor of the highest (consular) rank were established in a Roman province re-named *Provincia Syria Palaestina*. The *Legio Sexta Ferrata* (Sixth Legion) occupied a new region of military lands, this time east of Caesarea and north of Sebaste. The legionary camp at Capercotnei gave to the place its new name *Legio* (modern Lejjun), which later became a city-territory with the Valley of Jezreel as the veterans' lands (*campus maximus legionis*).

The Emperor Severus (AD 193-211) advanced Idumaea including En-gedi to city-status as Eleutheropolis (former Betogabris); also Lydda to Diospolis (the former Judaean districts of Lydda and Thamna). Soon afterwards in AD 220-1 Heliogabalus did the same for Emmaus, which became the city of Nicopolis. Thus by AD 221 the whole of Palestine, except for certain imperial estates, had been transformed into a net of larger and smaller city-territories as shown on the map. The estates remaining were in the Jordan Valley and Upper Galilee (Tetracomia). A similar development east of the Jordan turned the Nabataean kingdom into an imperial province, Provincia Arabia, which was rapidly 'urbanized'.

THE THREE PALESTINES
The province so constituted was then, following policies effected or promoted by Diocletian (AD 284-305), slightly adapted first to a separation of authority, then to a system of provincial sub-division.

Diocletian, here as elsewhere, divided the Roman legions into field-armies and frontier-troops. He set up a strip of military territory along the southern border of Idumaea, defined as *Limes Palaestinae*. This provided defensive forts connected by roads. At its western end it was later divided into *Saltus Constantiaces*, the city of Sycomazon and *Saltus Gerariticus*.

Diocletian divided civil from military command, creating the new army-rank of *Dux Palaestinae*. About AD 358 the Roman province was split at the *limes* (border), the area south of Beersheba being added as *Palaestina Salutaris* (*Palaestina Tertia*) with Petra as its capital. Then about AD 400 the area north of the *limes* was divided in two as *Palaestina Prima* (capital Caesarea) and *Palaestina Secunda* (capital Scythopolis). These late divisions are the overall frame within which the 6th and 7th century AD city-lists are given by Hierocles and Georgius Cyprius. Avi-Yonah's map does not extend to Byzantine developments.

THE ROAD-SYSTEMS
The milestones set up by Roman surveyors were the base for ancient maps, from which the *Onomasticon* of Eusebius and Jerome report accurate figures, assigning villages to city-territories. The Roman road-system was created quite late, largely produced by the presence of the legions, not the earlier auxiliaries of the procuratorial province. Only one section of road – along the coast – can so far be dated as early as Nero (AD 54-68); the other main periods of road-building are associated by inscriptions with Vespasian (AD 69-79), Trajan (AD 97-117) and Hadrian (AD 117-138). It seems likely that the Roman road between Caesarea and Jerusalem was begun soon after AD 70.

> 'POMPEY NEXT DEPRIVED THE JEWS OF THE TOWNS THEY HAD OCCUPIED IN COELE SYRIA, PUTTING THEM UNDER A ROMAN GOVERNOR SPECIALLY APPOINTED; THIS MEANT THAT THE NATION WAS CONFINED WITHIN ITS OWN BOUNDARIES. HE REBUILT GADARA, WHICH THE JEWS HAD RAZED TO THE GROUND, AS A FAVOUR TO A GADARENE AMONG HIS OWN FREEMEN. HE ALSO FREED FROM THEIR RULE ALL SUCH INLAND TOWNS AS THEY HAD NOT ALREADY DESTROYED – HIPPUS, SCYTHOPOLIS, PELLA, SAMARIA, JAMNIA, MARISA, AZOTUS AND ARETHUSA …'
> JOSEPHUS, WAR, BOOK 1

IN the late summer of 30 BC Octavian (Augustus) confirmed Herod as king and accorded him the lands Antony had assigned to Cleopatra, with the exception of Dora and Ascalon. In addition he gave him two of the Decapolis cities. Hippus and Gadara. Other cities of the Decapolis came under his jurisdiction in 23 BC when he was given the wild districts of Batanaea, Auranitis and Trachonitis. Now virtually all the territory around the Sea of Galilee was within his grasp, and he closed his grip on it when Augustus gave him Gaulanitis. The only land that Herod won by force of arms was the territory around Esbus, which he took from the Nabataeans in 32 BC.

Our knowledge of the boundaries of city territories and other divisions comes chiefly from Eusebius, other Church fathers, and Talmudic sources. Epigraphical evidence is important for the boundaries of Batanaea and its adjacent territories. Several divisions known to us originated after Herod's time, so some of the Herodian limits are conjectural. Recent archaeological research has shown that certain boundaries (Gaba, Narbattene and Ptolemais) require revision – the territory of Ptolemais because the main lines of the field divisions of the Roman veteran colony have recently been identified.

Herod's kingdom, which he received from Rome in 40/39 BC, consisted of Judaea, Galilee, Peraea, Samaria and Idumaea. Sometime between 37 and 36 BC Herod was compelled to cede Ituraea to Cleopatra VII, plus parts of Nabataea, Jericho and other areas in Syria and Judaea, also the cities of Joppa, Gaza and Samaria (later Sebaste). These he recovered after the battle of Actium (31 BC). Most of the lost territories were restored to him by Augustus; they included Strato's Tower (later Caesarea), Anthedon, Gadara and Hippus (Susita).

In 23 BC Herod received from Augustus Batanaea, Trachonitis and Auranitis, in 20 BC Hulata (the Lake Huleh area) and Paneas (later Caesarea Philippi). Ascalon remained independent, being a free city and ally of Rome.

Herod further owned vast estates derived from the Hasmonaean rulers, or confiscated from their supporters. A list of these areas cannot be included here; the largest were Trachonitis, Batanaea and Auranitis, much of the Plain of Esdraelon, the Plain of Jericho, the entirety of Peraea and probably much of the problematic 'King's Mountain Country' (in Judaea and southern Samaria). Recent archaeological surveys have shown further tracts in western Samaria and in western Narbattene. Another royal tract under military control may have extended to the east and west of Beersheba.

Herod's state was divided administratively into city territories and toparchies, the latter being areas lacking settlements of city status. The above units were grouped in five larger meridarchies, constituting respectively Idumaea, Judaea, Samaria, Galilee and Peraea.

On the death of Herod (4 BC) his dominions were divided among his three sons, Archelaus, Antipas and Philip. Archelaus received Judaea, Samaria and Idumaea; Antipas – Galilee and Peraea; Philip – Batanaea, Gaulanitis, Auranitis and Trachonitis. Most of Herod's royal estates seem to have been sold by the Roman government. Archelaus was deposed in AD 6 and his territory passed under direct Roman rule; Antipas was removed in AD 39. Gaza, Gadara and Hippus were transferred to the province of Syria. Scythopolis, though west of the R. Jordan, had belonged since Pompey's intervention to the Decapolis, and was administratively subject to Rome, as was Pella also.

References to populations in mixed areas are few and problematic. Samaria had been demographically mixed since the fall of the Israelite monarchy, and the records from the Wadi ed-Daliyeh cave in that area (late 4th century BC) refer not only to Samaritans but also to Idumaeans, Arabs, Moabites, Phoenicians and Babylonians. The populations of the maritime cities were no less cosmopolitan, and their more permanent elements were derived from Philistine, Phoenician, Greek and Jewish communities.

THE ECONOMY
Our economic information is based chiefly on sources not later than the 1st century BC. References to individual products relating to large areas are few; a more accurate distribution will only be obtained from forthcoming archaeological surveys. References to crops and industries in individual places are usual, but apt to be misleading, since given products (eg, cereals, wine, olives, olive-oil and figs) were obviously grown almost everywhere. Legumes were the chief substitute for meat among the greater part of the population, but there was an active fishing industry off the coast and around the Sea of Galilee, and fish salting was a flourishing industry. One of the successful industries in the

1st century was the growing of balsam (from which an aromatic resinous gum was extracted). It is clear that pottery was manufactured throughout the country. Flocks furnished the normal wool clothing of the population, and Nabataea perhaps produced the first fine white fleeces which ultimately became the refined wool of the Roman empire. The milk of sheep and goats served chiefly for the making of cheese. Recent excavations have revealed an extensive manufacture of flax at Gaba in the western plain of Esdraelon. The salt and asphalt of the Dead Sea were sought after, the latter being important for shipbuilding. The industries of the coastal cities are too little known; but the famous Tyrian purple was prepared all along the shore of Judaea; Ascalon produced grain, henna, onions and iron

PALESTINE UNDER THE ROMANS

HEROD'S KINGDOM

Rome was anxious not to expand her imperial administration beyond its limits and preferred to establish client kingdoms on the borders of the empire, which enjoyed some local autonomy, so long as loyalty to Rome was unquestioned. This was the situation in Palestine after Pompey's conquests and the Hasmonaean priests ruled for some time. However, the subsequent Herodian rulers – who as Idumaeans had no interest in Jewish nationalism – served the Roman interest better.

tools. Rice seems to have been grown in Judaea from Herod's time. Dates were exported, and Judaean fruit drinks were known to Pliny the Elder.

JUDAEA AFTER HEROD
Herod died in 4 BC. The bitterness with which his sons disputed his will was surpassed only by the violence of the Jewish repudiation of all three of them. Varus, with the legions from Antioch, had to suppress a bloody uprising; he had 2000 of the rebels crucified. It would have been more in character for Augustus to annex the kingdom, but after great hesitation he accepted the basic provisions of Herod's will, even though the division crippled a critical frontier state. He did, however, introduce a measure of direct Roman control by attaching the cities of Gaza, Hippus, Gadara and Esbus to the province of Syria. Philip, a wise ruler, died in AD 33 or 34 and his territory was joined to Syria, but in AD 37 was returned to Agrippa, a grandson of Herod the Great. Only because he had inherited a great portion of his father's cunning did Herod Antipas survive until AD 39, when he was banished to Gaul. Archelaus was dismissed and exiled by Augustus in AD 6. The emperor then put his territory under the direct control of a Roman governor of equestrian rank, who was only to some extent subordinate to the imperial legate in Syria.

> 'NOW WHEN JESUS WAS BORN IN BETHLEHEM OF JUDEA IN THE DAYS OF HEROD THE KING, BEHOLD, WISE MEN FROM THE EAST CAME TO JERUSALEM, SAYING, "WHERE IS HE WHO HAS BEEN BORN KING OF THE JEWS?" '
> MT 2.1

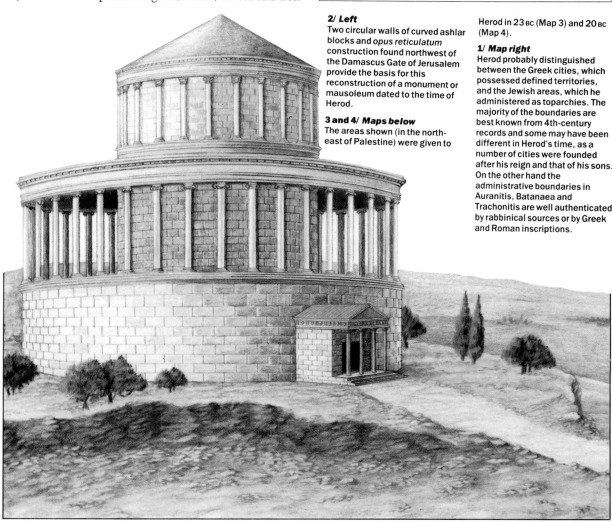

2/ Left
Two circular walls of curved ashlar blocks and *opus reticulatum* construction found northwest of the Damascus Gate of Jerusalem provide the basis for this reconstruction of a monument or mausoleum dated to the time of Herod.

3 and 4/ Maps below
The areas shown (in the north-east of Palestine) were given to

Herod in 23 BC (Map 3) and 20 BC (Map 4).

1/ Map right
Herod probably distinguished between the Greek cities, which possessed defined territories, and the Jewish areas, which he administered as toparchies. The majority of the boundaries are best known from 4th-century records and some may have been different in Herod's time, as a number of cities were founded after his reign and that of his sons. On the other hand the administrative boundaries in Auranitis, Batanaea and Trachonitis are well authenticated by rabbinical sources or by Greek and Roman inscriptions.

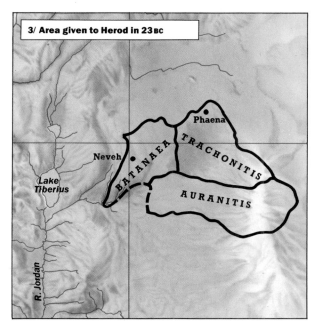

3/ Area given to Herod in 23 BC

Phaena
Neveh
BATANAEA
TRACHONITIS
AURANITIS
Lake Tiberius
R. Jordan

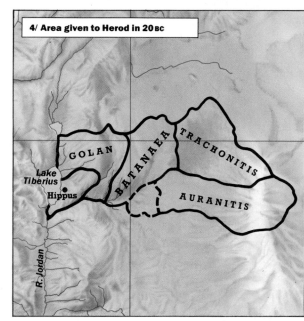

4/ Area given to Herod in 20 BC

GOLAN
BATANAEA
TRACHONITIS
AURANITIS
Lake Tiberius
Hippus
R. Jordan

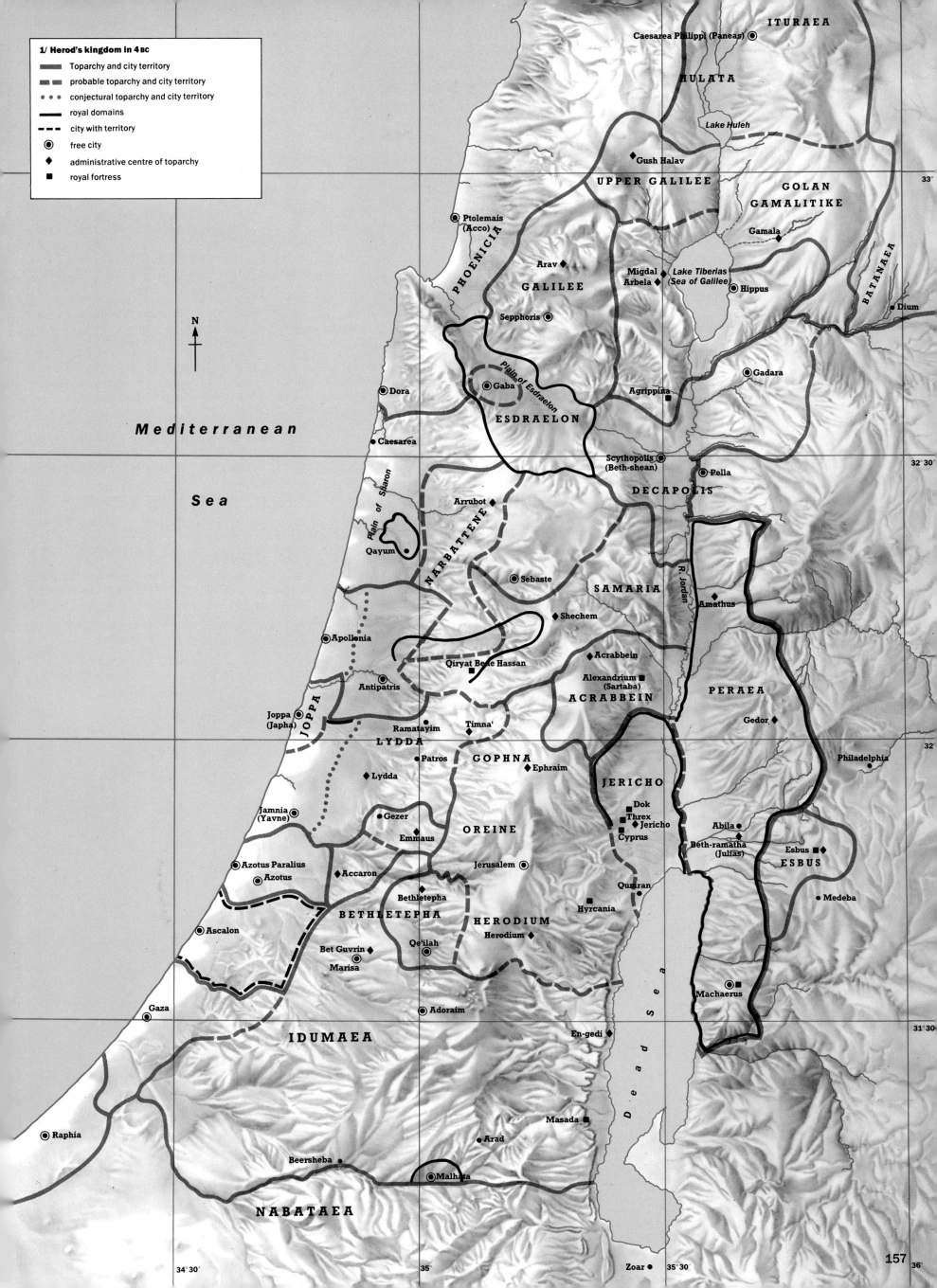

1/ Herod's kingdom in 4 BC

Toparchy and city territory
probable toparchy and city territory
conjectural toparchy and city territory
royal domains
city with territory
◉ free city
◆ administrative centre of toparchy
■ royal fortress

ITURAEA

Caesarea Philippi (Paneas) ◉

HULATA

Lake Huleh

UPPER GALILEE

GOLAN
GAMALITIKE

◆ Gush Halav

Ptolemais ◉
(Acco)

PHOENICIA

Arav ◆

GALILEE

Gamala ◆

BATANAEA

Migdal ◆ Lake Tiberias
Arbela ◆ (Sea of Galilee)

Hippus ◉

Dium ◉

Sepphoris ◉

Dora ◉

Gaba ◉ Plain of Esdraelon

Gadara ◉

Agrippina ■

ESDRAELON

Mediterranean

Caesarea ●

Scythopolis ◉
(Beth-shean)

Pella ◉

DECAPOLIS

Sea

Arrubot ◆

Plain of Sharon

NARBATTENE

SAMARIA

Qayum ●

Sebaste ◉

Amathus ■

Shechem ◆

R. Jordan

Apollonia ◉

Acrabbein ◆

PERAEA

Qiryat Bene Hassan ■

Alexandrium ■
(Sartaba)

Antipatris ◆

ACRABBEIN

Gedor ◆

Joppa ◉
(Japha)

Ramatayim ◆

Timna' ◆

JOPPA

LYDDA

GOPHNA

Philadelphia ●

Patros ●

Ephraim ◆

JERICHO

Lydda ◆

OREINE

Dok ■
Threx ■
Jericho ●
Cyprus ■

Abila ●

Jamnia ◉
(Yavne)

Gezer ●

Beth-ramatha ■
(Julias)

Esbus ■

ESBUS

Emmaus ◆

Jerusalem ◉

Azotus Paralius ◉
Azotus ◉

Accaron ◆

Qumran ●

Medeba ●

Bethletepha ◆

Hyrcania ■

Ascalon ◉

BETHLETEPHA

HERODIUM

Qe'ilah ◉

Herodium ◆

Bet Guvrin ◆
Marisa ●

Adoraim ◉

Dead Sea

Gaza ●

Machaerus ◉ ■

IDUMAEA

En-gedi ●

Raphia ◉

Masada ■

Arad ●

Beersheba ●

Malhata ◉

NABATAEA

Zoar ●

34°30'   35°   35°30'   36°

33°

32°30'

32°

31°30'

WHEREAS Syria in 27 BC was to become a regular imperial province, Palestine and the surrounding territories, which were equally embraced by Pompey's victories and had come within the Roman sphere of influence, were left under the supervision of local princes. Hence, the Hasmonaean dynasty continued until 37 BC, and, on its collapse, the Roman senate appointed Herod, son of Antipater, as king. Herod was an Idumaean – a people long antagonistic to the Jews, but conquered and forcibly Judaized by the Hasmonaeans. He is called the Great, partly to distinguish him from the many Herods belonging to his family and subsequently to bear rule, but chiefly because of the extent of his kingdom and the vast building programme he initiated.

Herod's building programme continued throughout his reign and points to a variety of motives. First, he was concerned for luxury, royal convenience and a reputation for grandeur, but a recognition of the vagaries of political power meant that royal residences often had a fortress-like appearance. As a result, many of the fortress-palaces were in more secluded parts of the country, which enabled him to plan in secret, and could provide refuge, should he need it. In this respect he followed the example of the Hasmonaean princes who had been only too conscious of the uncertainties of Jewish independence. These fortress-like edifices were in contrast with the elegant country estates established along the Jordan Valley, of which his winter palace just to the south of Jericho was a very good example.

In Jerusalem he built his central, elaborate palace and renovated the Hasmonaean citadel nearby, constructing three adjacent multi-storied towers, of which only the solid base of one (named Phasaeal after his brother) has remained. He also built another huge fortress (the Antonia) to the north of the Temple site, where a garrison could be lodged to protect the Temple precincts. A theatre and a hippodrome were also among his many, varied building projects.

To turn to Herod's palatial desert fortresses, all built in the top of mountains around the Jordan valley and the Dead Sea: the most famous of these fortresses were Alexandrion, Machaerus and Masada. At Masada Herod added to existing Hasmonaean buildings a series of huge water

PALESTINE UNDER THE ROMANS

HEROD THE GREAT'S BUILDING PROJECTS

The reign of Herod the Great is known mainly for its violence and bloodshed. It was, after all, this Herod who, according to the Bible, tried to kill the infant Jesus and was responsible for the 'slaughter of the innocents'. However, Herod was also a great builder and some truly remarkable structures date from his reign, such as the fortress-palaces of Herodium and Masada.

cisterns (to be filled by floods), food and ammunition store houses, fortifications and a unique palace, 'the Northern Palace', built on three natural rock terraces (see page 176). In Jericho Herod followed the Hasmonaeans in building (in three stages) an extensive winter palace with swimming pools and gardens. The most elaborate wing of the palace was a luxurious, well-designed complex built on both sides of the dry river Wadi Qilt (flowing only seasonally).

As he was alien from his origins, Herod was also concerned to show himself a zealous supporter of Judaism. The traditions of Hebron and Mamre went back to the time of Abraham, and the patriarchs were buried in that area, Herod accordingly built a monumental enclosure around the burial places.

However, among his projects the most famous was the Temple in Jerusalem, which replaced the small 'inglorious' building, constructed by the returned exiles after captivity in Babylon. The Temple itself (totally vanished today) was built in the middle of a huge sanctuary surrounded by colonnades of which the southern one, the 'Royal Basilicon' was the most extravagant. Only part of the outside retaining walls of this sanctuary survives, a living testimony to the Temple's splendour. This wall on the west side of the site was for long called the Wailing Wall and is now a Jewish synagogue. We have an account of Herod's Temple by Flavius Josephus who tells of the successive precincts, as one

went from the outer court of the gentiles gradually into the inner sanctum; gentiles were only permitted to enter the outermost zone.

Jerusalem has always been short of water and the preservation of a supply had been a concern in times of siege. Herod constructed an aqueduct which brought water from two springs south of Bethlehem.

One of Herod's outstanding projects was Herodium, where he chose to be buried and is the only site to carry his name. Here, on the edge of the desert, in the frame of a huge, harmonious architectural complex were incorporated a wide-spread summer palace (rich in water and gardens); the district capital; and the king's burial estate. The climax of Herodium was the Mountain Palace Fortress, a large rounded structure built on a hill which was encircled by an artificial cone-shaped mountain. The Mountain Palace Fortress served as a palace wing, a fortress and a monument (to be seen from long distances).

Next, motivated by political considerations, Herod engaged in the construction of public buildings and even cities. It was consciousness of his family traditions that led to new buildings in pagan Ascalon, his own birthplace, but he was most anxious to ingratiate himself with Rome. Two large cities were extensively rebuilt by Herod and named after the Emperor Augustus, his patron: Samaria-Sebaste and Caesarea-Maritime. Sebaste (the Greek form of Augustus) was built alongside Omri's capital city of Samaria which had been destroyed by the Assyrians in 722 BC. It included a temple built for the worship of the Emperor Augustus. Caesarea was built around a huge harbour built by Herod into the sea. This was Herod's largest engineering effort besides the Temple at Jerusalem and was built to serve as an important means of economic and political connection with the Roman world. Caesarea, carefully designed, also included a theatre, a hippodrome, a pagan temple and a promontory palace.

Whilst the most important part of Herod's kingdom had a Jewish population, there was a considerable gentile community. Herod accordingly sought to provide suitable religious and cultural centres. He gave instructions for the building of pagan temples, theatres, stadia and hippod-

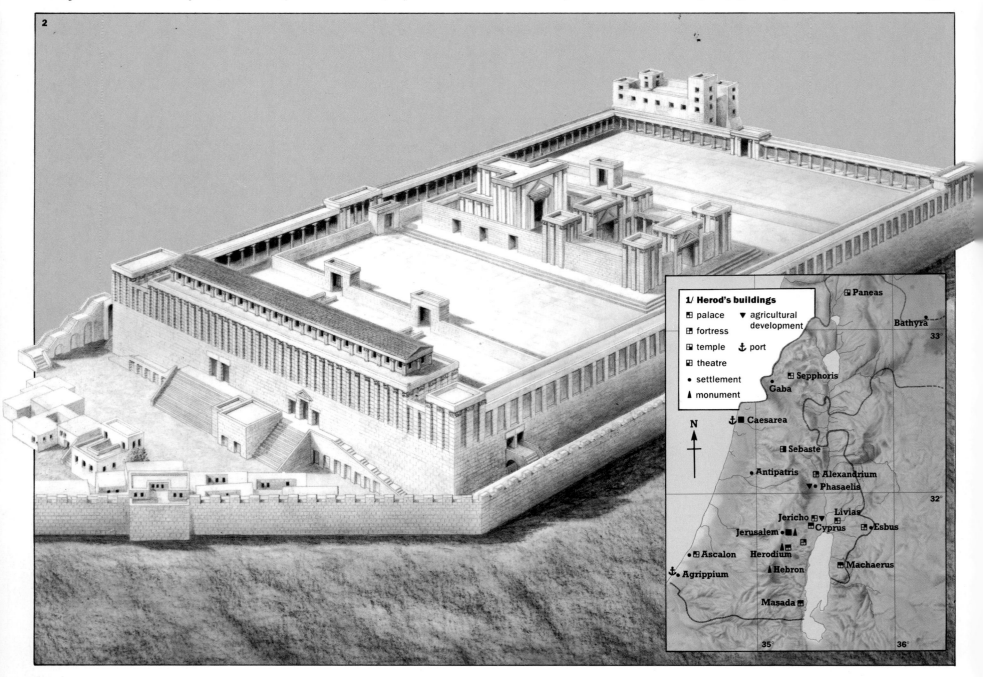

2

1/ Herod's buildings

⊞ palace ▼ agricultural development
⊞ fortress
⊞ temple ⚓ port
⊞ theatre
• settlement
▲ monument

N

⊞ Paneas
Bathyra
33°
⊞ Sepphoris
Gaba
⚓ ■ Caesarea
⊞ Sebaste
• Antipatris ⊞ Alexandrium
▼• Phasaelis
32°
Livias
Jericho ⊞▼■ ⊞ Esbus
Jerusalem •■▲ ⊞ Cyprus
•⊞ Ascalon Herodium
⚓ Agrippium ▲ Hebron ▲ Machaerus
Masada ■

35° 36°

romes in many areas – and particularly in the Decapolis, where the population was almost entirely composed of Greek-speaking gentiles.

Herod also initiated and donated buildings outside his kingdom's boundaries. Among these buildings in all the Mediterranean countries (from Palestine up to Western Greece) were theatres, stadia, gymnasia and a long colonnaded street (at the city of Antioch). The building activity abroad is known, so far, only from the writing of Flavius Josephus (see page 176). Josephus is also the main source, outside archaeology, for most of Herod's building projects in his own country. If it were not for him we would be ignorant of the grandeur that marked Herod's Palestine.

HAVING IMMORTALIZED HIS FAMILY AND FRIENDS HE DID NOT NEGLECT TO MAKE HIS OWN MEMORY SECURE. HE BUILT A FORTRESS IN THE HILLS FACING ARABIA AND CALLED IT HERODIUM AFTER HIMSELF, AND SEVEN MILES FROM JERUSALEM HE GAVE THE SAME NAME TO AN ARTIFICIAL HILL, THE SHAPE OF A WOMAN'S BREAST, ADORNING IT MORE ELABORATELY THAN THE OTHER. HE ENCIRCLED THE TOP WITH ROUND TOWERS, FILLING THE ENCLOSED SPACE WITH A PALACE SO MAGNIFICENT THAT IN ADDITION TO THE SPLENDID APPEARANCE OF THE INTERIOR OF THE APARTMENT, THE OUTER WALLS, COPINGS, AND ROOFS HAD WEALTH LAVISHED ON THEM WITHOUT STINT. AT VERY HEAVY COST HE BROUGHT IN AN UNLIMITED SUPPLY OF WATER FROM A DISTANCE...'

JOSEPHUS. WAR, BOOK I

1/ Map below left
The great variety and quantity of Herod's building projects is demonstrated by this map showing the distribution of Herodian buildings in Palestine.

2/ Below left
Herod's Temple was his greatest feat of construction, and work began in 19 BC. It may well be that Herod, an unpopular king of Idumaean descent whose rise to power had involved the systematic elimination of the Hasmonaean family, hoped to buy popularity by providing a splendid temple for the Jews. However, he was himself only a nominal Jew whose people steadfastly refused to be moved by his generosity.

3/ Below
The fortress of Herodium was a triumph of engineering skill. The illustration shown is based on the remains found by archaeologists (see inset photo below). The mound which encased the lower portion of the fortress was wholly artificial and helped to make the structure secure against attack. However, Herodium was not only a fortress – Herod furnished it magnificently and intended that it should also serve as a palace.

159

In the 1st century BC, immense revenues were generated by taxes levied on caravans. The cost of incense from Dhofar, pearls from the Persian Gulf, silk from China, spice and cotton from India doubled during transit through Nabataean-controlled territory.

Such wealth implied a degree of power which Augustus found unacceptable and he began an economic squeeze, whose effects became evident only a century later. The extent of Nabataean control of the Hauran fluctuated. Under strong kings of Judaea they were limited to a strip along the edge of the desert, but at other times they again controlled Damascus. The desert cities in the Negeb underwent their greatest development; efficient management of severely limited water resources made the desert bloom.

Long a vassal state and but a shadow of its former glory, Nabataea was annexed by Rome in AD 106. Bostra became the new capital and the headquarters of the legion stationed there to guard the Provincia Arabia, which had also absorbed the territories of the cities of the Decapolis. One of the first major works of the new administration was the construction of the Via Nova linking Syria and the Red Sea.

IRRIGATION TECHNIQUES
Only efficient water management permits life in the desert. Superlative skill was necessary to guarantee the agricultural productivity that sustained the relatively dense population of the Negeb in the Nabataean period. The Nabataeans may not have invented all the techniques, but their sophistication has left an indelible mark on the remains which are still available to be seen.

THE TERRACED WADI
From the air many tributary wadis look like staircases. In reality each step is a terrace created by a wall built at right angles to the wadi. These walls are 2-2½ft high as measured from the lower terrace and protrude 4-8in above the surface of the higher terrace; normally there are 5-7 layers of uncut stone. The walls are spaced 40-50ft apart.

The system works on 'runoff', ie, rainfall that is not absorbed by the soil on which it falls but runs off the hillsides to create the desert phenomenon of the flash flood. In tributary wadis such floods occur only on a very small scale. The water flows into a terrace. Some infiltrates the soil. More is ponded behind the terrace wall to penetrate the ground later. The surplus rainfall cascades over the wall to begin the same irrigation process in the terraces below.

THE RUNOFF FARM
Also located in a wadi bed, this system differs from the former in that the terraces are fenced. In addition the

management of the runoff is significantly improved by development of the catchment area.

The fence surrounding the farm is 5ft high. The terrace walls are 5-6ft high and consist of shaped stones; they protrude above their upper terraces by 1-1½ft. In the centre of each wall a drop-structure consisting of a set of stone steps controls the flow to the terrace below. Where-

as this was the only source of supply in the terraced wadi system, here it is only a safety measure to dispose of surplus water. Each field in fact has its own water supply.

The stones on the adjoining slopes were collected into heaps. This increased the runoff from light rains by 20-40%. The slopes were divided into sections by placing unhewn stones to form a loose embankment 6in high; the earth scraped from the upslope side to fill the spaces between the stones created a channel which directed the runoff from a particular section to a particular field. A special channel brought runoff to the cistern beneath the farmhouse; its overflow continued to one of the fields.

The ratio of catchment to cultivated area averages 20:1, which means that in an area with a rainfall of only 4in each field receives as much water as if the rainfall had been 12-20in.

The advantage of this system was that it extended the catchment area to the plateaux above the wadis. It also prevented destructive large flash floods by dividing the total runoff into small streams which could be controlled by simple engineering structures.

Documents from Nizzana dated to the 6th century AD indicates that the following were then produced locally: wheat, barley, figs, grapes, olives, almonds, pomegranates, and dates. The crops were unlikely to have changed since the Nabataean period.

> "...THEY HAVE TURNED ASIDE AND GONE AWAY. THEY DO NOT SAY IN THEIR HEARTS,"LET US FEAR THE LORD OUR GOD, WHO GIVES THE RAIN IN ITS SEASON, THE AUTUMN RAIN AND THE SPRING RAIN, AND KEEPS FOR US THE WEEKS APPOINTED FOR THE HARVEST". JER 5.23-24

THE NABATAEANS AND TRADE

First heard of in the Negeb in the 4th century BC, the Nabataeans quickly distinguished themselves from other Arab nomads by their sense of organized commerce. They collected the bitumen from the surface of the Dead Sea; it was used in Egypt for caulking boats and mummification. The weakness of the adjoining regimes in the 2nd century BC permitted them to develop into an independent state which, by 80 BC, surrounded the Jewish state and reached as far north as Damascus.

1/ Map below
The Nabataeans made their living by taxing international trade caravans. The map shows the caravan routes which covered the ancient Near East at that time. It also demonstrates the waxing and waning of Nabataean influence in the area over a period of some 500 years.

3a and 3b/ Below
These reconstructions show the irrigation methods described above. The terraced wadi (3a) is still used today by the bedouin. Remains of runoff farms (3b) can still by found throughout the Negeb. The example shown is based on one discovered in the vicinity of 'Avedat.

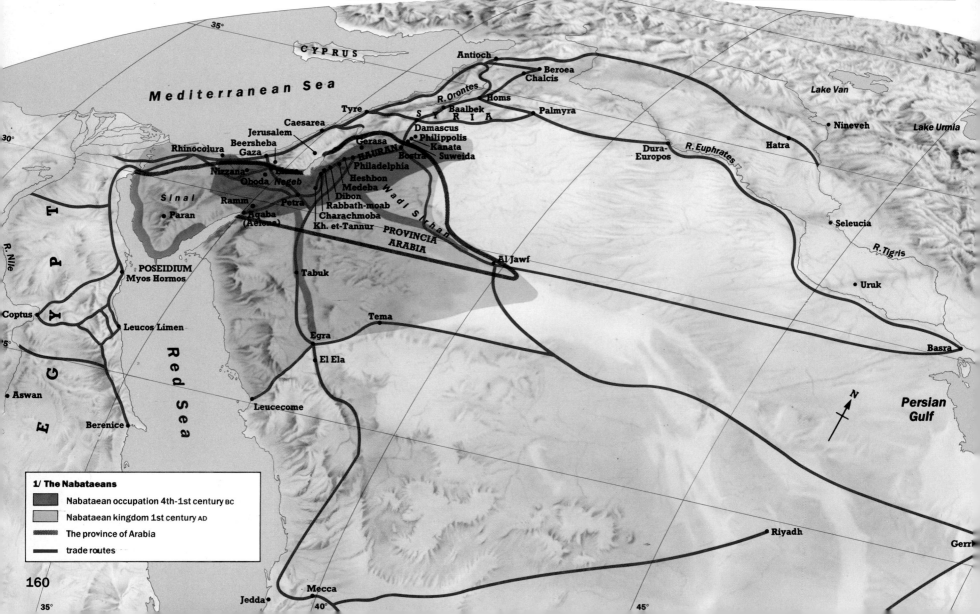

1/ The Nabataeans
- Nabataean occupation 4th-1st century BC
- Nabataean kingdom 1st century AD
- The province of Arabia
- trade routes

THE Essenes were a sect the origins of which are unclear but which some scholars believe may have originated in Babylon as a reaction against the religious laxity that had provoked the divine punishment of the exile in c587-538 BC. The members of this New Covenant dedicated themselves to the perfect observance of the exact interpretation of the Law. Since the Law was the reason for the community's existence it was studied around the clock: 'In the place where ten are, let there not lack a man who studies the Law night and day, continually concerning the duties of each towards the other. And let the Congregation watch in common for a third of all the nights of the year to read the Book and study the Law and to pray together.' (Rule of the Community 6.6-8).

In about 150 BC a faction of the Essenes split off from the main group and made their home at Qumran. Under the leadership of a deposed high-priest, who had taken the name of Teacher of Righteousness, they moved to the

THE DEAD SEA SCROLLS AND THEIR WRITERS

One of the most significant manuscript discoveries of the 20th century was the finding of the documents known as the Dead Sea Scrolls. These include copies of books of the Hebrew canon, commentaries on some prophetic books and texts which revealed the inner life of the Essenes, the Jewish sect that produced them. The scrolls threw unhoped-for light on the complexities of 1st century AD Judaism and on the social and religious context in which Christianity developed.

solitude of the desert to prepare for the advent of the Messiah. At first they numbered no more than 50, but an influx of new recruits in about 100 BC made imperative a considerable expansion of the earlier settlement. The buildings served only the religious, social and economic activities of the group. Their living-quarters were natural caves in the adjoining cliffs, tents and in underground chambers carved into the soft marl.

The Qumran sect provided their own food by farming the plain at the top of the cliffs and the oasis at 'Ain Fashkha, where they had a small settlement. This oasis is situated near a major spring and on the edge of a tract of land irrigated by other springs. Date palms were grown here and the reeds that grow wild were used for roofing and basketmaking. The rough grass on the littoral plain and the mountainside is still capable of supporting flocks of sheep, goats and camels. Salt was drawn from the Dead Sea, and from time to time the bitumen which floats to the surface in an almost pure state. Although control of bitu-

men was theoretically a Nabataean monopoly, it has been found at Qumran and a considerable quantity was deposited on one of the floors at 'Ain Fashkha.

The Essenes' dedication to strict observance of the Law meant that they had an obvious need for copies of the sacred books. Indeed their library contained copies of all the books of the Hebrew canon with the exception of Esther. Excavation in the Qumran caves has also unearthed a series of commentaries (*pesharim*) on prophetic texts, in which the Essenes wrote their history into the inspired word. Liturgical needs gave rise to a collection of beautiful hymns, and the requirements of discipline stimulated the development of a detailed rule covering all aspects of their community life.

When the news of the Roman advance preceded the tramp of the Tenth Legion down the Jordan valley in AD 68 the first concern of the Essenes was to hide their precious manuscripts. At the beginning they wrapped the rolls in linen and sealed them in jars, which were placed in remote caves. However, as time grew short they were forced to dump unprotected manuscripts in hiding places near the settlement, which degenerated into thousands of fragments.

THE ESSENES PROFESS A SEVERER DISCIPLINE: THEY ARE JEWS BY BIRTH AND ARE PECULIARLY ATTACHED TO EACH OTHER. THEY ESCHEW PLEASURE-SEEKING AS A VICE AND REGARD TEMPERANCE AND MASTERY OF THE PASSIONS AS VIRTUES. SCORNING WEDLOCK, THEY SELECT OTHER MEN'S CHILDREN WHILE STILL PLIABLE AND TEACHABLE, AND FASHION THEM AFTER THEIR OWN PATTERN ... CONTEMPTUOUS OF WEALTH, THEY ARE COMMUNISTS TO PERFECTION ...'

JOSEPHUS, WAR, BOOK II

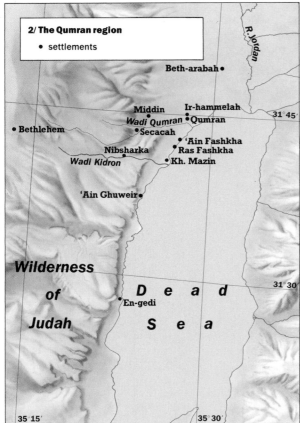

2/ The Qumran region
● settlements

R. Jordan

Beth-arabah ●

Middin ● Ir-hammelah
Wadi Qumran ● Qumran   31° 45'
● Bethlehem ● Secacah
Nibsharka ● 'Ain Fashkha
Wadi Kidron ● Ras Fashkha
● Kh. Mazin

'Ain Ghuweir ●

Wilderness

of   D e a d   31° 30'
● En-gedi
Judah   S e a

35° 15'   35° 30'

2/ Map left
In Judaea around 150 BC, a faction of the Essenes who may have come from Babylon, settled at Qumran. Excavations have shown that the Essenes farmed at 'Ain Fashkha and 'Ain Ghuweir, while members of the community lived in underground chambers and in caves in the cliffs.

4/ Below
Qumran was probably one of the six 'towns' located in the wilderness (JOSH 15.61-2), probably Ir-hammelah 'City of

Salt'. As this photograph demonstrates, excavation has shown that it was a very complex settlement. As demonstrated by the find of the Dead Sea Scrolls, the Essenes put great emphasis on study of Scripture, and archaeologists have uncovered a large 'scriptorium' at Qumran complete with bronze inkwells.

5/ Right
Part of the Isaiah Scroll, written on leather and hidden by the Essenes to protect it from the Roman advance in AD 68.

GALILEE, the northern province of Palestine, became a Roman administrative unit in 57 BC, when Gabinius reorganized the territory conquered by Pompey in 63 BC. The regional capital was first Sepphoris, about 3½ miles north-west of Nazareth, rebuilt at the time when Jesus was resident in Nazareth, and subsequently Tiberias, founded by Herod's son, Antipas (4 BC-AD 39) between AD 17-20. Its situation on the lake shore, close to hot sulphur baths and with easy access to the Hellenized territory of the Decapolis, provided a congenial setting for the court.

In Hellenistic and Roman times, Galilee was surrounded by Greek cities. Ptolemais, Tyre and Sidon lay on the Mediterranean coast; Caesarea Philippi (where Peter's confession took place according to MT 16.13; MK 8.27) was situated in the north; nine of the ten-city confederation, or Decapolis, were in Transjordan and the tenth, Scythopolis, was west of the Jordan; and Gaba was in the south. Yet despite these focal points of Hellenistic culture, the region was emphatically Jewish.

JOSEPHUS

Flavius Josephus, the 1st century AD Jewish historian, distinguishes between Lower and Upper Galilee (WAR* 3.39; cf also *Mishnah Shebiit* 9.2), the frontier between them being marked by the Bet Kerem valley and the deep gorge of the 'Ammud stream, which reaches the Sea of Galilee south of the town of Gennesaret.

Upper Galilee, because of its physical features and remoteness, ensured the persistence of a prosperous rural Jewish life. It also provided a haven for refugees from Judaea after the revolts of AD 66-70 and 132-135.

Lower Galilee is noted by Josephus for the fertility of its plain, west of the Sea of Galilee (WAR 3.516-21), a fertility matched by the eastern slopes of Transjordan (ie, Golan). Archaeological remains on both sides of the lake attest the same tools, utensils, technologies, etc, suggesting a population of identical culture, thus confirming the gospels' picture of an easy passage from one shore to the other.

At the start of the rebellion against Rome in AD 66, Galilee numbered, according to its governor, Josephus, 204 cities and villages (LIFE* 235). His terminology is, however, idiosyncratic for he suggests in one passage (WAR 3.43) that a 'village' consisted of at least 15,000 inhabitants, and he probably meant by 'city' the main centre of an administra-

---

* References to the works of Josephus should be read as follows:

WAR = *The Jewish War*;
LIFE = *The life of Josephus* (autobiography);
ANT = *The Antiquities of the Jews*.

Numbers following the book titles refer to chapters and individual lines.

2

THE CHRISTIAN ERA

GALILEE IN THE 1st CENTURY AD

Jesus was born during the reign of Herod the Great (37-4 BC). The gospels portray him as a Galilean who spent most of his life in the northern province of Palestine – Luke for example states that Jesus was from Galilee and subject to the jurisdiction of Herod Antipas who governed the province between 4 BC and AD 39 (LK 23.7). Galilee was surrounded at this time by Greek cities and indeed the Bible describes it as 'Galilee of the gentiles' (ISA 9.1, MT 4.15). However, even this considerable amount of foreign influence was insufficient to smother the underlying Jewish culture.

tive subdivision or toparchy of a region. The gospels also differentiate between city and village but not according to Josephus' criteria. Whereas Josephus refers to Capernaum and Nain as villages (LIFE 86.403), Luke (4.31; 7.11) calls them cities. Be this as it may, the literary sources supported by archaeological evidence characterize Galilee, apart from Sepphoris and Tiberias, as a rural area with a flourishing agriculture and a peasant ethos.

THE FISHING INDUSTRY

The Lake of Gennesaret (or Tiberias as it was called at this time) was famous for its fishing. The gospels regularly allude to fishermen, nets, boats and fish. Magdala, the Migdal Nunayya or Fish Tower of the Talmud, on the western shore, the presumed place of origin of Mary Magdalen, was the principal centre of the fishing industry. Its strength in the 1st century AD is indicated by the fact that Josephus was able to commandeer from there 230 (or according to a variant reading 330) small boats (WAR 2.635). The Greek name of the city Taricheae implies that the catch was salted. The Greek geographer Strabo notes that 'at the place called Taricheae, the lake supplies excellent fish for pickling'.

GALILEE UNDER HEROD

Galilee was the scene of the early exploits of the young Herod. On being appointed governor of the province by his father Antipater, he acquired notoriety by eliminating brigands from the northern limits of Upper Galilee bordering on Syria (ANT* 14.158). His achievements provoked the

1/ Map right
The province of Galilee at the time of Jesus.

2/ Below
This photograph showing the synagogue at Capernaum (see text), has been re-touched by an artist to eliminate modern structures which obscure the site from view.

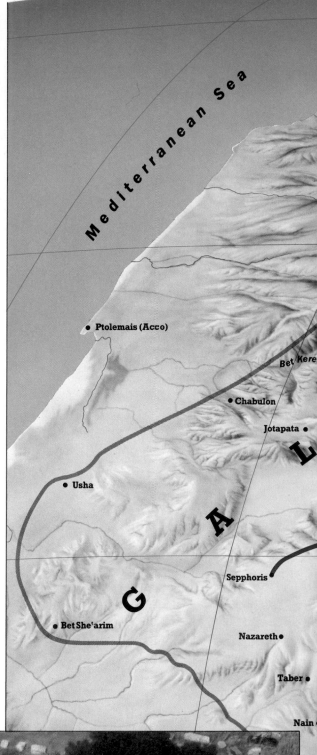

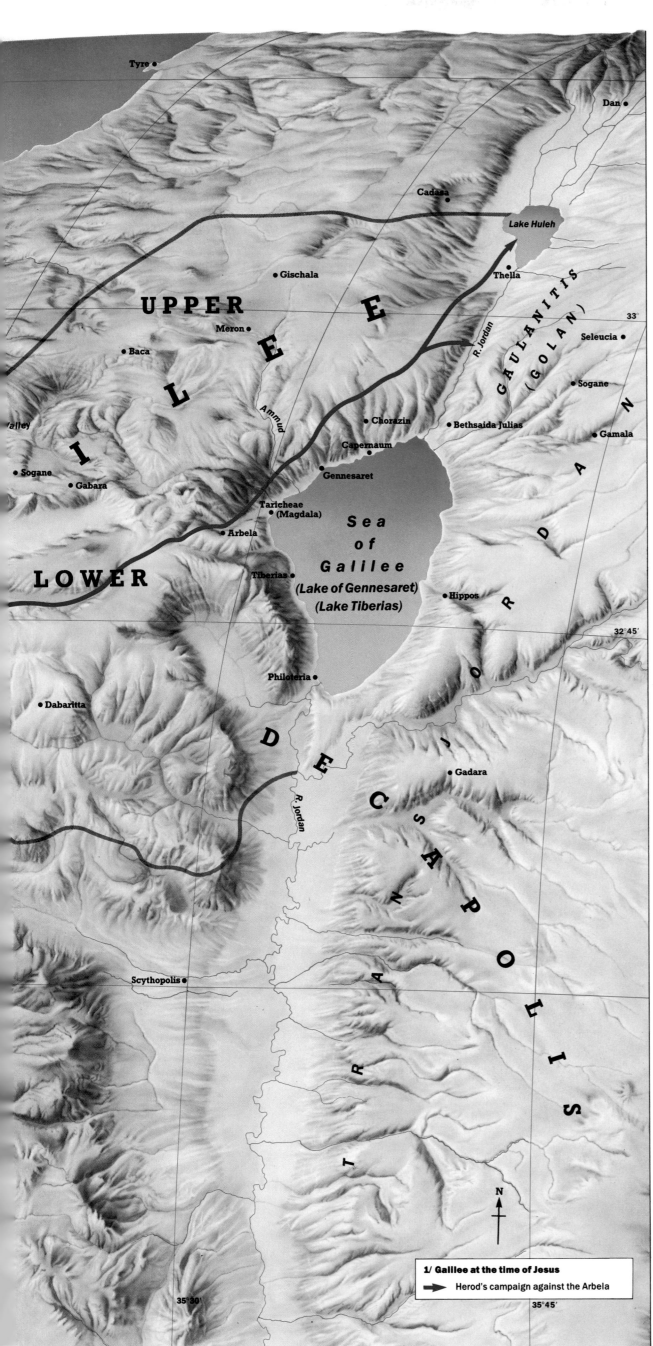

1/ Galilee at the time of Jesus

→ Herod's campaign against the Arbela

hostility of the Jerusalem aristocracy, who sought unsuccessfully to try him for summary killings (ANT 14.167f).

When in 40 BC he was appointed king by the Romans, Galilee opposed him, and the citizens of Sepphoris sided with his rival for the throne, the last Hasmonaean prince, Antigonus. Pursued by Herod, they fled from the city to the wild terrain and caves around Arbela; but he attacked them there, driving them once as far as the Jordan (ANT 14.416). The violence of their resistance was exemplified by an elderly fighter who chose to kill his wife and seven sons, and then to commit suicide, rather than surrender to Herod (ANT 14.421-30). Josephus also describes how the king's soldiers were lowered in cages to the cave openings and threw flaming brands inside among the fugitives.

When continued opposition resulted in the murder of his general, Pompey, Herod was obliged to return from Samaria to search out those rebels who had escaped to the marshes, probably around Lake Huleh. He destroyed their fortresses and imposed a heavy fine on their cities. Unfortunately, since Josephus fails to identify the places in question, the movements of this campaign cannot be outlined with any degree of certainty.

By contrast, the historian gives detailed information concerning Galilean frontiers and localities and of the cities and villages of the neighbouring territories. His familiarity with the topography of places such as Jotapata (WAR 3.158-60) and Gamala (414-18) can be ascertained by a visit to the sites. No boundary changes took place during the 1st century except that in AD 55 Taricheae (Magdala), Tiberias and Bethsaida Julias, together with their territories, were transferred by Nero to the control of Herod Agrippa II, ruler of Batanaea and Gaulanitis. From the point of view of a Jerusalem-based government, the term Galilee could loosely denote also the Golan region across the Jordan, although there is no evidence that in the 1st century AD it was administered as part of Galilee.

SYNAGOGUES
In view of the frequency of the references to synagogues in the literary sources, it is strange that archaeology has only uncovered five pre-AD 70 buildings that could have served this purpose, three of which are located in Galilee – Chorazin (now no longer to be identified), Magdala on the western lake shore, and opposite it about 6½ miles from the eastern shore of the lake, Gamala. This is in sharp contrast to the many basilica-style synagogues from the 3rd-5th century AD in Galilee, already mentioned. In all probability there was no fixed type of building for the earlier period, since even later there were considerable variations in style, depending on local circumstances. Public meeting places, if they existed at all, were probably multi-purpose, and it was only after the destruction of the temple that they took on fixed sacral features such as a Torah shrine, a *bēma* or podium and an orientation to Jerusalem with the entrance to the east. If there were Torah shrines in Jesus' day, they would in all probability have been mobile, on the basis of Nathan's rebuke to David, who had sought a fixed place for the Ark of the Covenant (II SAM 7.4-17).

Archaeological work begun at the turn of the century and still in progress does not yet permit the establishment of the size and plan of 1st century Capernaum (see photograph far left). The remains of a large synagogue on the site date to the late 4th or early 5th century, but there is apparently also evidence of an older building, possibly of the 1st century (cf LK 7.5). In addition, recent excavations in the adjacent area have uncovered rows of small houses clustered irregularly around little courtyards in the vicinity of the synagogue. One, with a limestone floor and plastered walls, later became the centre of a mid-5th century octagonal church with mosaic floors. It was probably regarded at that time as the house of Peter where Jesus healed Peter's mother-in-law (MK 1.31).

In the 1st century, Capernaum may have possessed some importance as a border town between the territories of Antipas (Galilee) and his brother Philip (Gaulanitis). It had a customs-post, with the future apostle Matthew at one time in charge (MT 9.9). A resident Roman centurion may have commanded a local garrison (MT 8.5-13). References in the gospels to fishing are brought vividly to life by the recent discovery of a jetty, though it was built at a later stage.

"'THE LAND OF ZEBULUN AND THE LAND OF NAPHTALI, TO-WARD THE SEA, ACROSS THE JORDAN, GALILEE OF THE GENTILES – THE PEOPLE WHO SAT IN DARKNESS HAVE SEEN A GREAT LIGHT, AND FOR THOSE WHO SAT IN THE REGION OF THE SHADOW OF DEATH LIGHT HAS DAWNED." MT 4.15-16

No precise date is given for the birth of Jesus. Matthew places it towards the end of the reign of Herod the Great (37-4BC), and Luke associates it with an otherwise unrecorded universal census ordered by the Emperor Augustus, linking this with the tax-registration organized by Quirinius, which occurred in AD6. Both agree on Bethlehem as the birthplace, but Matthew implies that Joseph and Mary resided there, whilst Luke brings them from Nazareth for the census. According to Matthew, the family fled to somewhere in Egypt, as Jesus' life was threatened by King Herod. With Herod's death the way was clear for a return to Palestine. Since Herod's son Archelaus was now ruler in Judaea, Joseph set out for Galilee. Hence both evangelists locate the family in Nazareth. Luke describes a visit to Jerusalem from Nazareth at Passover, when Jesus met the doctors of the Law in the Temple.

JESUS' MINISTRY IN THE SYNOPTIC GOSPELS

Jesus is introduced as a 'carpenter' or artisan, living with his mother, four named brothers and several unnamed sisters in Nazareth. From there he travelled to the southern reaches of the Jordan (MK 1.9) to receive baptism from John (LK 3.21), and preached at a site near Jericho, later identified with Beth-arabah. Jesus then departed to Galilee and began to preach, calling for repentance and proclaiming the imminent arrival of God's rule. Capernaum, on the northwestern shore of the Sea of Galilee, later renamed the Sea of Tiberias (JN 6.1) became the main centre of his activity and is described as 'home' (MK 2.1). Simon Peter also had a house there (MK 1.29). Chorazin and Bethsaida, neighbouring towns, were also places where he performed miracles, as was also Nain (south of Nazareth), where Jesus is reported to have resurrected a young man (LK 7.11-17). We have references to Magadan or Magdala, the town of Mary Magdalene, and Dalmanutha, possibly identical with Magdala.

THE CHRISTIAN ERA
THE MINISTRY OF JESUS

Information relating to Jesus comes mainly from the gospels, but they are not biographies in the modern sense and do not attempt to give a complete account of his life. They are not concerned with precise chronology and geographical references are sparse and imprecise. The evangelists concentrate on Jesus' public ministry and particularly on the crucial last week of his life. While Matthew and Luke refer to his birth, their accounts differ, and Luke alone provides a story from adolescence. Of his early manhood we know nothing. Mark, Matthew and Luke present the ministry as mainly Galilean and lasting little more than a year, whilst John points to a much longer ministry and indicates numerous and extended stays in Judaea.

There are also unnamed sites – the mountain where Jesus preached (MT 5.1), the place where he fed the multitude (MK 6.34) and the mountain of the Transfiguration (MK 9.2). Tradition sites the first two in the vicinity of Capernaum, whilst the third is identified as either Mt Tabor or Mt Hermon.

Jesus visited few towns outside Galilee. At Caesarea Philippi Peter voiced the disciples' belief that Jesus was the Messiah (MK 8.27-29; MT 16.13-16). Once we find Jesus casting out 'evil spirits' on the eastern lake-side, described as 'the land of the Gerasenes' (Gadarenes or Gergesenes), probably at Kursa (MK 5.1). As a result, his renown spread in the Decapolis (MT 4.25). Jesus also visited Tyre and Sidon (MK 7.24-30), delivering a gentile Syro-Phoenician girl from demonic possession.

The synoptists agree, then, that the ministry was largely conducted on the northern shore of the lake and the region about Nazareth. Jesus taught, healed and exorcized in synagogues (those in Capernaum and Nazareth are explicitly mentioned – MK 1.21; 6.2); in streets and squares and in the open country. He avoided the bigger cities. There is no reference to Sepphoris, Galilee's former capital, or to Tiberias, Herod's new capital. These were essentially gentile centres and Jesus confined his ministry to the Jews with a few exceptions. Apart from his early meeting with John the Baptist in the south, the synoptists take him to Judaea only once for the climax of his ministry in Jerusalem. Like most Galileans visiting Jerusalem, Jesus skirted the hostile Samaritan territory (MK 10.1; cf LK 9.51), crossing the Jordan and continuing south on the easter side of the river. He recrossed near Jericho, where he healed a blind beggar (MK 10.46-52). From Jericho he took the road to Jerusalem, passing the villages of Bethphage and Bethany (MK 11.1), and reached Jerusalem city by the Mount of Olives.

THE MINISTRY IN THE GOSPEL OF JOHN

The synoptic gospels allude to a single Passover in Jesus' ministry and portray him as 'the prophet Jesus from Nazareth' (MT 21.11). The fourth gospel, written later, presents a different chronology and scenario. It mentions several Passovers, implying a longer ministry, and his Galilean links are somewhat blurred.

John's gospel refers to the baptism of Jesus in the area of Bethany beyond Jordan (1.28) and then speaks of him in Cana of Galilee (2.1), a town of uncertain location. Jesus spends 'a few days' in Capernaum (2.12) and recruits his first disciples, but almost immediately sets out for Jerusalem for the Passover (2.13). There are then references to baptizing in Judaea (3.22) prior to a journey north through Samaria, when he spent two days (4.5) at Sychar (probably Shechem) and taught the Samaritans. He was warmly received in

1/ Map left
According to Matthew 1.18ff Jesus' family were forced to flee from Judaea into Egypt.

2/ Map below
The synoptic gospels represent the ministry of Jesus as being centred on the area around the Sea of Galilee.

3/ Map above right
John's gospel suggests that the ministry lasted for more than one year, including several visits to Jerusalem.

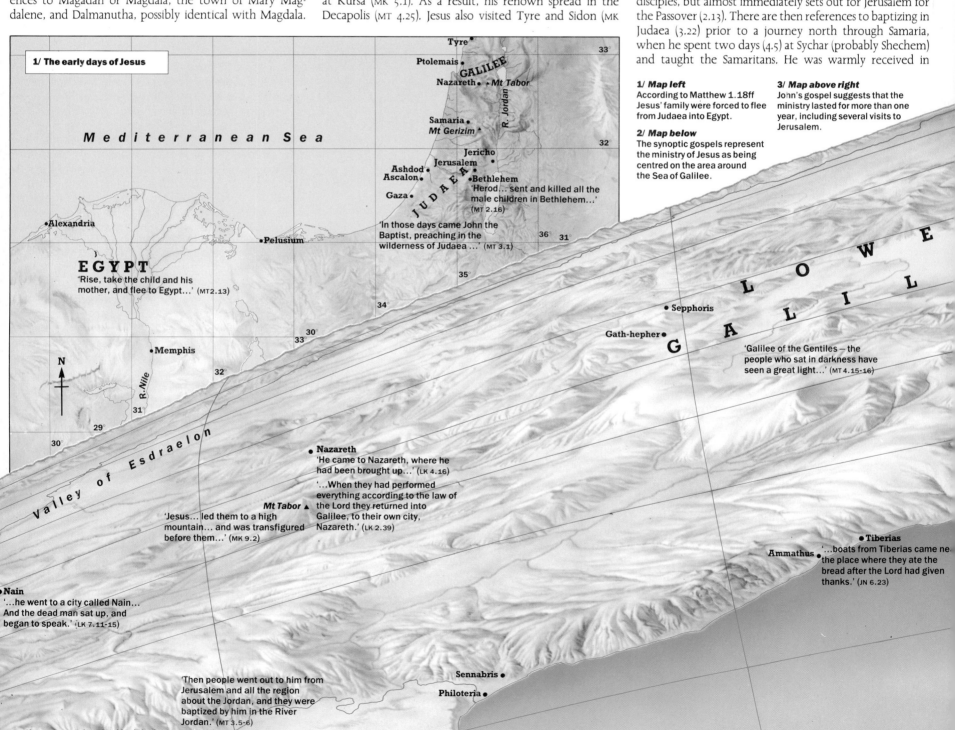

1/ The early days of Jesus

Tyre
Ptolemais
GALILEE
Nazareth • Mt Tabor
R. Jordan
Samaria
Mt Gerizim
Jericho
Jerusalem
Ashdod
Ascalon • Bethlehem
Gaza
JUDAEA
'Herod... sent and killed all the male children in Bethlehem...' (MT 2.16)
'In those days came John the Baptist, preaching in the wilderness of Judaea ...' (MT 3.1)

Mediterranean Sea

• Alexandria

• Pelusium

EGYPT
'Rise, take the child and his mother, and flee to Egypt...' (MT 2.13)

• Memphis
R. Nile
N

Valley of Esdraelon

GALOWE
GALILE
G
• Sepphoris
Gath-hepher •
'Galilee of the Gentiles – the people who sat in darkness have seen a great light...' (MT 4.15-16)

• Nazareth
'He came to Nazareth, where he had been brought up...' (LK 4.16)
'...When they had performed everything according to the law of the Lord they returned into Galilee, to their own city, Nazareth.' (LK 2.39)

Mt Tabor ▲
'Jesus... led them to a high mountain... and was transfigured before them...' (MK 9.2)

• Nain
'...he went to a city called Nain... And the dead man sat up, and began to speak.' (LK 7.11-15)

• Tiberias
Ammathus •
'...boats from Tiberias came near the place where they ate the bread after the Lord had given thanks.' (JN 6.23)

'Then people went out to him from Jerusalem and all the region about the Jordan, and they were baptized by him in the River Jordan.' (MT 3.5-6)
'Jesus ... was baptized by John in the Jordan.' (MK 1.9)
R. Jordan

Sennabris •
Philoteria •

GADARA

2/ The ministry of Jesus

Wadi Yarmuk

• Hippu

Galilee, revisited Cana and performed an act of healing in Capernaum (4.46-50). It is almost as if he were not a Galilean, but a visitor from Judaea (see 4.47, 54).

A little later, Jesus is back in Jerusalem for an unspecified feast (5.1), when he cures a paralytic. He is next seen to the east of the Sea of Galilee (6.1), shortly before a Passover (6.4). There is a visit to Capernaum (6.17) and Jesus remains in Galilee until the autumn Feast of Tabernacles (7.1-3). He is said to have gone secretly to Jerusalem for this festival (7.10) and to have stayed in Jerusalem or its environs until the Dedication Festival (Hanukkah) in December (10.22). Next we find him beyond the Jordan in the area where John the Baptist had worked (10.40-42). From there he travels to Bethany on the outskirts of Jerusalem and revives the dead Lazarus (11.1-44). Then he withdraws to Ephraim (Ephron), north of Jerusalem, because of a plot against his life (11.53-54) and spends a brief time in Bethany (12.1) before proceeding to Jerusalem. where he is to die.

'AND JESUS RETURNED IN THE POWER OF THE SPIRIT INTO GALILEE, AND A REPORT CONCERNING HIM WENT OUT THROUGH ALL THE SURROUNDING COUNTRY. AND HE TAUGHT IN THEIR SYNAGOGUES, BEING GLORIFIED BY ALL.' LK 4.14-15

Mediterranean Sea

Ptolemais
Dora
Caesarea
Apollonia
Joppa
Jamnia
Lydda
Cana
Sepphoris
Nazareth
GALILEE
Mt Tabor ▲
Dalmanutha (Magdala?)
Gennesaret Capernaum
Tiberias
Bethsaida
Sea of Galilee
Hippus

SAMARIA

Neapolis
Mt Gerizim ▲ Sychar (Shechem)
'So he came to a city of Samaria, called Sychar ... and so Jesus, wearied as he was with his journey, sat down beside the well.' (JN 4.5-6)

Scythopolis
Gadara
Salim
Pella

'That very day two of them were going to a village named Emmaus ... Jesus himself drew near and went with them.' (LK 24.13-15)

Ephraim (Ephron)

Emmaus
R. Jordan

'John answered them, "I baptize you with water; but among you stands one whom you do not know..." This took place in Bethany beyond the Jordan where John was baptizing.' (JN 1.26-28)

Jerusalem Bethphage
Bethany
'Six days before the Passover, Jesus came to Bethany, where Lazarus was, whom Jesus had raised from the dead.' (JN 12.1)

'It was the feast of the Dedication at Jerusalem ... and Jesus was walking in the temple...' (JN 10.22)

'"Go wash in the pool of Siloam"... he went and washed and came back seeing.' (JN 7-8)

Jericho
Beth-arabah

Dead Sea

Abila
Ptolemais

N

UPPER

GALILEE

Jotapata

Cana
'...there was a marriage at Cana in Galilee.' (JN 2.1)

'Jesus went about all the cities and villages, teaching in their synagogues.' (MT 9.35)

Arbela

Dalmanutha (Magdala?)
'And they ate, and were satisfied; ... And there were about four thousand people. And he sent them away ... got into the boat ... and went to the district of Dalmanutha.' (MK 8.8-10)

Gennesaret

'Seeing the crowds, he went up on the mountain.' (MT 5.1)

Chorazin
'Woe to you, Chorazin!' (LK 10.13)

Capernaum
'That evening ... they brought to him all who were sick or possessed with devils.' (MK 1.32)

'After this he went down to Capernaum...' (JN 2.12)

Sea of Galilee

(Sea of Tiberias)

'As he walked beside the Sea of Galilee he saw two brothers, Simon who is called Peter and Andrew his brother, casting a net into the sea for they were fishermen.' (MT 4.18)

Bethsaida
'Now Philip was from Bethsaida, the city of Andrew and Peter.' (JN 1.44)

R. Jordan

HIPPUS

Gergesa

'...to the country of the Gadarenes, two demoniacs met them...' (MT 8.28)

THE evangelists express the inevitability of Jesus' death. Mark portrays Jesus as 'the Son of man' who 'came not to be served but to serve, and to give his life as a ransom for many' (MK 10.45). Matthew writes of miraculous events accompanying the death of Jesus – the earth shaking, rocks splitting open and tombs opening (MT 27.51-54). Luke has Jesus asking, 'was it not necessary that the Christ should suffer these things and enter into his glory?' (LK 24.26), whilst, in John, Jesus is represented as saying to Pilate, 'You would have no power over me unless it had been given to you from above...' (JN 19.11). The crucifixion is a culmination, bringing all Jesus' activity to its completion (JN 19.28, 30 cf PS 69.21).

Jesus' last days began with his entry into Jerusalem from the Bethany-Bethphage area, little more than two miles from the city along the Jericho road. The approach on a donkey was seen as a self-conscious act in fulfilment of ZECH 9.9 – not a humble act, but rather the act of a king, coming in peace. The Galilean pilgrims to the feast of Passover are seen as enthusiastic supporters of Jesus, heralding his arrival into the city, but the Judaeans are seen as less welcoming, entering into dispute with him.

It appears that Jesus stayed overnight at Bethany, whilst continuing to preach in Jerusalem during the day. Gethsemane, on the Mount of Olives, was also frequented by Jesus and his disciples. A near riot in the Temple, resulting from Jesus' anger with the marketing allowed there, made the priestly leaders convinced that there would be trouble from the Roman authorities if he persisted in his ministry. Caiaphas, the High Priest, thought it expedient to have him executed by the Romans.

The sequence of events is not clear. The synoptic gospels speak of Jesus and his disciples celebrating the Passover in an upper room, whilst John describes the occasion of Jesus' subsequent trial and crucifixion as being the day before the Passover began (JN 18.28). It is likely that his chronology is correct as the holding of a trial on the first day of the festival would have been contrary to Jewish law, but John also has a theological motif – that Jesus was slain as the Passover lambs were being slaughtered in the Temple. We may take the Thursday evening meal to have been an anticipatory Passover feast or a fellowship meal.

The trial before the High Priest was concerned largely with Jesus' approach to the Temple and possible Messianic claims, but the charge before Pilate had to be couched in political terms. Crucifixion was the death meted out to rebels, and so Jesus is presented as a revolutionary, claiming to be King of the Jews (MK 15.2) and fomenting sedition all over the country (LK 23.5). The gospels seek to exonerate the Romans from responsibility for the death of Jesus

THE CHRISTIAN ERA

JESUS' LAST DAYS

The four evangelists are united in seeing the last week in Jesus' life as crucial to an understanding of his ministry. After his 'triumphal entry' into Jerusalem, he challenged the Temple authorities by raising a disturbance in the outer courts. This made it more important than ever for them to be rid of him – especially at the politically sensitive Passover season. The narrative moves on to betrayal, trial and crucifixion by order of the Roman procurator, Pontius Pilate.

– probably from a later apologetic interest-but the mode of execution indicates that the responsibility had to rest with the procurator. Luke suggests that Herod Antipas was consulted, as Jesus was technically under his jurisdiction, but Jesus was referred back to Pilate and sentence passed.

The location of the praetorium where Jesus was tried is disputed. At one time, it was linked with the fortress of Antonia, north of the Temple, where the troops keeping peace in the Temple were lodged, and the traditional 'Via Dolorosa', the route from the praetorium to Golgotha, where Jesus was crucified, begins there - most scholars would now see it as belonging to the citadel, first constructed by the Hasmonaeans and then enlarged by Herod the Great as his palace. It is likely that the procurator would

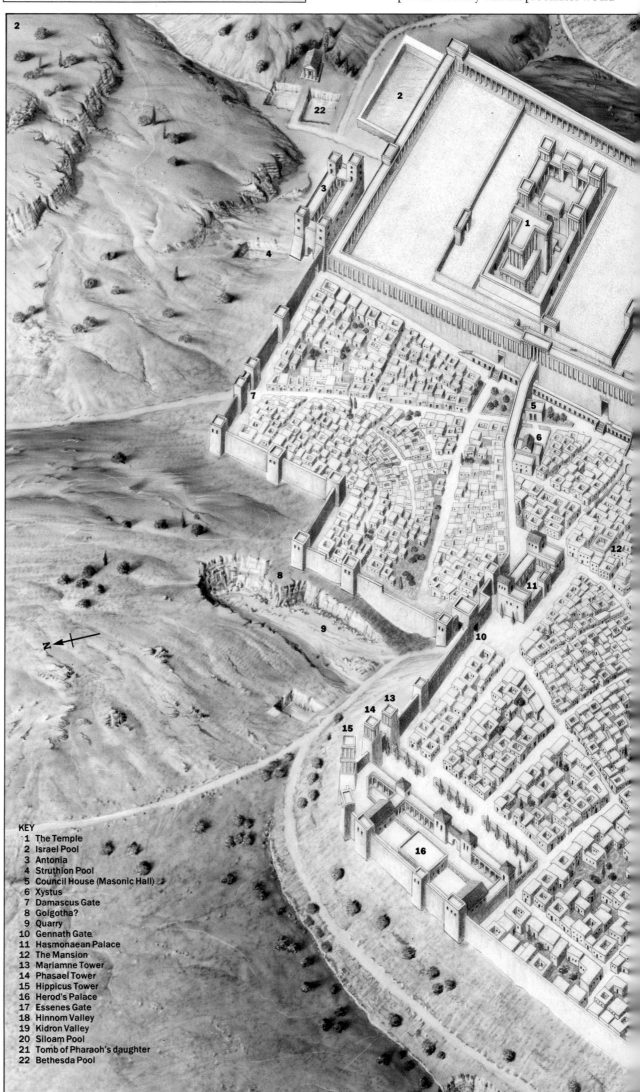

'... Jesus revealed himself again to the disciples by the Sea of Tiberias...' JN 21.1

Ptolemais
Capernaum · Bethsaida
Sea of Tiberias
(Sea of Galilee)
Sepphoris · Tiberias · Hippus
Nazareth
Mt Tabor
Gadara
Dora
Caesarea
Scythopolis
Ginae
32°30'

Samaria
Neopolis
Apollonia
Antipatris
Joppa
Gadara
32°

'While they were talking and discussing together, Jesus himself drew near and went with them.' LK 24.15

Ephraim

Jericho · Abila
Emmaus
Jerusalem
'Afterward he appeared to the eleven themselves as they sat at table...' MK 16.14

'Jesus said to her [Mary Magdalene], "Woman, why are you weeping? Whom do you seek?" JN 20.15

'And behold, Jesus met them and said, "Hail!" And they came up and took hold of his feet and worshipped him.' MT 28.9

'... Jesus himself stood among them. But they were startled and... supposed they saw a spirit.' LK 24.36-37

Then he said to Thomas, "Put your finger here, and see my hands..." JN 20.27

31°30'

1/ Appearances after the Resurrection

35° 35°30'

KEY
1 The Temple
2 Israel Pool
3 Antonia
4 Struthion Pool
5 Council House (Masonic Hall)
6 Xystus
7 Damascus Gate
8 Golgotha?
9 Quarry
10 Gennath Gate
11 Hasmonaean Palace
12 The Mansion
13 Mariamne Tower
14 Phasael Tower
15 Hippicus Tower
16 Herod's Palace
17 Essenes Gate
18 Hinnom Valley
19 Kidron Valley
20 Siloam Pool
21 Tomb of Pharaoh's daughter
22 Bethesda Pool

have used this palace on his visits from Caesarea to Jerusalem.

The place of execution was the site of a quarry just outside the city walls at that time. When Herod Agrippa (AD 41-44) extended the bounds of the city, the site was probably brought within the city limits. Jesus was buried in a rock tomb (MK 15.42-46) – in a location where other 1st century AD tombs still exist.

The four evangelists all agree that Jesus was later seen alive and that his tomb was found to be empty, but the sequence of events and appearances is uncertain. Luke locates all the appearances in Jerusalem and Judaea, whilst Matthew refers to a Galilean mountain (MT 28.16). John refers to appearances in Jerusalem (JN 20.11, 26-29) but adds a further story about an appearance of Jesus in Galilee, not on a mountain, but beside the shore of the Sea of Tiberias (Sea of Galilee).

THE PLACE OF CRUCIFIXION

Josephus, in his *The Jewish War* (5.136; 142-146), describes the 'three walls' by which the ancient city of Jerusalem was fortified. In the area formed by the angle of the First and Second Walls lies a quarry dating to the 7th century BC. The present-day Church of the Holy Sepulchre stands on the northern part of the quarry, but the southern section of the hill was left unquarried and Golgotha, (a name meaning 'the place of the skull') the site of Jesus' crucifixion, was here. Facing it are 1st century AD tombs, hewn out of the cliff. (A reconstruction of a rolling-stone tomb appears on page 77).

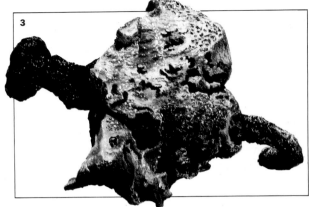

1/ Map far left
The gospels record the appearances of Jesus after the Resurrection.

2/ Left
A reconstruction of Herodian Jerusalem from archaeological findings.

3/ Above
The heel-bone, pierced by a nail, of Yehohanan, the crucified man of Giv'at HaMivtar.

CRUCIFIXION

Crucifixion is commonly associated with the Romans, but this form of death penalty did not originate with them. It appears to have been used by the Medes, and then by the Persians in the 5th century BC. Alexander the Great is also credited with using it at times – no doubt through his contact with Persia. In all likelihood the Romans adopted the practice of crucifixion from the Carthaginians who had their links with Phoenicia.

In Italy crucifixion was reserved for slaves and was extensively used after the crushing of the slaves' revolt under Spartacus. Elsewhere, in imperial times, rebels against Roman rule were condemned to this fate.

Death would occur quickly, if the body were allowed to hang without support. This would be through asphyxiation as the weight of the unsupported body would lead to the shutting off of the breathing passage. To prolong the agony the victim was provided with support for the feet and, at times, a seat peg as well.

A wooden pole was thrust into the ground, and the condemned man was then compelled to carry the top cross-piece which would then be fixed to the piece in the ground. When there were numerous victims, their arms would be simply roped to the cross-piece. In the case of the crucifixion of Jesus, our sources refer to only three being crucified at the same time. In that case, the victims were nailed both at the wrists – the nails passing between the radius and ulna – and at their feet. Nails would certainly not have been driven through the palms of the hand, as the hands could not take the weight of the body. Both JN 20.25 and Justin Martyr (writing in the second century AD) refer to nail wounds on the hands and feet of Jesus. (By 'hand' they would have included the wrist.)

In 1968 at Giv'at HaMivtar they unearthed an ossuary bearing the name 'Yehohanan' and containing the bones of a young man who had evidently been the victim of crucifixion. His are the only surviving remains of a crucified victim, but it is uncertain whether he was nailed or roped at his wrists. Tearing had occurred and his heels were certainly nailed. The nail which pierced the heel bone had evidently hit a knot in the wood and the tip had been bent so that the nail could not be withdrawn. It is this accident which is responsible for the survival of a remarkable piece of evidence. However, it would be dangerous to generalize from this single case.

The gospels refer to the custom of breaking the legs of victims. This would be done to accelerate death, as then removal of the lower support for the body would bring about speedy suffocation. In the case of those crucified with Jesus, it was important to remove their bodies before sunset, as the Jewish festival (a Sabbath, too) began then. Jesus had, of course, already died and so no action to accelerate death was required.

The gospels refer, also, to an inscription indicating the charge brought against Jesus (a claim to be King of the Jews). There is no external evidence of such a practice, but, had it been customary, the victim would have borne the plaque naming his crime, attached to the cross-beam of the cross.

> 'SO THEY TOOK JESUS, AND HE WENT OUT, BEARING HIS OWN CROSS, TO THE PLACE CALLED THE PLACE OF A SKULL, WHICH IS CALLED IN HEBREW GOLGOTHA. THERE THEY CRUCIFIED HIM, AND WITH HIM TWO OTHERS, ONE ON EITHER SIDE, AND JESUS BETWEEN THEM. PILATE ALSO WROTE A TITLE AND PUT IT ON THE CROSS; IT READ, "JESUS OF NAZARETH, THE KING OF THE JEWS."'
> JN 19.17-19

THE Emperor Tiberius (AD14-37) was anxious to strengthen the eastern frontiers of the empire in the face of the soaring power of Parthia. Accordingly, unstable vassal states were annexed, extending direct Roman control to the Euphrates. In AD18 Commagene was incorporated into Syria, and Cappadocia (including Lesser Armenia) became a Roman province. In AD23 eastern Pontus was linked to Bithynia (see page 150).

Emperor Gaius (AD37-41) reversed the policy, creating kingdoms for eastern princes who had been his companions in Rome. Herod Agrippa I, a grandson of Herod the Great, was a principal beneficiary under this policy. In AD37 Gaius gave him the tetrarchies of Philip and Lysanias and added the territory of his uncle Herod Antipas (Galilee and Peraea) in AD40.

Although Gaius was assassinated in AD41, his uncle Claudius (AD41-54) who succeeded him, rewarded Herod Agrippa I for his support by adding to his rule the area governed by the procurator of Judaea. He now controlled an area coextensive with that ruled by Herod the Great. His pro-Pharisee policy brought him into conflict with the young Christian community. For example, ACTS 12.1-23 describes how Agrippa had James put to death and had Peter imprisoned.

Agrippa I died suddenly at Caesarea in AD44. His heir was

only 17 years old, so Claudius transferred his entire kingdom to the control of a Roman procurator. This was the greatest extent of the province of Judaea, and it lasted only until AD53 when Claudius gave Abila, Arca, and the old tetrarchy of Philip (Gaulanitis, Batanaea, Trachonitis and Auranitis) to Agrippa II, who at this point surrendered Chalcis which he had ruled since AD50.

Sometime after Nero's accession to power in AD54 Agrippa's territory was increased by the grant of the cities of Tiberias and Taricheae with their districts, and in addition the city of Julias (Livias) in Peraea with 14 neighbouring villages. Agrippa would probably have been granted the remainder of his father's lands were it not for the outbreak of the 1st Jewish revolt in AD66 (see page 176). Agrippa II sided with the Romans and at first lost territory. It was quickly restored by Vespasian's victories in the north. As a faithful ally of Rome he was rewarded with new lands when the war ended. No details are given of their location, but the probability is that they lay to the north of his kingdom.

> 'ABOUT THAT TIME HEROD THE KING LAID VIOLENT HANDS UPON SOME WHO BELONGED TO THE CHURCH. HE KILLED JAMES THE BROTHER OF JOHN WITH THE SWORD...' ACTS 12.1-2

THE CHRISTIAN ERA
ROMAN RULE AFTER JESUS

In the 1st century AD the major political concern for the Roman governors of Judaea was to ensure stability within the province and the safety of their eastern borders. The borders of the kingdom at this time also reflect the emperor's desire to show favour to supporters. The reign of Agrippa I (AD41-44) was regarded as the last highspot for the Jewish nation before the disaster of the 1st Jewish Revolt in AD66.

1/ Map below
Claudius placed Judaea under Herod Agrippa I in AD 41 as a gesture of reconciliation after the cruelty of Gaius Caesar (Caligula). Agrippa II ruled the tetrarchy of Philip, Abila in Peraea and the tetrarchy of Abila in Damascus. Although he controlled the right to appoint the High Priests in Jerusalem, he did not control Judaea.

2/ Right
The chart lists all the Roman emperors (shown in yellow) and the governors of Judaea (in red). Also shown are the high priests of Jerusalem, most of whom came from four different families, which are indicated by a colour code.

ROMAN EMPERORS
AUGUSTUS (16 January 27 BC – 19 August AD 14).
TIBERIUS (17 September 14 – 16 March 37).
GAIUS (16 March 37 – 24 January 41).
CLAUDIUS (24 January 41 – 13 October 54).
NERO (13 October 54 – 9 June 68).
GALBA (10 June 68 – 15 January 69).
OTHO (15 January 69 – 14 April 69).
VITELLIUS (2 January 69 – 20 December 69).
VESPASIAN (1 July 69 – 24 June 79).
TITUS (24 June 79 – 13 September 81).
DOMITIAN (14 September 81 – 16 September 96).
NERVA (16 September 96 – 25 January 98).
TRAJAN (25 January 97 – 8 August 117).
HADRIAN (11 August 117 – 10 July 138).

ROMAN GOVERNORS OF JUDAEA (AD 6—135)
Prefects/Procurators subject to supervision by the Imperial Legate in Syria (AD6–66):
COPONIUS (6–9).
MARCUS AMBIBULUS (9–12).
ANNIUS RUFUS (c12–15).
VALERIUS GRATUS (15–26).
PONTIUS PILATE (26–36).
MARCELLUS/MARULLUS (36–41).
[**KING HEROD AGRIPPA I** (41–44).]
CUSPIUS FADUS (44–?46).
TIBERIUS IULIUS ALEXANDER (?46–48).
VENTIDIUS CUMANUS (48–c52).
ANTONIUS FELIX (c52–?60).
PORCIUS FESTUS (?60–62).
LUCCEIUS ALBINUS (62–64).
GESSIUS FLORUS (64–66).
[**JEWISH REVOLT** (66–70).]
Commanders of the Legio X Fretensis with praetorian rank (AD70–?120): Only isolated names are known:
SEX. VETTULENUS CERIALIS (70–?71).
LUCILIUS BASSUS (?71–73).
L. FLAVIUS SILVA (73–?).
CN. POMPEIUS LONGINUS (86).
SEX. HERMETIDIUS CAMPANUS (93).
ATTICUS (?99/100–?102/3).
C. IULIUS QUADRATUS BASSUS (102/3–104/5).
Q. ROSCIUS COELIUS POMPEIUS FALCO (105–107).
?TIBERIANUS (114).
LUSIUS QUIETUS (117).
Governors of consular rank when the Legio VI Ferrata was also stationed in Judaea (AD ?120–135):
Q. TINEIUS RUFUS (132).
C. QUINCTIUS CERTUS PUBLICIUS MARCELLUS (?).
SEX. IULIUS SEVERUS (135).

HIGH PRIESTS
Appointed by King Herod the Great (37–4 BC)
ANANEL (37–36, and again from 34 BC).
ARISTOBULUS III (35 BC).
JESUS SON OF PHIABI (to c 23 BC).
SIMON SON OF BOETHUS (c23–5 BC).
MATTHIAS SON OF THEOPHILUS (5–4 BC).
JOSEPH SON OF ELLEM (one day).
JOAZAR SON OF BOETHUS (4 BC).
Appointed by the Tetrarch Archelaus (4 BC–AD6)
ELEAZAR SON OF BOETHUS (from 4 BC).
JESUS SON OF SEE (to AD6).
Appointed by Quirinius, Legate of Syria (AD6).
ANANUS/ANNAS SON OF SETHI (AD6–15).
Appointed by Gratus, Procurator of Judaea (AD15–26).
ISMAEL SON OF PHIABI (c15–16).
ELEAZAR SON OF ANANUS (c16–17).
SIMON SON OF CAMITHUS (17–18).
JOSEPHUS CAIAPHAS (c18–37).
Appointed by Vitellius, Legate of Syria (AD35–39).
JONATHAN SON OF ANANUS/ANNAS (two months in 37).
THEOPHILUS SON OF ANANUS/ANNAS (from 37).
Appointed by King Agrippa I (AD41–44).
SIMON CANTHERAS SON OF BOETHUS (from 41).
MATTHIAS SON OF ANANUS/ANNAS (?).
ELIONAEUS SON OF CANTHERAS (44).
Appointed by Herod of Chalcis (AD44–48).
JOSEPH SON OF KAMI (?).
ANANIAS SON OF NEDEBAEUS (47–c59).
Appointed by King Agrippa II (AD50–?92).
ISMAEL SON OF PHIABI (c59–62).
JOSEPH CABI SON OF SIMON (61–62).
ANANUS SON OF ANANUS/ANNAS (three months in 62).
JESUS SON OF DAMNAEUS (c62–63).
JESUS SON OF GAMALIEL (63–64).
MATTHIAS SON OF THEOPHILUS (65–?).
Appointed by people during the Revolt (AD66–70).
PHANNIAS/PHANNI/PHANASOS SON OF SAMUEL (?).

| | House of Phiabi | | House of Ananus/Annas |
| House of Boethus | | House of Kamith |

Map labels
SYRIA
Chalcis · Abila
Damascus
Sidon
PHOENICIA
Tyre
Ptolemais ·
Caesarea Philippi
TRACHONITIS
GAULANITIS
BATANAEA
Nareh
Dium
Canatha
AURANITIS
Sea of Chinnereth (Sea of Galilee)
Hippus
Gadara
Taricheae
Tiberias
GALILEE
Diocaesarea (Sepphoris)
DECAPOLIS
Pella
Capitolias
Scythopolis (Beth-shean)
Maximianopolis
PERAEA
R. Jordan
Philadelphia
Gaba?
SAMARIA
Dora
Sebaste
Neapolis
Caesarea
Esbus
Julius (Livias)
Medeba
Jericho
NABATAEANS
Antipatris
Apollonia Sozusa
Machaerus
Salt Sea (Dead Sea)
R. Arnon
Aelia Capitolina (Jerusalem)
Diospolis
Nicopolis (Emmaus)
Joppa
JUDAEA
Jamnia
Masada
Areopolis
Charachmoba
Great Sea (Mediterranean Sea)
Azotus ·
Eleutheropolis
Ascalon ·
Gaza ·
Raphia ·

1/ The maximum extent of the kingdoms of Agrippas I and II
— Agrippa I's kingdom
— Agrippa II's kingdom

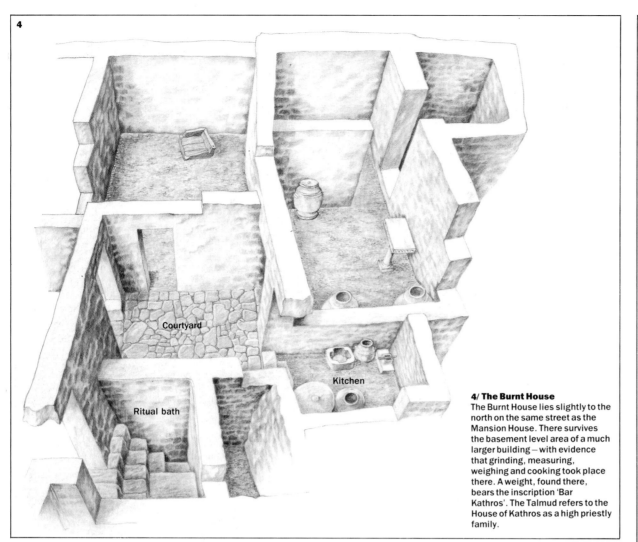

4/ The Burnt House
The Burnt House lies slightly to the north on the same street as the Mansion House. There survives the basement level area of a much larger building – with evidence that grinding, measuring, weighing and cooking took place there. A weight, found there, bears the inscription 'Bar Kathros'. The Talmud refers to the House of Kathros as a high priestly family.

THE THIRD WALL IN JERUSALEM
Whilst Herod the Great wished to rebuild much of Jerusalem – he only slightly extended the area of the city by the addition of the second wall. Accordingly, Golgotha was *outside* the walls at the time of Jesus' crucifixion (see page 166-7 for Herodian Jerusalem). According to Josephus (WAR, Book 5), it was Herod Agrippa I (AD 41-44) who laid the foundations of a new north wall, the Third Wall. It was completed during the First Revolt (AD 66-70). Josephus writes that the new wall began at the Hippicus Tower (one of Herod's towers to the Citadel), stretched north to the Psephinus Tower and then descended eastward, joining the older ramparts by the Antonia fortress and terminating in the Kidron valley. Archaeological evidence for the wall is inconclusive. Some think (see diagram 1) it followed a line co-terminous with the current Turkish north wall apart from the Sheep Market which was still outside the walls to the north of the Temple site, whilst others hold (see diagram 2) that the northern line was far to the north of the present north wall, enclosing all the nearby inhabited areas of the city in the 1st century AD. The city had gradually expanded in a northerly direction since the time of David. The fact that Titus ordered most of the walls to be razed in AD 70 and that there was further destruction in AD 135 accounts for the uncertainty in locating the Third Wall.

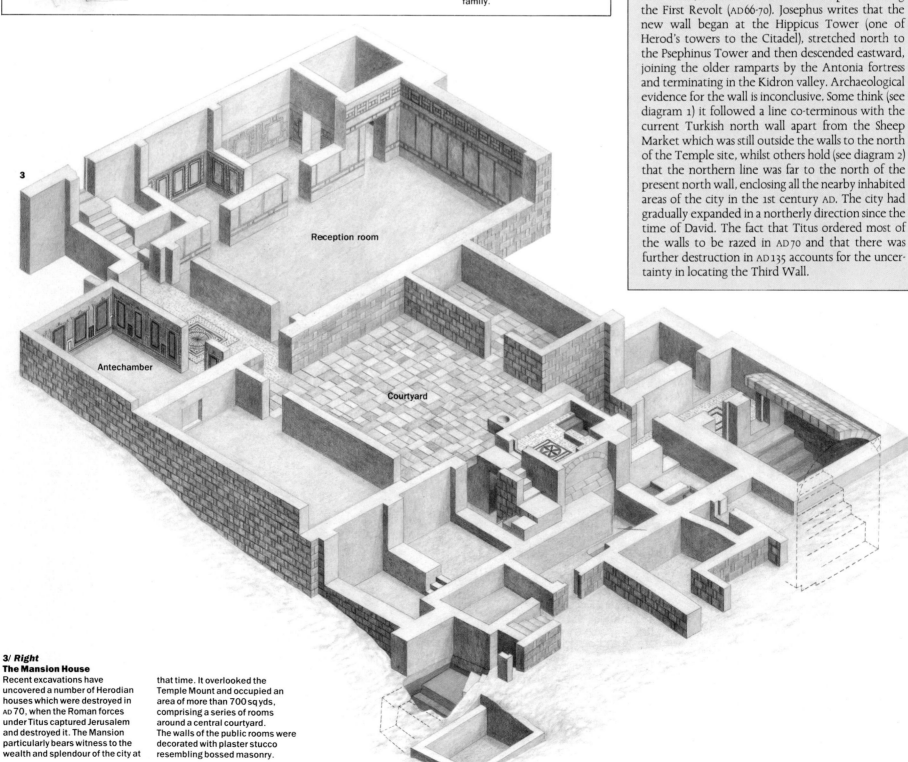

3/ Right
The Mansion House
Recent excavations have uncovered a number of Herodian houses which were destroyed in AD 70, when the Roman forces under Titus captured Jerusalem and destroyed it. The Mansion particularly bears witness to the wealth and splendour of the city at that time. It overlooked the Temple Mount and occupied an area of more than 700 sq yds, comprising a series of rooms around a central courtyard. The walls of the public rooms were decorated with plaster stucco resembling bossed masonry.

LARGE communities of Jews were first found outside Palestine in the late 8th and the 7th centuries BC, for it was then that, after the fall of the kingdoms of Israel and Judah, many captives were transported to Assyria and Babylonia. During the Persian period and after, this Mesopotamian diaspora remained a centre of Jewish life. A few Jews also moved from Judah to Egypt as mercenary troops of the Persian state, as the chance survival of the archive of a 5th century Jewish garrison at Elephantine in Upper Egypt has revealed. However, the great expansion of Jews outside Palestine occurred only after the conquest of the Persian empire by Alexander the Great in 332-323 BC (see page 138). Alexander's victory welded the lands of the Eastern Mediterranean and the Fertile Crescent into a single political unit and fostered the development of an homogeneous Hellenistic culture.

The causes of this diaspora were varied. Some Jews were carried off as war captives, not only to Assyria and Babylonia but also to Egypt by one of Alexander's successors, Ptolemy Soter (who reigned from 323-285 BC), and to Rome after the sieges of Jerusalem by Pompey in 63 BC and by Sosius in 37 BC. Others emigrated voluntarily, for Palestine was frequently an arena for warfare throughout the Hellenistic period and the hill country around Jerusalem was not very fertile, while growth in the Jewish population was not limited, as elsewhere in the ancient world, by infanticide or abortion. The political unification of the Near East by the Greek conquerors provided Jews with more enticing opportuni-

THE CHRISTIAN ERA

THE JEWISH DIASPORA IN THE 1st CENTURY AD

By the 1st century both Jewish and non-Jewish writers express astonishment at the extent of the Jewish dispersion over the Hellenistic world. The causes were varied but included emigration, exile, voluntary military service under foreign monarchs, and the sale into slavery of those captured after the fall of Jerusalem. This dispersion was to have profound consequences not only for the Jews but for the whole world.

ties abroad. Some settled in the cities founded by the Hellenistic monarchs. Others provided military service to the kings; best known of these are the Jewish mercenaries who served the Ptolemies of Egypt in the 2nd century BC, for their leader, the priest Onias, was permitted to found at Leontopolis a Jewish temple as a rival to the Temple of Jerusalem. Yet others settled as farmers in the lands adjacent to Palestine, as the survival of Jewish papyri from the Egyptian countryside amply documents. Those who sought a livelihood in the cities were usually occupied in crafts or local commerce, but by the end of the 1st century BC some Jews also became involved in more

long-distance trade; they were helped by the existence of Jewish communities in many of the cities along the coast of the eastern Mediterranean.

This huge diaspora was expanded still further when captives from the Judaean revolts of AD 66-70 and AD 132-135 were sold into slavery. By the 3rd and 4th centuries AD Jews were to be found in many places on the western Mediterranean coast. It is impossible to estimate how many Jews lived outside Palestine in the 1st century AD, though the Jewish philosopher Philo states that there were a million Jews in Egypt in his time. It is not known how much the natural increase of these diaspora communities was swelled by the inclusion of converts within their ranks.

There is not much literary evidence for the life of diaspora Jews in the 1st century AD, but a prime source is the New Testament itself, particularly the Acts of the Apostles, which frequently refer to Jews living in Syria, Asia Minor and Greece. The only Jewish author from the diaspora apart from St Paul whose writings survive in some quantity is Philo. His works, and fragments of Greek writings by other diaspora Jews in a variety of genres, were preserved only by the early Church.

Other evidence about the diaspora is more fragmentary. The historian Josephus, who was born in Jerusalem but ended his days after AD 70 in Rome and had contacts with the Jewish upper class in Egypt and Cyrene, frequently mentions the diaspora communities in passing. Non-Jewish writers, both Greek and Latin, make occasional, usually

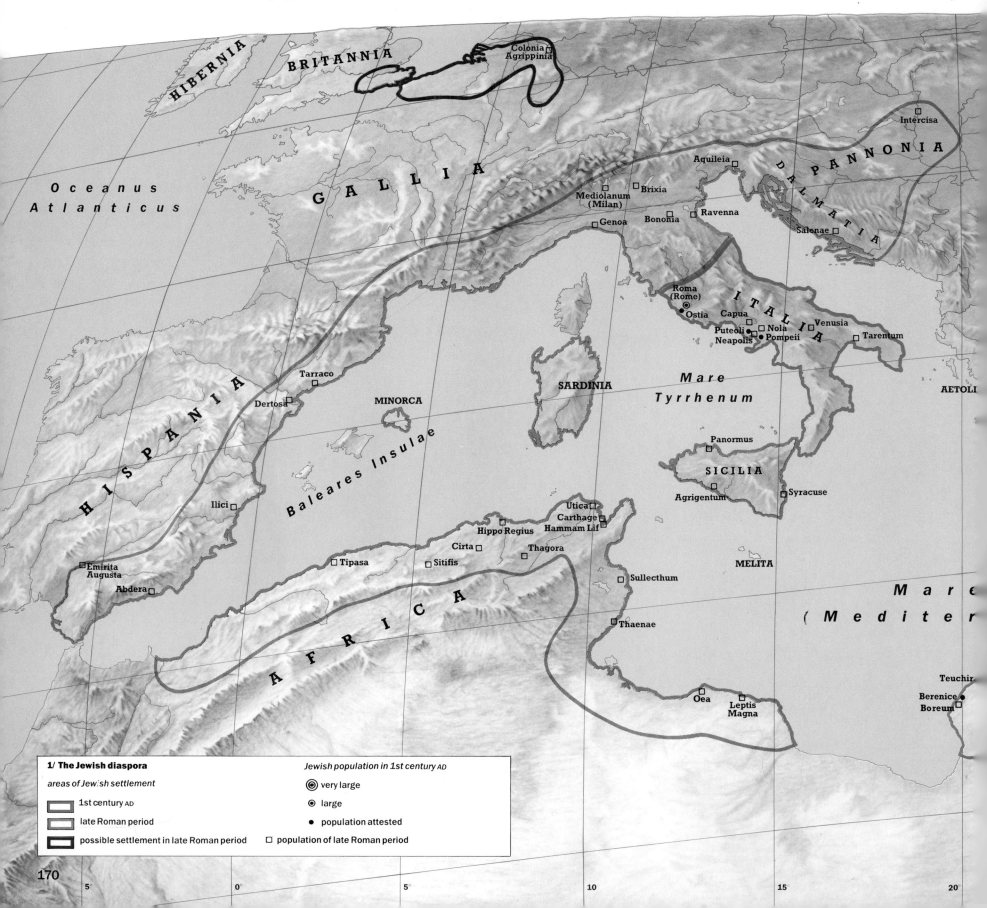

1/ The Jewish diaspora

areas of Jewish settlement

— 1st century AD
— late Roman period
— possible settlement in late Roman period

Jewish population in 1st century AD

◎ very large
◉ large
● population attested
□ population of late Roman period

ill-informed, remarks about the Jews in their midst. Many stone inscriptions survive, set up by Jews for funerary or honorific purposes, but most of these are from the late Roman period, and the mass of evidence found in the catacombs of the city of Rome itself is not paralleled elsewhere. The Jews of Egypt are particularly well recorded, both because of the political significance of the Alexandrian community and because of the survival in the desert sands of papyrus documents written by and about Jews. Archaeological evidence for synagogues is widely spread, though only a few of those buildings excavated are likely to have been in existence as early as the 1st century AD. Of those from later centuries the two most remarkable are the huge late Roman edifice at Sardis and the 3rd-century synagogue built at Dura-Europos on the Euphrates.

Diaspora Jews participated to a considerable extent in the surrounding culture. Most Jews in the Mediterranean lands spoke and wrote in Greek rather than in a Semitic tongue; Mesopotamian Jews used the local vernacular, Aramaic. In Greek areas some Jews may have participated regularly in the theatres and gymnasia, drawing a line only at participation in pagan cults, and in some cities Jews could become, at least by the late Roman period, councillors and magistrates. It is, however, not clear to what extent Jewish religion was also affected by the general notions of Hellenistic culture.

It is probable that Jewish worship in the diaspora was not very different from that in Palestine. Some scholars have claimed that Greek-speaking Jews were particularly prone to mystical interpretation of the Jewish Law, but this is not proven. Assimilation of pagan concepts into Jewish monotheism was in fact rare. Jews preferred to hold up their ethical supremacy for the emulation of gentile neighbours. Their own religious preoccupations were, as in Palestine, with the Temple and the Law. Most diaspora Jews recognized the supremacy of the Jerusalem Temple and respect for the sanctuary was regularly manifested by contributions to the Temple upkeep. As for the Law, it was as much upheld by Jews outside Palestine as within. All Jews preserved the traditional restrictions on food and observed the Sabbath as a day of rest.

The Law which enshrined this way of life was the focus of communal worship in the synagogue, where it was expounded. In the diaspora, synagogues were treated as sacred places worthy of fine buildings earlier than in Palestine, where sanctity was attributed to the Temple alone, and the importance of the diaspora synagogues was further enhanced by the way that the rulers of the synagogues acted not only in the religious sphere but also as magistrates in the imposition of community discipline. In many cities Jews managed their own affairs, settling their own disputes and shunning interference by the gentile authorities. In some places, this autonomy was formally recognized by the suzerain power. In others it was ensured by the *de facto* ability of the Jewish community to control deviants by the threat of excommunication. Perhaps not surprisingly, such self-isolation, combined with loyalty to a distant cult-centre in Palestine and the unsocial behaviour necessitated by Jewish dietary laws and prohibitions on intermarriage, made Jews less than popular in some cities. Anti-semitism is often expressed in Greek and Latin authors. The most hostile Greeks were those from Egypt. Especially virulent were the attacks by Alexandrian Greeks, who objected to the attempts by the Jews in their midst either to win the right to hold full citizenship of the city while refusing to participate in the city's pagan cults, or to free their community from all interference by the city authorities. The struggle in 1st-century Alexandria was long and often bloody. It culminated, in AD 117-119, in a great uprising by the Jews of Egypt, Cyrene and Cyprus, at the end of which the Jewish communities of these places were effectively obliterated. During these years and throughout the rebellions in Judaea the position of other diaspora Jews was less than happy, though only those settled closest to Palestine suffered massacre at the hands of their gentile neighbours in the vicious fighting in AD 66.

'...OF ALL THE TOWNS IN SYRIA THERE ISN'T ONE THAT HASN'T EXTERMINATED ITS JEWISH INHABITANTS... AS A SINGLE INSTANCE, THE DAMASCENES, THOUGH THEY COULDN'T EVEN FAKE A PLAUSIBLE EXCUSE, MADE THEIR OWN CITY ROCK WITH THE MOST LOATHSOME SLAUGHTER, BUTCHERING 18,000 JEWS...'

JOSEPHUS, WAR

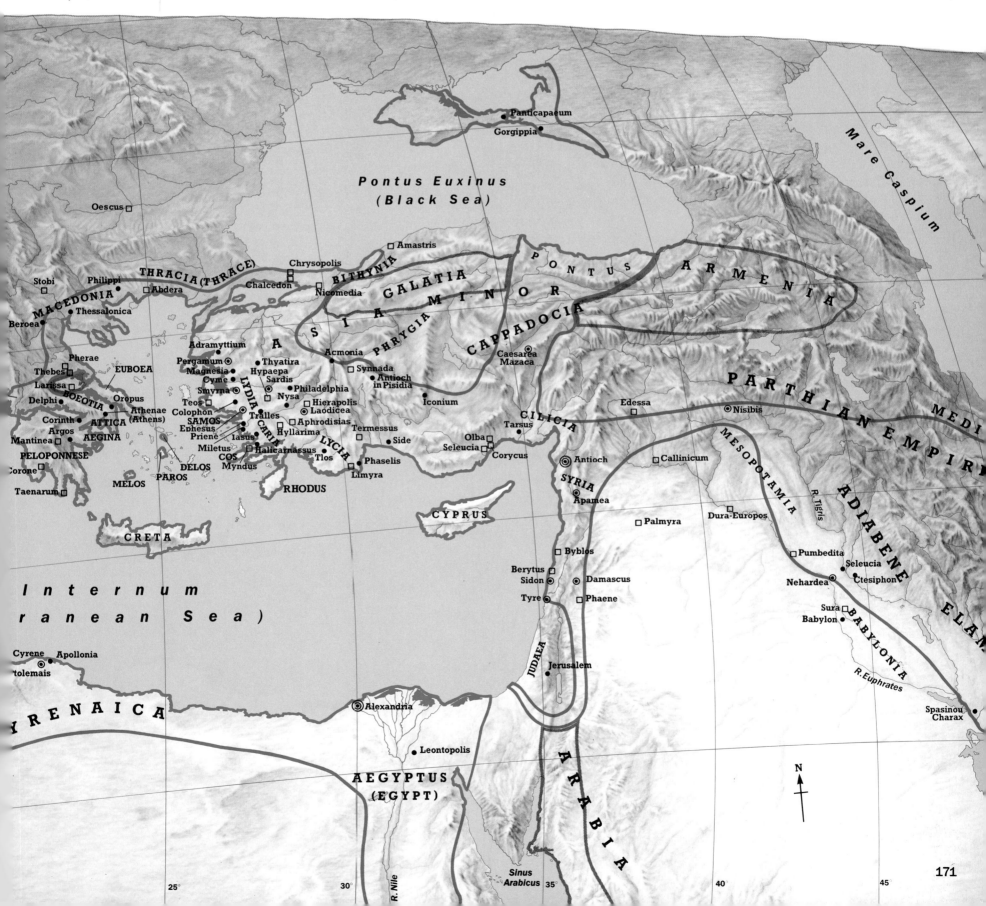

PAUL'S JOURNEYS

Paul was not the only believer to carry the faith beyond the borders of Palestine, but he has become the archetypal Christian missionary. After his conversion at Antioch he travelled extensively throughout the Mediterranean, covering well over 20,000 miles in his documented journeys. He also had plans to go as far afield as Spain. Paul's most significant religious contribution however, was not the number of churches he founded but his insight that Christianity could be separated from its parent Jewish culture. By paring faith to its essentials he enabled it to take root and to flower among the gentiles.

If a man's universe is the arena in which his mature energies are concentrated, the Aegean Sea was the centre of Paul's world, and the main centres of his activity were Corinth and Ephesus. Both were capitals of Roman provinces and enjoyed excellent communications. Not only could Paul travel easily in all directions, but the cities attracted visitors who could serve as ambassadors of the new faith in their homelands. As commercial centres they were more open to new ideas than smaller towns or conservative intellectual cities like Athens. Their size offered Paul anonymity which protected him from the Roman law against new religions. Their highly heterogeneous populations contained many energetic people whose ambitions were frustrated by religious and social factors; the paradoxes of Paul's theology found a powerful echo in the ambiguity of their lives. Others who had lost contact with their cultural roots and ancestral certitudes found in his words a message that gave meaning to existence. From Corinth the faith radiated throughout Achaia, but apart from Cenchreae (ROM 16.1) no community is named. The church of Ephesus evangelized the churches of Colossae, Hierapolis, and Laodicea in the Lycus valley.

FIRST JOURNEY

Paul's missionary work began sometime after AD 38, when he escaped from Damascus and made a visit to Jerusalem (II COR 11.32-33; GAL 1.17-18). His first journey (ACTS 13-14) was undertaken at the behest of the church of Antioch and under the guidance of Barnabas. They went first to Cyprus, which was the homeland of Barnabas (ACTS 4.36) where Salamis and Paphos had Jewish communities and in addition were respectively the industrial and political centres of the island.

The success of the mission in Cyprus persuaded Paul to go further afield. The conversion of the proconsul, Sergius Paulus (ACTS 13.7-12), is supported by the fact that they then went to Antioch in Pisidia (ACTS 13.14-52), because his family had a large estate further north, and he could have provided introductions to influential friends. From Pisidian Antioch they went east, presumably with the intention of making a circle back to Antioch-on-the-Orontes, but the opposition they encountered in setting up communities in Iconium, Lystra, and Derbe eventually persuaded them to retrace their steps, principally to give the infant communities an organized structure (ACTS 14.23). There being no need to return to Cyprus, they sailed directly from Attalia to Seleucia, the port of Antioch. This journey cannot be dated precisely, but it must have taken place in the early 40s AD.

SECOND JOURNEY

Immensely more ambitious than his first journey, Paul's second voyage (AD 48-51) led to the foundation of churches indelibly associated with his name. Luke places the second journey (ACTS 15.40-18.22) after the Jerusalem Conference (ACTS 15.1-30; GAL 2.1-10), but from Paul's letters it is clear that it must have taken place before this event. This time he worked independently, and his objective was Ephesus, but mysterious circumstances forced him north and then west (ACTS 16.6). An illness (GAL 4.13), caused him to winter in Galatia, where the estate of the Sergii Pauli was located. This gave him the opportunity to evangelize that region of wild Celtic tribes. The road system see (page 186) would have made it natural for him then to strike north into Bithynia, but again he was blocked (ACTS 16.7). He had little choice but to take the risk of cutting across the wild country in the north of Asia to Troas on the coast (ACTS 16.8).

At Troas, Paul made the momentous decision to carry the faith to Europe (ACTS 16.9-10). The first available boat probably determined the choice of Philippi as his landing-point (ACTS 16.12). From there it was natural to go west along the famous Via Egnatia to Thessalonica (ACTS 17.1). His intention may have been to go right through to the Adriatic Sea, but Jewish opposition forced him to seek refuge in Beroea (ACTS 17.10). When his adversaries followed him there, he decided on a long jump south to Athens (ACTS 17.13-34). A mistake in strategy having compromised his mission there, Paul cut his losses by seeking fresh pastures in Corinth, where the response was so favourable that he remained 18 months (ACTS 18.1-11).

Paul wrote three letters from Corinth. I Thessalonians was written during the founding visit in AD 50-51. The Pauline authorship of II Thessalonians is disputed, but if authentic it would have been written during the same period. On his third visit in the winter of AD 55-56 he wrote Romans 1-15 to prepare his visit to the capital of the empire.

In the summer of AD 51 Paul met the proconsul Lucius Gallio (ACTS 18.12), and this is the only key to dating this journey. Assuming that Paul spent one winter in Galatia and the following one in Philippi, he would have left Antioch in the spring of AD 48 at the latest. Given the northerly winds that prevail in summer, it was easiest to sail home. His brief visit to Ephesus (ACTS 18.19) was dictated either by the route of the ship or by the need to find a ship going to Caesarea (ACTS 18.22). This voyage would have taken place in August or early September AD 51.

THIRD JOURNEY

The following spring Paul set off on his third voyage (ACTS 18.23 – 21.16). His goal was Ephesus, and this time he reached it after having spent some time in Galatia (I COR 16.1). The capital of the Roman province of Asia became his base for 27 months (ACTS 19.8-10), roughly August AD 52 to October 55.

Of the five letters written from Ephesus three were directed to Corinth. Two of these letters have not been preserved, and only I Corinthians written in the spring of AD 54 remains. Philippians is a compilation of three letters, and it is not sure that all were written from Ephesus; one, at least, was written from prison. Their dates, and that of Galatians cannot be fixed precisely. II Corinthians is a

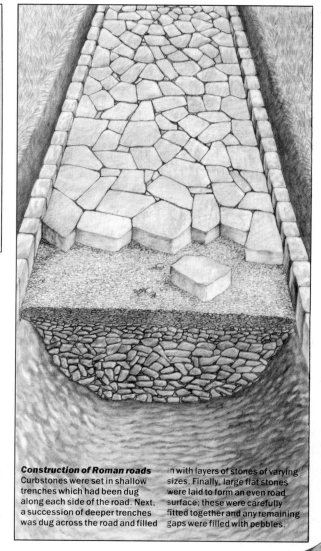

Construction of Roman roads
Curbstones were set in shallow trenches which had been dug along each side of the road. Next, a succession of deeper trenches was dug across the road and filled in with layers of stones of varying sizes. Finally, large flat stones were laid to form an even road surface; these were carefully fitted together and any remaining gaps were filled with pebbles.

3/ Above
'The roads were carried straight across the countryside, were paved with hewn stones and bolstered underneath with masses of tight-packed gravel; hollows were filled in, and torrents or ravines that cut across the route were bridged.' PLUTARCH.

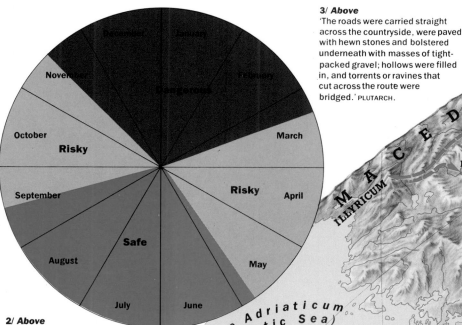

2/ Above
The seas were closed 11 November-10 March because of short days, dense cloud cover, poor visibility and strong winds. Snow and rain inhibited travel in mountainous areas during winter. Uncertain weather made sea travel risky 15 September-10 November and 11 March-26 May. The safe sailing season was 27 May-14 September.

compilation of two letters, both sent from Macedonia in the spring and late summer of AD55.

Problems in the Corinthian community forced him to make a visit there (II COR 13.2) in the summer of AD54. He returned overland to Ephesus via Macedonia (II COR 1.23-2.1). Mortal danger forced him to leave Ephesus for Troas in the autumn of AD54, whence he went to Macedonia, where he wintered either in Philippi or Thessalonica.

In the spring of AD55 Paul continued west, possibly as far as Illyricum (ROM 15.19), after having written II Corinthians 1-9. Sometime during the summer news reached him of a drastic deterioration of the situation at Corinth. His immediate response was to send II Corinthians 10-13, but he followed shortly after, (II COR 13.1-2; ACTS 20.2-3) and spent the winter of AD55-56 in Corinth, where he wrote Romans. The following spring he headed back to Macedonia, and celebrated Passover in Philippi (ACTS 20.6). They sailed down the coast of Asia (ACTS 20.6-21.1). The only ship sailing from Patara to Phoenicia brought them to Tyre, whence they walked to Jerusalem (ACTS 21.12-16).

FINAL JOURNEY

Paul's final recorded voyage was as a prisoner to Rome (ACTS 27.1-28.16). If the year is uncertain (AD58 or later), we are sure of the season; the time for safe sailing had passed (ACTS 27.9). The prevailing winds forced them to the north-west. They probably expected to winter in a port on the southern coast of Turkey, but a grain-carrier on the Alexandria-Rome run had been delayed and was still in Myra, and so they took passage on her (ACTS 27.5-6). At Cnidus, when they were no longer protected by the coast, they were forced to run south and under the lee of Crete. Fair-Havens being an unsuitable winter harbour they tried to make Phoenix, which was better protected (ACTS 27.8-12), but were driven to sea by a storm that eventually drove them ashore on Malta (ACTS 27.39-28.1). When the sailing season opened the following spring, they boarded another Alexandrian ship, which had wintered in Malta, and with stops at Syracuse and Rhegium they finally arrived at Puteoli (ACTS 28.11-16). They walked from Naples to Rome.

The letter to the Laodiceans (one of the 'Prison Epistles' written from Rome) is mentioned in Colossians 4.10, but has not been preserved. Philemon is the only letter that Paul wrote to an individual, and was probably sent together with Colossians.

'AND THEY WENT THROUGH THE REGION OF PHRYGIA AND GALATIA, HAVING BEEN FORBIDDEN BY THE HOLY SPIRIT TO SPEAK THE WORD IN ASIA. AND WHEN THEY HAD COME OPPOSITE MYSIA THEY ATTEMPTED TO GO INTO BITHYNIA, BUT THE SPIRIT OF JESUS DID NOT ALLOW THEM; SO PASSING BY MYSIA, THEY WENT DOWN TO TROAS.'
ACTS 16.6-8

4/ Left
A Mediterranean trading ship from the time of Paul, taken from part of a sarcophagus from Sidon. The safe sailing season ran from 27 May to 14 September.

1/ Map below
At Antioch Paul was first called upon to begin his missionary journeys (ACTS 13.1-2), which lasted for roughly 18 years, and took him right round the Mediterranean littoral, spreading the word, setting up churches and Christian communities.

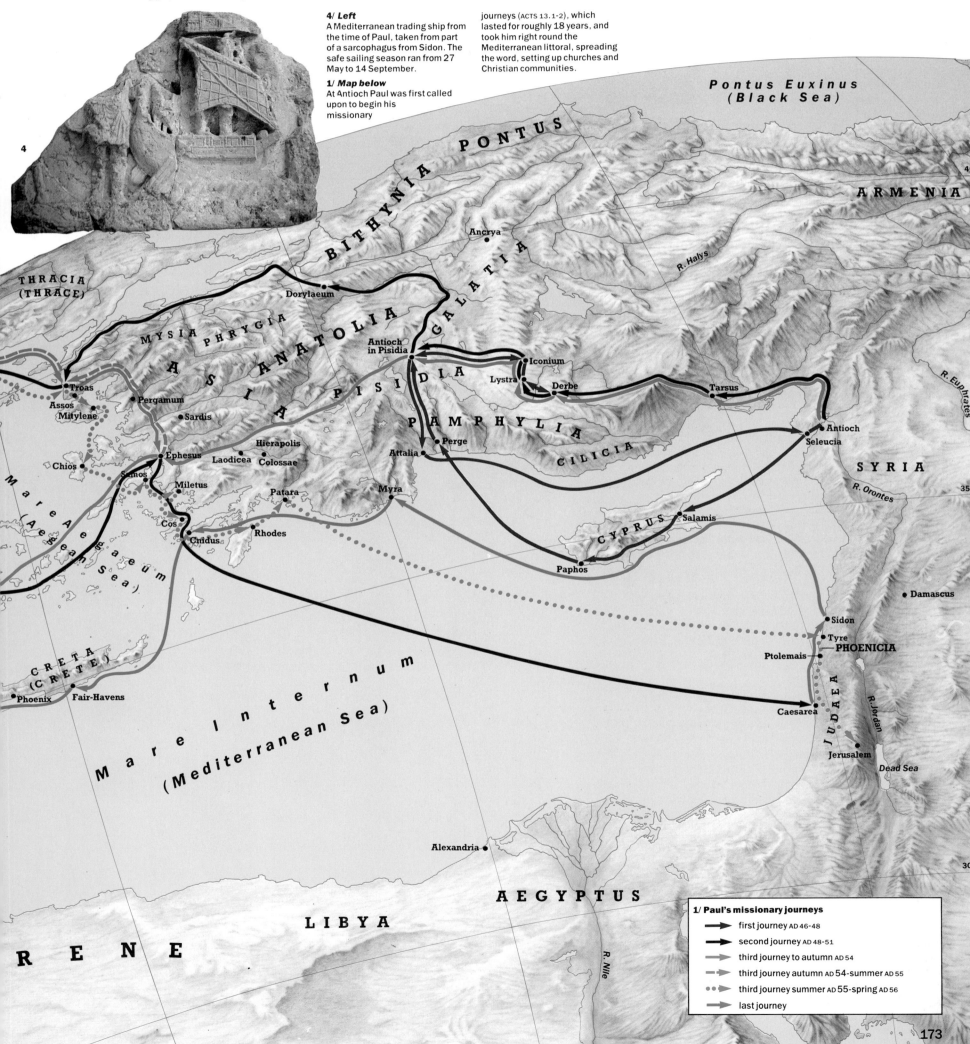

1/ Paul's missionary journeys
→ first journey AD 46-48
→ second journey AD 48-51
→ third journey to autumn AD 54
⇢ third journey autumn AD 54-summer AD 55
⋯ third journey summer AD 55-spring AD 56
→ last journey

173

IN ACTS Paul is twice recorded as saying that he was a citizen of Tarsus and once that he was born there, but nowhere in his letters does he refer to the fact – nor does he refer to his Roman citizenship.

Originally Anatolian, Tarsus, in Paul's day, had an odd mixture of Greeks, Romans and Jews. Cilicia had become a Roman province in 64 BC and Tarsus, an extremely ancient city, became its capital. It had a strategic position, controlling the narrow pass (the 'Cilician gates') between the mountains and the sea (see page 172). Under Augustus, Tarsus became a free city, enjoying local autonomy – with most citizens possessing Roman citizenship. Until the 3rd century AD it rivalled Athens and Alexandria as a centre of learning. The Roman geographer Strabo writes: 'the inhabitants of Tarsus have become so enthusiastic for philosophy and the whole area of education, that they have surpassed Athens, Alexandria and any other place you may mention as a seat of education and philosophy ... . You will also find various schools of rhetoric at Tarsus.' Although he was a Jew educated in Jerusalem and not a student of the Greek philosophical schools, Paul must have imbibed some Greek culture from his environment.

Tarsus was also famed for its leather work and, whilst Paul is described as a 'tent-maker', the word so translated often indicates a leather-worker.

ANTIOCH
In the Roman empire it is likely that only Rome and Alexandria surpassed Antioch in importance, both politically and culturally. Once the capital of the Greek empire, established by Alexander's general, Seleucus; under the Romans it was the capital of the province of Syria, where Roman government, Greek culture and oriental religion met. Many Jews had settled there during the Seleucid period, whilst Christianity reached there when the Greek-speaking Jewish Christians were scattered after Stephen's martyrdom (ACTS 11.19-26). It was there that the title 'Christian' was first applied to the followers of Jesus. It is likely that this term was used by gentiles. The Jews would have recognized the word 'Christ' as the equivalent of the Hebrew 'Messiah' (anointed one), but they would have been loath to recognize Jesus as God's anointed servant. By contrast, the gentiles would have found references to an 'anointed one' perplexing and so dubbed the followers of Jesus 'those who talk of anointing'.

After his conversion to Christianity and some years in Arabia, Paul had returned to his native Tarsus, but was summoned from there to Antioch by Barnabas. There, for the first time, he preached to gentiles. It was the Christian community which sent Paul and Barnabas on their first extended missionary journey (ACTS 13.1-2; 14.26). As the Christian community was made up of former diaspora Jews and gentiles, they would have been more concerned than the Jerusalem Christians with the need for on-going missionary expansion. It was there that Paul and Peter had their confrontation over the question of fellowship between Jewish and gentile Christians.

CORINTH
Corinth was a city of importance from the 7th century BC, controlling the Italian and Adriatic trade routes. It was famous for its bronze and pottery. According to Josephus, one of the gates of the Jerusalem Temple was of Corinthian bronze and more highly valued than those plated with silver or set in gold (WAR, Book 5). The city had been destroyed in 146 BC when the Romans conquered Achaia, but was refounded as a colony by Julius Caesar. When Augustus put the province of Achaia under senatorial control in 27 BC, Corinth became the capital of the province and the seat of the proconsul. In Paul's time its population and importance were far greater than those of Athens, although Athens was still the home of Greek culture. We can date Paul's first visit and 18-month stay to AD 51-56, because we are told that Gallio was proconsul (ACTS 18.12).

Strabo comments on the strategic importance of Corinth, straddling, as it did, the Isthmus – with a port on either side. Attempts to construct a canal proved vain, but small ships would be dragged across, whilst other cargoes could be taken overland. Cenchreae, one of the ports, looked towards Tasia, whilst Lechaeum – with a harbour three times the size of Cenchreae's – looked towards Italy. Hence Cenchreae harbour, linked with the city by two dirt roads, was full of ships from Egypt, Syria and Asia Minor, whilst Lechaeum's, connected with the city by long walls, had vessels from Spain, Italy and Sicily.

Because of these international contacts, Corinth became a very cosmopolitan city and, like many ports, had a reputation for immorality. 'To play the Corinthian' was to engage in loose living. The chief temple in the city was one

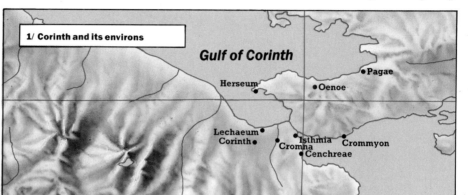

THE CHRISTIAN ERA

CITIES OF PAUL
As was evident from the account of Paul's missionary journeys we have reference to a large number of cities which he visited. Here we concentrate on Tarsus, his birthplace (see page 172); Antioch in Syria, where followers of Jesus had first been called 'Christians' and from where Paul went on his first great missionary journey; and then Corinth and Ephesus, both of which became focuses for his evangelistic activities.

dedicated to Aphrodite, the goddess of love.

The home of the Isthmian games (which alternated with the Olympic games), Corinth naturally attracted visitors from the whole of the Greek-speaking world.

In the excavations at Anaploga (part of Corinth) a villa has been unearthed dating to the time of Paul's residence in the city. As the church met in ordinary homes, the size of the villa is a pointer to the size of Christian congregations in Corinth. The *triclinium* (dining room), for example, would hardly have seated more than 12. The eucharist would have been celebrated at tables, but, with packed rooms, Paul found it necessary to speak of the need for 'decency and order' in worship and to remind the Christian community that, though meeting in a private house, they should act as

1/ Corinth and its environs

Gulf of Corinth

Pagae · Oenoe · Herseum · Lechaeum · Corinth · Cromna · Isthmia · Cenchreae · Crommyon

1/ Map left
Paul arrived in Corinth from Athens on his second missionary journey (see page 172) where he stayed for 18 months (ACTS 18.11). Corinth was an important trading centre in the 1st century AD, with ports on both sides of the Isthmus, Cenchreae and Lechaeum.

2/ Below
A reconstruction based on archaeological evidence of a Hellenistic villa recently excavated at Anaploga in Corinth. Christian congregations may have gathered in such houses to listen to Paul (see text).

in a public assembly.

It appears that the Eucharist took place at the conclusion of a meal, as the early Christians tried to pattern their ritual on what had happened at the Last Supper. The participants brought their own food to eat, and the nature of the food would have been a pointer to their social classes. Paul refers to discrimination between rich and poor. The more favoured would have had access to the *triclinium* and took occasion to dine and wine well prior to worship (see I COR 11.17-22). Paul, accordingly, suggests that they eat first in their own homes and only then come together for an act of worship.

EPHESUS

The importance of Ephesus for Paul is evident in the fact that he spent three years in the city. It was the leading city in Ionia, part of the Roman province of Asia and located on the main route from Rome to the east.

The chief fame of the city rested on the shrine of Artemis – not the virgin huntress of Graeco-Roman tradition, but the many-breasted Asian mother-goddess, the symbol of fertility. The cult was an ancient one – with the original statue probably of meteorite origin – but the temple in Paul's day dated to the 4th century BC and was regarded as one of the seven wonders of the world.

The site of the Artemisium has been excavated, as has the theatre where Paul had to face the mob, incited by the silver-smiths whose trade consisted largely in making figurines of the goddess (ACTS 19.29). The theatre, which was semi-circular in shape, backing on to a hall, could seat 20,000 spectators. The paved street from the theatre to the harbour has also been uncovered. Originally, it had shops on either side.

Much happened during Paul's three-year stay which is unrecorded. It is probable that Paul visited Colossae and Laodicea, as he later wrote letters to Christians in these cities. Ephesus, however, was the natural centre for the spread of Christianity in the whole province of Asia (see page 186). It is likely that the six other churches mentioned in REV 2-3 looked to Ephesus as their mother-church.

Many of the references and allusions in the account in ACTS of Paul's time in Ephesus are corroborated from other sources. There is reference to the destruction of books on magic. We know that Ephesus was so noted as a centre for the magical arts that books on the subject were often called 'Ephesian writings'. It is possible that Erastus (see ACTS 19.22) is to be identified with the Roman aedile of that name, known through an inscription from Corinth. The 'Asiarchs', mentioned as friends of Paul, had obviously been civic, public benefactors, as the title designated such in the Roman province of Asia.

> 'WHEN HE HAD LANDED AT CAESAREA, HE WENT UP AND GREETED THE CHURCH, AND THEN WENT DOWN TO ANTIOCH. AFTER SPENDING SOME TIME THERE HE DEPARTED AND WENT FROM PLACE TO PLACE THROUGH THE REGION OF GALATIA AND PHRYGIA.' ACTS 18.22-23

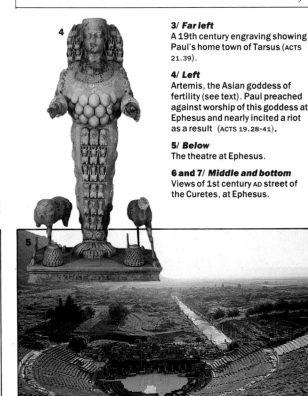

3/ Far left
A 19th century engraving showing Paul's home town of Tarsus (ACTS 21.39).

4/ Left
Artemis, the Asian goddess of fertility (see text). Paul preached against worship of this goddess at Ephesus and nearly incited a riot as a result (ACTS 19.28-41).

5/ Below
The theatre at Ephesus.

6 and 7/ Middle and bottom
Views of 1st century AD street of the Curetes, at Ephesus.

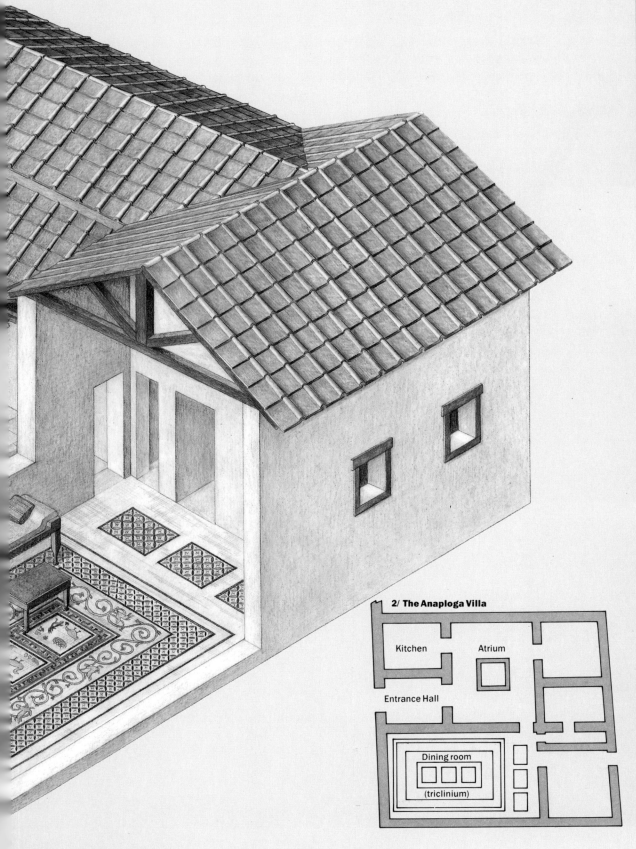

2/ The Anaploga Villa

Kitchen   Atrium

Entrance Hall

Dining room

(triclinium)

175

THE first war of the Jews against Rome was the outcome of an agitation nourished, ever since the subjection of Judaea to direct Roman administration in AD 6, by nationalist aspirations for independence mingled with messianic fervour. The venality and cruelty of the last two procurators of Judaea, Albinus (AD 62-64) and Gessius Florus (AD 64-66) further prompted the outbreak. The ultimate exacerbation came, however, in the late spring of AD 66 when Gessius Florus first seized a large sum of money belonging to the Temple and then, having obliged the reluctant Jerusalemites to welcome a Roman army contingent, instructed the soldiery to provoke the Jews and to turn their swords on whoever shouted insults at them.

The two main manifestations of the rebellion were the occupation by the revolutionaries (sicarii) of the fortress of Masada and the refusal by Eleazar, son of the High Priest Ananias, captain of the Temple, to offer sacrifice on behalf of the Roman emperor. When the civic leaders of the capital, assisted by king Agrippa II, proved unable to persuade the insurgents by amicable means, they resorted to force. This also met with no success. The fratricidal struggle in Jerusalem was accompanied furthermore by communal massacres in Palestinian cities with a mixed gentile-Jewish population (Caesarea, Ptolemais, Gabe, Samaria, Ascalon) and even in the Decapolis, Syria and Egypt (Alexandria).

The governor of Syria, Cestius Gallus (AD 63-66), failed to put down the revolt in Jerusalem and on his return was routed by the Jews near Beth-horon in October 66. Subsequently, the peace party of the Jerusalem notables was swept along into joining forces with the revolutionaries. Thus the first stage of the war was directed by high-ranking Sadducees and Pharisees (members of rival sects).

MILITARY DISTRICTS
The country was divided into military districts whose commanders are listed by Josephus in his book The Jewish War (II, 563-8). Jerusalem was entrusted to a former High Priest, Ananus son of Ananus, and Joseph son of Gorion. Two chief priests, Jesus son of Sapphias, and Eleazar, took charge of Idumaea. The region of Jericho was placed under Joseph son of Simon, the Transjordan (Peraea) under Manasseh. The north and west of Judaea (the districts of Thamna, Lydda, Joppa and Emmaus) were administered by John the Essene. John son of Ananias commanded northeastern Judaea (Gophna and Acrabeta), and both Galilee and the area of Gamala in Gaulanitis were allocated to Josephus son of Matthias, the author.

FORTIFICATION OF GALILEE AND GOLAN (AD 66)
Josephus set out at once in the winter of 66-67 to organize the defence of the territories under his command, despite the armed opposition to his leadership led by the extreme nationalist from Galilee, John from the town of Gischala. In Gaulanitis, Josephus sanctioned the repair of the walls of Gamala and fortified Seleucia and Sogane. In Upper Galilee, walls were erected around Jamnith, Meroth and Acchabare, and in Lower Galilee three cities, Taricheae, Tiberias and Sepphoris, were fortified, as well as a number of villages: the Cave of Arbela, Bersabe, Selame, Jotapata, Caphareccho, Japha, Sigoph and Mount Tabor (Josephus: Life 187-8; War II 573-4). Some of these fortresses were intended to block the road from Roman bases at Ptolemais (Sigoph, Caphareccho) and Scythopolis (Mt Tabor), or from the hostile Phoenicians in the north-west (Bersabe, Selame, Meroth) and from Agrippa's stronghold at Caesarea Philippi (Jamnith, Seleucia, Sogane). Others protected large population centres (Taricheae, Tiberias, Sepphoris, Japha). The rest of the fortresses were natural strongholds (Jotapata, Acchabare and Gamala).

ROMAN ATTACK ON GALILEE (AD 67)
In the spring of 67, Nero despatched Vespasian to put down the rebellion. He marched into Galilee from Antioch via Ptolemais, where his son Titus joined him from Alexandria. Together, they commanded 60,000 legionaries and auxiliaries, and the resolve of the Jewish forces cracked. Sepphoris joined the Romans at once. Josephus' army was assembled at Garis, but his untrained men scattered even before Vespasian's legions were seen on the horizon. The whole of Lower Galilee fell without a fight and Josephus fled with the remnant of his army to Tiberias, and then to the fortress of Jotapata. This in turn was captured in the early summer of 67 by Vespasian, and Josephus surrendered to him. The strongholds either opened their gates (Tiberias and Gischala), or were easily taken. Only Gamala put up fierce resistance before it was conquered. By the winter of 67, the whole of northern Palestine was in Roman hands.

CONQUEST OF PERAEA AND JUDAEA (AD 68-69)
The second stage of the war covered the period between

THE CHRISTIAN ERA

THE FIRST JEWISH REVOLT

The first Jewish war against Rome resulted from nationalist fervour and exacerbation caused by the misgovernment of the last procurators. In its first phase, the uprising was directed by high-ranking priests and Pharisees, among them the historian Josephus, commander of Galilee. The Romans under Vespasian, assisted by his son, Titus, easily conquered Galilee, Peraea and most of Judaea between AD 67 and 69, while in Jerusalem revolutionary parties, having replaced the aristocratic leaders, continued to fight among themselves. The capital was captured and destroyed by Titus in AD 70 after Vespasian's departure to Rome on his proclamation as emperor. Of the few remaining strongholds, Masada was the last to fall, in AD 74.

the subjugation of Galilee and the siege of Jerusalem. On the Jewish side it was characterized by a bloody civil war between the fanatical followers of John of Gischala allied to the Idumaeans, and the aristocratic leaders of the rebellion, who were accused of weakness in their resistance to Rome. Vespasian decided to let the Jewish factions destroy one another in Jerusalem and turned instead to Peraea, where he occupied the whole region as far south as the fortress of Machaerus, the site of John the Baptist's execution more than a generation earlier. By the late spring Antipatris, Lydda and Jamnia were seized. A legion was posted outside Emmaus, and after a march through Samaria the Romans entered Jericho.

Vespasian then travelled to Caesarea to prepare the siege of Jerusalem. The news of Nero's death reached him at this time, and he suspended all military action for almost 12 months whilst awaiting the outcome of the consequent internal strife of Rome. This ended with his own proclamation as emperor on 1 July 69. Shortly before, compelled by the exactions of a fresh rebel leader, Simon bar Giora, he

completed the conquest of Judaea, subjugating Gophna, Acrabeta, Bethel and Ephraim, as well as Hebron in the south. Only Jerusalem, Machaerus, Herodium and Masada remained in Jewish hands when he left Palestine first for Alexandria and finally for Rome, entrusting the settlement of the Jewish war to his son, Titus.

CAPTURE AND DESTRUCTION OF JERUSALEM (AD 70)

The struggle continued in Jerusalem between the three Jewish factions led by Simon bar Giora. John of Gischala and Eleazar son of Simon, the head of a splinter group detached from the party of John. The third group was soon eliminated, but persistent hostility between Simon and John ran parallel with the fight against the Romans from Passover until August/September 70, by which time the Temple had been reduced to ashes and much of the population had starved to death or been massacred. Others were captured and sent to the mines, or were paraded in Titus' triumph in Rome in AD 71.

MASADA – LAST REFUGE OF THE ZEALOTS

Lucilius Bassus, governor of Palestine (AD 71-74), proceeded to subdue the remaining centres of rebellion. Herod's fortress, Herodium, south of Jerusalem, surrendered, as did Machaerus on the eastern shore of the Dead Sea after some resistance. Only the rocky fortress of Masada, a sumptuous palace of Herod turned into a stronghold, held out for a while under the captaincy of Eleazar son of Jair, a descendant of Judas the Galilean, the founder of the party of the Zealots. But besieged by the armies of the new governor of Judaea, Flavius Silva (AD 73-81), it fell at last to the Romans after the mass suicide of the defenders in the spring of AD 74.

POLITICAL-MESSIANIC FIGURES IN 1st CENTURY PALESTINE

We learn from Josephus of a number of charismatic personalities claiming the power to call down divine intervention at this time. Theudas promised the Jews supernatural liberation under the procuratorship of Cuspius Fadus (AD 44-46), but was captured by the Romans and his followers were massacred (cf acts 5.36). Also, 'impostors and deceivers' pretending to possess miraculous talents appeared when Felix governed Judaea (AD ?52-60). Chief among these was an Egyptian 'prophet' who intended to destroy the walls of Jerusalem by the word of his command; but he, unlike most of his adherents, escaped the Roman cavalry and infantry. St Paul, when he was arrested in the Temple, was mistaken for him by a Roman officer (ACTS 21.38). Other unsuccessful prophets are mentioned as being active during the last phases of the siege of Jerusalem.

> "'MY LOYAL FOLLOWERS, LONG AGO WE RESOLVED TO SERVE NEITHER THE ROMANS NOR ANYONE ELSE BUT ONLY GOD, WHO ALONE IS THE TRUE AND RIGHTEOUS LORD OF MEN; NOW THE TIME HAS COME THAT BIDS US PROVE OUR DETERMINATION BY OUR DEEDS. AT SUCH A TIME WE MUST NOT DISGRACE OURSELVES. HITHERTO WE HAVE NEVER SUBMITTED TO SLAVERY, EVEN WHEN IT BROUGHT NO DANGER WITH IT; WE MUST NOT CHOOSE SLAVERY NOW, AND WITH IT PENALTIES THAT WILL MEAN THE END OF EVERYTHING IF WE FALL ALIVE INTO THE HANDS OF THE ROMANS.'"
>
> ELEAZAR'S SPEECH AT MASADA, JOSEPHUS, WAR, BOOK 7

1/ Map right
In response to the Jewish revolt in AD 66, the Romans under Cestius Gallus subdued Galilee and then marched to Judaea. Their attack on Jerusalem failed, and ended in retreat to the provincial capital at Caesarea. Vespasian in AD 67 subjugated Galilee, while his subordinates restored Roman control in Samaria and along the coastal plain. In 68 Vespasian conquered Peraea and moved into Idumaea, and between May and July 69 Roman control was tightened in northern Judaea and Idumaea. In 70 Titus advanced troops on Jerusalem from Emmaus, Jericho and Caesarea and after months of siege, the city was taken by assault. Finally after 70 the last strongholds of the rebels were methodically besieged and captured.

2/ Left
The fortress at Masada is described by Josephus in The Jewish War book VII. Situated on a rock surrounded by ravines, it became a last refuge for Jewish zealots after the Revolt had been quashed by the Romans. In AD 70, the Romans under Silva, besieged Masada, and heaped earth 300ft high, onto a rocky projection below the fortress. From this platform they then built a pier out of boulders, and a tower plated with iron. The Romans then hurled burning torches at the wooden walls of Masada, and were able to breach the Jewish defences, and climb into the fortress.

3/ Above left
Much of the information we have about this period comes from the historian Josephus. Born a Jew, he became a fighter against Rome, but was eventually captured and chose to accept service under the Romans.

4/ Below right
A shekel dating from the time of the First Revolt.

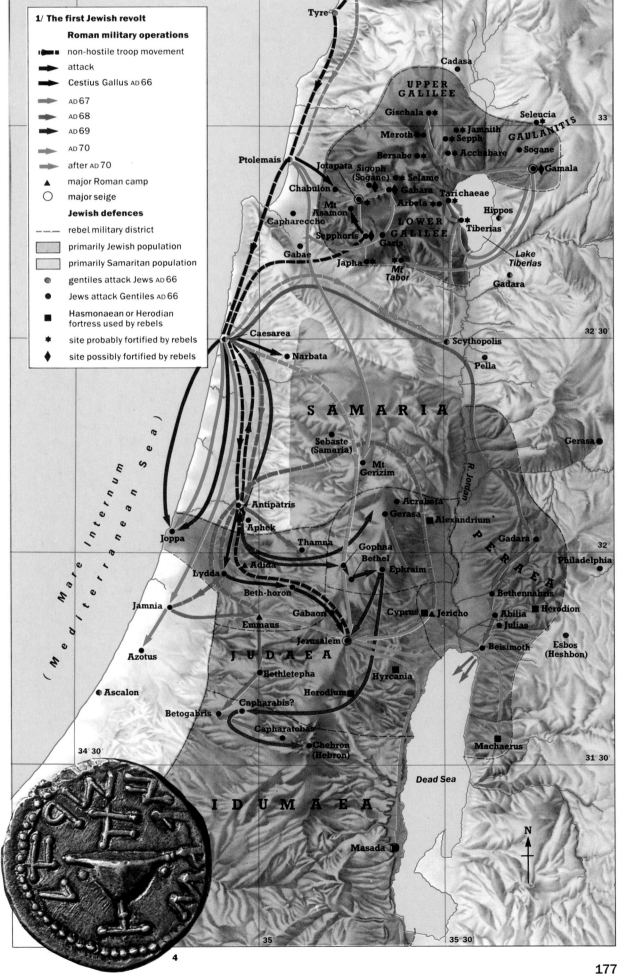

1/ The first Jewish revolt

Roman military operations
- non-hostile troop movement
- attack
- Cestius Gallus AD 66
- AD 67
- AD 68
- AD 69
- AD 70
- after AD 70
- ▲ major Roman camp
- ○ major seige

Jewish defences
- --- rebel military district
- primarily Jewish population
- primarily Samaritan population
- ● gentiles attack Jews AD 66
- ● Jews attack Gentiles AD 66
- ■ Hasmonaean or Herodian fortress used by rebels
- ✳ site probably fortified by rebels
- ◆ site possibly fortified by rebels

IN I COR and in ACTS we meet a Jew of Alexandria who travelled the eastern Mediterranean and told the story of Jesus wherever he went. One tradition says that he learned it in his native city, but how did the gospel first come to Alexandria? We can only guess.

Christianity was established in Rome before Paul arrived. In his letter, written three years before his arrival, he recognizes the Roman Christians as a mature community. Luke tells how Paul, journeying to Rome early in AD 60, was met by Christians who had come to greet him. But the beginnings of Christianity in Rome are as obscure as those in Alexandria. In both cities it started in the Jewish community. The 4th-century writer called Ambrosiaster (a name given to him by posterity for the sake of convenience as his true name is unknown) says that the Romans received the faith without apostles or miracles. This suggests that in Rome, as in Antioch (and probably also in Alexandria), Christianity was introduced by ordinary unnamed followers of Jesus.

On arrival in Rome, Paul spent two years under house

THE CHRISTIAN ERA

NON-PAULINE CHRISTIANITY IN THE 1ST CENTURY AD

The early history of Christianity is so dominated by St Paul, that it is often forgotten that in several areas, including Asia, Egypt, Rome, France and Spain, there were Christian communities whose founding had nothing to do with Paul's missionary work. The origins of such communities remain a mystery.

arrest; eventually he was probably executed. However, early tradition also associates St Peter with Rome. When Paul and Barnabas met the church leaders in Jerusalem it was agreed that they should undertake the evangelization of gentiles, while the Jerusalem leaders should concentrate

on preaching the gospel to Jews. However, the mission to Jews was not confined to Judaea – there were Jewish communities in all the major cities of the eastern Roman Empire, and in Rome itself.

Peter dominated the Jerusalem church for its first 15 years and then embarked on a mission to the Mediterranean Jews. However, they were not isolated from their gentile neighbours. In the mainly gentile church of Corinth Peter was well known – some liked his teaching more than Paul's, although Paul was their church's founder.

Peter's visit to Rome, where there was a large Jewish community, was inevitable. Emperor Claudius tried to expel the Jews from Rome in AD 49 but soon they were back, including some Christians. At the same time gentile Christians in Rome were increasing, and when Paul sent his letter to the Romans, early in AD 57, they evidently outnumbered the Jewish Christians. If the Jews returned to Rome about AD 54, this might have allowed Peter to help the Christian Jews among them.

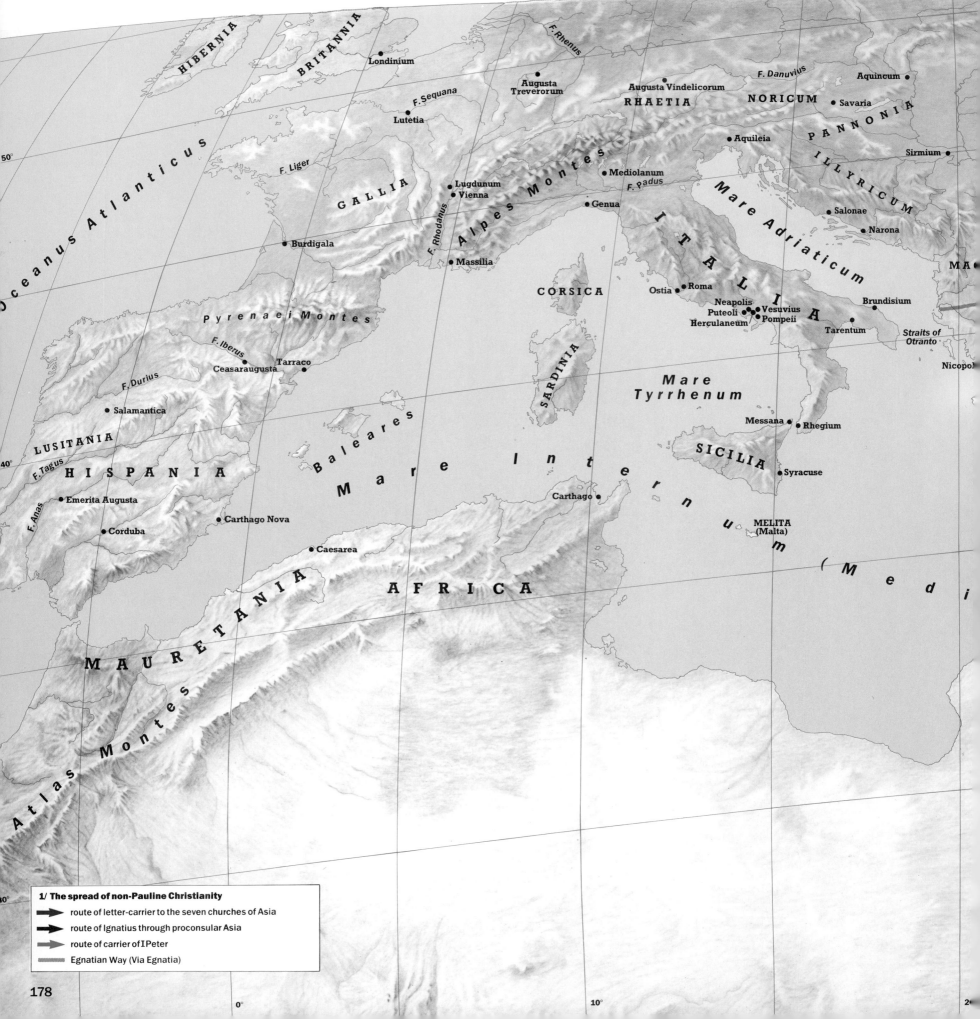

1/ The spread of non-Pauline Christianity

→ route of letter-carrier to the seven churches of Asia

→ route of Ignatius through proconsular Asia

→ route of carrier of I Peter

⟶ Egnatian Way (Via Egnatia)

Christianity arrived at an early date in other towns of south Italy. When Paul's ship from Malta put in at Puteoli in AD 60, local Christians entertained him. There were Christians in Pompeii and Herculaneum before their destruction by the eruption of Vesuvius in AD 79.

It is uncertain if Paul visited Spain, but others brought the gospel there if he did not. The first parts of Spain to be evangelized were those bordering on the Mediterranean.

In the 7th or 6th century BC a settlement was established on the Mediterranean coast of France by Greeks from Ionia; from there Greek civilization spread up the Rhône (Rhodanus) valley. It was natural, then, that in due course Christianity was brought there from the churches in Asia.

The NT includes a letter (I PETER) sent from Rome to the Christians of Asia Minor in the name of Peter. It could have been sent about the time of the persecution of Christians under Nero (AD 65), or when pressure was put on the Christians of Bithynia and Pontus by the younger Pliny (AD 111-112), or at some point between these dates. Two of

the provinces it mentions (Galatia and Asia) fell within the Pauline mission field, but by this time Paul was no longer free to visit them (if, indeed, he was still alive), and the Roman church was responsible for the Christians of those far-flung regions.

The seven churches of proconsular Asia are addressed at the beginning of Revelation. The order in which they are listed may suggest the route by which the book was taken. Although Asia was first evangelized by Paul and his colleagues when he was in Ephesus (AD 52-55), the churches there were influenced from c AD 66 onwards by Judaean immigrants.

Another visitor to Asia (c AD 110) was Ignatius, bishop of Antioch-in-Syria, who had displeased the authorities and was to be executed in Rome. We do not know by what route he went after passing through the Cilician Gates on the way from Antioch. Ignatius does not name cities through which he passed before Philadelphia. From there he was taken to Smyrna and then on to Troas. From there

he sent letters to the churches of Philadelphia and Smyrna, and a personal one to Polycarp, bishop of Smyrna. He then sailed to Neapolis; he was last heard of at Philippi. Presumably he was taken along the Egnatian Way and to Italy.

From Alexandria Christianity spread up into Egypt, to both Greek and Coptic speaking communities. One Greek-speaking community was at Oxyrhynchus where papyri have been unearthed. They include texts which bear witness to a Christian presence there. Among the earliest of these to be published were fragments of a collection of sayings of Jesus in Greek. More recently (1945) the complete collection, translated from Greek into Coptic (the so-called *Gospel of Thomas*), was identified among the Nag Hammadi papyri which date from the 4th century AD.

> AND SO WE CAME TO ROME. AND THE BRETHREN THERE ... CAME AS FAR AS THE FORUM OF APPIUS ... TO MEET US. ON SEEING THEM PAUL THANKED GOD ... AND WHEN WE CAME INTO ROME, PAUL WAS ALLOWED TO STAY BY HIMSELF, WITH THE SOLDIER THAT GUARDED HIM.'
> ACTS 28.14-16

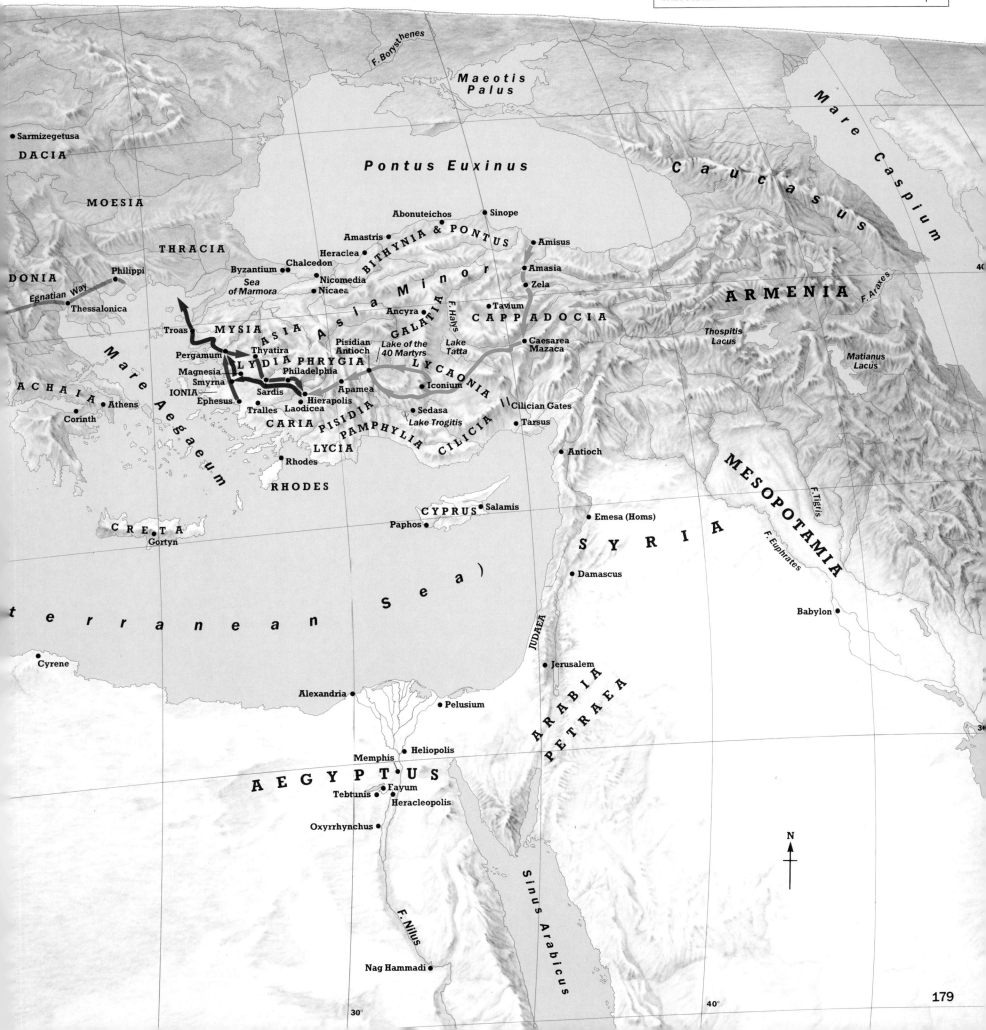

FOLLOWING the end of the First Jewish Revolt and the defeat of the revolutionaries by the legions of Vespasian and Titus, Palestine, designated Judaea, was administered by Roman military governors. Under their rule calm prevailed for several decades, even during the last years of Trajan (AD 115-117) when there was great unrest among the Jewish communities in Egypt, Cyrene, Cyprus and Mesopotamia. It was not until the reign of Hadrian (who became emperor in AD 117) that the Jews rebelled once more.

THE SEEDS OF DISCONTENT

The reasons for the new war, and the actual course of its military events, are not known with any certainty because of the scarcity of extant evidence, but the two chief causes of the outbreak appear to have been Hadrian's attempt to ban circumcision indiscriminately in all the subject nations, and to build a new pagan city, Aelia Capitolina, on the ruins of Jerusalem. The Jews were profoundly offended by both of the measures, and when Hadrian departed from the vicinity of Palestine – he was in Syria and Egypt between AD 129 and 131 – the standard of revolt was raised in an insurrection which lasted from AD 132 to 135.

THE REVOLT

The leader was Simeon, surnamed Bar Kokhba (son of the star = Messiah, cf NUM 24,17) by his friends, and Bar Koziba (son of the lie = false Messiah) by his enemies. His real name and title, preserved in documents discovered in the caves of the Wadi Murabba'at and Nahal Hever in the Judaean desert, are given as Simeon Bar Kosiba, Prince of Israel.

There was no Josephus to chronicle the Second Revolt. Nevertheless it must be assumed that Jerusalem, which was not at that time a fortified city but merely the camp of the Tenth Legion, was taken from Tinneius Rufus, the Roman governor, and held for two years. Coins struck by the revolutionaries commemorate not only the 'Freedom of Israel', but especially the 'Freedom of Jerusalem'. Hadrian then summoned from Britain one of his foremost generals, Julius Severus, to take charge of the war.

DOCUMENTARY EVIDENCE

From the evidence of the Bar Kokhba papyri found in the Murabba'at and Nahal Hever caves, it would seem that the main region held by the revolutionaries was that of the Judaean desert. The places mentioned include Herodium, Tekoa and the unidentified Beth Mashko. The latter, as well as Qiryat Arabayya and En-gedi, were centres of rebel military government.

The documents have preserved the names of several commanders: Joshua Ben Galgula, Judah Bar Manasseh, Jonathan Bar Ba'ayan and Masabala Bar Simon. According to Cassius Dio, the Roman historian who wrote a brief notice of the war, the legionaries, handicapped by the rugged terrain, were unable to engage the Jews in open battle. They had instead to hunt them down in small groups in the

caves in which they were hiding, and to starve them out by cutting off their food supplies. Some of these caves of refuge discovered in the wilderness of Judaea provide, with their skulls and skeletons, gruesome testimony of the 'annihilation, extermination and eradication' by the Romans of the last vestiges of the revolutionaries.

THE DEFEAT OF THE REBELS

The final battle took place in AD 135 at the mountain fortress of Bether, south of Jerusalem, where Simeon Bar Kosiba fell, and after three and a half years the rebellion collapsed. For the Romans, it was so costly a war that Hadrian, in his report to the senate, was obliged to omit the customary phrase, 'I and the legions are well'. For the Jews, however, the outcome was disastrous. 'Fifty of their most important outposts and nine hundred and eighty-five of their most famous villages were razed to the ground. Five hundred and eighty thousand men were slain in the various raids and battles, and the number of those who perished by famine, disease and fire was past finding out. Thus nearly the whole of Judaea was made desolate' (Cassius Dio). At the Hebron slave market, the price of a Jew dropped to that of a horse, and the supply still exceeded the demand, the surplus being transferred to Gaza, eventually to be shipped to Egypt.

CAVES OF REFUGE DURING THE SECOND REVOLT

Eighteen caves containing archaeological and manuscript remains dating to the Second Revolt have so far been identified in the Judaean desert. They lie, from north to south, in the Wadi Murabba'at, Nahal Hever, Nahal Mishmar, Nahal Harduf and Nahal Ze'elim.

The four caves situated in the northern wall of Wadi

THE CHRISTIAN ERA

THE SECOND JEWISH REVOLT

The Second Jewish Revolt, occasioned by the decree of the Emperor Hadrian (AD 117-137) prohibiting circumcision, and by his plan to build a Roman city on the site of Jerusalem, erupted in 132 and lasted three and a half years. Under the leadership of Simeon Bar Kokhba, the insurgents established themselves in Jerusalem and Judaea. Hadrian was obliged to summon Julius Severus from Britain to restore Roman rule. The last phase of the war consisted of guerilla fighting in the Judaean desert by small groups of Jews. A number of the caves in which they took shelter were discovered in 1951-52 and 1960-61. After his victory, Hadrian erected his new city on the ruins of the Temple and dedicated it to Jupiter Capitolinus. Thus Jerusalem, from which Jews were now excluded, became a gentile city.

Murabba'at have yielded, in addition to Hebrew, Aramaic, Greek and Latin manuscript fragments, jars, lamps, weapons, tools, domestic objects, sandals, cloth and dresses, as well as 19 coins, nine of which belong to the period of the Second Revolt.

The Cave of the Pool in Nahal Dawid, not far from En-gedi, must have sheltered a family for some time. It held a reservoir for water and huge jars for the storage of food.

In four of the five caves on the northern side of Nahal Hever household vessels were found and the bones of sheep and goats. The fifth, known as the Cave of Letters, preserved a good quantity of manuscripts and 19 human skeletons. In the cave on the south side, the so-called Cave of Horrors, it is clear that 40 persons, men, women and children, met their death by starvation. Apart from their skeletons, the cave held food containers, cooking vessels, lamps and the remains of the scroll of the Twelve Minor Prophets in Greek. A Roman camp on each side of the ravine in the neighbourhood of the caves rendered escape virtually impossible.

Two of the caves in the south wall of Nahal Mishmar were used as hiding places by several families. The third was for storage. Among the objects found in it were two fragments of papyrus, glass vessels, good quality pottery, lamps and stone utensils.

The single occupied cave discovered in the south side of Nahal Harduf contained a water reservoir and pottery but no human bones.

In the north wall of Nahal Ze'elim, in the Cave of Skulls, were found seven skeletons together with pottery and a coin of Trajan; in the Cave of Arrows, arrows and pottery; and in the Cave of Scrolls, fragments of a leather scroll, a phylactery and papyri, in addition to other objects.

JEWS IN PALESTINE AFTER AD 135

After the collapse of the insurrection, Hadrian's plan to build a Roman colony on the ruins of Jerusalem was put into effect. Aelia Capitolina was a pagan city inhabited by gentile settlers. On the southern gate, looking towards Bethlehem, was carved the image of a pig. A temple of Jupiter Capitolinus stood on the emplacement of the Jewish santuary. Jews were forbidden to reside there and were allowed into the city only on the anniversary of its destruction to lament on the site of the Temple. The Temple remains became one of the holiest Jewish sites.

Although Hadrian's successor, Antoninus Pius (AD 137-161), lifted the ban on circumcision in the case of the Jews, and Judaism became once more a legitimate religion, Judaea ceased to be its main homeland. It was therefore in Galilee that the rabbis, who first assembled in Yabneh after AD 70 to reshape Judaism, completed their work recorded in the Mishnah, the Palestinian Talmud and the remainder of early rabbinic literature.

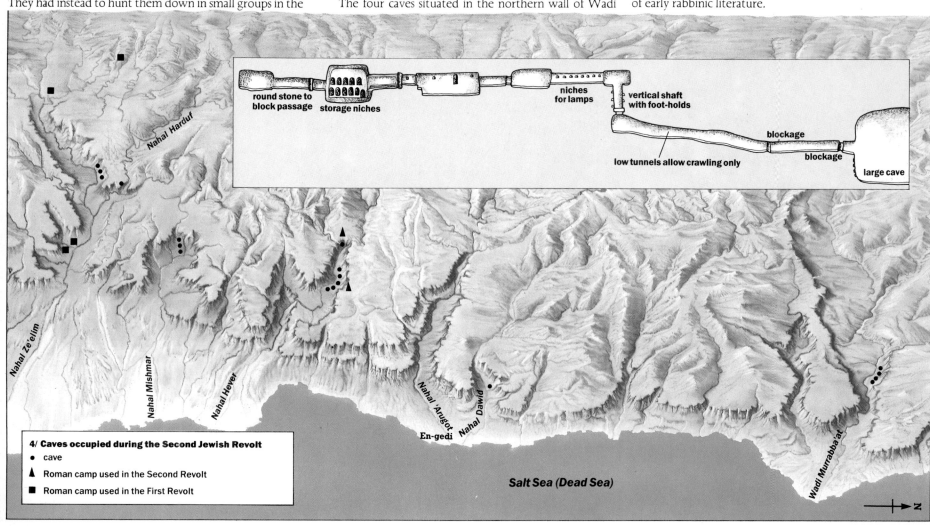

round stone to block passage
storage niches
niches for lamps
vertical shaft with foot-holds
blockage
blockage
low tunnels allow crawling only
large cave

Nahal Harduf
Nahal Ze'elim
Nahal Mishmar
Nahal Hever
Nahal 'Arugot
Nahal Dawid
En-gedi
Wadi Murabba'at

Salt Sea (Dead Sea)

4/ Caves occupied during the Second Jewish Revolt
● cave
▲ Roman camp used in the Second Revolt
■ Roman camp used in the First Revolt

1/ Map right

After the defeat of the Bar Kokhba rebels Judah ceased to be a Jewish area and Galilee became the main area of settlement. The Jews were excluded from Aelia Capitolina (Jerusalem) by order of Hadrian.

2/ Below left

A bust of the Emperor Hadrian, whose actions sparked off the Bar Kokhba revolt.

3/ Below

The two Roman coins, from the reign of Hadrian, on the left show Judaea personified as an enslaved woman and bear the legend 'JUDAEA CAPTA'. The silver Bar Kokhba coins on the right carry the inscriptions (top) 'Year Two of the Freedom of Israel' and (bottom) 'Shimeon.'

4/ Bottom left

The sites of known caves of refuge and Roman camps are shown. Inset is a cross-section through a tunnel found at Horbat Eitun.

5/ Bottom right

The Cave of Letters (shown here in horizontal cross-section so that the cave appears to have been scooped out of a flat surface) contained remarkable remains of the Bar Kokhba rebels. The cave is over 450ft long from the entrance to the innermost end, and for much of that length the low ceiling height makes entry difficult. A hoard of documents belonging to a woman named Babata was one of the most interesting finds.

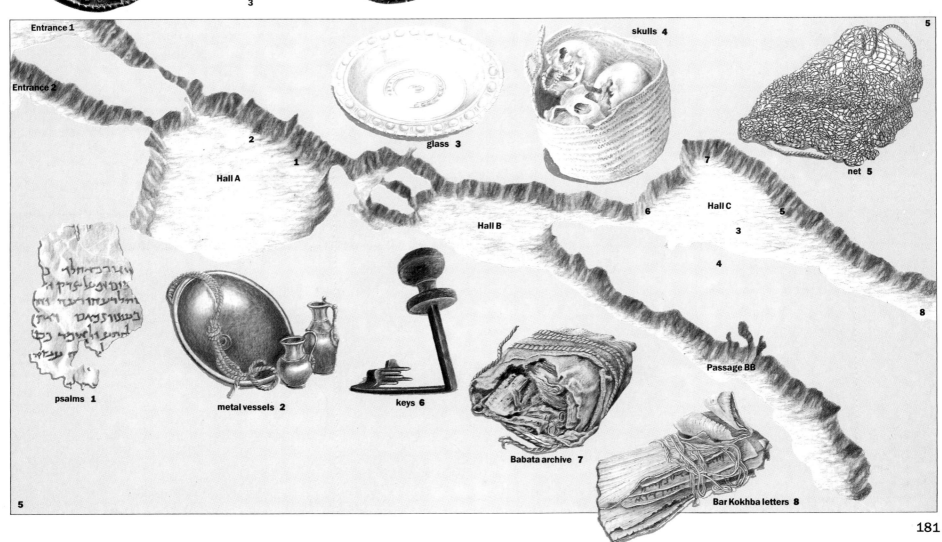

1/ Palestine after the Second Jewish Revolt

- area of Jewish settlement
- area from which Hadrian excluded the Jews

N

Tyre
Caesarea Philippi
Gischala
Ptolemais (Acco)
GOLAN
Naveh
Capernaum
Kefar Sikhmin
Ginnesar
Sea of Chinnereth (Sea of Galilee)
Shefar'am
'Arraba
Arbela
Cochaba
Sycaminum
Haifa
Sepphoris
GALILEE
BATANAEA
Husifa
Nazareth
Hammat Gader
Sennabris
Dora
Legio
JEZREEL
Daberath
Tsemah
Gadara
Scythopolis
Caesarea
Bet Alfa
Pella
Narbata
DECAPOLIS
Sebaste
Gerasa
SAMARIA
Neapolis
Apollonia
PERAEA
Acrabbein
Jaffa
Gedor
Ono
Philadelphia
Diospolis (Lydda)
Gophna
Na'aran
Bethel
Beth-nimra
Jamnia (Yabneh)
'En Tav
Emmaus
Aelia Capitolina (Jerusalem)
Jericho
Abel
Livias (Beth-ramatha)
Azotus
JUDAEA
Bethletepha
Bether
Bethlehem
Ascalon
Herodium
Eleutheropolis (Bet-Guvrin)
Tekoa
Antheden
Mamre
Gaza
Hebron
Maiumas
En-gedi
DAROMAS
Salt Sea (Dead Sea)
Bersabe
Rabbath Meba
Charachmoba

Great Sea (Mediterranean Sea)
R. Jordan

net 5
skulls 4
glass 3

Entrance 1
Entrance 2
Hall A
Hall B
Hall C
Passage BB

psalms 1
metal vessels 2
keys 6
Babata archive 7
Bar Kokhba letters 8

IN ROME the church went on increasing and its influence grew greater over the Mediterranean world, more because of the quality of its faith and practical Christianity than because of its position as the church of the imperial capital. Ignatius, bishop of Antioch in Syria early in the 2nd century AD, describes the Roman church as 'pre-eminent in love'; half a century later Dionysius, bishop of Corinth, writes appreciatively of its reputation for charity to fellow-Christians elsewhere and to others in need.

About AD96 Clement of Rome wrote to the church of Corinth to express his own church's concern at insubordination and division among the Corinthian Christians, similar to the situation which had called forth Paul's remonstrance 50 years before. Clement is traditionally listed among the early bishops of Rome, but he seems to have written this letter on behalf of the whole Roman church, as its foreign secretary. From about AD165 comes the record of the trial of a Christian philosopher named Justin, with some of his associates. The prefect of Rome expostulated with them for their 'superstition' and, when they refused to sacrifice to the state gods, had them executed. They were members of a house group in Rome, which was perhaps organized more like a Bible study class than an ordinary church. Until the end of the 2nd century the Roman church was mainly Greek-speaking; the first Latin-speaking Pope is said to have been Victor, about AD190.

ASIA MINOR

Asia Minor remained for many years one of the main centres of Christianity. Towards the end of the 1st century, some of the 'seven churches of Asia' (ie, of the province of Asia) received a sharp admonition in the Revelation of John, but they seem to have profited by it, to judge from the appreciation which Ignatius expressed for their help and love as he passed through that area about AD110 on his way to the arena in Rome. One or two years later the younger Pliny, Roman governor of Bithynia and Pontus, on the Black Sea coast of Asia Minor, reported that Christianity had been spreading so rapidly there that, because Christians had no part in blood sacrifice, there was an alarming decrease in the sale of fodder for sacrificial animals.

THE CHURCH IN THE 1st AND 2nd CENTURIES AD

Both in the Pauline mission field and beyond, Christianity continued to expand in the generations following the apostolic age. There was sporadic persecution in some areas, but throughout the 2nd century there was no concerted campaign of repression, and Christianity spread as far as the Indus. In the 2nd century the Bible was produced in the vernacular for the first time.

The province of Asia had one of its most illustrious martyrs in Polycarp, bishop of Smyrna, who was put to death at the age of 86 in AD155 or 156. However, the outbreak of Roman persecution in which he was killed was exceptional; he had served as bishop with no molestation that we know of for over 40 years.

The region of Phrygia gave birth about that time to the influential movement called Montanism – a charismatic movement which spread to other parts of the Mediterranean world and included among its converts such an illustrious person as Tertullian of Carthage.

GAUL

Relations between Asia Minor and south-east Gaul (France) remained close: it was from Asia Minor that Gaul was evangelized. When the churches of Lugdunum (Lyons) and Vienna, in the Rhône valley, suffered a severe persecution in AD177, it was to the churches of Asia Minor that the survivors wrote with details of the persecution; and it was from Asia Minor (probably from the vicinity of Smyrna) that the new bishop of Lyon was brought to replace the bishop who had died in the persecution. The new bishop,

Irenaeus, was a theological writer of the early church.

BRITAIN

The date when Christianity reached Britain is uncertain. It was probably carried by traders from Gaul. Tertullian, at the end of the 2nd century, testifies that Christianity had reached Britain by his time. Although this statement appears in a rhetorical passage it should not be put down to a flight of exaggeration.

NORTH AFRICA

In the Latin-speaking province of Africa (modern Tunisia and Algeria), especially around Carthage (which had been a Roman colony since 46BC), Christianity was firmly planted during the 2nd century. Tertullian of Carthage, the first Christian Latin author, was converted about AD180. In that

2

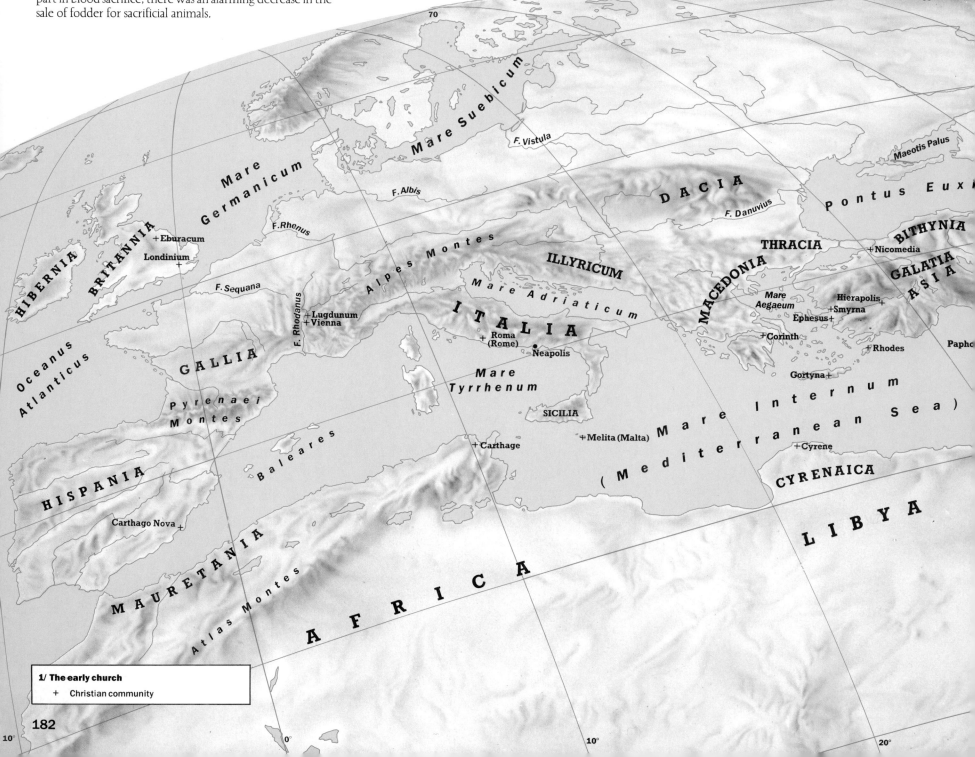

1/ The early church
+ Christian community

year, too, some humble people from the neighbouring town of Scilli were charged before the provincial governor with professing and practising Christianity. Since they refused to forswear their faith he ordered them to be executed. A box which was brought into court as evidence was said to contain 'books, and the writings of Paul, a just man'. This indicates that at least part of the Bible was available in Latin, and this conclusion is confirmed by Tertullian's biblical quotations. Visitors to Carthage today can still see the amphitheatre where Perpetua, a freeborn lady, and her slave-girl Felicitas, suffered martyrdom as Christians in AD 202.

EGYPT
The influence of the church of Alexandria was enhanced by the establishment of its catechetical school in the latter half of the 2nd century, under the leadership of Pantaenus. Eminent teachers at the school during the next two generations included Clement and Origen. In 202 the Alexandrian Church endured some persecution, to which Origen's father, Leonides, fell victim. However, it was short-lived, and the church enjoyed relative peace for 50 years.

PALESTINE
After Alexandria, Caesarea enjoyed high repute as a centre of Christian learning, especially after Origen took up residence there in AD 231. As for Jerusalem itself, a new city was founded on the ruins of the old by the Emperor Hadrian in AD 135. He named it Aelia Capitolina; it was a completely gentile city. A church was soon established there and called itself the church of Jerusalem. It was a gentile church (the original church of Jerusalem having been dispersed shortly before AD 70) but it fell heir to some of the prestige attaching to the name of the holy city.

MESOPOTAMIA
In Upper Mesopotamia the city of Edessa emerges as the chief centre of Christianity by the middle of the 2nd century. The kingdom of Edessa became the first Christian state with the conversion of its ruler Abgar IX (AD 179-216). The remains of a church there, destroyed by a flood in AD 201, form one of the oldest known church buildings. Another of the same date has come to light at Dura-Europos on the Euphrates.

A stabilizing influence in Mesopotamian Christianity was the production during the middle of the 2nd century of a Bible that was at least in part written in the vernacular. This was the Old Syriac version, of which two gospel manuscripts are known. Another popular edition of the gospels in those parts was the *Diatessaron*, a rearrangement of the contents of the four gospels so as to form one continuous narrative. This was the work of Tatian, a Mesopotamian Christian who returned to his native country after spending some time in Rome as a disciple of Justin Martyr.

INDIA
One difficulty in deciding how early the west coast of India was evangelized lies in an ambiguity about the term 'India'. Any territory bordering on the Indian Ocean, from the Persian Gulf eastward, might be so described. Traditionally the apostle Thomas (Mar Thoma) is credited with carrying the gospel to India: this probably means that India was evangelized by Syriac Christians who traced their spiritual ancestry back to Thomas.

Eusebius says that Pantaenus of Alexandria went on a mission to 'India' about 180, and found there a Christian community, converted allegedly under the preaching of the apostle Bartholomew, and possessing 'Matthew's writing in the script of the Hebrews'. It is likely that by the end of the 2nd century Christianity had reached the land around the mouth of the Indus.

> 'BUT I ASK, HAVE THEY NOT HEARD? INDEED THEY HAVE; FOR "THEIR VOICE HAS GONE OUT TO ALL THE EARTH, AND THEIR WORDS TO THE ENDS OF THE WORLD."' ROM 10.18

1/ Map below
In the 1st century AD the distribution of Christian communities in part reflects the missionary activities of St Paul (see page 172), but there were also many communities that existed independently from him (see page 178). Persecution of the Jews in the 2nd century AD, particularly after the 2nd Jewish Revolt (see page 180), encouraged Christianity to move away from its Jewish cultural matrix. Communities which by now were predominantly gentile, were set up in Britain, Gaul, Africa and Egypt.

2/ Above far left
The Colosseum at Rome, where Ignatius, bishop of Antioch, was probably exposed to wild beasts at the beginning of the 2nd century AD.

3/ Above left
The construction of the Colosseum was begun by Vespasian and finished under his sons Titus and Domitian. It was officially opened in AD 80 and measured 164ft high. It covered an area of c 7¼ acres and could hold up to 70,000 spectators.

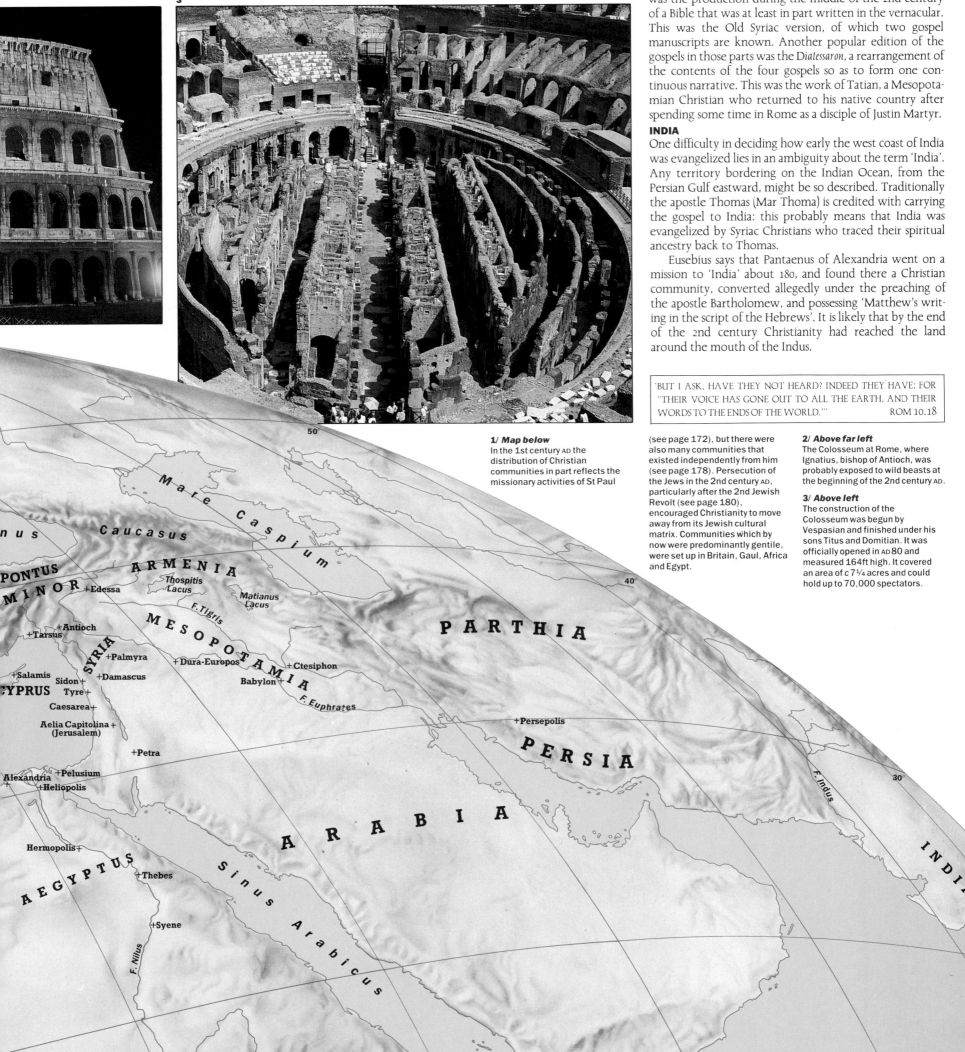

From the Emperor Constantine's reign at the beginning of the 4th century AD until 638 the three provinces of Palestine, Samaria, Galilee and Judaea, were ruled from the capital city of Byzantium, or as it was called in 327, Constantinople.

To start with the provinces were at peace, but late in the 5th century AD a civil war broke out when the Samaritans tried to become independent. Fifty years later they tried again, and caused a great deal of damage. More serious problems, however, lay ahead. In 614 a Persian army invaded Palestine and ousted Roman power. Their rule lasted until 628, when the Romans made a treaty. Ten years later Jerusalem surrendered to Caliph Umar el-Sharif, and was under Muslim rule until the Crusader invasion in 1099.

Apart from these wars, the Byzantine period in Palestine provided a longer time of peace than had ever been known beforehand, and an occasion when people could exploit trade and grow their own farm products with little interference. The fact that a large number of buildings of the Byzantine period can still be found in Palestine, and have not been subject to the ravages of war which beset other periods, shows that this was a period of peace and prosperity – though still disturbed by famines and ecclesiastical divisions.

To begin with the progress of conversion to Christianity took place mainly in cities, and was not completed until about half way through the 5th century when Palestine was filled with Christian buildings. In the late 3rd century Eusebius of Caesarea recorded seeing large churches being built in the cities, but of these buildings nothing remains, since they were all pulled down by an imperial edict in 303. However, map 1 also shows synagogues, some of which were built before 303.

The first church in Jerusalem was a 'house-church', Holy Sion, but with the coming of Constantine new churches were built at the principal places of pilgrimage. The impetus to build them came from Constantine, who sent his mother the Empress Helena to find Christ's tomb. Delighted with her success he ordered the building of the church of the Holy Sepulchre which surrounds it, and he

THE CHRISTIAN ERA

BYZANTINE PALESTINE

Palestine, as the Roman province was called, was from the reign of the Emperor Constantine ruled from Byzantium. For the three centuries which followed, Palestine mostly enjoyed peace, and many churches and synagogues were erected. Parish churches were built in Christian cities and villages, and over the old places of pilgrimage. Christian pilgrims even came from Spain and France, at the other end of the Empire. During the fifth century monastic life in Palestine attracted monks from many lands, and many monasteries were built. Jewish people were sometimes persecuted, but they too succeeded in building magnificently decorated synagogues, whose mosaics and marble are very like those of Churches.

and the Empress Helena built the churches at Bet Lehem (Bethlehem) and on the Mount of Olives. Since both places contained 'holy caves' they built holy places in the crypt, and the Holy Sepulchre had a building called 'The Anastasis' (Greek for 'resurrection') built over it.

The older religions of the area continued, however. The Jews, who had been excluded from the area round Jerusalem at the end of their war against Rome in the 2nd century, were in many cities, and in several villages in Galilee and south of Hebron, and their synagogues display much the same standard of ornamentation as the Christian churches. The Samaritans also continued, and the fact that archaeologists have not so far discovered many of their buildings is not a guide to their great strength in the Byzantine period.

MONASTERIES

Christian monasticism began in Palestine during Constantine's reign and was strengthened and regulated by Justinian, who legislated on many aspects of monasteries.

The first monastery was set up by a monk who had been trained home in Egypt, Saint Hilarion, who returned home

and set up a monastery near Gaza. When a donor founded a church they provided for the payment of the clergy, usually by giving land. Hence much of the country was in Christian hands by the late 5th century. Church officials were more important by then, since they were favoured by the exiled Empress Eudokia, who had fled from Constantinople, but maintained her own leadership over Palestine. She did not agree with the church Council of Ephesus in 431, which condemned Nestorius and justified the Cult of the Virgin Mary as Mother of God. But towards the end of her life she regretted the church divisions for which she was partly to blame, and sought advice from Simeon, the saint who lived on a pillar near Antioch. He referred her to the monk Euthymius, who was in a monastery four miles away from Jerusalem in the desert to the east. Empress Eudokia founded many church institutions, among them the church of St Stephen, in which when it came to the time of her death she was to be buried.

Emperor Justinian built some new churches, among them the church at Bethlehem, damaged by the Samaritans, and 'St Mary the New', the most spectacular church in Jerusalem. The Emperor died in 565, and very soon afterwards the Madaba map was made, showing the Holy Land with its shrines, and St Mary the New in Jerusalem.

The strength of the church was shown when a monk, Saint Saba, went on Palestine's behalf to ask the emperors in Constantinople for a remission of taxes.

'PAULA ENTERED JERUSALEM… AND STARTED TO GO ROUND VISITING THE HOLY PLACES. SHE DID SO WITH SUCH BURNING ENTHUSIASM THAT THERE WAS NO WAY OF TAKING HER AWAY FROM ONE UNLESS SHE WAS HURRYING ALONG TO ANOTHER. SHE FELL DOWN AND WORSHIPPED BEFORE THE CROSS AS IF SHE COULD SEE THE LORD HANGING ON IT. ON ENTERING THE TOMB OF RESURRECTION SHE KISSED THE STONE WHICH THE ANGEL HAD REMOVED FROM THE SEPULCHRE DOOR. THEN LIKE A THIRSTY MAN WHO HAS WAITED LONG AND AT LAST COMES TO WATER, SHE FAITHFULLY KISSED THE VERY SHELF ON WHICH THE LORD'S BODY HAD LAIN.'
ST. JEROME WRITING ABOUT HIS DISCIPLE, PAULA (LETTER 108.9)

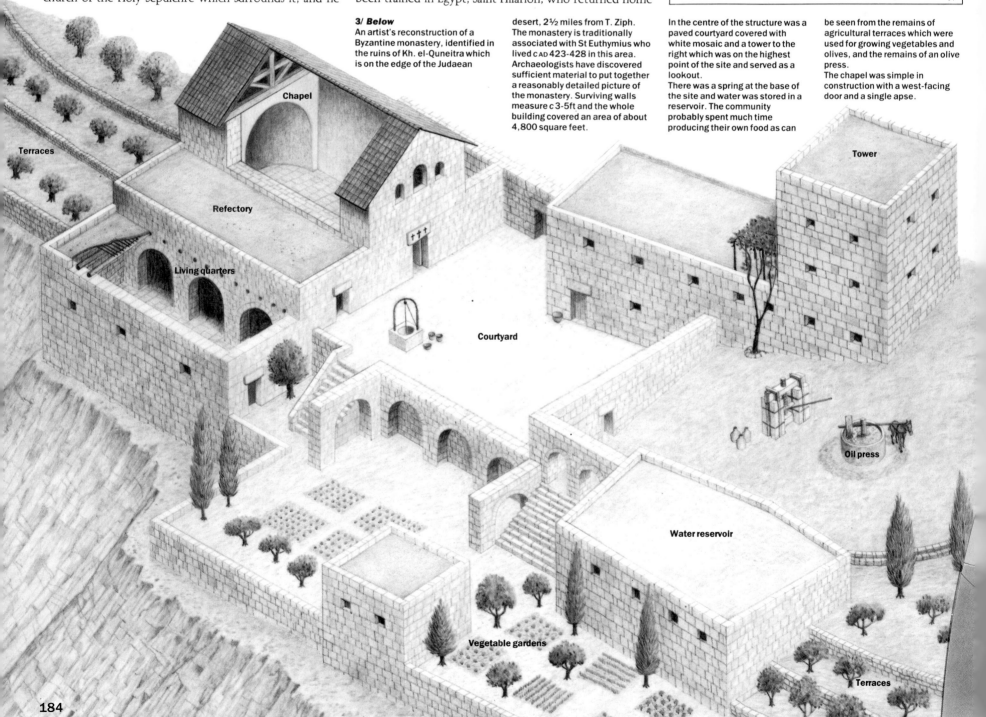

3/ Below
An artist's reconstruction of a Byzantine monastery, identified in the ruins of Kh. el-Quneitra which is on the edge of the Judaean desert, 2½ miles from T. Ziph. The monastery is traditionally associated with St Euthymius who lived c AD 423-428 in this area. Archaeologists have discovered sufficient material to put together a reasonably detailed picture of the monastery. Surviving walls measure c 3-5ft and the whole building covered an area of about 4,800 square feet.

In the centre of the structure was a paved courtyard covered with white mosaic and a tower to the right which was on the highest point of the site and served as a lookout.
There was a spring at the base of the site and water was stored in a reservoir. The community probably spent much time producing their own food as can be seen from the remains of agricultural terraces which were used for growing vegetables and olives, and the remains of an olive press.
The chapel was simple in construction with a west-facing door and a single apse.

Chapel

Terraces

Refectory

Living quarters

Courtyard

Tower

Oil press

Water reservoir

Vegetable gardens

Terraces

184

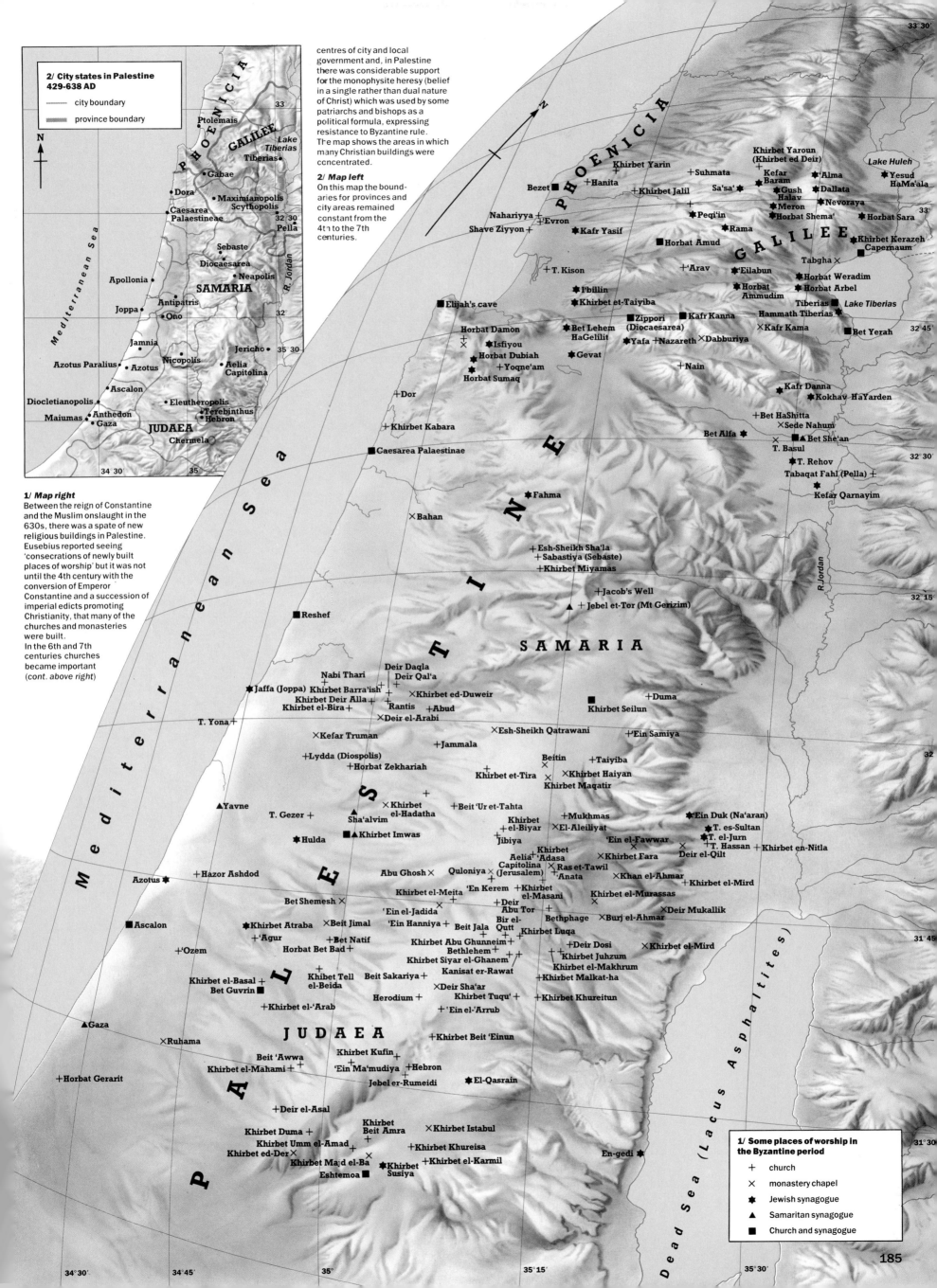

2/ City states in Palestine 429-638 AD

— — — city boundary

▬▬▬▬ province boundary

N

PHOENICIA

Ptolemais

GALILEE

Lake Tiberias

Tiberias

Gabae

Dora

Maximianopolis Scythopolis

Caesarea Palaestineae

Pella

Sebaste

Diocaesarea

Apollonia

Neapolis

SAMARIA

Joppa

Antipatris

Ono

Jamnia

Jericho

Azotus Paralius

Nicopolis

Azotus

Aelia Capitolina

Diocletianopolis

Ascalon

Eleutheropolis

Maiumas

Anthedon

Terebinthus

Gaza

Hebron

JUDAEA

Chermela

Mediterranean Sea

R. Jordan

centres of city and local government and, in Palestine there was considerable support for the monophysite heresy (belief in a single rather than dual nature of Christ) which was used by some patriarchs and bishops as a political formula, expressing resistance to Byzantine rule. The map shows the areas in which many Christian buildings were concentrated.

2/ Map left
On this map the boundaries for provinces and city areas remained constant from the 4th to the 7th centuries.

1/ Map right
Between the reign of Constantine and the Muslim onslaught in the 630s, there was a spate of new religious buildings in Palestine. Eusebius reported seeing 'consecrations of newly built places of worship' but it was not until the 4th century with the conversion of Emperor Constantine and a succession of imperial edicts promoting Christianity, that many of the churches and monasteries were built.
In the 6th and 7th centuries churches became important
(*cont. above right*)

PHOENICIA

Khirbet Yaroun (Khirbet ed Deir)

Lake Huleh

Khirbet Yarin

Suhmata

Kefar Baram

Alma

Dallata

Yesud HaMa'ala

Bezet

Hanita

Khirbet Jalil

Sa'sa'

Gush Halav

Nahariyya

'Evron

Peqi'in

Rama

Meron

Horbat Shema'

Horbat Sara

Shave Ziyyon

Kafr Yasif

Nevoraya

T. Kison

'Arav

'Eilabun

Horbat Amud

GALILEE

Khirbet Kerazeh

Capernaum

Tabgha

Horbat Weradim

Elijah's cave

I'billin

Khirbet et-Taiyiba

Horbat Ammudim

Horbat Arbel

Tiberias

Lake Tiberias

Horbat Damon

Bet Lehem HaGelilit

Zippori (Diocaesarea)

Kafr Kanna

Kafr Kama

Hammath Tiberias

Bet Yerah

Isfiyou

Yafa

Nazareth

Dabburiya

Horbat Dubiah

Gevat

Yoqne'am

Nain

Horbat Sumaq

Kafr Danna

Kokhav HaYarden

Dor

Bet HaShitta

Sede Nahum

Khirbet Kabara

Bet Alfa

Bet She'an

T. Basul

Caesarea Palaestinae

T. Rehov

Tabaqat Fahl (Pella)

Fahma

Kefar Qarnayim

Bahan

PALESTINE

Esh-Sheikh Sha'la

Sabastiya (Sebaste)

Khirbet Miyamas

Jacob's Well

Jebel et-Tor (Mt Gerizim)

Reshef

SAMARIA

Nabi Thari

Deir Daqla

Deir Qal'a

Duma

Jaffa (Joppa)

Khirbet Barra'ish

Khirbet ed-Duweir

Khirbet Seilun

Khirbet Deir Alla

Khirbet el-Bira

Rantis

Abud

Deir el-Arabi

T. Yona

Kefar Truman

Esh-Sheikh Qatrawani

'Ein Samiya

Jammala

Lydda (Diospolis)

Beitin

Taiyiba

Horbat Zekhariah

Khirbet et-Tira

Khirbet Haiyan

Khirbet Maqatir

Yavne

Khirbet el-Hadatha

Beit 'Ur et-Tahta

Mukhmas

'Ein Duk (Na'aran)

T. Gezer

Sha'alvim

Khirbet el-Biyar

El-Aleiliyat

T. es-Sultan

Hulda

Khirbet Imwas

Jibiya

'Ein el-Fawwar

T. el-Jurn

Khirbet Adasa

Khirbet Fara

T. Hassan

Khirbet en-Nitla

Aelia Capitolina (Jerusalem)

Ras et-Tawil

Deir el-Qilt

Hazor Ashdod

Abu Ghosh

Quloniya

'Anata

Khan el-Ahmar

Azotus

Khirbet el-Meita

'En Kerem

Khirbet el-Masani

Khirbet el-Murassas

Khirbet el-Mird

Bet Shemesh

'Ein el-Jadida

Deir Abu Tor

Deir Mukallik

Ascalon

Khirbet Atraba

Beit Jimal

'Ein Hanniya

Beit Jala

Bir el-Qutt

Bethphage

Burj el-Ahmar

'Agur

Bet Natif

Khirbet Abu Ghunneim

Khirbet Luqa

Deir Dosi

Khirbet el-Mird

'Ozem

Horbat Bet Bad

Bethlehem

Khirbet Juhzum

Khibet Tell el-Beida

Khirbet Siyar el-Ghanem

Kanisat er-Rawat

Khirbet el-Makhrum

Khirbet el-Basal

Beit Sakariya

Deir Sha'ar

Khirbet Malkat-ha

Bet Guvrin

Herodium

Khirbet Tuqu'

Khirbet Khureitun

Khirbet el-'Arab

'Ein el-'Arrub

Gaza

Khirbet Beit 'Einun

Ruhama

JUDAEA

Beit 'Awwa

Khirbet Kufin

Khirbet el-Mahami

'Ein Ma'mudiya

Hebron

Horbat Gerarit

Jebel er-Rumeidi

El-Qasrain

Deir el-Asal

Khirbet Duma

Khirbet Beit Amra

Khirbet Istabul

Khirbet Umm el-Amad

Khirbet Khureisa

Khirbet el-Karmil

En-gedi

Khirbet ed-Der

Khirbet Majd el-Ba

Eshtemoa

Khirbet Susiya

Dead Sea (Lacus Asphaltites)

1/ Some places of worship in the Byzantine period

+ church

× monastery chapel

✶ Jewish synagogue

▲ Samaritan synagogue

■ Church and synagogue

BY the reign of Vespasian (AD69-79), Asia Minor west of the Euphrates had been divided into six provinces, created at different dates: Asia (133 BC), Pontus and Bithynia (74 BC, enlarged AD 64), Galatia (25 BC), Cappadocia (annexed AD 17, attached to Galatia AD 76, and constituted as a province in its own right in c AD 107), Lycia and Pamphylia (AD 43) and Cilicia (constituted c 102 BC, attached to Syria c 30 BC, reconstituted AD 72). Several languages were spoken throughout the provinces although Greek was by far the most common.

The density of cities and towns in the western regions of Asia Minor (approximately west of longitude 32°) is in strong contrast to the sparseness in the east. On the other hand, the main lines of communication run eastwards (towards the River Euphrates) and southwards (towards Cilicia and Syria).

The paved roads which the Romans introduced into the western areas (in the 2nd and 1st centuries BC and into the eastern in the 1st century AD), facilitated the political, social and military requirements of an administration which was based on the urban centres. The most important town of each province became the provincial capital: Ephesus in Asia (in the west), Ancyra in Galatia and Caesarea in

THE CHRISTIAN ERA

ROMAN ASIA MINOR

Asia Minor, by the mid-1st century AD, had passed almost entirely into the Roman Empire. It was an area which possessed diverse but strong native cultures and allegiances. From 133 BC onwards the Romans dominated the country and there was a constant interplay between Roman administration and local autonomy. It was into this diverse but organized world that Christianity came and took root in the 1st century AD.

Cappadocia (in the centre), Perge in Lycia and Pamphylia and Tarsus in Cilicia (in the south), and Nicomedia in Pontus and Bithynia (in the north).

CITIES

The remaining cities, though often as ancient as the six provincial capitals, were grouped, primarily, according to provincial territories established and administered by the Romans. At the same time, the older loyalties – tribal,

religious, linguistic – although not always coinciding with the provincial boundaries – were nevertheless kept intact by the Romans and manipulated by them to the advantage of the empire. The grouping of cities by local allegiances was maintained, inter alia, by a system of regional assize-centres (conventus), or popular assemblies, symbolic perhaps but nevertheless important for official functions; the chief city of a region, known as a metropolis, focused the activities of minor urban centres.

The status of a city has been shown on the map by a system indicated in the key. As examples of a metropolis one may quote Isaura, metropolis for the Isaurians, a fierce and intractable people living in the Taurus mountains of southern Asia Minor; Laranda, metropolis for the Lycaonians, an ancient people who maintained their own language into the Roman period (ACTS 14.11). Greek had become the lingua franca of Asia Minor. Latin was the language of Roman provincial administration. The Phrygian language, and even Celtic, survived into early Byzantine times. Phrygia, however was not a Roman province. The land of the Celts, on the other hand, became Galatia. Synnada and Philomelium in the Roman administrative province of Asia were situated in the native region of Phrygia.

1/ Roman Asia Minor

- ■ colony
- ● city (coining)
- □ baths
- ○ city (non-coining)
- ▣ legionary centre
- ◉ conventus
- —— road (certain)
- ▲ metropolis
- - - - road (possible)

COIN PRODUCTION

The Romans allowed the production of coinage – usually bronze – by the cities of Asia Minor. Not all cities, or indeed colonies, minted their own coins but most did, even if sporadically. The major urban centres continued to produce their own independent coinage into the late 3rd century AD. The legends were in Greek, the symbols on the reverse side of the coins were chosen by the city. The concession made to the empire, however, was significant: the emperor's head and titles were almost invariably – the exceptions are minor – shown on the obverse.

ROADS

Roads had existed before Roman annexation. The paved roads introduced by the Romans did not by themselves open up Asia Minor to land traffic, but certainly the most effective consequence was to facilitate travel between cities by roads which came close to being all-weather methods of communication. It became easier, and perhaps safer, to travel along the new system of paved roads.

The network of paved roads which united and serviced the provincial cities and towns was not uniformly created in the very first days of Roman administration in Asia Minor. In the eastern provinces, in contrast to the western, the road-system probably came about in response to the need for military supply-lines, and was constructed between the years AD 76-82. On the other hand in the western province of Asia, a road network had been built in c 129 BC, immediately after Roman annexation (in 133 BC). These stone-paved roads serviced the major urban centres, Ephesus, Smyrna, Pergamum, Thyatira, Sardis, Philadelphia and Laodicea (the later Seven Churches of Asia), together with the lesser cities, Tralles, Magnesia ad Maeandrum and others.

In the province of Galatia, the stone-paved Via Sebaste, beginning at Cremna and running south to Comama, Antiochia, Iconium and Lystra, was built in 6 BC by the Emperor Augustus. Its function was to unite these newly founded colonies. The Via Sebaste was, moreover, linked to the road systems of the province of Asia. It is evident that anyone who joined the Via Sebaste at Lystra could have travelled westwards not only in Galatia from colony to colony but also in Asia from city to city, from metropolis to metropolis, from conventus to conventus, by a network of paved roads covering most of the coastal region of western Asia Minor – and yet Paul and Barnabas in their journey in Asia Minor (ACTS 13 and 14) did not do so (see page 172).

In his short story, *The Church that was at Antioch*, Kipling describes Paul as 'treading the Via Sebaste'. Here the author invokes one part of highway between the Roman colonies of Lystra, Iconium and Antiochia, but Paul's second journey into Asia Minor, to Derbe (ACTS 16.1) and 'throughout Phrygia and the region of Galatia', could have been made only along unsurfaced tracks or paths. The Romans did not begin the systematic paving of roads in Lycaonia and Galatia until AD 80.

After Derbe, Paul was constrained to travel not westwards to the major cities of Asia (principally Ephesus) but northwards into Galatia (perhaps to Ancyra and Pessinus) and northwestwards to Phrygia (perhaps to Philomelium, Dorylaeum and Cotiaeum): 'Now when they had gone throughout Phrygia and the region of Galatia, and were forbidden of the Holy Ghost to preach the word in Asia, ...' (ACTS 16.6). They passed through the more remote, perhaps roadless, hilly region between Asia and Bithynia and eventually came down to the coast where paved roads had certainly existed since 129 BC: '..., after they were come to Mysia, they assayed to go into Bithynia: but the Spirit suffered them not. And they passing by Mysia came down to Troas' (ACTS 16.7-8).

The spread of early Christianity throughout Asia followed the success of Paul's preaching (ACTS 19.10) at Ephesus, the leading city. Without doubt the dissemination of the faith and the creation of the Seven Churches of Asia (REV 1.4, 11) was facilitated by one of the great Roman achievements in Asia Minor during the 1st century BC, an established road network between the major urban centres of the province.

> 'I WAS IN THE SPIRIT ON THE LORD'S DAY, AND I HEARD BEHIND ME A LOUD VOICE SAYING, "WRITE WHAT YOU SEE IN A BOOK AND SEND IT TO THE SEVEN CHURCHES, TO EPHESUS AND TO SMYRNA AND TO PERGAMUM, AND TO THYATIRA AND TO SARDIS AND TO PHILADELPHIA AND TO LAODICEA."' REV 1.11

ARCHAEOLOGICAL field work may be divided into two main activities, in the horizontal and the vertical dimension: survey and excavation. The earliest surveys, aimed at identifying places mentioned in the Bible, were more in the way of exploration, eg, the two research trips made by Edward Robinson and Eli Smith in 1838 and 1853 (see page 73). The crowning achievement of 19th century Palestinography was the *Survey of Western Palestine* conducted by a team of Royal Engineers sponsored by the Palestine Exploration Fund. During the years 1872-1877 they drew up measurements for a 26-sheet set of maps covering the entire country. During the 1920s and 30s archaeologists began to base their survey analyses on the dateable potsherds collected from the surface of the ancient sites. Thus, some insight into the chronological settlement pattern could be obtained.

THE CHRISTIAN ERA

HISTORICAL GEOGRAPHY AND ARCHAEOLOGY

Archaeology is concerned with the retrieval and correct analysis of artefacts from the physical remains of human habitation which still survive. The goal of archaeological research is to elucidate the material way of life of ancient people, including their means of subsistence, social organization and technical and artistic achievements. Occasionally archaeology can produce information which has a direct bearing on a specific event in ancient history and events mentioned in the Bible.

public use such as temples, palaces, fortifications. Refuse disposal was a constant factor; some human debris simply accumulated on the floors and streets while pits were usually dug either within or near the dwellings. Structures may have had substantial foundations below the floor surface; in such cases, trenches were usually dug in which to lay the foundation stones. Residual space in those trenches could be filled with fresh soil and foundation deposits (cult objects, coins, etc). Later builders often dug up the stones of walls from ruined buildings which had been in use during earlier occupation periods; the resulting empty trench (so-called robbers' trench) would then be filled with fresh soil. Therefore, the main objective of the archaeologist as stratigrapher is to note the relationships which exist between the various artefacts and features found in the dig (sherds, bones, walls, pits, etc) and to reconstruct the

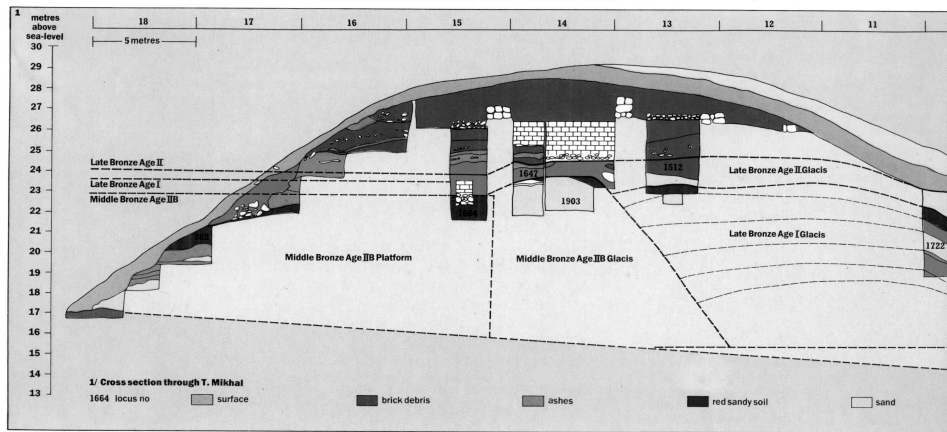

1/ Cross section through T. Mikhal

1664 locus no | surface | brick debris | ashes | red sandy soil | sand

1/ Above
A vertical view of a section at T. Mikhal, revealing a system of superimposed earthen ramparts dating from the MBA IIB—LBA II (c 1750-1200 BC). Each deposit uncovered in the excavation was designated separately according to its colour and composition. The thick black lines represent the upper surfaces of the various archaeological features dating from different periods. The broken lines represent the hypothetical continuation of these archaeological features.

2/ Right
A horizontal bird's-eye view of the superimposed architectural remains uncovered by archaeologists at T. Arad in the Negeb Desert.
The architectural remains shown in this plan represent different stages of the Iron Age fortress (c 1200-600 BC) with a square tower of Hellenistic date built above the earlier remains.

3/ Far right
A horizontal section at T. Beersheba.

Today, the surveyor must work on many planes, the location and character of each site is compared with the general pattern of settlement distribution over a given area, usually a distinct topographical unit which have common rock and soil traits. Ecological and anthropological factors play an important role in the process of analysis. Modern maps on the scale of 1:50,000 or 1:20,000 are used along with infra-red aerial photos and other techniques.

Scientific excavation can be said to have begun in 1890 when Sir Flinders Petrie conducted a stratigraphic excavation at T. el-Hesi. He demonstrated that the ancient mounds, or tells (Arabic *tell*, Modern Hebrew *tel*), were comprised of layers of debris deposited as the settlement was built and destroyed and later rebuilt down through the ages. The order of such an accumulation of debris layers is called *stratigraphy*. The vicissitudes of an ancient site over thousands of years have usually led to a complex situation where debris and artefacts from lower strata have been disturbed by intrusions from above and deposited on higher strata. Thus, stratigraphy must be defined as 'the three dimensional relationship between all the debris deposits in the mound.'

The elements uncovered as one digs a stratified mound are the result of both natural and human activity. Wind and rain may create deposits of soil between or above the decayed organic materials left by man. The inhabitants of the site usually constructed some sort of dwellings, storage installations and, in more advanced societies, buildings for

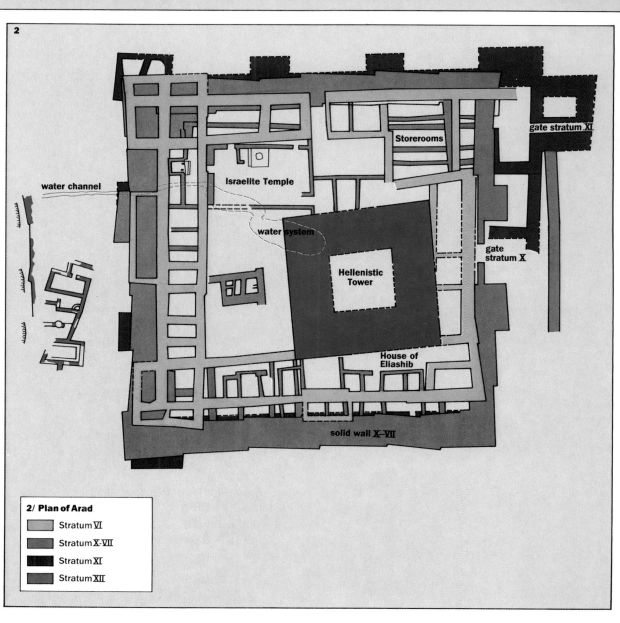

2/ Plan of Arad
Stratum VI
Stratum X-VII
Stratum XI
Stratum XII

'original' content of each stratum. This identification becomes the vital basis for any interpretation made concerning the site as a whole.

One of the most important tools for controlling stratigraphy is the recording system. Archaeological recording must overcome a fundamental problem of dimension. Excavating is a three-dimensional process; recording is on a flat surface, ie, it is two-dimensional. Photographs from various angles may preserve a three-dimensional perspective – but they cannot be made to reproduce an exact scale. However, vertical sections, cuts made through the layers of deposit covering the various occupation levels, can provide an accurate record of the *vertical* dimension, and they are an essential part of any excavation. However, vertical relationships between deposits and layers can, and usually do, vary greatly from place to place on the mound. One can

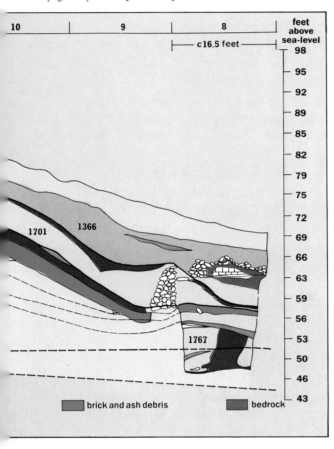

feet above sea-level: 98, 95, 92, 89, 85, 82, 79, 75, 72, 69, 66, 63, 59, 56, 53, 50, 46, 43

10   9   8

c 16.5 feet

1701   1366   1767

brick and ash debris   bedrock

never base his complete stratigraphic analysis on vertical sections alone. *Horizontal* plans of the excavated area, drawn to scale and marked wth the absolute heights of all significant features (walls, floors, pit edges and bottoms, etc) provide the best means of representing three-dimensional stratigraphy to an accurate scale.

In order to record the exact location of every find, serial numbers are assigned and the number is recorded on a plan along with a notation of the depth of the find. Thus, the three dimensions are placed on record. The various homogeneous pieces of space within the mound, such as fill layers, rooms, pits or other logical units, are also assigned numbers from an independent series. These units are called loci. The individual finds are assigned to their respective loci. The locus must be a logical, homogeneous piece of space. Within a locus, eg, a room, one may find several distinct layers of debris. When excavating these various deposits of debris and soil, their respective finds must be kept distinct, usually by the find/sherd basket numbers. It is preferable to reserve locus numbers for entities from real life, such as rooms, pits, etc. Every sherd basket number thus represents a subdivision of a locus.

The most common artefact recovered from an excavation of the site of an ancient settlement is the ceramic vessel, but these have usually been shattered into many fragments or potsherds. Because these were fragile and had to be replaced frequently, styles of construction and decoration were often changed by potters as they sought to sell their wares. Some pots can be reconstructed from sherds, but most cannot. Great quantities of potsherds remain as important evidence for not only the period of the settlement but for the type of activity which was carried on in a particular locus. The distinctive or diagnostic fragments – section of the rim or base, handles, or a decorated surface on the side of a pot – are classified according to type and recorded to provide the percentage of a type within a locus or stratum. From this quantative record of the change in style in the form and decoration employed by potters a trustworthy approximation of chronology can be had, even though only potsherds remain. Graphs of the frequencies of occurrence of ceramic types show that while change was gradual in public acceptance of the innovation of a potter, one style did replace another whether merely for the sake of vanity or for the purpose of utility. Classifying potsherds according to types of rim, base, handle and surface decoration can only be

done by staff members with a good eye for form. However, the processing of the data obtained by careful inspection in the field can be speedily processed into significant patterns by the computer.

Objects from stratified sites are utilized to reconstruct the typological sequence of artefact development. By noting similarities and differences, scholars are able to create type classes representing style changes through the passage of time, eg, the evolution in the shapes of pottery vessels, the layouts of houses, or the forms of letters in the alphabet. Such modifications in style are subject to the influences of many factors such as technical improvements or changes in function. Foreign influences and shifts in social status also play a role. The chronological classification of ceramic vessels has become a mainstay for the relative dating of occupation levels within a mound. In certain periods, there were recognizable imports, the geographical origin of which is known; these are often some of the most significant chronological indicators.

Similar chronological typologies have been and are being established for other types of artefacts such as metal tools and weapons, jewellery, ivory and bone carvings, etc. But the chronology is only a relative one. The initiative for coordinating archaeological finds with historical events is the province of the trained historian. One must admit, however, that it has been most difficult for archaeologists to reach a consensus on key issues such as the age of the patriarchs, the supposed destruction levels of the Israelite conquest, or even the stratum representing Solomon's fortifications of Megiddo.

In order to establish an absolute date for any archaeological find, it must be associated with some firmly dateable item. In later antiquity, coins are a useful indicator since the date of their minting is often known. In prehistory and in the earlier historical periods, the laboratory analysis of organic materials may supply an absolute date within margins of 100 to 150 years. In the Bronze and Iron Ages, dates may be established by correlation with neighbouring cultures such as those of Mesopotamia, Egypt or the Aegean. Artefacts of similar type found in one of these adjacent areas and also in Canaan/Israel (such as the Mycenaean pottery found at Amarna and also in Canaan) or dated imports (such as certain scarabs) are used as chronological pegs for absolute dating by virtue of their links with the established historical chronology of the other culture.

(continued on page 190)

3

(Continued from page 189)

The typology of artefacts has its own limitations and may not be pushed too far. A meaningful typological assemblage is obtained mainly in cities and forts which were destroyed by violent conquest and excavated on a broad site. Since such cases are limited, our typology contains, in the monarchical period, for example, well defined pottery groups of the late 10th, late 8th and early 6th centuries BC, corresponding to the destructions wrought by Shishak, Sennacherib and Nebuchadnezzar respectively. On the other hand, the pottery of the 9th century in Judah is practically unknown.

In the earlier practice of biblical archaeology, a synthesis was attempted between the historical data in the written sources and the archaeological data from excavations and surveys. Some of the problematic examples cited on the previous page (the Patriarchal Age, the Israelite conquest and the Solomonic fortifications) testify to the limitations of this method which 50 years of research have not yet been able to overcome.

More recently a new objective for archaeological research has appeared in the ancient Near East. Its usefulness has been demonstrated in New World and European archaeology. It is characterized by a social/anthropological paradigm. Anthropological archaeology shifts the focus from the object to the society, from description to explanation. It does not try to answer the old questions but rather it poses new ones. Archaeological research does not end with the uncovering of finds: the real work begins with the processing and analysis of the data retrieved.

Archaeological materials are seen as a unique source for the study of ancient society. Material culture preserves within itself an expression of general human culture, which is conceived as a society's means of adapting to its environment. Methods of human adaptation to a changing environment and the reciprocal relationships between people and their surroundings may be deduced from archaeological data in terms of the distribution of sites in a given region and the sources of food utilized by its population. The exploitation of faunal and floral resources reflected in an archaeological complex provides indications of climatic, geographical or geological changes.

Against the background of a changing environment one may test the economic base of a population, its means of sustenance (from agriculture, hunting, fishing, or outside support) and the factors (technological, social or political) that influenced them. Questions asked of the archaeological data are: was there a stratification in the society? To what degree was there a polarity between factions? What are the evidences for the accumulation of wealth, power and prestige? How did the ruling class guarantee the continuation of its superior position?

Answers to these questions may be found in the archaeological materials by the coordinated investigation of a clearly defined region and by the study of excavation data relevant to the questions of the environment, the economic base, the society and the realm of symbols and ideas.

Thus does social/anthropological archaeology stride forward into a new era.

HISTORICAL GEOGRAPHY AND PHILOLOGY

Other fields contribute to historical archaeology: biblical geography deals with the morphology and traits of the terrain, especially in relation to the ecological factors bearing on human existence. The landscape, the soils, the flora and fauna, the hydrology and the prevailing weather patterns must be taken into consideration. The graphic representation of all these factors, particularly in the form of maps, is also a speciality of the physical geographer. Many are the disciplines that contribute to this intricate endeavour, eg geology, cartography, aerial photography, zoology and botany, etc.

Historical philology is the analysis of ancient written documents, in this case those which contain geographical information. Not only the names of ancient places and features but also social, political and military data are of relevance. The main sources are the Bible itself, inscriptions discovered in the ancient Near East, Greek and Roman geographers and historians, the Church Fathers and the Rabbinic literature. Although they are a rich source of information, the historical documents may present a biased picture of ancient life. The principle point of view is that of the ruling elite. The way of life of the commoners is seldom represented. Moreover, most of these documents are clearly used as a means of maintaining the hegemony of the upper classes, by political propaganda and/or religious ideol-

1/ Map left
Maps showing the distribution of soils can be useful in determining the agricultural potential of lands surrounding ancient settlements. The circle encloses lands which are located within a radius of one hour's walk from T. Gerisa.

2/ Map below
Changing settlement patterns during the EBA and MBA.

3/ Above right
Wilson's Arch in Jerusalem, excavated 1869.

4/ Far right
Warren, who compiled the Survey of Western Palestine in the 1870s, climbing through rubble in the Tyropoeon Valley.

5/ Right
19th century excavation at Gezer.

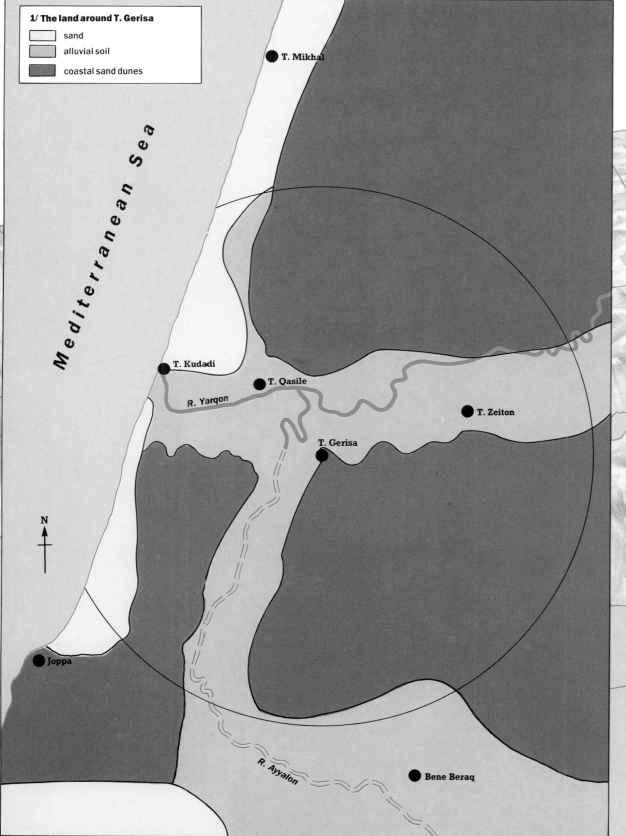

1/ The land around T. Gerisa
- sand
- alluvial soil
- coastal sand dunes

Mediterranean Sea

T. Mikhal

T. Kudadi

T. Qasile

R. Yarqon

T. Zeiton

T. Gerisa

N

R. Ayyalon

Joppa

Bene Beraq

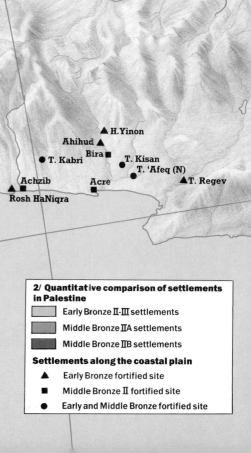

Sea of Galilee

H. Yinon

Ahihud

Bira

T. Kabri

T. Kisan

T. 'Afeq (N)

Achzib

Acre

T. Regev

Rosh HaNiqra

2/ Quantitative comparison of settlements in Palestine
- Early Bronze II–III settlements
- Middle Bronze IIA settlements
- Middle Bronze IIB settlements

Settlements along the coastal plain
- ▲ Early Bronze fortified site
- ■ Middle Bronze II fortified site
- ● Early and Middle Bronze fortified site

ogy. Each generation tended to rewrite its history, thus introducing a certain bias to each new edition. Geographical details are usually trustworthy, however, even in a propagandist text such as a boastful display inscription from some egotistical pharaoh or Assyrian monarch.

Toponymy, the study of place-names, is a highly technical field but can provide fascinating details about the language, psychology, religion and society of the ancient inhabitants. The preservation of numerous biblical and non-biblical toponyms down to modern times, albeit in Arabic dress, was one of the surprises awaiting western scholars who began to come in the wake of Napoleon's ill-fated Egyptian campaign in 1799. Most ancient sites have had more than one name or form of the original name, eg, Hebrew, Greek, Latin, Arabic, Anglicized (from the English Bible), etc. The choice of spelling to be used on an historical map such as those in this atlas, depends on the objective for which the map was designed.

'I WENT OUT BY NIGHT BY THE VALLEY GATE, ... AND I INSPECTED THE WALLS OF JERUSALEM WHICH WERE BROKEN DOWN AND ITS GATES WHICH HAD BEEN DESTROYED BY FIRE. THEN I WENT ON TO THE FOUNTAIN GATE AND TO THE KING'S POOL; BUT THERE WAS NO PLACE FOR THE BEAST THAT WAS UNDER ME TO PASS. THEN I WENT UP IN THE NIGHT BY THE VALLEY AND INSPECTED THE WALL; AND I TURNED BACK AND ENTERED BY THE VALLEY GATE, AND SO RETURNED.' NEH 2.13-15

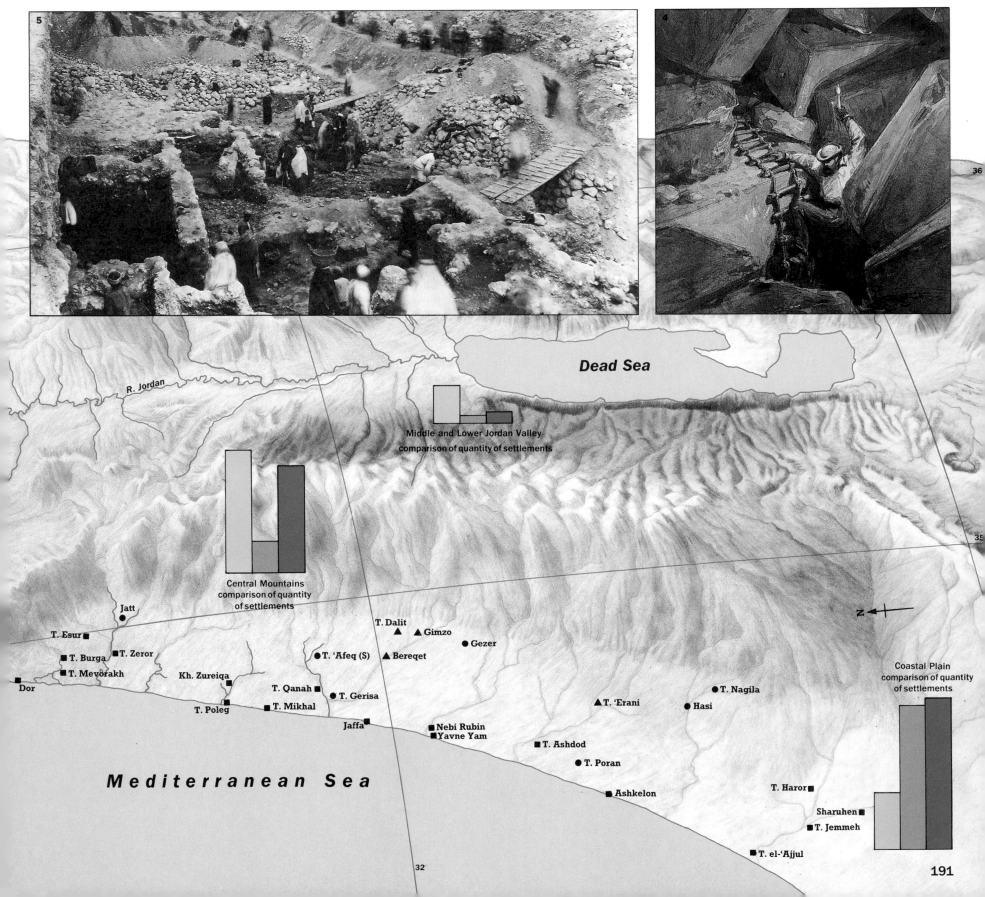

Dead Sea

R. Jordan

Middle and Lower Jordan Valley
comparison of quantity of settlements

Central Mountains
comparison of quantity
of settlements

Jatt

T. Esur

T. Burga   T. Zeror

T. Mevorakh   Kh. Zureiqa

Dor

T. Qanah

T. Poleg   T. Mikhal

Jaffa

T. Dalit

T. 'Afeq (S)   Gimzo   Gezer

Bereqet

T. Gerisa

Nebi Rubin
Yavne Yam

T. Nagila

Hasi

T. 'Erani

T. Ashdod

T. Poran

Ashkelon

T. Haror

Sharuhen

T. Jemmeh

T. el-'Ajjul

Coastal Plain
comparison of quantity
of settlements

Mediterranean Sea

ACKNOWLEDGEMENTS
AND ABBREVIATIONS

The publishers should like to thank the following people and institutions, all of whom have given advice and help at various stages in the production of this book:
Naama Arzi, Pauline Batchelor, Belinda Barratt, British Museum, Joan Candy, Orly Bat Carmel, Rupert Chapman, Trude Dothan, Israel Eph'al, Aya Eshet, John Ferguson, Shulamit Geva, Sandi Gibson, Shimon Gibson, Martin Goodman, Emanuel Hausman, Candida Hunt, Caroline Lucas, Palestine Exploration Fund, Aviva Rosen, H.W.F. Saggs.

The Scripture quotations contained herein are from the Revised Standard Version of the Bible, copyrighted 1946, 1952, 1971, by the Division of Christian Education of the National Council of the Churches of Christ in the USA, and are used by permission.

Those quotations for which no other attribution is given are taken from *Ancient Near Eastern Texts relating to the Old Testament* 3rd edition, 1969, by James B. Pritchard, and are reprinted by permission of Princeton University Press.

Quotations from *The Jewish War* by Josephus are reprinted by permission of Penguin Books, London.

The quotation on page 141 from *De Architectura* is reproduced by permission of William Heineman Ltd, London.

ABBREVIATIONS
The following abbreviations for the Books of the Bible have been used.

OLD TESTAMENT

Genesis	GEN	II Chronicles	II CHRON	Daniel	DAN
Exodus	EX	Ezra	EZRA	Hosea	HOS
Leviticus	LEV	Nehemiah	NEH	Joel	JOEL
Numbers	NUM	Esther	ESTHER	Amos	AMOS
Deuteronomy	DEUT	Job	JOB	Obadiah	OBAD
Joshua	JOSH	Psalms	PS	Jonah	JON
Judges	JUDG	Proverbs	PROV	Micah	MIC
Ruth	RUTH	Ecclesiastes	ECCLES	Nahum	NAHUM
I Samuel	I SAM	Song of Solomon	SONG	Habakkuk	HAB
II Samuel	II SAM	Isaiah	ISA	Zephaniah	ZEPH
I Kings	I KINGS	Jeremiah	JER	Haggai	HAG
II Kings	II KINGS	Lamentations	LAM	Zechariah	ZECH
I Chronicles	I CHRON	Ezekiel	EZEK	Malachi	MAL

APOCRYPHA/DEUTEROCANONICAL BOOKS

Tobit	TOB	1 Esdras	I ESD	I Maccabees	I MACC
Judith	JDT	II Esdras	II ESD	II Maccabees	II MACC
Additions to Esther	ADD ESTH	Letter of Jeremiah	LET JER	III Maccabees	III MACC
				IV Maccabees	IV MACC
Wisdom	WIS	Prayer of Azariah and the Song of the Three Young Men	SONG OF THR	The Prayer of Manasseh	PRAYER MAN
Sirach (Ecclesiasticus)	SIR				
Baruch	BAR				
		Susanna	SUS		
		Bel and the Dragon	BEL		

NEW TESTAMENT

Matthew	MT	Ephesians	EPH	Hebrews	HEB
Mark	MK	Philippians	PHIL	James	JAS
Luke	LK	Colossians	COL	I Peter	I PET
John	JN	I Thessalonians	I THESS	II Peter	II PET
Acts of the Apostles	ACTS	II Thessalonians	II THESS	I John	I JN
Romans	ROM	I Timothy	I TIM	II John	II JN
I Corinthians	I COR	II Timothy	II TIM	III John	III JN
II Corinthians	II COR	Titus	TIT	Jude	JUDE
Galatians	GAL	Philemon	PHILEM	Revelations	REV

NOTE: Since many of our readers may consider the Hebrew word for God too holy to pronounce, we have normally substituted 'the Lord'. However, in some direct quotations this has not been possible and we have therefore used the tetragrammaton Yhwh.

MAPS

We have pleasure in acknowledging:

p63 4 Based on *The Problem of Ai* by Z. Zevit in *Biblical Archaeological Review* Vol XI No. 2 page 58-67 1985

p79 4 Based on photograph courtesy of Sonia Halliday Photographs, Weston Turville, England

p96 2,3 Based on original material by Y. Aharoni, with permission of M. Aharoni, and Burns & Oates Ltd, Tunbridge Wells, England and The Westminster Press, Philadelphia

p152 1, 2 Based on information from *Ancient Synagogues Revealed* edited by L. I. Levine published by Israel Exploration Society, Jerusalem

p153-55 Based on original material by M. Avi-Yonah, and used by courtesy of the Israel Department of Antiquities and Museums, Jerusalem

p160 1 Based on original information by A. Negev, Jerusalem

p190-1 1 Based on Broshi and Gophna *Middle Bronze Age II Palestine – Its Settlements and Population* published in BASOR 261; 74-90 used by permission of American School of Oriental Research, Valpariso University, Indiana

Front end paper Based on information published in *Land of the Bible* by Y. Aharoni, and used by permission of M. Aharoni and Burns and Oates Ltd, Tunbridge Wells, England, and The Westminster Press, Philadelphia

ILLUSTRATIONS

Unless stated to the contrary, all the illustrations in this book are the work of the following artists: Irene Bates, Duncan Mackay, Rex Nicholls and Malcolm Swanston.

The publishers should like to thank the following museums, publishers and picture agencies for permission to base illustrations upon their photographs or to reproduce them. Where there is no such acknowledgement, we have been unable to trace the source, or the illustration is a composition by our illustrators and contributors.

p26 3, 5 Institute of Archaeology, University of London
     4 Professor B. Hennessy, Sydney, Australia
     6 Palestine Exploration Fund, London
     7 The British School of Archaeology, Jerusalem

p27 8 Professor B. Hennessy, Sydney, Australia

p28 2 Based on fig. 3 pages 224-225 of *Israel Exploration Journal* Vol 2 1952, published by Israel Exploration Society, Jerusalem
     3 Based on excavation of Arad, courtesy of Ruth Amiran, Director, Arad Expedition, sponsored by the Israel Museum and the Israel Exploration Society; and drawing by L. Ritmeyer, Jerusalem

p29 4 Based on excavation by W.F.M. Petrie, published by J.C. Hinrichs Verlag, Leipzig
     5 Based on excavation by R. De Vaux, published in *Revue Biblique* 69, 1962 planches XIX, XX and XXI, by Ecole Biblique et Archéologique Française, Jerusalem

p30 2 (Inset) Professor D. Wiseman, Epsom
     3 ET Archive, London

p31 (Inset) Michael Holford, London; courtesy of the Trustees of the British Museum, London

p32 4 ACL, Brussels

p34 2 Based on *Ebla: An Empire Rediscovered* by Paolo Matthiae, published by Doubleday & Company, New York
     3 Based on *Land des Baal*, published by Philipp von Zabern, Verlag, Mainz

p35 4 Based on *The Atlas of Ancient Archaeology* by Jaquetta Hawkes, Rainbird Reference Books, London; *Mission archéologique de Mari (Le Palais) (Vol II)* published by the Louvre, Paris.
     5, 6 Giraudon, Paris

p36 2, 3 Service des Antiquités, Cairo
     4 From *Late Middle Kingdom Papyrus* by William Hayes, published by Brooklyn Museum, New York

p37 6 Courtesy of the Oriental Institute of the University of Chicago

p38 2 Scala, Florence, Italy
     3 Based on information from *The Art and Architecture of Ancient Egypt* by W. Stevenson Smith, published by Penguin Books, London
     4, 6, 7 Courtesy of the Trustees of the British Museum, London
     5 Michael Holford, London; Courtesy of the Trustees of the British Museum, London

p39 8 Sonia Halliday Photographs, Weston Turville, England

p40 4 Peter Clayton, Hemel Hempstead, England
     5 Uni Dia Verlag, Munich

p42 2, 3, 4 Peter Clayton, Hemel Hempstead, England

p43 5, 6 Peter Clayton, Hemel Hempstead, England

p44 2 Based on *Ugaritica* IV figs 20-21 by Peter Schaeffer, published by Mission Archéologique de Ras-Shamra-Ougarit, Lyon, France
     3 Paolo Koch, Vision International, London
     4 Damascus Museum, Syria

p45 6, 7, 8 Paolo Koch, Vision International, London
     9 Cliché Musées Nationaux, Louvre, Paris

p46 2 Department of Antiquities, Israel Museum, Jerusalem
     3 Michael Holford, London; Courtesy of the Trustees of the British Museum, London
     4 ET Archive, London

p47 5 Werner Braun, Jerusalem
     6, 7 Michael Holford, London; Courtesy of the Trustees of the British Museum, London

p49 4 J. Vertut, France
     5 Giraudon, Paris

p50 3 Courtesy of the Trustees of the British Museum, London
     4 Peter Clayton, Hemel Hempstead, England
     5 National Museum of Antiquities, Cairo
     5a K.A. Kitchen, Liverpool

p53 3 Courtesy of the Trustees of the British Museum, London

p54 4, 5 Sonia Halliday Photographs, Weston Turville, England

p55 6 Courtesy of the Trustees of the British Museum, London

p60 2 The Ancient Art and Architecture Collection, London
     3 Based on information published in *Geography of Israel* by E. Orni and E. Efrat, 1964, Jerusalem

p61 4, 5, 7 The Ancient Art and Architecture Collection, London
     6 Michael Holford, London; by courtesy of the Trustees of the British Museum, London

p66 5 Werner Forman Archive, London

p67 3 Erich Lessing of Magnum Paris, the John Hillelson Agency, London
     4 The Ancient Art and Architecture Collection, London

p69 7 Department of Antiquities, Israel Museum, Jerusalem

p71 2 The Ancient Art and Architecture Collection, London; Britain/Israel Public Affairs Committee and United Press International, London; Z. Radovan, Jerusalem

p76 2 Z. Radovan, Jerusalem
     3, 4 Institute of Archaeology, University of London
     5 (illustration) Based on Jericho P19 tomb, excavated by Kathleen Kenyon, Courtesy of the Trustees of the British Museum, London
     5 (photograph) Courtesy of the Trustees of the British Museum, London

p77 6, 7 Department of Antiquities, Israel Museum, Jerusalem
     8 Z. Radovan, Jerusalem
     9 Based on information from *Painted Tombs in the Necropolis of Marisa* by Peters and Thiersch, published by the Palestine Exploration Fund, London
     10 (photograph) Sonia Halliday Photographs, Weston Turville, England

p81 3 Sonia Halliday Photographs, Weston Turville, England

p84 1 Courtesy of the Trustees of the British Museum, London
     2 Z. Radovan, Jerusalem
     3 Sonia Halliday Photographs, Weston Turville, England

p85 4, 6, 8, 11 Sonia Halliday Photographs, Weston Turville, England
     7 Department of Antiquities, Israel Museum, Jerusalem
     9 ET Archive, London
     10 Michael Holford, London; Courtesy of The Trustees of the British Museum, London
     12 Based on *Megiddo I seasons of 1925-34 Strata I-V* published courtesy of the Oriental Institute, University of Chicago

p86 1 Based on *The City Gate in Eretz-Israel and its Neighbouring Countries* by Z. Herzog, published by The Institute of Archaeology, Tel Aviv
     2 Based on *City of David I (Qedem 19)* by Y. Shiloh, published by the Institute of Archaeology, Hebrew University of Jerusalem
     3 Based on L.K. Townsend in H. Shanks' *The City of David After Five Years Digging* published in Biblical Archaeology Review 11,6:22-38

p87 4 Based on T.A. Busink *Der Tempel von Jerusalem von Salomo bis Herods* Vol I 1970, E.J. Brill, Leiden
     6 Based on *King Solomon's Palaces* by D. Ussishkin published in Biblical Archaeologist 36:78-105

p88 2, 2a   Based on figs 3 and 4 of *Tel Aviv* Vol VII 1980 published by The Institute of Archaeology, Tel Aviv University

3   David Harris, Jerusalem

4, 5   Based on figs 390 and 394 of *Megiddo* II, published by courtesy of the University of Chicago Press, Chicago

6   Department of Antiquities, Israel Museum, Jerusalem

7   David Harris, Jerusalem

8   Reproduced by permission of the British Academy, London and of the estate of Y. Yadin from the 1972 Schweich Lecture *Hazor* by Yigael Yadin

p89 9   Based on *Shechem – A biblical city* by G.E. Wright, published by Wilfred Laurier University, Ontario

10   Based on *Beth-shean* Vol II plate VI by E. Rome, published by the University of Philadelphia

11   Sonia Halliday Photographs, Weston Turville, England

12   Courtesy of Ruth Amiran, Director, Arad Expedition, sponsored by the Israel Museum and the Israel Exploration Society, Jerusalem

13   Z. Radovan, Jerusalem

14   W. Braun, Jerusalem

15   Published courtesy of the estate of Yigael Yadin, *Hazor*, vol 1, plate CLXX 1.1

16   A. Duncan, Mepha Photographs, London

17   Holle Verlag, Baden-Baden

p91 3, 4   Michael Holford, London; courtesy of the Trustees of the British Museum, London

p92 2, 3   Based on information in *History of Ancient Geography* by J. Oliver Thompson, 1948, published by Cambridge University Press, Cambridge

p93 4   Reproduced by courtesy of the Trustees of the British Museum, London

p96 4   Reproduced by courtesy of the Trustees of the British Museum, London

p97 5   Cliché Musées Nationaux, Louvre, Paris

6, 7   Courtesy of the Oriental Institute of the University of Chicago

p98 5   Based on information in *Samaria Sebaste 1: The Buildings* plates 1 and 2, by J. W. Crowfoot, K. M. Kenyon and E. L. Sukenik published by The Palestine Exploration Fund, London, 1942

p99 2   Michael Holford, London; courtesy of the Trustees of the British Museum, London

3   Based on *Revue Biblique* 58, 1952, published by Ecole Biblique et Archéologique Française de Jerusalem

p100 2   Cliché Musées Nationaux, Louvre, Paris

p102 2   F. Roulet, Biblical Institute Fribourg, Switzerland Department of Antiquities, Israel Museum, Jerusalem Z. Radovan, Jerusalem

3   Badisches Landesmuseum Karlsruhe, West Germany

p103 4   F. Roulet, Biblical Institute, Fribourg, Switzerland

5   Cliché Musées Nationaux, Louvre, Paris

6, 7, 8   Z. Radovan, Jerusalem

p105 6   By courtesy of the University Museum, University of Pennsylvania

p107 3   Based on information from *Solar and Lunar Eclipses of the Ancient Near East from 3000 BC*, published by Butzon und Bercker Verlag, Gmbh, Kevelaer I, West Germany

p110 1   Uni Dia Verlag, Munich

2, 3, 6, 7   Z. Radovan, Jerusalem

8, 9   The Ancient Art and Architecture Collection, London

10   Sonia Halliday Photographs, Weston Turville, England

p111 4, 5, 13, 14   Z. Radovan, Jerusalem

11   Cliché Musées Nationaux, Louvre, Paris

12   Sonia Halliday Photographs, Weston Turville, England

15   W. Braun, Jerusalem

p112 4   Z. Radovan, Jerusalem

5c   Paul Jordan, Norwich

p113 5a   Z. Radovan, Jerusalem

5b   Department of Antiquities, Israel Museum, Jerusalem

p115 6   Museo Civico, Turin

7   Holle Verlag, Baden-Baden

p116 1   Michael Holford, London; courtesy of the Trustees of the British Museum, London

p117 2, 3, 4   Michael Holford, London; by courtesy of the Trustees of the British Museum, London

6   Palestine Exploration Fund, London

p119 4 (Arad-rabbah fortress)   Based on *Ancient Arad* by Ruth Amiran and Y. Aharoni, used by permission of R Amiran, Z. Herzog, and M. Aharoni.

(Ezion-geber fortress)   Based on fig 9, vol 26-28 of *Biblical Archaeologist* 1963-65

(Kadesh-barnea fortress)   Based on information published by the Israel Museum, Jerusalem

p122 3a, 4, 5   Michael Holford, London; by courtesy of the Trustees of the British Museum, London

p123 1, 2, 6   Michael Holford, London; by courtesy of the Trustees of the British Museum, London

p128 4   Based on Israel Exploration Journal, 160, Vol 10, p130, published by Israel Exploration Society, Jerusalem

p129 2   Giraudon, Paris

3   Michael Holford, London

p130 2   Courtesy of Professor D. Wiseman, Epsom

p132 2   By courtesy of the Trustees of the British Museum, London

3, 4   The British Library, London

p133 5   The Bodleian Library, Oxford

6   Z. Radovan, Jerusalem

7   Mepha, London

p134 4   Sonia Halliday Photographs, Weston Turville, England

p135 3   Based on *Archives from Elephantine: The life of an ancient Jewish Military Colony* by B. Porten, published by University of California Press, California

p136 1   William McQuitty, London

2   Z. Radovan, Jerusalem

p137 3, 4 (Esther scroll)   Z. Radovan, Jerusalem

6, 7   Sonia Halliday Photographs, Weston Turville, England

5   Robert Harding, London

p138 2   Giraudon, Paris

p140 6   Based on information from William Dinsmoor perspective drawing of the Athenian Agora, Agora Excavations, American School of Studies, Athens

1   Sonia Halliday Photographs, Weston Turville, England

p141 2, 3, 4, 5   Sonia Halliday Photographs, Weston Turville, England

6 (coin)   By courtesy of the Trustees of the British Museum, London

p143 4   The Mansell Collection, London

5   By courtesy of the Trustees of the British Museum, London

6   The British Library, London

p144 3   The Mansell Collection, London

p148 2   Based on drawing by L. Ritmeyer, Jerusalem

p149 3   By courtesy of the Trustees of the British Museum, London

p152 2   Based on information in *Ancient Synagogues Revealed*, compliments of the excavator, Eric M. Meyers

p156 2   Based on a reconstruction by L. Ritmeyer and drawings by E. Netzer, Jerusalem

p158 2   Based on a reconstruction by L. Ritmeyer, Jerusalem

p159 3   Based on a reconstruction by E. Netzer, Jerusalem

p161 4   Sonia Halliday Photographs, Weston Turville, England

5   The Ancient Art and Architecture Collection, London

p162 2   Sonia Halliday Photographs, Weston Turville, England

p166 2   Based on a reconstruction by L. Ritmeyer, Jerusalem

p169 4   Based on *Discovering Jerusalem* by N. Avigad, published by Basil Blackwell, Oxford

p173 4   Sonia Halliday Photographs, Weston Turville, England

p174 2   Based on a reconstruction by L. Ritmeyer, Jerusalem

p175 3, 4, 5, 6, 7   Sonia Halliday Photographs, Weston Turville, England

p176 2   Based on a reconstruction by L. Ritmeyer, Jerusalem

3   N.Y. Carlsberg Glypotek, Copenhagen

4   Z. Radovan, Jerusalem

p180 4   Based on a reconstruction by L. Ritmeyer, Jerusalem

p181 2, 3   Z. Radovan, Jerusalem

5   Based on information from *The Bar Kochba Revolt* by Y. Yadin, published by Weidenfeld & Nicolson, London

p182 2   Werner Forman Archive, London

p183 3   Werner Forman Archive, London

p184 3   Based on a reconstruction by L. Ritmeyer, Jerusalem

p189 3   Sonia Halliday Photographs, Weston Turville, England

p191 3, 4, 5   Palestine Exploration Fund, London

PEOPLE OF THE BIBLE

The number of personal names mentioned in the Bible is enormous, and many of them are accompanied by no biographical details whatever. Any attempt to list them all would require a book in itself. The following glossary is, therefore, selective. The names chosen are those which figure prominently in the Atlas, with a strong emphasis on those people who play an important part in the 'action' of the Bible narrative. Minor characters have often been subsumed in the entries for major ones (eg, Bathsheba, *see* David). The characters of the Apocrypha have not been included, as many Bibles do not contain these books. However, readers who wish to find out more about the personalities of the Intertestamental period will find that many Bible references – particularly to Maccabees – have been included in the main texts accompanying the maps in that section. Those who seek further information on biblical characters are referred to the *Dictionary of Proper Names and Places in the Bible*, by O. Odelain and R. Séguineau published by Doubleday in the USA and Robert Hale in Great Britain.

Abdon (Judge)
JUDG 12.13-15 Abdon judges Israel for 8 years; dies; buried at Pirathon in territory of Ephraim

Abel (Son of Adam and Eve)
GEN 2.1-8 Born to Adam and Eve; killed by his brother Cain

Abijah (also called Abijam, King of Judah)
I KINGS 14.31 Succeeds Rehoboam as king
15.3 Does evil and is not loyal to the Lord
15.4 The Lord gives Abijah a son for David's sake and to keep Jerusalem secure
15.7 War between Abijah and Jeroboam
15.8 Abijah dies; succeeded by Asa

Abimelech (King of Gerar)
GEN 20.2 Has Abraham's wife Sarah brought to him believing that she is Abraham's sister
20.3 The Lord appears to Abimelech in a dream and threatens him
20.14-16 Gives Sarah back to Abraham

Abishag (the Shunammite chosen to comfort David in his old age)
I KINGS 1.3-4, 15 Ministers to King David
2.17 Adonijah asks Bathsheba to persuade Solomon to give him Abishag as his wife
2.19-22 Bathsheba asks Solomon on Adonijah's behalf

Abner (Saul's Commander)
II SAM 2.12-17 Abner and Joab pitch their men against each other at the Pool of Gibeon
3.27 Joab murders Abner in Hebron

Abraham/Abram (Patriarch)
GEN 11.27-32 Genealogy
12.1-9 God tells Abram to take the people to Canaan; God's promise
12.10-20 Abram goes to Egypt because of famine; Sarai is taken into Pharaoh's house
13.1-18 Abram and Lot leave Egypt and travel through the Negeb to Bethel and Ai before separating
14.13-24 Hears of Lot's capture; pursues the captors as far as Dan and then to Hobah
15.1-21 God's covenant with Abram
16.1-6 Sarai gives her maid, Hagar the Egyptian, to Abram
16.15 Hagar bears Abram a son, Ishmael
17.1-8 God speaks to Abram saying his name shall be Abraham
17.9-14 The covenant of circumcision
17.15-27 God says Sarai's name shall be Sarah and she will bear a son; the males in the household are circumcised
18.1-15 The Lord appears before Abraham and promises him a son
18.16-33 Abraham's plea for Sodom
19.27-28 Looks at the destruction of Sodom
20.1-2 Journeys towards the Negeb; dwells between Kadesh and Shur; sojourns in Gerar
20.9-18 Abimelech speaks to Abraham about Sarah
21.2-7 Sarah bears Abraham a son, Isaac
21.9-14 Casts Hagar and her son out into the wilderness at Beersheba
21.24 Swears not to deal falsely with Abimelech and Phicol
21.25-34 Complains to Abimelech about the well; they make a covenant at Beersheba; Abraham sojourns in the land of the Philistines
22.1-14 God tests Abraham by telling him to sacrifice his son, Isaac
23.2-20 Sarah dies at Hebron and is buried in the cave at the field of Machpelah, given to Abraham by Ephron the Hittite
24.1-9 Makes his servant swear that he will find Isaac a wife from his own people
25.1-2 Takes another wife, Keturah and she bears six children
25.7-10 Dies and is buried beside Sarah

Absalom (Son of David)
II SAM 3.3 Born to David and Maacah, the daughter of the King of Geshur
13.20 Takes his sister Tamar into his house after she is raped by Amnon
13.28-33 Tells his servants to kill his brother Amnon
13.34-38 Flees to Geshur
13.39-14.1 King David's heart goes out to Absalom
14.21-24 David asks Joab to fetch Absalom back
14.25-27 Absalom's beauty; the birth of his children
14.28-33 Uses Joab to reconcile with David
15.1-6 Speaks to every man who comes to David for judgement
15.7-14 Declares himself King of Hebron; David flees Jerusalem
15.34 David sends Hushai to be Absalom's servant
15.37 Absalom takes Jerusalem
16.16-23 Hushai asks to serve; Absalom seeks Ahithophel's counsel
17.1-4 Ahithophel advises; says he will pursue and kill David
17.5-7 Seeks Hushai's opinion
17.14 Considers Hushai's advice
17.18 Is told of sighting of Jonathan and Ahimaaz
17.20 His servants look for Jonathan and Ahimaaz
17.24-26 Crosses the Jordan and camps in Gilead
18.5 David asks that Absalom is dealt with gently
18.9-18 Killed by the servants of David; buried in a pit in the forest
18.29-32 David asks after Absalom
18.33 David weeps for Absalom
19.1-4 David mourns for Absalom
19.9-10 The tribes speak of his death
I KINGS 2.7 David speaks of his flight from Absalom

Achish (King of Gath)
I SAM 21.10-15 David flees to Achish and feigns madness
27.2-3 David dwells in his house
27.5-6 Gives Ziklag to David

27.10-12 Questions David about his raids
28.1-2 Makes David his bodyguard
29.2-11 Enters battle with David; sends him back to Ziklag

Adrammelech (King of Assyria)
II KINGS 17.31 Children sacrificed as burnt offerings to Adrammelech
ISA 37.38 Adrammelech and his brother Sharezer kill their father Sennacherib, King of Assyria

Agrippa (Herod Agrippa II; also see Paul)
ACTS 25.13 Arrives at Caesarea to welcome Festus
25.22 Asks to hear Paul speak
25.23-27 Awaits Paul in the audience hall; Festus speaks to him of Paul
26.1 Asks Paul to speak for himself
26.2-19 Paul replies to Agrippa

Ahab (King of Israel)
I KINGS 16.29-33 Reigns over Israel in Samaria for 22 years; serves Baal and provokes the Lord's anger
18.1-2 Elijah sets out to meet Ahab
18.3-6 Tells Obadiah to look for water; goes himself to end the famine
18.16-20 Ahab meets Elijah
18.44-46 Elijah tells Ahab to go home; rides to Jezreel
19.1 Ahab tells Jezebel, his wife, of Elijah
20.1-12 Ahab forced into war with Ben-Hadad of Syria
20.13-15 A prophet speaks to Ahab of battle and promises victory
20.21-22 The defeat of Syria by Ahab
20.34 Makes covenant with Ben-Hadad
21.2-27 Naboth refuses to sell his vineyard to Ahab; Jezebel orders Naboth's death; Ahab repents
22.20 The Lord calls for someone to entice Ahab to go up and fall at Ramoth-gilead
22.29-37 Goes up to Ramoth-gilead; killed in battle
22.51 Ahaziah, his son, reigns

Ahasuerus (also called Xerxes, King of Persia)
EZRA 4.6 The reign of Ahasuerus
ESTHER 1.1 Gives a banquet for all his princes and servants
1.10-22 Queen Vashti refuses to obey his command; Ahasuerus banishes her from his presence and decrees that women will honour their husbands
2.1-4 His servants plan to find maidens to please the King instead of Vashti
2.16-18 Pleased by Esther; makes her queen
3.1 Promotes Haman the Agagite
3.7-11 Haman suggests that the Jews be destroyed; Ahasuerus agrees
3.12 Sends out letters to his provinces ordering the destruction of the Jews
5.1-6 The king goes to a dinner prepared by Esther
6.3-11 Honours Mordecai
7.1-5 Feasts with Esther; she intercedes for the Jews
7.7-10 Orders Haman to be hanged on the gallows he had built for Mordecai
8.1-2 Gives the house of Haman to the Jews
8.3-13 Pleased with Esther; allows Esther and Mordecai to write an edict on the Jews in his name
10.1-3 Pays tribute to Mordecai

Ahaz (King of Judah)
II KINGS 16.1-4 Reigns over Judah; burns his son as an offering to idols
16.5-6 Rezin, king of Syria, and Pekah, king of Israel, wage war on Ahaz
16.7-8 Asks the king of Assyria to rescue him
16.10-18 Sees the altar of the king of Assyria; orders similar altar to be built
16.20 Dies; buried in Jerusalem

Ahaziah (King of Israel)
I KINGS 22.40 Reigns after his father, Ahab
II KINGS 1.2-4 Falls through the lattice in his chamber; sends messengers to ask the god of Ekron if he will recover
1.5 Messengers return with message from Elijah
1.9 Sends 50 men to bring Elijah to him
1.17 Dies after Elijah speaks the Lord's word to him

Ahaziah (King of Judah)
II KINGS 8.24-26 Reigns over Judah
8.29 Visits wounded king of Joram at Jezreel
9.16 Visits Joram
9.21 Goes to meet Jehu with Joram
9.23 Joram speaks of Jehu's treachery
9.27-28 Flees but is shot by Jehu; dies at Megiddo, buried in Jerusalem
10.13 Jehu slays the kinsmen of Ahaziah
II CHRON 22.7-10 Murdered by Jehu
22.10 His mother destroys the royal house of Judah

Amon (King of Judah)
II KINGS 21.18 Reigns instead of his father, Manasseh
21.19-26 Reigns wickedly and is killed by his servants

Amos (Prophet)
AMOS 1.1 The words of Amos, a shepherd from Tekoa
7.10-14 Amaziah tells Jeroboam that Amos has conspired against him
7.12 Amaziah tells him to flee
7.14 Amos replies to Amaziah

Archelaus (Son of Herod the Great of Judaea)
MT 2.22 Reigns over Judaea in place of his father Herod

196

II KINGS 1.3-4	Intercepts messengers who are going to ask Baalzebub, the god of Ekron, about Ahaziah's health
1.8	The messengers return and tell Ahaziah of their meeting with Elijah
1.9-12	Ahaziah twice sends a captain and fifty soldiers to fetch Elijah but they are struck down by fire from heaven
1.13-15	The captain of the third party of soldiers pleads for their lives so Elijah accompanies them to Ahaziah
1.16	He tells Ahaziah that he will die because he has forsaken the God of Israel
2.1-6	Journeys with Elisha from Gilgal; tells Elisha three times to go no further but Elisha will not leave him
2.6-8	They reach the R. Jordan; Elijah strikes the river with his cloak and the water parts so they cross over on dry ground
2.9-10	Asks Elisha what he can do for him before he departs; Elisha says he wishes to inherit a double share of Elijah's spirit
2.11-12	They continue on but are separated by a chariot of fire and Elijah is taken up to heaven by a whirlwind
2.13-14	Elisha takes Elijah's cloak and parts the waters of the Jordan
2.15	The sons of the prophets at Jericho say that 'The spirit of Elijah rests on Elisha'

Elisha (Prophet)

I KINGS 19.16-17	Elijah is told by the Lord to anoint Elisha, the son of Shaphat, to be prophet in his place
19.19-21	Is ploughing with oxen when Elijah comes up and throws his cloak over him; leaves the farm and his family to follow Elijah
II KINGS 2.1-6	Travels from Gilgal with Elijah
2.12	Sees Elijah taken up in a whirlwind to heaven
2.13	Takes Elijah's cloak and strikes the R. Jordan; the water parts and he crosses
2.15	The sons of the prophets at Jericho hail him as Elijah's successor
2.19	The men of Jericho complain that the water in the city is bad and the land unfruitful
2.20-22	Elisha makes the water wholesome again
2.23-25	Travels to Bethel; as he leaves Jericho he curses a group of children who are jeering at his bald head
3.11-14	The kings of Israel, Edom and Judah join forces to fight the Moabites; they ask Elisha for help when they run out of water
3.15-20	Elisha prophesies rain and a victorious battle
4.1	A widow comes to him saying her children are to be taken as slaves to pay creditors
4.2-7	He tells her to take her last jar of oil and use it to fill empty jars borrowed from neighbours; she does this and sells the oil to pay her debts
4.8-17	Goes to Shunem where a wealthy woman gives him food and shelter; he tells her that she shall bear a son
4.18-25	The boy is taken ill and dies; his mother sets out to Mt Carmel to find Elisha
4.26-37	She asks Elisha for help and he returns with her to Shunem and restores the child to life
4.38-44	Goes to Gilgal where there is famine and feeds the people from a pottage of herbs and wild gourds
4.42-44	Multiplies the provisions brought by a farmer to feed the people
5.8-16	Cures Naaman, commander of the Syrian army, of leprosy; refuses a reward
5.20-27	His servant, Gehazi, follows Naaman and takes the reward; Elisha tells Gehazi that he and his descendants will be lepers
6.1-7	Goes to the Jordan with the sons of the prophets
6.12-14	Stays in the city of Dothan; the city is surrounded by the Syrians
6.15-19	Asks the Lord to strike the Syrians with blindness and then leads them to Samaria
6.20-23	At Samaria their sight is restored and Elisha hands them over to the king of Israel
6.31-7.2	Samaria is besieged by the Syrians and there is a great famine; Elisha says that barley and meal will be found
8.1-6	Tells the woman whose son he restored to life to leave the land because there will be famine
8.7-9	Goes to Damascus; Ben-Hadad is ill and sends Hazael to ask Elisha if he will recover
8.10-14	Weeps and replies that Hazael will become king of Syria
9.1-3	Sends a man to Ramoth-gilead to find Jehu and anoint him king over Israel
13.14	Falls ill; Joash visits him and weeps
13.15	Tells Joash to fire arrows in an eastward direction; prophesies victories over the Syrians
13.20-21	Dies and is buried

Esau (see Jacob)

Ezra (A scribe)

EZRA 7.1-10	Ezra, the son of Seraiah, leaves Babylon for Jerusalem to study the law of the Lord
7.11	King Artaxerxes of Persia sponsors his journey
10.1-5	Prays and weeps before the house of God at Jerusalem; makes the Israelites take an oath to abandon mixed marriages
10.10-11	Addresses the Israelites telling them to abandon mixed marriages
10.16	Appoints men to examine the matter
NEH 8.1-6	Stands on a wooden pulpit and reads the laws of the Lord to the Israelites
8.9-10	Tells the people not to mourn or weep but to feast
8.13	Continues with his readings
9.6	Speaks to the Lord
12.1	Is a chief priest in Jerusalem in the days of Joshua
12.36	Attends the dedication of the wall of Jerusalem

Gideon (Judge; also named Jerubbaal)

JUDG 6.11-16	Is threshing wheat at Ophrah when an angel appears and tells him to save Israel from the Midianites
6.25-32	Pulls down the altar of Baal and builds an altar to the Lord; is given the name Jerubbaal
6.33-35	Gathers up an army from the tribes of Manasseh, Asher, Zebulun and Naphtali
6.36-40	Asks God for a sign of victory
7.1-3	Camps with his army by the spring of Harod; the Lord tells him to reduce his forces and 22,000 men return home but 10,000 stay
7.4-8	The Lord tells him to reduce his army further
7.9-14	Takes his servant and steals into the camp of Midianites
7.15-22	Returns to his camp and arouses his army; they attack the Midianites who flee
7.24-25	Sends messengers to the tribes in the hill country of Ephraim telling them to seize the waters of Beth-barah and Jordan to cut off the Midianites
8.1-3	The men of Ephraim are angry with him because they were not called to fight until the end of the battle
8.4-9	Crosses the Jordan in pursuit of the Midianites; asks at Succoth and Penuel for provisions but is refused
8.11-12	Goes via the caravan route east of Nobah and Jogbehah and attacks the Midianites
8.13-17	Returns from the battle via Succoth and Penuel
8.18-21	Questions the captured Midianite kings about whom they slew at Mt Tabor; kills them
8.22-28	Refused to become king; makes an ephod from the spoils of the battle and puts it in his home town, Ophrah
8.29-32	Has seventy sons; dies and is buried at Ophrah

Goliath (Philistine giant)

I SAM 17.4-7	Goliath, of Gath, the giant is the champion soldier of the Philistines in battle with the Israelites at the valley of Elah
17.8-10	He taunts the lines of Israelite soldiers that no one can defeat him
17.16	Takes his stand for forty days
17.23	David hears his words
17.24-27	The Israelites flee from him and are afraid
17.32-37	David tells Saul that he will fight Goliath and the Lord will deliver him
17.41-44	Speaks disdainfully to David because of his youth and says he will give David's flesh to the birds and beasts
17.48-51	Is struck on the forehead by a stone from David's sling; he falls and is beheaded by David
17.54	David takes the head of Goliath to Jerusalem
21.9	David takes Goliath's sword
22.10	Doeg speaks of seeing David with Goliath's sword

Hadadezer/Hadarezer (King of Zobah)

II SAM 8.3-4	Hadadezer, king of Zobah is defeated by David as he went to restore his power at the R. Euphrates
8.5-12	The Syrians comes to the aid of Hadadezer but are slain by David; David takes spoil from Betah and Berothai, the cities of Hadadezer
10.16	Gathers up Syrian troops at Helam and his commander, Shobach, leads them
10.19	His servants make peace with Israel after the defeat of the Syrians
I KINGS 11.23	God raises up Rezon, who had fled from his master Hadadezer, as an adversary to Solomon

Ham (Son of Noah)

GEN 5.32	Noah is 500 years old when he becomes the father of Shem, Ham and Japheth
10	The world is divided between the descendants of Ham and his brothers

Hazael (King of Aram)

I KINGS 19.15-17	The Lord tells Elijah to anoint Hazael king over Syria
II KINGS 8.8-10	Ben-Hadad, king of Syria is sick and tells him to meet Elisha in Damascus and ask if he will recover
8.11-12	Meets Elisha who weeps saying 'I know the evil that you will do to the people of Israel'
8.13	Elisha says he knows Hazael will be king of Syria
8.14-15	Returns to Ben-Hadad and murders him; becomes king
8.28-29	Ahaziah joins with Joram to make war against Hazael at Ramoth-gilead
9.14	Joram and the Israelites are on guard at Ramoth-gilead against him
10.32	Defeats the Israelites throughout their territory
12.17-18	Fights against and takes Gath; decides to go on to Jerusalem
13.3	Continues to defeat the Israelites
13.22	Oppresses Israel during all the reign of Jehoahaz
13.24-25	His son becomes king when he dies; Jehoash retakes the cities taken by Hazael

Herod the Great (King of Judaea)

MT 2.1	The wise men ask him where the king of the Jews has been born
2.3-8	Summons his priests and scribes asking them where Christ is born; also asks the wise men
2.12	The wise men are warned in a dream not to return to Herod
2.13-15	Joseph is warned in a dream of Herod's intentions towards Jesus
2.16	Is furious when he realises he has been tricked by the wise men; orders all male babies in Bethlehem to be killed
2.19	Dies; Joseph is told in a dream that he can return to Israel

Herod Antipas (King of Judaea)

MT 14.1-5	Seizes John the Baptist and imprisons him
14.6-7	The daughter of Herodias dances and pleases him; he promises her whatever she might ask
14.8-10	She asks for the head of John the Baptist; has John beheaded

MK 6.14-16	When he hears of Jesus he says 'John, whom I beheaded, has been raised'
6.17-28	The imprisonment and death of John the Baptist
8.15	Jesus warns disciples of 'the leaven of Herod'
LK 3.1	The word of God comes to John during Herod's reign as tetrarch of Galilee
3.19-20	Imprisons John
9.7-9	Hears of Jesus and seeks to see him
13.31	Jesus is warned by some Pharisees that Herod wants to kill him
23.7	Pilate sends Jesus to him
23.8-11	Meets Jesus and questions him at length; mocks Jesus and sends him back to Pilate
23.12	Becomes friends with Pilate that day despite their previous enmity
23.15	Pilate says neither he nor Herod found Jesus guilty
ACTS 13.1	Manaen, a member of the court of Herod, worships the Lord at Antioch

Hezekiah (King of Judah)

II KINGS 16.20	Reigns as king of Judah after the death of his father, Ahaz
18.1-2	Begins his reign at the age of 25
18.4-8	Breaks down altars to false gods; rebels against the king of Assyria and fights the Philistines as far as Gaza
18.9	In the fourth year of his reign, Samaria is besieged by Shalmaneser of Assyria
18.10	In the sixth year of his reign, the king of Assyria takes the Israelites captive
18.13	In the fourteenth year of his reign, Sennacherib, king of Assyria, takes the fortified cities of Judah
18.14	Sends a message to Sennacherib at Lachish saying 'I have done wrong; withdraw from me; whatever you impose on me I will bear'
18.15-16	Sennacherib asks for 300 talents of silver and 30 talents of gold and these are given him
18.17-18	Sennacherib sends an army from Lachish to Hezekiah at Jerusalem
18.19-31	Rabshakeh, an Assyrian, speaks to Hezekiah's household telling them to make peace with the Assyrians
19.1-7	When he hears of the meeting he sends a delegation to consult Isaiah for guidance
19.9-10	Rabshakeh sends messengers saying 'do not let your God on whom you rely deceive you . . .'
19.14-19	Receives the message and prays to the Lord to save the people
19.20-21	Isaiah promises the Lord's support
20.1	Is sick; Isaiah comes to him saying 'you shall die . . .'
20.2-11	Prays to the Lord; Isaiah returns saying he will recover by using a poultice of figs
20.12-13	Shows his treasures and storehouses to the envoys of Merodach-baladan, king of Babylon
20.14-19	Is questioned by Isaiah about the envoys; Isaiah predicts that Babylon will defeat Judah
20.20	Dies; Manasseh, his son, reigns in his stead

Hiram (King of Tyre)

II SAM 5.11	Hiram, king of Tyre, sends a trade mission to David
I KINGS 5.8-10	Hiram offers to supply Solomon with cedar wood
9.11-12	Solomon gives Hiram 20 towns in Galilee but Hiram does not like them and calls the area 'Cabul', meaning worthless

Hoshea (King of Israel)

II KINGS 15.30	Conspires against Pekah and murders him; reigns in his stead
17.3	Becomes subservient to the Assyrian king, Shalmaneser
17.4	Shalmaneser finds him treacherous and imprisons him
17.6	In the ninth year of his reign, Shalmaneser captures Samaria
18.1	In the third year of his reign, Hezekiah begins to reign in Judah
18.9-10	In the seventh year of his reign, Samaria is besieged by the Assyrians

Isaac (Patriarch)

GEN 17.19	The Lord tells Sarah that she will have a son, Isaac
21.3-5	Born to Sarah and Abraham
22.2-14	The Lord tests Abraham telling him to take Isaac to the land of Moriah and sacrifice him
24.4-5	Abraham tells his servant to find a wife for Isaac
24.62-67	Comes from Beer-lahai-roi to live in the Negeb; sees and marries Rebekah
25.9	Buries Abraham in the cave of Machpelah
25.11	Lives in Beer-lahai-roi
25.19-26	Is forty when he marries Rebekah; she gives birth to twins, Jacob and Esau
26.1	Goes to Abimelech, king of the Philistines, in Gerar
26.6-11	Dwells in Gerar; Abimelech says he will kill anyone who harms Isaac or Rebekah
26.12-16	Prospers in Gerar until Abimelech tells him to leave
26.17-22	Moves to the valley of Gerar and reopens the wells
26.23-25	Goes to Beersheba; builds an altar there
26.32-33	His servants dig a well which he calls Shibah
26.35	Is anxious about Esau's marriage to Judith
27.1-28.9	Wishes to bless Esau but is deceived by Rebekah into blessing Jacob
35.27-29	Jacob comes to him at Mamre; Isaac dies there

Isaiah (Prophet)

II KINGS 19.2-7	Hezekiah sends Eliakim to Isaiah, the son of Amoz
19.20-34	Prophesies against Assyria
20.1-11	Visits the dying Hezekiah; returns to cure him at the request of the Lord
20.16-18	Prophesies that Hezekiah's house and family will be taken into Babylon
ISA 20.3	The Lord tells him to walk naked as a sign against Egypt and Ethiopia
37.2-4	Eliakim is sent to him
38.1-22	Heals Hezekiah

Ish-Bosheth (Son of Saul)

II SAM 2.8-10	Taken by Abner to Mahanaim and made king of Israel
3.7-8	Angers Abner by alleging misbehaviour with Saul's concubine
3.14-15	Sends Michal, his sister, to David
4.1	His courage fails him when he hears of Abner's death at Hebron
4.5-12	Is murdered by Rechab and Baanah who take his head to David; buried in the grave of Abner at Hebron

Jacob (Patriarch)

GEN 25.26	Born to Isaac and Rebekah with his twin brother, Esau
25.27	Is a quiet man 'dwelling in tents'
25.34	Obtains Esau's birthright
27.1f	Rebekah deceives Isaac into blessing Jacob instead of Esau
27.42	Esau hates him because of the blessing and plans to kill him
27.43-45	Rebekah tells him to flee to her brother Laban in Haran
28.1-5	Isaac blesses him and sends him to Paddan-aram
28.10	Leaves Beersheba to go to Haran
28.11-22	Has a dream of a ladder going up to heaven; names the site of the dream Bethel
29.1	Continues his journey
29.10-12	Sees Rachel, Laban's daughter
29.13-25	Works for Laban for seven years to secure Rachel as his wife but is tricked into marrying her sister, Leah
29.26-31	Works another seven years and marries Rachel; she is barren
30.1-10	Leah bears him four sons; has four more sons by Bilhah and Zilpah
30.17-19	Leah bears him a fifth and sixth son
30.25-43	Strikes a bargain with Laban over his wages
31.1-16	There is ill-feeling between him and Laban
31.17-21	Leaves with his family to go to the land of Canaan; crosses the Euphrates and travels towards Gilead
31.22-55	Is pursued by Laban to the mountain of Gilead
32.1-2	Meets angels of God; calls the site of meeting Mahanaim
32.3-5	Sends messengers to Esau in the land of Seir to seek a reconciliation
32.13-21	Prepares gifts for Esau; sends his family across the ford of Jabbok
32.24-32	Wrestles with God; receives the name Israel; names the site Peniel
33.1-15	Sees Esau approaching with 400 men; they are reconciled
33.17	Journeys to Succoth and builds himself a house there
33.18	Comes to the city of Shechem in Canaan and builds an altar called El-Elohe-Israel
34.5-6	His daughter, Dinah, is raped by Shechem; speaks to Shechem's father, Hamor
35.5	Journeys to Luz in Canaan; builds an altar at El-Bethel
35.9-15	God appears to him again; restores the altar at Bethel
35.16-20	Journeys from Bethel to Ephrath; Rachel dies in childbirth on the way
35.21	Continues on and camps at Eder
35.27-29	Goes to Isaac at Mamre; buries Isaac there
37.1-2	Dwells in Canaan; his family history
37.12	Sends Joseph to his brothers at Shechem
37.34-35	Mourns for his son Joseph whom he assumes is dead
42.1-2	Sends his sons to Egypt to buy grain
42.29-38	The sons return with a message from Pharaoh's governor calling for Benjamin
43.1-15	Sends Benjamin to Egypt
45.25-28	Learns that Joseph is alive and in Egypt
46.1-7	Sets out from Beersheba to visit Joseph
46.8-27	The descendants of Jacob
46.28-30	Comes to the land of Goshen; is reunited with Joseph
47.7-10	Joseph takes him to meet Pharaoh; he blesses Pharaoh
47.27-31	Lives in Egypt for seventeen years; is 147 years old; gives instructions for his burial
48.1-49.28	Gathers his sons at his deathbed and blesses them
37.12-47.31	The story of Joseph (see Joseph)
49.29-33	Gives instructions for his burial at the cave of Mach-pelah in Canaan; dies
50.1-14	His body is embalmed and Joseph buries him in Canaan

Jael (see Barak)

Japheth (Son of Noah)

GEN 5.32	The son of Noah
10	The world is divided between the descendants of Japheth and his brothers

Jehoahaz (King of Israel)

II KINGS 10.35	Becomes king of Israel after the death of his father, Jehu
13.1-8	Reigns for 17 years but oppresses Israel and angers the Lord
13.9	Dies and is buried in Samaria
13.25	His son, Joash, recovers the cities of Israel

Jehoash/Joash (King of Israel)

II KINGS 13.9-13	Reigns over Israel in Samaria for 16 years
13.14-19	Visits Elisha on his deathbed
13.25	Recovers from Ben-Hadad the cities of Israel
14.8-27	Amaziah of Judah sends a challenge to Jehoash; defeats Amaziah and takes Jerusalem

Jeholachin (King of Judah)

I KINGS 24.6-9	Becomes king of Judah when he is 18 years old; reigns for three months in Jerusalem
24.12-17	Nebuchadnezzar takes him prisoner and exiles him to Babylon
25.27-30	King Evil-Merodach of Babylon frees him and treats him well

Jeholakim (King of Judah)

II KINGS 23.34	Pharaoh Nechoh appoints Eliakim (Jehoiakim) as king of Judah
23.35	Levies and pays taxes to Pharaoh
23.36-37	Reigns 11 years in Jerusalem
24.1-6	Rebels against Nebuchadnezzar; dies
II CHRON 36.4-8	His reign as king of Judah
JER 22.18-24	Jeremiah speaks the Lord's words concerning him
26.21-23	Fetches Uriah from Egypt and has him killed
36.20-32	Burns the scroll containing the Lord's words

Jehoram/Joram (King of Israel)

II KINGS 1.17	Becomes king of Israel
3.1	The son of Ahab; reigns over Israel in Samaria for 12 years
3.4-12	Asks the kings of Judah and Edom to help him fight Mesha, king of Moab
8.28-29	Battles against Hazael of Syria at Ramoth-gilead
9.14-16	Goes to Jezreel to heal his wounds; Jehu conspires against him
9.21-25	Is killed by Jehu and buried in Naboth's vineyard
II CHRON 22.5-7	Is visited at Jezreel by Ahaziah

Jehoshaphat (King of Judah)

I KINGS 15.24	Becomes king of Judah after the death of his father, Asa
22.1-4	Joins forces with the king of Israel to fight the Syrians at Ramoth-gilead
22.5-23	They call for the words of prophets before the battle; Micaiah's prophecy
22.29-33	Goes to Ramoth-gilead; is mistaken for the king of Israel
22.41-50	Reigns for 25 years; dies and is buried in Jerusalem
II KINGS 3.1-14	Joins with the king of Israel to fight Mesha, the king of Moab

Jehu (King of Israel)

I KINGS 19.16-17	The son of Nimshi; the Lord nominates him to be the future king of Israel
II KINGS 9.1-13	Is anointed king of Israel at Ramoth-gilead
9.14	Conspires against Joram
9.17-26	Travels to Jezreel to meet Joram; kills him
9.30-37	Kills Jezebel, the mother of Joram
10.1-11	Has Ahab's 70 sons killed; slays the remainder of the house of Ahab in Jezreel
10.12-14	Slays the kinsmen of Ahaziah at Beth-eked
10.15-17	Joins with Jehonadab; goes to Samaria and slays the house of Ahab there
10.18-31	Destroys Baal worship in Samaria
10.35-36	Dies and is buried in Samaria; his reign lasts 28 years

Jephthah (Judge)

JUDG 11.1	The illegitimate son of Gilead
11.2-3	Is cast out by his half-brothers and flees to Tob
11.4-11	The elders of the land of Gilead ask him to return and lead them against the Ammonites
11.12-28	Sends delegations to the Ammonites which go unheeded
11.30-31	Asks the Lord for victory and says he will sacrifice whoever comes first through the doors of his house
11.32-33	Defeats the Ammonites from Aroer to Minnith and Abel-keramim
11.34-35	Returns home to Mizpah. His daughter is the first person he sees
11.36-40	His fulfillment of his vow to the Lord leads to the death of his daughter
12.7	Judges Israel for six years; dies and is buried in Gilead

Jeremiah (Prophet)

II CHRON 35.25	Laments the death of Josiah
36.12	Zedekiah refuses to acknowledge him as prophet
36.22	Cyrus, king of Persia, implements the words of Jeremiah
JER 1.4-19	The Lord appoints him as prophet
7.1	Stands in the gate of the Temple and proclaims the Lord's word
18.1-6	Goes to the potter's house; compares the moulding of clay with the Lord's moulding of Israel
18.18	The people of Jerusalem plot against him
19.1-15	The Lord instructs him to take an earthenware jar to the valley of Hinnom and break the jar denouncing the practices of the people
20.1-6	Pashhur hears him speaking and puts him in the stocks at the upper Benjamin Gate; curses Pashhur on his release
21.1	Foretells the siege of Jerusalem
26.9-24	The people threaten to kill him because of his prophecies against the city
27.2-8	Speaks of the yoke of Babylon
28.10-16	Hananiah removes from him a symbolic yoke-bar
29.1	Sends a letter to the exiles in Babylon
32.2	Imprisoned in the palace of the king of Judah
34.6	Speaks to Zedekiah, king of Judah
36.1-32	Dictates the Lord's message to Baruch, the scribe
37.12	Travels from Jerusalem to the land of Benjamin
37.15-21	The princes imprison him
38.6	Is cast into the cistern of Malchiah, the king's son
38.7-13	Ebed-melech rescues him
38.14-16	King Zedekiah spares his life
39.11	King Nebuchadnezzar takes Jerusalem and orders that Jeremiah is protected
40.6	Goes to Mizpah
43.6-8	Journeys to Egypt; receives the word of the Lord at Tahpanhes
51.60-64	Prophesies the destruction of Babylon

Jeroboam I (King of Judah)

I KINGS 11.26-28	Assumes control of all the forced labour of the house of Joseph
11.29-39	Goes out from Jerusalem; meets Ahijah on the road who prophesies the future
11.40	Flees to Egypt to escape Solomon
12.2-4	Returns from Egypt to speak to the new king, Rehoboam
12.20	Made king of Israel after the rebellion against Rehoboam
12.25	Builds Shechem in Ephraim and lives there; also builds Penuel
12.28-33	Sets up golden calves at Bethel and Dan; appoints priests and holds feasts
14.1-3	Sends his wife to Shiloh to ask Ahijah about their sick child
14.6-16	Ahijah condemns Jeroboam and his house
14.20	Reigns for 22 years; dies
II CHRON 10.2-15	Returns from Egypt and speaks to Rehoboam
13.1-20	Wars with king Abijah of Judah

Jeroboam II (King of Israel)

II KINGS 13.13 and 14.16	Jeroboam succeeds his father, Joash, as king
14.23	Begins to reign in Samaria. Reigns for 41 years
14.24	Does what is evil in the sight of the Lord
14.25	Restores the border of Israel from the entrance of Hamath as far as the Sea of the Arabah
26-27	Because the afflictions of Israel are great the Lord uses Jeroboam to save the nation
AMOS 1.1	Amos prophecies during the reign of Jeroboam. Because of the prosperity of the nation under Jeroboam, Amos condemns the growing social injustice
HOS 1.1	Hosea prophecies during the reign of Jeroboam

Jesus Christ

MT 1.1-17	The genealogy of Jesus (LK 3.23-38)
LK 1.5-25	Zechariah and Elizabeth (from the hill country of Judah) receive the promise of a son
1.26-38	Mary (from Nazareth) is told she is to have a son
1.39-56	Mary visits her cousin Elizabeth and stays three months
1.57-58	Elizabeth gives birth to a son, called John (later the Baptist)
MT 1.18-25	Joseph (to whom Mary is betrothed) is informed of the circumstances of Mary's pregnancy and marries her
LK 2.1-6	Joseph and Mary go to Bethlehem for the census (MT 2.1)
2.7	The birth of Jesus in Bethlehem (MT 2.1)
2.8-20	The shepherds visit the infant Jesus
2.21	Jesus is circumcized (?in Jerusalem)
2.39	The parents of Jesus return (with him) to Nazareth
MT 2.1-11	The wise men seek for Jesus in Jerusalem and are sent to Bethlehem
2.13-15	Joseph is warned in a dream to take Jesus and Mary to Egypt. They stay there until the death of Herod
2.16-18	Herod has the male children of Bethlehem killed
2.19-23	The holy family returns from Egypt, but settles in Nazareth
LK 2.41-51	Jesus accompanies his parents to Jerusalem for the feast of the Passover at the age of 12; visits the Temple and then returns to Nazareth
MK 1.2-8	The ministry of John the Baptist (MT 3.1-12; LK 3.1-20; JN 1.6, 18, 19-28) in Bethany and beyond Jordan
1.9-11	The baptism of Jesus (MT 3.13-17; LK 3.21-22; JN 1.29-34)
1.12-13	The temptation of Jesus in the wilderness (MT 4.1-11; LK 4.1-13)
JN 1.35-42	Andrew and another disciple of John follow Jesus; Andrew introduces his brother Simon to Jesus
1.43-51	Jesus goes to Galilee, meets Philip of Bethsaida (a townsman of Andrew and Simon) and, through him, meets Nathanael
2.1-11	Jesus attends a marriage feast in Cana
2.12	Jesus goes to Capernaum with his mother, his family and disciples
2.13-25	In Jerusalem for the feast of the Passover
3.22-23	Jesus and his disciples baptize in Judaea, while John baptizes in Aenon near Salim
4.3-42	Jesus leaves Judaea for Galilee and passes through Samaria, stopping at Sychar
MK 1.14-15	Jesus begins his preaching in Galilee after the arrest of John the Baptist (MT 4.12-17; LK 4.14-15)
1.16-20	The call of the disciples by the Sea of Galilee (MT 4.18-22; LK 5.1-11)
1.21.38	Jesus' ministry and acts of healing in Capernaum (MT 8.14-17; LK 4.31-41)
1.39	Jesus travels throughout Galilee
JN 4.45	Jesus is welcomed in Galilee
4.46-54	Jesus in Cana and Capernaum
5.1-18	Jesus goes to Jerusalem for a Jewish festival and heals a paralytic by the pool of Bethzatha
MK 5.1-20	Jesus crosses the Sea of Galilee to Gerosa and heals a demoniac (MT 8.28-34; LK 8.26-39); he preaches in the Decapolis
5.21-43	Continuation of the preaching tour, recrossing the Sea of Galilee; acts of healing (MT 9.18-38; LK 8.40-56)
6.1-6	A visit to Nazareth, where Jesus is rejected (MT 13.53-58; LK 4.16-30)
6.7-13	Commissioning and instruction of the 12 disciples (MT 10.5, 15; LK 9.1-5)
6.14-29	Herod Antipas' reaction to Jesus; account of the death of John the Baptist (MT 14.1-12; LK 9.7-9)
6.45-52	Crossing to Bethsaida; Jesus walks on the water (MT 14.22-23; JN 6.16-21)
6.53-56	Crossing the Sea of Galilee to Gennesaret; general Galilee ministry (MT 14.34-36)
JN 7.1-9	Jesus remains in Galilee and will not go to Jerusalem for the feast of Tabernacles because the Jews seek to kill him
7.10-52	Secretly follows the disciples to Jerusalem
8.1-11	Events in Jerusalem and Judaean ministry; the Jews try to arrest him
10.40-42	Leaves Jerusalem and crosses the Jordan
MK 7.24-30	Jesus leaves Galilee for region of Tyre and Sidon (MT 15.21-28)
7.31-37	Return to the Sea of Galilee from Tyre via Sidon; visit to the Decapolis and healing of a deaf mute
8.1-10	Feeding of the four thousand (MT 15.32-38); crossing by boat to Dalmanutha
8.22-26	Healing of blind man in Bethsaida

8.27-33	Jesus goes with his disciples to Caesarea Philippi; Peter confesses that Jesus is the Messiah (Christ). (MT 16.13-23; LK 9.18-22)
9.2-8	The transfiguration of Jesus on a 'high mountain' (Tabor or Hermon) (MT 17.1-8; LK 9.28-36)
9.14-29	Healing of an epileptic boy at foot of the mountain (MT 17.14-21; LK 9.37-42)
9.30-32	Journeying through Galilee and discourse on the passion (MT 17.22-23; LK 9.43-45)
9.33-50	Arrival at Capernaum; discussion with disciples (MT 18.1-5; LK 9.46-50)
LK 9.51-62	Sets off for Jerusalem, travelling through Samaria
10.1-20	The mission of the 70 sent ahead of him
17.11-19	Heals the lepers, one a Samaritan
MK 10.1	Reaches the region of Judaea, having crossed the Jordan
10.46-52	Arrival in Jericho; healing of Bartimaeus (MT 20.29-34; LK 18.35-43)
LK 19.1-10	Jesus encounters Zacchaeus in Jericho and stays at his house
JN 11.1-44	Jesus goes to Bethany and raises Lazarus from death
11.45-57	The Pharisees and priests plan to kill him; Jesus travels to the hill country of Ephraim
12.1-8	Jesus revisits Bethany and is anointed by Mary (sister of Lazarus and Martha)
LK 10.38-42	Jesus in the house of Martha and Mary
MK 11.1-11	The triumphal entry into Jerusalem from the region of Bethphage and Bethany via the Mount of Olives (MT 21.1-11; LK 19.28-40;); return to Bethany for the night
11.15-19	Re-entry into Jerusalem and revisiting of the Temple; overthrow of the Temple bankers and merchants (MT 21.12-17; LK 19.45-48; JN 2.13-22)
JN 11.49-50	The chief priests, led by Caiaphas, plot the death of Jesus
12.20-23	He meets with Greeks, in Jerusalem for the Passover
MK 14.1-2	The chief priests and scribes seek for a chance to kill Jesus (MT 26.3-5; LK 22.1-2)
14.3-9	The visiting of Jesus by a woman in the house of Simon in Bethany (MT 26.6-13)
14.10-11	Judas Iscariot arranges the betrayal of Jesus (MT 26.14-16; LK 22.3-6)
14.12-25	The Last Supper (MT 26.17-29; LK 22.7-30; JN 13.21-29)
14.26-31	The walk to the Mount of Olives (MT 26.30-35; LK 22.31-34; JN 13.36-38)
14.32-52	Jesus prays in Gethsemane, is betrayed by Judas and seized by the Temple guards (MT 26.36-56; LK 22.39-53; JN 18.1-12)
JN 18.13	Jesus is led to the home of Annas
MK 14.53-72	Jesus is taken to the house of Caiaphas and tried by the Sanhedrin; the denial of Peter (MT 26.57-75; LK 22.54-62; JN 18.14-27)
15.1-5	Jesus is taken before Pontius Pilate (MT 27.1-2; LK 23.1; JN 18.33-19.16)
LK 23.6-12	Pilate sends Jesus to Herod Antipas, but Herod sends Jesus back to Pilate
MK 15.2-15	Jesus is questioned before Pilate and condemned to death (MT 27.11-26; LK 23.2-5, 13-25; JN 18.33-19.16)
15.16-20	Jesus is taken to the praetorium and prepared for the crucifixion (MT 27.27-31; JN 19.1-3)
15.21-41	The crucifixion at Golgotha (MT 27.32-56; LK 23.26-49; JN 19.18-37)
15.42-47	The burial of Jesus in the tomb of Joseph of Arimathea (MT 27.57-61; LK 23.50-56; JN 19.38-42)
16.1-20	The story of the resurrection (MT 28.1-20; LK 24.1-49; JN 20-21)
LK 24.50-53	The ascension

Jezebel (Wife of Ahab)

I KINGS 16.31	The daughter of Ethbaal; marries Ahab
18.4	Obadiah hides 100 of the prophets from Jezebel
18.13	Obadiah speaks to Elijah of how he saved the prophets from Jezebel
18.19	Elijah challenges the prophets of Baal and Asherah who eat at Jezebel's table
19.1-2	Learns that Elijah has slain the prophets; threatens to kill Elijah
21.5-15	Plans the death of Naboth so that her husband, Ahab, can acquire Naboth's vineyard
21.23	Elijah prophesies that she will be eaten by dogs at Jezreel
II KINGS 9.22	Jehu speaks of the harlotries and sorcery of Jezebel
9.30-37	Jehu has her killed; Elijah's prophecy is fulfilled

Joab (David's commander)

II SAM 2.13-14	The son of Zeruiah; confronts Abner at the Pool of Gibeon
2.24-28	Pursues Abner to the hill of Ammah
2.32	Marches towards Hebron
3.26-31	Kills Abner at Hebron
8.16	Commands David's army
10.7-14	David sends him to fight the Ammonites; returns to Jerusalem
11.6-7	David asks him to send Uriah, husband of Bathsheba, to him
11.14-15	David writes telling him to put Uriah in the front line of the battle
11.16-25	Undertakes David's instructions
12.26-27	Fights against and takes the city of Rabbah
14.1-22	Plans to reconcile David and Absalom
14.23	Goes to Geshur and brings Absalom to Jerusalem
14.29-33	Absalom asks to be taken to David
20.7-13	Fights and kills Amasa at Gibeon
20.14-22	Besieges Sheba in Abel of Beth-maacah
24.2-9	Travels the land taking a census of the people
I KINGS 1.7	Supports Adonijah's claim to be king
2.5	David speaks to Solomon condemning Joab's acts
2.28-35	Hears that Solomon is king and flees to the tent of the Lord seeking sanctuary; is killed by Benaiah
11.15-16	Slaughters the men of Edom
11.21	Hadad hears of the death of Joab
I CHRON 11.6	Becomes David's chief and commander
11.8	Repairs parts of Jerusalem
19.8-15	The defeat of the Ammonites
20.1	Besieges Rabbah
21.2-6	Undertakes the census of Israel

Joash/Jehoash (King of Judah)

II KINGS 11.2-3	Jehosheba hides him from Athaliah for six years
11.4-12	Is brought out of hiding and made king of Judah
11.21	Is seven years old when he begins his reign
12.1-2	Reigns for 40 years in Jerusalem
12.4-8	Orders repairs to the house of the Lord
12.18	Gives treasures to Hazael, king of Syria, to prevent him attacking Jerusalem
12.20-21	Is murdered by two of his servants on the road to Silla; buried in Jerusalem
II CHRON 24.22	Has Jehoiada's son killed
24.23-24	The Syrians war against him

John (the Apostle)

MT 4.21	Jesus sees him and James with their father, Zebedee, and calls him to follow (MK 1.19)
10.2	Named as a disciple (MK 3.17)
LK 22.8	Jesus sends him with Peter to prepare the Passover meal
ACTS 3.1-10	Goes with Peter to the Temple; the people marvel at them after a cripple is healed
4.13-20	The priests and the scribes command him not to teach
8.14	Goes to Samaria with Peter

John (the Baptist)

MT 3.1-12	Preaches in Judaea (MK 1.6-8, LK 3.2-20)
3.13-17	Baptizes Jesus in the River Jordan (MK 1.9-11, LK 3.21-22)
4.12	Jesus withdraws to Galilee on hearing of the arrest of John (MK 1.14)
9.14	His disciples question Jesus about fasting (MK 2.18)
11.2-3	Sends word to Jesus from prison (LK 7.17-23)
11.7-15	Jesus speaks to the crowds of John's greatness (LK 7.24-35)
14.2	Herod the tetrarch hears of Jesus and thinks he is John risen from the dead (MK 6.14-16, LK 9.7-9)
14.3-12	Is imprisoned and beheaded (MK 6.17-29)
16.14	Jesus is taken to be John the Baptist (LK 9.19)
17.13	Jesus speaks to the disciples of John
21.25-26	Jesus speaks of him to the priests and elders (MK 11.30-32, LK 20.4-6)
LK 1.13	An angel speaks to Zechariah and Elizabeth of John's birth
1.57-63	Born and named
11.1	Jesus' disciples ask to be taught to pray as John taught his own disciples
JN 1.19-34	The testimony of John
3.23	Baptizes at Aenon near Salim
5.33-35	Jesus speaks of his testimony
10.40	Jesus goes to the Jordan where he was baptized by John

Jonathan (see David)

Joram (see Toi)

Joseph (Patriarch)

GEN 30.23	Born to Rachel and Jacob
37.2	Gives bad reports of his brothers to Jacob
37.3	Is the favourite son of Jacob; Jacob gives him a special coat
37.5-11	Tells his brothers of his dreams
37.12-16	Jacob sends him to his brothers who are pasturing the flocks near Shechem
37.17-28	Follows his brothers to Dothan; they conspire to kill him but instead sell him to Midianite traders
37.29-36	The brothers tell Jacob he is dead; meanwhile the Midianites sell him to Potiphar, an officer of Pharaoh
39.1-6	Prospers in Egypt
39.7-20	Refuses the advances of Potiphar's wife; she has him imprisoned
40.5-23	Interprets the dreams of Pharaoh's butler and baker, who are also imprisoned
41.14-36	Pharaoh sends for him to interpret his dream
41.37-44	Pharaoh is pleased and rewards him by appointing him ruler over Egypt
41.46-52	Travels through Egypt and stores up grain; has two sons by Asenath, his wife
41.53-57	During the famine he sells the grain to the Egyptians
42.6-17	His brothers come to buy grain but fail to recognize him; he imprisons them
42.18-25	Allows them to have grain and return home if they bring him their youngest brother
43.15-34	They return with Benjamin
45.1-20	Makes himself known to his brothers and asks them to settle in Egypt
45.21-28	Gives them wagons to return to Canaan for their households; Jacob hears that Joseph is alive
46.28-34	Is reunited with his father in Goshen
47.13-26	Manages the food and land of Egypt
48.1-22	Takes his sons to be blessed by Jacob
50.14-26	Mourns for Jacob; leaves Egypt to bury his father in the cave of Machpelah
50.14-26	Dies aged 100 years and is buried in Egypt
EX 13.19	Moses takes his bones out of Egypt
JOSH 24.32	His bones are reburied at Shechem

Joseph (husband of Mary mother of Jesus)

MT 1.16	The son of Jacob
1.18	Is betrothed to Mary (LK 1.27)
1.19-21	The conception of Jesus; an angel appears to him in a dream
2.13	Is told in a dream to take Mary and Jesus to Egypt
2.19-23	Is told that they can return to Israel; goes to Galilee and dwells in Nazareth
LK 2.4	Goes to Bethlehem with Mary for inclusion in the census
2.16	The shepherds see him with Mary and Jesus
2.41-43	Takes Jesus to the feast of the Passover in Jerusalem
4.22	The congregation at the synagogue in Nazareth ask if Jesus is his son

Joseph (of Arimathaea)

MT 27.57	A rich man from Arimathaea who follows Jesus
27.58-60	Asks Pilate for the body of Jesus; places it in his own tomb (MK 15.43-46; LK 23.50-53; JN 19.38-42)

Joshua (also called Jehoshua and Oshea)

EX 17.8-13	Defeats Amalek in battle at Rephidim
24.13	Goes with Moses to Mount Sinai
32.17	Returns from the mountain and hears sounds of revelry from the Israelites' camp
NUM 13.8	Sent by Moses to spy out the land of Canaan
13.16	Moses changes his name from Hoshea to Joshua
14.6-8	Describes Canaan to the Israelites
14.30	The Lord says only Caleb and Joshua will see the promised land
27.22-23	Moses appoints him as his successor to lead Israel
32.28	Moses gives him instructions about the division of land
DEUT 1.38	The Lord says he will enter the promised land
3.28	Moses confirms the leadership of Joshua
31.23	The Lord commissions him as leader
34.9	The Israelites accept him as leader after the death of Moses
JOSH 1.1	The Lord tells him to take the Israelites across the Jordan
2.1	Sends two spies to Jericho
3.1	Sets out from Shittim with the Israelites and camps by the Jordan
3.6-13	Tells the priests to take the ark and lead the Israelites across the Jordan
4.1-10	Constructs a memorial to their crossing of the Jordan from 12 stones
4.19	Camps at Gilgal
5.2-8	Circumcizes all the male Israelites at Gibeath-haaraloth
5.13-15	Meets an angel of the Lord near Jericho
6.2	The Lord says he will give Jericho into Joshua's hand
6.8-21	As he commands, the people circle Jericho blowing trumpets; when they shout the walls collapse and the city is destroyed
6.26	Curses Jericho
7.2	Sends men to Ai to spy out the land
7.3-5	Attacks Ai but is repulsed
8.1-29	Captures the city of Ai
8.30	Builds an altar on Mount Ebal
9.3-15	The Gibeonites trick him into making a covenant with them at Gilgal
10.6-11	Defeats the Amorites and pursues them to Beth-horon, Azekah and Makkedah
10.15	Returns to his camp at Gilgal
10.16-27	Captures and kills the five kings of the Amorites at Makkedah
10.29-39	Captures Libnah, Lachish, Eglon, Hebron and Debir
10.40-43	Defeats the whole land; returns to Gilgal
11.6-10	Defeats Jabin of Hazor and his allies by the waters of Merom; pursues them to Great Sidon, Misrephoth-maim and Mizpeh
11.16	Takes all the land of Negeb, Goshen, Arabah and Israel
11.21	Wipes out the people of Anakim from the hill countries of Hebron, Debir, Anab, Judah and Israel
12.1-24	A list of the kings defeated by Joshua and the Israelites and the lands taken
13.1	Is old and advanced in years
14.1	Distributes inheritances of land to the people
14.13	Blesses Caleb and gives him Hebron
18.8-10	Is camped at Shiloh; casts lots for the division of land
19.49	Receives an inheritance of land from the people
20.2	The Lord tells him to appoint the cities of refuge
21.1-3	Gives cities and pasture land to the Levites
22.6	Blesses the Reubenites, the Gadites and half-tribe of Manasseh
23.1-13	Is old and about to die; charges the Israelites to obey the Lord
24.1-15	Gathers all the tribes of Israel to Shechem and addresses them
24.25	Makes a covenant with the people
24.29-30	Dies aged 110 years; is buried at Timnath-serah

Josiah (King of Judah)

I KINGS 13.2	His birth is foretold
II KINGS 21.24	Replaces his father, Amon, as king of Judah
22.1	Assumes the throne when he is eight years old; reigns 31 years in Jerusalem
22.8-10	His scribe reads to him from a book of the Law found in the restoration of the Temple
23.1-3	Reads the book of the Law to the scribes and elders and orders reforms
23.29-30	Killed at Megiddo by Pharaoh Nechoh; is buried in Jerusalem
II CHRON 33.25	Becomes king
34.1-33	The reforms undertaken in his reign
35.1-19	Keeps the Passover
35.20-24	His death and burial

Jotham (King of Judah)

II KINGS 15.5	Governs Judah for his father, Uzziah, who has leprosy
15.7	Becomes king when his father dies
15.32-33	Begins his reign when he is 25 years old; reigns for 16 years
15.38	Dies and is buried in Jerusalem
II CHRON 26.21	Governs Judah for his father
27.3-4	His reign includes building work on the wall of Ophel in Jerusalem and the building of cities in Judah

Laban (Father-in-law of Jacob)

GEN 24.29	The brother of Rebekah
27.43	Rebekah advises Jacob to escape from Esau and flee to Laban at Haran
28.2	Isaac tells Jacob to choose a wife from the daughters of Laban
29.13-20	Jacob works for him for seven years in return for Rachel as his wife
29.21-27	Deceives Jacob by giving him his daughter Leah
29.29	Gives Rachel, his daughter, a servant named Bilhah
29.30	Jacob serves him for another seven years
30.25-42	Strikes a bargain with Jacob over his wages
31.2	There is ill feeling between him and Jacob
31.12-13	The Angel of God speaks to Jacob of Laban's deeds and tells him to leave
31.22-25	Pursues Jacob to the mountain of Gilead
31.26-32	Confronts Jacob accusing him of cheating him and stealing his gods
31.33-35	Searches for the gods but cannot find them
31.36	Jacob is angry and upbraids him
31.43-54	They make a covenant
32.4	Jacob reports to Esau on Laban's visit

Leah (Wife of Jacob)

GEN 29.16	The elder daughter of Laban
29.17	Leah's eyes are weak
29.23-35	Laban substitutes her for Rachel in marriage with Jacob; she has four sons
30.9	Gives her maid Zilpah to Jacob as a wife
30.1-20	Bears Jacob his fifth and sixth sons
31.5	Jacob complains to her about his treatment from Laban
34.1	Her daughter, Dinah
35.23	Her sons who were born in Paddan-aram
49.31	Buried at Mamre in Canaan

Levi (Son of Jacob and Leah)

GEN 29.34	Born to Leah
34.25-31	Murders the men of Shalem
46.11	His sons are listed among the children of Israel
49.5	Jacob refers to the violence of Levi
EX 6.16	The names of his sons; lives to 137 years
NUM 16.7	Moses speaks to the sons of Levi
26.59	Genealogy
DEUT 10.9	Has no inheritance with his brothers
33.8	Moses speaks of Levi in his blessing for Israel
I CHRON 6.1-47	The sons of Levi
21.6	Joab excludes Levi and Benjamin from the census
EZEK 48.31	A gate of Judah is named after him
MAL 2.4	The Lord speaks of his covenant with Levi
2.8	The Lord accuses priests of corrupting the covenant

Manasseh (Son of Hezekiah - king of Judah)

II KINGS 20.21	Becomes king of Judah
21.1	Reigns for 55 years from the age of 12
21.2-18	He commits sacrilegious acts and murder during his reign
23.12	Josiah breaks the altars made by Manasseh
24.3	Judah is punished because of the sins of Manasseh
II CHRON 30.1	Hezekiah invites him to the House of the Lord in Jerusalem to keep the Passover
32.33	Becomes king after the death of Hezekiah
33.1-19	His evil reign
33.20	Dies; his son Amon succeeds him
JER 15.4	The Lord vows retribution because of Manasseh's evil actions in Jerusalem

Mary (Mother of Jesus; see Jesus)

Matthew (see Jesus)

Menahem (King of Israel)

II KINGS 16.17	Menahem becomes king of Israel and rules in Samaria for 10 years
16.18	Sins against the Lord
16.19	Gives the invading Pul (Tiglath-pileser III of Assyria) 1,000 talents of silver to support his claim to the throne
16.22	Dies

Merodach-baladan (The son of the king of Babylon)

II KINGS 20.12 and ISA 39.1	Sends envoys with letters and a present to Hezekiah

Mesha (King of Moab)

II KINGS 3.4	Mesha, king of Moab, is a sheep breeder who pays tribute to Israel
3.5	When Ahab dies, Mesha rebels against Israel
3.6-9	Jehoram of Israel, Jehoshaphat and the king of Edom make an alliance against Mesha
3.27	Mesha, on the verge of being defeated in battle, offers his son as a burnt offering; a disaster befalls the Israelite army which is forced to withdraw

Moses (Patriarch)

EX 2.10	Pharaoh's daughter accepts him as her son; names him
2.11-15	Kills an Egyptian in defence of a Hebrew; flees to Midian
2.20-21	Marries Zipporah, a daughter of a Midian priest; they have a son, Gershom
3.1-6	The angel of the Lord visits him by appearing in a burning bush
3.11	Questions the Lord's commission that he should deliver the Israelites out of Egypt
4.1-9	The Lord gives him signs so that the Israelites will follow him

4.14-16	The Lord suggests that Aaron should be spokesman in place of Moses
4.18	Asks Jethro, his father-in-law, to let him go
4.27-30	Meets Aaron at the mountain of God; they gather the elders and tell them of the Lord's words
5.1	Asks Pharaoh 'Let my people go . . .'
5.22	Asks the Lord the reason for the suffering of the Israelites
6.1-13	The Lord speaks to him
7.20-12.30	The ten plagues on Egypt
12.1-27	Institution of the Passover
12.31-32	After the last plague, Pharaoh summons him and says the Israelites may leave Egypt
13.1-2	God tells him that all first-born children shall be consecrated to the Lord
13.19	Takes the bones of Joseph with him as they leave Egypt
14.2	The Lord tells him to camp at Pi-hahi-roth
14.21-22	Parts the waters of the Red Sea
15	The Song of Moses
15.22-24	Leads the Israelites to Marah; they complain of thirst
16.2-33	The people 'murmur' against him because they are hungry; the Lord provides quail and manna
17.4	Appeals to the Lord because of the Israelites' complaints
17.8-16	Wars with Amalek at Rephidim
18.8	Tells his father-in-law, Jethro, of the journey out of Egypt
18.13-27	Sits in judgment on the people; on the advice of Jethro he appoints judges
19.2-19	The Lord speaks to him on Mt Sinai
20.1-17	The ten commandments
24.4	Builds an altar with 12 pillars to represent the tribes of Israel
24.18	Goes up into the cloud on Mt Sinai for 40 days and nights
25.10-22	The Lord instructs him to make the Ark and tabernacle
31.18	The Lord gives him two tablets of stone
32.1	The people appeal to Aaron when Moses fails to return
32.7	The Lord tells him to go down the mountain
32.11	Asks the Lord why he is angry with Israel
32.15-19	Goes down to the people; breaks the tablets when he sees them worshipping the golden calf
32.25-29	The Levites help him to slaughter the false worshippers
34.1-28	Is told to go up Mt Sinai again; the covenant is renewed
34.29-35	Returns; his face shines because he has been talking with God
35.1	Assembles the people to make the tabernacle
39.32-43	Approves the work on the tabernacle and blesses the people
40.1-15	The Lord instructs him on the erection of the tabernacle
LEV 8.1-9.22	Makes offerings to the Lord
10.4-20	Tells Uzziel's sons to remove from the tabernacle the bodies of Aaron's sons; speaks about offerings
NUM 1.1-3	The Lord tells him to take a census of the Israelites
7.1	Finishes setting up the tabernacle
10.29-32	Asks Hobab to come with him and the Israelites on their journey
11.2	Prays for the fire at Taberah to be put out
11.10-15	Asks the Lord about the heavy burden of responsibility he carries
12.1-2	Miriam and Aaron speak against him because of his marriage to a Cushite woman
13.3	Sends men from the wilderness of Paran to spy out Canaan
14.2-3	The people murmur against him and call to return to Egypt
16.1-50	Korah's rebellion against Moses
17.1-7	Deposits the 12 rods of princes in the tent of meeting
20.2-13	The Israelites complain about the lack of water in the Wilderness of Zin; produces water from the rock
20.14	Sends messengers from Kadesh to the king of Edom
20.23	The Lord speaks to him at Mt Hor
21.5-9	The people continue to complain about their flight from Egypt into the wilderness; makes a serpent of brass to protect them from snake bites
25.4	The Lord speaks to him of the Israelites' relationship with the Moabites and their gods
26.1-2	The Lord tells him to take a census
27.12	The Lord tells him to go up the mountain of Abarim
27.18-23	Commissions Joshua as his successor
31.1-54	Wars against the Midianites; the spoils are divided
32.5	The sons of Reuben and Gad ask for the land of Gilead
33.2	Lists all the journeys of the people of Israel
DEUT 31.2	Is 120 years old
31.14-15	The Lord tells him that he is about to die
31.23	The Lord commissions Joshua as Moses' successor
31.25-26	Commands the Levites to put the book of law by the Ark
32.1-43	The song of Moses
33	Gives a blessing to the Israelites
34.1-8	Dies in the land of Moab and is buried there

Nebuchadnezzar (King of Babylon)

II KINGS 24.1	Is king of Babylon; Jehoiakim rebels against him
24.10-16	His men besiege Jerusalem; takes king Jehoiachin of Judah prisoner and carries off many captives to Babylon
24.17	Puts Zedekiah on the throne
25.1-11	Zedekiah rebels against him; he again besieges Jerusalem
25.22	Appoints Gedaliah as governor of Judah
II CHRON 36.6	Captures Jehoiakim and takes him to Babylon
36.10	Brings Jehoiachin to Babylon
36.13	Zedekiah's rebellion
JER 21.2	Jeremiah prophesies the future of the war with Zedekiah
24.1	Takes the king, princes and craftsmen of Judah into exile
25.1	The first year of his reign
25.9	The Lord says he will bring Nebuchadnezzar against Judah
27.8	The Lord promises to punish any nation which will not accept the rule of Nebuchadnezzar
28.3	Hananiah says he will return the vessels taken from the Lord's house by Nebuchadnezzar
28.11-14	Hananiah says the Lord has said that he will break the yoke of Nebuchadnezzar

29.21	The Lord says he will deliver Ahab and Zedekiah into the hand of Nebuchadnezzar
32.1-2	In the 18th year of his reign, his army besieges Jerusalem
32.28	The Lord says he is giving Jerusalem into the hands of the king of Babylon
39.11-12	Tells the captain of his guard to look after Jeremiah well
43.10	The Lord says Nebuchadnezzar will set up his throne in Tahpanhes
50.17-18	The Lord says he will punish the king of Babylon for his wars against Israel
51.35	The judgement on Babylon
52.28-30	The numbers of Jews carried off by Nebuchadnezzar
EZEK 26.7-12	The Lord foretells the destruction of Tyre by Neuchadnezzar
29.18-19	The Lord gives the land, people and spoils of Egypt to him
DAN 1.1-4	Besieges Jerusalem and defeats Jehoiakim; brings Daniel and other Israelite youths into his court to be educated
2.1-11	Is troubled with dreams which his own wise men cannot interpret
2.12-16	Orders that all wise men are slain but Daniel says he can explain the dream
2.37-45	Daniel interprets the dream
3.1	Places a golden image in the plain of Dura
3.13-15	Is angry with Shadrach, Meshach and Abednego for not worshipping the image; says he will cast them into a fiery furnace
3.19-25	He casts them into the furnace but they are unharmed
4.10-17	His dream of a tree
4.28-37	Is walking on the roof of the royal palace of Babylon when he hears the Lord. After a long ordeal he acknowledges the Lord's dominion

Og (King of Bashan)

NUM 21.33	The king of Bashan fights against Israel at Edri
32.33	Moses allocates the land of Og
DEUT 1.4	Lives in Ashtaroth and Edrei
3.1-13	Wars with the Israelites at Edrei and is defeated
4.47	The Israelites take possession of the land of Og
31.4	Moses quotes the destruction of Og as an example of the Lord's protection of Israel
JOSH 2.10	Rahab speaks of the destruction of Og
12.4	Listed as one of the kings defeated by Israel
13.30-31	Moses divides the lands of Og

Omri (King of Israel)

I KINGS 16.21	The people of Israel are divided; half follow Omri and half follow Tibni. When Tibni dies Omri becomes king
16.24	Makes Tirzah his capital and reigns for six years
16.25	Does evil in the sight of the Lord by encouraging idolatry
16.28	Dies

Paul/Saul (Apostle)

ACTS 7.58	Is witness to the stoning of Stephen
8.1-3	Consents to the death of Stephen; attacks the church in Jerusalem
9.1-6	Continues to persecute the disciples; Jesus appears to him on the road to Damascus
9.8-9	He becomes blind for three days
9.17-19	Ananias meets him and restores his sight; Saul is baptized
9.23-25	Hears of a plot by the Jews to kill him and escapes
9.26-30	Joins the disciples and preaches in Jerusalem; is sent to Tarsus
11.25-26	Barnabas finds him in Tarsus and they go to Antioch
11.30	Goes to Judaea with Barnabas to take relief to famine victims
12.25	Returns from Jerusalem bringing John with him
13.1-3	With the prophets and teachers at Antioch; the Lord sets apart Saul and Barnabas for his work
13.4-12	Sails to Cyprus from Seleucia; preaches the gospel throughout the island
13.13-41	Sails from Paphos to Perga and travels on to Antioch of Pisidia; delivers a sermon in the synagogue
13.50-51	The Jews stir up persecution against him and drive him away; goes to Iconium
14.1-7	Preaches in the synagogue at Iconium but is forced to flee to Lystra
14.8-18	Heals a cripple at Lystra; the crowd believes he is a god
14.19	The Jews persuade the crowd to stone him; he is left for dead
14.20	Recovers and goes with Barnabas to Derbe
14.21	Returns to Antioch via Lystra and Iconium
14.24-26	Passes through Pisidia, Pamphylia and Perga; sails from Attalia to Antioch
15.1-4	Is sent to Jerusalem to discuss the question of circumcision with the elders
15.12	Tells the assembly the 'wonders God had done through them'
15.22	The church sends Barnabas and Silas back to Antioch with him
15.35	Remains in Antioch with Barnabas
15.36-41	Disagrees with Barnabas over who to take with them on a missionary journey; chooses Silas and travels through Syria and Cilicia
16.1-3	Comes to Derbe and Lystra; chooses Timothy to travel with him on a mission
16.6-10	They travel through Phrygia and Galatia to Troas; has a vision telling him to help people in Macedonia
16.11-15	Sails from Troas to Philippi in Macedonia; baptizes Lydia
16.16-24	Relieves a slave possessed by a spirit; her owners are angry and have him imprisoned
16.25-26	The prison doors are opened by an earthquake
16.35-40	Is freed; goes to Lydia
17.2-5	Enters the synagogue in Thessalonica and argues with the Jews over the scriptures; the Jews become angry

INDEX

INTRODUCTION TO INDEX

This atlas covers the Mediterranean World, the Near East and southwest Asia as they impinge on the history of the Holy Land over a period of several thousand years. The names on the maps, therefore, reflect the different languages involved over this time-span: ancient Egyptian, Akkadian, Greek, Latin, Hebrew and Arabic. In the interests of simplicity diacritics have been omitted in the transliteration of modern Hebrew and Arabic names, e.g. Zafzafot appears as Zafzafot, Taffūḥ as Taffuh.

This index includes the majority of the names shown on the maps. Entries are of four types:-

1 The names of Old and New Testament sites, given as they are spelled in the Revised Standard Version of the Bible. Variant spellings and forms of biblical names are given in column 3, together with earlier Egyptian and Akkadian and later Greek and Latin names by which the places were also known. In column 4 is given the modern Arabic name of the site (followed by a question mark if identity is uncertain). Column 5 gives the modern Hebrew name of the site if it has one. These places may be located on the end-paper maps by use of the six-figure grid reference given in column 6. The Palestine grid has been utilised (a system devised by the Ordnance Survey of Palestine during the period of the British Mandate and still widely used.) The grid co-ordinates should be read in the conventional manner; that is the first three numbers refer to the north-south axis and the second three numbers refer to the east-west axis.

2 The names of places outside the Holy Land are given a general geographical location in column 2 (eg Syria, Mesopotamia, SW Asia Minor). Variant forms of these names which may be helpful are given in column 3.

3 Where any variant name of a place appears in primary position on a map its identity with the biblical or principal name is indicated by the use of the equals sign =.

4 All other variant forms and spellings of names which are not found in primary position on any of the maps are cross-referred to main entries by the use of *see*.

ABBREVIATIONS

a/c	Also called
Akk.	Akkadian
Anc.	Ancient
Ar.	Arabic
a/s	Also spelled
Bibl.	Biblical
Eg.	Egyptian
Eng.	English
Gk.	Greek
G/L	Greek and Latin
H.	Horbat
Heb.	modern Hebrew
Kh.	Khirbet
Lat.	Latin
Mod.	Modern
Per.	Persian
T.	Tel (Hebrew)
	Tell (Arabic)

GLOSSARY OF GEOGRAPHICAL TERMS

'AIN (A)	spring
BE'ER (H)	well
BEIT (A)	house
BET (H)	house
BIR (A)	well
BURJ (A)	fort
'EIN (A)	spring
'EN (H)	spring
HAMMAM (A)	hot springs
HORBAT (H)	ruins
JEBEL (A)	mountain
KAFR (A)	village
KEFAR (H)	village
KHIRBET (A)	ruins
NAHAL (H)	river, stream
QAL'AT (A)	fort
QARN (A)	hill
QASR (A)	palace, fort
RAS (A)	headland, summit
ROSH (H)	headland, summit
RUJM (A)	mound, cairn
TEL (H)	mound
TELL (A)	mound
WADI (A)	watercourse

(A = Arabic,
H = Modern Hebrew)

NAME	AREA/COUNTRY	VARIANT NAMES	ARABIC NAME	MODERN HEBREW NAME	PALESTINIAN GRID REFERENCE	PAGE(S)
ABAR NAHARA	= Syria	a/c Province Beyond the River				135/1
ABDERA	NE Greece					138,142,170,171
ABDERA	S Spain	Mod. Adra				90,170
ABDON			Kh. 'Abdeh	T.'Avdon	165272	
ABEL	in Galilee		'Ain Ibl		188279	181
ABEL	in Gilead	a/c Abila, Seleucia	T. Abil		231231	
ABEL-BETH-MAACAH		a/c Abel-maim	Abil el-Qamh	T. Avel Bet Ma'akha	204296	66,114
ABEL-KERAMIM			Na'ur?		228142	68
ABELLA						143
ABEL-MAIM	see Abel-beth-maacah					
ABEL-MEHOLAH			T.Abu Sus		203197	69,98,113
ABEL-SHITTIM		a/c Shittim	T.el-Hammam		214138	
ABIEZER	clan district					69,112
ABIL		= Abel-beth-maacah				32/1,33/2
ABILA		= Abel				147,149,150,164,165
ABILA		a/c Abella				165/3,166
ABILA	Syria	a/c Abel Ar. Suq Wadi Barada				168
ABIL EL-QAMH	see Abel-beth-maacah					
ABILIA						177
ABILUM		= Abel-beth-maacah				33
ABIMAEL	tribe of S Arabia					93
ABONUTEICHUS	N Asia Minor					179,187
ABUD						185
ABU GHOSH		= Gibeah of Kiriath-jearim				26,185
ABU SHUSHEH	see Gezer					
ABYDUS	NW Asia Minor	a/s Abydos				142,186
ABYDUS	Upper Egypt	a/s Abydos				39,40/1
ACALISSUS	SW Asia Minor					186
ACCAD	see Akkad					
ACCARON		= Ekron				147,149,154,157
ACCHABARE		a/s Acchabaron				177
ACCILAEUM	W Asia Minor					186
ACCO		Akk. Akka, Eg. 'Akaya G/L Ptolemais, Eng. Acre	T.el-Fukhkhar	T.'Akko	158258	26,32,33,43,48,50,52,58,63,64,68, 83,96,97,122/1,128,134,138
ACHAIA	region of Greece	a/s Achaea				172,179
ACHSHAPH		Akk. Akshapa, Eg. Aksapa	Kh. el-Harbaj?	T.Regev	158240	58,62,63,64,50
ACHZIB	in Asher	Gk. Ecdippa	Ez-Zib	T.Akhziv	159272	32,33,64,96,103,122
ACHZIB	in Judah	a/c Chezib	Kh T.el-Beida?	H.Lavnin	145116	118
ACMONIA	W Asia Minor					171
ACRABBEIN		a/s Acrabeta, Acrabetta				155,157,177,181
ACRE	see Acco					
ACTIUM	NW Greece					151
ADAB	S Mesopotamia	Mod. Bismaya				30/2,102
ADADA	S Asia Minor					187
ADADAH	see Aroer					
ADAM			T.ed-Damiyeh		201167	96
ADAMAH		a/c Shemesh-adam	Qarn Hattin?	H. Qarne Hittim	193245	
ADAMI-NEKEB		a/c Adamim	Kh.et-Tell (ed-Damiyeh)	T. Adami	193239	
ADARUS		a/c Bucolon Polis				155
ADASA						147
AD DIANAM						153
ADER						33
ADIABENE	region of SW Persia					171
ADIDA		= Hadid				147,149,177
ADINNU						108
ADIR						103
ADORA		= Adoraim				143,147,149,150/2,154
ADORAIM		a/c Adora Heb. Adorayim	Dura		152101	58,96,118/1,157
ADOREN						42,43
ADRAMYTTIUM	NW Asia Minor					171,186
ADULLAM			Esh-Sheikh Madhkur	H.'Adullam	150117	62,75,118,147
ADUMMIM						50
ADURUN						50,51
AEGAE	W Asia Minor					186
AEGEAE	SE Asia Minor					187
AEGEAN SEA						142,172
AEGINA	E Greece					152,171
AEGYPTUS	Roman province of Egypt					92,151,171,179,183
AELANA	N Arabia	Mod. 'Aqaba				142,153,160

NAME	AREA/COUNTRY	VARIANT NAMES	ARABIC NAME	MODERN HEBREW NAME	PALESTINIAN GRID REFERENCE	PAGE(S)
AELIA CAPITOLINA		= Jerusalem				154,168,181,183
AELIA CAPITOLINA	city state					154
AENARIA	S Italy	Mod. Ischia				90
AENDOR		= En-dor				155
AENON					203138	
AEOLIS	region of NW Asia Minor					186
AETHIOPIA	country of E Africa					92
AETOLIA	region of Greece					171
AFRICA	Roman province					150,170,178,182
'AFULA		= Ophrah (in Abiezer)				26,28,52,59,67
AGADE	C Mesopotamia					29
AGRIGENTUM	Sicily	Gk. Akragas Mod. Agrigento				170
AGRIPPIAS		= Anthedon				154
AGRIPPINA		= Remeth				157
AGRIPPIUM						158
'AGUR		= Ajjur				185
AHLAB		a/c Mahalab	Kh. el-Mahalib		172303	64/1
'AHUMUTA						33
AI			Kh. et-Tell		174147	28,63,65,67
AIATH			Kh. Haiyan?		175145	
AIJALON		Akk. Ayaluna	Yalo		152138	26,62,64/2,80,96/2,97/1,118,125
AI KHANUM	Afghanistan					139,145
AIN			Kh. 'Ayyun?		212235	
AIN		a/c Ashan				80
'AIN EL-'ARUS						154
'AIN FASHKHA						161
'AIN EL-GHARABEH	see Beth-arabah					
'AIN GHUWEIR						161
'AIN HOD	see En-shemesh					
'AIN IBL	see Abel (in Galilee)					
'AIN JIDI	see En-gedi					
'AIN MALLAHA	see 'Eynan					
'AIN EL-QUDEIRAT	see Kadesh-barnea					
'AIN SAKHRI	see Beth-shemesh					25
'AIN SHEMS						52
'AIN ET-TANNUR						161
'AIN YARQA						154
'AKAYA		= Acco				33
AKKA		= Acco				46,59
AKKAD	N Mesopotamia	a/s Accad				31
'AKKO		= Acco				59
AKRAGAS	see Agrigentum					
AKSAPA		= Achshaph				33
AKSHAPA		= Achshaph				46
ALABANDA	SW Asia Minor					186
ALACA HÜYÜK	C Asia Minor					55
ALALAKH	Syria	Mod. Tell Atchana				35,41,45,53,55,
ALASHIYA		= Cyprus				30,41,45,48,55,128,130
'ALEIYAN	see Kedemoth					
ALEMA						147
ALEMETH		= Almon				73
ALEPPO		Lat. Beroea a/c Khalab Mod. Halab				29,35,41,42,51,55,101,108,109, 114-115,129
ALEXANDRIA	Lower Egypt					41,138,142,151,164,171,179,183
ALEXANDRIA AMONG THE PAROPANISADAE	Afghanistan					139
ALEXANDRIA ARACHOSION	Afghanistan	a/s Alexandria Arachoton Mod. Kandahar				139,145
ALEXANDRIA AREION	Afghanistan	Mod. Herat				139,145
ALEXANDRIA AD ISSUM		a/c Alexandria by Issus				145,187
ALEXANDRIA ESCHATE	C Asia					139,145
ALEXANDRIA IN CARMANIA	SE Persia					139,145
ALEXANDRIA MARGIANA	C Asia					139,145
ALEXANDRIA OXIANA	C Asia					139
ALEXANDRIA PROPHTHASIA	Afghanistan	Mod. Farah				139
ALEXANDRIA RHAMBACIA	SE Persia					139

NAME	AREA/COUNTRY	VARIANT NAMES	ARABIC NAME	MODERN HEBREW NAME	PALESTINIAN GRID REFERENCE	PAGE(S)
ALEXANDRIA TROAS	NW Asia Minor	a/c Troas				186
ALEXANDRIUM		a/c Sartaba Gk. Alexandrion				148,150,155,158,159,177
AL-HIBBA	S Mesopotamia	a/c Urukug				6/2
ALIA	W Asia Minor					186
ALI KOSH						26
ALINDA	SW Asia Minor					186
AL JAWF						160
'ALMA						185
ALMODAD	tribe of S Arabia					93
ALMON		a/c Alemeth	Kh. 'Almit		176136	80
ALMON-DIBLATHAIM		a/c Beth-diblathaim	Kh. Deleilat esh-Sherqiyeh?		228116	
AL-'UBAID	S Mesopotamia	a/c Tell el-Obeid				29
AMARNA	see El-Amarna					
AMASIA	NE Asia Minor	a/s Amaseia				179,187
AMASTRIS	N Asia Minor					171,179,186
AMATHUS						149,157
AMATHUS	Cyprus					91,157
AMBI						47
AMBLADA	S Asia Minor					187
AMIDA	E Asia Minor	Mod. Diyarbakir				31,109/1
AMISUS	NE Asia Minor	Mod. Samsun				179,187
AMMAN		= Rabbath-ammon				53
AMMATHUS		= Hammath				164/2
AMMON	country					30,56,64,70,74,96,97,99,101,113,114,118,122/1,126,128,130
AMMONITES	tribe					68
AMMONITIS	region					147,149
AMORITES	tribe					93
AMORIUM	W Asia Minor					186
AMURRU	region of Syria					47,48,109/3
AMYZUM	SW Asia Minor	Gk. Amyzon				186
ANAB			Kh. 'Anab es-Seghireh		145091	118
ANAHARATH		Eg. Anuhartu	T.el-Mukharkhash?	T.Rekhesh	194228	42,43
ANAMITES	tribe	a/c Anamim				92
ANANIAH		a/c Bethan	El-'Azariyeh		174131	134
ANAT	NW Mesopotamia	a/c Anatho, Anatu, Hana Mod. 'Anah				131
'ANATA						185
ANATHOTH			Ras el-Kharrubeh		174135	73,113
ANAZARBUS	SE Asia Minor					187
ANCYRA	W Asia Minor	Mod. Ankara				138,175,179,187
ANDEDA	SW Asia Minor					186
ANDREAS						26
ANEA						154
ANEMURIUM	SE Asia Minor					187
ANHARU						33
ANIM			Kh. Ghuwein et-Tahta	H. 'Anim	156084	118
ANTHEDON		a/c Agrippias				149,181,185
ANINETUS	W Asia Minor					186
ANTANDRUS	NW Asia Minor					186
ANTI-LEBANON						108,109
ANTIOCH	SE Asia Minor	Lat. Antiochia Mod. Antakya				141,142,160,171,173,179,183
ANTIOCH (OF PISIDIA)		a/c Pisidian Antioch				171,173,179,
ANTIOCHIA		a/c Edessa				145
ANTIOCHIA		= Hippos				144,147
ANTIOCHIA		= Nisibis				145
ANTIOCHIA		= Tarsus				145
ANTIOCHIA AD CRAGUM	SE Asia Minor					187
ANTIOCHIA AD MAEANDRUM	SW Asia Minor					186
ANTIOCHIA ON THE CHRYSORRHOAS		= Gerasa				147
ANTIOCHIA SELEUCIA		= Gadara				145,147
ANTIPATRIS		= Aphek				143,155,157,158,166,168,177,185
ANTIPATRIS	city state					155
ANTIPHELLUS	SW Asia Minor					186
ANUHARTU		= Anaharath				43
APA	see Upe					
APAMEA	SW Asia Minor					152,179,186
APAMEA	Syria					145,171

NAME	AREA/COUNTRY	VARIANT NAMES	ARABIC NAME	MODERN HEBREW NAME	PALESTINIAN GRID REFERENCE	PAGE(S)
APAMEA MYRLEA	NW Asia Minor					186
APERLAE	SW Asia Minor					186
APHAEREMA						147,149,155,157
APHEK	in Asher	a/c Aphik	T.Kurdaneh	T.Afeq	160250	64,68,72/1,130
APHEK	in Transjordan		Kh. el-'Asheq?	'En Gev	210243	99,113
APHEK	in Sharon	G/L Antipatris a/c Arethusa, Pegae a/s Pegai	Ras el-'Ain	T.Afeq	143168	28,32,33,43,45,52,58,62,72,73, 96/1,103,125
APHEKAH						118
APHRODISIAS	SW Asia Minor					55,171,186
APHRODISIAS	SE Asia Minor					187
APOLLONIA		a/c Sozusa				105/2,147,149,155,157,165/3,166, 168,181,185
APOLLONIA	city state					155
APOLLONIA	NW Greece					105/1
APOLLONIA	Libya					171
APOLLONIA AD RHYNDACUM	NW Asia Minor					186
APOLLONIA MORDIAEUM	S Asia Minor					186
APOLLONIA SALBACE	SW Asia Minor					186
APOLLONIERUM	W Asia Minor					186
APOLLONIS	W Asia Minor					186
APPIA	W Asia Minor					186
APQUM						33
APUM, NORTHERN & SOUTHERN	region of S Syria					33
AQABA, GULF OF		Lat. Sinus Aelanites				153
'AQLAYA		a/s 'Aqraya				33
AQUAE CALIDAE	SE Asia Minor					187
AQUAE GERMENAE	C Asia Minor					186
AQUAE SARUVENAE	E Asia Minor					187
AQUILEIA	N Italy					170,178
AQUINCUM		Mod. Budapest				178
ARAB						70,118
ARABAH	region					30,62,113,125
ARABAH, SEA OF	see Dead Sea					
ARABIA						83,135,145,151,160,171
ARABIA DESERTA	region					179
ARABIA FELIX	region					92
ARACHOSIA	country of S Asia					139,145
ARAD	Canaanite city	a/c Arad Rabbah	T.el-Milh	T.Malhata	152069	27,28,29,58,64,65,69,88,96,99, 125,128,134,154,157
ARAD	Israelite citadel	a/c Arad-jerachmeel	T.'Arad	T.'Arad	162076	130
ARADIUM	see Arvad					
ARAD-JERACHMEEL		= Arad				96
ARADOS	see Arvad					
ARAD-RABBAH		= Arad				96,119
ARADUS		= Arvad				91,134,135/2,145
'ARA'IR	see Aroer (in Reuben)					
ARAM		Mod. Syria				30,71,93,99,109
ARAMAEANS	tribe					83
ARAM-NAHARAIM	see Paddan-aram					
'ARAQ EL-EMIR	see Tyre of Tobiah					
'ARAV						157,185
ARBAILU		a/s Arbela, Mod. Erbil				114,126
ARBEL		= Arbela				152
ARBELA		Mod. Arbel				147,157,163,165/2,177,181
ARBELA		= Arbailu				138
ARCADIA	country of C. Greece					54
ARDATA	Syria					47
AREOPOLIS						168
ARETHUSA		= Aphek (Sharon)				149,150
ARGOS	S Greece					171
ARHABUM						33
ARHANU						33
ARIASSUS	S Asia Minor					186
ARIMATHAEA		a/c Ramathaim			151159	147,149
ARKITES	tribe of Caucasus					93
ARMENIA	country of E Asia Minor	Per. Armina				92,135,138,145,171,179,183
ARMENIA MINOR	province of E Asia Minor					187
ARNAM	Syria	Mod. Hermil				48-49,51
ARNEAE	SW Asia Minor					186

NAME	AREA/COUNTRY	VARIANT NAMES	ARABIC NAME	MODERN HEBREW NAME	PALESTINIAN GRID REFERENCE	PAGE(S)
ARNON, R.		Mod. W el-Mujib				64,96
AROER	in Reuben		'Ara'ir		228097	33,58,96/3,102,118
AROER	in Negeb	a/c Adadah	Kh. 'Ar'arah	H.'Aro'er	148062	124
ARPACHSHAD	Mesopotamia	a/s Arphaxad				93
ARPAD	Syria	Mod. Tell Erfad				28,109,114,115
ARPAD	region of Syria					109,114,115
ARQA	Syria					53,106,108,114
'ARRABA						180
'ARRABU						46
ARRAPKHA	N Mesopotamia	Mod. Kirkuk				114
ARRUBOT						157
ARSINOE	see Crocodilopolis					
ARSLANTAŞ	SE Asia Minor					91
ARUMAH			Kh. el-'Ormah		180172	
'ARUNA			Kh. 'Ara		157212	41,97
ARVAD	Syria	a/s Arwad, Akk. Awrada Lat. Aradus, Aradium Gk. Arados, Mod. Ruad				28,42,48,106,108,109,114,115, 123,126/1,129
ARVADITES	island people of Phoenicia					93
ARYCANDA	SW Asia Minor					186
ARZAWA	region of S Asia Minor					41,55
ASAMON, MT		Mod. Har 'Azmon				177
'AS'ANNU						33
'AS'APA						33
ASCALON		= Ashkelon				143,144,147,149,150,151,152, 154,157,164,177,181,185
ASCALON	city state					154
ASHAN		= Ain				118
ASHDOD		Gk. Azotus Ar. Esdud		T. Ashdod	117129	32-33,43,52-53,58,64,65,69,70, 88,96-97,112,114,118-119,123, 124,125,126,128,134,135,138
ASHDOD-YAM						119,123
ASHER	tribe					64,68,69
ASHKELON		Gk. Ascalon Eg. Asqalanu Akk. Ashqaluna	'Asqalan	T. Ashqelon	107118	37,41,45,48,51,52,53,56,64,70, 91,96,97,101,108-109,112,113,115, 123,125,126,128,130,134,138
ASHKENAZ	tribe of Asia Minor	a/c Scythians				93
ASHQALUNA		= Ashkelon				46
ASHSHUWA	region of NW Asia Minor					55
ASHTAROTH		Eg. As(ta)rtum Akk. Astartu	T.'Ashtarah		243244	33,58,96,97,99,103,104,105
ASHTEROTH-KARNAIM						35
ASHUR	C Mesopotamia	Mod. Sharqat a/c Qal'at Sharqat				29,30/2,41,105,109,114,126,127, 131
ASHUR	tribe of Mesopotamia					93
ASIA	Roman province of Asia Minor					41,151,173,179,183
ASIAB	SW Persia					26
AŞIKLI HÜYÜK						26
'ASIREH ESH-SHAMALIYEH	see Hazeroth					
ASLANLI HARABESI	C Asia Minor					186
ASOCHIS		= Hannathon				149,155
ASPHALTITES, LACUS	see Dead Sea					
ASPENDUS	SW Asia Minor					138,144,187
'ASQALAN,	see Ashkelon					
ASQALANU		= Ashkelon				33
ASRIEL	land					112
ASSALIEH						152
ASSOS	NW Asia Minor	a/s Assus				106,107,142,173,186
ASSYRIA	country					41,71,109,114,115,126,127
ASTARTU(M)		= Ashtaroth				33,46
ASTHEMOE						154
ASWAN	Upper Egypt					39,40/1,135,160
ATAROTH			Kh. 'Attarus		213109	64/2,73
ATHENS	Greece	Lat. Athena				44,53,54,135,138,140,142,151, 171,172,179
'ATHLIT		Heb. 'Atlit				91,134
ATHRIBIS	Lower Egypt					39,142
ATTALEA	S Anatolia	a/s Attalia				173,187
ATTICA	region of Greece					171
ATTUDA	SW Asia Minor					186
AUGUSTA	SE Asia Minor					187

NAME	AREA/COUNTRY	VARIANT NAMES	ARABIC NAME	MODERN HEBREW NAME	PALESTINIAN GRID REFERENCE	PAGE(S)
AUGUSTA TREVERORUM	Germany	Mod. Trier				178
AUGUSTA VINDELICORUM	Germany	Mod. Augsburg				178
AURANITIS	region					143,151/3,156,168
AURELIOPOLIS	see Tmolus					
AVARIS	see also Pi-Ramese	Bibl. Zoan, Eg. Ro-waty a/c Tanis				39,40,91
AVVITES	tribe	a/c Avvim				64-65
AWRADA	Syria	= Arvad				47
AYALUNA		= Aijalon				46
'AYYANU						33
AZA	see Azzah					
AZALLA	region of SE Asia Minor					109
AZEKAH			Kh. T.Zakariyeh	T.'Azeqa	144132	58,62,64/2,103,118,122/1,124
AZMAVETH		a/c Beth-azmaveth	Hizmeh		175138	
AZNOTH-TABOR			Kh. el-Jebeil?	T. Aznot Tavor	186237	
AZOR		a/c Azuru				24-25,26,67,91
AZOTUS		= Ashdod			114132	143,144,147,149,150,151,154,157 168,177,181,185
AZOTUS	city state					154
AZOTUS PARALIUS		a/c Hippenus				147,154,157,185
AZURU		= Azor				122/1
'AZZA	see Gaza					
AZZAH		a/s Aza	Zawata?		171183	112
BAALAH	see Kiriath-jearim					
BAALATH			El-Mughar?		129138	
BAALBEK	Syria					160
BAAL-HAZOR			T.'Asur		177153	72/2
BAAL-MEON	see Beth-baal-meon					
BAAL-ZEPHON	Sinai					57
BAB EDH-DHIRA						28,33
BABEL	= Babylon					93
BAB EN-NAQB						33
BABIRUSH	see Babylonia					
BABYLON		Heb. Babel				30-31,41,83,93,94,102,105,109/1, 114,115,126,127,131,135,138, 145,151,179,183
BABYLONIA		Akk. Karduniash Per. Babirush				31,70,83,102,109/1,114,126,127, 131,135,138,171
BACA						163
BACTRA	Afghanistan	a/c Zariaspa, Mod. Balkh				139,145
BACTRIA	country of SW Asia	a/c Bactriana				93,139,145
BAD	S Mesopotamia					29
BAGHDAD	Mesopotamia					109/1
BAGIS	W Asia Minor					186
BAHAN						185
BAHRAIN	see Dilmun					
BAITANATA						143
BALANEAE	Syria					145
BALATA		a/c El-Balata				28
BALBURA	W Asia Minor					186
BALU						103
BANIYAS		= Paneas				114
BAQ'ATUM						33
BARAK						68,69
BAR'AM						152
BARATA	C Asia Minor					187
BARGASA	SW Asia Minor					186
BARGYLIA	SW Asia Minor					186
BARIS	W Asia Minor					186
BARQA		a/s Barga				106,108,109
BARSIP	see Borsippa					
BASCAMA						147
BASHAN	see Batanaea					
BASILICA THERMA	NW Asia Minor					186,187
BASIR	see Bathyra					
BASRA	S Mesopotamia					160
BATANAEA	region of N Transjordan	a/c Bashan				58,151,168,181
BATHYRA		a/c Basir				158
BATRUNA		Ar. Batrun				47

215

NAME	AREA/COUNTRY	VARIANT NAMES	ARABIC NAME	MODERN HEBREW NAME	PALESTINIAN GRID REFERENCE	PAGE(S)
BAT YAM						91
BAYRAKLI	Asia Minor					55
BEERAIM						112
BEEROTH			Kh. el-Burj		167137	65,118
BEEROTH	see Beruta					
BE'ER RESISIM						33
BEERSHEBA		a/c Bersabe	T.es-Seba'	T.Be'er Sheva'	134072	27,28-29,30,32,34,56,58,64, 65,88,96,99,112/1,118,119,123, 125,128,134,157,160,181
BEHISTUN	NW Persia	a/c Bisitun				94,135
BEIDHA						25,27
BEIRUT		= Beruta				51
BEISAMUN						26
BEIT 'AWWA						185
BEIT DAJAN	see Beth-dagon					
BEITIN		= Bethel				52,185
BEIT JALA						185
BEIT JANN						103
BEIT JIBRIN	see Bet Guvrin					
BEIT JIMAL						185
BEIT LAHM	see Bethlehem					
BEIT NABALA	see Neballat					
BEIT NATIF		= Bethletepha				185
BEIT SAKARIYA						185
BEIT 'UR EL-FOQA	see Beth-horon, Upper					
BEIT 'UR ET-TAHTA	see Beth-horon, Lower					
BEKE KAPLICALARI	E Asia Minor					187
BEMESILIS						149
BENE-BERAK			Kheiriyeh (Ibn Ibraq)	H. Bene-beraq	133160	122/1
BENE BERAQ		= Bene-berak				26
BENJAMIN	tribe					64,69,72/2
BENJAMINITES	tribe					68
BEN SHEMEN						26
BEQA'A	valley in Lebanon					
BEREA						147
BERENICE	Libya					170
BERENICE		= Elath				143
BERENICE	Upper Egypt					142,160
BERENICE		= Pella				143,147
BEROEA		= Aleppo				91,145,160
BEROEA	N Greece					171,172
BERSABE		= Beersheba				153,154,177,181
BERSINYA	see Rogelim					
BERUTA		a/c Beeroth, Lat. Berytus Mod. Beirut				41,47,53,57
BERYTUS		= Beruta				134,144,171
BESARA						155
BESIMOTH		= Beth-jeshimoth				177
BET ALFA						152,181,185
BETA-SHAMSHU		= Beth-shemesh				33
BET DAGAN	see Beth-dagon					
BETEN			Kh. Ibtin?	H. Ivtan	160241	
BET GUVRIN		= Betogabris				152,157,185
BETHABARA						165/3
BETH-ANATH			Safed el-Battikh		190289	48,64
BETH-ANOTH			Kh. Beit 'Anun		162107	118
BETHANY		a/c Ananiah			174130	73,165/3
BETH-ARABAH			'Ain el-Gharabeh		197139	118,161,165/3
BETH-ARBEL			Irbid		229218	128,103
BET HASHITTA						185
BETH-AVEN	see Bethel					
BETH-AZMAVETH	see Azmaveth					
BETH-BAAL-MEON		a/c Baal-meon	Ma'in		219120	
BETH-BASI						147
BETH-DAGON			Beit Dajan	Bet Dagan	134156	122/1
BETH-DIBLATHAIM	see Almon-diblathaim					
BETH-EDEN	see Bit-Adini					
BETHEL		a/c Luz, Lat. Bethela a/c Beth-aven	Beitin		172148	28,33,34,62,67,69,72/2,73,94,99, 101,102,103,113,124-125,128, 147,181
BETH-EMEK			T. Mimas	T. Bet Ha-'Emeq	164263	64-65
BETHENNABRIS						177
BETHER		a/s Bethther	Kh. el-Yehud		162126	118

NAME	AREA/COUNTRY	VARIANT NAMES	ARABIC NAME	MODERN HEBREW NAME	PALESTINIAN GRID REFERENCE	PAGE(S)
BETH-GAMUL			Kh. el-Jumeil		235099	
BETH-HACCHEREM		a/s Beth-haccerem	Kh. Salih	Ramat Rahel	170127	96,118
BETH-HAGGAN		a/c Gina, Ginae	Jenin		178207	
BETH-HARAM		a/s Beth-haran	T. Iktanu		214136	
BETH-HOGLAH			Deir Hajlah		197136	
BETH-HORON	later divided into:-	Akk. E-dnin-ib				46,62,64,65,80,146,177
BETH-HORON, LOWER			Beit 'Ur et-Tahta		158144	96-97
BETH-HORON, UPPER			Beit 'Ur el-Foqa		160143	73
BETH-JESHIMOTH			T. el'Azeimeh		208132	
BETH-LEAPHRAH			Et-Taiyibeh?		153107	
BETHLEHEM	in Judah		Beit Lahm		169123	32,58,73,91,118,125,153,154,161, 164/1,181,185
BETHLEHEM	in Zebulun		Beit Lahm	Bet Lehem Hagelilit	168238	68
BETHLETEPHA		Mod. Beit Natif				154,157,177,181
BETH-NIMRAH		a/c Nimrah	T.el-Bleibil		210146	181
BETHOGABRI	see Betogabris					
BETH-PELET						91,118
BETHPHAGE					173131	185,165/3
BETH-RAMATHA		= Beth-saida				157,181
BETH-SAIDA		a/c Beth-ramatha, Julias Livias			209256	163,165,166
BETH-SHEAN		a/s Beth-shan, a/c Nysa Gr. Scythopolis	T. el-Husn	T. Bet She 'an	197212	26,28,33,34,46,48,50,53,60,64,66, 75,83,88,96,128,134,138
BETH-SHEMESH	in Naphtali	Eg. Beta-shamshu	Kh T. er-Ruweisi?	T. Tosh	181271	68
BETH-SHEMESH	in Issachar		Kh. Sheikh esh-Shamsawi?	H. Shemesh	199232	
BETH-SHEMESH	in Judah	a/c Ir-shemesh, Har-heres	T. er-Rumeileh	T. Bet Shemesh	147128	28,32,33/2,45,65,67,72/1,83/1,96, 97,122/1,124
BETH-TAPPUAH			Taffuh		154105	96,118
BETHTHER		= Bether				154,181
BETHUL						64-65
BETH-YERAH		a/c Philoteria	Kh. el-Kerak	T.Bet Yerah	204235	28,33
BETH-ZAITH		Ar. Zeita				147
BETH-ZECHARIAH						147
BETH-ZUR			Kh. et-Tubeiqeh		159110	33,64,67,91,96,118,124,125,134, 147
BET LEHEM HAGELILIT	see Bethlehem (in Zebulun)					185
BETOGABRIS		a/s Bethogabri a/c Eleutheropolis Ar. Beit Jibrin Heb. Bet Guvrin				151/3,177
BETONIM			Kh. Batneh		217154	
BET SHE'AN		= Beth-shean				58,152,185
BET SHE'ARIM						152,162
BET SHEMESH		= Beth-shemesh				185
BET YERAH		= Beth-yerah				152,185
BEYCESULTAN	Asia Minor					55
BEZEK			Kh. Ibziq		187197	74
BEZER			Umm el-'Amad?		235132	
BEZET		a/s Bezeth, Mod. Beit Zi'ta				185
BILEAM	see Ibleam					
BIR DEFIYYE						153
BIR EL-QUTT						185
BIRTA						143,147
BISITUN	see Behistun					
BIT-ADINI	region of Syria	Bibl. Beth-eden				109
BIT-BAKHIANI	region of N Mesopotamia					109/3
BITHYNIA	Roman province N Asia Minor					145,151/1,171,179,182,186
BITHYNIUM	NW Asia Minor	a/c Claudiopolis				186
BITIA	Sardinia					90
BITOLION						154
BIT-ZITTI						123
BLAUNDUS	W Asia Minor					186
BOEOTIA	region of C Greece					171
BOĞAZKÖY		Anc. Hattushash				53
BONONIA	N Italy	Mod. Bologna				170
BORIM			Kh. Burin	H. Borin	153203	97
BORSIPPA	C Mesopotamia	Akk. Barsip				30/2,102
BOSOR						147
BOSTRA	Syria					160
BOUQRAS	Syria	Mod. Buqrus				26

NAME	AREA/COUNTRY	VARIANT NAMES	ARABIC NAME	MODERN HEBREW NAME	PALESTINIAN GRID REFERENCE	PAGE(S)
BOZRAH	in Bashan	Akk. Busruna, Eg. Busranu Ar. Busra Eski-Sham				46,58,119
BOZRAH	in Edom	Ar. Buseirah				91
BRETANIA		Mod. Brittany				92
BRIA	W Asia Minor					186
BRITAIN						182
BRITANNIA	Roman province of Britain					178
BRIXIA	N Italy	Mod. Brescia				170
BROOK OF EGYPT						126
BRUNDISIUM	S Italy	Mod. Brindisi				178
BRUZUS	W Asia Minor					186
BUBASTIS	Lower Egypt	Bibl. Pibeseth				39,41
BUBON	SW Asia Minor					186
BUCEPHALA	NW India					139
BUCOLON POLIS	see Adarus					
BURDIGALA	SW France	Mod. Bordeaux				178
BURJ EL-AHMAR						185
BURJ EL-ISANEH	see Jeshanah					
BURQUNA						46
BUSEIRAH		= Bozrah				
BUSIRIS	Lower Egypt					39,135,142
BUSRA ESKI-SHAM	see Bozrah					
BUSRANU		= Bozrah				33
BUSRUNA		= Bozrah				46
BUTARTU						48/1
BUTO	Lower Egypt					39
BYBLOS		Bibl. Gebal, Akk. Gubla Mod. Jubail, Jebail, Jebeil				26,28,30,35,41,45,48,51,53,66,83, 91,94,101,113,126,129,130,134, 143,144,171
BYZANTIUM		later Constantinople Mod. Istanbul				55,92,135,151/1,179
CABIRA	N Asia Minor	a/s Cabeira, a/c Neocaesarea				186
CABUL	see Chabulon					
CADASA		= Kedesh				155,177
CADI	C Asia Minor					186
CADITIS	see Gaza					
CADYANDA	SW Asia Minor					186
CAESARAUGUSTA	N Spain	Mod. Zaragoza				178
CAESAREA		= Straton's Tower a/c Caesarea Maritime			140212	58-59,138,151/1/3,152,155,157, 160,165/3,166,173,177,183
CAESAREA	city state					155
CAESAREA	N Africa					178
CAESAREA GERMANICE	NW Asia Minor					186
CAESAREA MARITIME	see Caesarea					
CAESAREA MAZACA	E Asia Minor	Mod. Kayseri				171,179
CAESAREA PALAESTINAE						185
CAESAREA PHILIPPI		= Paneas			215295	155,157,168,181
CAESAREA PHILIPPI	city state					155
CAFERDAGO						155
CALAH	N Mesopotamia	a/s Kalah, Akk. Kalkhu Mod. Nimrud				31,83,93,107,109,114,131
CALLINICUM	E Syria					171
CALNEH	see Kullania					
CALYNDA	SW Asia Minor					186
CANA	in Galilee	a/c Kanah			178247	
CANA	C Asia Minor					149,165,187
CANAAN		Akk. Kina'ni, Eg. Retenu				28,33,37,41,43,47,48,53,56,62,93
CANATHA		a/c Kenath, Nobah Akk.Qanu, Ar. Qanawat				168
CANDYBA	SW Asia Minor					186
CAP BON	N Africa					90
CAPE GELIDONYA	S Asia Minor					44,91
CAPERNAUM		a/c Capharnaum			204254	103,152,163,165,166,181,185
CAPHARABIS						177
CAPHARECCHO						177
CAPHARNAUM		= Capernaum				155
CAPHARSALAMA						147
CAPHARTOBAS						177
CAPHTOR		= Cyprus				66

NAME	AREA/COUNTRY	VARIANT NAMES	ARABIC NAME	MODERN HEBREW NAME	PALESTINIAN GRID REFERENCE	PAGE(S)
CAPHTORITES	tribe of Egypt	a/c Caphtorim				92
CAPITALIAS						168
CAPPADOCIA	region of NE Asia Minor	Per. Katpatuka				83,135,151/1,171,179,187
CAPUA	C Italy					170
CARALIS	S Sardinia	a/s Carales, Mod. Cagliari				90
CARCHEMISH	NE Syria	Akk. Gargamish Ar. Jarabulus, Jerablus, Jerabulus, Jerabish				28,30,35,41,91,94,101,106,108, 109,114,115,126,127,129,131
CARIA	region of SW Asia Minor					138,142,171,179,186
CARMEL			Kh. el-Kirmil		162092	118
CARMEL, MOUNT		a/c Mt. User				41,51,58,128
CARNAIM		= Karnaim				147
CARTHAGE	N Africa	Lat. Carthago				82,83,90,94,150/1,170,178,182
CATHAGO NOVA	SE Spain	Mod. Cartagena				90,178,182
CASAE	SE Asia Minor					187
CASLUHITES	tribe of Egypt	a/c Casluhim				92
CASPHOR		a/c Chaspho				147
CASPIAN GATES						139
ÇATAL HÜYÜK	C Asia Minor					26
CAUNUS	SW Asia Minor	Gk. Kaunos				142,186
ÇAYÖNÜ						26
CEDRON		= Kedron				154
CELAENAE	W Asia Minor					135
CELENDERIS	SE Asia Minor					187
CELTS	tribe of W Europe					93
CENCHREAE	C Greece					172,174
CEPHALONIA	island of W Greece	a/s Cephallenia				54
CERAMUS	SE Asia Minor					186
CERASUS	N Asia Minor					186
CERETAPA	C Asia Minor	a/c Diocaesarea				186
CESTRUS	SE Asia Minor					187
CHABULON		a/c Cabul				162,177
CHAGAR BAZAR	NE Syria					29
CHALCEDON	NW Asia Minor					171,179,186
CHALCIS	Syria					160,168
CHALDAEA	region of Mesopotamia					115,131
CHARACHMOBA		= Kir-hareseth				160,168,181
CHARAX	S Babylonia					139
CHASALON		= Chesalon				154
CHASPHO	see Casphor					
CHEBRON		= Hebron				154,177
CHEPHIRAH			Kh. el-Kefireh		160137	118
CHEREM-HATTEL						112
CHERITH, BROOK OF						99
CHERMELA						185
CHESALON		a/s Chasalon	Kesla	Kesalon	154132	
CHESULLOTH		a/c Chisloth-tabor	Iksal		180232	
CHEZIB	see Achzib					
CHINNERETH		a/c Chinneroth	Kh. el-'Oreimeh	T. Kinrot	200252	32,63
CHINNERETH, SEA OF		= Sea of Galilee				
CHIOS	Aegean Sea					142,173
CHISLOTH-TABOR	see Chesulloth					
CHOMA	SW Asia Minor					186
CHORAZIN		Mod. Korazim			203257	152,163,165
CHORSIA	see Gergesa					
CHRYSOPOLIS	NW Asia Minor					171
CIBYRA	C Asia Minor					186
CIBYRA MINOR	SE Asia Minor					187
CIDRAMUS	SW Asia Minor					186
CIDYESSUS	W Asia Minor					186
CILICIA	country of SE Asia Minor	Akk. Que, Khilakku				45,47,126,134,142,144,151/1,171, 173,179,187
CILICIAN GATES						179
CIMMERIANS	see Gomer					92
CIRTA	N Africa					
CISALPINE GAUL	Roman Province of N Italy					150/1
CITIUM	Cyprus	Gr. Kition				91,140
CITY OF MOAB			Kh. el-Medeiyineh?		232076	
CITY OF SALT			Kh. Qumran?		193127	
CIUS	NW Asia Minor					186
CLAUDIOPOLIS	see Bithynium					

NAME	AREA/COUNTRY	VARIANT NAMES	ARABIC NAME	MODERN HEBREW NAME	PALESTINIAN GRID REFERENCE	PAGE(S)
CLAZOMENAE	SE Asia Minor					186
CNIDUS	SW Asia Minor					186,173
COCHABA		Mod. Kaukab				181
COELE-SYRIA	region					138
COLONIA AGRIPPINA						170
COLONIA ANTIOCHIA	S Asia Minor					187
COLONIA ARCHELAIS	E Asia Minor					187
COLONIA CLAUDIOPOLIS	SE Asia Minor	a/c Ninica				187
COLONIA COMAMA	S Asia Minor					186
COLONIA CREMNA	S Asia Minor					186
COLONIA GERMA	NE Asia Minor					186
COLONIA ICONIUM	C Asia Minor					187
COLONIA LYSTRA	C Asia Minor					187
COLONIA OLBASA	S Asia Minor					186
COLONIA PARLAIS	S Asia Minor					186
COLOPHON	W Asia Minor					171,186
COLOSSAE	SW Asia Minor					173,186
COLYBRASSUS	SE Asia Minor					187
COMANA	E Asia Minor					187
COMANA PONTICA	N Asia Minor					186
COMENAIS	district					155
CONANA	S Asia Minor					186
CONSTANTIA MAIUMAS		a/c Maiumas, Nea Gaza				154
COPTUS	Upper Egypt	Gk. Koptos, a/s Coptus				142,160
CORACESIUM	SE Asia Minor					187
CORDUBA	S Spain	Mod. Córdoba				178
COREAE						149
CORINTH	C Greece	Lat. Corinthus				54,91,151/1,152,171,172,174,179, 182
CORONE	S Greece					171
COROPISSUS	SE Asia Minor					187
CORSICA						105/1
CORYCUS	SE Asia Minor					171,187
CORYDALLA	SW Asia Minor					186
COS	Aegean	a/s Kos				142,171,173
COSSYRA		Mod. Pantelleria				90
COTENNA	S Asia Minor					187
COTIAEUM	W Asia Minor					186
CRATIA	NW Asia Minor	a/s Cratea, a/c Flaviopolis				186
CRETE		a/c Kaptaru, Lat. Creta				44,53,54,91,135,138,142,151/1, 171,173,179
CROCODILONPOLIS						134,147,155
CROCODILOPOLIS	Lower Egypt	a/c Arsinoe				142
CROMMYON	C Greece					174
CROMNA	C Greece					174
CTESIPHON	Mesopotamia					171,183
CUMAE	S Italy					90,94
CUNAXA	C Mesopotamia					135,138
CURIUM	Cyprus					91
CUSH	country of NE Africa	Akk. Kashi, Mod. Nubia				83,92
CUTHAEANS	tribe					151/3
CUTHAH	Mesopotamia					115
CYANEAE	SW Asia Minor					186
CYCLADES	islands of Aegean					52-53
CYDRARA	see Hierapolis					
CYME	W Asia Minor					171,186
CYNOPOLIS	Lower Egypt					41
CYPRUS		Gk. Cypros				158,177
CYPRUS		anc. Alashiya Bibl. Caphtor a/c Elishah				30,45,53,66,83,91,109,135,138, 142,144,173,179
CYRENAICA	region of N Africa					142,151/1,171
CYRENE	Libya					82,135,142,151/1,171,179,182
CYTHERA	island of S Greece					54
CYZICUS	NW Asia Minor					186
DABALOTH						149
DABARITTA		= Daberath				163
DABBESHETH			T.esh-Shammam?	T. Shem	164230	
DABBURA						152
DABBURIYA						181,185
DABERATH		a/c Dabaritta	Daburiyeh		185233	80,181

NAME	AREA/COUNTRY	VARIANT NAMES	ARABIC NAME	MODERN HEBREW NAME	PALESTINIAN GRID REFERENCE	PAGE(S)
DABIYA						152
DABURIYEH	see Daberath					
DACIA	Roman province of E Europe					179,182
DAHSHUR	Upper Egypt					40
DAK						147
DALDIS	W Asia Minor	a/c Flaviopolis				186
DALISANDUS	S Asia Minor					187
DALMANUTHA						165
DALMATIA	region of E Adriatic					170
DALTON		a/c Dallata				185
DAMASCUS	Syria	Mod. Esh-Sham, Dimashq Akk. Dimashqa				30,35,41,48,51,58,62,70,83,91,99, 100,108,109,113,114,115,126,129, 130,138,143,151/1,160,171,179,183
DAMASCUS	kingdom					99,109,114,128
DAN		a/c Laish	T.el-Qadi	T. Dan	211294	35,58,64,69,91,96,97,101,102, 103,128,163
DANITES	tribe					64,68,69
DAPUR						48,51
DARB EL-HAJJ	route across Sinai					57,91
DARB ESH-SHAWI	route across Sinai					57
DARDANUS	NW Asia Minor					186
DAROMAS	district					181
DASCYLIUM	NW Asia Minor					135
DATHEMA						147
DEAD SEA		a/c Salt Sea, a/c Sea of Arabah Heb. Yam HaMelah Lat. Lacus Asphaltites Ar. El-Bahr el-Mayyit				
DEBIR		a/c Kiriath-sepher	Kh. Rabud?		151093	62,65,69,81,96,118,124
DECAPOLIS	district of N Transjordan	a/c The Ten Towns				150,157,168,181
DEDAN	tribe of NW Arabia					91,93,135,181
DEIR ABU TOR						185
DEIR EL-ARABI						185
DEIR EL-ASAL						185
DEIR EL-'AZAR	see Kiriath-jearim					
DEIR EL-BALAH						52,67
DEIR DAQLA						185
DEIR DOSI						185
DEIR GHASSANEH	see Zeredah					
DEIR HAJLAH	see Beth-hoglah					
DEIR EL-MEDINA	Upper Egypt					39
DEIR MUKALLIK						185
DEIR QAL'A						185
DEIR EL-QILT						185
DEIR SHA'AR						185
DELOS	island of Aegean					142,152,171
DELPHI	C Greece					171
DENDRA	S Greece					54
DENIZLI	SW Asia Minor					55
DER'A	see Edrei					
DERBE	C Asia Minor					173,187
DERTOSA	NE Spain					170
DHAHR MIRZBANEH						77
DHIBAN	see Dibon					
DHIRA'						27
DIBON		a/c Dibon-gad	Dhiban		224101	48,56,58,64,91,96-97,99,103,104, 106,160
DIKLAH	tribe of S Arabia					91,93
DILMUN		Mod. Bahrain				107,109/1
DIMASHQA		= Damascus				47
DIOCAESAREA		= Sepphoris				155,168,185
DIOCAESAREA	city state					155
DIOCAESAREA	see Ceretapa					
DIOCAESAREA	SE Asia Minor					187
DIOCLEIA	W Asia Minor					186
DIOCLETIANOPOLIS		a/c Sarafia				154,185
DIOSPOLIS		= Lod				155,168,181,185
DIOSPOLIS	city state					155
DIOSPOLIS	Upper Egypt					142
DIUM		Gk. Dion				149,150,157,168
DJEFTY						41
DOCIMIUM	W Asia Minor					186

NAME	AREA/COUNTRY	VARIANT NAMES	ARABIC NAME	MODERN HEBREW NAME	PALESTINIAN GRID REFERENCE	PAGE(S)
DODANITES	*see* Rodanites					
DOKH						157
DOMITIANOPOLIS	*see* Sala					
DOR		a/c Dora Akk. Du'uru	Kh. el-Burj	T. Dor	142224	33,37,58,62,64,67,76,83,91,97, 113,128,134,138,143,147,149, 150,155,157,165,166,181,185
DOR		= Dor				
DORA	city state					155
DORYLAEUM	NW Asia Minor					58,173,186
DOTHAN			T.Dothan		172202	26,32,33,34,35,37,58,96,99,103
DRANGIANA	country of SW Asia					139
DUMAH	N Arabia		Kh. ed-Deir Domeh		148093	30,83,107,109/1,135,154
DURA	*see* Adoraim					
DURA-EUROPOS	Mesopotamia					141,145,152,160,171,183,185
DUR KURIGALZU	C Mesopotamia					30/2
DUR SHARRUKIN	N Mesopotamia					30/2,101
DUR UNTASHI	SW Persia					30/2
DU'URU		= Dor				114

NAME	AREA/COUNTRY	VARIANT NAMES	ARABIC NAME	MODERN HEBREW NAME	PALESTINIAN GRID REFERENCE	PAGE(S)
EBENEZER						72/1
EBLA	Syria	Mod. Tell Mardikh				28,29,30,34,35,45,94
EBURACUM	Britain	Mod. York				182
EBUSUS	W Mediterranean	Mod. Ibiza				90
ECBATANA	W Persia	Mod. Hamadan				31,127,135,139,145
ECDIPPA		= Achzib				134
EDESSA	SE Asia Minor					171,183
EDFU	Upper Egypt					40,135
E-DNIN-IB		= Beth-horon				46
EDOM	region	a/c Seir, Akk. Udummu				30,35,48,56,62,70,83,96,101,113, 114,118/3,122/1,123/2,126,130
EDREI			Der'a		253224	58,64
EFA		= Haifa				155
EFLATUNPINAR	Asia Minor					55
EGLAIM						149
EGLON			T.el-Hesi	T.Hasi	124106	62,65,96,118
EGRA	NW Arabia					160
EGYPT		Akk. Misri Per. Mudraya				30,37,40/2,41,45,48,50,53,55,57, 66,70,92,94,109/1,126,130,135, 138,142,144,160,173
EGYPT, BROOK OF		Mod. W.el-'Arish				113,122/1,123,126
'EILABUN						185
'EIN EL-'ARRUB						185
'EIN DUK		a/c Na'aran				185
'EIN EL-FAWWAR						185
EIN-GEV		a/c Nahal 'En Gev				25
'EIN EL-GHARABEH	*see* Beth-arabah					
'EIN GHAZAL						26
'EIN HOD	*see* En-shemesh					
'EIN HUSB	*see* Tamar					
'EIN IBL	*see* Abel					
'EIN HANNIYA						185
'EIN EL-JADIDA						185
'EIN JIDI	*see* En-gedi					
'EIN SAMIYA						185
EISEIBA						153,154
EITOUI						143/2
EKRON		a/s Eqron a/c Accaron	Kh. el-Muqanna'	T.Miqne	136131	64,65,66,69,70,72/1,96,102,103, 113,122/1,123,130
ELAEA	NW Asia Minor					186
ELAEUSSA	SE Asia Minor	a/c Sebaste				187
ELAH, VALLEY OF						78,79
ELAM	country of SW Persia	Per. Uwja				83,93,109/1,127,131,135,171
EL-'ABEIDIYEH	*see* Yenoa					
EL-ADEIMEH						26
EL-'AFFULEH	*see* Ophrah (in Abiezer)					
EL-'AL	*see* Elealeh					
EL-ALEILIYAT						185
EL-AMARNA	N Egypt					39,53
EL-ARISH						50
ELASA						146,147
ELATH		a/s Eloth, earlier El-paran Lat. Aela(na), Gk. Aila Mod. Elat				30,34,58,113,119,134

NAME	AREA/COUNTRY	VARIANT NAMES	ARABIC NAME	MODERN HEBREW NAME	PALESTINIAN GRID REFERENCE	PAGE(S)
EL-'AZARIYEH	see Ananiah					
ELEALEH			el-'Al		228136	
EL ELA	NW Arabia					160
ELEPHANTINE	Upper Egypt	a/c Yeb				40,135,138,142
ELEUTHEROPOLIS		= Betogabris				185,154,168,181
ELEUTHEROPOLIS	city state					154
ELEUTHERUS, R.	Syria					134
EL-HADATHEH	see En-haddah					
EL-HADITHEH	see Hadid					
EL-IBREIJ						154
EL-IFSHAR	see Hepher					
ELIJAH'S CAVE						185
ELIM	Sinai					57
EL-'IRAQ	see Horonaim					
EL-'ISAWIYEH	see Nob					
ELISHAH		= Cyprus				71,92
EL JIB		= Gibeon				53/2
EL-JUBEIHAT	see Jogbehah					
EL-KAB	Upper Egypt					39,135
EL-KERAK	see Kir-hareseth					
EL-KHALIL	see Hebron					
EL KHARGA	Upper Egypt					158
EL LABOUÉ	Syria					26
EL-LUBBAN	see Lebonah					
EL-LUDD	see Lod					
EL-MALHAH	see Manahath					
ELMATTAN		a/c Pirathon	Immatin		165177	112
EL MEDEIYINEH						103
EL-MUGHAR	see Baalath					
EL-QASRAIN						185
EL-QEREIYAT	see Kerioth (in Moab)					
EL-QUDS	see Jerusalem					
EL-PARAN	see Elath					
ELTEKEH			T.esh-Shallaf?	T.Shalaf	128144	80,122/1
EL-TUR	S Sinai					57
EL-'UBAID	see Al-'Ubaid					
ELUSA						154,160
EL-WAD						25
EL-YEHUDIYEH	see Jehud					
EMAR	Syria	a/c Meskene				28,55
EMERITA AUGUSTA	S Spain	Mod. Mérida				170,178
EMESA	Syria	Mod. Homs				145,179
EMIM	tribe of Transjordan					33
EMMAUS		a/s Emmaeus a/c Nicopolis			149138	147,157,165/3,166,177,181
EMPORIAE	NE Spain					90
'ENAN	see 'Eynan					25
EN-DOR		Lat. Aendor	Kh. Safsafeh	H. Zafzafot	187227	74,103
'EN DOR						152
ENGADDI		= En-gedi				154
EN-GANNIM			Kh. Beit Jann?		196235	
EN-GEDI		a/c Engaddi	'Ain Jidi (T.Jurn)	'En Gedi (T.Goren)	187097	27,28,32,58,65,88,96,103,118, 125,128,134,157,180,181
'EN GEDI						59,65,152,185
'EN GEV		= Aphek (in Transjordan)				91
EN-HADDAH			El-Hadatheh	T. 'En Hadda	196232	
'EN HAROD						68,69
'EN KEREM						185
ENKOMI	Cyprus					45,53,55,91
EN-NEBI YAQIN	see Kain					
'EN NESHUT						152
EN-RIMMON			Kh. Khuweilfeh	T. Halif	137087	
EN-SHEMESH			'Ain Hod		175131	
'EN TAV						181
'ENYA						33
EPHESUS	W Asia Minor					55,135,138,142,144,151/1,171, 173,179,182,186
EPHRAIM	city	a/c Ephron			181155	157,165/3,166,177
EPHRAIM	tribal area					64,72/2,128
EPHRAIMITES	tribe of Palestine					69
EPHRON	in Transjordan					147
EPHRON	in Judaea see Ephraim					
EPIPHANIA	SE Asia Minor					187

NAME	AREA/COUNTRY	VARIANT NAMES	ARABIC NAME	MODERN HEBREW NAME	PALESTINIAN GRID REFERENCE	PAGE(S)
EPIRUS	region of W Greece					151/1
EQRON	see Ekron					
ERBIL	see Arbailu					
ERECH	S Mesopotamia	Akk. Uruk, Mod. Warka				93,101
EREMMON						154
ERIDU	S Mesopotamia	Mod. Abu Shahrain				29,30/2,101
ERQ EL-AHMAR						25
ER-RAFEH	see Raphon					
ER-RAM	see Ramah (in Benjamin)					
ERYTHRAE	W Asia Minor					186
ESBUS		= Heshbon				149,150,151/3,157,158,177
ESDRAELON		= Jezreel				150,157
ESDRAELON, PLAIN OF		a/c Valley of Jezreel				41,97,128,164
ESDUD	see Ashdod					
ESHTAOL			Ishwa'	Eshtaol	151132	64,66,69,118
ESHTEMOA			Es-Semu'		156089	81,118,125,152,185
ES-SAFI	see Zoar					
ES-SEMU	see Eshtemoa					
ESH-SHAM	see Damascus					
ESH-SHEIKH MADHKUR	see Adullam					
ESH-SHEIKH QATRAWANI						185
ESH-SHEIKH SHA'LA						185
ES-SUR	see Tyre					
ETAM			Kh. el-'Khokh		166121	73,118
ETENNA	SW Asia Minor					186
ETHAM	Sinai					57
ETHER			Kh. el-'Ater	T.'Eter	138113	
ETRUSCANS	people of N Italy					90
ET-TAIYIBEH	see Beth-leaphrah, Hapharaim, Ophrah (in Benjamin)					
EUBOEA	region of N Greece					171
EUCARPEIA	SW Asia Minor					186
EUHIPPE	SW Asia Minor					186
EUMENEIA	SW Asia Minor					186
EUROMUS	SW Asia Minor					186
EVLAYIM	see I'billin					
'EVRON						185
EXALOTH		= Chisloth-tabor				155,163
'EYNAN		a/s 'Enan, a/c 'Ain Mallaha				
EZION-GEBER		Mod. Tell el-Kheleifeh				57,83,91,96,119
EZ-ZARAT	see Zereth-shahar					
ES-ZIB	see Achzib (in Asher)					

NAME	AREA/COUNTRY	VARIANT NAMES	ARABIC NAME	MODERN HEBREW NAME	PALESTINIAN GRID REFERENCE	PAGE(S)
FAHMA						185
FAIR HAVENS	Crete					173
FAIYUM	Lower Egypt					179
FAR'ATA	see Pirathon					
FASAYIL						25
FLAVIA JOPPA	see Joppa					
FLAVIA NEAPOLIS	see Neapolis					
FLAVIOPOLIS	SE Asia Minor see also Cratia, Daldis, Temenothyrae					187

NAME	AREA/COUNTRY	VARIANT NAMES	ARABIC NAME	MODERN HEBREW NAME	PALESTINIAN GRID REFERENCE	PAGE(S)
GABA						157,158,168
GABAE		a/c Hippeum Gk. Hippeon Mod. Sheikh Abreiq				155,157,177,185
GABAON		= Gibeon				177
GABLINI	E Syria					126
GAD	tribal area					64,68,69
GADARA		a/c Antiochia Seleucia				144,147,149,150,151,155,157, 163,165,166,168,177,181
GADARA	region of Transjordan					164/2
GADES		Mod. Cádiz				82
GAGAE	SW Asia Minor					186
GALAADITIS		= Gilead				149,163
GALATIA	province of C. Asia Minor					151,171,173,179,186
GAL'AZA		= Gilead				114

NAME	AREA/COUNTRY	VARIANT NAMES	ARABIC NAME	MODERN HEBREW NAME	PALESTINIAN GRID REFERENCE	PAGE(S)
GALIL						155
GALILEE	region	Lat. Galilae				128,143,147,149,150,151,157, 162,163,164,165,168,177,181,185
GALILEE, SEA OF		a/c Sea of Chinnereth, Lake of Gennesaret, Sea of Tiberias, Lake Tiberias, Ar. Bahr Tabariyeh Heb. Yam Kinneret				164,165
GALLIA	Roman province of France	= Gaul				170-178
GAMALA						149,152,157,163,167,177
GAMALITKE	district of S Syria					157
GANDHARA	C Asia	a/s Gandara				139
GANGRA	N Asia Minor	a/c Germanicopolis				186
GANJ DAREH	Persia					26
GARABA						155
GARGAMISH	see Carchemish					
GARGARA	NW Asia Minor					186
GARIS						177
GARU	region	= Gaulanitis				46
GATH	in Asher		Jett		172264	
GATH	in Sharon	a/c Gath-padalla Akk. Gitti-padella	Jett		154200	
GATH	in Philistia	Akk. Gitti	T.es-Safi	T.Zafit	135123	64,66,69,70,72/1,96,97,99,102,113, 119,122,123,
GATH-HEPHER			Kh. ez-Zurra	T.Gat Hefer	180238	64,113,164/2
GATH-PADALLA		= Gath				32,33,43,96
GATH-PAR'AN						112
GATH-RIMMON		Akk. Gitti-rimuni	T.Jerisheh?	T.Gerisa	132166	80
GATH-SHEMESH						58
GAUGAMELA	SE Asia Minor					138
GAUL		Lat. Gallia				182
GAULANITIS	region	a/c Caditis Akk. Garu, Bibl. Geshur				143,149,151,168,177
GÂVUR KALESI	Asia Minor					55
GAZA		Akk. Ghazzati a/c Pekena'an	Ghazzeh	'Azza	099101	32,40,41,43,46,48,50,51,62,69, 96,101,122,123,126,128,130, 134,140,147,150,151,152,154, 160,185
GAZA	city state					154
GAZARA		= Gezer				147,149
GAZRI		= Gezer				46
GEBA	in Samaria		Jeba'		171192	80,150,151
GEBA	in N Benjamin		Kh. et-Tell?		174158	112,125
GEBA	in Benjamin	a/c Gibeah, Gibeath-elohim	Jeba'		174140	73,128,157
GEBAL		= Byblos				45,130
GEBA-SOMEN		a/c Hill of Eight Ar. Tell el-'Amr Heb. Tel Me'amer				43
GEBELEIN		Upper Egypt				39
GEDOR	in Gilead		T.'Ain-Jedur		220160	151,157,181
GEDOR	in Judah		Kh. Jedur		158115	118
GEDROSIA	ancient country of SW Asia					139,141
GENNESARET					200252	147,165
GENNESARET, LAKE OF		= Sea of Galilee				
GENUA	N Italy	Mod. Genova, Eng. Genoa				170,178
GERAR			T.Abu Hureireh	T.Haror	112087	27,34,103
GERASA		a/c Antiochia on the Chrysorrhoas Mod. Jerash				144,147,149,150,152,157
GERGESA		a/c Chorsia			211248	165
GERIZIM, MT.						147,149,177
GERMANICOPOLIS	SE Asia Minor	see also Gangra				187
GERRHA	Persian Gulf					160
GESHER						26
GESHUR		= Gaulanitis				64
GESHURITES	tribe	a/c Geshuri				64
GEVAT						185
GEZER		a/c Gazara Akk. Gazri	T.Jezer (Abu Shusheh)	T.Gezer	142140	26,28,32,33,37,41,45,51,52,58, 62,64,66,67,78,80,86,87,96, 103,114,124,128,130,134,157
GHAZZATI		= Gaza				46
GHAZZEH	see Gaza					
GHURABA						26
GIBBETHON			T.Melat	T.Malot	137140	64,80,99,102,123

NAME	AREA/COUNTRY	VARIANT NAMES	ARABIC NAME	MODERN HEBREW NAME	PALESTINIAN GRID REFERENCE	PAGE(S)
GIBEAH		= Geba				64,72,74,78,96,118,124
GIBEAH OF KIRIATH-JEARIM		a/s Gibeath-kiriath-jearim	Abu Ghosh?		160134	72/1,73,118
GIBEATH-ELOHIM		= Geba				72/2
GIBEON		a/s Gabaon	El-Jib		167139	32,33,62,73,74,78,79,80,91,96, 118,124
GILAT						27
GILBOA, MT.						68
GILEAD	region of N Transjordan	Akk. Gal'aza				37,74,99,114,125,128
GILEADITES	tribe of Transjordan					68
GILGAL			Kh. el-Mefjer?		193143	62,69,74,99,128
GIMTU	see Gittaim					
GIMZO			Jimzu	Gimzo	145148	
GINA, GINAE		= Beth-haggan				155,166
GINNESAR						155,181
GIRGASHITES	tribe					93
GISCHALA		= Gush Halav				87,163,177,181
GITHTHAM						155
GITTAIM		a/c Gimtu	Ras Abu Humeid		140145	123
GITTI		= Gath				46
GITTI-PADELLA		= Gath-padalla				46
GITTI-RIMUNI		= Gath-rimmon				46
GIV'ATAYIM						26
GIZA	Lower Egypt					39
GLA	C Greece					54
GOBOLIS						149
GOLAN			Sahm el-Jolan?		238243	26,156
GOLAN	region of SW Syria					58,157,181
GOLGOTHA						166
GOMER	tribe of C Asia Minor	a/c Cimmerians				92
GOPHNA		Mod. Jifnah				73,147,155,157,177,181
GORDIUM	C Asia Minor	Gk. Gordion				55,138
GORGIPPIA	NW Caucasus					171
GORTYN	S Crete	a/s Gortyna				179,182
GOSHEN	Lower Egypt					37
GOZAN	see Guzanu					
GRANICUS, R.						138
GREAT SEA		= Mediterranean Sea				
GREECE						53,54,55,92
GUBLA		= Byblos				108,109,114,123,126
GURAN	Persia					26
GURGUM	region of E Asia Minor					109/1,114
GUROB	C Egypt					53
GUSH HALAV		a/c Gishchala				135,152,157
GUZANU	N Mesopotamia	a/s Gozan				115

NAME	AREA/COUNTRY	VARIANT NAMES	ARABIC NAME	MODERN HEBREW NAME	PALESTINIAN GRID REFERENCE	PAGE(S)
HACILAR						26
HADERA						26
HADID		a/c Adida	El-Haditheh	T.Hadid	145152	128
HADRACH	see Khatarikka					
HADRIANEIA	NW Asia Minor					186
HADRIANI	NW Asia Minor					186
HADRIANI	SW Asia Minor					186
HADRIANOPOLIS	NW Asia Minor see also Stratonicea					186
HADRIANOPOLIS SEBASTE	C Asia Minor					187
HADRIANUTHERAE	NW Asia Minor					186
HADRUMETUM	N Africa	Mod. Sousse				90
HAHHUM	W Asia Minor					30
HAIFA		a/c Efa				41,58,181
HALAH	region of N Mesopotamia					115
HALA SULTAN TEKKE	Cyprus					45
HALHUL			Halhul		160109	118
HALI			Kh. Ras 'Ali	T.'Alil	164241	
HALICARNASSUS	SW Asia Minor					44,55,171,186,135,138,143
HAM			Ham		226213	33
HAM	tribal grouping					92
HAMA		= Hamath				28,53
HAMADAN		= Ecbatana				31
HAMATH	Syria	Mod. Hama				35,91,108,109,114,115,126,129,130

NAME	AREA/COUNTRY	VARIANT NAMES	ARABIC NAME	MODERN HEBREW NAME	PALESTINIAN GRID REFERENCE	PAGE(S)
HAMATH		= Hammath				46,101
HAMATHITES	tribe of Syria					93
HAMAXIA	S Asia Minor					186
HAME TEVERIYA	see Hammath (in Naphtali)					
HAMMAM TABARIYEH		= Hammath (in Naphtali)				103
HAMMAM LIF	N Africa	= Naro				170,152
HAMMAT		a/c Hammat Teverya				152
HAMMAT GADER						152,181
HAMMATH	in Naphtali	a/c Ammathus, a/c Hammath Tiberias	Hammam Tabariyeh	Hame Teveriya	201241	50,185
HAMMATH	near Beth-shean	a/s Hamath	T.el-Hammeh		197197	
HAMMON			Umm el'Awamid		164281	64/2
HANIGALBAT	region of Mesopotamia					47
HANITA						185
HANNATHON		G/L Asochis Akk. Hinnatuna, Hinnatuni	T.el-Bedeiwiyeh	T.Hannaton	174243	46
HAPHARAIM			Et-Taiyibeh		192223	97
HARAMU						33
HARIMU						33
HARAN	Syria	Mod. Harran				30,35,101,108,109,115,126,127, 129,131
HAR-HERES		= Beth-shemesh				64,66
HARPASA	SW Asia Minor					186
HARRAN	see Haran					
HAR YEROHAM						33
HASA						33
HASORA		= Hazor				33
HASSAN						157
HASURA		= Hazor				47
HATRA	Mesopotamia					160
HATTI	country of C Asia Minor	a/c Hatti-Land				41,44,51,130
HATTUSHASH	C Asia Minor	Mod. Boğazköy				41,44,53,55,83,94
HAURAN	province	= Khaurina				109,114
HAVILAH	tribe of SW Arabia					93
HAWWARIN	see Ziphron					
HAYONIM						25
HAZARMOTH	tribal region of S Arabia					93
HAZAZU						109/3
HAZEROTH	in Samaria		'Asireh esh-Shamaliyeh?		175184	112
HAZEROTH	in Sinai					57
HAZEVA	see Tamar					
HAZOR		Akk. Hasora, Hasura	T.el-Qedah	T.Hazor	203269	30,32,33,43,45,50,53,56,58,62,63 64,67,68,83,88,91,97,99,103, 113,114
HAZOREA'						33
HEBRON		a/c Kiriath-arba Lat. Chebron	El-Khalil		160103	28,33,35,37,41,56,58,62,70,78,88, 97,101,103,122,124,125,128,134, 147,149,159,181,185
HELEK	clan district					112
HELENOPOLIS	city state					155
HELEPH			Kh. 'Irbadeh?	H. 'Arpad	189236	
HELIOPOLIS	Lower Egypt	a/c On				37,39,40,41,48/1,135,179,183
HELKATH			T.el-Qassis?	T.Qashish	160232	
HELLAS	S Greece					138
HEPHER			El-Ifshar?	T.Hefer	141197	62,112
HERAEUM	Greece					174
HERACLEA PONTICA	NW Asia Minor					186
HERACLEA SALBACE	SW Asia Minor	a/c Heraclea ad Latmum				186
HERACLEOPOLIS	Lower Egypt see also Sebastopolis					143,179
HERCULANEUM	C Italy					178
HERMOCAPELEIA	W Asia Minor					186
HERMOPOLIS	Lower Egypt					39,41,143,183
HERODIUM		Gk. Herodion				73,152,154,157,159,177,185
HERSEUM						174
HESBAN	see Heshbon					
HESHBON			Hesban		226134	45,58,64,96,97,103,118,160
HETH	tribe	a/c Hittites				93
HIBERNIA		= Ireland				178
HIERACONPOLIS	Upper Egypt					39
HIERAPOLIS	SW Asia Minor	a/c Cydrara				171,173,179,182,186
HIEROCAESAREA	W Asia Minor					186

NAME	AREA/COUNTRY	VARIANT NAMES	ARABIC NAME	MODERN HEBREW NAME	PALESTINIAN GRID REFERENCE	PAGE(S)
HIEROPOLIS	SW Asia Minor					186
HIEROPOLIS CASTABALA	SE Asia Minor					187
HIEROSOLYMA		= Jerusalem				150,151
HILEN	see Holon					
HINNATUNI		= Hannathon				46
HIPPO REGIUS	N Africa					90,150,170
HIPPOS		a/s Hippus, a/c Antiochia				147,149,151,155,163,165,166,168, 177
HIPPOS	city state					155
HIPPO ZARYTUS	N Africa	Mod. Bizerta				90
HISARLIK		= Troy				53
HISPANIA	Roman province of Spain					150,170,178
HITTITE EMPIRE						48/1
HITTITES		= Heth				71
HIVITES	tribe					93
HIZMEH	see Azmaveth					
HOGLAH	clan district					112
HOLON		a/c Hilen				81
HOMS		= Emesa				160
HORBAT 'ADULLAM	see Adullam					
HORBAT 'AMMUDIM						152,185
HORBAT AMUD						185
HORBAT 'ANIM	see Anim					
HORBAT ARBEL						185
HORBAT 'ARO'ER	see Aroer (in Negeb)					
HORBAT 'ARPAD	see Heleph					
HORBAT BENE-BERAQ	see Bene-berak					
HORBAT BET BAD						185
HORBAT BETER						27
HORBAT BORIN	see Borim					
HORBAT DAMON						185
HORBAT DIKKE						152
HORBAT DUBLAH						185
HORBAT GAMOM	see Hukkok					
HORBAT GERARIT						185
HORBAT IVTAN	see Beten					
HORBAT KANAF						152
HORBAT KISHOR						152
HORBAT LAVNIN	see Achzib (in Judah)					
HORBAT MARUS						152
HORBAT MATAR						27
HORBAT MIGDAL GAD	see Migdal-gad					
HORBAT NEVALLAT	see Neballat					
HORBAT QANA	see Kanah					
HORBAT QARNE HITTIM	see Adamah					
HORBAT QEDESH	see Kedesh (in Galilee)					
HORBAT RIMMON						152
HORBAT RIMONA	see Rimmon					
HORBAT RUMA	see Rumah					
HORBAT SANSANNA	see Sansannah					
HORBAT SARA						185
HORBAT SHEMA'						152,168,185
HORBAT SHEMESH	see Beth-shemesh (in Issachar)					
HORBAT SOKHO	see Socoh (in Shephelah)					
HORBAT SUMAQ						152,185
HORBAT SUSEYA						152
HORBAT TOV	see Kinah					
HORBAT 'UZZA	see Ramoth-negeb					
HORBAT WERADIM						185
HORBAT YA'ANIN	see Neiel					
HORBAT YATIR	see Jattir					
HORBAT YITTAN	see Moladah					
HORBAT YODEFAT	see Jotbah					
HORBAT ZAFZAFOT	see En-dor					
HORBAT ZANOAH	see Zanoah					
HORBAT ZEKHARIAH						185
HOREB, MT.		= Mt. Sinai				57
HORITES	tribe					33
HORMAH			Kh. el-Meshash	T.Masos	146069	62,64,119

NAME	AREA/COUNTRY	VARIANT NAMES	ARABIC NAME	MODERN HEBREW NAME	PALESTINIAN GRID REFERENCE	PAGE(S)
HORONAIM			El-'Iraq?		211055	149
HOSAH	see Uzu					
HUKKOK			Kh. el-Jemeijmeh?	H. Gamom	175252	
HULATA	region					157
HULDA						152,185
HULEH, LAKE		a/c Lake Semechonitis Lat. Lacus Semechonitis				
HUSAN	see Hushah					
HUSHAH			Husan?		162124	
HUSIFA						152,181
HYDE	C Asia Minor					187
HYDISUS	SW Asia Minor					186
HYLLARIMA	SW Asia Minor					171,186
HYPAEPA	W Asia Minor					171,186
HYRCANIA	city	Mod. Kh. el-Mird				149,150,157,177
HYRCANIA	country of S Caucasus	Per. Warkana				93,135,139
IALYSUS	SW Asia Minor					44
IASUS	SW Asia Minor					55,171,186
IBERIA		= Spain				92
I'BILLIN		Heb. Evlayim				185
IBLEAM		a/c Bileam	Kh. Bel'ameh		177205	64,32,33
IBN IBRAQ	see Bene-berak					
ICONIUM	C Asia Minor					135,171,173,179,143,147
IDUMAEA						150,151,155,157,177
IJON		Mod. Tel ed-Dibbin				58,66,88,114
IKSAL	see Chesulloth					
ILGIN KAPLICALARI	E Asia Minor					187
ILICI	E Spain	Mod. Elche				170
ILISTRA	C Asia Minor					187
ILIUM	NW Asia Minor	a/c Troy				186
ILLAHUN	C Egypt					39
ILLYRICUM	Roman province of SW Europe					150,172,178,182
IMMATIN	see Elmattan					
INDIA						139,183
INTERCISA	C Europe					170
IONIA	country of W Asia Minor	Per. Yauna				92,138,143,186
IOPPE	see Joppa					
IOTAPE	SE Asia Minor					187
IPSUS	W Asia Minor					144
IQRAT						33
IRA						25
IRBID	see Beth-arbel					
IRENOPOLIS	SE Asia Minor					187
IRQATA	Syria	Eg. 'Irqatum				28,33,47
IR-SHEMESH	see Beth-shemesh					
ISAURA	SE Asia Minor					187
ISAURA NOVA	S Asia Minor					186
ISAURIA	district of S Asia Minor					186
'ISFIYA		Heb. Husifa				185
ISHMAELITES	tribe					33
ISHWA'	see Eshtaol					
ISIN	C Mesopotamia	Mod. Bahriyat				30/2
ISINDA	SW Asia Minor					186
ISRAEL						51,70,72/1,89,96, 99,113
ISSACHAR	tribe					64,68
ISSUS	SE Asia Minor					135,138,145
ISTHMIA	Greece					174
ITALIA		= Italy				92,150,171,179
ITALY		Lat. Italia				55,172
ITJ-TOWY	Lower Egypt					37
ITURAEA	region					149,150,157
IULIA	W Asia Minor					186
IULIA GORDUS	W Asia Minor					186
'IYYE ZETA						27
'IZBET SARTAH						67

NAME	AREA/COUNTRY	VARIANT NAMES	ARABIC NAME	MODERN HEBREW NAME	PALESTINIAN GRID REFERENCE	PAGE(S)
JAAZER		a/s Jazer	Kh. es-Sar?		228150	
JABBOK, RIVER		Mod. Nahr ez-Zerqa				58,62-63,68,96
JABESH-GILEAD			T.el-Maqlub		214201	68,74,115
JABNEEL	in Naphtali		T.en-Na'am	T.Yin'am	198235	
JABNEEL	in Judah	a/c Jabneh, Jamnia	Yebna a/s Yibna		126141	
JABNEH		= Jabneel				58,113,118
JACOB'S WELL						185
JAFFA		= Joppa				52,67,185
JAHAZ		a/s Jahazah	Kh. el-Medeiyineh?		236110	
JAMMALA						185
JAMNIA		= Jabneel		Yavne		147,149,150,151,157,165/3,168, 181,185
JAMNIA	city state					154
JAMNITH		a/s Jamneith Ar. Khirbet Benit				177
JANAOTH						112
JANOAH	in Galilee		Yanuh		173265	
JANOAH	in Ephraim		Kh. Yanun		184173	
JAPHA						155
JAPHETH	tribal grouping					92-93
JAPHIA		= Joppa				64,177
JAPHO	see Joppa					
JARMO						26
JARMUTH	in Judah		Kh. el-Yarmuk	T.Yarmut	147124	62,118
JARMUTH	in Issachar see Remeth					
JATTIR		a/c Jethira, Lat. Iethira	Kh. 'Attir	H. Yatir	151084	81,118
JAVAN	region of the Aegean					92
JAZER		= Jaazer				64,147
JEBA'	see Geba					
JEBEIL	see Byblos					
JEBEL AQRA						114
JEBEL MUSA						92-93
JEBEL QA'AQIR						33
JEBEL ER-RUMEIDI						185
JEBEL ET-TOR		= Mt. Gerizim				185
JEBEL ZULEIQA						154
JEBUS		= Jerusalem				64
JEBUSITES	tribe					93
JEDDA	Arabia	a/s Jiddah				160
JEHUD			El-Yehudiyeh	Yehud	139159	
JEMDAT NASR	S Mesopotamia	a/s Jemdet Nasr, a/c Kidnun				29
JENIN	see Beth-haggan					
JERAH	tribal region of S Arabia					93
JERICHO		Lat. Iericho	T.es-Sultan		192142	25,26,28,37,45,52,56,62,77,88,99, 134,147,149,150/2,158,164/1,166, 177,185
JERUSALEM		a/c Jebus Eg. Urushalimum Akk. Urushalem Lat. Aelia Capitolina, Hierosolyma	El-Quds	Yerushalayim	172131	28,52,56,70,73,77,78,88,99,101,104, 122,123,126,128,130,134,147,149, 158,164/1,165/3,166,169,173,177
JESHANAH				Burj el-Isaneh	174156	
JESHUA			T.es-Sa'weh?	T.Jeshu'a	149076	
JETAN		= Juttah				154
JETHIRA		= Jattir				154
JETT	see Gath					
JEZREEL		a/s Jezrael, a/c Esdraelon	Zer'in	T. Yizre'el	181218	64,68,99,103,155,181
JEZREEL, VALLEY OF						52,68,70,114
JIBIYA						185
JIDDAH	see Jedda					
JIFTLIK						26
JIMZU	see Gimzo					
JISR EL-HASERA						26
JISR QULEID						26
JOBAB	tribal region of S Arabia					93
JOGBEHAH			El-Jubeihat		231159	69,74
JOKMEAM			T.el-Mazar?		195171	
JOKNEAM			T.Qeimun	T.Yoqneam	160230	32,62,68,93,103
JOKTANITE	tribe of S Arabia					93
JOPPA		a/c Japho, Japhia, Flavia Joppe Akk. Yapu, Eng. Jaffa Lat. Ioppe	Yafa	Yafo	126162	30,32,37,58,96,97,114,122,128,134, 147,149,150,151,157,177

NAME	AREA/COUNTRY	VARIANT NAMES	ARABIC NAME	MODERN HEBREW NAME	PALESTINIAN GRID REFERENCE	PAGE(S)
JOPPA	city state					155,157
JORDAN, FORDS OF THE						69
JORDAN, RIVER		Heb. HaYarden Ar. Nahr al Urdunn				
JOTAPATA		= Jotbah				155,162,165/2,177
JOTBAH		a/s Jotbath a/c Jotapata Lat. Iotapata	Kh. Jefat	H. Yodefat	176248	
JOTBATHAH		Ar. Tabeh?				57,119
JUBAIL	see Byblos					
JUDAEA		= Judah				58,72/1,143,147,149,150,151,154, 157,168,177,181,185
JUDAH		Lat. Judaea				68,69,70,74,96,97,99,113,122,123, 124,125,126/1,128,138
JULIAS		= Beth-saida				177
JUTTAH		a/c Jetan Lat. Ietan	Yatta		158095	81,118

NAME	AREA/COUNTRY	VARIANT NAMES	ARABIC NAME	MODERN HEBREW NAME	PALESTINIAN GRID REFERENCE	PAGE(S)
KABRI						28
KABUL	Afghanistan	= Ortospana				139
KABUL			Kabul		170252	
KABZEEL						118
KADESH-BARNEA		a/s Qadesh-barnea Mod. 'Ain el-Qudeirat? Heb. Qadesh-Barnea'				33/2,34,57,58,62,64, 65,96/2,119,125,134
KAFR 'ANA	see Ono					
KAFR DANNA						185
KAFR KAMA						185
KAFR KANNA						152,185
KAFR YASIF						185
KAIN			En-Nebi Yaqin?		165100	118
KALKHA	see Calah					
KAMID EL-LOZ		a/c Kumidi				45,53
KAMON			Qamm?		218221	68
KANAH	in Asher		Qana		178290	64
KANAH	in Galilee	a/c Cana	Kh. Qana	H. Qana	178247	48/2
KANAH, BROOK OF						64
KANATA	Syria					160
KANESH	W Asia Minor	a/s Kanish, Mod. Kültepe				30,94
KANISAT ER-RAWAT						185
KAPTARU		= Crete				55
KARANA	N Mesopotamia					31
KARATEPE	SE Asia Minor					91,94
KARDUNIASH		= Babylonia				47
KARKAR	see Qarqar					
KARKISHA	region of W Asia Minor					55
KARNAIM		a/s Carnaim	Sheikh Sa'd		247249	33,113,128
KARNAIM	province, see Qarnini					
KARNAK	Upper Egypt					39,46,106
KARTHAN	see Rakkath					
KAR-TUKULTI-NINURTA	Mesopotamia					30/2
KASHI		= Cush				46
KASHPUNA	Syria					114
KATO ZAKRO	Crete					44
KATPATUKA	see Cappadocia					
KAUNOS	see Caunus					
KEBARA						25
KEDARITES	tribe of N Arabia	a/c Qedar Arabs or Qedarites				135
KEDEMOTH			'Aleiyan?		233104	
KEDESH	in Galilee		Kh. Qedish	H. Qedesh	202237	68
KEDESH	in Naphtali	a/c Kedesh-naphtali, a/c Cadasa,	T. Qades	T. Qedesh	199279	62,64,68,97,114,147
KEDRON		a/s Kidron, Cedron				147
KEFAR BAR'AM						185
KEFAR HANAYAH						155
KEFAR QARNAYIM						185
KEFAR SIKHNIN						181
KEFAR TRUMAN						185
KEILAH		Akk. Qilti	Kh. Qila		150113	118,157
KENATH		= Canatha				58
KEPHALLENIA	see Cephalonia					

NAME	AREA/COUNTRY	VARIANT NAMES	ARABIC NAME	MODERN HEBREW NAME	PALESTINIAN GRID REFERENCE	PAGE(S)
KERIOTH	in Moab		El-Qereiyat		215105	
KERIOTH	in Negeb		Kh. el-Qaryatein	T.Qeriyot	161083	
KERMANSHAH	Persia					109/1
KESALON	see Chesalon					
KESLA	see Chesalon					
KHALAB		= Aleppo				30,42,55
KHAN EL-AHMAR						185
KHANIA	Crete					53
KHARGA OASIS	Egypt					40,135
KHASHABU	Syria					42,47
KHASHI	Syria	Mod. T.Hizzin?				47
KHATARIKKA	Assyrian province	a/c Hadrach				114
KHAURINA	Assyrian province	a/s Hauran				114
KHEIRIYEH	see Bene-berak					
KHEREIBET EL-WATEN	see Moladah					
KHILAKKU	country of Asia Minor					109/1,126
KHIRBET 'ABBAD	see Socoh (in Shephelah)					
KHIRBET 'ABDEH		= Abdon				103
KHIRBET ABU GHUNNEIM						185
KHIRBET ABU SUKHEIBAN						154
KHIRBET ABU TABAQ		= Middin				124
KHIRBET 'ADASA						185
KHIRBET 'ALMIT	see Almon					
KHIRBET 'ANAB ES-SEGHIREH	see Anab					
KHIRBET 'ARA	see 'Aruna					
KHIRBET 'AR'ARAH	see Aroer (in Negeb)					
KHIRBET EL-ARAB						185
KHIRBET EL-'ASHEQ	see Aphek (in Transjordan)					
KHIRBET EL-'ATER	see Ether					
KHIRBET ATARAB						185
KHIRBET 'ATTARUS	see Ataroth					
KHIRBET 'ATTIR	see Jattir					
KHIRBET 'AYUN MUSA	see Nebo					
KHIRBET 'AYYUN	see Ain					
KHIRBET BARRA'ISH						185
KHIRBET EL-BASAL						185
KHIRBET BATNEH	see Betonim					
KHIRBET BEDD FALUH	see Netophah					
KHIRBET BEIT AMRA						185
KHIRBET BEIT 'ANUN	see Beth-anoth					
KHIRBET BEIT 'EINUN						185
KHIRBET BEIT JANN	see En-gannim					
KHIRBET BEIT NESIB	see Nezib					
KHIRBET BEL'AMEH	see Ibleam					
KHIRBET EL-BIRA						185
KHIRBET EL-BIYAR						185
KHIRBET BURIN	see Borim					
KHIRBET EL-BURJ	see Beeroth, Dor					
KHIRBET DEIR ALLA						185
KHIRBET ED-DEIR DOMEH	see Dumah					
KHIRBET DELEILAT ESH-SHERQIYEH	see Almon-diblathaim					
KHIRBET DELHAMIYEH						26
KHIRBET ED-DER						185
KHIRBET DIMNEH	see Madmen					
KHIRBET DUMA						185
KHIRBET ED-DUWEIR						185
KHIRBET FAGHUR	see Peor					
KHIRBET FAHIL	see Pella					
KHIRBET FARA						185
KHIRBET GHAZZAH	see Ramoth-negeb					
KHIRBET GHUWEIN ET-TAHTA	see Anim					
KHIRBET EL-HADATHA						185
KHIRBET HAIYAN		= Aiath				185
KHIRBET HAMIDEH	see Rabbah					
KHIRBET EL-HARBAJ	see Achshaph					
KHIRBET IBTIN	see Beten					
KHIRBET IBZIQ	see Bezek					
KHIRBET IMWAS						185

NAME	AREA/COUNTRY	VARIANT NAMES	ARABIC NAME	MODERN HEBREW NAME	PALESTINIAN GRID REFERENCE	PAGE(S)
KHIRBET 'IRBADEH	see Heleph					
KHIRBET ISKANDER						28, 33
KHIRBET ISTABUL						185
KHIRBET JALIL						185
KHIRBET EL-JEBEIL	see Aznoth-tabor					
KHIRBET JEDUR	see Gedor					
KHIRBET JEFAT	see Jotbah					
KHIRBET JEL'AD	see Ramath-mizpeh					
KHIRBET EL-JEMEIJMEH	see Hukkok					
KHIRBET JUDUR						52
KHIRBET JUHZUM						185
KHIRBET JUL	see Ramah (in Naphtali)					
KHIRBET EL-JUMEIL	see Beth-gamul					
KHIRBET KABARA						185
KHIRBET EL-KARMIL						185
KHIRBET EL-KEFIREH	see Chephirah					
KHIRBET EL-KERAK	see Beth-yerah					
KHIRBET EL-KHASIF						154
KHIRBET EL-KHOKH	see Etam					
KHIRBET KHUREISA						185
KHIRBET KHUREITUN						185
KHIRBET KHUWEILFEH	see En-rimmon					
KHIRBET EL-KIRMIL	see Carmel					
KHIRBET KUFIN						185
KHIRBET EL-LAHUN						103
KHIRBET LUQA						185
KHIRBET EL-MAHALIB	see Ahlab					
KHIRBET EL-MAHAMI						185
KHIRBET MA'IN	see Maon					
KHIRBET MAJD EL-BA						185
KHIRBET MAKHNEH EL-FOQA	see Michmethath					
KHIRBET EL-MAKHRUM						185
KHIRBET MALKAT-HA						185
KHIRBET EL MAQARI	see Nibshan					
KHIRBET MAQATIR						185
KHIRBET EL-MASANI						185
KHIRBET EL-MEDEIYINEH	see Jahaz, Moab, City of					
KHIRBET EL-MEFJER	see Gilgal					
KHIRBET EL-MEITA						185
KHIRBET EL-MEJDELEH	see Migdal-gad					
KHIRBET EL-MESHASH	see Hormah					
KHIRBET EL-MIRD						185
KHIRBET EL-MISHASH						154
KHIRBET MIYAMAS						185
KHIRBET EL-MUQANNA'	see Ekron					
KHIRBET EL-MURASSAS						185
KHIRBET EN-NITLA						185
KHIRBET EL-'OREIMEH	see Chinnereth					
KHIRBET EL-'ORMAH	see Arumah					
KHIRBET QANA	see Kanah					
KHIRBET EL-QARYATEIN	see Kerioth (in Negeb)					
KHIRBET QASYUN	see Kishion					
KHIRBET QEDISH	see Kedesh (in Galilee)					
KHIRBET QILA	see Keilah					
KHIRBET QUMRAN	see Salt , City of	= Qumran				161
KHIRBET EL-QUNEITIREH	see Rakkath					
KHIRBET QUSIN	see Kozoh					
KHIRBET RABUD	see Debir					
KHIRBET RADDANA						67
KHIRBET RAS 'ALI	see Hali					
KHIRBET RUHEIBE						154
KHIRBET ER-RUMEH	see Rumah					
KHIRBET T.ER-RUWEISI	see Beth-shemesh					
KHIRBET SAFSAFEH	see En-dor					
KHIRBET SALIH	see Beth-haccherem					

NAME	AREA/COUNTRY	VARIANT NAMES	ARABIC NAME	MODERN HEBREW NAME	PALESTINIAN GRID REFERENCE	PAGE(S)
KHIRBET SAMMUNIYEH	see Shimron					
KHIRBET ES-SAMRAH	see Secacah					
KHIRBET ES-SAR	see Jaazer					
KHIRBET SEILUN		= Shiloh				185
KHIRBET ESH-SHAMSANIYAT	see Sansannah					
KHIRBET SHEIKH ESH-SHAMSAWI	see Beth-shemesh (in Issachar)					
KHIRBET SHUWEIKEH	see Socoh (near Mt. Judah)					
KHIRBET SHUWEIKET ER-RAS	see Socoh (in Sharon)					
KHIRBET SITT LEILA	see Zephath					
KHIRBET SIYAR EL-GHANEM						185
KHIRBET SUSIYA						185
KHIRBET TAIYIB	see Kinah					
KHIRBET ET-TAIYIBA						185
KHIRBET TANA EL-FOQA	see Taanath-shiloh					
KHIRBET ET-TANNUR						160
KHIRBET TATRIT	see Madmannah					
KHIRBET ET-TELL	see Ai, Geba (in N Benjamin)					
KHIRBET TELL EL-BEIDA		= Achzib (in Judah)				185
KHIRBET ET-TELL (ED-DAMIYEH)	see Adami-nekeb					
KHIRBET TELL EL-FAR'AH	see Tirzah					
KHIRBET TELL ZAKARIYEH	see Azekah					
KHIRBET TEQU'	see Tekoa					
KHIRBET TIBNAH	see Timnath-serah					
KHIRBET ET-TIRA						185
KHIRBET ET-TUBEIQEH	see Beth-zur					
KHIRBET TUQU'						185
KHIRBET UMM EL-AMAD						185
KHIRBET YA'NIN	see Neiel					
KHIRBET YANUN	see Janoah (in Ephraim)					
KHIRBET YARIN						185
KHIRBET EL-YARMUK	see Jarmuth (in Judah)					
KHIRBET YAROUN		a/c Khirbet ed-Deir				185
KHIRBET EL-YEHUD	see Bether					
KHIRBET YEMMA	see Yaham					
KHIRBET ZANU'	see Zanoah					
KHIRBET ZEITUN ER-RAMEH	see Ramah (in Naphtali)					
KHIRBET ZUREIKIYEH						33
KHIRBET EZ-ZURRA'	see Gath-hepher					
KHIROKITIA						26
KHORSABAD	Mesopotamia					107
KHUME	country of E Asia Minor					130
KINAH			Kh. Taiyib	H. Tov	163081	118
KINA'NI		= Canaan				47
KING'S HIGHWAY						57,58,59,83
KIR-HARESETH		a/c Kir of Moab, Kir-moab, Charachmoba	El-Kerak		217066	103
KIRIATBENE HASSUN						157
KIRIATHAIM			Qaryat el-Mekhaiyet?		220128	
KIRIATH-ANAB			T.esh-Shihab?		241233	
KIRIATH-ARBA	see Hebron					
KIRIATH-BAAL	see Kiriath-jearim					
KIRIATH-JEARIM		a/c Kiriath-baal, Baalah, Baale-judah	Deir el'Azar	T.Qiryat Ye'arim	159135	72/1,73,96,118
KIRIATH-SEPHER	see Debir					
KIR-MOAB		= Kir-hareseth				99,101
KIRŞEHIR	E Asia Minor					187
KISH	S Mesopotamia	Mod. Tell el-Oheimir				29,30/2,102
KISHION		a/s Kishon	Kh. Qasyun	T.Qishyon	187229	
KISHON		= Kishion				80
KISHON, R.						41,52,68,97
KITION	Cyprus	Lat. Citium				45,53,55
KITTIANS	tribe of S Asia Minor	a/c Kittim				92
KIZZUWADNA		= Cilicia				55
KNOSSOS	Crete	Lat. Cnossus				44,53,94

NAME	AREA/COUNTRY	VARIANT NAMES	ARABIC NAME	MODERN HEBREW NAME	PALESTINIAN GRID REFERENCE	PAGE(S)
KOKAB EL-HAWA	see Remeth					
KOKHAV HAYARDEN		= Remeth				152,185
KOMMOS	Crete					53
KOPTOS	see Coptus					
KORAZIM	see Chorazin					
KORESIA	Aegean					142
KOUKLIA	Cyprus					45
KOZOH		Kh. Qusin			167182	112
KUDISOS						143
KULLANIA		a/c Calneh				114
KÜLTEPE	see Kanesh					
KUMIDI		Ar. Kamid el Loz, a/c Merneptah in Pi-Aram				47,48,51,53
KUMMUKH	Assyrian province of E Asia Minor					114
KUNTILLET 'AJRUD						57,91
KUNULA	N Syria					109/3
KUPNI	Syria	a/s Kubni				33/3
KUR						112
KURKH	Mesopotamia					107
KUSHU	district					33/3
KYTHERA	see Cythera					

NAME	AREA/COUNTRY	VARIANT NAMES	ARABIC NAME	MODERN HEBREW NAME	PALESTINIAN GRID REFERENCE	PAGE(S)
LABANA	see Lebo-hamath					
LABRAUNDA	C Asia Minor					186
LABWE, WOOD OF						48,49
LACHISH		Akk. Lakishi	T.ed-Duweir	T. Lakhish	135108	28,33/2,37,51,52,62,64,67, 88,91,96/3,103,118,122,123, 124,134
LACONIA	region of S Greece					54
LAERTES	SE Asia Minor					187
LAGASH	S Mesopotamia	Mod. Tello				29,30/2,101
LAGBE	SW Anatolia					186
LAISH		a/c Dan, Leshem				33,35,66
LAKANA	Syria					143
LAKISHI	see Lachish					
LAMPSACUS	NW Asia Minor					186
LAMUS	SE Asia Minor					187
LAODICEA	Syria					141
LAODICEA	SE Asia Minor					142
LAODICEA	SW Asia Minor					171,173,178
LAODICEA AD LYCUM	SW Asia Minor					186
LAODICEA COMBUSTA	C Asia Minor					187
LARANDA	C Asia Minor					187
LARISSA	C Greece	a/s Larisa				171
LARISSA	Syria					141
LARSA	S Mesopotamia	Mod. Senkereh				29,30/2,101
LEBANON						108,109
LEBEDUS	SE Asia Minor					186
LEBO		= Lebo-hamath				42
LEBO-HAMATH		a/c Lebo, Labana Mod. Lebweh				113
LEBONAH			El-Lubban		173164	58
LEBWEH	see Lebo-hamath					
LECHAEUM	Greece					174
LEGIO	city state					155
LEGIO MAXIMIANOPOLIS		a/c Legio, Capercotnei, Mod. Lejjun				115,181
LEHABITES	a people of Egypt	a/c Lehabim				92
LEILAN	Syria					29
LEMBA						149
LEONTOPOLIS	Lower Egypt					142,171
LEPTIS MAGNA	N Africa					170
LESBOS	Aegean Sea					44,142
LESHI						33
LEUCECOME	Red Sea					142,160
LEUCOS LYMEN	Egypt					142,160
LIBNAH			T.Bornat?	T.Burna	138115	62,81,118,122,128
LIBNATH			T.Abu Huwam?		152245	103
LIBYA	country of N Africa					92,93,130,138,173,182
LIDEBIR	see Lo-debar					
LIFTA	see Nephtoah, Waters of					
LIMYRA	SE Asia Minor					171,188

NAME	AREA/COUNTRY	VARIANT NAMES	ARABIC NAME	MODERN HEBREW NAME	PALESTINIAN GRID REFERENCE	PAGE(S)
LINDOS	Rhodes					91
LITANI, R.						58
LIVIAS		= Beth-saida				158,181
LIXUS	NW Africa					82,90,150
LOD		a/c Lydda, Gk. Diospolis	El-Ludd	Lod	140151	58,103,128,134
LO-DEBAR		a/c Lidebir	Umm ed-Dabar?		207219	113
LONDINIUM		Mod. London				178,182
LOWER GALILEE						164/2
LOWER SEA		= Persian Gulf, = Red Sea				131
LUBA	Egypt					33
LUCENTUM	E Spain	Mod. Alicante				90
LUDU	country of Asia Minor	= Lydia				130
LUGDUNUM	C France	Mod. Lyon				178,182
LUHUTU	region of Syria					109/3
LUKKA	S Asia Minor					41
LUSITANIA	Roman province of Portugal					178
LUTETIA	N France	Mod. Paris				178
LUXOR	Upper Egypt					39
LUZ	see Bethel					
LYCAONIA	country of SE Asia Minor					151,179,186
LYCIA	country of SW Asia Minor					55,135,142,151,171,179,182, 186
LYDDA		= Lod				26,147,149,157,165/3,166, 177,185
LYDIA	country of W Asia Minor	Akk. Ludu Per. Sparda				82,109/1,126,130,135,171,179
LYDITES	people of Egypt	a/c Lydians, Lud				92
LYSINIA	SE Asia Minor					186
LYSTRA	SE Asia Minor					173

NAME	AREA/COUNTRY	VARIANT NAMES	ARABIC NAME	MODERN HEBREW NAME	PALESTINIAN GRID REFERENCE	PAGE(S)
MA'AN						59/3
MAA-PALAIOKASTRO	Cyprus					53
MA'BAROT						33
MABARTHA	see Neapolis					
MACEDONIA	country of N Greece					91,135,138,142,151,171,172,179, 182
MACHAERUS						149,150,157,158,168,177
MACHIR	tribe					68
MACHMAS		= Michmash				154
MADA	see Media					
MADAI		= Medes				93
MADEBA	see Medeba					
MADMANNAH			Kh. Tatrit		143084	
MADMEN			Kh. Dimneh?		217077	
MADON						63
MAEONIA	W Asia Minor					186
MAEOTIS PALUS		= Sea of Azov				182
MAGDALA		a/c Magadan				165
MAGIDDU		= Megiddo				46
MAGIDDU	Assyrian province	= Megiddo				114
MAGNESIA	W Asia Minor	a/c Magnesia ad Maeandrum				171,179,186
MAGNESIA AD SIPYLUM	W Asia Minor					186
MAGOG	tribe of Caucasus					93
MAGUR	Syria					51
MAGYDUS	S Asia Minor					187
MAHALAB		a/c Ahlab				123
MAHANAIM			T.edh-Dhahab el-Gharbi		214177	35,64,96
MAHOZA	see Muhhazi					
MA'IN	see Beth-baal-meon					
MAIUMAS		a/c Constantia Maiumas				181,185
MAIUMAS ASCALON						154
MAKED	N Transjordan					147
MAKKEDAH						62
MAKTULYA						33/3
MALACA	S Spain	Mod. Malaga				90,150
MALATHA		= Moladah				154,157
MALLIA	Crete					53
MALLUS	SE Asia Minor					187
MALQATA	Upper Egypt					39
MALTA		a/c Melita				172

NAME	AREA/COUNTRY	VARIANT NAMES	ARABIC NAME	MODERN HEBREW NAME	PALESTINIAN GRID REFERENCE	PAGE(S)
MAMPSIS						154
MAMRE		G/L Terebinthus				181
MANAHAT	see Manahath					
MANAHATH			El-Malhah	Manahat	167128	118
MANASSEH	tribe					64,69
MANNAEANS	tribe of NW Persia	a/c Minni, Mannai				109/1
MANSATU	Syria					42
MANSUATE	region of Syria					109/4,114
MANTINEA	S Greece					171
MAON			Kh. Ma'in		162090	152
MA'OZ HAYYIM						152
MARACANDA	C Asia	Mod. Samarkand				139
MARAH	Sinai					57
MARALAH			T.Thorah?	T.Shor	166228	64/2
MARASH	E Asia Minor	Mod. Maraş				91
MARATHON	C Greece					135
MARATHUS	W Syria					134
MARESHAH		G/L Marisa, a/s Marissa				64/2,118/1,2,124
MARI	N Mesopotamia	Mod. Tell Hariri				29,31,35,45,94,101
MARISA		= Mareshah				77,91,138,139,149,150,157
MARSIH-KI (N&S)						33
MASA	region of S Asia Minor					55
MASADA		Heb. Mezada				58,103,149,150,152,154,157,158, 168,177,181
MASHA						33
MASSILIA		Mod. Marseille				178
MASTAURA	W Asia Minor					186
MASWALA						33
MAURETANIA	province of NW Africa					178,182
MAXIMIANOPOLIS						168,185
MECCA	W Arabia		Makkah			160
MEDEBA			Madeba		225124	64,103,118,147,149,157,160,168
MEDES	people, N Persia	a/c Madai				93
MEDIA	country of N Persia	Per. Mada				109/1,115,127,131,135,139,145 171
MEDIAN WALL	C Mesopotamia					131
MEDINA	see Yatribu					
MEDIOLANUM	N Italy	Mod. Milan				170,178
MEDITERRANEAN SEA		a/c Great Sea , Lat. Mare Internum				
MEGIDDO		Akk. Magiddu	T.el-Mutesellim	T.Megiddo	167221	26,28,33,41,45,48,50,56,58,62, 63,64,67,68,83/1,88,96,97, 100,113,114,126,128,134
MELID	country of E Asia Minor					109/1,114
MELITA		= Malta				90,170,178,182
MELITENE	E Asia Minor	Mod. Malatya				55
MELOS	Aegean					171
MELUKKHA	region of Egypt	a/c Nubia				46
MEMPHIS	Lower Egypt	Bibl. Moph, Noph				37,39,40,41,45,53,83,109/1,126, 135,138,142,179
MENDES	Lower Egypt					39
MEPHAATH			T.Jawah?		239140	
MERNEPTAH IN PI-ARAM		= Kumidi				51
MERNEPTAH, WELLS OF						51
MEROM		a/c Meroth	T.el-Khirbeh?	Meron	190275	48
MEROM, WATERS OF						63
MERON		= Merom				103,152,163,185
MEROTH	see Merom					
MERSIN	SE Asia Minor					55,91
MESER		Heb. Mezer				26
MESHECH	tribe of S Asia Minor	a/c Mushki				92
MESKENE	see Emar					
MESOPOTAMIA						29,31,35,83,100,101,131,151, 171,179
MESSANA	Sicily	Mod. Messina				178
MESSENIA	region of S Greece					54
METHANA	SE Greece					142
METROPOLIS	C Asia Minor					186
METROPOLIS	W Asia Minor					186
MEUNITES	tribe of Sinai					113
MEVASSERET ZIYYON	see Mozah					
MEVO DOTAN						26
MEZADA	see Masada					
MEZAD HASHAVYAHU						91,96/3,128,130

NAME	AREA/COUNTRY	VARIANT NAMES	ARABIC NAME	MODERN HEBREW NAME	PALESTINIAN GRID REFERENCE	PAGE(S)
MEZER		= Meser				28
MICHMASH		a/s Michmas, a/c Machmas	Mukhmas		176142	73,74,147
MICHMETHATH			Kh. Makhneh el-Foqa		175176	64,112
MIDAEUM	W Asia Minor					186
MIDDIN			Kh. Abu Tabaq?		188127	118,161
MIDIAN	region of NW Arabia					30,57
MIDIANITES	tribe					33,68
MIGDAL						157
MIGDAL-GAD			Kh. el-Mejdeleh?	H. Migdal Gad	140105	
MIGDOL	Egypt	Akk. Magdalu				47,57,126,135
MILETOPOLIS	NW Asia Minor					186
MILETUS	W Asia Minor					44,53,55,135,138,152,171,173, 186
MINNI	see Mannaeans					
MINORCA	W Mediterranean					170
MIKHMORET						91/2
MINET EL-BEIDA	Syria					45
MINET EL-QAL'AH		Heb. Ashdod-yam				96/3
MIRA-KUWALIYA	region of W Asia Minor					55
MIRUS	W Asia Minor					186
MISHAL			T.Kisan	T.Kison	164253	
MISHREFA						154
MISREPHOTH-MAIM						63
MISRI		= Egypt				46
MITANNI	country of N Mesopotamia					31,41,42,47
MITYLENE	NW Asia Minor					173
MIZPAH	in Benjamin	a/s Mizpeh	T.en-Nasbeh		170143	72,73,96,118,124,125,130,134, 147
MIZPAH	in Gilead	= Ramath-mizpeh				33
MIZPAH-GILEAD		= Ramath-mizpeh				68
MIZPEH	see Mizpah					
MIZPEH, VALLEY OF						63
MIZRAIM	a people of Egypt					92
MOA						153,154
MOAB	region					30,48.56,62,64,70,96,97,99, 101,103,113,114,119,122,123, 126,128
MOAB, PLAIN(S) OF						56
MOABITES	tribe					69
MOABITIS	region					143,147,149
MOAHILE						153,154
MODIN		a/s Modein				138,147,149,157
MOESIA	province of SE Europe					179
MOHENJO-DARO	N India					95
MOLADAH		a/c Malatha	Khereibet el-Waten	H.Yittan	142074	118
MOPH	see Memphis					
MOPSUESTIA	SE Asia Minor					152,187
MOREH, HILL OF						69,74
MORESHETH-GATH		Akk. Mu'rashti	T.el-Judeideh?	T.Goded	141115	113,118,124
MOROCCO	country of N Africa					90
MOSTENE	W Asia Minor					186
MOTYA	Sicily					90
MOUKHTARA	Syria					26
MOULIANA	Crete					55
MOZAH			Qalunyah	Mevasseret Ziyyon	165134	118,134
MUDRAYA	see Egypt					
MUHHAZI		a/s Mu'khazi, a/c Mahoza	T.Abu Sultan	T.Mahoz	125147	
MUKAWIR						103
MU'KHAZI		= Muhhazi				46
MUKHMAS		= Michmash				185
MUNHATTA						26
MURASHRASH						153
MU'RASHTI		= Moresheth-gath				46
MUREYBIT	Syria					26
MUSA, JEBEL		= Mt. Sinai				57
MUSHKI	country of Asia Minor	Bibl. Meshech				115
MUSUR, NAHAL		= Brook of Egypt				130
MUTARA						33
MYCALE	W Anatolia					135
MYCENAE	S Greece					44,53,54,82,91
MYLASA	SW Asia Minor					142,186

NAME	AREA/COUNTRY	VARIANT NAMES	ARABIC NAME	MODERN HEBREW NAME	PALESTINIAN GRID REFERENCE	PAGE(S)
MYNDUS	SW Asia Minor					171,186
MYOS HORMOS	Egypt					142,160
MYRA	SW Asia Minor					173,186
MYRINA	NW Asia Minor					186
MYSIA	country of NW Asia Minor					179
NAARAH		a/s Naaran, Naarath Heb. Na'aran, Lat. Neara	T.el-Jisr		190144	
NA'ARAN		= Naarah				152,181
NABATAEA	region	a/s Nabatea				143,149,150,151
NABATAEANS		a/s Nabateans				157,160,168
NABESHA	Egypt					39
NABI THARI						185
NABLUS	see Neapolis					
NACOLEIA	W Asia Minor					186
NACRASA	W Asia Minor					186
NAG HAMMADI	C Egypt					179
NAGIDUS	SE Asia Minor					187
NAHAL 'ARUGOT						180
NAHAL DAWID						180
NAHAL 'EN GEV	see Ein-Gev					
NAHAL GERAR						33
NAHAL HARDUF						180
NAHAL HEVER						180
NAHAL MISHMAR						27,60,180
NAHAL OREN						25,26
NAHAL RABBA						26
NAHAL SHIQMA						33
NAHAL ZE'ELIM						180
NAHARINA	region of N Syria	a/s Naharima a/c Naharaim				42,47
NAHARIYYA						88,185
NAHR EL-KALB		a/c Dog River				48
NAIN		a/s Naim			183226	155,162,164,/2,185
NAKHL	Sinai					57
NAPHTALI	tribal area					27,64,68,128
NAPHTUHITES	a people of Egypt	a/c Naphtuhim				92
NAPLES		= Neapolis				172
NARBATA						147,155,177,181
NARBATTENE	city territory of Narbata					155,156,157
NARBONENSIS	province of S France					150
NAREH	= Naveh					168
NARO	NW Africa	Mod. Hammam Lif				152
NARONA	Yugoslavia					178
NAUCRATIS	Lower Egypt					41,135
NA'UR	see Abel-keramim					
NAVEH			Nawa		248255	168,181
NAWA	see Naveh					
NAZARETH					178234	103,162,164,165,166,181,185
NEA GAZA	see Constantia Maiumas					
NEAPOLIS		a/c Mabartha, a/c Flavia Neapolis Mod. Nablus				155,165/3,168,181,185/2
NEAPOLIS	city state					155
NEAPOLIS		= Naples				150,170,178,182
NEAPOLIS AD HARPASUM	SW Asia Minor					186
NEARA		= Naarah				154
NEBALLAT			Beit Nabala	H. Nevallat	146154	
NEBO			Kh. 'Ayun Musa?		220131	103,128
NEFRUSY	Lower Egypt					40
NEGEB	desert of Middle East	a/s Negev				57
NEHARDEA	Mesopotamia					171
NEIEL			Kh. Ya'nin	H. Ya'anin	171255	
NEOCLAUDIOPOLIS	N Asia Minor	a/c Phazimon				186
NEPHTOAH, WATERS OF			Lifta	Me-Neftoah	168133	
NESANA						160
NETANYA						59
NETOPHAH			Kh. Bedd Faluh?		171119	
NEVORAYA						185
NEWE UR						26

NAME	AREA/COUNTRY	VARIANT NAMES	ARABIC NAME	MODERN HEBREW NAME	PALESTINIAN GRID REFERENCE	PAGE(S)
NEZIB			Kh. Beit Nesib		151110	118
NIBRU	see Nippur					
NIBSHAN			Kh. el-Maqari?		186123	118,161
NICAEA	NW Asia Minor					139,186
NICOMEDIA	NW Asia Minor					171,179,186
NICOPOLIS		= Emmaus				154,168,185
NICOPOLIS	city state					154
NICOPOLIS	N Asia Minor					186
NICOPOLIS	N Greece					178
NIMRAH	see Beth-nimrah					
NIMRUD	N Mesopotamia	Akk. Kalkhu, Bibl. Calah				107
NINA	see Surghul					
NINEVEH	N Mesopotamia	Akk. Ninua, Mod. Quyunjiq				29,31,41,83,93,94,101,105,107, 108,109,114,115,127, 135,160
NINICA	see Colonia Claudiopolis					
NIPPUR	S Mesopotamia	Akk. Nibru, Mod. Nuffar				29,30-31,101,131
NISIBIS	E Asia Minor	a/c Nisibin, Akk. Nasibina				108,109,115,171
NIYI	Syria	Mod. Qal'at el-Mudiq				42,47,48/2
NOAH	clan district					112
NOB			El-'Isawiyeh?		173134	
NOBAH	see Canatha					
NOE						143
NOLA	S Italy					170
NOPH		= Memphis				28,66
NORA	Sardinia					54,90
NORICUM	province of C Europe					178
NUBIA	see Melukkha					
NUGASSE		= Nukhashshe				42
NUKHASHSHE	region of Syria	a/s Nugasse				41,47
NUZI	N Mesopotamia	a/s Nuzu, Mod. Yorghan Tepe				29
NYSA		= Beth-shean				147
NYSA	W Asia Minor					171,186
OAK IN ZAANANNIM						68
OBODA		a/s Obodo				103,160
OEA	N Africa					170
OENOANDA	SW Asia Minor					186
OENOE	C Greece					174
OESCUS	SE Europe					171
OLBA	S Asia Minor					171,187
OLBIA	Sardinia					90
OLIVES, MOUNT OF					173132	73
OLYMPUS	SW Asia Minor					186
OLYMPUS, MT.						54
ON	Lower Egypt	a/c Heliopolis				37,126,130
ONO		Lat. Onus	Kafr 'Ana	Ono	137159	128,181,185
ONUS	city state	= Ono				155
OPHIR	tribal region of S Red Sea area					83,93
OPHRAH	in Abiezer		El-'Affuleh?	'Afula	177223	68
OPHRAH	in Benjamin		Et-Taiyibeh		178151	72/2,73
ORCHOMENUS	E Greece					54
OREINE	province					157
ORONTES, R.						40,48,49,129
OROPUS	E Greece					171
ORTHOSIA	W Syria	Akk. Ullaza				134,145
ORTHOSIA	SW Asia Minor					186
ORTOSPANA	Afghanistan	Mod. Kabul				139
OSTIA	C Italy					152,170,178
OXYRHYNCHUS	Lower Egypt					142,179
'OZEM						185
PADDAN-ARAM	region of Mesopotamia	a/c Aram-Naharaim				35
PAGAE	C Greece					174
PALAEOBEUDUS	W Asia Minor					186
PALAESTINA TERTIA	province					153,154
PALESTINE		Lat. Palaestina				58,59
PALMAHIM						33/2
PALMYRA		a/c Tadmor, Mod. Tudmur				79,83,101,109,145,151,160 171,183

NAME	AREA/COUNTRY	VARIANT NAMES	ARABIC NAME	MODERN HEBREW NAME	PALESTINIAN GRID REFERENCE	PAGE(S)
PAMPHYLIA	country of SE Asia Minor					142,151,173,179,187
PANEAS		Gk. Paneion, a/s Panion a/c Caesarea Philippi Mod. Baniyas				142,144,147,150,151,155,158
PANNONIA	province of C Europe					170,178
PANORMUS	Sicily	Mod. Palermo				90,170
PANTICAPAEUM	S Russia					171
PAPHLAGONIA	country of N Asia Minor					135
PAPHOS	Cyprus					82,91,142,160,173,179
PAPPA	SW Asia Minor	a/c Tiberia				187
PARALIA	region					147
PARAN, WILDERNESS OF						33
PARIUM	NW Asia Minor					186
PAROS	island of Aegean					171
PARSA	see Persis					
PARTHIA	country of N Persia					135,139,145,183
PARTHIAN EMPIRE						171
PASARGADAE	W Persia					135,139
PATARA	SW Asia Minor					142,173,186
PATHRUSITES	a people of Egypt	a/c Pathruhim				92
PATINA	region of N Syria					109/3
PATROS	Greece					157
PATTALA	NW India					139
PEGAE		= Aphek				143,147
PEHEL		= Pella				33
PEHELI		= Pella				46
PEKENA'AN		= Gaza				46
PELLA		a/c Pehel, Akk. Peheli Eg. Pililum, G/L Berenice Ar. Kh. Fahil				25,46,58,96,103,143,147,157, 165/168,177,181
PELLA	NE Greece					138,140,149,150,185
PELOPONNESE	region of S Greece					54,171
PELUSIUM	Lower Egypt					135,142,151,164,179,182
PENUEL		a/s Peniel	T. edh-Dhahab esh-Sherqiyeh		215176	35,69,96,97
PEOR			Kh. Faghur		163119	118
PEQI'IN		Ar. Buqei'a				185
PERAEA	region					117,147,150,151,156,157,168,181
PERGA		a/s Perge				145,173,186
PERGAMUM	NW Asia Minor	Gk. Pergamon				138,144,171,173,179,186
PERGE		= Perga				26
PERPERENE	NW Asia Minor					187
PERSEPOLIS	W Persia					95,135,145,183
PERSIAN GULF		a/c Lower Sea				31
PERSIS	country of E Persia	Per. Parsa				135,139,145
PERTA	C Asia Minor					187
PESSINUS	C Asia Minor					186
PETHOR	Syria					79,108
PETRA						58,94,143,151,153,160,183
PETRA TOU LIMNITI	Cyprus					26-27
PHAENE	Syria	a/s Phoena, Lat. Phaestus				171
PHAISTOS	Crete					53,94
PHARATHON						147
PHASAELIS						158
PHASELIS	SW Asia Minor					138,144,171,186
PHAZIMON	see Neoclaudiopolis					
PHELLUS	SW Asia Minor					186
PHERAE	N Greece					171
PHILADELPHIA		= Rabbath-ammon				143,144,147,149,150,157,160,168, 177,181
PHILADELPHIA	Lower Egypt					142
PHILADELPHIA	W Asia Minor					171,179,186
PHILIPPI	N Greece					171,172,179
PHILIPPOPOLIS	Syria					160
PHILISTIA	country					70,72/1,78,97,99,104,105,113 119,125,128
PHILISTINES	tribe					33,64,66,68,69,92,113,114
PHILOMELIUM	SW Asia Minor					187
PHILOTERIA		= Beth-yerah				143,149,155,163,164/2
PHOCAEA	W Asia Minor					186
PHOENICIA						71,91,99,101,104,105,125, 126,138,143,145,151,157, 168,185
PHOENIX	Crete					172

NAME	AREA/COUNTRY	VARIANT NAMES	ARABIC NAME	MODERN HEBREW NAME	PALESTINIAN GRID REFERENCE	PAGE(S)
PHRYGIA	country C Asia Minor					135,138,144,151,171,173,179, 182,186
PHYLAKOPI	Greece					53
PIBESETH	see Bubastis					
PIHILUM		= Pella				33
PINARA	SW Asia Minor					186
PIONIA	NW Asia Minor					186
PI-RAMESSE	Lower Egypt	Bibl. Rameses, Mod. Qantir				39,48,50,51,57
PIRATHON		a/c Elmattan	Far'ata		165177	68
PIRIDDU	country of E Asia Minor	a/s Pirindu				130
PI-SAPT	Lower Egypt					41
PISIDIA	country of SW Asia Minor					151,173,179,186-187
PISIDIAN ANTIOCH	see Antioch (in Pisidia)					
PITANE	NW Asia Minor					186
PITHOM	Lower Egypt					39
PODALIA	SW Asia Minor					186
POGLA	SW Asia Minor					186
POMPEII	S Italy					170,178
POMPEIOPOLIS	N Asia Minor					186
POMPEIOPOLIS	see Soli					
PONTUS	province of N Asia Minor					145,151,171,173,179, 183,186
POSEIDIUM	region of S Sinai					160
POSIDIUM	NW Syria					135,145
PRAENESTE	C Italy					90
PRIENE	W Asia Minor					152,186
PROSTANNA	SW Asia Minor					186
PRUSA	NW Asia Minor	a/c Prusa ad Olympum Mod. Bursa				44,55,186
PRUSIAS AD HYPIUM	NW Asia Minor					186
PRYMNESSUS	W Asia Minor					186
PTOLEMAIS		= Acco			157258	142,144,149,150,151,155,157, 162,164,165,166,168,177,181, 185
PTOLEMAIS	city state					155
PTOLEMAIS	N Africa					171
PUMBEDITA	Mesopotamia					171
PUNON						58
PUTEOLI	S Italy					170,172,178
PYLA- KOKKINOKREMNOS	Cyprus					53
PYLOS	S Greece					44,53,54,94,103
PYTHIA THERMA	NW Asia Minor					186

NAME	AREA/COUNTRY	VARIANT NAMES	ARABIC NAME	MODERN HEBREW NAME	PALESTINIAN GRID REFERENCE	PAGE(S)
QADESH	Syria	Akk. Qidsha Bibl. Kadesh Mod. Tell Nebi Mend				28,35,41,42,45,47,48,49,51,53, 114,130
QADESH	see Kedesh					
QADESH-BARNEA	see Kadesh-barnea					
QAHLAMU						33
QAL'AT EL-MUDIQ	see Niyi					
QAL'AT SHARQAT	see Ashur					94-95
QALUNYAH	see Mozah					
QAMM	see Kamon					
QANA	see Kanah					
QANAWAT	see Canatha					
QANAYA	Egypt					33
QANTIR	Lower Egypt	a/c Pi-Ramesse				39
QANU		= Canatha				46
QARN HATTIN	see Adamah					
QARNINI	province	a/c Karnaim				114
QARQAR		a/s Karkar				108
QARQARUM						33
QARYAT EL-MEKHAIYET	see Kiriathaim					
QASR ED-DIL						153,154
QASR EL-'ABD						153,154
QASR EL-JUHEINIYE						154
QASR EZ-ZUWEIRA ET-TAHTA						154
QASR UMM BEGHEQ						154
QASR WADI ES-SIQ						153,154

NAME	AREA/COUNTRY	VARIANT NAMES	ARABIC NAME	MODERN HEBREW NAME	PALESTINIAN GRID REFERENCE	PAGE(S)
QATNA	Syria	Mod. Tell el-Mishrifeh				28,30,35,41,42,46,53,101
QAYUN						157
QAZRIN						152
QIDSHA		= Qadesh				47
QILTI		= Keilah				46
QISYON						155
QUE	country of SE Asia Minor	= Cilicia				46,83,109/1,114
QUMRAN		Heb. Qumeran Ar. Kh. Qumran				149,157,161
QURAMATI	Syria					131
QUYUNJIQ	see Nineveh					

NAME	AREA/COUNTRY	VARIANT NAMES	ARABIC NAME	MODERN HEBREW NAME	PALESTINIAN GRID REFERENCE	PAGE(S)
RAAMAH	tribal region of S Arabia					93
RABBAH	in Judah	a/c Rubute Akk. Rubbuti	Kh. Hamideh		149137	96,118
RABBAH	in Ammon	= Rabbath-ammon				35,78-79
RABBATH-AMMON		a/c Rabbah, Rabbath-bene-ammon G/L Philadelphia	'Amman		238151	30,58,66,68,70,74,88,101,103, 113,114,128,134
RABBATH-MOAB		a/s Rabbathmoba				160,181
RACHGOUN	NW Africa					90
RAKEFET						25
RAGAHA						33
RAGES	see Rhagae					
RAKKATH		a/c Karthan?	Kh. el-Quneitireh	T.Raqqat	199245	
RAMAH	in Naphtali	Heb. Rama	Kh. Zeitun er-Rameh (Kh. Jul)		187259	185
RAMAH	in Benjamin		Er-Ram		172140	72/2,73,118
RAMATAYIM						157
RAMATHAIM		a/c Arimathaea				147
RAMATHAIM-ZOPHIM						73
RAMATH-MIZPEH		a/c Mizpah-gilead	Kh. Jel'ad?		223169	64,128
RAMAT MATRED						96
RAMAT RAHEL		= Beth-haccherem				58,91,124
RAMESSES		= Pi Ramesse				56
RAMESSES IN EDOM						160
RAMM						160
RAMOTH		= Remeth				83
RAMOTH-GILEAD			T.Ramith		244210	58,64,68,99,113,114,128
RAMOTH-NEGEB			Kh. Ghazzah	H.'Uzza	165068	125
RANTIS						185
RAPHIA			T.Rafah		077079	50,58,96,144,149,154,157,168
RAPHIA	city state					154
RAPHON		a/c Raphana	Er-Rafeh		258255	147
RAPIHU		= Raphia				114,122,123,126
RAS ABU HUMEID	see Gittaim					
RAS EL-'AIN	N Syria					28
RAS EL-'AIN	see Aphek (in Sharon)					
RAS EL-KHARRUBEH	see Anathoth					
RAS ET-TAHUNEH	see Zemaraim					
RAS FASHKHA						161
RAS SHAMRA		= Ugarit				26,53
RAS WADI ROMAN						153
RAVENNA	N Italy					170
RAYATA						33
RED SEA		Heb. Yam Suf				30,37,45
REED SEA	see Red Sea					
REGIO JERICHO	city state					154
REHOB	in Galilee		T.el-Balat?		177280	
REHOB	in Asher		T.el-Bir el-Gharbi?	T.Bira	166256	64,68
REHOB	near Beth-shean		T.es-Sarem	T.Rehov	197207	46,50,97
REHOBOTH						33
REHOBOTH-IR	N Mesopotamia					93
REHOV		= Rehob				152
REKEM		Ar. Umm el Bayyareh?				119
REMETH		a/c Ramoth, Jarmuth, Agrippina	Kokab el-Hawa	Kokhav-Hayarden	199222	
REPHAIM	people	a/c Zamzummim				33/2
REPHAIM, VALLEY OF						78
RESEN	N Mesopotamia					93
RESHEF						185

NAME	AREA/COUNTRY	VARIANT NAMES	ARABIC NAME	MODERN HEBREW NAME	PALESTINIAN GRID REFERENCE	PAGE(S)
RETENU		= Canaan				33,41,50
REUBEN	tribe					64,69
REZEPH	E Syria					129
RHAETIA	province of C Europe					179
RHAGAE	W Persia	Bibl. Rages, Mod. Rai				139
RHEGIUM	S Italy	Mod. Reggio Calabria				172,178
RHINOCOLURA	Lower Egypt	a/s Rhincorura				142,143,149,160
RHODES	E Mediterranean	GK. Rodhos, Lat. Rhodus				44,91,135,138,142,144,151,171, 173,179
RHODIAPOLIS	SW Asia Minor					186
RIBLAH	Syria		a/c Shabtuna			129,130
RIMMON			Rummaneh	H.Rimona	179243	118
RIPHATH	tribal region of N Asia Minor					92
RIYADH	Arabia					160
RODANITES	people of Rhodes	a/c Rodanim, a/c Dodanites, Dodanim				92
ROGELIM			Bersinya?		223215	
ROME		Lat. Roma				94,150,170,178,182
ROSH HANIQRA						28,33,82,190
ROSH HORESHA						25
ROSH ZIN						25
RO-WATY	Lower Egypt	a/c Avaris, Tanis, Bibl. Zoan				37
RUBBUTI		= Rabbah				46
RUBUTE	see Rabbah					
RUHAMA						185
RUJM EL-KHADRA						153
RUJM MEKRI HADID						153
RUMAH			Kh. er-Rumeh	H. Ruma	177243	128
RUMMANEH	see Rimmon					
SABASTIYA		= Samaria				185
SABTAH	people of S Arabia					93
SAFADI		Heb. Horbat Zafad				27
SAFED	see Zefat					
SAFED EL-BATTIKH	see Beth-anath					
SAFFARIN	see Sepher					
SAGALASSUS	SW Asia Minor					186
SAHAB						26
SAHM EL-JOLAN	see Golan					
SAIDA		= Sidon				53
SAIDE	Syria					25
SAIS	Lower Egypt					39,83,135,151
SAITTAE	W Asia Minor					186
SAKMEMI						33/3
SALA	W Asia Minor	a/c Domitianopolis				186
SALAMANTICA	N Spain	Mod. Salamanca				178
SALAMIS	Cyprus					135,142,144,173,179,183
SALAMIS	S Greece					135
SALIBIYA						25
SALIM					202197	165/3
SAL'KHI	Syria					47
SALONAE	Adriatic					170,178
SALT, CITY OF						118
SALT SEA		= Dead Sea				
SALTUS CONSTANTINIACES	district					154
SALTUS GERARITICUS	district					154
SAMAGA						149
SAM'AL	country of SE Asia Minor					114
SAMARIA		a/c Sebaste a/s Sabastiya	Sebastiyeh		168187	58,96,97,99,102-103,108,109, 113,128,135,147,149,150,151
SAMARIA	region	a/c Samaritis, Akk. Samerina				113,114,115,122,147,149,154, 157,165/3,177,181,185
SAMARITANS						157
SAMARITIS		= Samaria				150,151
SAMARRA	C Mesopotamia					29
SAMERINA	Assyrian province	= Samaria				114,126
SAMOS	Aegean Sea					91,159,171,173
SAMU'ANU						33/3
SANAUS	SW Asia Minor					186
SANSANNAH			Kh. esh-Shamsaniyat	H. Sansanna	140083	118

NAME	AREA/COUNTRY	VARIANT NAMES	ARABIC NAME	MODERN HEBREW NAME	PALESTINIAN GRID REFERENCE	PAGE(S)
SA'PUM						33
SAQQARA	Lower Egypt					39,130,135
SAR'A		= Zorah				46
SARABIT EL-KHADIM						48,94
SARAFAND		= Zarephath				52
SAR'AH	see Zorah					
SARDINIA						55,90,94,150,170
SARDIS	W Asia Minor	a/s Sardes				55,135,138,152, 171,173,179,186
SAREPTA		= Zarephath				53,91,50,134
SARID			T.Shadud		172229	
SARMIZEGETUSA	E Europe					179
SARTABA	see Alexandrium					
SA'SA'		Heb. Sasa				152,185
SAVARIA	C Europe	Mod. Szombathely				178
SAVATRA	C Asia Minor					186
SCEPSIS	NW Asia Minor					186
SCYTHIA	country of SE Europe					138
SCYTHIANS	tribe of the Caucasus	a/c Ashkenaz				93
SCYTHOPOLIS		= Beth-shean				143,144,149,155,157,163,165/3, 166,168,177,181,185/2
SCYTHOPOLIS	city state					155
SEBA	people of NE Africa					93
SEBASTE		= Samaria				155,157,158,177,181,185/2
SEBASTE	SW Asia Minor					186
SEBASTE	see Elaeussa					
SEBASTIYEH	see Samaria					
SEBASTOPOLIS	SW Asia Minor					186
SEBASTOPOLIS	N Asia Minor	a/c Heracleopolis				186
SEBENNYTUS	Lower Egypt					142
SECACAH			Kh. es-Samrah?		187125	118,161
SEDASA	S Asia Minor					179
SEDE NAHUM						185
SEFUNIM						25
SEIR	region	a/c Edom, Akk. Sheri				48
SELA						58
SELA'IM						51
SELAME						177
SELBIT	see Shaalbim					
SELEUCIA						149,163,177
SELEUCIA		a/c Abila				147
SELEUCIA	Mesopotamia	a/c Selucia-on-the-Tigris				145,151,160,171
SELEUCIA	SE Asia Minor	a/c Seleucia Pieria				142,144,171,173
SELEUCIA AD CALYCADNUM	SE Asia Minor					187
SELEUCIA SIDERA	SW Asia Minor					186
SELEUCID EMPIRE						144-145
SELGE	SW Asia Minor					186
SELINUS	SE Asia Minor					187
SEMECHONITIS, LACUS		= Lake Huleh				155
SENNABRIS						155,164/2,181
SEPHARVIM	see Sippar					
SEPHER			Saffarin		160185	112
SEPPH						177
SEPPHORIS		a/c Diocaesarea Heb. Zippori				149,150,151,152,157,158,162 164,165,166,177,181
SESTUS	NW Asia Minor	Gk. Sestos				142
SEVAN, LAKE						127
SEXI	SE Spain	Mod. Almuñécar				90
SHAALBIM		a/s Shaalabbin	Selbit	T.Sha'alvim	148141	66
SHA'ALVIM						152,185
SHA'AR HAGOLAN						26,33/3
SHABTUNA		= Riblah				48,49
SHAHR-I SOKHTA	W. Persia					95
SHAKMI		= Shechem				46
SHALAM-'IL						33
SHAMASH-ADAM						43
SHAMIR						68
SHAM'UNA		= Shimron				46
SHANGAR		= Shinar				47
SHARIYANU						33
SHARON, PLAIN OF						41,62,96,99,112,113

NAME	AREA/COUNTRY	VARIANT NAMES	ARABIC NAME	MODERN HEBREW NAME	PALESTINIAN GRID REFERENCE	PAGE(S)
SHARUHEN			T.el-Far'ah	T.Sharuhen	100076	37,40,41,64,96,191
SHASU	tribe	a/c Habiru				46
SHAVEH-KIRIATHAIM						33/2
SHAVE ZIYYON						185
SHAWI, MT						51
SHEBA	tribal region of SW Arabia					83,93
SHECHEM		a/c Sekmen, Akk. Shakmi	T.Balatah		176179	30,32,33,37,45,50,58,62,64,66, 68,70,74,83,88,91,96,97,99, 102,103,112,144,147,149,157
SHEFAR'AM						181
SHEIKH ABU ZARAD	see Tappuah					
SHEIKH 'ALI						26
SHEIKH EL-AREINI						67
SHEIKH SA'D		= Karnaim				48
SHELEPH	tribal people of S. Arabia					93
SHEM	trival grouping					93
SHEMESH-ADAM	see Adamah					
SHEMIDA	clan district					112
SHEPHELAH	region					62,64,125
SHERI		= Seir				46
SHIANU	W Syria					108,114
SHIKIMONAH			T.es-Samak	T.Shiqmona	146247	
SHIKKERON			T.el-Ful		132136	
SHILOH		Ar. Kh. Seilun				33,64,65,66,72/1,74,96,103
SHIMRON		Akk. Sham'una a/s Shim'on a/c Simonias	Kh. Sammuniyeh	T.Shimron	170234	58,62,64
SHINAR		= Babylonia				93
SHIQMONA		= Shikimonah				91
SHITTIM	see Abel-shittim					
SHUFAH	see Siphtan					
SHUNEM			Solem	Shunem	181223	58,64,75,97,99,164-165
SHUQBA						25
SHUR	region of Sinai					34
SHURINA, VALLEY OF						42
SHURUPPAK	Mesopotamia	Mod. Tell Fara				29,30/2
SHUTU	region					33
SIBIDUNDA	SW Asia Minor					186
SICILY		Lat. Sicilia				55,150,170,172,178
SIDDIM, VALLEY OF						33/2
SIDE	S Asia Minor					138,142,144,171,186
SIDON		Akk. Siduna, Mod. Saida				41,43,53,62,66,83,91,99,108, 109,113
SIDONIANS	tribe					66,113
SIDUNA		= Sidon				47
SIDYMA	SW Asia Minor					186
SILANDUS	W Asia Minor					186
SILE	Egypt					40,41,50
SILLYUM	S Asia Minor					186
SIMEON	tribe					64,69
SIMIRRA	province of Syria	Bibl. Zemer, a/s Simyra				114
SIMONIAS		= Shimron				162
SIMYRA		a/s Simirra, Sumur(a) a/c Simyra of Ramesses				48,51,115
SINAI						30,37,45,50,57,130
SINAI, MT		= Mt. Horeb				57
SINDA	Cyprus					45
SINITES	tribe					93
SINOPE	NE Asia Minor					135,179,187
SINZAR	Syria					42,47,68
SIPHTAN			Shufah?		157186	112
SIPPAR	C Mesopotamia	a/c Sepharvaim				101,115
SIRHAN, WADI						160
SIRMIUM	C Europe	Mod. Sremska Mitrovica				178
SITIFIS	N Africa					170
SIWA OASIS	Egypt					135,138,142
SIYANNU	Syria					42
SMYRNA	W Asia Minor	Mod. Izmir				44,55,82,91,171,179,186
SOCOH	in Sharon		Kh. Shuweiket er-Ras		153194	32,43,58,83/1,96/2,112
SOCOH	in Shephelah		Kh. 'Abbad	H. Sokho	147121	118
SOCOH	near Mt. Judah		Kh. Shuweikeh		150090	124
SODOM						59/3

NAME	AREA/COUNTRY	VARIANT NAMES	ARABIC NAME	MODERN HEBREW NAME	PALESTINIAN GRID REFERENCE	PAGE(S)
SOGANE						163,177
SOGDIANA	country of C Asia					93,139,145
SOLEM	see Shunem					
SOLI	SW Asia Minor	a/c Pompeiopolis				138,140,187
SOZUSA	see Apollonia					
SPAIN						182
SPARDA	see Lydia					
SPARTA	S Greece					53,54,135,138,142
SPASINOU CHARAX	Mesopotamia					171
STECTORIUM	SW Asia Minor					186
STOBI	SE Europe					152,171
STRATONICEA	SW Asia Minor					186
STRATONICEA	W Asia Minor	a/c Hadrianopolis				186
STRATO'S TOWER		a/c Straton's Tower a/c Caesarea				58,143,144,147,149,150,157
SUBA	see Zobah					
SUBARTU	region of N Mesopotamia					31
SUBERDE						26
SUCCOTH			T.Deir 'Alla		208178	33,58,65,69,96,102,103,125
SUCCOTH	Lower Egypt					57
SUEZ						160
SUHMATA						185
SULCI	Sardinia					90
SULLECTHUM	N Africa					170
SUMER	country of S Mesopotamia					29,31
SUMUR(A)		a/c Simyra				41,47
SUPITE	Assyrian province of Syria	Bibl. Zobah				114
SUQ WADI BARADA	see Abila					
SURA	Mesopotamia					171
SURAYA						33
SURGHUL	Mesopotamia	Anc. Nina				30/2
SURRI		. = Tyre				46
SURUDANU						33
SUSA	S Persia	Mod. Shush				29,30,31,83,94,109/1,127,135,139, 145
SUSIANA	country of N Persia					139
SUWEIDA	Syria					160
SUWEIMA						26
SYCAMINUM						181
SYCHAR					177180	165/3
SYCOMAZON	city state					154
SYEDRA	SW Asia Minor					187
SYENE	Upper Egypt					135,183
SYNNADA	SW Asia Minor					171,186
SYRACUSE	Sicily	Lat. Syracusae				90,150,170,172,178
SYRIA						41,101,130,138,142-143,145,149, 151,160,171,173,179
TAANACH		Akk. Ta'(nuk)a a/s Thaanach	T.Ti'innik		171214	28,41,43,45,52,58,62,64,67,68 96,97,83/1
TAANATH-SHILOH			Kh. Ta'na el-Foqa		185175	112
TABAE	SW Asia Minor					186
TABAL	tribal region of SE Asia Minor	Bibl. Tubal				109/1,114,122,127
TABALA	W Asia Minor					186
TABAQAT FAHL						26,53,185
TABEH	see Jotbathah					
TABIGHA						185
TABOR						162
TABOR, MT						69,149,164,165,166,177
TABUK	Arabia					160
TADMOR		= Palmyra				35,30,129
TAENARUM	S Greece					171
TAFFUH	see Beth-tappuah					
TAIYIBA		a/s Taibé				25,185
TAKHSI	region of Syria					42,47,51
TAKRIT	Mesopotamia					125
TAMAR		Ar. 'Ein Husb Heb. Hazeva				58,96,119
TAMINTA	region of Syria					51
TANANIR						88
TANIS	Lower Egypt					39,45

NAME	AREA/COUNTRY	VARIANT NAMES	ARABIC NAME	MODERN HEBREW NAME	PALESTINIAN GRID REFERENCE	PAGE(S)
TA'NUKA		= Taanach				46
TAPHNITH			Tibnin		188288	
TAPIKA	E Asia Minor	Mod. Maşat				55
TAPPUAH			Sheikh Abu Zarad		172168	62,64,112
TARBISU	Mesopotamia					126
TARENTUM	S Italy	Mod. Taranto				170,178
TARICHEAE						149,163,168,177
TARRACO	E Spain	Mod. Tarragona				170,178
TARSHISH	a people of the Mediterranean					92
TARSUS	SE Asia Minor	a/c Antiochia				55,91,109,135,138,142,145,151, 171,173,179,183,187
TAVIUM	NE Asia Minor					179
TAXILA	NW India					139,141
TEICHOS DYMEION	E Greece					54
TEIMA'	see Tema					
TEKOA			Kh. Tequ'		170115	113,118
TEL ABIL	see Abel (in Gilead)					
TEL ADAMI	see Adami-nekeb					
TEL 'AFEQ		= Aphek				67,190,191
TEL AKHZIV	see Achzib (in Asher)					
TEL 'AKKO	see Acco					
TEL 'ALIL	see Hali					
TEL 'ARAD		= Arad (Israelite Citadel)				91
TEL ASHDOD		= Ashdod				191
TEL 'ASHIR						33
TEL ASHQELON	see Ashkelon					
TEL 'AVDON	see Abdon					
TEL AVEL BET MAAKHA	see Abel-beth-maacah					
TEL AVIV						26,28
TEL 'AZEQA	see Azekah					
TEL AZNOT TAVOR	see Aznoth-tabor					
TEL BATASH		= Timnah				27,52
TEL BE'ER SHEVA'		= Beersheba				67,103
TEL BET HA-'EMEQ	see Beth-emek					
TEL BET MIRSHAM	see Tell Beit Mirsim					
TEL BET SHE'AN	see Beth-shean					
TEL BET SHEMESH	see Beth-shemesh (in Judah)					
TEL BET YERAH	see Beth-yerah					
TEL BIRA	see Rehob (in Asher)					
TEL BURGA						33,191
TEL DALIT						191
TEL DAN		= Dan				67,88
TEL DOR						185
TELEILAT EL-GHASSUL						26,28,77,88,161
TEL 'EN HADDA	see En-haddah					
TEL 'ERANI						28,124,191
TEL ESHDAR						65
TEL ESUR						33,191
TEL 'ESTER	see Ether					
TEL GAMMA	see Yurza					
TEL GAT						28
TEL GAT HEFER	see Gath-hepher					
TEL GERISA		= Gath-rimmon				33,191
TEL GEZER		= Gezer				185
TEL GODED	see Moresheth-gath					
TEL HADID	see Hadid					
TEL HALIF	see En-rimmon					
TEL HANNATON	see Hannathon					
TEL HARASHIM						33
TEL HAROR		= Gerar				191
TEL HASI	see Eglon					
TEL HAZOR	see Hazor					
TEL HEFER		= Hepher				28
TEL 'IRA						124
TEL JESHU'A	see Jeshua					
TEL JEZER	see Gezer					
TEL KINROT	see Chinnereth					
TEL KISON		= Mishal				67,185
TEL LAKHISH	see Lachish					

NAME	AREA/COUNTRY	VARIANT NAMES	ARABIC NAME	MODERN HEBREW NAME	PALESTINIAN GRID REFERENCE	PAGE(S)
TEL MA'ARAVIM						67
TEL MAHOZ	see Muhhazi					
TEL MALHATA		= Arad (Canaanite city)				33
TEL MALOT	see Gibbethon					
TEL MARESHA	see Mareshah					
TEL MASOS		= Hormah				33,67
TEL ME'AMER	see Geba-somen					
TEL MEGADIM						91
TEL MEGIDDO	see Megiddo					
TEL MEVORAKH						33,52,88,91,96/3,190
TEL MIKHAL						33,52,60,96,190,191
TEL MIQNE		= Ekron				67
TEL MOR						52,96/3
TEL NAGILA		= Tell Najileh				190-191
TEL POLEG						33,91,96,190,191
TEL PORAN						33,191
TEL QASHISH	see Helkath					
TEL QEDESH	see Kedesh (in Naphtali)					
TEL QERIYOT	see Kerioth (in Negeb)					
TEL QIRYAT YE'ARIM	see Kiriath-jearim					
TEL QISHYON	see Kishion					
TEL RAQQAT	see Rakkath					
TEL REGEV		= Achshaph				190
TEL REHOV		= Rehob				185
TEL REKHESH		= Anaharath				33
TEL ROSH	see Beth-shemesh (in Naphtali)					
TEL SERA'	see Ziklag					
TEL SHA'ALVIM	see Shaalbim					
TEL SHALAF	see Eltekeh					
TEL SHARUHEN	see Sharuhen					
TEL SHEM	see Dabbesheth					
TEL SHIMRON		= Shimron				33
TEL SHIQMONA		= Shikimonah				37
TEL SHOR	see Maralah					
TEL YAHAM	see Yaham					
TEL YARMUT	see Jarmuth (in Judah)					
TEL YIN'AM	see Jabneel (in Naphtali)					
TEL YIZRE'EL	see Jezreel					
TEL YONA						185
TEL YOQNEAM	see Jokneam					
TEL YOSEF						33
TEL ZAFIT		= Gath				33
TEL ZEFI	see Zephath					
TEL ZEROR		= Migdal				33,52,60,67,96,191
TEL ZIPPOR						33,67
TEL ZOR'A	see Zorah					
TEL ZOVA	see Zobah					
TELL ABU HABIL						26
TELL ABU HAWAM		= Libnath, a/s Tell Abu Huwam				52,91,96
TELL ABUE HUREIREH		= Gerar				33
TELL ABU HUREYRA	Syria					26
TELL ABU SELEIMEH	see Laban					
TELL ABU SULTAN	see Muhhazi					
TELL ABU SUS	see Abel-meholah					
TELL AHMAR	E Syria	= Til Barsip				28
TELL 'AIN-JEDUR	see Gedor					
TELL 'AITUN						67
TELL EL-'AJJUL		= Beth-eglain				28,33,37,52,60,67,191
TELL EL-'AMR		= Geba-somen				33
TELL 'ARAD	see Arad (Israelite Citadel)					
TELL 'AREINI						
TELL 'ARQA	see 'Arqat					
TELL 'ASHTARAH	see Ashtaroth					
TELL 'ASUR	see Baal-hazor					
TELL ATCHANA	see Alalakh					
TELL EL-'AZEIMEH	see Beth-jeshimoth					
TELL EL-BALAT	see Rehob (in Galilee)					
TELL BALATAH		= Shechem				52
TELL BASUL						185

NAME	AREA/COUNTRY	VARIANT NAMES	ARABIC NAME	MODERN HEBREW NAME	PALESTINIAN GRID REFERENCE	PAGE(S)
TELL EL-BATASHI	see Timnah					
TELL EL-BEDEIWIYEH	see Hannathon					
TELL BEIT MIRSIM		Heb. Tel Bet Mirsham				28,33,37,52,67,96/3,121,122,124
TELL EL-BIR EL-GHARBI	see Rehob (in Asher)					
TELL EL-BLEIBIL	see Beth-nimrah					
TELL BORNAT	see Libnah					
TELL BRAK	E Syria					29,30
TELL BURNA	see Libnah					
TELL ED-DAMIYEH	see Adam					
TELL DEIR 'ALLA		= Succoth				53,67
TELL EDH-DHAHAB EL-GHARBI	see Mahanaim					
TELL EDH-DHAHAB ESH-SHERQIYEH	see Penuel					
TELL EDH-DHURUR	see Migdal					
TELL ED-DIBBIN	see Ijon					
TELL DOTHAN	see Dothan					
TELL ED-DUWEIR	see Lachish					
TELL EL-FAR'AH (NORTH)		= Tirzah				28,29,33,52,91,99
TELL EL-FAR'AH (SOUTH)		Bibl. Sharuhen Heb. Tel Sharuhen				33,37,52,67,91,134
TELL EL-FUKHKHAR	see Acco					
TELL EL-FUL						67,124
TELL EL-FUL	see Shikkeron					
TELL EL-GHASSUL						53,161
TELL HALIF						28,33,124
TELL EL-HAMMAM	see Abel-shittim					
TELL EL-HAMMEH	see Hammath (near Beth-shean)					
TELL HARIRI	see Mari					
TELL HASHBEH	see Khashabu					
TELL HASSAN						185
TELL EL-HESI		= Eglon				28,33,52,67,130,191
TELL HIZZIN	see Khashi					
TELL EL-HUSN		= Beth-shean				33
TELL IKTANU		= Beth-haram				26,33
TELL ISDAR						27
TELL JAWAH	see Mephaath					
TELL JEMMEH		= Yurza				33,67,91,119,134,191
TELL JERISHE		= Gath-rimmon				52,67
TELL EL-JISR	see Naarath					
TELL JOKHA	see Umma					
TELL EL-JUDEIDEH	see Moresheth-gath					
TELL EL-JURN						185
TELL KABRI						33,190
TELL EL-KHELEIFEH		= Ezion-geber				91
TELL EL-KHIRBEH	see Merom					
TELL KISAN		= Mishal				28,33,52,67,91,96/3,190
TELL KITTAN						88
TELL KUDADI						91,96,190
TELL KURDANEH	see Aphek (in Asher)					
TELL EL-MAQLUB	see Jabesh-gilead					
TELL MARDIKH	see Ebla					
TELL EL-MASKHUTA	Lower Egypt					135
TELL EL-MAZAR	see Jokmeam					
TELL MELAT	see Gibbethon					
TELL MEVORAKH						101
TELL EL-MILH	see Arad (Canaanite city)					
TELL MIMAS	see Beth-emek					
TELL EL-MUKHARKHASH	see Anaharath					
TELL MUSA						26
TELL EL-MUTESELLIM	see Megiddo					
TELL EN-NA'AM	see Jabneel (in Naphtali)					
TELL EN-NAHL						103
TELL NAJILEH		Heb. Tel Nagila				33,52
TELL EN-NASBEH		= Mizpah				28,67,77
TELL NEBI MEND		= Qadesh				53
TELL QADES		= Kedesh (in Naphtali)				103
TELL EL-QADI	see Dan					
TELL QANAH						33,191

NAME	AREA/COUNTRY	VARIANT NAMES	ARABIC NAME	MODERN HEBREW NAME	PALESTINIAN GRID REFERENCE	PAGE(S)
TELL QASILE						65,66,83,88,91,96/3,190
TELL EL-QASSIS	see Helkath					
TELL EL-QEDAH	see Hazor					
TELL QEIMUN	see Jokneam					
TELL QIRI		a/c Hazorea				67
TELL RAFAH	see Raphia					
TELL RAMAD						26
TELL RAMITH	see Ramoth-gilead					
TELL RASHIDIYEH	see Usu					
TELL ER-RATABA	Lower Egypt					39
TELL EL-REQEISH						91
TELL ER-RUMEILEH	see Beth-shemesh (in Judah)					
TELL ER-RUWEISEH						33
TELL ER-RUWEISI		= Beth-shemesh (in Naphtali)				33
TELL ES-SAFI		= Gath				52,37,67
TELL ES-SA'IDIYEH		= Zaphon				26,53,91,96/3
TELL ES-SALIHIYEH						53
TELL ES-SAMAK	see Shikimonah					
TELL SANDAHANNAH	see Mareshah					
TELL ES-SAREM	see Rehob					
TELL ES-SA'WEH	see Jeshua					
TELL ES-SEBA	see Beersheba					
TELL SHADUD	see Sarid					
TELL ESH-SHALLAF	see Eltekeh					
TELL ESH-SHAMMAM	see Dabbesheth					
TELL ESH-SHARI'AH		= Ziklag				52,67
TELL ESH-SHEMDIN						26
TELL ESH-SHIHAB	see Kiriath-anab					
TELL SUKAS	Syria					91
TELL ES-SULTAN		= Jericho				103,185
TELL TA'YINAT	Syria					91
TELL THORAH	see Maralah					
TELL TI'INNIK	see Taanach					
TELL TURMUS						26
TELL EL-'UBAID	S Mesopotamia					30/3
TELL 'UBEIDIYEH						33
TELL UMM HAMAD	see Zarethan					
TELL UMM HAMMAD EL-GHARBI						33
TELL UMM HAMMAD ESH-SHARQI						26
TELL 'UQAIR	C Mesopotamia					29,30/3
TELL EL-YAHUDIYEH	Lower Egypt					39,45,91
TELL ZIF	see Ziph					
TELMESSUS	SW Asia Minor					186
TEMA	NW Arabia	a/s Teima'				30,83,109/1,127,135,160
TEMAN						119
TEMENOTHYRAE	W Asia Minor	a/c Flaviopolis				186
TEMNUS	NW Asia Minor					186
TEN TOWNS	see Decapolis					
TEOS	W Asia Minor	a/c Teus				171,186
TEPE GAWRA	N Mesopotamia					29
TEPE YAHYA	Persia					95
TEPHON						147
TEREBINTHUS		= Mamre				185
TERMESSUS	SW Asia Minor					142,171,186
TERMESSUS MINOR	SW Asia Minor					186
TETRACOMIA		= Upper Galilee				155
TEUCHIRA	N Africa					171
TEUS	see Teos					
THAANACH		= Taanach				155
THAENASE	NW Africa	a/s Thenae				170
THAGORA	NW Africa					170
THAMARA						154
THAMNA		= Timnath-serah				155,177
THAPSACUS	Syria					135,138,141
THAPSUS	N Africa					90
THARRUS	Sardinia					82,90
THASOS	NE Greece					91
THEBES	Upper Egypt					39,40,83,109/1,126,135,138,142,183
THEBES	C Greece					53,54,171
THELLA						154,163

NAME	AREA/COUNTRY	VARIANT NAMES	ARABIC NAME	MODERN HEBREW NAME	PALESTINIAN GRID REFERENCE	PAGE(S)
THEMISONIUM	SW Asia Minor					186
THERA	Aegean Sea					44,53,91,142
THERMA	E Asia Minor					186
THERMAE THESEOS	W Asia Minor					186
THERMOPYLAE	C Greece					135
THESSALONICA	region of N Greece					171,172,179
THONA						149
THRACE	region of N Greece	Lat. Thracia				135,138,142,171,173,179,182
THREX						157
THYATIRA	W Asia Minor					171,179,186
TIBERIA	see Pappa					
TIBERIAS					201242	103,155,157,163,164,165,166, 177,185/2
TIBERIAS	city state					155
TIBERIAS, LAKE	see Sea of Galilee					
TIBNIN	see Taphnith					
TIL BARSIP	E Syria	Ar. Tell Ahmar				108,109,114,115
TILMEN HÜYÜK	SE Asia Minor					55
TILUM	Syria					28
TIMBRIADA	C Asia Minor					187
TIMNA'	Sinai					27,48,124,147
TIMNAH			T.el-Batashi	T.Batash	141132	69,122
TIMNATH-SERAH		a/c Timnath Gk. Thamna	Kh. Tibnah		160157	147,157
TINGIS	NW Africa	Mod. Tangier				90
TIPASA	NW Africa					170
TIRAS	tribal people of NE Greece					92
TIRAT ZEVI					152	
TIRYNS	S Greece					53
TIRZAH			Kh. T.el-Far'ah		182188	58,62,74,96/3,99,102,103,112
TISHBE						99
TJEBU	Lower Egypt					41
TJEKKER	tribe					66
TLOS	SW Asia Minor					171,186
TMOLUS	W Asia Minor	a/c Aureliopolis				186
TOB, LAND OF						68
TOGARMAH	tribal region of NE Asia Minor					93,109/1
TOMARIS	W Asia Minor					186
TOR ABU SIF						25
TRACHONITIS	region of N Transjordan					151,156,168
TRALLES	SW Asia Minor					171,179,186
TRANSJORDAN	region of Middle East					
TRAPEZOPOLIS	SW Asia Minor					186
TRAPEZUS	NE Anatolia	a/c Trebizond Mod. Trabzon				55,135,138,151,187
TREBENNA	SW Asia Minor					186
TREBIZOND	see Trapezus					
TRIANDA-IALYSOS	SW Asia Minor					53
TRICOMIAS	city state					154
TRIPOLIS	W Syria					135,141,142
TROAS	NW Asia Minor	a/c Alexandria Troas				173,179
TROAS	region of NW Asia Minor					186
TROY	NW Asia Minor	Lat. Ilium, Mod. Hisarlik				44,53,55,138
TUBUL		= Tabal				93
TUL						112
TUNIP	Syria					41,42,47,48
TUTUL	W Mesopotamia					29
TYANA	C Asia Minor					135,138
TYRE		Akk. Surri Lat. Tyrus	Es-Sur		168297	41,48,66,83,91,99,101,109, 114,123,126,130,134,138 171,177,183
TYRE OF TOBIAH			'Araq el-Emir		222148	
TYRUS	city state	= Tyre				151,155

NAME	AREA/COUNTRY	VARIANT NAMES	ARABIC NAME	MODERN HEBREW NAME	PALESTINIAN GRID REFERENCE	PAGE(S)
UDUMMU	see Edom					
UGARIT	Syria	Mod. Ras Shamra				28,30,41,42,45,47,49,51,53,55, 83,94,101
ULATHA	region					155
ULLAZA	Syria	a/s Ullasa, a/c Orthosia				33,47
ULLUBU	region of N Mesopotamia					114

NAME	AREA/COUNTRY	VARIANT NAMES	ARABIC NAME	MODERN HEBREW NAME	PALESTINIAN GRID REFERENCE	PAGE(S)
UMMA	Mesopotamia	Mod. Tell Jokha				29
UMM EL-'AMAD	see Bezer					
UMM EL 'AWAMID	see Hammon					
UMM EL-BAYYAREH	see Rekem					
UMM ED-DABAR	see Lo-debar					
UMM EZ-ZUWEITINA						25
UNQI	country of NW Syria					109/1,114
UPE	region of Syria	a/c Apa				47,48
UPPER GALILEE	region	a/c Tetracomia				157,165/2
UR	Mesopotamia	Mod. El-Muqaiyar				29,31,94,101,131
URARTU	country of E Asia Minor					109/1,126,131
URUK	Mesopotamia	a/c Unug, Bibl. Erech, Mod. Warka				29,30/2,94,131,160
URUKUG	see Al-Hibba					
URUSHALEM		= Jerusalem				46
URUSHALIMU(M)		= Jerusalem				33
USANATU	Syria					108
USHU		= Uzu				123
USNU	W Syria					114
UTICA	N Africa					82,170
UWJA	see Elam					
UZAL	tribal people of S Arabia					93
UZU		Akk. Ushu, a/c Hosah				46,50
VALLEY OF ANTIOCHUS						149
VASADA	S Asia Minor					187
VENUSIA	S Italy					170
VERBE	SW Asia Minor					186
VESUVIUS	S Italy					178
VIA MARIS						58,75,83
VIA NOVA						56
VIENNA	C France	Mod. Vienne				179,182
VOLOS	N Greece					53,54
WADI EL-'ARISH		Eng. Brook of Egypt				126
WADI HASA						103
WADI MUJIB						103
WADI MURABBA'AT						180
WARKANA	see Hyrcania					
WERADIM						152
XALOTH		= Exaloth				163
XANTHUS	SW Asia Minor	a/s Xanthos				138,142,186
XOIS	Lower Egypt					142
YABILYA						33
YABRUD						25
YADANU		= Cyprus				126
YAFA		= Joppa				185
YAFA	see Joppa					
YAFO	see Joppa					
YAHAM		= Yehem				96
YALO	see Aijalon					
YAM SUF	see Red Sea					
YAMU'ARU						33
YANOAM	see Yenoam					
YANUH	see Janoah (in Galilee)					
YA'NUQA						33
YAPU		= Joppa				46
YARIMUTA						33
YARUN	see Yiron					
YAS'APA						33
YASHUB		Ar. Yasuf?				112
YASID	see Yazith					
YASUF	see Yashub					
YA'TIR	see Yattir					
YATRIBU	NW Arabia	Mod. Medina				127

NAME	AREA/COUNTRY	VARIANT NAMES	ARABIC NAME	MODERN HEBREW NAME	PALESTINIAN GRID REFERENCE	PAGE(S)
YATTA	see Juttah					
YATTIR			Ya'tir		181284	
YAUNA	see Ionia					
YAVNE		= Jabneel (in Judah)				27,185
YAVNE YAM						33
YAZITH			Yasid		176189	112
YAZUR	see Azor					
YEB	see Elephantine					
YEBNA	see Jabneel (in Judah)					
YEHEM		a/s Yaham, Ar. Kh. Yemma				41,43
YEHUD	see Jehud					
YENOAM		a/s Yanoam	El'Abeidiyeh		202232	51
YESUD HAMA'ALA						185
YIBNA		= Jabneel				37
YIRON			Yarun		189276	64
YISHUR						157
YOQNE'AM						185
YORGHAN TEPE	see Nuzi					46,94
YURZA		Akk. Yursa, Ar. Tell Jemmeh? Heb. Tel Gamma				96/3,125

NAME	AREA/COUNTRY	VARIANT NAMES	ARABIC NAME	MODERN HEBREW NAME	PALESTINIAN GRID REFERENCE	PAGE(S)
ZACYNTHUS	SE Greece	a/s Zakynthos				54
ZAKRO	Crete					53
ZAMZUMMIM	see Rephaim					
ZANOAH			Kh. Zanu'	H. Zanoah	150125	118
ZAPHON			T.es-Sa'idiyeh		204186	64,68,96
ZAREPHATH		G/L Sarepta, Mod. Sarafand				45,99,123
ZARETHAN						91,96
ZAWATA	see Azzah					
ZEBULUN	tribal region					64,113
ZEBULUNITES	tribe					68
ZEFAT		Ar. Safed				59/3
ZEITA	see Beth-zaith					
ZELA	NE Asia Minor					179,187
ZEMAH						181
ZEMARAIM			Ras et-Tahuneh?		170147	96
ZEMARITES	tribe of S Syria					93
ZEMER	see Simirra					
ZEPHATH			Kh. Sitt Leila	T.Zefi	150215	
ZEREDAH			Deir Ghassaneh		159161	
ZERETH-SHAHAR			Ez-Zarat?		203111	
ZER'IN	see Jezreel					
ZEUGMA	SE Asia Minor					187
ZIKLAG			T.esh-Shari'ah?	T.Sera'	119088	64,118
ZINJIRLI	SE Asia Minor	a/s Zincirli				55,91
ZIPH			T.Zif		162098	64,118,124
ZIPPORI		= Sepphoris				185
ZOAN	see Avaris					
ZOAR		Ar. Es-Safi				33,119,149,157,
ZOBAH		Akk. Supite	Suba?	T.Zova	162132	80,118
ZORAH		Akk. Sar'a	Sar'ah	T.Zor'a	148131	64,66,69,118
ZUMIMRA						152
ZUZIM	region					33

NEW TESTAMENT SITES
[For Old Testament sites see front endpapers.]

To take account of all NT material would require a map of the whole of the eastern half of the Roman Empire. This map of the Holy Land, where Christianity began, indicates the parallels, and contrasts with the OT period. Many sites are shared by the two Testaments, but newer centres of government required new cities, such as Caesarea, built by Herod the Great, and Tiberias built by his son Herod Antipas. Greek rule had already meant the establishment of new cities almost entirely gentile in their population. These can be found in Upper Galilee and the Decapolis.

The depopulation of Judaea after the failure of the Bar Kokhba revolt in AD 135 and a parallel depopulation of Galilee during Turkish rule (AD 1516-1918) means that the location of many sites is uncertain. Both archaeology and the stories of pilgrims' journeyings have helped in locating most sites. *The Holy Land* by Jerome Murphy-O'Connor (N.P. 1986) clearly indicates changes through the centuries. A modern pilgrim needs to remember that modern centres of population do not always reflect what the ancient location was like. For example, Bethlehem and Nazareth were small villages in NT times, but are now bustling towns. By contrast, the peaceful surroundings of the north end of the Sea of Tiberias were once busy centres of trade and commerce.